Knowing The Song

This book is dedicated to

John and Shirley Murray
1929-2017 and 1931-2020

Knowing The Song

A Companion to the Publications of the New Zealand Hymnbook Trust from 1993 to 2009

Together with the New Zealand Supplement to With One Voice (1982)

By
Colin Gibson

The New Zealand Hymnbook Trust
in association with
Philip Garside Publishing Ltd

Copyright © 2021 Colin Gibson
All rights reserved.

This book or any portion thereof may not be reproduced or used in any manner whatsoever without the express written permission of the publisher except for the use of brief quotations in a book review.

Email Colin at:
colin.gibson22@icloud.com

Published by:
The New Zealand Hymnbook Trust
in association with
Philip Garside Publishing Ltd

International print edition 2021
ISBN 978-1-98-857280-2

PDF, Kindle and ePub editions also available

Produced and distributed by:
Philip Garside Publishing Ltd
PO Box 17160
Wellington 6147
New Zealand
books@pgpl.co.nz — www.pgpl.co.nz

Front cover photograph:
Pohutukawa tree blossom
Alexander Garside—Garside Imaging

Contents

Acknowledgements 6

Introduction 8

The Appendices 10

Standard Abbreviations and Short Titles 11

The Hymns 13

The People 273

Appendix — 1
A Finding List of New Zealand Hymn Writing 376

New Zealand Publications 376

New Zealand Hymns Published Overseas 388

Appendix — 2
Writing About New Zealand Hymns and Hymn writers ... 399

Books 399

Articles and Reviews 400

Theses 406

Appendix — 3
The New Zealand Hymnbook Trust 407

Part One: 1979-2000 407

Part Two: 2000-2014 412

Coda: 2014-2021 418

Indexes 419

Hymn Names and First Lines 419

Scripture 428

Tune Names 437

Acknowledgements

The compiler of any Companion of this nature owes much to others, without whose help it could not have been prepared.

John and Gillian Thornley, joint Managers of The New Zealand Hymnbook Trust, and the Editorial Board of the Trust agreed to commission this Companion in 2010, and since that time John and Gillian have been in continuous communication, offering information from Trust files and sharing the pleasures and challenges of the work. In the final stages of the book they provided invaluable close editorial oversight. Earlier files of the Trust were also readily made available to me by its previous chairperson, John Murray. In many ways, the Companion is a tribute to the Trust and its leaders, under whose dynamic direction a large and significant body of creative work by New Zealand poets and musicians, together with a representative selection of Māori and Pacific Islands religious choral music, has been assembled and brought to publication. David Bush, former General Secretary of the Methodist Church of Aotearoa New Zealand – Te Haahi Weteriana O Aotearoa, was instrumental in securing financial backing for publication from the F.A. Parker Bequest.

I further owe a large debt of gratitude to those many writers, composers, translators, arrangers and family members who have responded to requests for biographical and other information. New Zealand hymn writers Marnie Barrell, Jillian Bray, Barry Brinson, Felicia Edgecombe, Bonnie Low, Shirley Erena Murray, Rosemary Russell and Bill Wallace have been particularly generous in this respect. Without their help it would have been impossible to construct any adequate record of contemporary New Zealand hymn writing as represented in the publications of the Trust.

All hymnbook Companions draw on the work of earlier scholars. For overseas hymn writers and the hymn writers of the past, most of them appearing in the New Zealand Supplement to *With One Voice,* I have drawn on many Companions prepared for other hymnals as primary sources of information. In particular I want to record my appreciation of the comprehensive and detailed scholarly work of Professor Wesley Milgate, author of *Songs of the People of God: a Companion to the Australian Hymnbook/With One Voice* (Collins Liturgical, 1982) and its sequel – and much-thumbed – *Companion to Together In Song: Australian Hymn Book II,* by the Reverend Dr D'Arcy Wood (The Australian Hymn Book, 2005), which built on Milgate's materials. Of almost equal importance has been Carlton R. Young's *Companion to the United Methodist Hymnal* (Abingdon Press, 1993) and Dr I-toh Loh's pioneering *Hymnal Companion to Sound the Bamboo: Asian Hymns in their Cultural and Liturgical Contexts* (GIA, 2011). Other American, Canadian and English Companions I have consulted in preparing this one are listed in the appendix, **Writing about New Zealand Hymns**.

An important additional resource has been *The Canterbury Dictionary of Hymnology,* launched on-line in 2013, whose materials I have been able to access during its compilation, thanks to the generosity of Professor Dick Watson, its genial General Editor, with Co-Editor Dr Emma Hornby. And like most hymn book editors and commentators I have occasionally drawn on the first great scholarly history of hymn writing, John Julian's monumental *Dictionary of the Origin and History of Christian Hymns of all Ages and Nations* (revised edition, John Murray, 1907). Although his *Oxford Dictionary of New Zealand Music* makes practically no mention of church music, John Mansfield Thomson's *Biographical Dictionary of New Zealand Composers,* Victoria University Press (1990), has been a useful resource for some New Zealand hymn composers. So too has *A Panorama of Christian Hymnody,* by Erik Routley, edited and expanded by Paul A. Richardson, GIA Publications (2005).

It would have been impossible to create adequate entries for the hymns of Shirley

Erena Murray, unquestionably New Zealand's greatest hymn writer and richly represented in the publications of the Trust, without the assistance of her American publishers, Hope Publishing Company and its management and editorial staff. The company has generously granted The New Zealand Hymnbook Trust permission to reprint information about the writing and content of individual hymns supplied to them by the author and published in the collections of Shirley Murray's hymns brought out by Hope Publishing (see under Individual Author Collections in the Appendix, **A Finding List of New Zealand Hymnody**).

The staff of the Hewitson Library, Knox College, Jo Smith, archivist for the Methodist Church of New Zealand, Stuart Strahan, former Librarian, and the staff of the Hocken Library, University of Otago, the archival staff of the University of Otago, and the staff of the Dunedin Public Library, which holds a major archive of New Zealand and world-wide hymn writing, have responded patiently and generously to my many requests. Christina Schneider (USA) supplied photocopies of an out-of-print Hymn Society of America pamphlet. I owe a special debt of gratitude for the support of Anthony Tedeschi, former Chief Reference Librarian at the Dunedin Public Library. The SOUNZ Centre for New Zealand Music website has provided an invaluable and reliable database of New Zealand composers' biographies and lists of their works.

A number of university students, friends and acquaintances have contributed information or carried out research on my behalf. They include Marguerite Bennet, Janet Newdick, Alice Peterson, Colin Scarf, Wayne te Kaawa and Leah Taylor. John and Jillian Thornley and more recently Marnie Barrell have scrupulously exercised the tedious but vital task of checking the accuracy of the text and Philip Garside has brought the publication to completion with praiseworthy professional efficiency. But my chief debt of gratitude is to my wife, Jeanette Gibson, who uncomplainingly surrendered hours of her husband's time to the completion of this book and played a significant role in the unrewarding business of proofreading its contents. To her this book and the labours which brought it into existence are dedicated.

Colin Gibson
August 2021

Introduction

A Companion of this kind is only as useful as its readers find it to be, so this Introduction sets out to provide guidance and advice to those seeking the information it provides.

First, a word of warning. Since this is the first time such a comprehensive Companion to a large body of New Zealand writing and musical composition has been prepared it will inevitably have deficiencies and contain errors. It is intended to be an on-going source of information, and the Editor will gratefully receive any new information or corrections, as well as suggestions for additions. These may be sent to Professor Colin Gibson, 28 Mitchell Avenue, Mornington, Dunedin 9011, New Zealand, or emailed to colin.gibson22@icloud.com.

Abbreviations and Short Titles

Standard English print abbreviations – such as *cf.* for 'compare,' or *e.g.* for 'for example' – have been kept to a minimum to make the reading of much information as pleasant an experience as possible.

But to save space and avoid unnecessary duplication, in the body of any entry the names of writers, translators, composers and arrangers are given in a shortened (and often more familiar) form and are set in bold font to facilitate cross-referencing. So **Shirley Murray** instead of **Shirley Erena Murray** and **Nigel Eastgate** instead of **Nigel Onslow Eastgate**; **Willow Macky** instead of **Willow Katherine Faith Macky** and **Bill Wallace** instead of **William (Bill) Laurence Wallace**. **Giovanni Francesco di Bernadone (St Francis)** is listed in the Index of Names as such, but appears as the better known **St Francis** in the body of the text. Titles indicating rank or status—such as New Zealand public honours or membership of a religious order—are not used.

Hymnbook titles, too, are given in a shortened form within entries on a hymn or its writer or composer. So *Alleluia Aotearoa* rather than *Alleluia Aotearoa: Hymns and Songs for all churches*. The full form of any such hymnal title will be found in the *Finding List of New Zealand Hymn Writing*, which forms one of the appendices to this Companion. Within such entries the year of publication is given to avoid confusion between otherwise identical titles: to differentiate, for instance, *In Every Corner Sing* (1987) Shirley Murray's privately published collection of 16 hymns published in Wellington, from the larger American collection of 84 of her hymns, *In Every Corner Sing: The Hymns of Shirley Erena Murray*, published in 1992 by the Hope Publishing Company, Carol Stream, Illinois.

A list of all standard abbreviations used in the Companion will be found later in this section.

Biblical quotations

It is evident that although by one definition hymns are religious poems independent of the scriptures – being in this respect different from praise and worship songs, which versify or duplicate Biblical textual material – the imaginations and memories of most of the writers who appear in this Companion are full of the Biblical passages which they have read or heard repeated regularly in the liturgy, the singing and the preaching of the Church.

Older writers have such aural and visual memories of the standard 1611 King James version of the Bible. Modern and contemporary writers draw on a huge variety of later translations, and since hymn texts are poems, not academic statements, their creators are not required to and seldom indicate which translation they may have used or recall as they write. Only once have I found a writer naming her source translation, in this case, the *Good News Bible*.

Apart from the numbering of the Psalms, there is virtually no disagreement between versions of the Bible about book, chapter and line reference systems, so I have chosen a modern edition of the Bible with some claim to being recognized as a standard one. This is the *New Revised Standard* version, published by William Collins, New York, Glasgow and Toronto (1989). All references to and quotations from scripture in this Companion (unless otherwise specified) relate to the text of that edition.

The Biographies

The names of more than two hundred authors, translators, composers and arrangers appear in the six hymnbooks which are covered by this Companion, *With One Voice* (1982), *Alleluia Aotearoa* (1993), *Carol our Christmas* (1996), *Faith Forever Singing* (2000), *He Came Singing Peace* (2002) and *Hope is our Song* (2009). Each has been given a biographical account, which includes their life story and their work with hymns. Many of them are New Zealanders whose biography has never been previously recorded or who have received only casual reference in formal sources. Following each entry the hymns associated with them are listed in bold: more information will be found in the entries dealing with those hymns.

Hymn Titles and Tune Names

Separate indexes list all hymn titles and tune names as they appear in the hymnbooks covered by this Companion.

Normally, hymns are listed under the first line of their text, but where authors or editors have given texts a separate and different title both are listed in strict alphabetical order. So Shirley Murray's 'Carol our Christmas' is found under both 'Carol our Christmas' and Upside Down Christmas. Where hymn titles are identical with other hymn titles, as with the three Māori hymns which begin 'E te Ariki,' the Index gives an extended line to differentiate among them. So 'E te Ariki, he ataahua koe' can be distinguished from 'E te Ariki kia aroha mai.' The seven 'Alleluia Aotearoa' texts (this forms the complete text) are differentiated only by their numbering in Alleluia Aotearoa (1993).

Tune names are listed in strict alphabetical order. Where no tune name has been created by the composer, the editor of this Companion has invented one, placing it within square brackets. So Felicia Edgecombe's unnamed tune for her carol 'O he is born' is listed as [O HE IS BORN]. Occasionally two tunes have been supplied for one hymn text; in that case, both are listed and differentiated as (i) and (ii).

Wherever possible, the meaning or significance of a tune name is explained. Tune names in a language other than English are glossed: so, RANGI RURU (Māori=wide sky shelter) and SACRA (Latin=sacred things).

Paging and Numbering

In the first three of the Trust's publications, *Alleluia Aotearoa*, *Carol our Christmas* and *Faith Forever Singing*, several poems without musical settings and occasional prose materials were introduced without numbering. In this Companion they are given the reference number of the hymn facing them, distinguished with an asterisk. So in *Faith Forever Singing*, Shirley Murray's poetic text 'Easter New Zealand' is printed on the page opposite the third hymn in the collection, 'As we walk along beside you.' The poem, referenced both by its title and its first line, is identified as *F3**.

Sources and Themes

Wherever possible, the sources of a hymn text are identified, and the occasion for which it was written, along with its earliest appearances in print. Alterations to the text, whether made by the author or subsequent editors, are noted, along with any existing comments made by the writer or composer about their own work. In this respect, Shirley Murray's annotations on her own hymns offer a unique and extensive personal commentary on the work of a poet, theologian, and passionate advocate for enlightened religious and social change.

Attention is given to the literary and musical qualities of the hymns, together with their themes and the development of thought they offer. Musical arguments are traced as well as theological ones. Such critical analysis is, of course, the work of the Editor, whose opinions should not be attributed to the authors or composers of the body of creative work discussed in this Companion.

The explanation of allusions to persons, places and things has frequently proved to be easier than tracing the richness of biblical quotation or allusion in these texts. A few of the hymns are virtual or intentional paraphrases of specific biblical passages, but in most cases it would do little justice to these rich texts to define them as commentaries on or expositions of a single biblical passage. Consequently, although a simple page-referenced list of Biblical allusions in the hymns is provided under the index heading SCRIPTURE, there is no index of scriptural themes or topics of the kind provided in a number of major hymnals. The reader is advised to refer to the indexes of seasonal, liturgical and other themes complied by the editors of the various volumes published by the New Zealand Hymnbook Trust. Only one hymnbook, *Hope is our Song*, carries a comprehensive Biblical Index.

The Appendices

The creation of this Companion has involved assembling a great deal of hitherto ungathered information about the appearance of New Zealand hymn writing in national hymnbooks not published by the Trust as well as in overseas publications. It is evidence that New Zealand hymn writers have enriched the hymn vocabularies of Christian communities throughout the world and penetrated international markets for religious choral music to a degree never before realized.

The New Zealand Hymn Book Trust

The full history of hymnwriting in New Zealand, which must now take into account Māori and Pacific translations as well as original language hymns, is yet to be written. But the work of the New Zealand Hymnbook Trust stands out as the first ecumenical attempt to foster and collect for publication contemporary writing in English supported by New Zealand musicmakers. In this Companion the pioneering work of the Trust members and their successive editorial boards is recorded in the words of the two chairmen who led the enterprise from 1978 to 2009 and beyond, the period covering the publication of the New Zealand supplement to the Australian hymnbook, *With One* Voice in 1982 to the last of six remarkable collections of contemporary New Zealand hymnwriting, *Hope is our Song*, in 2009.

Finding List of New Zealand Hymnody

This is the first attempt to map the publication and world-wide spread of New Zealand hymn writing, taking into account denominational and other hymnbooks, single author collections and occasional printings in journals and similar publications. Inevitably items will have gone unrecorded; in particular, it has not been possible to comprehensively research Christian music resources in Europe, Africa and South America for appearances of New Zealand hymns. However, it is the Editor's hope that any discoveries in New Zealand collections and libraries as well as in international publications will be reported so that they can be added to an on-going finding list.

Reports would usefully include the full title of a publication, the publisher, place and date of publication, together with the titles and authors concerned and a position reference. Early New Zealand hymn writers often published their work in England or America, and our poets wrote many hymns texts now buried among other writing. Church publications such as newsletters, newspapers and journals, are other potential sources which need to be examined. And it should be stressed that hundreds of hymns which have not got beyond manuscript or local use in service sheets, have gone unrecorded in this list, which has had to be confined to printed copies or scores. It has become clear to the

Editor that New Zealanders are as fertile and creative a people in their religious lives as in their secular lives and that hymns, religious songs and carols are used in community ways far beyond the limits of church walls, from Christmas petrol station free booklets of carols to school song books. The broadcasts of hymn performances over radio and television channels, as well as commercial recordings on vinyl records, cassette tapes, CDs and DVDs, and online digital music services, also lie beyond the scope of this list.

Writing about New Zealand Hymns and Hymn writers

This is a similar first attempt to recognise the scholarly work done on our hymn writers and their hymns, a significant area of our national artistic creativity which is only beginning to receive the attention it deserves. This bibliography lists national and international publications gathered alphabetically under Books, Articles and Reviews and Theses. Like the Finding List it is a work in progress, and the editor would be grateful for further information.

Note: Following modern print practice, macrons (as in Māori) signifying the lengthening of certain sounds have been used in Māori language quotations through this Companion, but the original hymns texts were all published by the Trust without macrons, before this practice began.

Standard Abbreviations and Short Titles

Bible references are given in the short form 'Genesis 1:15-16,' and the text quoted is normally that of the New Revised Standard Version (*The Holy Bible, containing the Old and New Testaments, New Revised Standard Version*. Anglicized Edition. Oxford: Oxford University Press, 1995).

Personal names are given in a shortened form (first name and surname only), except in the biographies, where they are given in full in the heading to an entry.

The following abbreviations and short forms of hymnbook titles are frequently used in this *Companion*. For the reader's convenience, dates of publication are regularly supplied in each individual entry for a hymn.

A or **Alleluia Aotearoa** *Alleluia Aotearoa: Hymns and Songs for all Churches*. Christchurch: The New Zealand Hymnbook Trust (1993)

A Place at the Table *A Place at the Table: New Hymns written between 2009 and 2013*. Shirley Erena Murray. Carol Stream, IL.: Hope Publishing (1996)

C or **Carol our Christmas** *Carol our Christmas: A Book of New Zealand Carols*. Raumati: The New Zealand Hymnbook Trust (1996)

Every Day in Your Spirit *Every Day in Your Spirit: New Hymns written between 1992 and 1996*. Shirley Erena Murray. Carol Stream, IL.: Hope Publishing (1996)

Faith Forever Singing *Faith Forever Singing: New Zealand Hymns and Songs for a New Day*. Raumati: The New Zealand Hymnbook Trust (2000)

Faith Makes the Song *Faith Makes the Song: New Hymns written between 1997 and 2002*. Shirley Erena Murray. Carol Stream, IL.: Hope Publishing (2003)

HP or **He Came Singing Peace** *He Came Singing Peace: Songs to overcome Violence*. Raumati: The New Zealand Hymnbook Trust (2002)

H or **Hope is our Song** *Hope is our Song; New Hymns and Songs from Aotearoa New Zealand*. Palmerston North: The New Zealand Hymnbook Trust (2009)

In Every Corner Sing (1987) *In Every Corner Sing: New Hymns to Familiar Tunes in Inclusive Language by Shirley Murray.* Wellington: Shirley Erena Murray (1987)

In Every Corner Sing (1992) *In Every Corner Sing: The Hymns of Shirley Murray.* Shirley Erena Murray. Carol Stream, IL.: Hope Publishing (1992)

New Zealand Praise *New Zealand Praise: A Book of Contemporary New Zealand Christian Songs and Hymns written by and for the people of New Zealand.* Comp. David R.S. Dell. Hastings: New Zealand Christian Resource Trust (1988)

Reading the Signature *Reading the Signature: New Hymns and Songs by Colin Gibson.* Carol Stream, IL.: Hope Publishing (1994)

Servant Songs *Servant Songs: Psalms, Hymns and Spiritual Songs for God's People,* Compiled by Guy E. Jansen and Felicia Edgecombe. Sutherland, Australia: Albatross Books (1987)

Singing Love *Singing Love: A Collection of New Hymns and Songs and Carols for Today's Church.* Colin Gibson. 143pp. London, Auckland and Melbourne: Collins Liturgical (1988)

Songs for a Rainbow People *Songs for a Rainbow People: New hymns and Songs by Colin Gibson.* Carol Stream, IL.: Hope Publishing (1998)

Touch the Earth Lightly *Touch the Earth Lightly: New Hymns written between 2003 and 2008.* Shirley Erena Murray. Carol Stream, IL.: Hope Publishing (2008)

W or **With One Voice** *With One Voice: A Hymn Book for all the Churches, with New Zealand Supplement.* London and Auckland: Collins (1982)

Other abbreviations used are:

The Hymn *The Hymn: A Journal of Congregational Singing.* Richmond (formerly Boston): The Hymn Society in the United States and Canada (formerly the Hymn Society of America), volume 1, number 1, 1922-

Klusmeier *The Music of Ron Klusmeier. Volume Two, featuring words by Shirley Erena Murray: A Five-Volume Collection of Hymns and Songs Composed from 1972 to 2012.* Parksville, British Columbia: Musiklus (2012). 67 texts by Shirley Murray.

Music in the Air *Music in the Air: Song and Spirituality* (later *Exploring Spirituality in the Creative Arts*), numbers 1-40, Summer 1996-Winter/Spring 2015. Palmerston North.

SOUNZ Centre for New Zealand Music, Marion Square, Wellington 6141.

The Hymns

A child was born in Bethlehem C1
Metre: 12.12.14.10

This dancing carol was written by Dominican Sister **Cecily Sheehy**, one of a number of religious songs for children she contributed to the monthly magazine of the Catholic Family Living Programme between 1980 and 1985.

There is a model for the text in the 15th century Latin carol, 'Puer natus in Bethlehem, Alleluia' (A boy was born in Bethlehem, Alleluia), found in the *Piae Cantiones [Pious Songs]* of 1592, but probably of earlier origin still. In the English translation offered in the *Oxford Book of Carols* (1928) the fourth verse addresses Christ's humanity: 'Then praise the Word of God who came / To dwell within a human frame.' There are traces of this carol in the New Zealand poem in the opening line, the repeated alleluias and the reference to Christ as Emmanuel (the Romanized form of a Hebrew word meaning 'God is with us,' found in Isaiah 7-8 and quoted in Matthew 1:22-23). But the carol soon develops other themes dear to this writer.

Christ is repeatedly said to be reborn in every new human birth (verse 1, 'A million times a day the Christ is born'), a trope affirming the infinite worth of every human child. Equally, the natural world is praised and human spoliation of the earth is called to the (adult) singer's urgent attention. In verse 1 the divine birth is replicated in every 'blade of grass, a seed, a rose'; in verse 2 anguish is expressed in the cry, 'But oh, my friends, what have we done to life on planet earth?' while verse 3 calls for 'reverence for all people, and for every living thing,' and in verse 4 New Zealand (Aotearoa) is praised for its unspoiled 'green, the oceans clean' a claim increasingly challenged by modern environmentalists.

[BETHLEHEM] Originally written as a melody with guitar accompaniment, the setting is the work of Cecily Sheehy herself. The joyful text is supported by a skipping 3/4 rhythm spiced with time-shortened bars for the alleluias. In the rises and falls of the melody, experienced carol singers will hear echoes of other Christmas tunes, PUER NOBIS ('Unto us a boy is born, / King of all creation,' and IN DULCI JUBILO ('Good Christians all rejoice and sing'). The harmony is grounded in the celebratory key of D major, with a mid-point shift into the dominant key of A major.

A great and mighty wonder W639
Metre: 7.6.7.6 D

The text is a fresh translation by **Colin Gibson** of an ancient Christmas hymn, 'Mega Kai Paradoxon Thauma,' sung in the services of the Greek Orthodox Church since the eighth century and attributed to **Germanus of Constantinople** (c.645-740). It was first translated into English by John Mason Neale (1818-1866), who published his version in his *Hymns of the Eastern Church* (1862).

The words draw heavily on Luke 1 and 2 for their references to Jesus' birth to a virgin mother in a manger at Bethlehem and the song of the angels heard by shepherds. The first two lines of the chorus quote Luke 2:14. For Jesus as the Word (verse 2) and the triumph of light over darkness (verse 5) see John 1:1-14. The imagery of verse 3 is derived from Psalm 98. The breaking of idols (verse 5, line 1) echoes Ezekiel 6:4, but it also alludes to the eighth-century controversy in the Eastern Orthodox Church over the veneration of icons.

MIRACULUM MAGNUM (Latin=great wonder) This hymn tune was one of two composed in 1964 by **Geoffrey Butcher** for a new folk mass. At the time Butcher was a student at the General Theological Seminary, New York, and with three fellow students wrote *The Rejoice Mass*, which was performed in St Peter's Episcopal Church, New York, because the Dean of the Seminary thought its folk idiom inappropriate for the Seminary's chapel. The mass containing Butcher's hymn was recorded, issued on disc and published in the same year. The tune was later included in a collection of hymns in Spanish, *Albricias*, published by the National Hispanic Office of the Episcopal Church in 1987. There it was named RIO GRANDE, since its composer was working in the diocese of Rio Grande at the time. Here it is named after the Latin version of the first line of Germanus' hymn, and has been freshly arranged by **Guy Jansen** for its inclusion in the New Zealand supplement to *With One Voice* (1982). Another well-known musical setting for the text of this hymn is the 1609 four-part arrangement by Michael Praetorius (1571-1621) of the melody 'Es Ist Ein Ros,' written by an unknown earlier German composer.

A pinch of salt H1
Metre: Irregular

The original title of this hymn was 'Salty Christians'; it was written in 2007 by **Colin Gibson** when his minister, the Reverend Stuart Grant, to whom it is dedicated, publicly rued the fact that he could not find a sufficiently salty hymn to go with his sermon on the text 'You are the salt of the earth' (Matthew 5:13). The endeavour was encouraged by frequent meals provided by a friend who was an excellent and experimental cook, as well as by male bewilderment at recipes which prescribed a 'pinch' of salt. The song first appeared in *Hope is our Song* (2009); the durability of its recipe is yet to be tested.

The theme of the text is the necessity for faith, hope and love in the world; but at the same time, with an eye on the over-zealous, the writer warns against too much of these good things. The metaphor of cookery ingredients is worked out in detail throughout the text, from 'tasteless stew' to the 'baking / making' of Christ's kingdom.

Verse 1 includes Jesus' charge to his disciples to be both salt and light in the world (Matthew 5:13-14). Verse 2, emphasising a 'drop' of hope, opens up the Pauline theme of faith, hope and love as abiding and necessary virtues (1 Corinthians 13). But it warns against excessive hope in terms of the pillar of salt Lot's wife was turned into when she chose to look back at the city of Sodom from which her husband had taken her (Genesis 6:19). Verse 3, focusing on a 'grain' of faith, describes the effects of any excess in terms of a sea of brine (the Dead Sea) or the Bonneville salt flats of western Utah, the scene of many attempts on world speed records. Verse four reiterates the need for just a 'pinch' of salt, a 'drop' of hope, a 'grain' of faith and a 'touch' of love to bring about Christ's kingdom in the making.

SAL (Latin=salt) The author's own perky tune to which these words are set is named after the item which inspired its creation. Set in F major, the melody takes brief excursions into B flat and C major before recovering its senses and closing in F.

A stranger met by chance H2
Metre: 10.10.10 D

This hymn text, suitable as a communion hymn or for general use, was written in 1997 by **Marnie Barrell**. It was first published with the present setting in *Hope is our Song* (2009); it is also on the *Oremus* website.

Although it is based on the Emmaus Road encounter between the risen Christ and two of his disciples (Luke 24:13-35) and follows the threefold structure of the biblical original closely, the hymn turns this historic event into a contemporary experience, as 'Christ the Lord…walks with us on our Emmaus Road' (verse 1). Verse 2 connects modern congregations gathered to celebrate communion ('Companions at the table, faithful friends') with the original meal at which Cleopas and his unnamed companion recognized Jesus as he 'took the bread and blessed and broke it and gave it to them.' The third verse focuses on the disciples' excited return to Jerusalem to report the news of Jesus' resurrection. But it also universalizes the historical event as the impulse to proclaim the good news to the contemporary world. The final line alludes to Christ's commission to his disciples, Mark 16:15-16 and Matthew 28:19-20.

EMMAUS ROAD The tune name refers to the biblical story on which the hymn text is based. In this setting, written by **Colin Gibson** in 2002, the melodic line is imitated and 'caught up with' by the bass line in a way that suggests the meeting as it is recorded by Luke. The original music chosen for this hymn was **William Henry Monk**'s UNDE ET

MEMORES ('And now, O Father, mindful of the love').

A Wedding Song *facing A25*

This is an extract from a much longer poem originally published in 1989 in *Zealandia*, a tabloid newspaper brought out by the Catholic Bishop of Auckland. The full text was later included in the collection known as *Aotearoa Psalms: Prayers of a New People*, published by Pleroma Christian Supplies, Otane: 2004. It was written by the distinguished New Zealand novelist, children's writer, poet and Catholic commentator **Joy Cowley**.

The poet boldly begins by melding the opening statement in Genesis, 'In the beginning, God…' with 1 John 4:7-8, 'Love comes from God… God is love.' In the following lines she develops a mythic narrative of how Love, 'being the Creator,' fashions a creature in its own image, a Beloved other with which it plans to bring into being 'an eternity of loving.' But in order to do so through such a being 'bound by space and time in another dimension' Love divides the creature in half and sets the halves apart on the earth. Knowing their incompleteness, the two halves 'roam the earth, looking for each other'… seeking 'to become one again.'

Readers of the Greek philosopher Plato's *Symposium*, written c.385-70 BCE, will recognize that this New Zealand Catholic poet has adapted the fable accounting for the nature of human love put into the mouth of the comic dramatist Aristophanes – love is the irresistible impulse driving two halves separated by a divine being to fuse together to discover 'the wholeness of Love within themselves' (cf. Luke 16:18, 'they shall become one flesh').

In this way, the poet fuses biblical and classical thought in a way that ancient writers within both traditions would have found quite familiar.

A'ou manatu ifo nei *W647*
Metre: 8.8.8.8 and refrain

This text is a translation into the Samoan language of **Isaac Watts'** famous hymn 'When I survey the wondrous cross.' The translator's name is unknown, as is the date, but it is probably the work of an English missionary. Under John Williams, the London Missionary Society began evangelising in 1830, though a Wesleyan mission team had previously arrived in 1828 to find some Samoans already converted to the new faith through the teaching of Europeans already present on the island. In 1834 the Society is known to have brought in hymnbooks in the Samoan language, printed in the Society Islands. Whatever its origin, the hymn is now perceived to be a traditional Samoan version of Watts' famous original. Cf. the entry for **Ka tirohia te ripeka** W646.

LEULUMOEGA FOU This vigorous tune, intended for unaccompanied singing, was composed about 1950 among the boys of the Leulumoega Fou High School, Western Samoa (now the Leulumoega Fou College and University). The College is one of the six operated by the Congregational Christian Church of Samoa.

Abba, Matua, we ask you (Song of Letters) *H3*
Metre: 8.7.8.7.8.7.7

This Advent or invocatory hymn was written in 2007 by Anglican vicar **Timothy Hurd** for his All Saints, Dunedin, congregation and first published in *Hope is our Song* (2009).

The text takes the unusual form of an acrostic poem* in which the first letter of each line of the poem spells out a word or name or letter pattern of some significance. As the title of the hymn, 'Song of Letters,' indicates, the first letter of each line follows in descending order the first 21 letters of the alphabet: the whole ingenious and unified construction of the hymn might be thought of as an answer to the dislocation of modern life referred to in verse 2 ('our dislocated voices').

But the body of the text is also highly allusive, with frequent echoes of the Lord's Prayer, other biblical passages and other hymns, notably Charles Wesley's Advent hymn, 'Come, thou long expected Jesus,' with which it shares several key words as well as its basic metrical pattern. Verse 1 opens with a Hebrew-Māori version of 'our Father' (literally, 'father-parent'); verse 2 echoes the Lord's Prayer ('hallowed be thy name') and references the feeding of the five thousand (Matthew 14:13-21, Mark 6:30-44, Luke 9:10-17, John 8: 1-14). For verse 3 see Ephesians 1:7-9, Augustine, *Confessions*, Book 1 ('our hearts are restless until they find their rest in thee'), and 1 Corinthians 13:12 ('Then I will know fully just as I also have been fully known').

ACROSTIC The tune name acknowledges the poetic form of the hymn text. The setting was written in 2008 by **Marnie Barrell** for *Hope is our Song*. The original musical setting chosen by the author was DIVINUM MYSTERIUM also known as CORDE NATUS, one of the most beautiful of the plainsong tunes, with a probable origin in the Byzantine Church and frequently matched with 'Of the Father's love begotten,' another possible source for some of the words and ideas in this richly allusive text. Marnie Barrell's melody itself imitates the phrasing and step movement of such a plainsong melody.

> *The writer notes that his acrostic hymn follows 'an ancient pattern, using (as does Psalm 119) the letters of the alphabet to give shape to thought and song.'

Above the peaks the angels sing C2
Metre: 8.8.8.8.8.4.4

This summer Christmas carol was written by **Colin Gibson** in 1994 to celebrate the birth of his second English-born grandchild, Ronan Jack, to his daughter Philippa and her husband Desmond Shanahan. The manuscript carries a dedication to Desmond. Although the carol was not published until 1996 in *Carol our Christmas*, it had already received a number of public performances, notably by the City of Dunedin Choir in the Dunedin Town Hall.

The narrative recasts the biblical account of Christ's nativity in New Zealand terms. The angels sing above the snow-clad mountain peaks of the Southern Alps; the shepherds become New Zealand sheep musterers looking to find a small country town rather than a Palestinian village (verse 1). In verse 2 the imminent birth of Christ is signalled by the appearance of two New Zealand trees which flower red in summer, the forest rata and the coast-loving pohutukawa (also known as the New Zealand Christmas tree), while golden sands and sea-shells whitening in the strong sunlight signify the beaches thronged with holiday-makers over the Christmas season, which in this country stand in for the arid sands of a Middle Eastern desert. Verse 3 translates the journey of the Magi into the familiar return home of many New Zealanders rejoining their families for the Christmas celebrations. They are led not by a single star (as in Matthew 2:9), but by the distinctive southern hemisphere constellation the Southern Cross, headed by two stars known appropriately as the Pointers. In the final verse the singers join the ancient traditions of Christianity, and 'take the road' (cf. the Way) to discover the 'summer Child' born in their hearts and minds.

MARYLANDS The tune name refers to the East London district of Maryland, in which the composer's English family were living at the time. The melodic line is constructed to imitate the geographic movement of the first verse of the text, which takes the singers to the Alpine heights, then down to a small country town, only to climb expectantly once more. The harmonic structure rests on a sustained F tonic bass note, until the final bars rapidly modulate 'upwards' to close in a joyful D major chord.

Advent I *facing C48*

This is the first of a cycle of three poems written in 1995 by **Shirley Murray** to a commission by **Peter Godfrey** and his Kāpiti Choir. Written for an unaccompanied SATB choir, with solos in the second text for high soprano and bass, it was set by the New Zealand composer **Christopher Marshall** and first performed by the Dunedin Southern Consort of Voices directed by Jack Spiers in May 1996. A further performance followed in December 2007, given by the choir of St Paul's Anglican Cathedral, Dunedin, under the direction of David Burchell. The full score was published in 1995 by Vaia'ata Print, Dunedin; a copy is held by the National Library of New Zealand.

This poem introduces themes found elsewhere in Murray's writing: the God / Christ potential in every new human birth (see H49), and the urgent need for peace and an end to conflict (see F75 and H28). Her constant advocacy for women is lightly touched on in verse 2, lines 3-4: 'What daughter or what son / may be the coming One?' The writing also shows her gift for striking imagery, as in verse 3, lines 2-3, 'in creation's womb / the Word has made a home,' a reworking of John 1:14.

In light of verse 3, lines 5-6, 'the seed for summer bloom / within the earth is breaking [open],' it may be necessary to explain that in New Zealand the season of Advent coincides with the height of the summer season.

Advent Triptych III *facing C35*

See above for the general context of this poem by **Shirley Murray**, set to music by **Christopher Marshall** in 1995.

As its refrain taken directly from John 1:5 shows, this text concentrates on one dominant image of light, an obvious connection with the fierce light typically flooding this country in summer. But Murray's concerns for social justice (in verse 2) and peace (verse 3) also surface, as does her understanding of the life of Christ as challenging the self-satisfied attitudes of her countrymen and women in a 'favoured country' (verses 1 and 3). New Zealand's current freedom from the Covid pandemic currently raging through the world beyond its shores might also be taken as more recent evidence of such favour.

Agaaga Tapu *W649*
Metre: 9.6.8.6 and refrain

While this invocation to the Holy Spirit, popular among Niuean faith communities in New Zealand as well as on the Pacific island of Niue, is described as 'traditional'; neither its authorship nor date of writing has been established. However, its melodic and harmonic structure as well as its catechistic text suggest that it is a local version of an early missionary song, brought by London Missionary Society workers, who reached Niue in 1856 (see especially verse 2, 'convert our stubborn hearts').

The theme of the hymn is evangelical: the singers are to acknowledge their sinfulness (verses 2-3) and pray for conversion to belief in the Christian Holy Spirit as against the spirits of older pagan belief. The ideas in the text are biblical in origin: for the Spirit's gift of a new birth (verse 1) see John 3:3, for the Holy Spirit as 'comforter' (refrain) see John 14:26, for the conversion of 'stubborn hearts' see Ezekiel 36:26, and the prayer for loving unity echoes Jesus' famous prayer 'that they may be one' (John 17:22).

AGAAGA TAPU (Niuean=Holy Spirit). The melody was transcribed by **Guy Jansen** from congregational singing. Whatever its origin, it now has a thoroughly Western musical shape, harmony and rhythm.

All over creation *C3*
Metre: 6.5.9.6.5.12

Originally titled 'Peace Carol II,' this carol, written in 1995 by **Shirley Murray,** came into being in the following circumstances: 'The tune ELIZABETH was sent to me [Shirley Murray] by Jillian Bray. Its gentle movement suggested a peace carol, and the last line of the music had a wistful note which I have tried to capture in the words of the first and last verses. I was writing this when our first granddaughter, coincidentally named Elizabeth, was born.'

The idea of worldwide peace, personified as a mother figure kissing the earth, nursing creation and spreading her wings, frames the whole text a little wistfully, but the tone of the carol is generally joyful and upbeat ('This child will bring freedom' / this child will release wellsprings of compassion'). Only in verse 3 – 'this Christ will confront us / when, children no more, / we plunder our planet, crying from want and war' – does the writer briefly raise issues of environmental damage, poverty and war. The descriptive formula which structures the two middle verses, 'This child will...' is derived from the Song of Simeon, 'Behold, this child is set for the fall and rising of many in Israel' (Luke 2:34).

ELIZABETH Originally named for the mother of John the Baptist by its composer **Jillian Bray**, this melody, written in 1995, has the feel of a joyful jig with its 9/8 time signature and generally cheerful E major tonality. But there are harmonic excursions into B major and the flattened chords in the second last bar give rise to the 'wistful' feeling Shirley Murray responded to. There is another setting by Canadian composer **Ron Klusmeier** (Klusmeier 37).

All poor men and humble W641
Metre: 6.6.8 D

Although usually described as a traditional Welsh carol, it is more accurate to say that this is a carol by an unknown Welsh writer. The English version of the carol now in common use is by **Katharine Emily Roberts** (1877-1962), and was made for the *Oxford Book of Carols* (1928). It was described there as a 'free' translation and it is; as one scholar has said, there is almost no point of direct correspondence between the Welsh and English words other than the general theme of welcoming the Christ Child. However, Roberts' words have become familiar, largely through their association with the beautiful melody of the original Welsh carol. There have been various unsuccessful attempts to make the text less gender-exclusive.

OLWEN There is no evidence of authorship or publication of this melody before 1910, when this tune was recorded from the singing of a Mr Jones of Croeswian, Caerwys, Flintshire, and printed in the *Journal of the Welsh Folk Song Society*. It was harmonized by **Caradog Roberts** for the *Welsh Congregational Hymnal* (1921), and that version was taken over for the *Oxford Book of Carols* (1928) and is used in *With One Voice*. The tune name is still unexplained, and seems to have been given to Roberts' elaborate chorale-like setting in the *Welsh Methodist Hymnbook* in 1929. Welsh hymnbooks continue to use the name O DEUED POB CRISTION, taken from the first line of the words accompanying the tune.

All who would see God's greatness
C4 (i) and (ii)
Metre: 7.6.8.7.8.8

Written by **Marnie Barrell** in about 1994, this Nativity hymn was first published in *Carol our Christmas* (1996). The writer says that her imagination was first prompted by hearing Herbert Howells' setting of G. K. Chesterton's poem 'Here is the little door' [The text begins, 'Here is the little door, lift up the latch, oh lift!…Bend low about his head, for each he has a gift']. She refers to 'The mental picture of having to approach through a small opening and get down as low as possible to see what God has done. And that the smallness, poverty and nakedness of the Little Lord is all God has to say about power, wealth, etc.…I liked the meditative tone of it, and the sharpness of words like "violence" or "naked" which usually belong to quite different contexts. I'm one who enjoys the contrast of hushed, sombre and thought-provoking hymns with the manic jolliness of most Christmas favourites…And I tried to imitate the way the beloved carols place us in the scene in a vivid, sensory way, ox and ass and all, while still voicing the theological meanings – "Here in our hands for holding is Love that upholds all things."'

It is a compelling modern reworking of the ancient paradox implicit in the Christian belief that in the person of a helpless, naked baby born into a poor and powerless peasant family God, the creator of the universe and 'God of all,' dwelt among us. There are also many echoes in this hymn of the *Magnificat*, Mary's song prophesying the confusion of the rich, the downfall of the powerful of this world and the exaltation of the poor (Luke 1:47-55).

The verses successively address four attributes of God: God's greatness made small, God's richness 'made so poor,' God's power, subjected to violence and imprisonment, and God's love and glory present even among the singers. In verse 1, 'bend down' (an echo of the Chesterton poem) suggests both the traditional gesture of obeisance to a ruler and the need to bend to see the tiny, hidden child (a reminder of the many religious paintings which represent Jesus as small and laid below the watchers' eye level). Verse 2 ends with a recollection of Charles Wesley's hymn 'This, this is the God we adore,' with its extravagant praise of God's love and power [which] 'neither knows measure nor end.' Verse 3 reminds its singers of both Herod's attempt to destroy the child at birth (Matthew 2:16-18) and Christ's peaceful surrender to those coming to arrest him in the garden of Gethsemane (Matthew 26:51-54) followed by his submission 'to all our violence.' Verse 4 suggests the ritual of communion in which the elements representing Christ are placed, 'here in our hands for holding.' It introduces another paradox, of song heard in 'the holy silence,' a reference to the song of the angels (Luke 2:13-14) and to the familiar Christmas hymn, 'O little town of Bethlehem,' which the author describes as 'a fairly direct source.'

OBEISANCE The tune name is derived from the second line of the hymn, 'draw near, bend down.' This piano setting was written in 1995 by **Ian Render** for *Carol our Christmas*. An alternative arrangement for organ by **Jillian Bray** was written at the same time; all three composers, Render, Bray and Gibson (see ASHBURTON), were members of the editorial committee engaged in preparing the hymnal.

ASHBURTON The tune name is derived from the South Canterbury town where the Methodist minister Gordon Abernethy and his wife Anne, to whom the 1995 piano setting by **Colin Gibson** is dedicated, were living at the time. Both Render and Gibson place the meditative text in a predominantly minor setting (D minor and A minor respectively), though Gibson closes with a D major cadence). In interestingly different ways their melodies and harmonies reflect the idea of height descending to lowness, using pitch as the musical equivalent to convey the concept of God's greatness brought 'down' from heaven and made so small and humble.

All will be well A2
Metre: 5.5.5.5

This four-part round, written in 1968 and published by **Betty Wendelborn** in her privately printed collection *Sing Green; Songs of the Mystics. Words and Music [by] Betty Wendelborn*, Auckland (1988), takes as its text a saying by the 14th century English mystic **Julian of Norwich** (1342-1416), 'All shall be well, all shall be well, and all manner of thing shall be well.' It appeared in her *Sixteen Revelations of Divine Love* (long version), Chapter 27, Revelation 1, written 20 years after she experienced a series of visions in May 1373. Julian claimed that these words were spoken to her by God: they perfectly express her profound theology of hope.

JULIAN The melody, by **Betty Wendelborn,** is named after Julian of Norwich. The words may be sung as a response or declaration of faith; or sung with the voices entering as marked for as many repetitions as required.

All will be well H4
Metre: 4.5.4.5.4.5.4.5

This hymn was written by Christchurch-based **Bill Wallace** shortly before its publication in his American collection *The Mystery Telling: Hymns and Songs for the New Millennium by William L. Wallace* (New York: Selah, 2001). It reached New Zealand congregations in *Hope is our Song* (2009).

The text is based on a saying by the 14th century English mystic **Julian of Norwich** (1342-1416), 'All shall be well, all shall be well, and all manner of thing shall be well.' It appeared in her *Sixteen Revelations of Divine Love* (long version), Chapter 27, Revelation 1, written twenty years after she experienced a series of visions in May 1373. Julian claimed that these words were spoken to her by God: they perfectly express her profound theology of hope. Another setting of the same words by **Betty Wendelborn** will be found in **A2**.

In this hymn Julian is twice quoted, but the following poetic text defining and describing her vision of wellbeing is constructed from original patterns of words and images: in verse 1, *peace*, as a profound, deep-water dream [note the repetition of 'deep' in this text], *light*, as a primary attribute of divinity, *love*, as a healing stream (see Ezekiel 47). In verse 2, paradox dominates: of pain yielding delight, grief yielding joyful songs, wounds nurturing light. In verse 3 lists of nouns ('time, time, moment, day') and verbs (dance, discern, know') form a patterned structure. At the close of the third verse the Julian quotation is displaced by the pictorial image of a smiling God tenderly holding the believer – perhaps derived from a Buddhist sculptural pose, though the pair of lovers pictured in the Song of Solomon 2:6 may equally be a visual source.

JULIAN The tune name is that of the mystic whose words are quoted in the text. The music was composed by Bill Wallace's fellow Christchurch musician **Alison Carey**. The harmonies remain grounded throughout in a reassuring D major tonality.

Alleluia Aotearoa! *A1*

This is the first of seven short acclamations published in Alleluia Aotearoa (1993), written in 1992-3 by members of the editorial board of the New Zealand Hymnbook Trust at the prompting of the Chairman of the Board, John Murray, as a way to celebrate and affirm the title of the new hymnbook.

'Alleluia' is a Hebrew term meaning 'give praise to Jahweh.' Aotearoa is a Māori term meaning 'long white cloud' and has been taken into common use as the Māori name for New Zealand, with which title it is now often linked. The reference is said to be to the first appearance of the islands of New Zealand as canoes approached them from the Pacific Ocean. The whole phrase means, 'Let the people of Aotearoa/New Zealand give praise to God.'

This setting is by **Shirley Murray**, and is the only musical composition by this prolific hymn text writer in the books published by the Trust.

Alleluia Aotearoa! *A13*

See the entry for **Alleluia Aotearoa!** *A1.*

This unison setting in A major is by Murray's close friend Jillian Bray. The joyfully syncopated, off-beat melody plays against a steady bass line pattern of stressed crochets and quavers, and the underlying harmonic structure modulates through a circle of keys to conclude as it began. An acclamation only for confident, relaxed singers.

Alleluia Aotearoa! *A34*

See the entry for **Alleluia Aotearoa!** *A1.*

This four-part vocal setting in E flat is by **Colin Gibson**; it may be repeated as often as the singers wish.

Alleluia Aotearoa! *A53*

See the entry for **Alleluia Aotearoa!** *A1.*

This two-part setting in F major is by **Colin Gibson**; it is intended to reflect a Pacific style of melody and should not be sung too quickly.

Alleluia Aotearoa! *A92*

See the entry for **Alleluia Aotearoa!** *A1.*

This exuberant setting for unison voices supported by four-part harmony in the celebratory key of D major is by **Colin Daley**, an equally accomplished musician and typesetter for all the New Zealand Hymn Book Trust publications. Its unusual 7/8 time signature is perfectly suited to the text and will not be found difficult for congregations willing to swing with it. It is one of Daley's two compositions published by the Trust.

Alleluia Aotearoa! *A121*

See the entry for **Alleluia Aotearoa!** *A1.*

Richly harmonised, this accompanied setting for unison voices is by **Guy Jansen.** Beginning in E minor it reaches E major mid-way, then repeats the harmonic pattern, closing on an E major chord which leaves the singers with the sense of an open ending, an invitation to repeat an endless alleluia.

Alleluia Aotearoa! *A131*

See the entry for **Alleluia Aotearoa!** *A1.*

This accompanied setting for unison voices was written by **Ian Render**. An attractive feature of the musical fabric is the running melodic line shared between the alto and tenor, which might be played on an accompanying instrument above the more measured chords supporting the melody. The harmonic centre is always secure on the F major tonic chord, but there is rich harmonic movement circling round it.

Alleluia Aotearoa! *A163*

See the entry for **Alleluia Aotearoa!** *A1.*

The three-part vocal setting in G major is by **Cecily Sheehy**; the voices begin by imitating each other but even within a very small scale each soon develops its own identity and shape, symbolizing individual singers coming together in a joyful celebration.

Alleluia, alleluia *W674 (i)*
Metre: 4.4.4.4

This simple Alleluia was created in the 20th century within Chevetogne Abbey, also known as the Monastery of the Holy Cross, a Roman Catholic Benedictine monastery dedicated to Christian unity located in the Belgian village of Chevetogne. Its inspiration is the ancient plainchant melodies of the medieval Roman Catholic Church.

In its original form – intended for unaccompanied male voices – the melody is set a sixth lower, in the key of G minor. The version in *With One Voice* (1982) may be sung in any convenient key and is intended for congregational use. It may be supported by an instrument, but unaccompanied song is its truest expression.

Alleluia, alleluia, give thanks to the risen Lord (Alleluia No 1) *W674 (ii)*
Metre: 8.8 and refrain

This hymn was written by **Donald Fishel** in the summer of 1971, at a time when the writer was studying the flute at the University of Michigan School of Music and, as a member of the Word of God community in Ann Arbor, Michigan, was experiencing the charismatic revival which swept the United States at that time. It was first published in the *New Life Songbook* (1972) and record album, and soon became widely popular.

The text is a mosaic of biblical quotations: sources identified include Psalm 35:28, Psalm 96:2-3, Matthew 28:19, Luke 1:46-7, Romans 6:4, 8, 1 Corinthians 15:3, 2 Corinthians 5:17, Galatians 2:20, Ephesians 1:10, 20-22, and Colossians 1:15-17. Fishel describes the hymn as having been written 'in a time of prayer,' and says that he included verse 3 in memory of his own baptism in 1970. The original words of verse 4, 'God has proclaimed the just reward, / Life for all men, / Alleluia,' have been omitted in a number of hymnals, or altered as they have been for *With One Voice* (1982). The author himself now prefers 'God has proclaimed his gracious gift.'

ALLELUIA NO 1 This setting was so-named by the composer, Donald Fishel, because it was the first hymn he had ever written. It has become known as 'Jesus is Lord of all the earth.' The original music published in the *New Life Songbook* (1972) has since undergone several arrangements; the one used in *With One Voice* is by New Zealand musician **Jillian Bray**.

See the entry for **Alleluia Aotearoa!** *A1.*

This unison vocal setting in A major is by **Jillian Bray**; syncopation enlivens the melody and the composer uses a powerful bass line to drive the music towards D major, then reset it to A major.

Alleluia, Jesus, saviour *W674 (iii)*
Metre: 8.8.8.7

This song of adoration was first published in *Sound of Living Waters: Songs of Renewal*, edited by Betty Pulkingham and Jeanne Harper (London: Hodder and Stoughton, 1974), where it is described as the work of an anonymous writer, probably modern

American, since the copyright is held by Maranatha! Music, a United States publisher of praise song material. It is directed to be sung 'With quiet adoration.' The original text consists of 6 verses, each repeated 8 times over and consisting of a simple phrase: 'Alleluia,' 'How I love Him,' 'Blessed Jesus,' 'My Redeemer,' 'Jesus is Lord,' 'Alleluia.' The edited text published in *With One Voice* (1982) is worked by **Colin Gibson**, and was written in 1980.

[ALLELUIA] The melody is named after the word used as the first and last verse of the original. It appears in an arrangement by **Betty Pulkingham** published in *Sound of Living Waters*, to which New Zealand musician **Guy Jansen** has added a descant. Confusingly, in the melody-only edition of *With One Voice*, the descant is referred to but not printed.

Alofa mai ia, afio mai *A3*
Metre: 9.8.9.8 and refrain

The probable original of this Samoan hymn text is a hymn of invocation to the Holy Spirit by Methodist preacher and scholar **Thomas Powell** (1791-1850). The Samoan text of the hymn is reprinted from *O Pese ma Viiga Le Atua*, the hymnal of the Congregational Christian Church of Samoa (1894 and subsequent editions). The translation from English into Samoan is by an unknown writer, probably an early missionary.

Verse 1 recalls the ancient (9th century) hymn text by Rabanus Maurus, *Veni creator spiritus*. For verses 2-3 see Romans 8:26-27; verse 4 references John 14:25-27.

[SAVIOUR'S NAME] Although it is not given a title in *Alleluia Aotearoa*, the tune is usually called SAVIOUR'S NAME. It was composed by **William Henry Rudd** (1869-1963) and is Rudd's setting of a hugely popular gospel song by Frederick Whitfield (1829-1904), 'There is a name I love to hear' (also known as 'O how I love Jesus'). Whitfield was the author of a number of hymns collected in his *Sacred Poems and Prose* (1861) and *The Christian Casket* (1864). Julian's *Dictionary of Hymnology* (1892) says that the hymn with its setting by Rudd was published in 1855 'in hymn-sheets and leaflets in various languages... and set to special music.' Rudd's setting is printed in many hymnals, from *Redemption Songs* (1889) to *Complete Mission Praise* (1999), and a choral performance of the hymn was recorded by the Southern Singers of the Salvation Army in 1967. The arrangement printed in *Alleluia Aotearoa* is attributed to Samoan musician **Va'alotu Solofa**.

Always there's a carol *H6*
Metre: 6.5.6.5.6.5 and refrain

This cheerful Christmas carol was written in November 2001 by **Shirley Murray**, 'for our U.S.A friends, to offer a sense of hopeful cheer for Christmas 2001.' Its original title was 'Carol for a Dark Night,' explained as the work of a New Zealand writer for whom Christmas is a summertime experience sent to a country where Christmas takes place in winter. It was first published in 2003 in the author's American collection, *Faith makes the Song*, then in *Hope is our Song* (2009).

The song acknowledges traditional associations with the festival – carols, candles and the Christ-child, and refers to the biblical account of the 'Christmas star' (Matthew 2:9) and the angelic chorus (Luke 2:13-14). But it also expresses themes important to this writer: the enfolding presence of God 'where we are' (verse 2), peace 'countering the strife,' and concern for deprived children 'crying for a life' (verse 3).

BALLYHERKIN The Irish-jig style setting by **Colin Gibson**, written in 2001, was a response to a cheerful request from the author for music for 'a little diversion,' received after he had returned to New Zealand following a stay with his daughter at Ballyherkin, the name of her home in southern Ireland. The optional descant is particularly suitable for a flute or violin. Canadian composer **Ron Klusmeier** (Klusmeier 14) has written an alternative setting.

And did you see him, little star *A4, C5, W644*
Metre: 8.4.8.4 D

The circumstances of the writing in 1973 of this Christmas song by Wellington poet **Helen Clyde** are described by the editor of the December 2010 *Messenger* of St John's in the City, the Presbyterian church where she was for many years a member: 'Helen Clyde lived for many years in Kelburn Parade, above the University. Late one night, just prior to Christmas, Helen Clyde looked out of one of her windows towards the Orongorongos [a range of hills east of Wellington and across the harbour]. It was a perfect Wellington night. A particularly bright star caught her attention. As she looked at the star Helen Clyde wondered. She wondered if this was the very star that shone down on the manger and led the three Wise Men to Jesus. A little later on, Helen Clyde wrote a poem about that night.' The poem remained unpublished until it was set by the composer **Colin Gibson** in 1972, and included in his collection of hymns and carols, *Singing Love* (1988), under the title of 'Children's Christmas Hymn,' as well as the New Zealand supplement in *With One Voice* (1982), *Alleluia Aotearoa* (1993) and *Carol our Christmas* (1996).

STARSIGHT The setting is named after the implication of the first line of the poem. It was written by **Colin Gibson** in 1972 as a simple unison melody in C major with piano accompaniment. The carol is recorded in a performance by the Kiwikids under the direction of Radha Wardrop on the CD *Carol our Christmas: Contemporary New Zealand Carols* (1996).

And Jesus said *F1*
Metre: 8.8.8.8.8

This hymn was written in 1998 by **Shirley Murray** to send to a terminally-ill friend in Canada. She describes it as 'An interpretation of the first verses of John 14.' It was first published in *Faith Forever Singing* (2000), then in Murray's American collection, *Faith Makes the Song* (2003).

The theme of the hymn, powerfully reiterated in all three verses, appears in the first line, 'And Jesus said, don't be afraid' (cf. John 14:1, 'Let not your heart be troubled, believe in God, believe also in me'). The principal direct borrowing from John appears in the final verse in the order John 14:6 ('I am the way, and the truth, and the life'); and 2-3 ('In my Father's house are many rooms…I go to prepare a place for you').

The positive tone of the hymn is largely created through the strong verbs that structure each verse: 'I've come…I know…I hear,….I'll heal…I am…You have.' But not to be missed are the moving contrasts between high terms such as 'the deep' (cf. Genesis 1:1 and Psalm 42:7) and familiar ones, such as 'God's home.'

LACE This tune was written in the same year as the text (1998) by **Jillian Bray,** who says of her choice of name, 'One may think "Lace" an odd title for a hymn tune, but the idea evoked for me something crafted – predominantly of the past – beautiful – having a "folk" culture – created.' Bray's music follows the text attentively and flexibly, moving through some time signature and key changes (notably into A flat in bar 4). The second half of the hymn setting engages in a falling movement, as if towards sleep; this is never completed with a return to the tonic chord, but comes to rest on a dominant chord – as if prepared for a fresh beginning. In *Faith Makes the Song* the words are associated with a tune by American composer Donald Hustad named DAISY HILL.

Arahina, e Ihowa *W661*
Metre: 8.7.8.7.4.7 extended

This is a translation by an unknown writer into Māori of the first two verses of the Welsh hymn popularly known by its first line as 'Guide me, O thou great Jehovah,' though the Welsh actually means, 'Lord, lead me through the wilderness.' The original 5-stanza hymn was published by the Welsh Methodist preacher-poet **William Williams** in his *Hallelujah* (Bristol 1744/5), with the heading 'Strength to pass through the

Wilderness.' The first translation into English (of stanzas 1, 3 and 5 only) was printed in the Reverend Peter Williams' *Hymns on Various Subjects* (1771) and the first complete English translation of the text as we know it now appeared as an undated leaflet (?1771/2), titled *A Favourite Hymn sung by the Countess of Huntingdon's Young Collegians* (that is, at the College at Trevecca, Wales, founded by the Countess in 1768 for six Methodist students expelled from an Oxford college, the first such institution to be established for the training of ministers of religion). The hymn quickly spread into Methodist use through George Whitfield's *Psalms and Hymns* (1773), became widely popular among all denominations and is now one of the most famous of all hymns in Welsh or English. It was probably brought to New Zealand by early Methodist missionaries.

CWM RHONDDA The tune name means the valley of the Rhondda river, a coal-mining area in South Wales. The composer first called it RHONDDA, but added CWM (valley) after discovering that another tune had been named after the place. The melody was written by **John Hughes** for a 1907 Baptist singing festival at Pontypridd, composed, so it is said, while Hughes was attending worship in Salem Baptist Chapel in LLantwit Fardre, Wales. Although it was immediately popular among the singers – by 1930 it had been sung at more than 5,000 such festivals – it is in few Welsh hymnals and was slow to enter mainstream English hymn books. It has been suggested by Alan Luff (*Welsh Hymns and their Tunes*, 1990) that it was resisted by editors for many years 'because of the tune's great vigour and what can be best be called its vulgar appeal – not necessarily a bad thing.' Despite such matters of musical taste, Māori congregations and their pākehā counterparts have long enjoyed its martial rhythm and the florid extension of the melody, vying in holding for as long as possible the pause in the third last bar.

As sisters, brothers, called by Christ (A Hymn for Church Meetings) H5
Metre: 8.6.8.6

This hymn text was written by **Jocelyn Marshall** in 1994 for the congregation of the Cathedral Church of St Peter's, Hamilton, and published in her collection of hymn texts, *An Occasional Faith* (1995), followed by *A Singing Faith* (1996), and *Hymns for All Seasons* (2007). It reached *Hope is our Song* in 2009. Although it is titled 'Synod Hymn' in her own hymnbooks, the author's note explains that it was 'Written for any church gathering – not just a synod – and dedicated to Bishop David Moxon [Bishop of the Cathedral Church of St Peter's from 1993-2005] whose ministry emphasises inclusiveness in the contemporary Church.'

The hymn is structured as a prayer for 'wisdom, grace, / respect for human worth,' 'charity,' courage and openness of mind. The theme of the unity of the community of Christ and respect for all others runs through this 6-verse hymn, imaged as an 'outstretched hand of fellowship' (verse 2), and membership of 'one family' (verse 5). The hymn also contains an appeal for the recognition of difference and openness of mind (verses 3-5).

ST PETER [also known as CHRIST CHURCH] is indicated as the suggested musical setting, following the writer's practice of naming well-known tunes in *Hymns Ancient & Modern*, revised edition (1950). This hymn tune was written by **Alexander Robert Reinagle** (1799-1877), organist of St Peter's Church in the East, Oxford, England, and first published in his *Psalm Tunes for Voice and Pianoforte* about 1836. In his *Companion to Together in Song* (2000), Dr D'Arcy Wood describes it as 'not great music, but a popular and useful tune.'

As the sun beats down (A Song in Times of Drought) F2
Metre: 10.7.10.7

Written as a reflection both on the harshness of dry conditions (natural or spiritual) that seem to have no end in sight, and about a God who provides hope in time of loss, this hymn was written in the late 1980s when the author, **Bill Bennett**, was vicar of Dannevirke in rural southern Hawke's Bay. It was first published in *Faith Forever Singing* (2000).

Bennett says, 'The 1990s and early years of the 21st century saw farmers in New Zealand and Australia having to cope with devastating droughts. But farmers have a philosophical approach to climate and weather events – a sense that nature will somehow bring balance and restoration to the created order. The rains that eventually fall following big dries become a parable of resurrection hope.' Bill Bennett believes that the dynamics of faith have starting points in the real and human experiences of the world around us. Thus faith is an affirmation that eventually the grass will be replenished by life-saving rain and stock will survive.

Verse 2, line 3, requires a comma after 'restores' to clarify the sense. Verse 3 alludes to John 6:35, 'Jesus said to them, "I am the bread of life."' In Verse 4, 'still blue' means remaining blue, that is with no sign of rain clouds. Verse 5 recalls God's promise never to again destroy the earth through flood (or, by implication, drought); see Genesis 9:8-17.

[IN TIMES OF DROUGHT] The setting, in D minor, is by the author. It moves into a major key as the text refers to hope and restoration. The melody follows the thought closely, too, descending as 'the sun beats down' and turning upwards to express hope and faith.

As the wind-song through the trees
H7
Metre: 7.7.9.7.7.9.6.5.9.7.7.9

A hymn text written by **Shirley Murray** in 2004 in response to 'an engaging tune sent to me without a theme by composer friend Swee Hong Lim of Singapore.' The text and its melody were first published in *Touch the Earth Lightly* (2008), then in *Hope is our Song* (2009).

The hymn is constructed from an imaginative succession of images, both biblical and drawn from the natural world, exploiting the triple senses of the Hebrew word *ruach*=wind, breath and spirit. Verse 1 interfuses these senses with the image of 'the wind-song in the trees' and 'the stirring of the breeze,' adding two more instances to the more than 80 biblical passages in which the Spirit is described as wind. In lines 3-4 John Wesley's conversion experience of 'the heart made strangely warm' (fire is another constant symbol of the Holy Spirit) is matched with Elijah's experience of 'the voice within the storm' (1 Kings 19:9-18). Lines 7-8 recall Jesus' account of the uncontrollable wind of the Spirit (John 3:8). Acts 1:8 refers to the 'power' of the Holy Spirit (line 9), and Acts 2 records the 'tongues as of fire' (line 10) that rested on each of the disciples at Pentecost. Verse 2 recalls the Genesis flood story (Genesis 9:12-17) and echoes Revelation 21:5, 'Behold I make all things new.' In lines 9-11 the gifts of the Spirit (1 Corinthians 12:7-11), Jesus' parable of the yeast (Matthew 13:33) and the wedding at Cana (John 2:1-11) are all referred to.

WAIRUA TAPU (Māori=Holy Spirit) This tune name for music associated with a text characterising the nature and work of the Holy Spirit was suggested by the author at the composer's request. The music was sent to Shirley Murray, by her friend Singaporean composer **Swee Hong Lim**; she says of it, 'Its lyricism gave me a feeling of the movement of the Spirit, both gentle and powerful.' The A-B-A form of the melody contributes to this doubleness; the middle section expresses the power of the Spirit with its sudden lift into E minor, while the opening and closing sections of the melody, set in G minor, with their limited pitch range and rising-falling back motif suggest a gentler aspect of the Holy Spirit. There are interesting likenesses between this setting and another by Canadian composer **Ron Klusmeier** (Klusmeier 38) though each is quite independent of the other.

As we walk along beside you *F3*
Metre: 8.8.8.11

This communion hymn text was written in 1981 by **Michael Perry**, then vicar of

Bitterne in Southampton, England. It was first published in *Hymns for Today's Church*, which he edited for the Jubilate group in 1982. When the text was set in 1981 by Norman L. Warren to his tune BURNING HEART, the composer prefaced the original text with two alleluias. These are gathered to form a fourth verse in the *Faith Forever Singing* version.

The text positions the singers as the anonymous disciples who encountered Jesus on the road to Emmaus (Luke 24:1-35, with particular verbal borrowings from verses 29-32 and 35). The author's own framing of the story appears in verse 1, line 2 ('we hear you speak of mercy') and verse 3, where the present-time act of communion ('we reach for you believing') and post-communion commission to proclamation ('we go to love and serve you') displace the original gospel version, which ends with the physical appearance of Jesus to the gathered disciples.

RECOGNITION The tune is named after the event described in Luke 24:31, 'And their eyes were opened and they recognized him.' Coincidentally, the music is by a New Zealand Anglican vicar, **Ian Render**, who set his English counterpart's words in 1998 for the committee preparing *Faith Forever Singing* (2000). The ideas in the text are closely imitated in the music, which has a relaxed, 'ambling' rhythmic movement suggesting a quiet walk together. The twice-repeated move in bars 1-4 from a minor key (E) to a major one (G) suggests the displacement of doubt and sadness by the joyful and positive act of recognition. The melodic line is tightly constructed from variations of the initial 8-note figure, from which F, G, E are drawn to create the double final cadence.

Au, e Ihu, tirohia W631
Metre: 8.7.8.7 and refrain

This translation into Māori of a well-known Methodist hymn is by an unknown writer, probably a late 19th century evangelist. The source hymn is 'Jesus, lover of my soul,' by **Charles Wesley**, written shortly after his conversion experience in 1738. It first appeared in print in the Wesleyan hymnal, *Hymns and Sacred Poems* (1740), but it was left out of John Wesley's definitive collection, *Hymns and Spiritual Songs Intended for the Use of Real Christians of all Denominations* (1753), and included only in a later (1797) edition published after John's death. It has been suggested that the delay in acceptance was because of Wesley's dislike of terms of intimate fellowship (like 'lover of my soul') applied to God.

The translation omits the third verse of the original; an instructive comparison between translation and original can be made easily since all four verses of 'Jesus, lover of my soul' are printed as number 139 in *With One Voice*.

MY REDEEMER This tune was written in 1877 by **James McGranahan** (1840-1907) a 19th century American evangelist and gospel music writer, as a setting for the words of a hymn by fellow American evangelist **Philip Paul Bliss** (1838-1876), 'I will sing of my Redeemer and his wondrous love to me,' composed after Bliss's sudden death in a train accident. There has been some minor adjustment of the melodic line to accommodate the translation. McGranahan toured England, Scotland and Northern Ireland twice and published two collections of his music in England, so it is possible that whoever made this translation and chose this setting for it encountered it at a gospel meeting in one of the many towns McGranahan visited, from London to Edinburgh, from Glasgow to Belfast.

The music has the driving triple rhythms, the rising and falling melodic line, the strong beating and long-held notes typical of the emotional gospel music of its time, but it is unusual (and true to the original) in changing from a 3-beat time for the verses to a 4-beat time for the refrain. It is interesting to consider that by this date in England both Parry's ABERYSTWYTH and Dykes' HOLLINGSIDE, now considered the standard settings for Wesley's hymn, had been published.

Aue te tu aroa A5
Metre: Irregular

This hymn text was written by distinguished Cook Islander **Taria Kingstone** (1961-2006). Nothing has been discovered about the particular circumstances or date of its composition.

Verses 1-2 and the refrain have their source in a gospel chorus written in 1914 by **Charles Austin Miles** (1868-1946), a pharmacist turned gospel writer, and editor and manager of the United States Hall-Mack publishing company for 37 years:

> Wide, wide as the ocean,
> high as the Heaven above;
> Deep, deep as the deepest sea
> is my Saviour's love.
> I, though so unworthy,
> still am a child of His care;
> For His Word teaches me that His love
> reaches me everywhere.

Verse 3 draws on 1 John 3:1; verse 4 draws on Psalm 100:4,' For the Lord is good; his steadfast love endures forever and his faithfulness to all generations.'

NGA TUPUNA (Cook Island Māori=The Ancestors) The music is original and was written by the author-composer for four-part harmonized singing in Cook Islands style, probably unaccompanied.

Autumn comes in all its fullness H8
Metre: 8.7.8.7 and refrain

This meditative text on the season of Autumn was written by **Bill Wallace** and published in his *Sacred Earth, Holy Darkness* (1990), the first of the books constituting his *Singing the Circle* trilogy. The text printed in *Hope is our Song* (2009) represents a major revision of the original four-verse poem, which is given below* for purposes of comparison and explication.

The text treats the Autumn season of the natural year both literally and metaphorically as a period in the human life-span, contemplating the ancient paradox that 'Every death brings hope of birthing, / every birth enfolds life's end.' The author writes of this hymn, 'For southern hemisphere Christians the marriage of Autumn and Easter requires a new understanding of Easter – the potential of Spring hidden in the tomb, rather than the expression of its actuality.'

HAMILTON AVENUE The first printing of the hymn listed HYFRYDOL and BITHYNIA as possible tunes. HAMILTON AVENUE, was written by Bill Wallace himself and arranged by **Barry Brinson** in 2008 for *Hope is our Song*. It was named after the composer's Christchurch address at the time of writing.

> *Autumn comes in all its fullness,
> Harvest of the land and heart.
> Autumn has its birth in Winter
> In the stillness where life starts.
>
> > *Every death brings hope of birthing,*
> > *Every birthing heralds death,*
> > *For the patterns framed by nature*
> > *Form the seasons of our hearts.*
>
> Autumn calls for deep reflection
> On the choices that bear fruit,
> How we sow and how we nurture
> All our just and vain pursuits.
>
> Buried in Autumnal endings
> Lies the greening of the tomb,
> For the letting go in Autumn
> Gives the entry to life's womb.
>
> God of March and April Autumn,
> God of Northern Autumn too,
> May Christ's life and Nature's seasons
> Be as one instead of two.

Ave lou ola A6
Metre: 11.10.11.10 and refrain

This is a translation into the Samoan language of the classic English hymn 'Take my life and let it be' by **Frances Ridley Havergal,** written in 1874 and first published in the 1874 Appendix to Charles Snepp's *Songs of Grace and Glory* (1872). The attribution in *Alleluia Aotearoa* to **John Marriott**, an earlier English hymn writer (1780-1825), is incorrect. Havergal's hymn consists of six stanzas from which the unknown adapter has taken the first three stanzas, using the final stanza as a refrain. The print source of this Samoan hymn is given as *O Pese ma Viiga i le Atua*, the hymnal of the Christian Congregational Church of Samoa* (1894, and subsequent editions), but it is not present in the first edition of the hymnal. The date of its entry into Samoan hymnody is unknown.

Frances Havergal, the daughter of a clergyman and an accomplished singer and pianist, was widely read and wrote poetry from an early age. She also learned six foreign languages, including Greek and Hebrew, so it is not surprising that her hymn text has a strong scriptural basis in Isaiah 6:8, Philippians 1:20-21, Romans 12:1 and Luke 21:2-3.

[AVE LAU OLA (Samoan=Take my life)] This original setting by New Zealand composer and ethnomusicologist **Richard Moyle** is one which sympathetically interprets the choral singing style of Samoan congregations; it was created for a Samoan choir competition held in Auckland in 1991-2. Havergal's own preferred tune was PATMOS, written by her father, but the setting CONSECRATION, written by **William Herbert Jude** (1851-1922) and named after Havergal's own description of her hymn as 'Self-Consecration to Christ,' became a favourite among the Victorians.

*The title of the Church is incorrectly given in *Alleluia Aotearoa*.

Awake before sunrise C6
Metre: 11.11.11.11

This Advent carol was written by **Bill Bennett** in the late 1980s, when the author was vicar of Dannevirke Parish in the Southern Hawke's Bay district. It was first published with a setting by David Dell in the first update to *New Zealand Praise* (1990), followed by publication with the writer's own setting in *Carol Our Christmas* (1996) and *Gradual Praise* (2010).

Bill Bennett describes the personal experience which provides the context for his carol: 'Christmas is a busy time for sheep farmers. It is the season for the main wool shear. [I] have,

from childhood, often been in a local farmer's woolshed, assisting the 'rousie' [person employed to do odd jobs in a shearing shed], getting stock into the inside pens and watching the shearers at work. The wool is gathered up, sorted and pressed into woolpacks. Meanwhile, the shepherds are busy outside. Some mustering other sheep from the hilltops, while others are driving the newly-shorn back to pasture.'

This context supplies a setting for a carol that is typical of a summertime Christmas sheep-shearing scene in Aotearoa/New Zealand. The author imagines the shearers and shed-hands pausing for 'smoko' (morning or afternoon tea break), while someone takes a guitar and sings about the Christ child. The baby lies on a bed of wool. Not only is this a special moment for all in the woolshed. Those with their sheep dogs (distinguished as huntaway and heading dogs) on distant hills admire and reflect on the beauty and openness of God's creation and the reality of the baby in their midst, God's incarnation.

While the account in Luke 2:8-20 of Palestinian shepherds present at the nativity of Christ lies behind this carol, the characters have been completely re-imagined and localised. The refrain plays on the paradox of a child as 'our Shepherd' (see John 10.11) and 'Head' (=leader, as in the leader of a shearing gang – a New Zealand equivalent for 'Lord'). Verse 2, line 1, 'go muster'=go off to gather in the sheep; 'hunt away'=are directed to seek and locate sheep. Verse 3, line 1, 'give pride'=give pride of place/take pride in.

[AWAKE BEFORE SUNRISE] This setting by Bill Bennett consciously adopts a folk-song style. The melody consists of variations on the first four-bar phrase, supported with simple modulations from E flat major to the related keys of B flat and A flat major. There is an alternative setting by New Zealand composer **David Dell** in the first update to *New Zealand Praise* (1990), where it is given the title 'Woolshed Carol.'

Be still my heart F4 (i) and (ii)
Metre: 6.4.6

The text of this centering prayer was written by **John Murray** in 1999 as one of a set of brief prayer texts modelled on those in the Iona Community's collection *A Wee Worship Book* (1999) and was first published in *Faith Forever Singing* (2000). The biblical source is Psalm 46:10.

[BE STILL] The tune names for both of these settings derive from the theme of the set text, and each was written in 1998 by a member of the editorial committee preparing *Faith Forever Singing*. **Cecily Sheehy** composes a two-voice choral setting, with the text repeated to bring the setting to its quiet conclusion in the tonic key of C.

STILLNESS This tune was named and the simple arching unison melody written by **Colin Gibson**. The setting is in B flat major.

Be their names remembered F5
Metre: 6.5

This short liturgical text was extracted from a six-verse 'Litany for sisters of the Christ'* written in 1998 by **Shirley Murray**. One of several such texts prepared for *Faith Forever Singing* (2000), it was intended to accompany the recital of names on such memorial occasions as funerals, church family days or Anzac Day.

SOROMUNDI This setting is by **Jillian Bray**, and was also written in 1998. The tune is named after a famous Oregon, United States, women's choir founded in 1989, whose mission was and is to support diversity and a strong and visible gay and lesbian community. The tune name, adapted from Latin *sorores mundi*, means 'sisters of the world.' (It is also the name of a main-belt asteroid, discovered in 1979.)

>*The opening verses of the Litany read:
>
>Sisters of the Christ,
>you who nursed the truth,
>gave him to be blessed,
>wrapped him in your love.

>Be your names remembered
>in the heart of God.
>
>Women at the birth,
>women at the death,
>you who washed the body,
>found the Jesus life.
>Be your names remembered
>in the heart of God.

Beautiful presence H9
Metre: 10.10.10.10.9.9.10.10

The text of this hymn is a poem written by **Joy Cowley** in December 2006 and first published in 2009 in *Hope is our Song*.

The theme of the poem is praise of Christ as one who escapes all verbal definition (cf. Brian Wren's hymn 'Bring many names, beautiful and good'). Some of the ascriptions used here are biblical: see Colossians 3:11, 'Christ is all and in all' for verse 1, line 2; and Galatians 2:20, 'It is no longer I who live but it is Christ who lives in me; and the life I now live in the flesh I live by faith in the Son of God,' for the refrain, line 4. The phrase 'ocean of love' is not biblical but is found in the Muslim poet Rumi (1207-73) and the Sufi mystical tradition; 'soft as a dove' refers to both Jesus' gentle dealings with others and his association with peace and love, which the bird commonly symbolizes. Verse 2, line 4, elaborates an idea found elsewhere in Joy Cowley's writing: 'We need to own our darkness. It is our growing point, the point of transformation. In our darkness there is always the seed of light ready to burst open into spiritual growth' ('The Green Season,' 2007 Pompallier Lecture for the Auckland-based Catholic Institute of Theology*).

BEAUTIFUL PRESENCE The tune name is taken from the first line of the Joy Cowley poem. This setting was written by **Barry Brinson** in 2007 for this text. The composer describes it as 'in the style of a contemporary worship song rather than a formal hymn.' The accompaniment is keyboard-based; the 9/8 dotted crochet rhythm is reminiscent of such older hymns as 'Morning has broken' and 'Blessed assurance,' but, says the composer, 'I really have tried not to plagiarise these old favourites. When placing a new tune before singers and congregations it's not a bad strategy to give them a feeling that they might have heard it before.' Stephen Foster's 1864 parlour song 'Beautiful dreamer' is another possible melodic influence.

> *There are a number of echoes of this poem in the text of the lecture. Compare, for instance:
>
> I discovered in that place [Easter Island] the Presence I had always known (verse 1). Let's talk about Jesus. In this celebration of faith that's where we begin and that's how we journey – through him, in him, with him – the Word made flesh who dwells among us (Refrain). There are times when we feel diminished by our failure. Our dear hearts so hunger for goodness that we try to separate our light from our darkness. But we need to own our darkness (verse 2). Jesus calls us away from our egocentric nature. He helps us to break down the walls of the small prison of self, to step out into the larger reality of God's love in creation (verse 3).

Because you came *facing F19 (ii), H10*
Metre: 9.8.10.9

This hymn, written by **Shirley Murray** in 1991, was first published in her second American collection, *Every Day in Your Spirit* (1996) as a stand-alone text, then in *Faith Makes the Song* (2003), where it is set to the music of American Lutheran composer **Amanda Husberg**. It reached New Zealand publication in *Faith Forever Singing* (2000, text only) and *Hope is our Song* (2009).

The text originated in an Iona Community prayer* which Murray found in the *Worship Book* of the World Council of Churches Assembly at Canberra in 1991. She says of it, 'Its words seemed to put into contrasting focus the beauty of the world and the arrogance of human behaviour. Its final part begins with the words I used to open my hymn: "Because you came among us and sat beside us"… It shows Jesus as the fully human person who does care to come and sit with us, listens to us, is ignored by us, heals us, but is hurt and finally violated by us, yet overcomes our inhumanity and hatred. I took and expanded some of [its] images, sharpening the contrast between our love of status and money, our violent natures and love of power, set against the lifestyle of Jesus. A lifestyle of simplicity, laughter and self-giving, with an insistent mission to create peace at all costs.'

This beautifully structured hymn takes the form of a solemn confessional, concluding in a refrain asking for forgiveness and finally offering hope and praise. Verse 1 alludes to Jesus' companionship with 'sinners and tax collectors' (Mark 2:15), to the many occasions on which the gospel writers record conversations with members of the crowds and his own disciples, and to the crowd's rejection of him when offered his release by Pilate. Verse 2 alludes to Christ's praise of children (Mark 10:14). Verse 3 speaks of Jesus weeping 'to see us war.' Jesus is not recorded as weeping at human conflict, though he did weep over the death of Lazarus and Jerusalem, the city that first welcomed then rejected him; here as elsewhere the writer's own passion for peace comes through. Verse 4 is remarkable for its independent theology of the crucifixion and death of Christ: instead of the traditional Atonement theory, here Christ's love 'absorbs' our sin, and our acts of cruelty 'wound us.' Verse 5 returns to the words of the first verse ('Because you came') and lists three later 'comings' of Christ – in the Easter garden, at the Pentecost event and in the person of the Holy Spirit (John 14:18, 'I will not leave you desolate; I will come to you'). Shirley Murray comments, 'the final verses make connections between what we understand the Cross, resurrection and the Spirit to mean.'**

FORGIVENESS. The melody in the 'sad' key of E minor takes its name from the repeated word in the refrain. This setting was written by **Colin Gibson** in 1996. Over a steadily sinking bass line and with repeated falling figures, the melody, itself dropping towards the tonic note, powerfully expresses the grieving aspect of this text. **Amanda Husberg's** tune, MAUJER

STREET, is used in Murray's American collections *Faith Makes the Song* (2003) and *Singing the Faith* (2011).

> *The full version of the original prayer is printed in Morning Liturgy B, *A Wee Worship Book* (Glasgow: Wild Goose publications, 1999 and successive editions).
>
> **See further 'Hymn for Easter,' by John Thornley, *Touchstone*, April 2009, page 5.

Because you live, O Christ A7
Metre: 6.11.6.11.6.6.6.6

Shirley Murray, the author of this resurrection hymn text, explains that 'the irritant* to write this came from the outdated words in our parish hymn-book and my love of this great tune VRUECHTEN. I wanted a fresh expression of community joyfulness with light, colour, and the vision of the covenant rainbow through the Resurrection.' The text was written in 1984 and first appeared in the author's privately published collection, *In Every Corner Sing* (1987). It then appeared in her American collection of the same name (1992) and reached a New Zealand audience in *Alleluia Aotearoa* (1993).

Verse 1 alludes to the garden of Gethsemane in which Mary encountered the risen Christ (John 20:11-16). 'Flooded' (line 4) implies light rather than water (cf. 'floodlight'). Verse 2 refers to 'the spirit bird of hope': both the dove released by Noah (Genesis 8:8-11) and the dove, symbolic of the Holy Spirit (Matthew 3:16). In the final verse the rainbow of God's covenant (Genesis 9:8-17) becomes an arch of peace spanning the whole creation, and the final lines reference John 12:32, 'As for me, if I am lifted up I will draw all people unto me.' The refrain refers to the mysterious rolling away of the stone blocking the mouth of Jesus' burial place recorded in all the gospels (Matthew 28:2, Mark 16:3-4, Luke 24:2, John 20:1). That this text is a response to Woodward's hymn appears most clearly in the refrain, as comparison with the earlier text will show:

> Had Christ, that once was slain,
> Ne'er burst his three-day prison,
> Our faith had been in vain:
> But now hath Christ arisen,
> Arisen, arisen, arisen!

CRASHAW The setting was written in 1988 by **Roy Tankersley,** and is named after Brian Crashaw, Deputy Mayor of Gisborne and at the time acting Mayor of the town. The 3/4 melody is both dance-like and celebratory, rising three times to a high note at points of climax. The harmonies modulate in a way reminiscent of medieval dance forms. VRUECHTEN (*With One Voice*, 302) was the original recommended tune; it was used again for the 1987 American collection of Shirley Murray's hymns.

> *Of the two hymns in the Presbyterian *Church Hymnary* (third edition) for which this tune is used, George Woodward's 'This joyful Eastertide' and Percy Dearmer's 'How great the harvest is,' the Easter hymn is most likely the 'irritant' of which Murray writes.

Beyond all accidents of chance and change H12
Metre: 10.10.10 D

This hymn, entitled 'A Hymn for Older Christians' in the original manuscript, was written in 1987 by **Colin Gibson**, following a chance meeting before a service at Knox Church, Dunedin, with the Reverend Doctor Frank Nichol, former Professor of Systematic Theology and Christian Ethics at the Presbyterian Theological Hall, Dunedin. Nichol had been the Principal of the College from 1972 until his enforced retirement in 1985 due to a stroke, which had left him in ill health and confined to a wheel chair pushed by his wife Beth.

The thought of the hymn text was occasioned by the contrast between Frank Nichol's still cheerful character, bright mind and strong faith, and the body now so evidently crippled and helpless – a condition not uncommon among older people.

Verse 1 draws on Job 19:26, 'though my flesh may be destroyed yet in my body I shall see God.' The image of 'all-devouring time' comes from Shakespeare's Sonnet 19, a poem which acknowledges the defeats of time yet declares its defiance of the losses brought about by age: 'Yet, do thy worst, old Time; despite thy wrong / My love shall in my verse live ever young.' Verse 2 draws on **Isaac Watts**' hymn, 'O God, our help in ages past,' in particular the line, 'time, like an ever-rolling stream bears all its sons away.' The thought in the final line of this verse is that after death God continues to bear witness to the life and character of every human being. Verse 3 echoes Psalm 16:1 and Deuteronomy 33:27 ('The Eternal God is your refuge, and underneath are the everlasting arms'), as well as Mary B. Peters' hymn, 'Through the love of God our Saviour…all will be well.' The final image in the fourth verse derives from 1 John 1:7 ('walk in the light'), but also from pictorial images of souls after death walking forward into a great tunnel filled with light.

The suggested tunes are SONG 1, by the 17th century English composer Orlando Gibbons (1583-1625), or FINLANDIA, from music by the Finnish composer Jean Sibelius (1865-1957).

Blessings on the buildings *H11*
Metre: 6.5.6.5.6.5.6.5 D

Written in September 2005 by **Colin Gibson** to mark the centenary of the Glenaven Church, Dunedin, and the experience of its modern congregation, the hymn text moves from a cheerful enumeration of the physical features of the church and its hall, then to those of the people within it and finally to the typical varieties of age and character to be found there.

Although the text is couched in general terms, suitable to any long-established Christian church and its congregation, it acknowledges the special history of the community, which under the leadership of the Reverend Dr David Bromell (1986-1993), the first 'openly gay' minister in New Zealand, became one of the first in New Zealand to declare itself an inclusive church (that is, accepting gay and lesbian people, lay or ordained, as full members of its congregation) at a time when the matter was under fierce debate in the national Methodist Church – and among other denominations. The Jesus bus referred to in verse 1 was run at Glenaven by a fully public company, rather than a private one of the kind still found today among the many Christian systems of transport. And this congregation is still 'holding on' (verse 3, line 14) to the principles it embraced at the beginning of the controversy.

BLESSINGS The derivation of the tune name is from the rain of blessings mentioned in the text. The setting was written by **Colin Gibson** in 2005: both the simple triadic melody and fundamental harmonic structure are intended to allow for a mood of happy celebration.

Blow through the valleys and sing in the rimu *F6*
Metre: 12.11.12.11 and refrain

This hymn was written by **Bill Bennett** in the late 1980s, while the author was vicar of Dannevirke Parish in the Southern Hawke's Bay district. It was first published in *Faith Forever Singing* (2000).

Bill explains that he frequently went tramping into the Ruahine mountain ranges immediately south of Dannevirke, a place with a reputation for strong winds, 'normally westerlies that rush over the high peaks and sweep across the countryside, sometimes blowing farmers off their horses, toppling shelter belts and lifting roofs.' The hymn is 'a fond reflection on the power of that wind, reminding the writer of the rush of Pentecostal wind [see Acts 2:7]. It was also written during a time of profound economic change for rural communities, the result of policies known as "Rogernomics" [after the reforms of Roger Douglas, Minister of Finance from 1984 to 1988 in the Fourth Labour Government, which suddenly and brutally exposed the country to a global economy.] This market-driven government policy caused much headache among farmers and small rural communities, so there is a strong social justice consciousness reflected in the words.'

There are parallels between this refrain and Sister Miriam Winter's 1965 hymn 'Spirit of God in the clear running water, / blowing to greatness the trees on the hill,' with its refrain, 'fill the earth, bring it to birth,' but the New Zealand character of this text is established both by its sharp social focus (see especially verse 1 and 2) and by its language. *Rimu* (refrain, line 1) is a native tree renowned for its superb, reddish-grained wood and its beautiful drooping, frond-like leaves in its first years of growth. Verse 2 insists on the importance of the concept of partnership between races, here Māori with *pākehā* as the use of the Māori term *whenua* (=the land) suggests. The word in this context, explains Bill Bennett, refers to the land and landscape and to the deep connections people have with that land. *Aroha* (verse 3) is another Māori word meaning love expressed in relationships, the ultimate principle of unity in the universe.

RUAHINE Bill Bennett's tune is named after the mountain range under which Dannevirke rests. The composer recalls 'camping in the bush-clad valleys and hearing the gathering roar of enormous gusts of wind bearing down on the valley floor from the tops of the main ridge, and leaning grimly on the side of his small pup-tent to ensure it also didn't blow away into the far beyond.' The melody has a relaxed folk-song character, though the shift to minor tonalities in the verse setting suggests the more serious concerns expressed there for a rejection of market values, and the recovery of compassion, justice, racial harmony and fresh hope. The arrangement of the tune in *Alleluia Aotearoa* is by **David Dell**.

Born in the night, Mary's child
W642
Metre: 4.3.6 D

This text was written in 1959 by English Methodist minister **Geoffrey Ainger**, during Ainger's ministry at Loughton, Essex, as part of a play for teenagers, placing the Nativity in a contemporary setting. It was first published in his *Songs from Notting Hill* (1964). It achieved wider circulation through its inclusion in the British Methodist supplementary hymnbook, *Hymns & Songs* (1969). It has become a standard modern carol.

Although the theology of this text, which presents Jesus Christ as 'light of the world,' 'truth of our life,' 'hope of the world' and finally 'king of the earth,' is conventional, the ideas are energized by its form as a direct conversation between the singers and 'Mary's child.' Jesus is presented as one of the homeless city children Ainger knew through his own ministry to the poor, 'born in a borrowed room,' and named simply as an anonymous human baby, 'Mary's child' (repeated eight times). The imagery of a night-time birth (for which there is no biblical authority) for one who is to be the light of the world, and dawn, sun-like, on 'our darkened day' draws on much traditional Christian art and symbolism. The final line owes something to Frank Mason North's 'O tread the city's streets again,' in his 1903 hymn 'Where cross the crowded ways of life.'

MARY'S CHILD This setting was composed for his own text by Ainger, and first published as a single melodic line with guitar chord indications. The regular strummed chords both carry and contrast with the relatively laid-back rhythms of the melody.

Bring in your new world *H13*
Metre: 9.10.4 D

'In 2005, the shadow of the war in Iraq* was the context of this Advent carol,' says **Shirley Murray**, its author. 'With a world of others I felt a longing for a leader who would bring us out of the horrors of that conflict. My words are an attempt to meld the joy of the Incarnation and the human hope for a new leader, with the profile of Jesus as prophet for peace.' The hymn was first published in *Touch the Earth Lightly* (2008), followed by *Hope is our Song* (2009).

The theme of the hymn is a plea for a 'new world' to replace 'our sad world' plunged into the darkness of war. Christ is addressed as the source of light (enlightenment), as a world leader from the east, the author of a new vision of peace, justice and freedom, and as a vulnerable human child symbolising God's compassion and kindness towards all creation, the triumph of light over darkness and life over death. The first verse is dominated by the metaphor of light shining forth (see John 1:4-5). Verse 2 refers to the turmoil of the political scene into which Christ was born (a Jewish insurgency directed against the Roman occupying forces) and the perceived threat posed both by his challenge to the orthodox religious leaders of his time and his championing of the poor. Verse 3 describes Christ's vision of a peaceable kingdom, using imagery from Isaiah's visionary account of a new leader: Isaiah 11:3-9. Verse 4 focuses on the hopes raised by the simple human birth ('child of our earth') celebrated at the season of Advent.

SALISBURY STREET The tune is named after the Dunedin address of a recently arrived Korean Methodist minister's family, David and Susan Ahn and their new-born child Daniel, to whom the setting, written by **Colin Gibson** on Christmas Day 2005, is dedicated. The 3/4 time signature of this melody gives it a joyful dance-like rhythm, supported by the lifting figure in the bass and enhanced in *Touch the Earth Lightly* by the provision of a descant line for flute, violin or similar instrument which employs skipping arpeggios and scalic runs to decorate the melody and express the emotion of sheer joy.

There is another 2005 setting of this hymn by **Jillian Bray**, named LOFTIS after Deborah Carlton Loftis, President of the Hymn Society of America and Canada at the time. There are also settings by at least two American composers: NEW WORLD CHILD, by **Jane Marshall**, and an untitled setting by **Jim Strathdee**.

> *The invasion of Iraq in 2003 by forces of the United States and the United Kingdom aiming to remove the government of President Saddam Hussein led to a war followed by a long drawn-out insurgency against the newly-installed Iraqi government and the western forces supporting it. With United Nations agreement, the attack was authorised by American President George Bush and British Prime Minister Tony Blair, both of whom have since left office. In February 2009, the newly-elected President of the United States, Barak Obama, announced the withdrawal in 2011 of the last of the coalition's combat troops.

Bring peace to us *F7 (i) and (ii)*
Metre: 4.4.4

This short liturgical prayer text was written by **John Murray** in 1999. It is based on the *dona nobis pacem* phrase (Latin=grant us peace) found in the ancient Agnus Dei section of the Roman Catholic Mass and probably derived from John 14:27, 'My peace I give you.'

[BRING PEACE (i)] This setting by **Cecily Sheehy**, written in 1999, takes the form of a three-part round in the key of D major.

[BRING PEACE (ii)] In this alternative setting by **Colin Gibson**, also written in 1999, the composer has chosen to hang the melody above discordant, unpeaceful chords in C minor which resolve on a final C major chord with the third repetition of the word 'peace.'

Broken the body *F8*
Metre: 10.8.10.6 and kyries

This powerful text, in part communion hymn, in part confessional, was written by **Shirley Murray** in 1985, prompted by the reception of a new tune from **Jillian Bray**. 'I wrote this as a song of despair and penitence at what I see to be the fragmentation of our church, and our lack of courage to deal with fundamentalism in the light of the contemporary world.' The hymn first appeared in her American collection *Every Day in your Spirit* (1996), and then in *Faith Forever Singing* (2000).

Its theme is the 'brokenness' of the modern body of the Christian church, matching the physical body of Christ 'broken' on the cross and the bread symbolically broken during Holy Communion. The writer's passionate and despairing mood is communicated through forceful language: 'Broken, scattered, frozen, fractured, faltering, losing our nerve, bloodless (that is, lacking any passion or emotion), crumbled, weak, small.' Through such words we are made to 'feel our broken life' (verse 4).

Underlying the text are two key biblical passages: Christ's prayer for the unity of his followers (John 17:21) and Paul's elaborate metaphor for the Christian community as requiring the co-operative action of the body (1 Corinthians 12:12). But there are other allusions, biblical and non-biblical in this richly allusive text. Verse 1 recalls the crucifixion of Christ between two thieves (Matthew 27:38); and alludes to Mark Gibbs and Ralph Morton's famous 1964 book, *God's Frozen People*. Verse 3 speaks of denominations competing for 'customers' in terms of Luke 7:31-32; verse 5, line 2, draws on Jesus' words on the cross (Luke 23:34); and the hymn closes with a fourfold repetition of the ancient Christian prayer for forgiveness, *Kyrie eleison*, 'Lord, have mercy.'

MIRIAM The tune name does not relate to Shirley Murray's text, having been written before it, but refers to the prophetess Miriam, sister of Aaron and Moses, who hid her baby brother to protect him from Pharaoh's soldiers and later sang a Victory Song after the loss of Pharaoh's army in the Red Sea (Exodus 2, 15). 'I was currently naming tunes after Biblical women I admire,' says **Jillian Bray**. The music was composed in 1995 and sent to Shirley Murray for words to fit it, with the suggestion that a communion hymn would be suitable. Jillian Bray says that she was overwhelmed by the resultant text; because 'I felt passionately about the disintegration of the Church.' Later a descant was added 'to intensify the words.'

Brother, sister, let me serve you (The Servant Song) *A8*
Metre: 8.7.7.8

Written in 1976-7 by **Richard Gillard**, this hymn began as a verse (now the third verse of the text) and a tune jotted down in 1976 when the author was returning from travel overseas, then further developed in 1977. Richard Gillard says, 'in the back of my mind was the passage in John's Gospel [John 13:2-9] where Jesus washes the disciples' feet, and the re-enactments of that moment I had witnessed and experienced in the Maundy Thursday services at St Paul's [Anglican Church, Auckland]. Also influential were sermons and discussions I heard at St Paul's on the subject of Christian service and servant-hood.'

The first line of the text has been subject to much editorial attention to make its address gender-inclusive. The original first line, 'Brother, let me be your servant,' retained in earlier printings, has been changed to 'Brother, sister, let me serve you' (the author's preferred alteration) or more simply, 'Will you let me be your servant?' The editors of *Voices United* (1997) made even more radical changes, starting the hymn with the original second verse (in which they exchange 'Fellow-travellers' for 'We are brothers'), and substituting 'Sister' for 'Brother' at the start of the new second verse.

The hymn was gifted to David and Dale Garrett, creators of the New Zealand Scripture in Song organisation, who issued it on an LP recording, *Father make us one* (1978), and published it in their *Songs of the Kingdom* (1981). Gillard's home church, St Paul's, Auckland, had earlier published it in *New Harvest* (1979) as one of the songs 'emanating from our corporate worship,' and issued it on a later LP recording by the St Paul's Singers. It first reached international attention through its publication in the Celebration hymnal *Cry Hosanna* (1981), with an accompanying recording by the popular folksong group, the Fisherfolk. It was then taken into national and international mainstream hymnals to the point where it can now be regarded as an iconic New Zealand hymn. It is also well represented in evangelical hymn and praise songbooks such as *Green Book Choruses 28*, *The Promise Keepers' Songbook*, *Spring Harvest* and *New Song*. As a representative New Zealand hymn it was reprinted (words only) in *A Panorama of Christian Hymnody*, by Erik Routley and Alan A. Richardson (Chicago: GIA, 2005).

What distinguishes this hymn from many other journeying hymns is the intimate and moving dialogue between its male and female voices (there is a strong intentional sense of family and family relationships present in the text) and the detailed working out of the idea of loving service and companionship offered mutually as well as to others 'on the road.' Verse 2 offers a particularly rich assemblage of classical Christian religious images: life is a pilgrimage, a road to be travelled in company (see the road to Emmaus story, Luke 24:13-27) and walked, bearing the load (see Matthew 5:41 and Galatians 6:2).

[SERVANT SONG] The melody for this hymn was written by its author, Richard Gillard, for the guitar; the piano arrangement in *Alleluia Aotearoa* is by **Val Fleetwood,** taken from *New Harvest* (1979). Gillard's own not very different but somewhat simpler setting is found in *Songs of the Kingdom* (1981). The melody has received a number of arrangements by later composers; **Betty Pulkingham's** chordal setting is found in several hymnbooks, including *Evangelical Lutheran Worship* and the Brethren and Memnonite *Hymnal: A Worship Book* (1992). Paul Westermeyer provides a detailed discussion of the musical and textual implications of such settings in his *Hymnal Companion to Evangelical Lutheran Worship* (Minneapolis: Augsburg Fortress, 2010, pp 509-10).

Carol our Christmas (Upside down Christmas) A9, C7
Metre: 6.5.6.4 D

This carol was written by **Shirley Murray** in 1986, and first published in Colin Gibson's first English collection, *Singing Love* (1988), followed by David Dell's first New Zealand collection, *New Zealand Praise* (1988). It was then published in Shirley Murray's first American collection, *In Every Corner Sing* (1992).

In an introductory note in *In Every Corner Sing* the author wrote, "'Upside down Christmas," as this carol is known, is a carol for our part of the world 'down under' [i.e. in the southern hemisphere], where high summer makes unreal the imagery of reindeer and robins in the snow.' 'Upside down Christmas' alludes to the *Antipodes*, the northern hemisphere term for countries on the opposite side of the globe. The word's root meaning comically suggests upside-down walkers whose feet meet the feet of 'right side up' walkers.

The first two verses elaborate the idea of 'a nativity summer can reach.' Verse 3 translates the traditional shepherds and wise men into New Zealand terms: these shepherds and musterers (an Australasian term for farm workers employed to search for and assemble sheep for shearing) hear no angelic songs (as described in Luke 2:8-14) because they are busy shearing, while the New Zealand equivalents of the Magi (Matthew 2:1-2) are forever travelling, engaged in the search for 'signs of the truth to be born.' The final verse suggests that another Nativity occurs at every human birth, and the traditional gifts of the Magi, gold, frankincense and myrrh (Matthew 2:11), are replaced by hope and love, 'the Jesus gift.'

REVERSI The tune name refers to a then popular board game (also known as Othello) in which black and white counters are turned over to reveal their reverse colour in the course of match play. This carol was set in 1986 as a unison song by **Colin Gibson**, using a cheerful 3/4 dance rhythm. The carol, sung by the Wellington Youth Choir, is recorded on the CD *Carol our Christmas: Contemporary New Zealand Carols,* published by the New Zealand Hymnbook Trust in 1996.

Celebrate each generation A10
Metre: 8.7.8.7

Written in 1985, this hymn by **Shirley Murray** was created for a baptism in her home church, St Andrew's on the Terrace, Wellington. It was listed under the title 'Hymn for a Child's Baptism' in the first collection of her own work, *In Every Corner Sing* (Wellington, 1987). It then appeared in David Dell's *New Zealand Praise* (1988) before reaching an international audience in the first American collection of her work, *In Every Corner Sing* (1992), followed by *Alleluia Aotearoa* (1993).

She says of it, 'Few baptismal hymns for me express the utter wonder of "the miracle of birth." I wanted, here, to include the congregation or godparents who promise to care for the faith of the growing child [see verse 3].' Accordingly, the text both celebrates the joy of a child's birth as 'a bud of hope,' prays for a faith-filled and secure environment in which the child may grow up and acknowledges the sacred ritual of baptism.

In Shirley Murray's earlier hymns, the expression of the author's ideas is often compressed, its sense to be fully understood by the singers in the context of the hymn. So here verse 1 might be expanded to 'let every birth of a child in the world be an occasion for joy; in this church let us solemnly dedicate to God this baby and all concerned with the utter wonder represented by the birth of this child.' 'Touch of living water' (verse 2, line 3) refers to the ritual of signing the cross on the forehead of a child with a finger first dipped in the baptismal font, but the phrase also alludes to John 4:14. 'Be the Christ' (verse 3) means 'May the spirit of Jesus Christ be present'; 'flower within the certain future' (verse 4) means 'grow up and flourish within the security of a reliable and loving environment.' The final image of the poem, the newborn child as a 'bud of hope within the wood,' is derived from Job 14:7-9.

BUD OF HOPE The name of this tune by **David Dell** is taken from the final line of the text. The music was written in 1987 and first published in Dell's own hymnal *New Zealand Praise* (1988). The words were first sung to the English folk melody SHIPSTON, found in *With One Voice* (1982) as the setting for John Arlott's hymn 'God whose farm is all creation,' but originally collected by Lucy Broadwood in 1893 and popularised through the arrangement given it by **Ralph Vaughan Williams** for his *English Hymnal* (1906). In the American collection *In Every Corner Sing*, the setting used is GENERATION, written by distinguished American church composer Allan Pote (b. 1945).

David Dell's melody begins as a compression in 3/4 time of the opening bars of SHIPSTON, which is in a 4/4 metre, but its subsequent development is original, and although both tunes are in E flat major their harmonies and rhythmic flow differ considerably. The simplicity of the drop of a third to close on the tonic note is a special pleasure of the New Zealand melody.

Child of blessing, child of promise
A11
Metre: 8.7.8.7

This baptismal hymn was written by **Ronald Cole-Turner** and first published in *Everflowing Streams: Songs for Worship* (Cleveland: Pilgrim Press, 1981). It was composed for and sung at the baptism of the author's daughter, Rachel Elizabeth, on 13 June 1982. It has since been published in several American and Canadian hymnals, including *The United Methodist Hymnbook* (1989), the *Presbyterian Hymnal* (1990), *Voices United* (1996) and *Worship and Rejoice* (2001). The original text of verse 4 begins 'Child of God, *the* loving Parent.' An alternative to verse 1 is provided for congregations which bless rather than baptize infants:

> Child of blessing, child of promise,
> Consecrated and assigned
> To the care of God who claims you
> Unto love and grace divine.

The hymn generally alludes to Christ's blessing of the children brought to him (Luke 18:16-17, Mark 10:14, Matthew 19:14, 1 John 3:1) and to Acts 2:39. Appropriately, the word 'love' occurs in various forms no fewer than 7 times.

BLESSING The tune name is derived from the first line of the hymn. The setting in *Alleluia Aotearoa* is the work of **Colin Gibson**, who wrote it in 1987 for a baptismal service in his own Mornington Methodist Church. The preferred tune in America is the very four-square German melody STUTTGART.

Child of Christmas story (Small Carol) A12, C8
Metre: 6.5.6.5

Written by **Shirley Murray** in 1988, this carol was first published in 1990 in the Christian Conference of Asia hymnnal *Sound the Bamboo,* set to the tune IXTHUS by Taiwanese composer **I-to Loh**,* then in *In Every Corner Sing* (1992) and *Alleluia Aotearoa* (1993). In the author's own words, the text was intended to evoke 'the heart-melting vulnerability of a tiny baby in our arms. It asks whether, even now, we recognize the meaning of the Incarnation.' The title 'Small Carol' refers to the tune name of a setting by the New Zealand composer **Nigel Eastgate** given to Shirley Murray as a Christmas gift in 1990 and used in the American collection.

Although its language and verse form are of the utmost simplicity, the carol offers a succession of compelling images and strong contrasts, beginning with 'straw and star' (verse 1), and continued with a baby's finger curled around our own, who has come to 'melt our hearts and change the world' (verse 2). The same baby then appears as the unifying child of the whole divided human race (verse 3), and finally as the boy born of an ordinary human mother's birth pangs, yet bringing hope to the whole world (verse 4). The question posed in the second to last line of the carol, with its allusion to Matthew 16:15, is left open-ended for the singer to imagine other possible answers than the obvious one, Jesus the Christ.

INCARNATION was composed in 1983 by **Richard Madden** for the choir of St Paul's Cathedral Church, Dunedin, as a setting (dedicated to his wife Robyn) of the famous early English Marian lyric, 'I sing of a maiden.' The music printed in *Alleluia Aotearoa* is a simplified version of the original, which was scored for treble solo, SATB choir and organ. There is an interesting contrast between the admiration for Mary's human courage and endurance of pain expressed in the final verse of Shirley Murray's carol and the more theological praise of Mary as the Mother of God, in the first and fifth verses of the earlier poem: 'I sing of a maiden who is matchless; / King of all kings as her son she chose… / Mother and maiden, there was never anyone such as she; / Well may such a lady God's mother be.' This carol, set to Richard Madden's melody, is recorded on the CD *Carol our Christmas: Contemporary Christmas Carols*, published by the New Zealand Hymnbook Trust.

*For an Asian perspective on the carol, see I-to Loh's *Hymnal Companion to Sound the Bamboo: Asian Hymns in their Liturgical and Cultural Contexts*, Chicago: GIA (2011) 363. IXTHUS, from a Greek word meaning 'fish,' forms an acrostic in which the letters can be read as the initials of the Greek words meaning 'Jesus Christ, Son of God, Saviour.' The sign of a fish was used by early Christians as a secret symbol of their faith.

Child of joy and peace A14 (i) and (ii), C9
Metre: 5.5.8.8.5.5

'Hunger Carol was written as a protest at our consumer society,' says author **Shirley Murray**, 'and has been used [in New Zealand] for the annual Christmas Appeal of Christian World Service.' The text was written in 1987 and published in the Asian hymnal *Sound the Bamboo* (1990) and the author's American collection *In Every Corner Sing* (1992) before reaching *Alleluia Aotearoa* (1993) and being reprinted in *Carol our Christmas* (1996).

Fired by indignation, the text steadily extends and sharpens its assault on the secular Christmas carnival of lavish spending and commercial greed, moving from an acknowledgement of the universal homage given to the Christ child and the social values of joy and peace associated with his nativity to a climax which labels the behaviour of Christmas merchants and shoppers as a denial of Christian values and a form of crucifixion of the poor, as represented by the 'Son of poverty' (cf. the title 'Son of Man').

Verse 1 draws on Matthew's account of the wise men following the star and offering gifts (Matthew 2); its reference to 'East and West' would have had a particular resonance in the Asian hymnal in which it was first published. Verse 2 sharpens Luke's account of the birth (Luke 2:6-7) with a crying baby symbolizing 'our tears and our anger' at such treatment of the poor. Verse 3 shifts focus to the breaking and sharing of bread at the communion table (see Luke 22:19) and the obligation to feed the world. Verse 4 frames Christmas social behaviour as another rejection of loyalty to Christian values and a veritable crucifixion on a Christmas 'tree' (see Luke 22-3).

JENNIFER'S GIFT This setting in 4/4 time was written by **Ian Render** in 1992. It received its name when one of the composers' parishioners at the Newlands-Paparangi parish where Ian Render was Vicar at the time – named Jennifer and herself a musician – brought together the separate chord structure and melody which Render was working on, in a piano arrangement which he transcribed and duly named JENNIFER'S GIFT.

UTRECHT In *Alleluia Aotearoa*, this title displaces the original tune name HUNGER (used in *In Every Corner Sing*) which picks up the theme of the poor left to go hungry while Christmas merrymakers lavish money on expensive gifts. UTRECHT points rather to the 'Child of joy and peace' praised in the first line of the carol, and is associated with the famous peace treaty signed in 1713 in the Dutch town of that name, which brought an end to the Wars of the Spanish Succession (1701-14) and was celebrated by Handel with a famous Te Deum and Jubilate. Under either name, the music is by **Douglas Mews** and was written in 1987. Shirley Murray comments that [this] 'was one of the first texts in which I worked with eminent New Zealand composer and devout Roman Catholic, Dr. Douglas Mews.' But the original musical setting was the sober German chorale melody ARNSTADT (SEELINBRAUTIGAM), written by Lutheran pastor Adam Drese (1620-1701) and first published in *Geistreiches Gesangbuch* (1698). Murray also praises as 'a fine alternative in an Asian mode,' I-toh Loh's tune SMOKEY MOUNTAIN, published in *Sound the Bamboo* (1990). This name is derived from a huge garbage dump on the outskirts of Manila, where thousands scavenge through the waste to make a living. (See further I-to Loh's *Hymnal Companion to Sound the Bamboo: Asian Hymns in their Cultural and Liturgical Contexts*. Chicago: GIA (2011), 370-1.)

Christ ascends to God! (A Hymn for Ascension) *H14*
Metre: 8.7.8.7.8.7

This hymn was written in 1999 by **Marnie Barrell** to celebrate the Feast of the Ascension of Jesus Christ, an ecumenical festival usually celebrated on a Thursday, the 40th day of Easter (following the count established by Acts 1:3-11), although some Roman Catholic provinces have moved the observance to the following Sunday.

The language of the hymn, spiced with cries of 'alleluia!' (Hebrew=give praise to God), is high and celebratory, ('unimagined – that is, unable to be imagined or as yet undreamed of – powers enfold him'), the imagery royal ('mortals worship at his feet, reign in his own right, throned in splendour, Universal Lord'). Although the account in Acts of Christ's ascension ('he was lifted up, and a cloud took him out their sight') provides the basis for the narrative of the hymn, it is enriched with phrases and images from Revelation (for instance 19:10, 'I fell down at his feet to worship him,' cf. verse 1, line 4). Ephesians 3:7-10 contributes the 'mystery' of God and the 'powers' of heaven (verses 1-2).

The argument of the hymn takes a sudden turn in verse 3, 'He is with us. Do not seek him / throned in splendour far above.' This, too, is biblical in basis (see Matthew 28:20 and Revelation 21:3-4), but the argument takes one further turn in verse 4, where Christ as 'the Universal Lord' is identified as 'creation's heart' (line 6), to be found 'in nature's smallest part,' 'time and space [his] work of art.' Here the writer echoes contemporary eco-theologians like Teihard de Chardin, and Brian Swimme, bringing the ecstatic praise of the risen Christ to a presence in the cosmos itself.

MICHAELMAS The tune is named for another Christian festival in the Western Church, the feast of St Michael the Archangel, celebrated on 29 September. The 4-part choral setting (with an effective unison moment) was written in 2001 (revised in 2003) by **Barry Brinson**, to replace the grand English melodies with which the text had been previously associated, REGENT SQUARE, GRAFTON and ST HELEN'S.

Every opportunity is taken to illustrate the idea of ascent, from a bass line surging upwards and climbing inner part scalic phrases (as in bars 18-21) to harmonic sequences shifting upwards and a melody that climbs gradually to a peak on E flat (probably the highest note modern congregations can reach) 4 bars from the end. The rhythm is a majestic but pulsing 3/4, and the melody carries echoes of other triumphal tunes: the initial downward movement compressing the energy of the line, allowing for an ever-expanding and upwards drive to the triumphant climax is also found in VULPIUS (*With One Voice* 287(i); and the final 4 bars imitate the close of REGENT SQUARE (which is also in the MICHAELMAS key of B flat major).

Christ has changed the world's direction *H15*
Metre: 8.7.8.7.6.7

This hymn by **Shirley Murray** was commissioned by the Presbyterian Church of the United States for its General Assembly held at Columbus, Ohio, in 2002, and was written shortly after 11 September 2001. It was first published in her American collection *Faith Makes the Song* (2003), before its appearance in *Hope is our Song* (2009).

The given theme of the hymn is 'Ambassadors for Christ,' taken from 2 Corinthians 5:20, 'So we are ambassadors for Christ, since God is making his appeal through us.' The poet finds alternative versions of the biblical image of ambassadors: 'agents of the new creation' in verse 1, and 'Envoys of a High Commission' in verse 5. The phrase 'High Commission' plays on the double sense of 'a commission from on high (God) and 'the overseas embassy of one nation to another.' There is similar word play in verse 2 on 'common wealth and common state,' where the political terms 'commonwealth' and 'state' play against the sense of 'wealth and status held in common.' Verse 3 refers to the initiative developed in 2000 for the relief of poverty by the cancellation by rich nations of the debts owed to them by poorer nations. Olive trees are ancient symbols of peace in both Greek and Jewish culture; see Isaiah 9:5 for soldiers' boots. Verse 4 opens with an allusion to 2 Corinthians 3:1 'Do we need…letters of recommendation to you, or from you?' Verse 5 recalls 2 Corinthians 5:20, 'God, who through Christ reconciled us to himself and gave us the ministry of reconciliation.' Christ as 'our internet of care' is a strikingly modern image, meaning 'Christ is our connective system, making possible our contact with and care for each other.'

NEW DIRECTIONS The tune name is taken from the first line of the hymn, and the setting is by **Barry Brinson**, who chooses a 4/4 march-like style, perhaps influenced by his long-time work with choirs and brass bands. Note the division of the music into unison and harmony sections, differentiated tonally – F major, moving into G minor, then returning to F major. There are echoes here of Handel's sturdy tune GOPSAL.

Christ is alive (Easter Song) *A15*
Metre: 13.12.13.7.6.11

Jillian Bray, the composer of the tune HEARTBEAT, explains the circumstances of the writing of the hymn text: 'I sent this tune to Shirley on 11 July 1988. By 21 July she had responded with her text, titled Easter Song.' The song gained immediate popularity when it was printed in *Alleluia Aotearoa* in 1993, so much so that author **Shirley Murray** included it in her second American collection, *Every Day in your Spirit* (1996).

The first verse has parallels with an earlier hymn by Irish church educator Pamela Stotter, 'Christ is alive, with joy we sing,' published in *The Australian Catholic Worship Book* (Melbourne, 1985):

> Christ is alive, with joy we sing;
> we celebrate our risen Lord,
> praising the glory of his name.
> *Alleluia, alleluia, alleluia.*

But such parallels are probably fortuitous, given the nature of the theme, the celebration of Christ's resurrection, and there are a number of hymns that begin in this way.

The refrain of Shirley Murray's hymn is sourced in Luke 24:2 ('They found the stone rolled away'), but in verse 1 there is also an echo of Job 38:7 ('When the morning stars sang together and all the Sons of God shouted for joy'). Verse 2, lines 1-2 echo George Matheson's famous hymn, which opens with 'O love that wilt not let me go,' but Romans 8:38-39 is heard in the third line ('Nor height, nor depth, nor anything else in all creation will be able to separate us from the love of God in Christ Jesus our Lord'). Verse 3, line 2, echoes Romans 6:53 ('God's grace has set us free').

[HEARTBEAT] Jillian Bray's melody received its name HEARTBEAT in the American collection *Every Day in your Spirit*; it is taken from verse 2, line 2, 'the heartbeat of Love.' The composer says of her work, 'This is only one of a handful of tunes I would consider God-given. Certainly it has stood the test of time, unlike others. I can remember sitting at the piano composing this one…Now it is probably my best-known tune, having been broadcast, televised, recorded and sung in numerous services.' Set in the celebration key of D major, the melody has the classic shape of a steady rise to a top E, followed by a steeper fall to the tonic note.

Christ is our peace *A16*
Metre: 8.8.10.8

This text was written for the ninth General Assembly of the Christian Conference of Asia, held in Manila in 1990, with the general theme, 'Christ, our Peace: Building a Just Society.' This is a text showing a poet playing with a set of key words: 'peace,' 'health,' 'wealth.' It was written by Shirley Murray in 1985, stimulated by the beauty of the Irish melody SUANTRAI. The author says of it, 'I have always been drawn to the strength and simplicity of Celtic prayers and songs,' and she attempts to create a text with similar qualities. Her hymn was first published in *Sound the Bamboo* (1990) where it is set to **I-to Loh's** tune SAM KIAP,* before appearing in *In Every Corner Sing* (1992), where it is set to PEACELIFE by American composer **Jane Marshall**, and *Alleluia Aotearoa* (1993).

Focusing on the search for peace, one of Murray's constant themes, each verse reiterates the key word – 7 times altogether. Verse 1 begins with a quotation from Ephesians 2:14, 'For he himself is our peace,' then alludes to John 1:14, Christ as the Word made flesh. Verse 2 perhaps presses the metaphor 'open-handed' (here meaning 'opened to truth and the demands of love' rather than 'generous') too far. Its second couplet takes an unexpected direction by introducing the idea that those who follow Christ in the search for peace must expect to face his experience of physical violence and brutality. Presumably the bright flower and burst seed[pod] refer to the flowering and spread of peace. Verse 3 offers a gnomic statement of the ideas that began the hymn.

SUANTRAI (Gaelic=lullaby) This melody, of unknown date and authorship, appeared in C.V. Stanford's edition of *The Complete Petrie Collection of Ancient Irish Music* (London, 1902), where it is described as a lullaby or nursery song. It was taken into *Leabhar Iomann* (1961), the Gaelic hymnbook of the Church of Ireland, and has since been used in *New Hymns for all Seasons* (1969), a collection of Scottish Jesuit priest James Quinn's hymns. The arrangement used in *Alleluia Aotearoa* is by Thomas Henry Weaving (1881-1966), and was originally made for *Leabhar Iomann*.

*For a moving account of this setting and its name see I-to Loh's *Hymnal Companion to Sound the Bamboo: Asian Hymns in their*

Liturgical and Cultural Contexts, Chicago: GIA (2011) 363-4.

Christ of darkness, Christ of light
C10
Metre: 7.7.7.8

This carol was written in 1989 by **Colin Gibson** for the Mornington Methodist choir; the manuscript carries the title 'Not a Christmas Carol.' It was published in *Carol our Christmas* in 1996, but with inaccuracies in several places. The original first verse reads:

> Christ of darkness, Christ the light
> Burning undiminished, bright;
> High above, a million stars
> Shine down upon you, child of night.

The original final line of verse 3 read 'In this her travail here on earth.' The first line of verse 4 originally read 'Christ for whom the angels sang.'

The words originated in a reflection on the theme of darkness and light in John 1:1-10. The first verse matches the biblical image of Christ as the light of the world, with the historical Jesus as a baby looking up at the stars in the night sky above him. Verse 2 presents Jesus as both the child of a poor family and the one through whom in John's words 'the world was made.' Verse 3 translates this idea into the birth of Jesus when 'all creation comes to birth in this travail here on earth.' Verse 4 recalls Luke's account of the angelic song that heralded Jesus' birth (Luke 2:13-14) and John's phrase 'the true light' (John 1:9).

[DARK CHRIST] The setting by **Colin Gibson**, also written in 1989, represents the oppositions of dark and light, heaven and earth, helpless child and creator of the universe in musical terms, by moving in both melody and bass lines through the extreme range of an octave or more from very low notes to very high notes and back again. The key likewise shifts upwards and downwards from G minor through several keys before coming to rest in B flat major.

Christ of the sad face F9, HP2
Metre: 9.9.9.9

This powerful penitential Easter hymn was written by **Shirley Murray** in 1992. She says of it, 'This hymn finds its source in the Gospel readings for Holy Week (Matthew 24, Luke 13). The words reflect on our slowness to be caught up in Jesus' passion for justice and peace.' The text was first published in Murray's American collection (1996) *In Every Corner Sing*, then in *Faith Forever Singing* (2000).

The words of the text reflect the biblical accounts of the weeks leading up to Christ's arrest and execution, but they are also informed by Shirley Murray's commitment to the work of Amnesty International and the reports of political persecution and oppression regularly circulated by that organization. Verse 1 directly references Luke 13:34 ('Jerusalem, Jerusalem, the city that kills the prophets and stones those who are sent to it'), but it also images Christ as the Man of Sorrows, acquainted with grief (Isaiah 53:3) and alludes to the machinations of the Jerusalem religious authorities scheming the death of Jesus. Verse 2 projects the sufferings of Christ onto the modern world where 'torture and terror darken the light' and justice itself is 'imprisoned' (that is, people are unjustly imprisoned). Verse 2 resumes the reference to Luke 13:34 ('How often have I desired to gather your children together as a hen gathers her brood under her wing'). The final verse strongly reiterates the theme of peace. The second line references Matthew 10:13 ('And if the house is worthy, let your peace come upon it'), but also John 14:27. The phrase 'peace without tears' (line 3) was a newspaper headline at least as early as 1959 during the Cold War between Russia and America; it means 'reaching an agreed peace without the necessity of a war to bring it about.'

CAMBRIDGE The tune name refers to the English university city of Cambridge, where the composer, **Colin Gibson** was taking sabbatical leave when the text reached him. In keeping with the somber words of the hymn, the melody line repeatedly uses falling appoggiaturas to convey the idea of suffering and grief. The harmonic structure moves through minor keys, B minor, F sharp minor, B minor, with a throbbing bass pattern and frequent discords. The final cadence resolves on a B major chord to contrast the suffering in the world with the peace of 'a spirit centred in God.' There is a further setting by Canadian composer **Ron Klusmeier** (Klusmeier 5).

Christ, let us come with you *A17*
Metre: 6.5.5.5.5.6

This hymn of invocation was written in 1991 by **Shirley Murray**, who explains its occasion as '[having been] written after I returned home from the World Council Assembly held in Canberra [Australia, 1991]. It gathers up my feelings about a communion which is still divided by our different traditions.' It was first published in her American collection, *In Every Corner Sing* (1992) before reaching *Alleluia Aotearoa* (1993).

The argument of the hymn is explained by its background; the author's disappointment at the inability of Assembly members to celebrate together the central Christian feast of communion forms the substance of verse 3 ('forgive us all'), while the remaining verses articulate the ideas of making peace (verse 1), becoming one (verse 2), and openness to each other (verse 4). As usual, biblical allusions seam the text. In verse 1, Mark 14:15 and Luke 22:12 refer to the large upper room where the Last Supper took place; John 14:27 refers to the peace given (here 'made') by Christ. Verse 2 draws on John 15:14, 'You are my friends…no longer do I call you servants,' and on John 17:21, 'that they may all be one…so that the world may believe that you have sent me.' Verse 3 reiterates the reference to Christ's prayer for the unity of believers in John 17. Verse 4, line 1, alludes to Psalm 145:16; line 4, refers to Mark 16:7, 'he is going ahead of you.'

WROSLYN ROAD **Colin Gibson** wrote this setting for the hymn in 1991. Murray comments, 'He sensed my mood immediately.' The prevailing subdued mood is established by the D minor tonality, though the music resolves on a final optimistic D major chord. The tune is named after the street in the village of Freeland, Oxfordshire, England, where the composer was living at the time of writing.

Christians are all kinds of people *H16*
Metre: 8.8.12.8.8.8.8.11.8.8

This cheerful account of the people of God was written by **Stan Stewart** in 2005. Verse by verse the writer incorporates an increasingly varied list, making the point that 'God uses all kinds of people.' The chorus-like final lines are a quotation from a 1914 chorus written by American evangelist **Charles Austin Miles** (1868-1946) and based on Romans 8:35:

> Wide, wide as the ocean,
> high as the heavens above,
> Deep, deep as the deepest sea
> is my Saviour's love.
> I, though so unworthy,
> still am a child of his care,
> For his Word teaches me that his love
> reaches me everywhere.

OOM-PAH-PAH The tune is named for the 'four hearty, tuba-like "Oom Pah Pah's"' which the writer directed should precede each verse. The original manuscript offers only a melody line with chord indications. The version in *Hope is our Song* was prepared by **Barry Brinson** in 2008. The melody swings along with a kind of music-hall gaiety that reflects the cheerful inclusiveness and confidence of the text, and the arranger has added some brass-band stylistic flourishes of his own.

Christmas in the picture book *A18*
Metre: Irregular

This hymn text is based on a poem written before 1947 by **Dorothy Neal (Ballantyne) White** which probably reflects her own happy times at the beach with her two daughters, Vicky and Kerry. Originally titled 'Carol for a New Zealand Child,' the poem was first published in 1947 in an American journal of literature for younger readers, *The Horn Book*, then reprinted in *Told under the Christmas Tree: An Umbrella Book*, published in England in 1948 by Macmillan, where it came to the attention of the composer, **Colin Gibson**, and with its setting was first published in his *Singing Love* (1988). The repetitions of the seventh line of each verse were introduced by the composer.

White was an outstanding children's librarian, working at the Dunedin Public Library from 1937 to 1974, and familiar with the many children's picture books retelling the Christmas story. The first verse describes a typical illustration from one of these books, showing a northern hemisphere winter crossing of the desert as the three Kings travel to Bethlehem (Matthew 2:1-12). The archaic word 'rime' (frost) implies both the antiquity and the 'otherness' of the biblical scene. In the second verse this cold world is contrasted with a contemporary New Zealand summer scene at the beach, where laughing children playing in the breakers offer 'a Christmas hymn.' The north-west wind ('a nor'west day') in eastern parts of New Zealand is a warm wind bringing hot dry weather (cf. William James' Australian carol, 'The north wind is tossing the leaves').

THEO The tune is named after and dedicated to the composer's first grandchild, Theo Barrett Gibson (born 1982), to whom, with his parents, the poem with its four-part setting was given as a Christmas gift. Although the tonic key is F major, in bars 3 and 7 minor chords hint at the snows and the strange Kings mentioned in the first stanza. Having reached its peak in bar 10, the melody moves down towards the tonic note in a series of sequential phrases that take the music through F, D and C major to the final cadence.

Church of the living Christ (Hymn for the Church after Easter) *A19*
Metre: 6.6.6.6.8.8

Written in 1985 by **Shirley Murray** for her Wellington, St Andrew's on the Terrace, Presbyterian church, this hymn was 'intended to generate energy from the Resurrection story, and refocus our congregation on mission.' It first reached print in the author's private publication *In Every Corner Sing* (1987), carrying the title 'A Hymn for the Church after Easter,' then in her first American collection, *In Every Corner Sing* (1992), before appearing in *Alleluia Aotearoa* (1993).

The forceful language ('burst the tomb apart,' 'no patching up old schemes') and the imperative tone of the text ('speak to the Man,' 'sharpen every nerve') generate their own verbal energy, and as usual there is a running subtext of biblical allusion. The striking phrase in verse 1, 'the Man who walks' – the metre dictates a break here – suggests the resurrection appearances of Christ, in particular the disciples' encounter with him on the road to Emmaus (Luke 24:13-35), and this idea is carried forward into verse 2 ('Christ's presence sets the pace'). But 'walk free' also has connotations of release from a judicial sentence or a prison (cf. 1 Peter 3:18-20). Verse 2 paraphrases the parable of the wineskins and the patched cloth (Matthew 9:16-17), and verse 4 recalls 1 Corinthians 12:27, 'Now you are the Body of Christ,' and Isaiah 30:21, 'This is the way, walk in it.' Line 3 of the final verse recalls Mark 6:15 ('Go forth and preach the gospel'); for Jesus himself as the Word see 1 John 1:1-2. The final line of the hymn points forward to Pentecost.

RESURRECTION The tune name of the setting used in *Alleluia Aotearoa* refers to the theme of the hymn; this strong, vigorous, march-like music was written by **Jillian Bray** in the late 1980s. However, the hymn was first sung to the tune CHRISTCHURCH, written in 1858 by **Charles Steggall** (1826-1905), and widely regarded as one of the finest tunes of the 19th century. In *In Every Corner Sing* the text was matched to a setting named DIVERSITY by the American composer **Jack Schrader**. In both *Alleluia Aotearoa* and *In Every Corner Sing*, LITTLE CORNARD, by English composer **Martin Shaw** (1875-83), is suggested as an alternative tune; it was named after the small Suffolk village where the composer enjoyed his honeymoon.

'Click, click,' how the needles fly (Caring) A20
Metre: 7.10.8.9

This children's hymn was written by **Colin Gibson** in 1986. It was intended to provide children with an alternative to the prevailing concept of God as male-gendered. Each verse elaborates on one of Jesus' own 'maternal' images of God: verse 1 draws on Matthew 11:28-30, Luke 12:27-28; verse 2 on Mark 10:13; verse 3 on Matthew 23:37, Luke 13:34; and verse 4 on Luke 13:20-21. Each of these images is translated into a contemporary equivalent intelligible to a child: knitting a jersey, cuddling a baby, a hen gathering its chickens, a mother preparing dough to make bread and feed a family.

CARING This simple unison tune with its cheerful syncopated rhythms was written for these words by **Colin Gibson** in 1986. The tune name refers to the theme of the hymn, God's caring and protective love for all of humanity.

Clippety-clop, clippety-clop C12
Metre: Irregular

This was the third song written by **Jackie Wise** for the annual Nativity services held at St Cuthbert's school, Epsom, Auckland, for the 5 to 7 year-old (Year 1-3) girls there. Jackie Wise says of her carol, 'We had sung the same donkey song for many years, and in 1994 we felt it was time for a change! So I tried to think about the trip to Bethlehem from the donkey's point of view. What would he be thinking as they all journeyed? What would he hear Mary and Joseph talking about? And the donkey realized, before Mary and Joseph ever arrived in Bethlehem, that their hopes for rest and comfort at the end of the trip would probably not be fulfilled. But, thankfully, someone *was* kind.'

There is no mention in the gospels of Mary riding on a donkey to Bethlehem, but it is a very early Christian tradition, mentioned in the second-century Christian writing, *Protoevangelium of James*, chapter 17: 'And they came into the middle of the road, and Mary said to him: Take me down from off the ass, for that which is in me presses to come forth. And he took her down from off the ass, and said to her: "Whither shall I lead you, and cover your disgrace? For the place is desert." And he found a cave there, and led her into it; and leaving his two sons beside her, he went out to seek a midwife in the district of Bethlehem.'

Jackie Wise's text is actually spoken by the donkey – historical or not. It contrasts Joseph and Mary's cheerful expectations of their arrival at Bethlehem with the donkey's doubts (confirmed by our knowledge of their actual reception as described in Luke 2:7).

[CLIPPETY-CLOP] The tune name and the music refer to the sound of the donkey's hoofs striking regularly on the hard surface of a road (the word appears c.1925 with this sense), and both repetitive melody and rocking bass line suggest the tedium of the journey – at least from the donkey's point of view.

Colour me free! A21
Metre: Irregular

This happy children's song, introducing in a simple way the concept of racial tolerance and harmony, was written in 1985 by Dominican Sister **Cecily Sheehy** as one of a series of such songs for children published in the Catholic magazine *Family Living*. Its first hymnbook appearance was in *New Zealand Praise* (1988), in an arrangement by **David Dell** for spoken as well as singing voices, which was used for publication in *Alleluia Aotearoa* (1993).

The opening line of the chorus employs a 1962 United States slang expression 'colour me,' meaning 'see me,' or 'let me present myself.' Although the origin of the phrase suggests that behind it lies the search for freedom from racial bigotry and oppression in American terms, this text takes a more positive view of skin colour and ethnic difference as 'the gifts of the world to me' and further elaborates 'colour' in terms of art and painting. (The writer herself enjoys practising her own skills as a painter.) Consequently, the opening phrase may be taken to mean 'colour me in with the hues and tones appropriate to a free and independent person.' The final vision is of 'a great pattern of harmony,' which neatly unites the concepts of musical and artistic beauty and wholeness with the idea of 'harmonious' social relationships.

[COLOUR ME FREE] As the composer, **Cecily Sheehy** herself, indicates, this lively syncopated song is conceived of as a sung chorus, with its two intervening verses spoken rather than sung, though the verses can be sung to the chorus tune with minor adjustments of note values.

Come and find the quiet centre F10 (i) and (ii)
Metre: 13.12.13.12 D

This hymn of invocation was written in 1989 by **Shirley Murray** for a New Zealand Presbyterian Women's conference on the theme of 'Making Space.' The author comments, 'It has always surprised me how much use these words have had, even to being used in the Chaplain's devotions in the White House [Washington, USA].' The hymn was first published in Shirley Murray's initial American collection, *In Every Corner Sing* (1992), where it was set to Benjamin White's tune BEACH SPRING for the gospel song 'Come, ye sinners, poor and needy' (*The Sacred Harp*, 1844), arranged by **Jack Schrader**, Hope's musical editor at the time. Shirley Murray has described this tune as 'appropriately serene.' As a representative New Zealand hymn it was reprinted (words only) in *A Panorama of Christian Hymnody*, by Erik Routley and Alan A. Richardson (Chicago: GIA, 2005).

Typically, the text is organized round a dominant space / room metaphor, reflecting the Conference theme, as in the second verse, 'lifting shades to show the sun' (with the common word play on Christ as the Son of God) or the conclusion of the text, 'In the Spirit's lively scheming / there is always room to spare.' In verse 2, 'touches base' carries the meaning 'makes contact, gets in touch with us.' In verse 3 'unravel' means 'lose their knots and tangles,' an image drawn from the craft of knitting. Shirley Murray directs attention to Psalm 46:10 ('Be still and know that I am God'), 1 Kings 19:12 ('After the earthquake a fire, but the Lord was not in the fire, and after the fire a sound of sheer silence') and to Matthew's account of the Transfiguration of Jesus (17:1-8).

GAELIC TRADITIONAL MELODY This gentle, lilting folk melody from the Island of Lewis is printed in an arrangement by **John Bell**, of the Iona Community. It figures in worship performed in Iona Abbey as a setting for the John Bell-Graham Maule hymn 'Jesus calls us here to meet us' (number 66 in the *Iona Abbey Music Book*, Glasgow: Wild Goose Publications, 2003). This melody responds well to the genial tone of the hymn, characterized by the final line of the hymn, 'In the Spirit's lively scheming there is always room to spare.'

SANCTUM The editorial committee for *Faith Forever Singing*, aware that the text had already been set by several non-New Zealanders, sought to redress this, and **Jillian Bray** offered her alternative tune in 1996. The tune name suggests the retired, quiet 'inner sanctum'; the 'quiet centre' mentioned in the first line of the hymn text. Bray's music offers a quite different setting for Shirley Murray's words, one that resonates well with the idea of quiet centering. Where the Lewis melody is set in F major in 3/4 dance time, Jillian Bray chooses a D minor tonality in a steady 4/4 time, with a more flexible harmonic progression. However, both melodies rise to a middle peak, then sink back to a quiet close on the tonic note.

Come celebrate the gift of life H17
Metre: 8.8.8.8 D

This hymn, written by **Margaret Bond** in 1995, was first published in *Hope is our Song* (2009). It came out of her reading of cosmologist-theologians Teihard de Chardin, Thomas Berry and Brian Swimme (b. 1950, founder of the Centre for the Story of the Universe). At the time, she says, 'I became particularly interested in exploring where and how the stories of our tradition melded with the everyday experience of living in the world as we were coming to understand it.' It is rare to find a modern hymn that celebrates our universe in the light of contemporary scientific discoveries about its origin. While acknowledging the existence and presence of a creating God, this text praises God's gift of life in both individual human souls and within the flow of the vast universe in which we live.

Verse 1 describes the 'big bang,' as it is now known, as the 'first great flaring forth of light' in response to 'God's word of power' (Genesis 1:3, 'Let there be light'). Hebrews 4:2, 'For the word of God is living and active,' forms the basis of the second half of the verse. The second verse acknowledges the 'inborn needs of self' (in modern biological understanding, for survival, reproduction and gratification) at the same time as it praises the potential of the supreme gift of unselfish love (see 2 Corinthians 5:17). Verse 3 celebrates the gift of human consciousness, endowing us with the capacity to 'see creation as a whole' (line 4) and know the presence of God-life 'in all things' (lines 5-6). The hymn closes with a prayer for human life to 'reflect the joy creation sings' (cf. the similar injunction in Psalm 95:1, 'Come, let us sing for joy to the Lord').

GIFT OF LIFE The tune name is derived from the first line of the hymn. The setting in A major was written by **Colin Gibson** in 2006. The emphatic nature of the music was suggested by Scottish psalm settings. Its open ending (on an E major chord) corresponds to the stress in the text on the 'flow,' 'potential' and 'possibility' of the universe it describes.

Come in, come in, New Year C13 (i) and (ii)
Metre: 6.6.6.6.8.8

'Not just a carol for the New Year celebration, but a song for Epiphany and the universalizing of the Gospel,' says **Shirley Murray**, who wrote this carol in 1993. It was first published in 1996 in both *Carol our Christmas* and the author's American collection *Every Day in Your Spirit*. In the latter, where it is titled 'Song for the New Year,' the seasonal description 'shining summer day' (verse 1) is allowed to be changed to 'sparkling winter day,' though the alteration is not admitted to the printed text. The chosen setting for American singers is ST JOHN (also known as ADORATION), a tune which was first published in *The Parish Choir* (1851) and is possibly by **Frances Ridley Havergal** (1836-79).

Some of Murray's familiar themes are repeated in this text. January is an open door allowing for renewed hope; it is characterised as a time to risk change and take a new direction. In the experience of Simeon and Anna (Luke 2:21-38), whom the author describes as 'the sometimes forgotten personages in this part of the story,' the infant Jesus is seen as 'the child who rules all time to be,' and this theme is developed in the following verse which closes with a prayer for 'a year of peace' – unsurprisingly, since in 1992 bloody civil wars had broken out in Afghanistan and Bosnia. They continued into 1993, when new outbreaks of civil violence occurred in Burundi and Nagaland.

SARABAND AVENUE Named after the address of Christchurch Anglican friends, Bill and Lois Ball, and dedicated to them, this melody was written in 1993 by **Colin Gibson.** This is a hearty medieval-sounding tune with echoes of drums and pipes, and although the key signature is A flat minor, with irrepressible optimism the harmony keeps breaking towards F major and succeeds in doing so in the final bar.

NEW YEAR SAMBA Also written in 1993, **Ian Render**'s setting, in E flat major, picks up the theme of hopeful jollity by adopting the musical form of a samba, a popular South American dance, though the frequent use of diminished chords carries through a strain of unresolved melancholy – or is it anxiety? There is a further setting of this carol by Canadian composer **Ron Klusmeier** (Klusmeier 2).

Come into the streets with me (Palm Sunday Song) A22
Metre: 7.7.7.7 and refrain

As **Shirley Murray** explains, her Palm Sunday Song was written in 1989 as an action song for a children's procession celebrating Palm

Sunday at her home church, St Andrew's on the Terrace, Wellington. It was initially published in the first American collection of her work, *In Every Corner Sing* (1992). New Zealand publication followed in 1993 in *Alleluia Aotearoa*.

This is no simple song of celebration. The first two verses closely follow the gospel accounts of Jesus' entry into Jerusalem (Matthew 21:6-11, Mark 11:1-10, Luke 19:28-40, John12:12-15). But verse 3 alludes to the disciples' betrayal of Jesus at the time of his arrest (Matthew 27:47-56, Mark 14:43-50, Luke 22:47-53, John 18:1-12) and verse 4 refers to the resurrection appearances of Jesus to his disciples. The refrain is based on the children's rhyme, 'Follow my leader,' but with an echo of Jesus' call to his first disciples (Matthew 4:18-19, Mark:16-17).

SEE SAW SACCARA DOWN A traditional English folk melody, as arranged by **Charles Strange**. It had already been used in 1983 as a setting for Brian Wren's children's hymn, 'I am going to Calvary.' There is an original setting by Canadian composer **Ron Klusmeier** (Klusmeier 3).

Come now where we least expect you C15
Metre: 8.7.8.7.3.3.7

Written by **Marnie Barrell** in 1995, this Advent song was first published in *Carol our Christmas* (1996) and is included on the Oremus website.

The scripture-rich text takes its beginning from Matthew 24:44: 'Therefore you must be ready, for the Son of Man is coming at an hour you do not expect.' That 'we still reject you' alludes to Isaiah 53:3, 'he was despised and rejected, a man of sorrows.' The phrase 'sacred ground,' in this context meaning 'within the Christian Church,' derives from Exodus 3:5. Verse 2 works around Jesus' declaration, 'the last shall be first' (Matthew 20:16), but the writer substitutes 'the least' for 'last,' using another Jesus expression, 'the least of these.' Verse 3 addresses the Christmas Christ-child, but the imperative verb 'come' prompts thoughts of another manifestation of Christ, described in the formulation of the Apostles' Creed as seated at the right hand of God the Father almighty; 'from thence he will come to judge the living and the dead.' This is followed by a reference to Christ as the Word of God made flesh (John 1:14) and as the expression of the divine love (John 3:16). Finally, Jesus is invoked as Lord (1 Peter 3:15).

AUCKLAND The tune name refers to the New Zealand city where Marnie Barrell was living at the time of writing. **Colin Gibson**, its composer, dedicated his setting, written in 1996, to a young couple of his acquaintance, Margot Gibson and William Pope, who were later married. A cheerful, sometimes syncopated melody in A major, the music shifts to C major to mark the change of direction in the text at the words 'Look around, Christ is found far beyond our sacred ground,' then reassuringly shifts again back to the tonic key. On the Oremus website Herbert Howell's MICHAEL (see *With One Voice* 464(ii)) is given as an alternative tune.

Come now, Lord Jesus (Carol for Advent) W645, A23 (i) and (ii), C14 (i) and (ii)
Metre: 5.5.6.6

This very popular carol was written by **Shirley Murray** in 1980, and first published in the New Zealand Supplement to *With One Voice* (1982). It then appeared in *New Zealand Praise* (1988) and her first American collection, *In Every Corner Sing* (1992), followed closely by *Alleluia Aotearoa* (1993) and *Carol our Christmas* (1996). Shirley Murray later wrote, 'This Advent carol was the first of my texts ever officially published. It appeared in *With One Voice* (Collins, 1982) as a last-minute inclusion. It was also the first to be recorded, sung to the Zulu tune which I had heard on an album of the King's Singers and which had originally inspired it…This was the first occasion, too, when I had struggled over the title "Lord" and found myself unable to do away with it.'

The carol takes the form of a bidding prayer invoking the presence of Jesus in 'our Christmas' as the singers contemplate 'a new-made manger,' probably in front of them. The successive verses stress both the simplicity and deprivation of the circumstances into which this 'cold and crying' baby was born and Christ's divinity ('Son…of our own Creator'). In the fourth verse there is an allusion to the crucifixion ('your body feeling hurt'), and in the final line of the carol to the burial of Jesus ('myrrh will yet anoint you'). Myrrh, a fragrance derived from a tree resin and one of the gifts of the Magi, among many other purposes was used for embalming (see John 19:39). Besides the familiar elements of the Nativity story – a manger, 'born of a woman' (cf. the creedal statement, 'born of the Virgin Mary'), 'no place to receive you' (Luke 2:7), gifts and a star pointing the way – there are other biblical references in this deceptively simple text. Verse 4, 'our flesh your temple,' refers to 1 Corinthians 6:19; verse 5, 'bread to be broken,' alludes to the ritual words of Holy Communion, reflecting 1 Corinthians 11:24.

[MEWS] This unnamed setting of the text is by **Douglas Mews** and was written in 1992. It features two alternating melodies, set in the related keys of C major and E minor.

LALA MNTWANA (Zulu=Sleep now, child) This tune is named after the Zulu song which inspired the writing of Murray's text. It was made famous by the English unaccompanied choral group the King's Singers, formed by six Cambridge University choral scholars in 1968. With the participation of Stanley Glasser, a South African-born ethnomusicologist, they recorded the song in a collection titled *Street Songs*. The setting used in W645 is an arrangement of the original melody by **Shona Murray**; an alternative setting by **Roy Tankersley** is used in *A23 (ii)* and *C14 (ii)*.

Come on this wedding day (Hymn for a Wedding) *A24*
Metre: 6.6.11.6.6.11

This wedding hymn was written by **Shirley Murray** in 1985. It was first published privately in *In Every Corner Sing* (1987, then appeared in the first American collection of Shirley Murray's work, *In Every Corner Sing* (1992). New Zealand publication followed in 1993 in *Alleluia Aotearoa*.

Shirley Murray says, 'Close friends asked for a hymn at their marriage service, and this was offered on the understanding that it would be read, not sung, if a tune could not be found. In the event we used DOWN AMPNEY [by **Ralph Vaughan Williams**] but my feeling is that this tune is properly wedded to "Come Down, O Love Divine" and so I hope for a new setting.'

'Christ of Cana' (verse 1, line 2) refers to Christ's presence at the marriage of friends at Cana in Galilee (John 2:1-11). The opening lines of verse 2 echo the words of the marriage service, and verse 3 references Paul's famous praise of love as the greatest of the Christian virtues, in a passage often read at marriages (1 Corinthians 13:13).

DOWN AMPNEY See above. This famous tune, named after the composer's birth-place near Cirencester in Gloucestershire, was written by **Ralph Vaughan Williams** for the hymn 'Come down, O love divine,' and published in his *English Hymnal* (1906). A new setting of the kind hoped for by Shirley Murray has not yet emerged.

Come, teach us, Spirit of our God *F11*
Metre: 8.6.8.6

Written in 1990 by **Shirley Murray**, this text was her response to an American Hymn Text search for texts to be used in an educational establishment. (She comments wryly that 'In the event I didn't feature in the "mention" list.') The search led her to 'play with images of creativity.' The result was first published in 1992 in Murray's first American collection, *In Every Corner Sing* (1992), set to the tune PITYOULISH by Reginald Barrett-Ayres (1920-81), a prolific Scottish composer and Haydn scholar, who taught at the University of Glasgow from 1951 to 1981, becoming

Reader and Head of the Department of Music there. The tune was named after a lake in the Scottish Highlands. When the hymn was published in 1995 in the American United Church of Christ *New Century Hymnal* it was given a fresh tune by Arthur G. Clyde, named MURRAY in honour of Shirley Murray, and this tune with Murray's text was reprinted in her second American collection, *Every Day in your Spirit* (1996). When the hymn finally reached New Zealand publication in *Faith Forever Singing* (2000), **Jillian Bray** provided an indigenous tune, EDUCARE, written in 1999.

The text shows a creative writer at play with images and language. The Holy Spirit is invited to behave like any good teacher – to teach, excite, engage, inspire and delight minds, wits, spark (the word carries a play on 'soul,' 'fiery energy' and 'flash of light') and hearts – and is finally manifested as an aspect of the character of God. A similar facility inspires Shirley Murray's choice of no fewer than 14 verbs of activity, which close in worship and learning 'compassion's code.'

EDUCARE This invented tune name plays with 'Education' and 'Care' (it is now the brand name of several New Zealand commercial educational services and institutions). Fitting the text it supports, Jillian Bray's music is set in the harmonic frame of a major key (F), and the melody, with its kaleidoscopic note values, leaps about energetically. There is a further setting by Canadian composer **Ron Klusmeier** (Klusmeier 4).

Come to a wedding A25
Metre: 10.9.10.9

Shirley Murray, the author of this wedding hymn written in 1988, comments, 'This [text] was written for the marriage of our youngest son, Rob, to Christine, and set to the over-used BUNESSAN because it was a tune everyone could sing. BUNESSAN will always be, for me, the Gaelic 'Child in a manger.' The last line is left open for Christian names to be added, or [to be sung as] 'Now to you both....'

Before appearing in *Alleluia Aotearoa* (1993), the hymn was published in Murray's American collection *In Every Corner Sing* (1992). There it appeared with BUNESSAN, identified only as 'a traditional Gaelic melody,' in an arrangement by **Jack Schrader** (b. 1934, then musical editor with Hope Publishing). In *Alleluia Aotearoa*, the same matching was presented, but the tune, now given its common name, appeared in an arrangement by **Jillian Bray**.

The first verse prudently allows for the fickle weather patterns of New Zealand; the second verse celebrates both love expressed in social relationships and centred in God (1 John 4:8), whose love is without end (1 Corinthians 13:8, the opening of a passage frequently used as a reading for a marriage service). The same passage is the source of the idea of love as a gift (Verse 3, line 1), but as the next line shows the writer is also thinking of the giving and exchange of rings, usually made of gold, symbolizing the precious nature of the new relationship formalised in the marriage service. 1 Corinthians 13:5 and the account of the miraculous turning of water into wine by Jesus at a wedding at Cana (John 2:1-11) contribute to the final lines of this verse.

BUNESSAN This tune is a Scottish highland melody collected by Alexander Fraser and first published in 1888 in Lachlan Macbean's *Songs and Hymns of the Gaels* as a setting for Mary Macdonald's carol 'Child in a Manger.' It is named after Mary Macdonald's birthplace near Bunessan on the Isle of Mull off the west coast of Scotland. The arrangement by Jillian Bray provided for *Alleluia Aotearoa* is described by the musician herself as 'drawn from several sources.'

Come to our land A26
Metre: 8.8.9.9 and refrain

Shirley Murray wrote this invocation in 1990. She describes it as 'an attempt to interweave the spirituality of the original people of New Zealand with the European, at a time when the justice of land rights and social equity were in question.* It is also a prayer for the precious and beautiful environment we share.' It was first published in Murray's American collection *In Every Corner Sing* (1992), then in *Alleluia Aotearoa* (1993).

The verses have a solemn liturgical pattern, 'Come...bring, Come...teach, Come...speak,' with much repetition, including the refrain. Māori terms are used to affirm the 'interweaving' of the two cultures of which the author speaks. *Wairua tapu* is the Holy Spirit, the single focus of this prayer. *Aotearoa* (=land of the long white cloud) is a Māori name for New Zealand: it has since become officially recognized as a name for the country. The attributions of the Spirit listed in the first two verses – peace, truth, life, new birth – are biblical in origin; they become indigenous in verse 3 as the poet thinks of the dense forests ('bush') of New Zealand and the famously rich bird life they contain. The refrain celebrates the national and universal unifying power of the Holy Spirit, almost in North American Indian terms, as the 'Great Spirit of God.'

HAEREMAI (Māori=welcome). The tune name suggests the respectful coming together of two cultures, and their languages. The music of the verses is given a gentle, Māori-style rhythm, but swells to a stronger theme and a more emphatic rhythm as the text declares 'And all our people will sing together' (symbolized in musical terms by the introduction of unison phrases). The setting was written by **Colin Gibson** in 1990 and this hymn was one of the earliest collaborations between these two artists, developed as they worked together on the editorial board for *Alleluia Aotearoa*.

> *1987 had seen the introduction by the then National Government of the Māori Affairs Amendment Act, which allowed greater government interference in Māori landholding rights and was vigorously opposed as yet another European land grab. It became one of the catalysts for a national Māori protest movement. By the mid-1990s a new wave of activism over land ownership and Treaty of Waitangi issues challenged the idea that New Zealand was a comfortable, unified society, 'God's own country,' as a popular phrase put it.

Come to the celebration *A27*
Metre: 12.11.12.11

This joyful approach to communion hymn was written by **Marnie Barrell** in 1989 and first published in *Alleluia Aotearoa* (1993); it has also been published on the Oremus website.

The theme of the hymn is the celebration of the Eucharist as a wedding feast at which Christ is the bridegroom and his Church the bride. It follows Matthew 22:1-10, but is enriched with additional resonances. The traditional invitation to the Jewish feast of the Passover is 'Let all who are hungry come and eat' (cf. verse 1, line 1). 'The best wine' alludes to John 2:10. 'Here he comes' refers to the parable of the wise and foolish marriage attendants (Matthew 25:1-10). Verse 2 begins with a reference to Matthew 8:22, 'Follow me and let the dead bury their own dead.' Luke 14:23 refers to those brought in from the 'roadsides' to share the wedding feast. Verse 3 incorporates the Jesus saying, 'the last shall be first and the first shall be last' (Matthew 20:16), and in Matthew 22 the feast is given by a king for his son (cf. 'Royal guests of honour,' line 3). Verse 4 introduces the ancient metaphoric conception of the Church as the bride of Christ, based on such scriptural passages as John 3:29 and Revelation 19:7. The final verse reverses Old Testament injunctions against appearing 'empty-handed' before God (Deuteronomy 16:16, Exodus 24:20); it also references Jesus' encounter with the Samaritan woman at the well, 'Whoever drinks of the water that I shall give him will never thirst' (John 4:14) and closes with a phrase from Psalm 100:5, 'The Lord is good, his steadfast love endures for ever.'

CANA The tune name refers to the wedding at Cana in Galilee, which Jesus attended and where he performed his first miracle (John 2:1-11). The music, by **Marnie Barrell**, is patterned on the Northumbrian folk dance tune THE KEEL ROW* and was arranged for *Alleluia Aotearoa* by **Douglas Mews**. Although the text is a long one of five verses, the strong dotted rhythms and springing melodic line carry the words along with infectious gaiety, with scarcely a pause for breath. On the Oremus website, ST CATHERINE'S COURT by Richard Strutt (1848-1927) is given as an alternative setting.

> *This tune was popularised in New Zealand in association with Michael Hewlitt's 1969 Christmas carol 'When God almighty came to be one of us.'

Come to the feast H20
Metre: 6.9.6.6.9

This communion hymn was written by **Rob Ferguson** in 1993 during a lay ministry course the author was facilitating, in response to an exercise about being invited to the banquet of God.

The text stresses the simplicity and openness of God's invitation to the divine banquet (an idea that draws on both Isaiah 25:6 and Luke 24:15-24). There are other biblical echoes, too: in verse 1, 'let a child show the way' (Isaiah 11:6, echoed in Luke 1:76), 'be at peace' (Mark 9:50), and verse 2, 'taste and see' (Psalm 34:8). Verse 2 identifies the divine feast as Christian communion, associated with drinking wine and the breaking of bread (verse 2, 'There's a chalice of wine, break the bread and we'll dine'). A chalice is a drinking cup or goblet, in particular, the special cup used for the Eucharist.

BECKENHAM The tune name refers to the suburb of Christchurch where Rob Ferguson was stationed as a Methodist minister when he wrote the hymn text. This unison melody was composed by **Colin Gibson** in 2005 for this text. Its relaxed 6/8 rhythm is meant to suggest both the ease and simplicity referred to in the text (verse 1, 'Be at peace, you need do nothing more') and the celebratory nature of the occasion (verse 3, 'Take my hand, dance along').

Come to this Christmas singing
A28, C16
Metre: 7.7.7.6 D

Author **Shirley Murray** describes this carol, written in 1983, as 'an early experiment in contextualisation ['making this child our own']…written when the season was high summer and the wealth of our islands' resources seemed to contrast with much of the rest of the world. At this time, too, New Zealand was working towards declaring our country "Nuclear Free."'* The words were first published in 1987 in her own first collection of her work, *In Every Corner Sing* (1987) before reaching American publication in the similarly titled *In Every Corner Sing* (1992) and the New Zealand collections *New Zealand Praise* (1988), *Alleluia Aotearoa* (1993) and *Carol our Christmas* (1996).

The carol reworks the biblical story of the gifts brought by the Magi to the infant Jesus (Matthew 2:1-11). The gifts celebrated are those of 'our country.' 'Beauty of shell and stone' refers to the iridescent paua (abalone) shells common along New Zealand's coastline, and the deposits of greenstone (jade) sacred to Māori. The 'riches of race and culture' (verse 2, line 2) are the different cultural heritages brought by Māori, European and later ethnic groups who have settled in New Zealand. Verse 2, line 5, alludes to the controversy surrounding national policy on the deployment of nuclear arms: this was the period of the so-called Cold War between the United States and Russia and their allies. *Aroha*** (verse 2) is 'the Māori concept of warm, all-embracing love' (the author's words). Verse 3 contrasts the summertime Christmas world in New Zealand (at the time a major exporter of primary produce) with the northern hemisphere winter Christmas. 'Quicken' carries the meanings of 'inspire, stimulate' and 'hurry.'

GERALDINE The name refers to a prosperous farming community in South Canterbury where the composer **Colin Gibson** was enjoying a Christmas holiday when he wrote this setting in 1987: it appeared in his own first collection of hymns and carols, *Singing Love* (1988). The variously skipping and lilting melodic line reflects the joyful tone of much of Shirley Murray's text. But there is a sudden shift from E major into A minor in bar 19 to capture the reminder at the end of this carol of cold, poverty and winter. There is another setting of the words by New Zealand composer **Douglas Mews**. Named AROHA, it has a lively rhythm and an interesting harmonic structure. The Taiwanese musicologist and composer I-to Loh*** comments that Mews has 'skilfully brought together the various tonalities like gifts, matching the spirit of the text.'

> *In 1984, the then Prime Minister of New Zealand, David Lange, barred nuclear-powered or armed ships from using the country's ports or entering its territorial waters. In 1987, under the New Zealand Nuclear Free Zone, Disarmament and Arms Control Act, New Zealand became a nuclear-free zone. This position has since been enshrined in foreign policy.
>
> ** This key term, which appears frequently in New Zealand hymn writing deserves a fuller explanation of its meaning, which is given here by Māori teacher and *tohunga* (wisdom-keeper) Ruth Makuini Tai. 'The word *Aroha* holds a premier position within the Māori language of Aotearoa New Zealand. Māori language and practice holds the memory of a time when the force of *Aroha* was understood and respected by all. *Aroha* is the creative force behind all dreams. *Aroha* defines great leadership, ensures personal success, inspires us to go the extra mile. *Aroha* means Love. However, when we explore its roots *Aroha* yields a profound message about love that is not widely understood. *Aro* is thought, life principle, to pay attention, to focus, to concentrate; *ro* is inner, within, introspection; *ha* is life force, breath, energy; *oha* is generosity, prosperity, abundance, wealth. *Aroha* may be described as the binding force of all that is.'

***For a detailed analysis of the text and Colin Gibson's setting of it, see I-to Loh, *Hymnal Companion to Sound the Bamboo: Asian Hymns in their Liturgical and Cultural Contexts*. Chicago: GIA (2011), pages 364-6.

Come, fill our cup with the water of life *H18*
Metre: 10.10.11.10

In 2005 **Bill Bennett** began to write hymns and songs for each of the gospel readings chosen for the Three-Year Revised Common Lectionary, eventually publishing the complete set as *Gradual Praise* (2010). This song, written in 2004 for the second week in Epiphany (Year C), was first published in *Hope is our Song* (2009), then in *Gradual Praise*.

The author comments, 'Many of the stories about Jesus' ministry are set around times of meal-sharing. And many of his parables make reference to times of feasting and celebration. This song has a Trinitarian flow – speaking of the profusion of God's over-brimming love, the generosity of Christ's hospitality at the communion table, the passion and fire of the Holy Spirit and the fullness of God, Lord of all.'

The text takes its beginning from John's story of Jesus' first miracle performed at a wedding held at Cana in Galilee (John 2:1-11); there are also verbal echoes of the story of Jesus' meeting with the Samaritan woman at a well (John 4:7-15). Verse 2, line 1, refers to John 6:35, 'I am the bread of life.' *Aroha* (line 4) is 'the Māori word commonly used for love, especially the familial, all-encompassing love that brings people together' [author's note]. Verse 3 identifies the Holy Spirit with breath (so Genesis 2:7) and fire (Acts 2:3). For the 'fullness' of God (verse 4, line 2) see Colossians 1:19 and Ephesians 3:16-19.

WHAKAKI (Māori=fullness). The tune is named after a large coastal estuary known as Lake Whakaki, near Wairoa in Hawke's Bay. It regularly fills with tidal water, and is also full of fish, which help sustain the local communities.

Bill Bennett says of his own melody, 'This is a song that encourages the warmth of welcome, the joy of togetherness and fellowship, with a lilt that could almost lead to dancing.' The lilt derives in part from the echo of the modern (20th century) song by Hugh S. Roberton, 'Westering home and a song in the air,' which in turn is probably derived from the Irish Gaelic song 'Trasna na dTonnta' (Across the waves).

Companions, let us pray together
H21
Metre: 9.8.9.8 and refrain

This unison hymn was written by **David Clark** and **Witi Ihimaera** in 1991 for the first National Gay Christian Conference held in Auckland in June of that year. The Conference sought to affirm the integrity of gay and lesbian people in the church, to share common insights and experiences, and to explore issues related to the subject.

The words of the hymn express themes of solidarity and God's loving acceptance of the singers 'as we are.' The many biblical references to the presence of God with the believer and the believing community (as in Psalm 23:4) are caught up in lines 3-4 of the first verse. References in verses 2-3 to Christ's crucifixion and resurrection appearance to the disciples (John 20:19) as well as to 'breaking bread' and 'poured out wine' make this an appropriate general hymn for a communion service. The refrain also suggests a reaching for the freedom which Christ has won for all (cf. 1 Corinthians 9:24 and Philippians 3:14). *Whanau*=an extended family group; *in aroha*=with love towards each other.

COMPANIONS The accomplished musical setting was written in 1991 by the major New Zealand composer **David Hamilton**. The relaxed rhythm of the melody, with its characteristic offbeat phrase-openings, conveys something of the idea of freedom itself. In the opening bars of the refrain an unexpected harmonic shift upwards from E major to A major expresses the aspiration of the singers to claim kinship with the Son.

Singers need to be aware that verses 2, 3 and 4 begin on a one-syllable upbeat.

Creation sings H29
Metre: 11.10.11.10

This hymn text was written in 2000 by **Shirley Murray** for a Hymn Search by the American Presbyterian Association of Musicians to celebrate the gift of music. It was first published in 2003 in the writer's United States collection, *Faith Makes the Song* (2003), with a setting by American composer Hal H. Hopson which he named CREATION SINGS, then as a poem without a musical setting in *Hope is our Song* (2009).

While there is some biblical precedent for a singing universe (see Job 38:37), the poetic idea that creation is 'resonant with music' (verse 2, line 3), that the movement of the celestial bodies in our galaxy constitutes an inaudible but divine harmony, is derived from the ancient philosophical concept of *musica universalis* (also known as the music of the spheres) that regarded mathematical proportions in the movements of the planets and the stars as giving rise to a unique form of actual music. Pythagoras, Plato and Boethius gave the idea their authority and it continued to appeal to thinkers about music until the end of the Renaissance. Shakespeare's *Merchant of Venice*, Act V, Scene 1, extended the life of the idea, adding a further romantic resonance.

Here a modern poet revives the same imaginative conception in verses rich with musical terminology,* as a general metaphor for the 'energy and art' of God (verse 1, line 2), reflected not only in human musical expressions and in the social 'harmony' of peace and beauty (verse 3, line 3) but in the existence of all forms of life: 'the universe is resonant with music, / the smallest creature dances to its play' (verse 2, lines 3-4). In verse 1, line 3, there is an allusion to angelic song, drawing on traditions that have developed around passages in Luke and Revelation. In verse 3, line 1, Shirley Murray modifies Romans 8:22, which describes creation as groaning in the pangs of birth; her creation groans with dismay at 'our discordant clashing.' In verse 4, line 2, St Francis' famous prayer, 'Make me an instrument of your peace,' is also adapted to the theme of the hymn.

> *All the following terms can carry a musical connotation: 'sing, song, movement, litany, resonance, music, dance, play, groans, discord, harmony, melody, silence, instrument.'

Creator God, we give you thanks (A Hymn of Thanks for our Pets) H22
Metre: 8.8.8.8.8.8

Responding to a request from a member of his Mornington Methodist congregation, animal lover and trainer Beverley (Bev) Sutherland, for a new hymn to use in a Pets Sunday service, **Colin Gibson** wrote this text in 2007. It was first published in *Hope is our Song* (2009).

No modern understanding of the processes of creation now attributes to the direct action of a god the existence of the swarming animal, bird and insect life on earth. But, with the understanding that creation is a deeper, more mysterious thing than either science or religion has so far understood, the hymn addresses the Genesis Creator (Genesis 1:20-25) to express human gratitude for the multitude of creatures we have made our companions as pets. Cecil Frances Alexander's 1848 hymn, 'All things bright and beautiful, / all creatures great and small,' can also be considered an influence on the text.

Each verse makes a serious point about pets: in verse 1, that all living forms exist in connection within the planetary system of life; in verse 2, that the astonishing variety of life is to be valued and respected; in verse 3, that larger lessons about caring for the whole of creation may be learned through the exercise of loving care for pets; while verse 4 is a prayer for the recovery of the Edenic vision of Genesis, giving due attention to the rights to shelter, respect and care for 'every creature, everywhere,' whether they are animal rights or human rights. Underlying the whole text is a rejection of the ancient biblical concept of divinely authorised human domination of creation, replaced by a more modern understanding of the responsibilities and privileges of stewardship of the natural world.

GOD'S CREATURES The tune name is self-explanatory: the phrase is a common one and appears, for instance, in the title of *God's Creatures: A Biblical Understanding of Animals*, by Susan Bulanda (2008). The music, written by author **Colin Gibson,** is a deliberately simple setting in D major. A pause on the third note in bar 9 allows singers to take breath before moving into the reflective half of the hymn.

Deep in the human heart H19
Metre: 6.6.8.6 D

This hymn text took its present form in 1977, when Methodist minister **Bill Wallace** revised an earlier version to be sung at a People's Night for the combined Methodist and Presbyterian congregations of Christchurch. The hymn was premièred in the city's Town Hall. The text was first published, without a setting, in the author's *Something to Sing About* (1981), followed by a reprinting in his *Singing the Circle*, Book 1 (1990), where it appeared with an original tune, PATATAG*, by Philippines composer Francisco Feliciano. It was simultaneously published with the same tune in the Asian hymnal *Sound the Bamboo* (1990). In 1995 it was included in the international ecumenical hymnbook *Thuma Mina* (Strube Verlag, Munich and Basel) and in 2009 in *Hope is our Song*.

A bold, declarative text, this hymn is a call to a vision of 'a world renewed.' Bill Wallace describes it as 'an affirmation that within each human being there is a sense of justice. However, it appears that only a minority of the rich and powerful are prepared to be in touch with this. If they were, it would necessitate that they share their wealth and their power. Injustice is not just a product of individual selfishness, but of institutional oppression. The call to Christians is to take our stand with the poor and the oppressed.'

Verse 1 draws on Luke 4:18-19, where Jesus reads in the synagogue of Nazareth a passage from Isaiah 61 announcing a radical social programme. Verse 2 lists the goals of such a programme in the modern world. Verse 3 calls for a 'step of faith' into 'the future's world' to bring 'new hope and fuller life / to all humanity.' 'Radical concern' (verse 1, line 4) carries the meaning, 'a deeply-rooted concern addressing fundamental problems.' The final lines of the hymn have as their sub-text Jesus' declaration, 'I came that they may have life and have it abundantly' (John 10:10).

DIADEMATA The suggested tune, usually associated with 'Crown him with many crowns,' was written by **George Elvey** (1816-93); it first appeared in the 1868 Appendix to *Hymns Ancient and Modern*.

> *PATATAG is the name of a musical that depicted Christian involvement in the struggle for human rights and democracy in the Philippines. For information on the tune see I-to Loh's *Hymnal Companion to Sound the Bamboo: Asian Hymns in their Liturgical and Cultural Contexts*, Chicago: GIA (2011) 366.

Do this in remembrance of me A29
Metre: 8.8.9.8

This scriptural communion song was written by American singer and country and gospel songwriter **Valerie (Val) Cash** in 1984. **David Dell's** adaptation of the original lyric was first published in this country in *New Zealand Praise* (1988). The original words as published in *Lift Every Voice & Sing II: An African American Hymnal* (published by the Episcopal Church of America in 1993) are:

> Do this in remembrance of me.
> Do this in remembrance of me.
> I hung out on a tree for thee, for thee,
> Do this in remembrance of me.
>
> Eat this in remembrance of me.
> Eat this in remembrance of me.
> I hung out on a tree for thee, for thee,
> Eat this in remembrance of me.
>
> Drink this in remembrance of me.
> Drink this in remembrance of me.
> I hung out on a tree for thee, for thee,
> Drink this in remembrance of me.

Both versions of the text are drawn from Luke 22:19-20 (King James version) with little alteration.

[DO THIS IN REMEMBRANCE] The original music for this chorus was created by Val Cash; it was first arranged by **David Dell** for *New Zealand Praise*, and further arranged for *Alleluia Aotearoa* by Wellington musician **Jillian Bray**.

Don't tell anyone C17
Metre: Irregular

This unison Advent song was written in 1992 by **Colin Gibson** in Cambridge, England, for the Sunday School children of a small English Methodist church. It was first published in *Carol our Christmas* (1996).

The text was created to introduce the main characters in the biblical Nativity story in an enjoyable way, with the young singers imagining themselves revealing the open secret by whispering on a playground to a school friend ('cos you're my friend I'll just tell you'). The biblical references include Matthew 2 for the star (verse 1), Herod and the three Kings (verse 3), and Luke 2 for the song of the heavenly host, the shepherds, the innkeeper, Mary's baby and 'old Simeon's eyes' (verses 2 and 4). In a later performance by the children of the writer's own Methodist church in Dunedin the letters forming the secret words were printed on large cards and held up one after the other in a row.

When this song was taken up by an American publishing house the words were adjusted to remove any idea of a shared secret among children – to allay the potential fears of anxious parents (!). So much for the fate of comedy in a hyper-sensitive society.

[IT'S A SURPRISE] The setting was composed by the author to maximize the fun of performing it for both singers and listeners, and a number of additional dramatic and musical possibilities are suggested in C17.

Dream a dream (Carol of Dreams)
F12 (i) and (ii)
Metre: 7.8.8.6

This carol, written by **Shirley Murray** in late 1996, was first published in *Faith Forever Singing* (2000), then in *Faith makes the Song* (2002), where Murray describes the circumstances of its creation: 'Carol of Dreams is one of two carols designed for a tune [LULLABY CAROL] by Professor **Peter Godfrey**, who asked for a "grown-up's" version and one for small children.' In the event, Murray's Lullaby Carol was matched to the Godfrey tune (see F46), and 'Dream a Dream' was sent to Dunedin composer **Nigel Eastgate** as a Christmas gift.

The theme of the carol may owe something to the famous song, 'I dreamed a dream,' in the 1985 West End musical *Les Misérables*. The verses articulate Shirley Murray's most prominent social themes: the search for peace and the promotion of social harmony, the abolition of war, poverty and hunger, and the protection of the natural environment. There are some biblical underlays: verse 2 alludes to Isaiah's vision of swords beaten into ploughshares (2:4); verse 3 refers to the creation of man (Genesis 2:7); verse 4 refers to Luke's account of the angelic presence at the nativity of Christ (Luke 2:8-14). 'The greening of the earth' (verse 3) is a phrase much used in the then current scientific debate about the effects of the burning of fossil fuels on the earth's atmosphere: a famous 1992 television film was titled *The Greening of Planet Earth*. However, Murray uses the phrase to suggest the general vision of a regenerated planet, protected rather than exploited by its human inhabitants.

CAROL OF DREAMS This tune, written by **Nigel Eastgate** in December 1996, and sent as a reciprocal Christmas gift to Shirley Murray, offers a gentle melody of child-like simplicity moving steadily above shifting harmonies (E minor, D major, C major) which leave and then return safely to the home key of G major. The tune name heads the manuscript of Dr Eastgate's setting, carrying the date 22 December 1996.

[DREAM A DREAM] This alternative tune was written in 1999 by **Charlotte Murray**, then a student at Tawa College, where her mother, **Shona Murray**, was Head of Music. When the text of Shirley Murray's 'Dream a dream' was brought to the editorial committee preparing *Faith Forever Singing* (2000), while it was agreed that the Eastgate tune fitted Murray's words well, it was decided that a livelier, more up-to-date style of music needed to be introduced to balance the number of tunes of a conventional kind appearing in the collection. Shona Murray offered her daughter's musical services, and the present second piano setting of the hymn, with shifting harmonies beneath its rhythmic and lyrical melody, was the excellent result. There is a further setting by Canadian composer **Ron Klusmeier** (Klusmeier 29).

E aere rekareka mai *W627*
Metre: 8.7.9.5 and refrain

This hymn, by an unknown early missionary, has become part of the body of Cook Islands hymnody. It probably dates from soon after 1821, when the first London Missionary Society workers reached the islands and began their work of converting the population from their indigenous animism. Although the hymn is associated with the then popular American gospel writer **John Harrison Tenney**, no exact match has been found by the compiler of this Companion, and the refrain, translated as 'We have been living in darkness in these islands,' and both verse 1 ('pray to the true God') and verse 3, 'Let us all accept in our hearts [God's] spirit of goodness,' suggests that this is a fabricated missionary text aimed at conversion, rather than a translation of any American gospel song.

There are frequent biblical allusions: verse 1, line 1, 'Come with great joy' (cf. Luke 2:10), line 4, '[God] gives us life' (Genesis 2:7); verse 2 derives from Matthew 4:16 ('the people who sat in darkness have seen a great light'); verse 3 refers to the goodness of God, as praised in Psalm 107:1, and the gift of the Holy Spirit (John 14:16-17).

TENNEY This tune now known as TENNEY is associated with the hymn 'Ever will I pray' by Annie Cummings, published in 1875 with music by Tenney. However, comparison of Tenney's setting of the Cummings hymn with the melody printed in *With One Voice* does not suggest any relationship, and the tune name may have been given in a general way. The precise hymn tune remains to be discovered among Tenney's many popular gospel melodies.

E Ihoa Atua W677, A51

(Today usually rendered as *E Ihowā Atua*.) See the entry for **God of nations, at thy feet**.

E te Ariki (Lord, have mercy) F13
Metre: 10.10.10

This Māori language version of the ancient Greek liturgical formulation *Kyrie eléison, Christe eléison, kyrie eléison* is of unknown date and authorship, though the Kyrie was probably introduced to Māori converts by early Anglican or Roman Catholic missionaries.

The Kyrie petition may have had its origin in the tax-collector's prayer in Jesus' parable of the Pharisee and the Tax-collector (Luke 18:9); it is part of the earliest divine services which were celebrated in the Greek language in both the Western and Eastern traditions of Christianity. It is usually part of any musical setting of the Mass, and settings exist in styles ranging from Gregorian chant to contemporary folk idioms.

NEWLANDS ROAD This setting was written in 1998 by Anglican vicar **Ian Render** for his congregation at St Michael and All Angels, Newlands Road, in the Wellington diocese. Ian describes it as 'a way of encouraging the congregation to begin to use some *Te Reo* [Māori language] in worship. This seemed like a very easy entry point, made even easier by the cantor/congregation echo format.'

E te Ariki A30
Metre: 10.10.10.10

Lines from this Māori *waiata* or song were recorded on the Kokiri *marae* (community gathering place) at Maungarei (Mount Wellington) in 1983, but the song is probably much older than that. It appears to be a fusion of love lyric sentiment with a Trinitarian formula honouring Father, Son and Holy Spirit. The image of 'bright star' has possible Marian overtones; Jesus as 'the way' derives from John 14:6, as does the association of the Holy Spirit with 'everlasting life' ('I am the way, the truth, the life').

[HE ATAAHUA KOE] Neither the composer nor the author of this gentle song of praise are known. The melodic line hovers quietly around the tonic note C.

E te Ariki H23
Metre: Irregular

This short liturgical text, not to be confused with **E te Ariki** (F13), is of unknown date and authorship. Simply described as 'traditional' in *Hope is our Song* (2009), it is perhaps the product of missionary activity among Māori in New Zealand (beginning with Samuel Marsden in 1814). Although the version printed in *Hope is our Song* emerged from within the Māori Division of the Presbyterian Church, Te Aka Puaho a Te Ahorangi, this plea for divine recognition is also included in Roman Catholic liturgies – it is now a rosary hymn – and, more widely still, used on formal religious and cultural occasions of suitable gravity. It has further been taken up by schools and Māori singers.

The translation supplied in *Hope is our Song* is a general one only, paying no attention to its detail or its rhetorical repetitions.* The opening invocation to God to hear and see those present is based on an identical formula found in the Psalms (e.g. Psalm 39:12, Psalm 61:1-4) and elsewhere in the Bible. Nehemiah 1:6 supplies both the eye-ear formula and the characterisation of the speakers as God's children – here the children of Israel, a popular identification later made by Māori themselves. Lines 8-12 constitute a creedal statement of belief in God as Father, Son and Holy Spirit, which in turn incorporates a fourfold expression of contrition, 'Auē, auē, auē, auē' (two repetitions are used in the *Hope is our Song* version).

In current performance of the song, dance and gesture may be employed, and the lines may be divided between men and women.

[E TE ARIKI] (Māori=O Lord God) **Wi-Patena Te Pairi** is the composer of this chant-like melody, which became a signature tune for one his touring bands, sung to round off their concerts. It has since become adopted as a Māori folk melody, coming to life on the *marae* (the formal gathering place of a community) and at Māori worship occasions, often with guitar accompaniment. The arrangement for piano is by **Roy Tankersley**, working in collaboration with the composer. Roy Tankersley has also arranged the song for mixed choir and piano accompaniment. The song was also recorded by Steve Apirana for his album *No Turning Back* (1992) and Dennis Marsh for the album *Māori Songs 2* (Sony Music, 2015). The latest recording (2018) is by Māmā Mihirangi and the Māreikura, a contemporary Māori female group advocating for indigenous cultural values.

> *A literal translation of the Māori text:
>
> Lord, listen to me there
> and to us all
> Lord, look at me there
> And at us all
> Here we [are] your children
> We believe in you
> Alas, alas, alas, alas!
> The Father, the Son and the Holy Spirit
> The Father, the Son and the Holy Spirit

E te Atua *A31*
Metre: 9.9.9.7.7

This translation into the Māori language of a popular 1960s religious song, 'Kum Ba Yah,' is of unknown date and authorship. Now an equally popular Māori hymn, it was published in *Alleluia Aotearoa* (1993), and in other printed hymn collections.

The simple text consists of three prayers for divine love, blessing and assistance, unrelated to the original text of 'Kum Ba Yah,' 'Someone's crying, Lord, kum ba yah…'

KUM BA YA (Pidgin English=Come by here) Modern scholarship has traced this tune, previously thought to be an African spiritual, to its apparent origins in the southern states of America. Its first appearance in a major hymnbook was in the *New Catholic Hymnal* (1971), followed by *New Church Praise* (1975) and *Come and Praise* (1978); however, it had already reached New Zealand in *Songs of Faith* (1966). The arrangement in *Alleluia Aotearoa* is by **Nicola** and **Guy Jansen**.

E te Atua, kua ruia nei *W650*
Metre: 9.6.9.6

The Māori text of this hymn is by an unknown author, probably an Anglican or Methodist missionary writing for converts. Essentially its focus is on the 'good seed' referred to in Jesus' parable of the Sower (Matthew 13:1-23). Its singers are called to abandon the 'evil deeds' of the past, and receive a 'new heart' (see Ezekiel 36:26, 'I will give you a new heart and put a new spirit into you').

The Māori term *Atua* (line 1) referring to the one god of Christian theological thought is a Polynesian word meaning 'Power, strength.' Māori mythology envisaged a number of tutelary gods, such as Tane, the creator of all living things such as animals, birds and trees and Tangaroa, god of the sea, but no single supreme god. Missionary activity led to the choice of *Atua* as the most appropriate term for the Christian concept of 'God as supreme being,' and it has since been widely adopted by the Māori- language speaking community.

FOR ALL THY MERCIES This tune is better known as CONTEMPLATION, and although it is described in *With One Voice* as a traditional Māori melody, there is nothing to justify that description. The music was actually written by the English composer **Frederick Ouseley**

(1825-89) for the well-known hymn 'When all thy mercies, O my God' by Joseph Addison, and first appeared in the 1889 Supplement to the 1875 edition of *Hymns Ancient and Modern*. Ouseley – more properly Sir Frederick Arthur Gore Ouseley, Baronet – was an infant musical prodigy who eventually became Professor of Music at Oxford University. He was ordained in 1849, and after serving several curacies became Precentor of Hereford Cathedral. A major figure in the mid-19th century revival of English church music, and the composer of a large quantity of church and chamber music, he was closely associated with the first edition of *Hymns Ancient and Modern*. Ouseley's hymn tune became popular among Māori as well as pākehā congregations; it was arranged for the New Zealand supplement to *With One Voice* by **Jillian Bray**.

E te Iwi *A32*
Metre: Irregular

Like 'Whakatau mai te Atua' (A15) this text, which dates from the 1980s, is the work of a group of senior Māori; the circumstances of its composition are unknown, though it is a new work, not a traditional Māori hymn. The authors' names are Moni Riini, Hoki Tawa, and Kitty Temara, about whom no information has come to light.

There are a number of gospel songs with a similar theme to this text, which is addressed to the singers representing the people (cf. the French carol, 'People, look east, the time is near') and calls for a renewed focus on the Cross as the object of pious contemplation and the treasured symbol of salvation. Behind the dramatised voice from the Cross, 'Come back to me,' stand the words of Jesus, 'Come unto me' (Matthew 11:28).

[E TE IWI] The tune published with this text is a co-operative work composed by an unnamed group of musicians led by Mona Riini. It is a melody of the utmost simplicity, with a basic range of three notes barely straying from the tonic note C. Such a song, whose authentic Māori rhythms are faithfully recorded in the print notation, should if possible be sung without accompaniment or with guitar. It is a purely vocal melodic line.

E te Matua *H24*
Metre: 9.9.9.8

In 2005 **Bill Bennett** began to write hymns and songs for each of the gospel readings chosen for the Three-Year Revised Common Lectionary, eventually publishing the complete set as *Gradual Praise* (2010). This song, written in 2004 for Trinity/Pentecost Sunday (Years A-C), was first published in *Hope is our Song* (2009), then in the author's collection *Gradual Praise* (2010).

The area of Aotearoa New Zealand where Bill Bennett lives [Hawkes Bay] has in parts Māori populations. 'Most European or *pākehā* clergy are expected to have some cultural knowledge of Māori customs, as well as a knowledge of formal language and of some prayers and liturgies,' says Bill Bennett, who writes out of that context.

The hymn adopts a liturgical mode, three times addressing each member of the Trinity in turn, then joining in supplication to all three together. The author comments on the language of the hymn: 'While each tribal Māori area may have their own distinctive language differences, generally the language (*te reo*) is understood by all Māori speakers throughout the land. The version created here acknowledges the usage common in the Hawkes Bay area, the area of the Ngāti Kahungunu tribal group.' The translation into English is provided as an explanation of the words sung; it is not for singing purposes.

TOKOTORUTAPU (Māori=Holy Trinity). The composer remarks that 'In Māori contexts the people usually sing their hymns in unaccompanied natural harmony, or with guitar accompaniment. This hymn tries to replicate this tradition.' It should be sung in a measured way, in harmony if possible, respecting the metronomic indication.

Easter New Zealand *facing F3*

The date of writing of this poem by **Shirley Murray** is unknown: it was probably created towards 2000 for inclusion in the hymnbook *Faith Forever Singing*.

Implicit throughout the text is a comparison between the deciduous trees of the northern hemisphere, with their annual (and spectacular) loss of leaves in autumn and equally spectacular recovery in spring, marking the church season of Easter, and in the southern hemisphere the evergreen forests of New Zealand, where Easter takes in autumn, with no visible change in the natural world. Choosing as her symbol of death and resurrection the continual emergence of fresh coiled fern leaves from their clumps of previous and now decayed vegetation, she is able to claim that resurrection is 'evergreen,' always present in this country.

Ephphatha, be opened my soul *H25*
Metre: 8.6.8.6 and refrain

This hymn text was written by **Colin Gibson** in 2003, with a dedication to the Reverend Ken Russell, whose sermon on the text, 'Ephphatha, be opened' (Mark 7:34) prompted its writing. It was first published in *Hope is our Song* (2009).

Ephphatha (pronounced 'ef-far-tha') is an Aramaic word meaning 'be opened.' It is a significant word, not only because of its meaning in its context, the story of Jesus' healing of a deaf man, recorded in Mark 7:31-7, but also because it is one of the very few surviving words of his own language which we can be sure was spoken by Jesus. The refrain allows the singers to savour the word by its repetition.

In this hymn, the singers are asked to put themselves in the place of the deaf man yearning for healing and seeking release from their own 'disabilities.' The biblical story relates to physical deafness, but the text expands the idea of 'opening' to include using the faculties of hearing, sight and speech to open ourselves to and express our sense of 'the daily beauty of the world' and 'the precious quality of life, / the worth of every soul.'

EPHPHATHA The music was composed in 2003 by **Colin Gibson**, as a unison setting for this text. The tune is named after the Aramaic word which heads the hymn. Different melodic phrases distinguish the refrain from the verses and the use of a major key (F) for the former and a minor key (D) reinforces the distinction. The effect is to highlight the unique word which is the whole text of the refrain.

Eternal God, beyond the reach of mystery *H26*
Metre: 12.12.11.14

This hymn was written in 2006 by **Colin Gibson**, and was the outcome of a series of open-ended discussions of the Christian faith led by the Reverend Rod Mitchell of Knox Church, Dunedin, to whom it is dedicated, together with the members of his Marcus Borg Seminar. The hymn was first published in *Hope is our Song* (2009).

The long-lined verses are themselves an expression of the idea that however we formulate our concepts of 'God' the reality remains beyond the grasp of human modes of expression and thought, and certainly remains beyond definition or capture within church or creed. The first three verses address the traditional trinity of God, Christ and the Holy Spirit; the fourth adds the mystery of 'grace' which sets us 'free to choose the pathway of our soul.' Verse 1 uses the metaphor of God as the ocean of being: an image at least as old as the 1891 revivalist hymn by Albert Simpson, 'The mercy of God is an ocean divine, / A boundless and fathomless flood. / Launch out in the deep, cut away the shore line, / And be lost in the fullness of God.' Verse 2 alludes to the story of Christ as fellow traveler on the road to Emmaus (Luke 24:13-35). Verse 3 uses the familiar image of the Holy Spirit as the unpredictable force of wind (John 3:8 and Acts 2:1-13).

NORTHVIEW The name of the Reverend Rod Mitchell and his wife's Dunedin home when this hymn was written, with its view of the high hills surrounding the town on its northern border. The D minor setting and relatively low-pitched melodic line are intended to convey a sense of mystery. The final larger gesture (bars 13-17) represents a grasping for the infinite.

Eternal Spirit of the living Christ A33
Metre: 10.10.10.10

Widely regarded as his finest hymn, this text was written in 1974 by Swedish-American Presbyterian minister and poet **Frank von Christierson**, and first published in *New Hymns, Songs and Prayers for Church and Home* (1974) by the Hymn Society of America and Canada in that year. It was revised by the author for the Society's *Hymns Published for Special Occasions and on Special Subjects 1942-79* (1979). The original version of stanza 3 (where revision took place) is used in *Alleluia Aotearoa*; the later version reads:

> Come with the strength I lack,
> bring vision clear
> Of human need; O give me eyes to see
> Fulfillment of my life in love outpoured,
> My life in You, O Christ, Your love in me.

A number of scriptural references have been noted: they include Romans 8:26-27, and Luke 11:1-4. Gilbert Doan, in his *Companion to the Presbyterian Hymnal 82*, describes the text as 'unvarnished, simple (mostly monosyllablic), and direct, not to say intimate; it petitions without groveling, aspires without presuming. It moves from private need to a vision of cosmic redemption – then comes to a conclusion that ties up all the loose ends.'

ARGYLE STREET The tune name refers to the Dunedin street where the dedicatee of this hymn setting, Andrew Doubleday, was living at the time. The music was written by **Colin Gibson** in 1986 as a gift to Doubleday, who was seeking ordination in the Methodist Church and eventually became its President in 2021. There are several other modern settings, anthems and organ preludes by American composers.

Even if you're small (You can Walk Tall) A35
Metre: Irregular

This cheerful children's song, introducing in a simple way the concepts of repentance and forgiveness, was written in 1980 by Dominican Sister **Cecily Sheehy** as one of a series of such songs for children published in the Catholic magazine *Family Living*. Its first hymnbook appearance was in *New Zealand Praise* (1988), in an arrangement for piano and voice by **David Dell**, followed by publication in *Alleluia Aotearoa* (1993).

The phrase 'Walk tall,' meaning 'have pride and confidence in oneself,' dates back to the mid-1900s, but it was revived after the 1973 American film *Walk Tall* was shown on New Zealand screens. As recently as 2013 it entered the title of a life-skills for children programme developed by the Dunedin Methodist Mission, 'Wise Up, Walk Tall, Tamariki' [Māori=children]. Lines 3-5 reassure the singers that adults are just as capable of any faults that children may acknowledge, using nursery rhyme words like 'horrid' and 'nasty' to describe behaviour adults might call 'sinful.' The final line opens up the possibility of a 'fresh start.'

[WALK TALL] The happy, syncopated unison melody, with its attractive long pause marking the text break 'THEN' before the music develops its second theme of 4 rising notes, was composed by the author of the text as a unison melody with guitar, and given a piano accompaniment by **Douglas Mews**. To symbolize the possibility of a new beginning, the composer prescribes at least one repetition of the song.

Every day I will offer you A36
Metre: 8.7.8.7.7.8

Written by **Shirley Murray** for a Presbyterian Women's Conference held in Wellington in 1991, this hymn addressed the theme 'Let's Step out of the Boat,' which the author found initially 'rather unprepossessing.' Line 5 of the first verse originally read 'Help me see I'm your daughter,' but 'daughter' was changed to 'image' 'for the sake of inclusiveness' before the hymn was published in her first American collection, *In Every Corner Sing* (1992). The text was virtually rewritten for its appearance in *Alleluia Aotearoa* (1993), and the textual differences are so considerable that the original version is given here.

> Every day
> I will offer you, loving God,
> my heart and mind
> every way I discover You
> in the work your hand has signed;
> help me see I'm your image,
> and you have dreamed what I might be–
>
> every day
> in your Spirit, I'll find the love and energy!
>
> Every day
> I will focus on Christ, and lift my courage high
> through the tides and the tossing of waves that drown,
> and hopes that die;
> help me see stepping out of the boat,
> I'll learn what risk might be–
>
> every day
> in your Spirit, I'll find the love and energy!
>
> Every day

The Matthew passage behind the Conference theme reads, 'He said, "Come." So Peter got out of the boat and walked on the water and came to Jesus.' The text correspondingly speaks of dedication and life-long commitment. Verse 1 alludes to the Genesis creation story 1:26, 'Then God said, "Let us make man in our image," but the concept of God's dream of 'what I might be' is original and one to which this writer returns: 'In each of us God dreams a dream' (**God was in Christ**, H49). The original 4-verse version remains much closer to the Matthew passage throughout.

LYNNEFRITH This setting, written in 1991 by **Colin Gibson** for the revised text, is named after the Rev'd Dr Lynne Frith, the minister in charge of the Mornington Methodist Church congregation at the time. It translates the 'energy' repeatedly mentioned in the refrain into a modern popular style, with the bass line surging up and down energetically beneath the word itself. The is another setting by Canadian composer Ron **Klusmeier** (Klusmeier 21).

Every hair upon your head H27
Metre: 7.7.11 D and refrain

This hymn was written in 1994 by **Colin Gibson**, as a contribution to the United Nations Year of the Family. Although on the surface a comic song, it addresses the serious theological idea of God's all-inclusive family. It was first published in Gibson's second American collection, *Songs for a Rainbow People* (1998); its first New Zealand publication was in *Hope is our Song* (2009). In the author's words, 'The text was the result of a search for a mark of our common humanity as we gather within the loving embrace of such a parent; its starting point found in Jesus' declaration that "Even the hairs of your head are all counted" (Matthew 10:30). This biblical insight was connected with a moment of inspiration in a church service when sunlight picked out the beautiful hair of a nearby choir member.

Verse 1 elaborates on Matthew 10:30 by listing some of the various hair colours, natural or artificial, to be seen on the streets. Verse 2 adds to the idea of human variety and difference by referring to various hair styles in vogue at the time of writing. 'Cherokee' (also known as 'Mohican') was a haircut that left a narrow crest of hair on the top of the head with either side shaved bald. The last two lines refer to the hair of the elderly and new-born babies. Verse 3 deals with the prejudices and animosities aroused even today by unusual haircuts (representing society's intolerance of those thought of as 'different'). Verse 4 uses the language of professional hairdressers to stress the comprehensiveness of God's love: a follicle is the sheath surrounding the root of every single hair; 'split end' refers to the damaged condition when the hair loses its outer cuticle and literally splits apart (known scientifically as *trichoptilosis*). It is usually dealt with by cutting off the offending hair.

HAIRSONG This unison tune was named after the literal subject of the text. Written by the hymn writer in the same year (1994), the musical setting of the verses is jazzy and light-hearted, but the syncopated rhythms of the melody give way to an emphatic sequence of chords for the refrain which spells out the theme of the hymn. This hymn has been recorded on CD. It has also been arranged for male quartet (TTBB) by Matt Melchert, leader of the Hamilton Glory Boys, with an added 'Prelude' and independent text.

Every star shall sing a carol W640
Metre: 8.7.8.7 and refrain

This carol was written by **Sydney Carter** in 1961 and first published in *Nine Carols or Ballads* (1964) with the typical disclaimer, 'Here are the words and tunes of 9 songs as they stand in April 1964.* But I seldom sing them the same way twice, so I expect they will go on altering as they have been doing ever since they started.'

After its conventional beginning with an allusion to the star of the nativity and Job 38:7 ('Where were you when I laid the foundation of the earth…when the morning stars sang together?') followed by praise of the 'King of Heaven,' the carol announces its true theme in the words 'By whatever name you know.' Carter has written at length about the occasion of the carol, an experience of a wave-like revelation at a time of despair and rejection of 'the Christian label.' 'This wave had a more than human personality. Male or female? Both, neither, all together: it did not speak to me but let me see that I was not alone. Nobody was alone: we were alone together, travelling. We were safe, beyond our danger; whole, beyond our being broken. What had I become aware of? I rejected the glib label 'God.' I did not want to compromise the truth of this experience. The name of Jesus did not seem appropriate, though he was surely riding in the wave as well. Critically, I began to ask myself: 'Do I have this experience, or do I just imagine it? Is it nothing but possibility, like a song that is asking to be written?' If that is all it is, I feel, that is good enough for me' (*Green Print for a Song*, Sydney Carter, London: Stainer & Bell, 1974, page 62).

Verse 3 shows Carter as the iconoclastic theologian, who posits the explosive possibility of other such nativities (and crucifixions) in worlds beyond planet earth – a potential for human-like life elsewhere, with which scientists are even now grappling. 'Milky Way' suggests both the constellation at the limits of 'our' universe, and the nursing of the child Jesus. Verse 4 introduces the notion of other time dimensions and still other incarnations of Jesus ('crosses still to come or long ago).' Verse 5 images the historical Jesus as blood-brother ('Brother of my blood and bone'), though the New Zealand connotations of 'blood and bone' as a type of natural fertilizer, caused the editors of the New Zealand Supplement to *With One Voice* to replace the phrase with 'flesh and bone.' The chorus of the carol reiterates the traditional view of Christ as both divine and human, but insists on the validity of the singer's own conception of Christ, whatever that may be.

EVERY STAR The tune name is drawn from the first line of the carol. Carter usually wrote out only the melody line of his songs; this harmonization may be by Donald Swann. Like the words of the carol, the music has the attractive simplicity and dance-like rhythm of folk music.

*It was recorded by Donald Swann in 1964 on Argo EAF 48, *Songs of Faith and Doubt*.

Everything that has voice (Sing for Peace) H28
Metre: 6.6.6.6.7.7.6.3

One of **Shirley Murray's** many Peace hymns, this was written in August 2003 and first published in her American collection *Touch the Earth Lightly* (2008) before appearing in *Hope is our Song* (2009). The text is carefully worked and the manuscript shows evidence of extensive alteration. In verse 3, 'every tenant of the earth' (line 4) expresses the modern understanding of humanity as temporary occupants of this planet and guardians of its resources rather than its overlords as in Genesis 1:28.

This plea for united action to promote peace is rhetorically organized into three sets (verses). The first introduces a string of verbs of action focused on expressing (voicing) the call to peace; the second clusters round verbs of desire for peace (longing); the third develops a set of synonyms exhorting everyone to take action for peace.

ROYAL TERRACE Named for a Dunedin street, the home address of a friend, this dancing tune with a descant for solo instrument was written by **Colin Gibson** in 2003. *Touch the Earth Lightly* prints a different setting by American composer Marty Haugen, named SING FOR PEACE and written, as the author records in *Touch the Earth Lightly*, shortly after a visit to the Murray's home at Raumati.

Faafetai i le Atua W629
Metre: 8.7.8.7 and refrain

No information about the date or authorship of this Samoan hymn has been found. The writer was probably a 19th century missionary, as its simple Trinitarian theme of thanks to God, Jesus and the Holy Spirit – to which is added a refrain consisting of an alleluia and an instruction to give thanks – suggests. The three verses draw on basic biblical concepts: God is the giver of life (Genesis 2:7) and the one who freely loves us (John 4:10); Jesus is the one from heaven (John 6:38) who protects us against suffering (cf. 2 Thessalonians 3:2); the Holy Spirit is the helper (John 14:26).

O LE FAAFETAI The composer and date of composition is unknown, but the music is in the style of a gospel hymn, and like many other Samoan 'traditional' hymns probably has its source among the hundreds of such late 19th century American gospel hymns which were spread by travelling evangelist-singers and became hugely popular on both sides of the Atlantic before reaching the Pacific.

Faith has set us on a journey F14
Metre: 8.7.8.7.D

Written in 1986 by **Shirley Murray**, this hymn was first published in her privately printed collection *In Every Corner Sing* (1987), then in her first American collection with the same title (1992). It reached New Zealand publication in *Faith Forever Singing* (2000).

The theme is a traditional one, the Christian life as a journey of faith – with Abraham's departure from Haran (Genesis 12:1-4, cf. verse 1, line 5) as its paradigm, but as usual Murray puts a distinctive stamp of modernity on it. She writes, 'Themes of pilgrimage and journeys through the desert sand seem unreal in a world of air travel and insurance policies, hence the contemporary imagery.' Equally distinctive is her comical description of the community of faith, the 'Body' of Christ (verse 3, line 2), as a 'company of clowns and cripples,' with the prophets as their travel agents and their road laid by 'gospel makers.' Differences in tone and content make comparison between this hymn and Joy Dine's 'God who sets us on a journey' (F32) instructive.

'The Word that tells us 'Go!'' (verse 1, line 4) is a compressed double allusion to John 1:14 (Christ as the Word of God), and Mark 16:15, 'He said to them, "Go into all the world and proclaim the good news to the whole creation." The 'swags of easy conscience' (verse 2, line 1) are wanderers of no fixed loyalties (strictly tramps carrying their possessions rolled into a swag or bundle) and no strong moral convictions either. The 'Book' (verse 2, line 4) refers to those who take the Bible as their sole religious and moral guidebook.

The author notes that the line 'Love the Christ and leave the Church' (verse 2, line 8) 'has aroused [hostile] reaction from those who cannot conceive of people leaving the Church and still loving Jesus Christ! The word "leave" has, in one instance, been changed to "serve," thus deflecting any impact from the reality.'

VENTURE The rising, steady, march-like progression of the tune so named is intended to match the determined, adventurous journeying theme of the text. This setting was written in 1986 by **Colin Gibson**. As indicated in *Alleluia Aotearoa*, the text may also be sung to **Martin Shaw**'s 1915 hymn tune, MARCHING.

Fancy Noah sailing in the ark (Rainbow People) F15
Metre: 9.9.7.7.7.9.10.8.7.9

This hymn version of the story of Noah's landing on Ararat (see Genesis 8:6-19) was written in 1996 by **Colin Gibson**, and dedicated to a New York friend, B.J. Adams, a remarkable textile artist, 'maker of rainbows.' It was first published in Gibson's second American collection, *Songs for a Rainbow People* (1998), where it supplies a title and an epigraph, then in *Faith Forever Singing* (2000).

While the narrative of the hymn is biblically-based, its theme is the joyous, unqualified acceptance of all humanity before the face of God. The vision it offers is of a rainbow world populated by rainbow people of every shade of 'colour,' including, by implication, every kind of sexual orientation, since the rainbow is both the symbol of God's covenantal relationship with all life on earth and the adopted sign of the movement for equality for gay people within and outside the Church.

Verse 1, line 1, 'Fancy' means 'imagine'; line 8 refers to the dove carrying an olive leaf (a symbol of peace) which brought proof of the end of the Flood (Genesis 8:10-11). Verse 2 addresses the folk who 'want a world of 'this and that,' in other words, of discrimination, rejecting their attitude for the unlimited 'harmony of all things,' symbolised by the appearance of the rainbow arch and God's covenant with humanity (Genesis 9:8-17). Verse 3 returns to the absolutism practised by those who demand a world of 'black and white' morality; against their narrowness is set 'God's delight in the multitudinous colours of a multifarious world' (=a world characterised by variety) – as evidenced by Genesis 1:3. The description of rainbow people as 'children of the light' derives from 1 Thessalonians 5:5. Verse 4 rejects the concept of Hell and the terrors of the Last Judgement (Matthew 25:41) for the non-judgemental love of God as described by Jesus in Matthew 5:44-45. The hymn closes with the visual image of the rainbow shining through the rain, 'pledge of seed and harvest times,' and a vision of joyful people filling the earth with 'the love and grace and laughter of a plenitudinous (=bountiful, super-abundant) God.'

DURHAM STREET The tune, written in 1996 by composer / writer **Colin Gibson**, is named for a Christchurch Methodist church where a reconciling ministry was being practised by a congregation led by the Reverend Doctor David Bromell. The music catches something of the salty flavour of a sailor's sea-shanty (as the introductory phrase suggests), to match the nautical nature of the biblical source-story.

First set your mind on the kingdom of God W635
Metre: Irregular

This is one of the most popular and widely sung of the many praise songs which came out of America in the 1970s. It was written by **Karen Lafferty** in 1971 under circumstances she herself has described. 'I had quit my entertainment job and was trying to support myself with teaching guitar lessons. I had three students! When my savings were all gone, and I had no money to make my car payments, I became very discouraged and confused. One evening I went to a Bible study at church, and we talked about Matthew 6:33. I was tremendously encouraged and challenged by the words about Christ's kingdom. So I went home, wrote the tune, recorded it on a tape recorder, and then sang this little descant part [in another account Karen says that as she listened to the tape she discovered an 'alleluia' counter-part that 'fitted nicely']. I taught the song at church the next week and it caught on right away.' The first independent New Zealand publication to reprint this song (in its one-verse form) was *Songs of Praise*, third edition, 1973, a year after the song had been copyrighted.

The original version (which begins 'Seek ye first the kingdom of God') consisted only of the Matthew 6:33 saying in the King James' version, 'Seek ye first the kingdom of God and his righteousness, and all these things shall be added unto you,' but a second verse based on Matthew 7:7 ('Ask, and it will be given you; seek, and you will find; knock, and it will be opened to you') soon entered a number of songbooks, followed by a third verse based on Matthew 4:4 ('It is written man shall not live by bread alone, but by every word that proceeds from the mouth of God' [quoting Deuteronomy 8:3]). The New Zealand hymn writer **Colin Gibson** modernized these three verses for the New Zealand supplement to *With One Voice* (1982).

SEEK YE FIRST Karen Lafferty's melody, here in an arrangement made in 1974 by the New Zealand musician **Janet Elder** for the Christchurch choral group the Celebration Singers, is now named after the text it supports. It appeared in the Australian publication *Together in Song* (1999) in a different arrangement by Canon Lawrie Bartlett. In its present form faint-hearted congregations can sing it as a standard verse-refrain hymn; bolder singers will enjoy it in the form it first took, as a canon in which the *alleluia* counter-melody acts as a descant to the primary melody.

Fofoga mai ma Iesu *W651*
Metre: 8.7.8.7.4.7 extended

This Niuean hymn of invocation to the Trinity was written after 1846, when missionaries from the London Missionary Society began their work on Niue, displacing the indigenous religion of the Niueans, who are thought to have reached the island more than a thousand years ago and had a religious culture of ancestral spirits. It is by an unknown writer, no doubt an early missionary, and seems to have been created to introduce gatherings for Christian worship or other purposes. Its doxology-like structure may have been suggested by the opening of Horatius Bonar's hymn: 'Glory be to God the Father, / Glory be to God the Son, / Glory be to God the Spirit, / Great Jehovah, Three in One,' but it is interesting that the Spirit is addressed as the second person of this Trinity, which may reflect the cultural world the missionary author was addressing.

The familiar association of the Holy Spirit with light shining into darkness and the warmth of fire derives from Matthew 4:16 (ultimately from Isaiah 9:2), and the Pentecost story. Though the matching of this text with REGENT SQUARE has become traditional on the island, some awkward slurrings are required to fit words and music together.

REGENT SQUARE This hymn tune was originally composed by **George Thomas Smart** as a setting for Horatius Bonar's hymn, 'Glory be to God the Father,' and was first published in the Presbyterian hymnal *Psalms and Hymns for Divine Worship* (London,1867), for which Smart was the musical editor. Smart had been the organist at St Philip's Presbyterian Church, Regent Square, London, where Dr James Hamilton, the words editor of *Psalms and Hymns for Divine Worship* was the minister, hence the tune's name as a tribute to his former church and his collaboration with Hamilton. The soaring melody rapidly became widely popular, and it was used for a number of other hymns, as it has been here.

Follow the Way *F16*
Metre: 9.6.9.6

When this text by **Shirley Murray** was published in *Faith Makes the Song* (2003), its author described it as 'a short response which could be used in a litany, or between readings for a Holy Week service. The first Christians were called "People of the Way."' It appeared there set to a tune written in 2001 by New Zealand composer **Jenny McLeod**. It had already been published in 2000 in *Faith Forever Singing*, and was actually written in 1995, with the sub-title 'Refrain for a Litany,' to fit a tune offered to her by her friend Jillian Bray in that year.

The key phrase, 'the Way of the Cross,' is the name of a devotional ritual probably initiated by St Francis of Assisi, in which the worshipper moves physically past a set of 'stations' – there are usually 14 of these – each representing an event in Jesus' progress towards and through his crucifixion to his death, as recorded in the gospels and made vivid by artistic representations in paintings or sculpture.

GETHSEMANE The music by **Jillian Bray** was written in 1995; the name of the tune refers to the garden at the foot of the Mount of Olives in Jerusalem where Jesus prayed with his disciples and was arrested prior to his trial and execution (Matthew 26:36, following Mark 14:32). *Gethsemane* is an Aramaic word meaning 'the place of the oil press.' The E minor key (though it briefly modulates to D major) and the bass line dropping towards B minor create a strong sense of sadness, reinforced by the slow descent of repeated phrases in the melody, echoed by the tenor line beneath. The piece is constructed to allow for as many repetitions as required.

Food is given for us all (Grace before Meals) A37
Metre: Irregular

Cecily Sheehy is the writer/composer of this grace, which takes the musical form of a round for two voices. It was first printed, with instructions for the singers, in *Alleluia Aotearoa* (1993).

Genesis 1:29 is the scriptural basis for the first line of the round, to which is added 'and for us to give to others,' together with the whole of the second line, and the chorus of thanks. The effect is cheerful, even comical: a good preparation for a hearty meal at which the singers first acknowledge the needs of others less well provided than themselves.

For all small children (Litany for a Spirit-filled Planet) A38
Metre: Irregular

This litany, or prayer, that along with the fauna and flora of the natural world children may be respected and 'find a place,' was written by Dominican Sister **Cecily Sheehy** as one of a series of such songs for children published in the Catholic magazine *Family Living* between 1980 and 1985. Its first hymnbook appearance was in *Alleluia Aotearoa* (1993).

This inventive and imaginative litany, with its double lists of – by implication – inanimate elements and animate beings at risk of being polluted or 'crowded out' by the ever-increasing human population of the planet, expresses a deep concern for the environment developed by Cecily Sheehy, a concern which eventually took her to study Creation Spirituality under Matthew Fox and the staff of the Institute in Culture and Creation Spirituality, Holy Name College, California, inspiring her to write several more religious songs about our obligation to care for the planet and its creatures.

The initial and prayerful invocation of the Holy Spirit is at least as old as the ninth century AD (cf. the plainsong hymn 'Veni Creator Spiritus'). But this text delightfully mixes such ancient ritualistic language with imaginative and suggestive phrases like 'small fast insects' (fleas come to mind) and 'crawlers and creepers.' 'Pets and children' comically suggests their common status in the eyes of disapproving adults. Yet references to 'pure clean water' and 'whales and dolphins' call serious attention to potentially much more serious concerns about water pollution and the survival of some of earth's largest and most intelligent marine mammals.

[LITANY] Though it is not much more than a short repeated chant, this melody by Cecily Sheehy herself is pleasingly syncopated, and climbs easily and stepwise to a musical climax on B resolved by a step down to the tonic note G.

For everyone born, a place at the table F17, HP3
Metre: 11.10.11.10.11.10.11.7

This hymn was written in 1996, at a time when its author, **Shirley Murray**, was involved with work for Amnesty International, and was unable to find any hymn reflecting a broad overview of human rights.

The hymn was first published in 2000 in *Faith Forever Singing*, and reached American congregations in 2003 with its inclusion in *Faith Makes the Song*. It gave the title to the collection *For Everyone Born: Global Songs for an Emerging Church*, published in 2008 by the New York-based General Board of Global Ministries, and was published in 2013 in *Community of Christ Sings*, with translations into French and Spanish. In her own fifth American collection, *A Place at the Table* (2013), the hymn text both gives the book its title and is given an additional verse, 'because there are still Christian people not welcome at the communion table or at the common table of society.'

> For gay and for straight, a place at the table,
> a covenant shared, a welcoming space,
> a rainbow of race and gender and colour,
> for gay and for straight the chalice of grace,
> and God will delight
> when we are creators of justice and joy,
> compassion and peace…

The dominant image of the poem – sharing a place at a meal table as a sign of inclusion, has both domestic and religious resonance. Shirley Murray writes, 'What is this table? In my mind it began as the table of the world in the peaceable kingdom, an imaginary place of justice and joy, where everyone gathers and is fed. But inevitably it was taken up as a communion hymn, in the context of the Holy Table….And in places where exclusion by the Church is a source of injustice and pain, as with the gay and lesbian communities, it has been used to ask for a place at the table, along with every other believer.'

As the author explains, 'I have used some of the very basic ideas of the Universal Declaration of Human Rights – the right to shelter, safety, food, and later [verse 5], the right to a job, to freedom of speech and worship. I've tried to put them into a context which relates directly to the Gospel, but without excluding those who are not of the Christian faith…But in a more specific way, and to me an authentic one, it relates deeply and immediately to the manifesto of Jesus and all that he taught.'

The fourth verse has proved problematic for some singers, with its inclusion of the 'unjust' and the 'abuser' among those at the table. Again the author says, 'I wrote the "tough" verse 4 because I knew, under the manifesto of Jesus, that even the worst abuse has to be dealt with and faced, and forgiveness requires singing about here' (quoted in 'For Everyone Born, a Place at the Table,' Lauren Hall, *The Hymn* 63.3, Summer 2012, 42-4).

MENSA (Latin=table). This setting was written by **Colin Gibson** in 1996 in response to the sharing of her text by its author. The natural rhythm of the long lines of the verses called for an equally rhythmical melodic setting – in F minor to match the serious nature of the argument, but with a lift to D flat major in the refrain to suggest God's delight and joy at justice done and inclusiveness honoured. A different setting, FOR EVERYONE BORN, written by American composer Brian Mann in 2000, is used in *A Place at the Table*, and there is another setting published by Canadian composer **Ron Klusmeier** (Klusmeier 30).

For the bread and wine and blessing *A39*
Metre: 8.8.8.8

This communion-centred hymn of celebration was written by **Shirley Murray** in 1989. She says that it originates from the worship practices of the congregation of St Andrew's on the Terrace – her home church in Wellington from 1975 to 93 – 'where, in the Reformed tradition, we often celebrate Communion all standing around the table. As we pass the bread and wine to one another, we sing simple responses such as those of Taizé or Iona.' This hymn first appeared in *In Every Corner Sing* (1992), then in *Alleluia Aotearoa* (1993). In the American publication it is set to the tune WECK, by composer Jane Holstein.

The hymn is conceived as a set of simple response of the Taizé or Iona kind. Verse 2, line 3 refers to 1 Timothy 1:1, 'Christ Jesus our hope.' The Hebrew word *alleluia* (verse 4) means 'give praise to Jahweh.'

BREAD AND WINE This setting, named from the first line of the text for which it was written, was composed by **Guy Jansen** in 1989. Its 3/4 waltz-like rhythm and scalic melody make for easy singing, but it has some rhythmic complexity, with a mid-section change to 4/4, and there are several harmonic shifts.

For the crowd another busy day (Easter City) *F18*
Metre: 9.9.10.10.10.15

This hymn was written in 1998 by **Colin Gibson**, at the request of the Reverend Doctor David Bromell, after whom its tune is named, for a hymn on the theme of 'Christ in the modern city,' as part of a Lent-in-the-City programme organized by the inner-city churches of Christchurch. It was first published in *Faith Forever Singing* (2000).

The text places the scene of Christ's crucifixion on the streets of a modern city, and closes with the sober reminder of how much work remains to be done in any large urban centre to bring the spirit of Christ to its lifestyle. Verse 1 contrasts the gospel record of cheering crowds at Christ's entry into Jerusalem (as in Mark 11:1-11) with a modern crowd's casual interest. For the jeering crowd, see Mark 15:29-32. The second verse describes the events surrounding the resurrection, from Mary's meeting with the resurrected Christ to his appearance to the disciples in the locked room (John 20). The 'peaceful garden' recalls both the Garden of Gethsemane and the famed civic Botanic Gardens of Christchurch – and most major cities. Verse 3 alludes to the behaviour of the passers-by in the story of the Good Samaritan (Luke 10:29-37). In the final verse, there are echoes of New Zealand poet R.A.K. Mason's poem about an exhausted swagman, *On the Swag* (1962): 'Let the fruit be plucked and the cake be iced, / Let the bed be snug and the wine be spiced in the old cove's nightcap, / For this is Christ,' and the close of John Bunyan's *Pilgrim's Progress* (1678), 'and all the trumpets sounded for him on the other side.'*

BROMELL Named for the then Superintendent of the Christchurch Methodist City Mission, the melody is set in D minor to fit its sombre theme, with brief excursions into G minor, and F major.

*For a fuller account of this hymn see 'Easter City: "For the crowd another busy day," a hymn for Easter,' Colin Gibson, *Music in the Air* 22 (Winter 2006).

For the hurt that I create *F19 (i) and (ii)*
Metre: 7.6.7.6.8.6.8.6

One of a set of short original texts created by **John Murray** in 1999 for the publication *Faith Forever Singing* (2000). A prayer for forgiveness, with echoes of Romans 7:19.

SUPPLIANT The tune name means 'one who humbly begs' – in this case, for forgiveness. This unison setting was composed by **Jillian Bray** in 1999 for this text. The E minor key is chosen to reflect the confessional nature of the prayer.

FIVE SCRUPLES A scruple is a thought that troubles the mind or conscience: five such thoughts are listed in the prayer. This alternative unison setting, composed by **Ian Render** in 1999, increases the emotional power of the words by playing the rising melodic line against a descending chromatic scale in the key of F minor.

For the man and for the woman *A40*
Metre: 8.7.8.7.8.7.8.7

This hymn was written by **Colin Gibson** in 1987, as an invited offering, at Makiling, near Manila in the Philippines, on the occasion of the 1987 Asian Workshop on Liturgy and Music organised by the Asian Institute for Liturgy and Music. It was first published in 1993 in *Alleluia Aotearoa*, followed by *Reading the Signature: New Hymns and Songs* by Colin Gibson (Carol Stream, Illinois, Hope Publishing, 1994).

Colin Gibson writes that the hymn was conceived 'as a response to the kaleidoscope of artistic expressions of the Christian faith and the huge diversity of cultures present at the Workshop, affirming the wholeness and unity of human life and art in the presence of God.' Its strategy is to reject the usual separation into polar opposites common in Western civilisation and Christian thought for lists of unifying pairings, such as man and woman, person and people, doubt and belief, rock and flower, circle and line. In the final verse, dedicating the arts of dance, poetry, music, painting and theatre, the singers offer their combined praise to the great Creator, 'light of light and fire of fire.' In verse 3, 'the language of the hands' refers to the beautiful hand-gesturing used in many Asian dance forms.

MAKILING This tune name refers to the place of composition; the setting is by the hymn writer, **Colin Gibson**.

For the music of creation A41
Metre: 8.7.8.7 D

This splendid tribute to music as an expression of the nature of God was written by **Shirley Murray** in 1988 for a Festival of Praise in celebration of the Arts, at an ecumenical event in the Wellington Civic Centre. It was first published in the author's American collection *In Every Corner Sing* (1992), then in *Alleluia Aotearoa* (1993). A number of settings have since been written by composers eager to honour their own art; they include Milburn Price, Larry Harris, Sally Ann Morris, Lloyd Larsen, David Haas and Colin Gibson. The text has also been the subject of several hymn searches.

This poem assembles an astonishing number of musical terms – nearly 30 of them – with several of them, such as 'composer, discord, division' and 'harmony,' carrying an additional non-musical sense. The metaphoric heart of the text is the conception of God as supreme musician, matched with the Platonic idea of human musical activity as an echo of the divine voice.

There is no exclusive focus on religious music: lullabies and love songs appear with hymns and carols; likewise gesture and dance (ballet, American musicals and Indian musical expression come to mind) are celebrated, together with purely musical modes. While the conception of the creation of the world as taking place in some way through music is found in *Job* and in the writings of J.R.R. Tolkien and C.S. Lewis, this author rises to original poetry in her concept of 'All the voices of the ages' meeting 'in transcendent chorus' as part of the 'song of God that cannot cease.'

[MUSIC OF CREATION] The music chosen for the first performance of this text was Beethoven's W679 (a melody taken from the composer's Ninth Symphony). Shirley Murray said of the linkage, 'I hope it is never repeated!' However, the several references in the text to joy and rejoicing make such a connection at least plausible. Shirley Murray herself proposed the use of **C.H.H.** Parry's tune RUSTINGTON, composed in 1897 and named after the English town in Sussex where the composer lived for 40 years, and that was the melody published with the text in the 1992 publication *In Every Corner Sing*.

Douglas Mews was the New Zealand composer whose unnamed setting was chosen for *Alleluia Aotearoa*. His music, written shortly before 1993, provides a vigorous march-like melody, with unison and four-part sections and mid-melody harmonic shifts from G to D and A major, reminiscent in overall structure of M.L. Wostenholm's stirring 1908 hymn tune 'There's a light upon the mountain.' There are other settings by the New Zealand composer **Colin Gibson** and American and Canadian composers, including one by Canadian **Ron Klusmeier** (Klusmeier 1).

Forgive us, O God F21
Metre: 5.4.6.10.6

Written by **Colin Gibson** in 1999 out of a sense of deep grief and disappointment at the quarrelling over the admission of gay people to full membership and leadership that was creating deep divisions in the Methodist Church to which he belonged, this text was first published in *Faith Forever Singing* (2000) after a compromise had been reached. However, it still addresses the frequent doctrinal and other differences that from time to time have brought dissension to the body of Christ that is the Christian Church. It seeks forgiveness for such betrayal of the unity for which Christ prayed (John 17:21).

The first verse frames such dissension as analogous to the soldiers quarrelling at the foot of the cross over the division of the crucified Christ's clothing (John 19:23-25). The second verse addresses the practice of selecting scriptural texts to use as intellectual weapons against the beliefs of fellow Christians. For 'the undivided Word' see John 1:1-3 and 14. Verse 3 contrasts the cold unyielding positions that frequently characterise profound theological disputes with the sacrificial love symbolised by the broken jar of costly ointment used to anoint the head of Christ shortly before his arrest and execution and accepted by him as a supreme gesture of love (see Mark 14:3-9). Verse 4 is a plea for change (cf. Revelation 21:5) and a prayer for 'life made whole, made peaceful, kind and true' – that is, authentically Christ-like.

RIVERTON The name of a small coastal town in Southland, New Zealand, the home of a friend caught up in the dissension affecting the Methodist Church and other denominations at the time of composition. It contains a pun on 'rive,' meaning 'split, separate.' The music is by the writer and musician **Colin Gibson** and was composed for this text. Grounded in A major, and unified by the repetitions and variations on the opening phrase with its 'dropping' interval signifying disappointment, the music closes in F minor, signifying a muted hopeful outcome.

Forgive, forgive us, Holy God *F20, HP4*
Metre: 8.8.8.8

This powerful plea for God's forgiveness, originally titled 'Lament,' was written by **Shirley Murray** in 1994, 'While John, my husband, was in South Africa as an Ecumenical peace Monitor at the elections there. While South Africa provided some good news, Bosnia and Rwanda offset this by escalating horror. This hymn expresses my feeling of numb helplessness.' The events to which she refers were the civil war (1992-5) between Serbian forces in Bosnia and the country's Croat and Muslim inhabitants, culminating in a horrendous massacre at Trebinjska. Genocide and ethnic cleansing was also a feature of the 1994 conflict in the African republic of Rwanda, between the Hutu and Tutsi peoples. Verse 3 refers to the accumulating nuclear arsenals of America and Russia, resulting from the so-called Cold War (1947-91).

The text was first published in Shirley Murray's American collection *Every Day in your Spirit* (1996); later in *Faith Forever Singing* (2000).

The hymn begins and ends with references to the Lord's Prayer, which is also alluded to in verse 2 and in the reiteration of 'Forgive us.' 'Household gods' suggest the Roman practice of keeping a domestic shrine containing the gods thought to protect the home and its inhabitants. In this context, the phrase suggests the real self-interested values that may hide behind public professions of concern for others.

LACRIMAE RERUM (Latin='Tears are at the heart of things') The text name is a quotation from the Latin poet Virgil's epic poem, *The Aeneid*, Book 1, line 462. In context, the line is spoken by a Roman hero as he looks on depictions of the Trojan War and is overwhelmed by a sense of the futility and suffering of war. The musical setting was written in 1994 by **Colin Gibson**. The key chosen for its somber tone is C minor, where it remains apart from a brief modulation into

G minor. The melody rises to a pitch of grief, then sinks steadily downwards to the tonic note of C. There is another setting by Canadian composer **Ron Klusmeier** (Klusmeier 7).

Friend in Christ H30
Metre: 10.8.9.10.8

This unison song was written in 2003 by **Colin Gibson** and first published in *Hope is our Song* (2009). It was intended as a simple song of welcome to be sung by a congregation to any visitors, expressing the idea of an inclusive community centred on Jesus Christ (cf. Galatians 3:28). They are imagined sharing their life-stories, the common behaviour of church groups both before and after a service.

AMICITIA The Latin tune name means 'friendship.'

From pastures green C18
Metre: 8.7.8.7.D and refrain

This now iconic New Zealand Christmas carol text was written in 1965 by **Bing Lucas** (see under **Percy Hylton Craig (Bing) Lucas**) for the Linden-Tawa Baptist Church congregation, and first published by that church in 1966. Commercial publication began with *Servant Songs* (1987), followed by *Carol our Christmas* (1996). There are many textual and musical differences between these two publications (in each case *Servant Songs* preserves the original.) In verse 1, 'How bright the Southern Cross' becomes 'At night the Southern Cross'; in verse 2 'the sea' becomes 'when sea'; in verse 3 'to manhood youth is growing' becomes 'from childhood youth is growing,' 'to man compassion' becomes 'to all compassion,' 'how Christ's blood was shed' becomes 'Christ whose blood was shed' and 'his love to God repaying' becomes 'his love for us displaying.' In the refrain 'with us' replaces 'with man.'

Although the text fondly recalls the traditional elements of the nativity stories in Matthew and Luke, they are seen from a New Zealand vantage point, and the imagery is drawn from contemporary rural New Zealand life. (It is worth remembering that the writer was a committed conservationist with a deep love for New Zealand's natural landscapes.) Verse 1 establishes the summer setting of a New Zealand Christmas with its sheep-sheering, irrigated pastures and high-country dry tussock* ground. At this time, too, the southern-hemisphere star constellation known from its configuration as the Southern Cross appears. Verse 2 celebrates the world-wide tradition of giving gifts on Christmas Day, but it also addresses the New Zealand population's summer holidaying at the country's many beaches or, for the more vigorous, mountain-climbing in the Alps. The rata tree mentioned in verse 3 produces blood-red blossoms in summer, a southern analogue to the northern holly berries, both of them symbolizing the blood spilt in Christ's Passion. The theological commentary in the refrain recalls John 3:16.

[PASTURES GREEN] **Alex Duncan** is the composer for the setting combining melody and guitar accompaniment used in *Servant Songs*; the arranger of the more elaborate setting for congregation and choir in *Carol our Christmas* remains anonymous.

As with the text, there are considerable differences between the settings in *Servant Songs* and *Carol our Christmas*. The pitch is lowered by a key change from C to B minor, and the parts are laid out in *Carol our Christmas* to more clearly distinguish the melody from the choral and (rewritten) piano accompaniment.

> *Tussock is a hardy grass that grows to a considerable height and often forms the only plant covering for the rocky mountain terrain known as the high-country.

From the apple in the garden (Hymn for Bible Sunday) A42
Metre: 8.7.8.7.7

Shirley Murray wrote this hymn for Bible Sunday, 1991. It was first published in her American collection *In Every Corner Sing* (1992), then in *Alleluia Aotearoa* (1993).

The author says, 'When I wrote this text I had been reflecting on the material provided [by the Bible Society] for this year's "Bible

Sunday," and the fact that our society, once called "Christian" but now highly secular, is mostly "unchurched" and Biblically illiterate.'

The verses traverse key events in the Bible, balancing Old and New Testament stories with each other. Verse 1 contrasts the story of the Fall (Genesis 2-3) and God's promise to Noah (Genesis 8) with the story of Christ's nativity (Matthew 2); verse 2 links the manna provided to Moses' people (Exodus 16) with both the breaking of bread at the Last Supper (1 Corinthians 11:23-25, and the Synoptic Gospels) and the Supper at Emmaus (Luke 24); verse 3 refers to imprisoned prophets (1 Kings 22:27 [Micaiah], Jeremiah 32:3, Mark 6:17 [John the Baptist]), the darkness following the crucifixion (Mark 15:33, Luke 23:44) and the resurrection of Christ (Mark 16:1-4, Luke 24:1-2); verse 4 contrasts 'the curse of Eve and Adam' (Genesis 2:17-19) with the blessing of Christ, and the (evil) spirits of discord (1 Corinthians 1:10-17) with the presence of the Holy Spirit.

FRANKLIN WEST Named after the Co-operating Parish in Waiuku, near Auckland, this setting was written by **Colin Gibson** in 1991 for Shirley Murray's words and dedicated to the Reverend David Alley, then Methodist minister at West Franklin Church. The setting in F major contrasts a flowing melodic line used for the verses with an emphatic chordal movement for the refrain, with the inner parts echoing the previous fluid lines.

From the waiting comes the sign
A43
Metre 7.6.76.76.12

This hymn, subtitled 'Invocation to the Spirit,' was written by **Shirley Murray** in 1989 and first appeared in the American publication *In Every Corner Sing* (1992), then in *Alleluia Aotearoa* (1993).

The author says that this gnomic text was envisaged as a meditation for the theme of the World Council of Churches Assembly held in Canberra, Australia, in 1991, 'Come, Holy Spirit.' It takes the form of a prayer of invocation constructed as two sets of mystical paradoxes, with the final line of each stanza summarizing the gifts of the Spirit. Both verses draw on the most famous biblical manifestation of the Holy Spirit, the day of Pentecost (Acts 2:1-28). The biblical text refers to signs (verse 19), presence (verse 28) and fire (verse 3), with 'song' substituted for the 'utterance' mentioned in verse 4. Verse 2, lines 1 and 3, 'In the spending is the gift…In the breaking is the life,' rework the saying recorded in all three synoptic gospels, 'Whoever loses his life for my sake and the gospel's will save it. For what does it profit a man to gain the whole world and forfeit his life?' (Mark 8:35-36). Line 5 also recalls 'this is my body broken for you' (1 Corinthians 11:24).

The responsive phrase and the theme of the Assembly, 'Come, Holy Spirit,' is the opening of a medieval devotional poem or sequence prescribed in the Roman Liturgy for the Mass for Pentecost. Its authorship is uncertain; Pope Innocent III and Stephen Langton, Archbishop of Canterbury, have both been mentioned as possible candidates.

SIGNUM (Latin=sign). This setting was composed by **Colin Gibson** in 1989. While it can be sung as a unison melody, it is constructed as a series of musical phrases in which a cantor-like unison melody receives a choral response from the congregation, 'Come, Holy Spirit, come.' Its D minor tonality and plainsong melodic style is intended to reflect the liturgical solemnity of the words.

From this holy time *H31*
Metre: 5.5.5.5.6.5.6.5

This hymn text, intended as an end-of-service hymn 'to bridge the gap between the worship / ritual frame of mind and our everyday life and ministry," was written by **Marnie Barrell** in November 1993, with a dedication to close friends Vicar Lawrence and Elizabeth Kimberley, and their son (the hymn writer's godson) Aidan. It was first published in *Hope is our Song* (2009).

The hymn is a profession of dedication to Christ and to a life imitating his example, 'to love as he loves / and work for God's reign.' Verse 1 references John 14:8, 'I am the way, the truth and the life.' Its two final lines form a refrain for all three verses, drawn from Micah 6:8: '...what does the Lord require of you, but to do justly, and to love mercy, and to walk humbly with your God?' Marnie Barrell says of these words, 'I wanted to underline a memorable take-home summary of our mission [as Christians]. Although the phrase is from Micah rather than Jesus himself, he of course exemplified and taught [it] so I portray it as his way. I always liked the phrase, and thought it could hardly be bettered as a summary of the religious life – one of those First Testament phrases with rich content for Christians as much as Jews.'

Verse 2 focuses on the life of the resurrected Christ: line 1 references John 20:26; line 2 alludes to Acts 1:9-11; line 3 references 1 John:1-7. Verse 3 refers to the *parousia*, the Second Coming of Christ – for the phrase 'till Christ comes again,' see Matthew 16:28. 'God's reign' is the establishment on earth of the kingdom of God (more commonly in the gospels 'the kingdom of heaven').

HOLLY LEA The tune is named after a retirement village in Fendalton, Christchurch, adjacent to St Barnabas's Anglican Church, with which the composer **Barry Brinson** has been associated. The four-part choral setting was written in 2007. Although it is composed in a standard 'hymn-tune' style, the directness and coherence of the melody (constructed entirely of variations on the initial 5-note phrase by repetition, inversion and extension) well suits the simplicity and brief phrases of the text. Modulations quickly move the tonality away from D major to A major then G major before returning to the home key, and the quotation from Micah is given prominence by the higher pitching and wider intervals of the melody in the final bars. Marnie Barrell says of it, 'Barry's tune is quite successful, I think. I like a bracing and vigorous tune to go out to.' The original tune envisaged was HANOVER, by William Croft (1708).

Gentle God A44, HP5
Metre: 8.7.8.7.7.7

Written in 1991 by **Shirley Murray**, this text was one of a number inspired by the writer's commitment to the international Peace movement. She herself recognised its theme as being unusual: 'Peace hymns, for me, do not often express the difficulty of dealing with anger, and the strength needed to be non-violent on both personal and global levels.' It was published in her first American collection, *In Every Corner Sing* (1992), then in *Alleluia Aotearoa* (1993).

Verse 1 uses the contemporary military and political phrase 'hawk and dove' for those ready to go to war and peace-seekers, and urges non-violent resistance to provocation in Jesus' words, 'turn the other cheek' (Matthew 5:39). 'Smear' in verse 2 suggests hurting or demonising an enemy with lies or propaganda. Verse 3, line 4, paraphrases Jesus' 'Love your enemies, do good to those who hate you' (Luke .6:27). Verse 4 opens with an allusion to the Lord's Prayer, Luke 11:4, 'forgive us our sins as we forgive those who have sinned against us,' and closes with a reference to Galatians 5:22, 'the fruit of the Spirit is...peace.'

TAWA Named after the Wellington suburb in which she was living at the time, this melody was written in 1991 in circumstances described by the composer, **Jillian Bray**: 'the text was tabled as requiring a tune at an editors' meeting [of the New Zealand Hymnbook Committee] at St Andrew's on the Terrace [Wellington], with several others. Shirley Murray invited the music editors to each select a text and gave us about 40 minutes to write a setting. I was amazed to complete a rough draft at the time as I was not used to composing under pressure. An elaborate piano accompaniment was later added for the *Alleluia Aotearoa* tape.' In this subdued setting in D minor, the varying line lengths of the text are accommodated with time shifts between 3/4 and 2/4.

Gentle is the way of Jesus *F22, HP6*
Metre: 8.7.8.7 D

This hymn was written by **Shirley Murray** in January 1999, in response to a hymn tune offered to her by her friend Jillian Bray in December 1998. It was first published in *Faith Forever Singing* (2000) with Jillian Bray's setting, then as a plain text in *He Came Singing Peace* (2002), a publication to support the World Council of Churches' announcement of a Decade to Over. the character of the text later fitted to the music. There is another setting by Canadian composer **Ron Klusmeier** (Klusmeier 31).

Get up, get up, no time to yawn *C19*
Metre: 8.8.8.8 and refrain

This carol was written by **Colin Gibson** on Christmas Day 1983, during a family holiday at Anaura Bay, one of the most beautiful of the East Coast beaches north of Gisborne. It was first published in his collection *Singing Love* (1988), before reaching *Carol our Christmas* (1996).

The features of sunrise at Anaura Bay are successively recorded in the verses and made symbolic of the spiritual life, as in the traditional association of the risen sun with Christ the Son of God (verse 4). In each verse the light of a new day is contrasted with the darkness of the preceding night, and the carol ends in the full blaze of day. The final line of verse 1, 'the world begins its Christmas Day,' refers to the fact that because of their country's position relative to the international dateline New Zealanders are among the first people on Earth to celebrate Christmas Day and do so in mid-summer (verse 2, 'the summer flowers proclaim delight'). The refrain invites the singers to join the traditional biblical figures of the shepherds and kings who attended Christ's nativity.

ANAURA BAY The musical setting by **Colin Gibson** is named after the bay where the carol was composed, in a world actually 'filled with light.' The 6/8 time signature indicates the joyful dance rhythm of the music.

Give thanks for life *A45*
Metre: 10,10.10 and alleluias

This text was written by **Shirley Murray** in 1986 as a funeral hymn. It was first published privately in *In Every Corner Sing* (Wellington, 1987). It then appeared in the first American collection of Shirley Murray's work, *In Every Corner Sing* (1992). New Zealand publication followed in 1993 in *Alleluia Aotearoa*.

Shirley Murray describes it as follows: 'I wrote this as a celebration for someone who [had] lived a full life, though it has now become used for other occasions of thanksgiving and commemoration.' The final verse draws on John 12:24. *Alleluia* is a Latin transliteration of the Hebrew word meaning 'Praise Yah (God).'

[THANKS FOR LIFE] This untitled setting was written in 1992 for this text by **Douglas Mews**. It fits music to the rhythms of the text in a masterly way, modulating effortlessly through B and A major before returning to the affirmative key of D major. The original setting chosen by the author was the well-known SINE NOMINE, by **Ralph Vaughan Williams**. In the American edition of *In Every Corner Sing* the hymn is set to ENGELBERG, by American hymn writer and composer **Jim Strathdee**.

Gloria *C20*
Metre: Irregular

In 1995 John Murray, leader of the editorial board preparing *Carol our Christmas* invited composer members of the board to contribute settings of the ancient Latin text *Gloria in excelsis deo, et in terra pax hominibus* ('Glory to God in the highest, and on earth peace among all people,' literally 'men') because of its association with the Christmas season. The text derives from Luke's account of the song of the angels at the time of Jesus' birth (Luke 2:14).

Jillian Bray writes a choral work for four voices, using an English language translation of the Latin. In the key of G, it sets the text syllable by syllable, with the piano (or organ) contributing an independent display of enriched chords reaching higher than is possible for voices (see especially the setting of 'highest heaven'). The first loud section is contrasted with the second piano section as the melody drops towards the final tonic note denoting 'earth.'

Gloria *C21*
Metre: Irregular

See **Gloria** *C20* for the circumstances of composition of this piece.

Colin Daley, responsible for preparing the print versions of many of the New Zealand Hymn Book Trust's publications and a musician in his own right, sets the Latin text for four-part choir, sometimes sub-dividing the parts to create a rich vocal texture in the style of high renaissance church music

The work is divided into two sections, each using half of the text. The opening key is C, the extreme parts move in opposite directions, the bass dropping steadily in a chromatic succession to a low F before recovering to C while the soprano line climbs steadily higher until it reaches and tops a final C chord with a high G. In the second *pax in terra hominibus* section, marked optional and completed with a return to the first section, the key moves through a succession of downward harmonic sequences to reach a final D major chord while the melody slowly drops in similar motion (towards 'earth'). The volume increases steadily from an extreme pianissimo to an excited double forte in the first section, while the second 'peaceful' section remains moderately soft.

Gloria *C22*

See **Gloria** *C20* for the circumstances of the composition of this piece.

Colin Gibson chooses to set the text in a format that allows the music to be used as a chant, canon or chorale (see the instruction to singers). The language choice is equally open and optional, offering Latin, English and Māori versions of the full text.

The key choice is C, and the four-part text setting is syllabic, with no dynamic indications. As the bass drops steadily down from C the melody line rises then falls in an arch-like structure. Multiple repetitions are possible in the style of a Taizé chant, and the piece comes to a close with a collapsing arch that closes on the tonic 'earth' note C.

Gloria in excelsis *C23*

See 'Gloria' *C20* for the circumstances of the composition of this piece.

Here **Colin Gibson** uses a Latin and English version of the *Gloria* text and a format that allows for repetition as a congregational chant, performance by a choir, or performance by a congregation with participation from a three-part choir of high voices (see the instruction to singers). The *Gloria in excelsis* phrase repeats throughout, with increasing decoration and elaboration, closing in a triple rendition of the word *Gloria* matched with rising inversions of the tonic chord in both voice and instrumental accompaniment. The effect is cumulative as further voices are added over the repeated chant motif, with only a brief excursion into F and G and a change of melody for the 'peace' section interrupting the steady climb towards the final extremely spread chord.

Glorious are you *H33*
Metre: Irregular

The text of this hymn is based on a religious poem written 'as a personal Gloria' by Joy Cowley in 2007, which has become part of many modern liturgies in New Zealand churches. It was first published in full in *Hope is our Song* (2009). However, a shortened and altered version had previously been published in the author's *Come and See: Reflections on the Life of Jesus among us* (Otane, Central Hawkes Bay: Pleroma Christian Supplies, 2008). There are substantial and literal differences between the two texts that warrant the printing of the poet's second version in full.*

The original *Gloria*, the traditional Christian prayer of adoration on which both these texts are based, is an ancient hymn of praise to the

Trinity that has been in use in the Christian Church since the second century. It was written in Greek in the second century and was introduced to the Western Church by St. Hilary of Poitiers (d. 368).

Joy Cowley, while retaining the Trinitarian formula of the original, develops that formulation in her own unique and distinctive way. God is addressed in verse 1 as 'the Mystery of Life,' and portrayed in terms of images of the natural creation ('dawn on mountain peaks'), using inherited metaphors of music (the music of the spheres) and light to symbolise the harmonious, symphonic structure and movement of the universe as it has been discovered by modern science ('you are the music of the atoms within us'). Human activity ('farm,' 'rush of the city') is briefly mentioned, and the poet uses 'human' imagery – the embrace of love – to describe the relationship between the mystery that is God and the universe as the expression of God's nature.

Verse 2 portrays Jesus as 'cosmic love in human flesh' (cf. John 3:16); the one who teaches us to dance to the music, not of time – as in Nicolas Poussin's 1636 painting or Anthony Powell's sequence of novels (1951-75) – but of love. There are allusions to events recorded in the gospels (see Matthew 14:22-33, 9:20-22, Luke 24:13-25 and Philippians 2:8), but the emphasis falls on their deeper significance for modern lives ('revealing that cross and resurrection are one on the road to freedom'). 'You graced the smallness of time and space' parallels 'Our God, contracted to a span, / Incomprehensibly made man,' from **Charles Wesley**'s 1744 hymn, 'Let earth and heaven combine.'

The verse dealing with the Holy Spirit rapidly scans traditional definitions and images (see John 16:13, Ephesians 1:17, Genesis 2:7 and Acts 2:1-4), but Joy Cowley adds the novel image of the Holy Spirit as a compass needle steadily pointing to 'the true North' (with echoes of Shakespeare's Sonnet 116) and a final image of a 'sacred dance into the mystery of life' (cf. line 1 of this poem, and the concluding picture of the Dance of Death in Ingmar Bergman's film, *The Seventh Seal*).

MYSTERY The tune name picks up on the poet's definition of God as 'mystery of life' (line 1). The music, by **Colin Gibson**, was written in 2007, and takes up on the repeated image of dancing used in the text. It is conceived as a stately sacred dance, a kind of formal minuet. The modality is predominantly in C major, but there is a later modulation to F major, A minor and D minor before the melody finally settles on F major, permitting an easy return to the C major beginning, but also allowing for an ending with the third verse on an 'open' F major chord, as the singers / dancers move 'into the mystery of life.'

*In *Come and See*, p23, the text is titled 'Trinity' and carries an epigraph from John 14:15-17. The body of the text is headed 'Gloria.'

Glorious are you, O Mystery of Life,
essence of all creation.
You are the symphony of stars and planets.
You are the music of the atoms within us.
Forest and farm, the rush of the city,
everything is held in your love.
We rejoice as we sing our gratitude.

Glorious are you, O Jesus Christ,
cosmic love in human flesh,
our brother, teacher and friend.
You make your home in our lives,
daily revealing that cross and resurrection
are one on the road to freedom.
We rejoice as we sing our gratitude.

Glorious are you, O Spirit of Truth.
You are the needle of the inner compass
always pointing to true North,
guiding us in the dance of love
that takes us to the heart
of the Mystery of Life.
We rejoice as we sing our gratitude.

Glory be to the Father W675
Metre: Irregular

This version of the text of an ancient Christian doxology based on Matthew 28:19-20 was written by **Richard Avery** and **Donald**

Marsh and first published in their *Hymns Hot and Carols Cool* (Carol Stream, IL.: Hope Publishing, 1967).

GLORIA The original lively and syncopated melody composed by Avery and Marsh for their text, in a modern popular idiom completely typical of their refreshing church music, was arranged in 1981 for the committee preparing the New Zealand Supplement to *With One Voice* (1982) by **Shona Murray**, then Head of Music at Tawa College, Wellington.

Glory to God *F23*
Metre: 13.13.13.10

One of a set of short original texts created by **John Murray** in 1999 for the publication *Faith Forever Singing* (2000).

The untitled unison setting for this text was composed by **Cecily Sheehy** in 1999.

Glory! Glory! *C24*
Metre: 11.10.7.6.10

This ascription of praise was written by author and composer **Jillian Bray** in 1995. It was first published in *Carol Our Christmas* (1996).

The words are derived from the song of the angels at the time of Christ's nativity (Luke 2:14), though the initial 'sing it' belongs to the gospel song leader's exhortation to the congregation. 'Good news' is a phrase from Luke 2:10, though, ironically, in modern times the phrase 'Good news is here to stay' has become a media headline cliché. 'Glory from highest heaven falling on earth and sea' reworks Luke's 'Glory to God in the highest and on earth peace' (Luke 2:14). John 16:14 is the source for the final phrase.

SPONTANEITY The tune name describes the work as an act of spontaneous praise on the part of both the writer and the singers. The syncopated melodic line with a strong underlying rhythmic beat suggests informality and spontaneity in a modern popular style. The largely independent piano accompaniment literally illustrates the verbal text, rapidly rising and falling in pitch between 'heaven' and 'earth' and finally leaving the words behind to fling upwards to a top G, supported by chords shifting up from C major through D major to E major.

Go gently, go lightly *H35 (i) and (ii)*
Metre: 6.6.6.6.5 D

This simple song of blessing and dismissal was written by **Shirley Murray** in 2001 and published in her American collection *Faith Makes the Song* (2003). There it is set to the tune ROSEMARY, composed by **Carlton Young**. Other settings have been written by Americans Lori True and David Haas, and Canadian **Ron Klusmeier**, and the text has been translated into German by Hardmut Handt for a 2017 hymnal.

This text touches with equal lightness on its biblical sources. The key terms, 'gently' and 'lightly,' have scriptural associations: see Matthew 11:30, 'For my yoke is easy and my burden is light,' and Galatians 5:22-23, 'And the fruits of the Spirit are…gentleness.' This passage is again alluded to in verse 2, lines 1-2. The injunction to live simply derives from Jesus' instructions to his disciples (Mark 6:8-11, 'Take nothing for the journey except a staff…').

LENITER (Latin=lightly) LENITER was composed by **Marnie Barrell** in 2008. The melody, in 6/8 time, moves quickly and lightly, an effect supported by a repeated dotted three-note figure. The harmonic base shifts upwards from D major to G before sequencing down to close on the tonic.

LEGÈRE (French=lightly) This fellow setting was also written by **Colin Gibson** in 2008. The melody, set in F major and in 3/4 time, twice moves steadily upwards before falling back, then steps carefully down to close on F. There is a canonic imitation in the bass line. The text is then repeated in a four-voice choral arrangement. Another setting by Canadian composer **Ron Klusmeier** (Klusmeier 22) moves the melody through several key changes.

God be in, around, above me H36
Metre: 8.7.8.7 D

This Celtic-style hymn of invocation was written by **Marnie Barrell** in 2001 and first published in *Hope is our Song* (2009). The theme of the hymn is the span of the believer's developing life within the family of God, from the state of childhood to that of maturity in the faith. Its occasion was the confirmation of the writer's goddaughter, Eve Daniell, and the hymn carries a dedication to Eve Daniell, dated June 2001. The original setting chosen was ODE TO JOY, the famous melody taken from Beethoven's Ninth Symphony.

The first verse addresses the persons of the Trinity in personal and intimate terms, seeking individual presence, protection and guidance. In keeping with the theme, the believer sings to God as mother and father, creator and friend. Verse 2 shifts the focus to Christ as 'elder brother through my growing' and as 'anchor, still [always] the same.' The episode in Jesus' life where he declares his brotherhood with his followers (Mark 3:35, picked up in Hebrews 2:11) is the source of both the 'elder brother' image and the familiar use of the term 'brethren (brothers)' to describe all Christians – as is done throughout Hebrews. (That Christ also addressed his followers as his 'sisters' has largely been ignored.) The anchor is an ancient Christian symbol derived from Hebrews 6:19, 'We have this [hope in Jesus] as a sure and steadfast anchor of the soul.' Verse 3 claims the Church throughout history as the singer's extended family ('here I claim as family'), closing with an image of Christ's people (in both senses as 'followers' and 'relatives') gathered round the communion table 'everywhere.' Verse 4 completes the 'family' theme: the family unites in the praise of Christ, it inherits blessings from God (possibly suggested by 1 Peter 3:9), and works for justice, peace, freedom, inclusion and the achievement of God's kingdom on earth. The final lines echo the Lord's Prayer (also known as the family prayer of the Church, 'Thy kingdom come, thy will be done').

DANIELL The tune is named after Marnie Barrell's goddaughter. The music was written by **Colin Gibson** in 2008. In keeping with the large theme of the hymn, the main melodic phrase is a broad sweeping one, moving in two repetitions from a tonic chord in D major to an A major chord; then modulating briefly through B minor and A major before closing with a return to the opening melodic phrase, now cadencing in D major.

God bless our land H37
Metre: 11.11.10.5.5

This hymn was written by **Shirley Murray** to celebrate Waitangi Day, 2005. As she explains in her American collection *Touch the Earth Lightly* (2008), where this hymn was published before appearing in *Hope is our Song* (2009), 'Waitangi Day, February 6, is remembered as New Zealand's national day, celebrating the Treaty of understanding between people' [signed in 1840 between the British Crown and representatives of the indigenous Māori population at Waitangi, in the Bay of Islands, and at other centres in the country].

The text invokes God's blessing on a country which has seen the arrival of many ethnicities, from the Pacific, Europe, Asia and more recently Africa. Verse 1 refers to 'our islands,' which comprise three main islands, the North, South and Stewart Islands, together with off-shore islands extending east to the Chatham Islands and south to Campbell Island near Antarctica. *Whenua* is the Māori word for ground, country and that which binds us to it (literally, placenta). *Aotearoa* is a Māori name for this nation, popularly translated as 'land of the long, white cloud,' describing what the first Māori saw as they approached these shores in their ocean-sailing canoes.

Verse 2, line 2, 'treasures, baskets,' allude to the Māori words *taonga*, 'cultural treasures,' and *kete*, 'food baskets.' The 'wrongs of history' are the acts of land seizure which are still causes of grievance and are being dealt with in a slow process of negotiated settlements by the Crown. Verse 4, line 2, 'freedoms daily granted,' probably refers to the rights granted under the

Treaty of Waitangi; cf. the repeated description in the National Anthem of New Zealand as 'our free land.' *Aroha* (line 3) is the Māori word for love and understanding.*

WAITANGI DAY The tune name acknowledges the occasion of the hymn. The author says of this setting, '**Barry Brinson** has given this [text] a feeling of serious grandeur and hopefulness suited to the occasion.' The strong chordal progression of the music over a steadily advancing bass line has affinities with **Ralph Vaughan Williams'** majestic SINE NOMINE ('For all the saints'), as does the off-beat commencement of the tune and the melodic shape of the final 'Aotearoa.'

> *For a fuller account of this key word in Māori culture and contemporary New Zealand religious thought see the entry for 'Come to this Christmas singing.'

God comes to us as one unheard (God in Everything) H42
Metre: 8.6.8.6

This hymn text was written by **Jocelyn Marshall** and first published in her collection *A Singing Faith* (1996), before appearing in *New Glory: Hymns, Psalms and Songs for a New Century* (Kevin Mayhew, 1999) and the author's own enlargement and revision of *A Singing Faith, Hymns for All Seasons* (2007). Though it is not to be regarded as a source, there is a hymn similar in thought and metre written in 1984 by Bishop Timothy Dudley-Smith, 'He comes to us as one unknown, / A breath unseen, unheard.'

The theme of the hymn is the unrecognised presence of God in all things. Verses 1-2 instance the divine presence in moments of silence, sound and beauty, including 'the miracle of birth.' This poet's special appreciation of music ('marvel of a symphony, / sublimity of sound') is expressed elsewhere in her hymn 'God, composer and conductor' (H34). Verse 3 draws on the Emmaus experience of the disciples (see Luke 24:13-50). Verse 4 acknowledges the divine presence 'when strength and faith are weak' in the assistance and support offered by friends. Verse 5, line 2, recalls the title of the book by C.S. Lewis, *Surprised by Joy* (1955); lines 3-4 reference John 1:5. The final verse logically concludes the hymn with a request to be taught to recognise the presence of the spirit of God everywhere (cf. John 14:17).

Jocelyn Marshall notes that this hymn 'was sung at Scott Base, Antarctica, on November 28, 2004, at the memorial service held on the 25th anniversary of the crash on Mount Erebus of an Air New Zealand plane in which 257 people perished, including four of my relations.'

The suggested tunes for this hymn text are NEWBURY, an early English carol tune introduced into the *English Hymnal* (1906) by **Ralph Vaughan Williams**; BELMONT, by a still unidentified composer and first published in something like its present form in *Islington Psalmody* (1854); or IRISH (also known as DUBLIN) likewise by an unidentified composer and first published in *A Collection of Hymns and Sacred Poems,* printed at Dublin in 1749.

God gave to man the woman A46
Metre: 6.6.6.5.6.6.6.6 and refrain

The wedding in 1982 of 'two very good friends' of the author-composer **Felicia Edgecombe**, became, in her words, 'an occasion for me to reflect on the nature of love – its attractiveness, powerfulness and challenge. Somehow human love and unity with all its paradoxes, helps us to understand a little better the mystery of God's love. He is LOVE in essence and in source.' This hymn, written in 1982, was first published in *Servant Songs* (1987) edited by Guy Jansen and Felicia Edgecombe, then in *Alleluia Aotearoa* (1993), and was reprinted in *Songs of Life*, by Felicia Edgecombe and Rosemary Russell (Wellington: Festivity Productions, 1996), with the melody separated and given an independent piano accompaniment by Glenys Chiaroni.

This wedding song offers a commentary on the account of the creation of human beings in Genesis 2:21-24, which forms the basis of the refrain. For the thought of verse 1 see the writer's ideas expressed in the previous paragraph. For the concept of love as 'a mystery' (line 1) see Ephesians 5:32-3. Verse 2 provides a blessing on the couple to be married, with an allusion to 1 Corinthians 13:8, 'Love never ends.' Verse 3 draws substantially on the famous description of the nature of love in 1 Corinthians 13:4-6, frequently quoted in marriage services

[GOD'S GIFT] In its original version, this hymn to human and divine love was given a four-part choral arrangement by the composer, marked 'Moderate speed, gently flowing,' with the first three bars sung as a unison melody above hummed chords. *Alleluia Aotearoa* provided a hymn-style four-part choral arrangement throughout. In *Songs of Life* the setting was changed to a unison melody throughout with piano accompaniment. In the refrain, there is much use of off-beat phrase openings and syncopation, contrasted with steadier, more emphatic crochet beating in the verses. The supporting harmony remains in a G major tonality for the thematic statement of the refrain, then moves with the melody through a rising succession of minor keys to a first D major focal point, then rather more chromatically downwards to a second D chord preparing for a repetition of the refrain.

God in the darkness *F24*
Metre: 11.11.11.5

This text was written by Australian **Elizabeth Smith** and published in her first collection of hymn texts, *Praise the God of Grace: Hymns for Inclusive Worship* (1990). As well as appearing in Colin Gibson's *Songs for a Rainbow People* (1998), and *Faith Forever Singing* (2000), the text has been reprinted in Erik Routley and Paul Richardson's *Panorama of Christian Hymnody* (2005) and L. William Countryman's *Run, Shepherds, Run: Poems for Advent and Christmas* (2005).

Elizabeth Smith says of her text, 'Many of our hymns celebrate light – and so they should. But worship also needs to acknowledge that there are times God meets us in the darkness and stays with us there.' The concept of God as existing in darkness is itself scriptural: see Psalm 18:11 and Psalm 97:2 and a significant earlier passage in 1 Kings 8:12, repeated in 2 Chronicles 6:1. The text is structured as a series of appeals for renewal to such a 'God in the darkness,' characterised as 'beyond our knowing,' and capable of drawing us 'past the limits of believing.' In verse 1 this God is imaged in traditional biblical terms as patient creator, seed, rock and flowing water. In verse 2 God is characterised as present in our grieving, friend of our tears and loyal companion. In the final verse, God, as Spirit of truth (line 3), is praised as the object of 'holy dreaming,' hope-giver, pledge of redemption, 'our memory and meaning.' Such calls for renewal are at least as old as 1 Samuel 11:14 and Lamentations 5:21 and as recent in scripture as Revelation 21:5, but are seldom given such extended and eloquent divine attributions.

TRARALGON This name of a small town in the Gippsland region of Victoria, Australia, is possibly derived from the language of the Gunai aboriginal people who have inhabited the La Trobe Valley area for more than 2,000 years, and means 'river of small fish.' The tune takes its name from the town because it was there that the composer, **Colin Gibson**, first came across Elizabeth Smith's work as a hymn writer.

Written in 1991, and first published in the composer's American collection *Songs for a Rainbow People* (1998), the music commences in the 'dark' key of C minor but soon modulates to A flat major and bridges to the 'bright' key of E flat major to reflect the search for renewal which closes each verse of the hymn.

God is the One whom we seek together *A47*
Metre: 6.6.6.6 and refrain

This text was written by **Colin Gibson** in 1978 as a contribution to a competition promoted by the Dunedin Council of Churches seeking texts suitable for multi-faith worship. It was first published under the title 'Godpoint' in the author's English collection, *Singing Love*

(1998), before reaching *Alleluia Aotearoa* (1993).

The theme is the centrality of the 'Godpoint,' 'the One' as the focus of spiritual search in all religions. The unity of God is a central tenet of the Jewish, Christian and Islamic faiths; it is also found in the Bahai faith and elements of Buddhism. God is further described as ultimate Life, Truth, Mystery, Love, Joy and Eternity: terms to which mainstream religions would generally subscribe. Members of other faith communities are acknowledged as fellow seekers, walking a common road, a common Way. John 14:6, 'I am the way, the truth, the life,' has contributed to the hymn text, but such images and concepts are found in many other sacred scriptures (see, for instance, the Koran 59:24, and 11:55-6).

GODPOINT This tune name is derived from the textual image of God as 'point' or 'mark' (though there is also a play on 'pointing towards God'). The musical setting, by the author, uses unison phrases as a metaphor for spiritual unity – its expansion into 4-part textures suggests the many ways to God taken by different faith communities – and a melodic structure that insistently arches upwards as if searching for the divine. The key is a minor one (A minor), fitting the idea of the mystery of God, but the final bars celebrate the ideas of love, joy and wholeness by breaking into four-part harmony.

God is working his purpose out
W652
Metre: irregular

This hymn by **Arthur Campbell Ainger** was written in 1894 at a time when Ainger was an assistant master at Eton College, and was intended for public school singing. It carried a dedication to Edward White Benson, the then Archbishop of Canterbury. It was first published in the Church Missionary Society's *Hymn Book* (1899) and reached the 1904 edition of *Hymns Ancient and Modern* and the 1933 *Methodist Hymn Book* as well as other main denominational hymnbooks.

It is an ironic fact that a major European war broke out only 20 years after the writing of the text, but the words are not simply an expression of misguided Victorian optimism. The refrain is based on Habakkuk 2:14, 'For the earth shall be filled with the knowledge of the glory of the Lord, as the waters cover the sea,' but where Habakkuk speaks of waiting passively for the fulfillment of the promise ('the vision is yet for an appointed time…thought it tarry, wait for it, because it will surely come, it will not tarry'), Ainger calls for immediate human action – though it is action of a kind that involves the blessing of God (verse 4, 'All we can do is nothing worth / Unless God blesses the deed'). Further, the context of the verse from Habakkuk is a warning of the terrible price to be paid for the implementation of the vision through the destruction of evil individuals and nations.

The editors of the New Zealand supplement to *With One Voice* omitted the second verse of Ainger's text. It is given here for the sake of completeness:

From utmost East to utmost West,
where'er man's foot hath trod,
By the mouth of many messengers
goes forth the voice of God:
'Give ear to Me, ye continents;
ye isles give ear to Me,
That the earth may be filled with the glory
of God, as the waters cover the sea.'

The second line references Psalm 19:4, quoted in Romans 10:18.

PURPOSE The original tune used for this hymn, BENSON, was composed by Millicent Kingham, organist of St Andrew's church, Hertford, whose rector was Grainger's brother-in-law. PURPOSE was composed for the same text by Dr Martin Shaw (**Martin Edward Fallas Shaw**) and was first published in his *Additional Tunes in Use at St Mary's, Primrose Hill* (1915), St Mary's being the London church where from 1908 to 1920 Shaw worked with Percy Dearmer to improve the quality of the liturgy and lift the standard of church music and hymn singing.

God of ages, times and seasons H39
Metre: 8.7.8.7 D

This hymn text was written in 1998 by **Jocelyn Marshall** as a contribution to the worship of the congregation of the Cathedral Church of St Peter, Hamilton. It was first published in her collection *Hymns for All Seasons* (2007) before reaching *Hope is our Song* (2009).

The theme of the hymn is the enduring presence and action of God throughout time (verse 4, 'God, the Alpha and Omega'): the dimensions of past, present and future provide the setting for each verse. Scriptural passages are referenced – John 1:4-5 ('the light that shines through all'), John 3:16 ('yours the sacrificial giving'), John 1:14 ('Word made flesh in Christ'), Revelation 22:13, 21 ('the Alpha and Omega...the ultimate AMEN'), Song of Solomon 8:6 ('the love that conquers death') – however, the power of the text resides in its steadily accumulating references to God's power and action in time ('You, the past that makes our present'), leading to the final triumphant line, 'God, our ultimate AMEN,' meaning that God both gives to and receives from humanity a final affirmation or endorsement of being, 'so be it.'

MILLENNIUM 1 This hymn tune setting for four-part singing was written in 1998 by Jocelyn Marshall's son, composer **Christopher Marshall**, and was first published in his mother's collection *Hymns for All Seasons* (2007). It was named after the approaching Millennium 2000 celebrations. There is every evidence of a professional composer at work, particularly in the variety of melodic step and scalic passages, crafted repetitions of the first two-bar phrase pattern and the shifting harmonic soundscape. A strong, march-like melody set in A minor is carried into E minor in the middle section of the tune, returning to A minor with a closure in the major key, but not before a surprising late movement into F major. In *Hymns for All Seasons* the nominated tune is AUSTRIA, by **Franz Joseph Haydn**; MILLENNIUM 1 is provided as an alternative tune.

God of all beauty A48
Metre: 5.7.5.6 4.7.4.6

Written in 1992 by **Marnie Barrell,** this hymn was first published in *Alleluia Aotearoa* (1993).

Each verse follows a similar pattern: an aspect of the nature of God is described and praised, then responded to by the singers ('here where you dwell / we know you and rejoice'). Verse 1 follows contemporary theology in declaring the beauty of the created universe, and the earth in particular: 'holy is your world, / you made it for your pleasure' (see Genesis 1:31). Verse 2 discovers God in the experience of grief. The language draws on Old Testament images of the throne of God as in Psalm 97:2, as well as echoing **Isaac Watts'** hymn, 'O God our help in ages past...beneath the shadow of thy throne.' Silence and darkness are traditional and biblical manifestations of sorrow (see Isaiah 47:5). Verse 3 praises God as author of new life – the term 'creators' has a wide range of meanings here. The opening lines echo a modern version of the Lord's Prayer from *A New Zealand Prayer Book* (1989, 181). Lines 5-9 draw on Genesis 1:26 ('Let us make man in our image') and Revelation 21:5 ('Behold, I make all things new'). Verse 4 invokes the life-giving presence of God ('God of compassion' addresses a God who treats humanity with compassion); as the phrase 'living waters' suggests, its imagery draws on John 7:38. Ezekiel 33:11 ('Let the wicked turn from their way and live') is the scriptural basis for the final, much more positive declaration, 'All humankind shall turn to you and live.'

BRITTANY The tune is named after the north-western province of France from which came this Breton folk tune. Marnie Barrell explains that she found the melody hand-written with the title 'Breton Tune' in a choir director friend's material and that she wrote the text to fit it and created the harmony to go with it. It was arranged by **Douglas Mews** in 1992 as a piano setting for the hymn. The melody has the lively 3/4 rhythm of a danced carol, and typically oscillates between minor and major modes (here A minor and C major) before it closes in A minor – not the best match with the strong positive final lines of each verse of the text.

God of all time A49
Metre: 11.10.11.10

Shirley Murray wrote this hymn for her St Andrew's on the Terrace, Wellington, congregation in 1988, intending it as a hymn of approach to communion, and with **Richard Terry's** 1933 hymn tune HIGHWOOD in mind. It was first published in Murray's American collection *In Every Corner Sing* (1992), followed by *Alleluia Aotearoa* (1993).

The opening verses of this hymn address the theme obliquely. In verse 1 praise is offered to the 'God of all time,' drawing on one of this poet's favourite images of human life as a spark, brought into being and protected by the greater 'blaze' of divinity (cf. Alexander Pope's 'The Dying Christian to his soul,' 'Vital spark of heavenly flame'). Verse 2 acknowledges the heritage of faith 'in this place' and the congregation's responsibility to pass on 'your hope, your truth.' Verse 3 focuses on the giving of the peace as a ritual act before communion; there are echoes of the Emmaus meeting with Christ (Luke 24:28-31). Verse 4 is an astonishing piece of imaginative writing in which poverty is defined as an insufficiency of care for others, starvation as a failure to share love with others, and the congregation is invited to be broken open (as the physical body of Christ was 'broken' on the cross) to 'receive your healing.'

INFINITE The tune name is drawn from the first line of Shirley Murray's text; the music was composed by **Douglas Mews** in 1990 for *Alleluia Aotearoa* (1993). It is one his finest hymn settings, with a measured forward progression and a melodic line that is expertly constructed from three variations on the initial 2-bar melodic phrase. Harmonic shifts give the four-part choral texture an unusual richness: the key, beginning in D major, shifts through F sharp minor and E major before returning to the home key signature. This setting was also used *In Every Corner Sing* (1992), in each case in an adapted form prepared by **Jack Schrader**, music editor for Hope Publishing.

God of diversity H40
Metre: 11.11.12.11

This important hymn of praise for the diversity and difference that characterises the whole of creation was written in 1994 by **Margaret Bond** and first published in *Hope is our Song* (2009). She says of it, 'accepting Diversity is what it is all about.'

Like many such phrases (cf. 'God of nations,' 'God of concrete, God of steel,' 'God of ages,' 'God of growth and recreation'), the opening address to 'God of diversity' has many senses, including 'God who presides over a world marked by diversity,' 'God present in the sacred diversity of things' and 'divine patron of diversity.' Verse 1 focuses on the 'extravagant' diversity present in nature, tacitly endorsing modern scientific understanding of the evolutionary ramification of life on earth. In the final line of this verse there is an echo of the answer to the catechism question, 'What is the chief end of mankind? To glorify God and enjoy him forever.' Verse 2 honours the cultural and religious diversity of humanity, tacitly endorsing multi-cultural and multi-faith acceptance and mutual respect. Verse 3 addresses human interdependence, drawing a parallel between early recognition of the complex organism of the human body (lines 1-2 are sourced in 1 Corinthians 12:14-26) and modern awareness of the increasing interdependence of the human world population ('this globe-become-village'), using a phrase probably coined by Marshall McLuhan in *Understanding Media* (1964), 'Since the inception of the telegraph and radio, the globe has contracted, spatially, into a single large village.' Verse 4 puts a final appeal for tolerance and respect for 'our different perspectives on things that are true' (see Philippians 4:8), as we come to know more deeply 'the God in Christ Jesus' (see 2 Corinthians 5:19).

MARGARET The tune was named by the composer **Colin Gibson** for the hymn writer.

Written for this text in 2006, the music, taking the form of a celebratory dance in 3/4 time, begins in D minor – suggesting an Israeli modality – but finds its way to F major and B flat major before closing decisively on the word 'joy' and subsequent key words with a D major chord.

God of freedom, God of justice
A50, HP7
Metre: 8.7.8.7.8.7

The author of this hymn, **Shirley Murray**, describes it as 'One of my first "gap-fillers." I wrote it for Amnesty International's campaign against torture when I could find nothing relevant to sing at a service for Prisoners of Conscience.' The hymn, written in 1981, first appeared in her privately printed collection *In Every Corner Sing* (Wellington, 1987). It then appeared in the Australian hymnbook *Sing Alleluia* (1987), the American publication *In Every Corner Sing* (1992) and *Alleluia Aotearoa* (1993). It has since been frequently reprinted in American and English hymnals.

The theme of the hymn is the reflection of Christ's sufferings in the modern world of political imprisonment and the use of torture on prisoners of conscience. In particular the verses allude to Christ's abuse at the hands of Herod's or Pilate's soldiers – the Gospel accounts differ – ('you who knew the dark of prison'), and his actual crucifixion ('you whose hands were nailed to wood'). Verse 2, line 4, blends the accounts of Christ's tears over Jerusalem (Luke 19:41-44) and the flow of blood from his dead body (John 19:34).

Verse 1 takes from *The Song of Solomon* 8:6 the idea that 'love is strong as death.' Verse 5, 'Make in us a captive conscience,' is not just an ingenious self-identification with prisoners of conscience. The phrase is taken from Martin Luther's famous expression of defiance before the Diet of Worms (1521), 'Unless I am convinced by the testimony of the Holy Scriptures or by evident reason – for I can believe neither pope nor councils alone, as it is clear that they have erred repeatedly and contradicted themselves – I consider myself convicted by the testimony of Holy Scripture, which is my basis; *my conscience is captive to the Word of God*.' In this way the writer associates the stand of modern protesters against state oppression with Luther's against the religious establishment of his own day.

PICARDY The suggested tune for this hymn tune at its first printing is named after the French province where it was first recorded; memorably, for New Zealanders, the scene of some of the most savage fighting during World War 1. Although its minor key and chant-like melody give it a fitting gravity, it is a French carol melody, probably written in the 17th century, and was printed in *Chansons populaires des provinces de France* (Paris, 1860), where it is titled 'La Ballade de Jésus Christ.' The harmony is probably by **Ralph Vaughan Williams** and is taken from his *English Hymnal* (1906).

[TREDEGAR] Without naming the tune, the editors of *Alleluia Aotearoa* printed a setting by **Guthrie Foote,** named for a market town in Monmouthshire, Wales, and first published in *The English Hymnal Service Book* (1962), where it was intended as a unison setting for a hymn by George Hugh Bourne, 'Lord, enthroned in heavenly splendour.' Shirley Murray comments that although she herself first chose PICARDY as the setting for her hymn the later tune 'provides a stronger support for the text.' Commencing in E minor, it soon modulates to G major where it optimistically remains. It has the character of an affirmative and vigorous march., less responsive than PICARDY to the darkness of human behaviour unflinchingly recorded in the text.

God of growth and recreation H41
Metre: 8.7.8.7 D

This hymn was written by Anglican vicar **Timothy Hurd** in 2004. The original score is titled 'Celebrating Sport and Recreation,' and the musical indication given is 'Jaunty.' It was first published in *Hope is our Song* (2009). The writer notes that it was 'composed for an Olympics, when I was particularly aware that with a former International

Olympics Committee member as part of our congregation we were connected, but not very good at celebrating as a Church anything related to sporting endeavour.'

The theme of the hymn is a celebration of God-given athletic prowess and grace displayed in the exercise of sport and recreational activities. There are biblical allusions bedded into the text: for verse 1 the main reference is to Paul's famous account of his own Christian life as an athletic contest, 'I press on toward the goal for the prize of the calling of God in Jesus Christ' (Philippians 3:14). But Genesis 1:26 and Isaiah 43:4 are also drawn on. Verse 2 uses the vocabulary of sport – 'fit,' 'competing,' 'an active world' – to celebrate the energy, beauty and passion of sportsmen and women, but it also calls for compassion and imagination on the part of athletes and closes with a verbal play on physical activity and social peace and harmony.

GAELIC AIR The tune name reflects the source of the melody, a folk melody from the Island of Lewis, off the coast of Scotland. The same tune has been used for Shirley Murray's 'Come and find the quiet centre' (F10 (i)). See the entry on this hymn for further information.

God of nations, at thy feet (God defend New Zealand) A51, W677
Metre: 7.7.7.6 D

Now one of the two national anthems of Aotearoa New Zealand – the other is 'God save the Queen' – this poem, titled 'God Defend New Zealand,' was written by **Thomas Bracken** in the early 1870s. Bracken offered a prize of ten guineas for the best musical setting for his words, and a competition was held in 1876 by his co-owned Dunedin newspaper *The Saturday Advertiser*. The winner of the competition – entries were sent to Melbourne, Australia, and judged by three eminent musicians there – was **John Joseph Woods**, an Otago schoolteacher, and as a song the poem was first sung at the Queen's Theatre, Dunedin, on Christmas Day 1876. A number of arrangements appeared in the following years, and in 1978 Maxwell Fernie (1910-99), a Wellington composer, organist, teacher and choral director, prepared an alternative official four-part choral arrangement for massed singing.

In the following years of the 19th and early 20th centuries 'God Defend New Zealand' became increasingly popular; in 1940 the New Zealand government bought the copyright and made it the country's national hymn in time for that year's centennial celebrations. From 1950 it was used at the British Empire Games as the national song, and from 1972 it was played at the Olympic Games for New Zealand teams and their successes. In 1977 it was adopted as the country's second national anthem, with words in English accompanied by an official version in Māori made by Thomas H. Smith, a Judge in the Native Land Court. This was not a literal translation, and in 1979 a back-translation into English was made by former Māori Commissioner Professor Timoti Karetu.

The original text consists of five verses* and until the 1990s only the first verse in English was commonly sung. In *With One Voice* (1977) four verses were printed, together with the official Māori translation, with Wood's music arranged for the hymnbook by **Guy Jansen**. After 1999 the practice developed of singing both the Māori and English first verses one after the other; this was anticipated in the printing in *Alleluia Aotearoa* (1993).

Bracken's text is a prayer for divine protection and guidance; unusually among national anthems, it extols the virtues of love (in its sense of compassionate social and community relationships), peace, tolerance, the moral exercise of power ('From dissension, envy, hate / and corruption guard our state'), freedom and faith in God, who is asked to make our country 'good' as well as 'great' (verse 2). Similarly, Bracken sees New Zealand as 'in the nations' van [the foremost position of an army] / preaching love and truth to man, / working out thy glorious plan.'

Psalm 47:9 is the likely source of the first line of the anthem, and the repeated requests for blessings (especially the blessings of peace and plenty), protection and guidance resonate with the Book of Psalms and other scriptural passages. Verse 1, line 5, has exercised some discussion: 'by 'Pacific's triple star' Bracken probably meant the three largest islands of New Zealand, North, South and Stewart Island, but other suggestions have ranged from the three stars on the heraldic shield of the Anglican Church of New Zealand (less likely since Bracken, an Irishman by birth, was a Roman Catholic in religious sympathies) to the Māori political and religious leader Te Kooti's flag with its three stars (probably an emblem of the Trinity). The image of God as defender against 'the shafts [arrows] of strife and war' derives from Psalm 76:3, 'There he broke the flashing arrows, the shield, the sword, and the weapons of war.' While there is some conventional imagery, such as 'crown her with immortal fame,' the real poet in Bracken is seen in his fortress image of New Zealand (verse 4): 'May our mountains ever be / freedom's ramparts on the sea,' as anyone who has witnessed New Zealand's precipitous coastlines backed by snow-clad alpine ranges and peaks will agree.

GOD DEFEND NEW ZEALAND The tune takes its name from the final line of each stanza. The music was written in 1876 by **John Joseph Woods**, who reportedly composed the melody in a single sitting in the evening after finding out about the competition (for more details see the Companion entry under Woods' name). Although the outline of the tune is now known by heart by most New Zealanders, its alpine features of downward rushing quavers, steady upward climbs to high D and E peak-notes and occasional dizzying bungy-jumping leaps (bar 3) make it less than easily sung. But such soaring sky-climbing suits most of the intensely emotional occasions on which it is sung, and the harmonic structure rooted in its tonic key provides such a rock-solid foundation that it could be described as an iconic musical image of New Zealand's finest landscapes.

*The omitted verse of Bracken's original poem is supplied here, together with its official Māori translation:

Peace, not war, shall be our boast,
But, should foes assail our coast,
Make us then a mighty host,
God defend our free land.
Lord of battles in Thy might,
Put our enemies to flight,
Let our cause be just and right,
God defend New Zealand.

Tōna mana kia tū!
Tōna kaha kia ū;
Tōna rongo hei pakū
Ki te ao katoa.
Aua rawa ngā whawhai
Ngā tutū e tata mai;
Kia tupu nui ai
Aotearoa.

God of our every day A52
Metre: 6.6.7.10.7 D

'The realities of unemployment and depression affecting our family and friends provoked this text,' says its author, **Shirley Murray**, who wrote the hymn in 1989. It appeared in her first American collection, *In Every Corner Sing* (1992), closely followed by *Alleluia Aotearoa* (1993).

In what was to become a typical hymnic strategy for this writer, God is first addressed and defined as 'God of our every day' (with a play on 'each day / ordinary'),' 'friend,' 'light,' 'meaning,' home,' 'power and peace,' then invoked to take action: to 'be,' 'speak,' 'lift,' 'shine,' 'break through' and 'live.' Such an imperative tone is itself affirming, and the hymn, which has begun with a focus on the small world of the every day ends with a suddenly expansive vision of divine 'power and peace' flowing through all creation.

Occasional biblical allusions underpin the text: verse 1, line 2, suggests the walk to Emmaus (Luke 24:13-32); God as light (verses 1 and 3) is a biblical commonplace; verse 2, line 4, hints at the parable of the buried talent (Matthew 25:14-39), while line 6 recalls

Genesis 1:26, 'Let us make man in our image.' In the final verse, the phrase 'little deaths' is stripped of its original sexual sense (French *'petite mort'*) to mean crisis points in human development – in this context the experience of unemployment and consequent depression.

JANSEN The tune is named after **Guy Jansen** by its composer **Colin Gibson**, who wrote this setting for Shirley Murray's hymn in 1989. At the time, all three of these people were working as co-editors of the New Zealand Hymnbook Committee preparing the hymnbook *Alleluia Aotearoa*, which was to have appeared in 1990, but in the event was published in 1993. The harmonic progression of the music shifts upwards from G major with each repetition of the initial melodic phrase (which itself rises a tone) until it reaches a still more confident resolution in the home key. This is a case of music attempting to imitate the affirmative action of the text it carries.

God of our island home *H43*
Metre: 6.6.7.10.7 D

This prize-winning song was written in 1993 by **Chris Skinner** and published first in his song album *Chants for Silence* (1994) then in his 2008 collection, *Truly Blessed under Southern Skies*. The original distribution of verses is more logical than in *Hope is our Song*, where two verses (verse 2 and 3) are conflated to form the second verse, and the first verse is repeated to form a new verse 3.

The comparison between the sea (actually an ocean) and God's love is hinted at in Psalm 136:13, but it is a New Zealand poet who perceives it as completely surrounding 'our island home'. The same may be said of the poet's praise of the 'compelling' beauty of the high mountain chains which form the backbone of both major islands (compare Isaiah 52:7, 'How beautiful upon the mountains are the feet of him who bringeth good tidings'). The surfaces of New Zealand's deep-water lakes are imagined as reflecting the face of God, presumably at moments of complete calm and stillness. Such striking natural images go some way to explaining why this song won the 1993 Aotearoa Spirituality songwriting competition.

[ISLAND HOME] The music is also by **Chris Skinner**, in the form of a melody with guitar chording. Coming as it does from a book of chants, and set in D minor (it insistently returns to a D minor chord), it is directed to be sung 'moderately slowly,' creating the effect of intense meditation, with a narrow tonal range that suggests Russian or Greek Orthodox chanting. It has been filled out for *Hope is our Song* in an arrangement for piano and flute by New Zealand musician **Roy Tankersley**.

God of our workplace *H44*
Metre: 10.9.10.9.6.7.7.5.10.7

In 1999 the Presbyterian Church of St John's in the City, Wellington, commissioned **Colin Gibson** to write a cantata to celebrate the imminent new Millennium and the continuing presence of the Spirit of God in New Zealand. Titled *The Spirit Within*, the work was premièred at St John's on Pentecost Sunday, 11 June 2000, and has since received performances in several other New Zealand cities. The libretto included a number of poems by eminent New Zealand poets both living and dead, and this text was commissioned from **Shirley Murray** by the composer, her longtime friend and collaborator. Taken from the score as an independent hymn, it was first published in Murray's third American collection *Faith Makes the Song* (2003) and later in *Hope is our Song* (2009). At least two recordings have been made on CD.

The assigned theme was 'The Spirit in the City,' and the text supplies a vivid account of busy modern life in the capital city of New Zealand ('business and banking, government office'). The extremes of commercial wealth ('marketplace mindsets,' 'high where the power-brokers play') and street-level poverty ('street kids,' 'food banks') are exhibited, but civic recognition of religious values and the presence of ordinary human values ('kindness / seen in the struggle') is also acknowledged*. The first line introduces the thought of God whose presence is to be found in our workplace and city, and this is pursued in the description of the Spirit of God blowing where it will through the complexities of urban existence. The reputation of Wellington as a windy city jostles with the biblical manifestation of the Holy Spirit as 'the rush of a mighty wind' (Acts 2:2) in such a phrase as 'there goes the Spirit, / here blows the Spirit,' and the writer puns on the secular as well as the religious sense of 'spirited people' (Holy Spirit-filled people / lively, energetic people). The Pentecost event – introduced in verse 4 with an eye on the occasion of the première of the cantata – allows the writer to imagine a reconciliation of power with compassion, and the emergence of a 'new language' (cf. Acts 2:5-11), culminating in the vision of the 'City of God come indeed,' referring to both John's vision of 'the holy city, the new Jerusalem, coming down out of heaven' (Revelation 21:1-2) and St Augustine's magisterial book *The City of God* (*De Civitate Dei*) written about 420.

VIVACE (musical term=in lively fashion). This tune, by **Colin Gibson**, aims to capture two different motions: the bustling activity of city life and the silent movement of the Holy Spirit. Begun in F major (to reflect the optimism of the text), it modulates through a number of keys to close in B flat major, a musical restlessness which again imitates the ever-changing scene of city life. The use of jazzy syncopations in the melodic line is a further reflection of urban secularity.

> *It is an interesting fact that during the 2020 Covid outbreak in New Zealand, Jacinda Ardern, the Prime Minister of the country, exhorted New Zealanders to be 'kind to each other.'

God of solemnity, God of festivity (The Many-Faceted God) H47
Metre: 12.10.12.10

This hymn text was written for her Waikato Cathedral Church of St Peter congregation by **Jocelyn Marshall**, and first published in her collection *A Singing Faith* (1996), followed by the revised and enlarged edition of that work, *Hymns for All Seasons* (2007).

The theme of the hymn is indicated by its title, 'The Many-Faceted God,' though successive verses focus on opposed facets of God, Jesus, the Holy Spirit and the Church. Anglican in its stress on balance, moderation and a life lived out by the principles of the gospel, it seldom reaches for metaphor or simile, preferring to list moral virtues or human activities. Unusually, there is a possible play on 'solemnity' and 'festivity' (line 1), both terms commonly used to refer to important Church occasions.

WAS LEBET This melody, found in *Hymns Ancient & Modern* (1939 edition), is recommended as the setting for her words by the author. It was first written down in a tune-book belonging to Johann Heinrich Reinhardt at Üttingen, Germany, in 1754. There it is laid out in two musical versions, suggesting that it was a traditional European melody much older than the 18th century.

God of the ages, by whose hand W662
Metre: 8.8.8.8

This hymn, written by **Elisabeth Havens Burrowes** at the age of 73, was composed in 1958 and first printed in the Hymn Society of America's journal, *The Hymn*. It then appeared in both the 1966 United States *Methodist Hymnal* and the 1972 United States Presbyterian *Worshipbook, Services and Hymns* before being collected in the Society's anthology of *Hymns published for Special Occasions and On Special Subjects, 1942-1979* (1979). The first line, 'God of the ages' is printed incorrectly in the words-only edition of *With One Voice*.

The text may owe something to Daniel C. Roberts' popular 1876 patriotic hymn 'God of the ages, by whose almighty hand,' but it addresses not the beauty of the created world and the experience of 'divine love [which] hath led us in the past,' which is Roberts' subject, but still-current anxieties about the future and the mysteries of a universe of 'dark uncharted space, / With worlds on worlds beyond our sight.' It is a remarkable hymn of confident faith, which anticipates not a final Day of Judgement but a new primal act of creation, 'Let there be light' (verse 4).

Verse 1 acknowledges **Philip Doddridge**'s 1736 hymn, 'O God of Bethel, by whose hand your people still are led,' before establishing its own theme. Verse 2 recalls Romans 8:35-9; verse 3 begins with a quotation from Montague Butler's 1812 hymn, 'Lift up your hearts, we lift them, Lord, to thee.' The fourth verse concludes with a quotation from Genesis 1:3.

HEREFORD Named after Hereford Cathedral, where the composer, **Samuel Sebastian Wesley** was organist from 1832-5, this hymn tune was first published in Wesley's *The European Psalmist* (1872). It is one of his finest, originally the setting for a version of Psalm 103, beginning 'The Lord abounds with tender love.'

God of the Bible (Fresh as the Morning) F25

Metre: 10.9.10.9 and refrain.

The text of this hymn was written in 1995 by **Shirley Murray**, at the request of Dr I-to Loh, to address the theme of the 10th General Assembly of the Christian Conference of Asia, held in Colombo, Sri Lanka, 'Hope in God in a Changing Asia.' Murray explains that each stanza is woven round the six chosen Bible studies for Assembly members, one verse for each day. The full text of these studies was later published as *Hope in God in a Changing Asia: Six Bible Studies: Biblical and Theological Reflection on the Theme of the 10th General Assembly, Christian Conference of Asia, Colombo, Sri Lanka, 10-14 June, 1995* (Hong Kong: Christian Conference of Asia, 1995). The refrain is drawn from Lamentations 3:22-23 ('The steadfast love of the Lord never ceases, his mercies never come to an end; they are new every morning, great is your faithfulness').

The verses reflect the Assembly's concern with the rights of women (verse 3, 'Those without status…midwives of justice'), the Asian cultural background (verse 4, 'small paper lanterns lighting the way'*), and the contemporary tense security situation in the country (verse 5, 'through all our turmoil, terror and loss'). Verse 2 employs the ancient Christian symbol of the pelican, which was reputed to feed its young by wounding its own breast. It became a symbol of Christ's Passion, but is here associated with the 'mothering Spirit' (see also Luke 13:34). Verse 4 refers to divine intervention to change the world order as the finger of God: Exodus 8:19 relates that when God struck the Egyptians with a plague of gnats to force them to release the Hebrews, the wizards of Pharaoh, unable to match the feat, described it as the work of God's finger.

HYDE PARK The tune name refers to the famous London park, near which the composer's family was living at the time of writing this setting. The music by **Colin Gibson,** written in 1995, contrasts the glad affirmation of the refrain, set in a high register in D major, with the darker subject matter of the verses set in a low register and with harmonic shifts from a muted opening in D major down through a succession of minor keys before returning to the tonic key. There is another setting, COLOMBO, including both Sri Lankan and Indian musical elements, written in 1995 by **I-to Loh**, and Canadian composer **Ron Klusmeier** has written a further setting (Klusmeier 22).

> *Shirley Murray has described this as her favourite image, drawn from a sight familiar in Asia by night: 'Small paper lanterns which, though seemingly ineffectual, flicker through the darkness of the world and give us hope to keep going.'

God of the galaxies (Honour the Earth) A54, HP8

Metre: 10.10.10.12

Shirley Murray, who wrote this hymn in 1988, describes it as 'one of my first efforts to grapple with the theme of environmental disaster and our care of the environment.' It first appeared in the Christian Churches of Asia hymnal *Sound the Bamboo* (1990), before reaching Murray's first American collection, *In Every Corner Sing* (1992), closely followed by *Alleluia*

Aotearoa (1993). The author says, 'its reception [in the 1990 edition of *Sound the Bamboo*] encouraged me to continue writing "green" hymns, especially in view of New Zealand's sensitivity to environmental matters. It has been said that our true spirituality is rooted in our land and its landscape.'

The refrain employs the biblical Garden of Eden (Genesis 1:27-31 and more importantly Genesis 2:8-15) as a familiar metaphor for the original unspoiled condition of the whole planet. Verse 3, 'bleeds in its clay,' creates a vivid image of erosion brought about by agricultural abuse of the land. Verse 5, 'life is a holy thing,' may be an echo of Jack Kerouac's 'Life is a holy thing and every moment is precious' (*On the Road*, 1957).

CHEAM The tune is named after the composer's birthplace, the town of Cheam in Surrey, England. The music was written in 1988 by **Douglas Mews,** then a member of the Editorial Committee for *Alleluia Aotearoa*. The bold and compelling shape of the melody carrying the verse – a downward arpeggio pressure followed by a rising scalic passage – is followed by a refrain which sustains the notes for the key words, 'honour' and 'garden.' The harmony presents an enriching sequence of key shifts through G, F and A flat major before travelling back to the home key, E flat. In *Sound the Bamboo* the tune is given the name HONOUR THE EARTH.

God of the northerlies *H45*
Metre: 10.10.4.4.10

Written in 1996 by **Bill Bennett,** this hymn was first published in *Hope is our Song* (2009), then in the author's *Gradual Praise* (2010), where it is included as 'a reflection on the gospel reading for Low Sunday, John 20:19-31; a comment on the wind of change that blew through doubting Thomas's life.'

This hymn is a comprehensive reflection on the actualities of New Zealand wind conditions* as well as the spiritual significance of wind. Where the author lives, in Hawkes Bay on the eastern coast of the North Island, 'northerly winds have a sub-tropical feel; easterlies inevitably bring rain; westerlies are fine dry-weather winds, and southerlies bring the chill of sub-Antarctic latitudes, often accompanied by snow on the high mountains and hills.' Given that wind is a powerful symbol of the Holy Spirit, Bennett says that he has tried to evoke a spiritual dimension for each of the winds experienced – 'the northerly warmth that encourages growth, the easterly that replenishes and renews, the westerly that shakes us out of our torpor and inaction, and the southerly that challenges our prejudice.'

MATANGI (Māori=the blowing wind) The composer, again Bill Bennett, remarks that he was tempted to use another Māori word, *porangahau,* meaning 'crazy, swirling, unpredictable wind,' the name of a small settlement in Hawkes Bay where his forbears first lived. The tune has the lilt and something of the melodic shape of the old Scottish folksong 'Westering home and a song in the air,' and its rising and falling suggests the swirling of wind, imitated by similar patterns in the accompaniment.

*Bill Bennett supplies this note on the winds sweeping New Zealand: 'Being a collection of three main islands in the southern Pacific Ocean and characterised by mountain chains running the length of both main islands, Aotearoa New Zealand is at the mercy of the elements, especially the winds. Depending on the time of the year and the progression of anti-cyclones and depressions within the great westerly wind belt that encircles the globe in the southern latitudes, the wind patterns change each week. Canterbury is renowned for the strong, hot, tiring winds known locally as 'nor-westers.' Each wind brings a different weather pattern, and each farmer looks skyward each day or checks computer information to determine what the weather might bring. The constancy of wind has been utilized nationally to provide electricity through the erection of wind farms in many parts of the land.'

God of the past F26
Metre: 8.8.4.4.8

This is a hymn written in 1995 by **Judy Mills**, wife of Bishop Murray Mills, as a pseudonymous submission to a hymn competition held as part of preparations by the Waiapu Diocese to celebrate the Millennium. In the event, it was awarded first equal place with a hymn sent in by **Bill Bennett**, and published in *Faith Forever Singing* (2000). (See further Bill Bennett's 'We praise our country's saints of old,' H143).

The hymn devotes one verse each to the past, present and future, acknowledging God's constant presence. Verse 1, lines 5-6, 'beckoned us / the Jesus way' is a compression of 'encouraged us' – rather than called us as Jesus would – 'to follow the Way of Jesus (the reference is to John 14:6, 'I am the way, the truth and the life'). Verse 2, 'songs for sighing' might mean 'songs to cheer us when we are sad' or 'songs to express our sad feelings.' In verse 3, 'Spirit who moves on waters' refers to the creation story in Genesis 1:2. For 'lift up our hearts' (line 4) see Lamentations 3:41 and Henry M. Butler's 1881 hymn 'Lift up your hearts, we lift them, Lord, to thee.' For the general thought of the hymn, cf. **Elizabeth Havens Burroughs**' 'God of the ages' (W662).

WHANAU O WAIAPU (Māori=the family/people of Waiapu) The reference is to the Anglican diocese of Waiapu in the central North Island. The author of the hymn is the composer (a fine pianist herself). In two complementary 4-bar phrases, the melody twice climbs to D, suggesting progress on 'the Jesus way,' then descends to a cadence. The harmonic shifts in bars 5-6, supported by a bass that steps upwards, perhaps symbolise the 'changes, choices, / journeys made.'

God of unexplored tomorrows F27
Metre: 8.7.8.7

Written in 1998 by **Beverley Jones** for a hymn-writing competition held as part of the 150th celebrations of the arrival of the first Scottish settlers in the South Island, this hymn combines the biblical journey to the promised land described in Exodus with an appreciation of the rocky desert-like landscapes, deep gorges and powerful rivers of the Central Otago area in the South Island of New Zealand. 'The opening line,' says the writer, 'evoked the great unknown into which those pioneers travelled.' It was first published in *Faith Forever Singing* (2000).

The hymn had a second life in England. In 2003, now Mayoress of Clitheroe in Lancashire, Beverley Jones was invited to offer a song for a civic service held on the Mayor's Sunday. 'The Clitheroe town motto, *stabit saxum, fluet amnis* [Latin=the rock will stand, the river will flow] came to mind as a relevant theme, with several layers of meaning…It had a personal significance for me as only six months previously I had left my native New Zealand to settle in the United Kingdom, having re-married. At a time when my immediate family were all on the opposite side of the world from me, the future truly did seem "unexplored."'

Two older 'desert' hymns haunt this text: **Elizabeth Cecilia Clephane's** 'Beneath the cross of Jesus' (1872) and **William Williams'** 'Guide me, O thou great Jehovah' (1744/5). But in a quite original way the hymn consistently works on two basic images, 'rock' (refuge, foundation, landmark, shelter) and 'river' (flowing way, cleansing, quenching [thirst], irrigating, disturbing, moving current), as principal religious symbols. The writer suggests that the imagery is a pictorial representation of our relationship with God, and the need for us to focus on God both as firm foundation and as transforming power. The rock represents history and settled tradition; the flowing river avoids stagnation by moving forward.

Verse 2, line 2, alludes to Matthew 7:24-27; line 3, 'landmark through the haze of doubting,' hints at the Exodus pillar of fire (Exodus 13:21). Verse 3 alludes to Jesus' encounter with the Samaritan woman at the well (John 4:7-15). However, the references to irrigation, shallows and current come from the Central Otago world of the powerful Clutha river. The verse 4 play on 'land of promise' and 'promised land' ultimately derives from Genesis 15:18-21.

CROMWELL The tune is named for the town – itself named after Oliver Cromwell, the great English Puritan leader (1599-1658) – located at the confluence of the Clutha and Kawarau rivers, then the home of the hymn writer Beverley Jones. The setting, written in 1999 by **Colin Gibson**, takes its cue from the words 'God of rock and flowing river' (verse 1), seeking to imitate in music the thought of travelling into the future, with God as the underlying 'rock' and the flow of the river as its musical metaphor for journeying. Set in C major for the first 4 bars, in bar 5 the key suddenly shifts into E major to suggest the unexpected newness of the future. Each stanza but the last ends with an interrupted cadence in E major – no rest there – but the final C major chord brings to a determined finish the long fall of the melody. The supporting bass remains fixed on C until bar 3, when, like the melody, it begins a long march before moving up to the tonic note.

This hymn was originally written to be sung to the tune MARCHING by **Martin Shaw**, first published in *Additional Tunes and Settings in use at St Mary's, Primrose Hill, London* (1915), as a setting for Bernard Severin Ingemann's 1925 hymn 'Igjennem Nai og Traengael,' translated from the Danish in 1867 by Sabine Baring-Gould (1834-81) as 'Through the night of doubt and sorrow.' The hymn text contains the line 'Marching to the promised land,' which, as D'Arcy Wood in *A Companion to Together in Song* (2000) comments, 'gives the tune its name.' Wood goes on to remark on the theme of pilgrimage – present in both the Danish and the New Zealand hymn – which, as he says, 'increasingly in the modern world, is an adventure of the mind, of the understanding and of the imagination' (page 114).

God of work and rest and play H46
Metre: 7.8.8.8.8.7.8.7 and refrain

In 2005, Workplace Support, the southernmost of the four regional centres of the National Interchurch Trade and Industry Mission organisation, commissioned a hymn to express their ethos as industrial chaplains. Working closely with hymn writer and composer **Colin Gibson** they developed together a four-verse text, which Gibson set in the same year. It was first published in *Hope is our Song* (2009).

The dominant theme of the hymn is the companionable presence of God in the daily workplace environment of the chaplains. Phrases such 'I ground my sense of self in you, / as servant and companion too,' or 'I'll help to spread the rumour / that you hold within your care...' were contributed by the chaplains themselves. 'What you have written has exactly captured who we are and what we do; it reflects our mission outlook most particularly,' wrote the organisation's Chief Executive. There are few overtly religious expressions, though 'I dare to take your pilgrim way' and 'God forever making new' have scriptural bases in John 14:6 and Revelation 21:5.

OUTRAM The tune is named after the township of Outram outside Dunedin where Trish Patrick, one of the chaplains, lived at the time. The melody, written in the comfortable key of C with few harmonic adjustments, uses syncopation and phrase repetitions to provide an easily accessible and 'catchy' song.

God our father, mother, lover H48
Metre: 8.7.8.7 D

Written in 1998 by **Jocelyn Marshall** as an entry for the Millennium Hymn Competition sponsored by St Paul's Cathedral, London, this hymn was first published in her collection *Additional Hymns* (1999), then in her *Hymns for All Seasons: A Singing Faith Revised and Enlarged* (2007) before appearing in *Hope is our Song* (2009). There the original fourth verse associating it with the competition is omitted.* In that verse the reference to 'this jubilee' and 'on the road to unity' were, in the author's words, 'an acknowledgement of the forthcoming millennium Jubilee celebrating 2000 years of history and looking forward to greater unity in Church and government in the years that lay ahead.'

The first three verses of the text printed in

Hope is our Song celebrate the three persons of the Trinity by naming some of their significant attributes and enlisting them in support of the aspirations of the singers. What emerges is a vision of the Christian Church engaged both in the rituals of worship and at work in the world. A modern view of God is offered which incorporates both masculine and feminine aspects of the divine, acknowledges divine power but focuses on gentler manifestations of the Godhead such as love, life-source, the natural world of wind, wave and flower, security (cf. Psalm 18:2) and the singers' search for justice, wholeness and peace.

There are biblical sources for most of these aspects but they are kept in the background. Similarly, Christ is praised in creedal terms as 'human yet divine,' but the emphasis falls on Jesus as founder of the Christian Church, his 'ultimate self-giving' remembered at the Eucharist, and his life as an inspiration to his 'pilgrim people' as he leads them on. The work of the Holy Spirit is also defined in terms of the support and guidance offered to the same pilgrim people as they are assailed by loss of nerve and doubt but continue to dream of liberation, yearn for equality and strive to 'recreate society.'

MILLENNIUM 2 In keeping with the writer's practice of setting her hymn texts to well known and traditional hymn tunes, the tune suggested for this text in *Additional Hymns* (1999), was HYFRYDOL (Welsh=Good cheer), written by **Rowland Hugh Prichard** about 1830. The present setting was composed in 1998 for his mother's text by **Christopher Marshall**. It was not originally named but acquired its title from the proximity of the Millennial year 2000. It was first published in *Hymns for all Seasons* (2007 edition). Marked *dolce* (Italian=gently, softly) in the original score, the four-part choral setting with its undemonstrative grandeur, shows every sign of professional composition. The melody is wholly constructed from extensions of the initial two-bar phrase, rising in a series of arches to a top D; the second half of the hymn tune begins with a repetition of the first half (beautifully and differently harmonised) then leads the singers through variations of the first phrase safely back to G major.

*The fourth verse is given here in full:

God, you call us, you empower us,
Love us though we fail or fall;
May we spread that love to others,
Answering the gospel call.
Let us blaze a trail for freedom,
Celebrate this jubilee,
With Christ's cross as sign and compass,
On the road to unity.

God rest us *F28*
Metre: 3.3.8.11.5.6. and Amen

This poem, by Australian poet and cartoonist **Michael Leunig**, was originally published in the *Sunday Age* newspaper, then collected in *The Prayer Tree* (North Blackmore, Victoria: Collins Dove, 1991). In his preface to the collection, Leunig speaks of mornings and evenings as 'the traditional times for prayer and the singing of birds, times of graceful light whereby the heart may envisage its poetry and describe for us what it sees.' He then suggests the need to 'find the mornings and evenings within,' with '…their gentle atmospheres and small miracles.' His poem evokes such an inner world, which corresponds to yet differs from the normal physical patterns of sleep and waking. A paradoxical world in which the sleeping part of the soul is to be awoken – an idea which may be traced to Ephesians 5:14; a world in which God is both 'asleep' (unrecognised?) within us and the one seeking to awaken us.

RESTING This setting of the poem by **Colin Gibson** was written in 1995, and originally conceived of as a four-part choral benediction, written for his own choir and dedicated to his wife, Jeanette.

God speed you on your way (Godspeed Song) *F29*
Metre: 6.6.6.6

Written by **Shirley Murray** in 1999 as 'A cheerful goodbye for someone about to travel, move away or take a new direction in life,' this text was first printed in *Faith Forever Singing* (2000), then in her American collection, *Faith Makes the Song* (2003). The origin of the song may be found in the dedication of *Faith Makes the Song* to the author's granddaughters Isabella, Anna and Rachel, 'to find a faith worth singing.' It carries a recurring Shirley Murray theme, the need to allow for freedom to change and journey on in the Christian life. 'God speed you' is an old (Middle English) form of blessing to someone departing, or setting out on a journey, short for 'May God prosper you, grant you success.' It has come to be a general expression of good wishes for a person's safety as well as their success.

STAFFORD This musical setting was written by **Shona Murray** for *Faith Forever Singing* (2000). It is named after a much-loved caretaker at Tawa College, Ken Stafford, who died of cancer at the age of 40. The music, by a distinguished musician and choral leader, allows for a descant in the third verse and within 8 bars manages to incorporate two harmonic shifts into A minor and E minor (the musical equivalent of the changes mentioned in the text) before returning to the 'home' key of G major. In *Faith Makes the Song* the text is set to the tune SARAH ALEXANDRA, by the American composer **Rusty Edwards**, and there are several other settings.

Shona Murray says that her setting, given a choral arrangement, has become a Tawa College anthem, sung at funerals, farewells and welcomes. 'The choir have sung it overseas at festivals, for weddings and for various community functions.' It was recorded by the Tawa College Dawn Chorus on their CD 'Making Tracks.'

God was in Christ *H49*
Metre: 4.4.4.4

Taking the form of a deceptively simple creedal statement, this hymn text was written by **Shirley Murray** in 2008 and first published in *Hope is our Song* (2009).

The hymn is one of several by this author which urge the greatest respect for every human individual, arguing here that each person contains the nature and goodness of God (implicitly rejecting the doctrine of Original Sin). The text begins with a direct quotation from 2 Corinthians 5:19, which it proceeds to explore in a logical way. Verse 2 draws out the implication that since Christ came as 'a human child,' all human beings (children) must contain 'all that God is,' a nature defined first as 'the will to good, the well* of peace,' followed by the God-spark of creation and the human experiences of joy and the sad aftermath of 'passion' (the only negative mentioned and referencing perhaps the after-effects of sexual passion). In verse 4, the God-bearing child of verse 1 is reincarnated in each new member of the human race, and a fresh image is introduced: 'in each of us God dreams a dream' (that is, we are God's vision of possibility). The final verse echoes the first, but the time shift is crucial: 'God *is* in us,' brought into existence by human love and believed in by an act of faith.

CORNELIA The tune, written by **Colin Gibson** in 2008, is named after Cornelia Grant, the Methodist (former Lutheran) minister of religion and friend to whom it was dedicated. The simple but profound nature of the hymn subject suggested the choice of F minor, closing in the final verse in F major as the words climax on the positives of 'conceived… born…believed.' The melodic shape consists of a quiet, curving rise and fall around the tonic note.

> *The image of a well or deep source of peace may have been suggested by the 1984 Peace Well project of the United States Institute for Peace, though the image appears elsewhere.

God weeps *F30*
Metre: 6.4.8.10

This extraordinarily powerful hymn was written by **Shirley Murray** in 1996. She describes it as 'A protest at violence of every kind, especially that inflicted on the totally vulnerable – children, women, and the created world.' It was first published in *Faith Forever Singing* (2000), then in her American collection *Faith Makes the Song* (2003). As a representative New Zealand hymn it was reprinted (words only) in *A Panorama of Christian Hymnody*, by Erik Routley and Alan A. Richardson (Chicago: GIA, 2005).

The hymn may have been prompted by recorded levels and particular cases of the sexual and physical abuse of children and domestic violence against women in New Zealand at the time, but the text generalizes as a hymn must do. The focus is almost completely on human society; the irrational ('causeless') destruction of animal and other species is briefly referred to in verse 3.

The theological view presented here is that God, though sharing the sufferings of the creation, will not directly intervene but patiently waits for human beings to comprehend the message of active love and compassion lived out by Jesus. The rhetorical structure of the hymn, centred on the figure of a grieving, suffering divinity – no passionless God here – with its accusatory lists of human violence and abuse, comes to a climax in an implied demand for redress and change. The manifestations of God weeping, bleeding, crying out, suggest the sufferings of Christ (cf. John 11:35, Luke 19:34 and Matthew 27:46), whose name finally appears in the final verse. In the last verse, Ezekiel 36:26 lies behind line 2, and James 3:18 behind line 3. Line 4 is compressed: it means 'hearts large enough to recognize and show compassion for the need of others' (see Galatians 6:2).

EMPATHY The tune name suggests the core idea of the hymn. The music was composed by **Ian Render** in 1999. It takes the form of a slow but agonizing 3/4 dance (created by discordant chords in the accompaniment), set in the 'suffering' key of D minor and remaining there to the end. American composer **Jim Strathdee**'s setting, written in 1998 (*Pieces of our Lives*, Carmichael, Cal: Caliche Records) uses a descending sequence in 4/4 time grounded in G minor, but closing on a hopeful major chord.

God who births us fully gifted *H51*
Metre: 8.7.8.7.8.7

This hymn was written by **Rob Ferguson** in 1997 for the induction into the Methodist ministry at Hamilton of his brother-in-law, Mark Gibson, in response to Mark's request for 'some words that were relevant to the way he works'. The author comments, 'This hymn has been used more than my other hymns… largely because there are so few Induction hymns.'

The theme of the hymn is the God-given gifts (verse 1) of all members of the community, their hidden strengths (verse 2). These are to be added to (verse 3), renewed (verse 4) and shared in loving service (verse 5). Paul's account of the various gifts of the Holy Spirit (1 Corinthians 12:1-11) stands behind this text with its broadly-scoped account of Christian ministry

NEW BEGINNINGS The tune name is taken from the third line of the first verse. This unison setting in 6/4 time was composed by **Colin Gibson** for the hymn in 2006.

The original hymn tune used in 1997 was REGENT SQUARE, named as an alternative tune in *Hope is our Song*. REGENT SQUARE was written in 1867 for Horatius Bonar's hymn, 'Glory be to God the Father,' by **Henry Smart**, organist at St Philip's Presbyterian church, Regent Square, London, from 1838 to 1844. At the time, Smart was the musical editor of a new hymnbook, *Psalms and Hymns for Divine Worship*, and he named his tune to honour his fellow-editor and friend, Dr James Hamilton, then minister at the Regent Square church. Rob Ferguson notes, 'Recently a friend in England wrote to tell me she is using this hymn for her ordination / induction to the United Reformed Church in Wales in July 2011. Regent Square church was where she met her husband!'

God who carved this timeless landscape F31
Metre: 8.7.8.7 D

Although the first line of this hymn contains two poetic fictions, that it was God who sculpted the land forms which the hymn describes and not the natural forces of ice, rain, fire and sun, and that the landscape is 'timeless,'* this text eloquently conveys the writer's spiritual sense of the stark beauty of the sub-alpine landscapes of New Zealand and the devoted 'calendar' of daily life for those who live and worship there. The text, originally titled 'Byways of North Otago,' is the work of **Douglas Grierson**; it was written in 1999 and was first published in *Faith Forever Singing* (2000) with several textual changes. In verse 1, 'plains' became 'plain,' in verse 2 'tears or laughter' became 'tears and laughter,' in verse 3 'nineties' wind' became 'history's wind' and 'Still widespread' became 'Scattered are.'

Verse 1 takes its shape from Psalm 121, mediated through the metrical psalm version 'I to the hills will lift mine eyes' in the 1650 *Scottish Psalter* (cf. 'Raise our eyes and you are found'); its principal image is of God as creator-artist. Line 3 refers to the water channels ('races') constructed by miners and farmers in the area and to the principal river, the powerful Waitaki, in volume second only to the Clutha River, the largest in New Zealand. Line 7 refers to the displays of the *aurora australis*, popularly known as the Southern Lights, and the spectacular sunsets regularly seen in these skies. Verse 2 acknowledges the rhythms of the farming year and the trials and triumphs of the farming community ('Nature's balance' is the key phrase here). The religious dimension is sustained in the reference to the Nativity ('Manger setting ever near' – in the woolsheds and stables on the area's farms) and the understated final line, 'Lord, with you, we're understood' (also a hint of the frequent animosity between town and country). Verse 3 focuses on the historical and present life of typical New Zealand rural Christian communities. 'Village life' suggests both the human closeness and geographical remoteness of the early farming settlements; 'tussock track' refers to the simple tracks between thick clumps of native tussock grass (the only vegetation clothing the high country) which pre-dated formed roads. The final 3 lines describe the shared ministry characterizing the life of modern rural congregations; 'each' here means every individual member of the congregation.

DANSEY The hymn was originally set to STRINGER, by Harold Cameron. No information has been found about either the musical setting or the name of the composer, though the Cameron family is widely represented in the South Island of New Zealand. The present tune is named after Danseys Pass, the high South Island mountain pass from which, at an elevation of 935 metres, a magnificent view of the Southern Alps is obtained. The name was given to his music by composer **Colin Gibson**, who wrote the setting for *Faith Forever Singing* in 2000. The music seeks to represent the quiet nobility of rural Christianity as well as the spectacular magnificence of these landscape by taking the character of a restrained but determined march forward. Commencing in A major, the harmonic progression is towards E major, with touches of C sharp minor to symbolize the elements of struggle and difficulty the text openly and honestly acknowledges.

*'Timeless' is an adjective frequently applied to New Zealand's iconic high country landscapes, as in *Timeless Land*, a now classic volume of essays, poems and paintings by Owen Marshall, Brian Turner and Grahame Sydney (1995).

God who granted faith and vision H50
Metre: 8.7.8.7 D

The words of this impressive hymn were written by **Marnie Barrell** in 1992 for the 125th anniversary of St Mary's Anglican Church, Christchurch, New Zealand. It was first published in *Hope is our Song* (2009) and appears on the Oremus website.

The three verses address the anniversary in terms of the church's past, present and future. Verse one acknowledges previous generations of faithful members of the church. The second verse addresses the three persons of the Trinity. It echoes Jesus' prayer for the unity of his followers (John 17:22) and in the phrase 'blood and body of your son' (line 4) both calls the congregation to show forth the life of Christ in their own lives and reflects words commonly spoken in the celebration of the central sacrament of the Church, the celebration of the Eucharist. See John 14:23-26 for the presence of the Holy Spirit 'in the world you call your own.' Verse 3 addresses God as the light that 'shines out before us' (see Exodus 13:21 and John 1:5) and sees the present congregation passing on 'the story of your love in action here' to future generations.

RUSTINGTON The standard hymn tune assigned to this text in *Hope is our Song* is by **Hubert Parry** (1848-1918). It was contributed to *The Westminster Abbey Hymn Book* (1897) for Benjamin Webbe's 'Praise the rock of our salvation,' then taken into *Hymns Ancient and Modern* (1904) as a setting for 'Through the night of doubt and sorrow.' The tune is named after the town of Rustington in Sussex, to which Parry moved in 1878 after spending holidays and summers there for 40 years. He probably wrote this setting in Rustington and it was at Rustington that he died on 7 October 1918.

God who sets us on a journey F32
Metre: 8.7.8.7 D

This popular hymn was written by **Joy Dine** in 1993 in circumstances best described by her husband, Mervyn Dine: 'During 1993 I took study leave to prepare for the 1993 Methodist Conference when I would be inducted as President of the Methodist Church. Joy offered to write a hymn for the occasion and so we talked about the possible theme for my Presidential address. We decided on the title *Journeying together in faith and compassion*. It was the 10th Anniversary of the decision made by the Church to embark on its bi-cultural journey...Another issue was the acceptance of persons other than those of a heterosexual orientation to be received into full connexion [as] presbyters within the Methodist Church...I felt the Church, whether people liked it or not, was on a journey, and when you journey you often find yourself in places you've never been in before, and it can be an exciting and challenging experience. So the Presidential address was born, as was this exciting hymn challenging the Church to realize that constant change is here to stay' ('God who sets us on a journey: the life, liturgy and hymns of Joy Dine, *Music in the Air* 16 (Winter 2003), 8-13).

The sustained theme of the hymn is the journey of God's people into the unknown and the text references the Bible at several points, particularly the journey from Ur by Abraham (Genesis 12) and the desert wanderings of the Hebrews led by the pillar of fire (Exodus 13:21-22). For verse 1 see Genesis 12:1 and Mark 2:30-31. For the Jesus light (verse 2) see John 8:12; the phrase 'mindful of your grace' echoes the Methodist Communion service. Verse 3, 'treasure that will last' alludes to Luke 12:32-34. The final verse alludes to Genesis 12:8 and Philippians 3:14, while the phrase 'keep us travelling in the knowledge that you are always at our side' recalls **Sydney Carter**'s 'keep me travelling along with you' from his popular hymn, 'One more step along the world I go,' with which the New Zealand hymn shares the common theme of journeying and some of its imagery.

CANVAS The tune name alludes to the material of a wanderer's tent (cf. verse 4, line 1, and the phrase 'under canvas'=camping, or living in a tent). This setting was composed by **Jillian Bray** in 1998 to provide a New Zealand alternative to the original and still popular choice of HYFRYDOL, by Welsh composer **Rowland Huw Prichard** (1811-87). Both settings provide a melody with plenty of swinging forward motion in 6/8 time. Jillian Bray's setting also modulates through G minor and F major to create a sense of changing or 'wandering' harmonic experience – 'the places you've never been before' – though it finally returns to the tonic key of B flat.

God who weeps H52
Metre: 8.7.8.7 D

This hymn was written by **Marnie Barrell** in 2001 in response to the terrorist attack on 11 September 2001 on the Twin Towers in New York. The writer, who belonged to an email group of American preachers at the time, recalls that 'A lot of what I was reading there was utter rage and calling on God to smite the enemy, understandably enough.' She says that 'I wanted to contribute to the American churches' struggles to process what had happened, and tried to say something credible and non-preachy, to acknowledge the pain of the situation, but place God on the side of suffering rather than vengeance, and point to the strength of Jesus' own refusal to meet violence with violence.' The hymn was first published in *Hope is our Song* (2009).

One of several New Zealand hymns which attribute to God – a weeping God – the qualities of pity and compassion, this text, addressed to the three persons of the Trinity, is a plea for tolerance, reconciliation and compassion. Verse 1, addressing God as creator, divine lover and friend, uses the words of the funeral service to commit into God's keeping 'those who suffer, struggle, fall.' Verse 2 describes Christ's behaviour under arrest, trial and crucifixion as providing a model for non-violent response to 'hate and violence.' Verse 3 invokes the power of the Holy Spirit to enable the worshippers to 'rise above retaliation' and 'live the peace we long to hear.' Verse 4 calls on God's help in building a new world of 'safety, peace and plenty.'

LACRIMOSA (Latin=pitiful, tearful) Named after the *lacrimosa* ('Ah! What weeping') movement in the Requiem Mass, this unison setting was written in 2008 by Marnie Barrell's fellow Christchurch musician **Barry Brinson**. The composer says, 'in searching for inspiration for a long (8.7.8.7 D) tune, I kept coming back to two traditional melodies – a Welsh hymn tune BRYN CALFARIA [Welsh=Mount Calvary, by William Owen, 1854], and a medieval Polish carol melody, 'Infant holy, infant lowly' ['W żłobie leży! Któż pobieży,' translated in 1920 by Edith Margaret Gellibrand Reed (1885-1933)]. Without blatantly quoting from these melodies, the rhythmic pattern seemed to flow with Marnie's words very well. Another important factor is the hint of a "minor/major" harmonic shift between the first half of each verse and the second, which I think gives expression to the contrasting moods (variously pensive/reflective/positive) within the verses.'

God within our deepest thought H53
Metre: 7.7.7 D

It is rare to find a hymn written about modern communion (in the sense of interpersonal communication), the media and truth, which is the sub-title of this hymn, written by **Shirley Murray** in 2004 and first published in her collection *Touch the Earth Lightly* (2005), before reaching *Hope is our Song* (2009).

Shirley Murray says of her text, 'This is a hymn about the media, and the way truth is often spun or twisted [that is, distorted, given a false interpretation]. It is also about our own discernment, learning to listen and to have a standard by which we judge what we see and hear.' The argument of the hymn is drawn out over its four stanzas: it invokes the God-presence within each human soul ('God within our deepest thought') to assist humans taking in the frequently inadequate, obscure and sometimes falsified and unbelievable words and pictures broadcast by the media to discern the realities behind them. But it goes further, encouraging the rejection of 'pictures that distort and tease' (political propaganda, pornography and commercial advertising come to mind) and encouraging the values of appreciation of quality programming ('treasures old and new') and tolerance of 'another's truth' (verse 3) as well as *aroha-love** of the kind Jesus taught, 'translated for our day,' that is, expressed in modern terms (verse 4) as a crucial standard of judgement. John 14:6, 'I am the way, the truth and the life,' stands behind much of the language of the hymn-writer here. Note the expressive word-play on 'play…ploy' (verse 2) which contrasts innocent human activities, such as games and recreational sport, with cunning, cruel activities and deceitful stratagems.

VERITAS (Latin=truth) *Touch the Earth Lightly* does not assign a tune to this text, which was set by **Colin Gibson** in 2008 for *Hope is our Song*. The melody, set in D major, has a 'dying fall,' representing the confusions and distortions described in the text. Beneath it, the sustained bass note represents the God-given awareness of truth 'in our deepest thought,' and carries down into the depths before rising steadily to the keynote D with which it began.

> *For an expansive explanation of this Māori term, see 'Come to this Christmas singing.'

God, come now to explore my heart
H38
Metre: 8.6.8.6 D

This self-reflexive, confessional hymn was written by **Marnie Barrell** in 2008, and first published in *Hope is our Song* (2009). It is now on the SongSelect website. She says of it, 'the thing that prompted it really was a felt need for a Lenten hymn that I wanted to sing! Not too abjectly grovelling, but frankly acknowledging sin/failure and the need for restoration, and with some hopeful mention of the good God has placed in us.'

Introspective and meditative hymns have not figured largely in modern New Zealand writing, which has often focused on social, environmental and justice issues. But in this hymn text, as singers we are taken within ourselves and set out on an interior journey of the soul. The traveller descends a quiet path, is bathed in a 'gently searching light' (cf. Matthew 11:29) and begins to build trust and learn how to face the 'dread of having all revealed.' Then the 'I' of the hymn takes full control of the process of self-examination, freely surrendering the 'keys to doors kept hidden from others' sight.' And alongside the negative discoveries ('needs ignored, faults denied, grief and guilt') there are balancing positives: the good seen by God, the 'unsuspected gifts placed there from the start,' the 'treasures in my heart'; even 'the missing parts of your design entrusted to my care.' Finally, the journeyer is led back, to complete this act of self-examination in loving service and a sharing of all that he or she has now found within themselves. There are some biblical resonances – the quiet path (John 14:6), faults denied (John 18:15-27), mending the broken (Psalm 147:3), called by my name Isaiah 49:1), gifts (1 Corinthians 12:1-11) – but this is a strikingly new poetic formulation of an ancient concept, the journey of the soul towards a deeper understanding of itself.

MYLOR The name of a small Australian town near Adelaide, where the hymn was written. The composer of the 4-part choral setting is **Marnie Barrell** herself, who chose the key of F minor for this thoughtful, meditative text. The music has a steady 'walking' rhythm (matching the inner journey described in the text) and a dark tone – a combination which recalls Welsh hymn tunes like EBENEZER ('Through the night of doubt and sorrow'). Mid-way there is a harmonic 'lift' to A major, but with the downward trajectory of the melody F minor resumes its sway.

> *For a fuller account of the argument of this hymn, see 'God, come now to explore my heart' [by Colin Gibson]. *Word & Worship*, 8.2, Autumn 2010, 24-6.

God, companion of our journey (New Beginnings) *H32*
Metre: 8.7.8.7

This hymn text was written in 2004 by **Jocelyn Marshall** on commission from the Reverend Vivienne Hill, to whom it is dedicated. It was first published in the writer's in-house collection *11 Hymns* (2004), then in her *Hymns for all Seasons* (2007), before reaching *Hope is our Song* (2009). The author explains that in 2004 the Reverend Vivienne Hill, an Anglican priest and former vicar of St Barnabas, Glenfield, Auckland, decided to set up a ministry for pets and their owners. 'She asked me if I could write a hymn specifically for this particular outreach, which she has named "Pet

Rites"; she takes services for pet owners in their times of celebration and mourning. The title "New Beginnings" refers to the novelty of this ministry for animals.'

The text reflects the new ministry for which it was written; it is essentially a prayer for divine help and guidance, followed by a dedication to fresh ways of service. Verse 1, line 1, alludes to the Emmaus Road story, Luke 24:13-25; line 2 to Psalm 46:1. For the Holy Spirit as comforter see John 24:16. Verse 2, line 3, echoes Psalm 23:3. Verse 3 focuses directly on the new ministry. It begins with a formulation frequent in hymn lyrics: cf. 'All things praise thee, Lord most high, / heaven and earth and sea and sky' (Henry Smart, 1866) and sustains that idea in the description of 'great and little things, / creatures furred and feathered' as knowing God. The New Zealand bellbird or *korimako* (line 4) is a bush bird, famed for its song, which the explorer Captain Cook described as being 'like small bells exquisitely tuned.' Verse 4, line 1 is a devotional commonplace, based on Nehemiah 9:6 and Romans 14:11. For the full meaning of the Māori word *aroha* (line 3), 'the love that unifies and sustains the universe,' see the entry for '**Come to this Christmas singing.**' Line 4 references Acts 17:18.

The tunes suggested by the writer for this text are SUSSEX or CROSS OF JESUS. SUSSEX is a traditional English folk song from the county of Sussex arranged by **Ralph Vaughan Williams** and first published as a hymn tune in the *English Hymnal* (1906). CROSS OF JESUS is a melody originally composed by John Stainer for his oratorio *The Crucifixion* (1887).

God, composer and conductor (Creator God) *H34*
Metre: 8.7.8.7.8.7

This hymn text, invoking and praising God, was written by Hamilton poet **Jocelyn Marshall** between 1996 and 1998 and dedicated to Dr Christopher Hainsworth, a renowned New Zealand concert organist and harpsichord player, former Associate Professor and Head of the Department of Music at Waikato University, Director of Music at St Peter's Cathedral, Hamilton, 'and a dear friend over many years.' It was first published in the writer's collection *Additional Hymns* (Hamilton, 1999).

Hainsworth's status as a musician and his skill as an arranger and improviser on the organ explains the opening stanza's praise of God as 'composer and conductor of earth's matchless symphony.' A pupil of Maxwell Fernie at St Mary's of the Angels, Wellington, Hainsworth studied French and music at Victoria University and completed a doctorate in music at the University of Toulouse. He held academic positions in both New Zealand and France, and became Director of the Beziers Conservatoire and organist of Beziers Cathedral in the region of Languedoc-Roussillon in his adopted country of France.

The poem pursues the theme of creativity throughout: God is praised in verse 2 as 'architect and artist of earth's colours, textures, forms.' Verse 3 praises God in the identities of scientist, healer and teacher, freeing us 'from the limits that restrain us.' Finally, verse 4 invokes God's presence as 'creative spirit in us…now, and to the end of time.'

This hymn text has not yet received a setting; the poet recommends the use of **Henry Thomas Smart**'s REGENT SQUARE (1867) or **Henry Purcell**'s WESTMINSTER ABBEY (c.1760), both of them grand and majestic tunes fitting both the theme of the text and the musical abilities of the dedicatee.

God's grace upon this house (A Blessing for a House) *H54*
Metre: 8.8.8.8.8.6

This blessing for a house was written by **Colin Gibson** in 2000, as an expression of gratitude following a brief stay at the hospitable home of two friends, Stuart and Cornelia Grant (a notable cook). It was first published in *Hope is our Song* (2009), then in the American collection *New Hymns of Hope* (2010).

There are biblical resonances in this short text: line 3 recalls both the hospitality Jesus himself received at the home of Martha and Mary, and Matthew 25:40, 'Just as you did it to one of the least of these….you did it to me,' while line 5 recalls Luke 10:5 and Jesus' instruction to his disciples, 'Whatever house you enter, first say "Peace to this house!"'

ROSETTA ROAD The tune is named after the then Palmerston North street address of Methodist ministers Stuart and Cornelia Grant. Written by **Colin Gibson**, the setting is in B flat major, and the melody is constructed from variants of the initial 9-note musical phrase, which play out over a harmonic tone-scape of closely related keys to give an impression of quiet benediction. The text is suitable for the blessing of new as well as established dwellings.

Grace before Meals *facing F61*

This set of three short Graces, differing in theme and in style, comes from **Joy Cowley**'s collection *Psalms Down-under* (Catholic Supplies: Wellington, 1996).

Great and deep the Spirit's purpose
A55
Metre: 8.7.8.7 D

This powerful hymn to the Holy Spirit was written in 1988 by **Marnie Barrell** and first published in *Alleluia Aotearoa* (1993), then in the fourth edition of the *Church Hymnary* (2005), where it is set to LUX TREMENDAE by American composer **Alfred Fedak**. As a representative New Zealand hymn it was reprinted (words only) in *A Panorama of Christian Hymnody*, by Erik Routley and Alan A. Richardson (Chicago: GIA, 2005). The text is also published on the Oremus website.

The text is embued with hope and optimism (cf. verses 1 and 3); and such joyful expectation is extended into the theme of the preciousness of children (children of God), each one 'uniquely loved and known' (verse 4), ultimately sharing in a final ecstatic vision of Christ's return in glory at the end of time (see Mark 13:26-27 and 1 Corinthians 15:23).

The narrative structure of the hymn text displays a grand progression from the mysterious but joyful promise of the work of Nature (verse 1), through the expanding proclamation of Christ and further exploration of 'the Word' (verse 2), to the perfection of human life throughout the earth (verse 3) and a final unimaginable ('unimagined') unification and perfection of all things – the words 'all' and 'every' are repeatedly used – at the coming of Christ in glory.

The language of the text is rich with biblical terms and phrases – for instance, cf. verse 1, line 7, with 1 Corinthians 13:12, verse 2, line 7, with 1 Corinthians 2:9, or verse 3, line 6, with Habakkuk 3:18; but the major biblical springboards are 1 Corinthians 2:7-10, 'We impart a secret and hidden wisdom of God…the Spirit searches everything, even the depths of God,' and Hebrews 2:3 on God's 'great salvation'. However, the writer's own imaginative power is expressed in the imagery of the Spirit as creative artist (verse 1), universal participation in 'the everlasting dance' (verse 4) and the vision of 'all God's children brought to birth, / freed from hunger, fear and evil.'

BRUNEL This tune, composed by **Colin Gibson** in 1989, was named after the Mornington, Dunedin, street address where Alan Upson and Lynne Frith, the ministerial team serving the composer's parish at the time and to whom it is dedicated, had their parsonage. It was first published in *Alleluia Aotearoa* (1993), then in the composer's American collection *Songs for a Rainbow People* (1998). Written in chorale style, it imitates the 'unfolding' of the Spirit's purpose by climbing in sequential patterns from the tonic key of G major to D major at mid-point; then illustrates the 'wealth of rich invention' with a series of harmonic modulations moving through A minor, G major, E minor and D major (bar 8), to close in a fresh series of climbing phrases which take the melodic line through C major, D minor and E minor before it settles back on the tonic note of G. In 2003 an even more elaborate version was created to give the men of the Mornington Methodist Church choir a more challenging singing role. That version was dedicated to another of the ministers serving the parish and singing in the choir, the Reverend Craig Forbes.

Great is the Love A56
Metre: Irregular

While she was studying in 1986 at the Institute of Culture and Creation Spirituality at Oakland, California, **Betty Wendelborn**, composer of this setting of a text by the 13th century German mystic **Mechthild of Magdeburg** (1210-1280), was, she says, 'so captivated by the beautiful songs of the mystics that I immediately set to work to translate them into musical settings.' This song, along with 63 others by various authors, was the result, first published in the collection *Sing Green: Songs of the Mystics* (Auckland, 1988).

The saying set to music here appears in Book 7 of Mechthild's *Fliessende Licht der Gottheit*, a title usually translated as *Flowing Light of the Godhead*; the material in Book 7 was written down during the 1270s. In a more literal translation the saying reads, 'Great is the overflowing of Love Divine, for it is never still. Always ceaselessly and tirelessly it pours itself out, so that the small vessel which is ourselves might be filled to the brim. So we are always Love even without knowing it' (Book 7, Revelation 55).

[GREAT LOVE] The setting is by **Betty Wendelborn** and was composed in 1986 and published in 1988. The time values of the original setting are halved for *Alleluia Aotearoa*. This is a religious song which may be sung slowly several times over, in the manner of a mantra, following the rising and 'spilling over' of the melodic line, which closely follows the text it serves.

Great ring of light A57
Metre: 4.7.4.7.4.8

This hymn text was written by **Colin Gibson** in 1986, following a visit to a Yorkshire friend, an amateur astronomer, who was looking in vain through cloudy Yorkshire skies to see Halley's Comet on its passage near Earth in that year. It was first published in *Singing Love* (1988), followed by *Alleluia Aotearoa* (1993) and Gibson's first American collection, *Reading the Signature* (1994).

The world-wide interest roused by the visit of the comet started a train of thought about God's presence in the world as manifested in light, reinforced by familiar images found in such biblical passages as the opening of St John's gospel. Although the comet strictly follows an elliptical course through space, verse 1 begins with traditional circular images of eternity and a light beam unrefracted through prism or water, followed by an allusion to John 1:5, 'The light shines in the darkness, and the darkness did not overcome it.' Verse 2 refers to the death and resurrection of Christ (see Matthew 27:46, Mark 15:34 and Luke 23:46). The Trinitarian structure of the hymn is completed with verse 3, where the Holy Spirit is imaged as fire (Acts 2:3) and 'comforter' (John 14:26). The final verse reiterates the Trinitarian theme in personal terms: 'I receive the life, the joy, the loving.'

HALLEY The tune name is that of the comet named after Edmond Halley the English astronomer who in 1705 correctly predicted its return in 1758. (It will next return in 2061.) The grandeur of the theme has suggested a Bach-style setting for organ, with a slowly descending pedal bass.

Greetings, little child of Bethlehem C25
Metre: 9.11.6.7.9

Written as a contribution to a Catholic Family Living Programme magazine by **Cecily Sheehy**, this Christmas song may be sung as a two-part round. After its initial publication it was printed in *Carol our Christmas* (1996).

The text opens with a phrase derived from Matthew 2:16, the 'child of Bethlehem,' who is immediately identified with every new-born child. Verse 2, line 2, alludes to Mark 16:15; line 3 to Mark 10:13-16 (see also Matthew 18:1-4, 19:13-15 and Mark 9:36-37).

But the writer's interest in creation spirituality also appears in lines 1 and 4: 'Planet Earth' is a coded phrase, now commonly used to refer to the precious natural environment of our planet (the 'every living creature' of verse 3). Verse 3 continues to extend the scope of the song: Christmas greetings are offered to 'each culture, and every living creature,' as well as to the 'child of Bethlehem.'

[GREETINGS] The charmingly simple rising and falling melody by the writer-composer allows space for modulations to two related keys (G and E minor) before returning to the home key C major.

Hail Mary, full of grace A58
Metre: 6.6.8.5.8.8

This Marian hymn was written by **Marnie Barrell** in 1987, published in *Alleluia Aotearoa* (1993) and later revised in 2001 for the Oremus website. There the lines are re-divided to form a 12.12.8.8 stanza form and stanza 1, line 4, becomes, 'in her holiness,' stanza 3, line 7, becomes 'God lifts the weak, puts down the strong'* and stanza 4, line 2, begins with 'that.' The text is now headed 'A hymn to Mary.'

One of the earliest of Marnie Barrell's hymns, it was written at a time when she was attending St Mary's Anglican Church, Addington, Christchurch, where she was impressed with the Marian devotions used there, and began to read around the subject. 'The hymn literature on the subject was feeble, and we were always stuck for something suitable to sing on feast days of Mary, the patronal festival, and so on; "Hail Mary, full of grace" was written to fill an obvious gap.'

The hymn is resonant with echoes of passages from the gospels of Luke 1:27-30, 46-53 and John 1:14, the Hail Mary prayer that forms the basis of the Rosary prayer in the Roman Catholic tradition, the Basque carol *Berjina gaztettobat zegoen* paraphrased by **Sabine Baring-Gould** (1824-1934) as 'The angel Gabriel,' and the familiar Christmas hymn 'O little town of Bethlehem' by **Philip Brooks** (1835-93). Verse 2 also refers to the legend that heaven and earth stood still at the moment of Christ's nativity (see James Kirkup's poem, 'The Eve of Christmas,' in *A Single Star: An Anthology of Christmas Poetry*, ed David Davis, London: Bodley Head, 1973). But the hymn is much more than pious pastiche. The underlying theme of the text is praise of the courage, strength and vitality of an autonomous young woman, 'virgin and alone,' 'our sister,' who 'freely chose the will of God / and made it her own,' by so doing becoming a model for later Christians who in love and faith 'receive Christ still and make him room' (that is, become Christ-bearers themselves).

AVE [Latin=hail!] This setting was written by **Douglas Mews** for the editorial committee of *Alleluia Aotearoa*. Set in F major, the opening unison phrase of the melody is crafted to suggest the determination, courage and strength celebrated in the poem (see verse 3); the following long-breathed phrases are carried over several modulations before the melody returns to the tonic key. The hymn was originally set to LOVE UNKNOWN, written for Samuel Crossman's 'My song is love unknown' by the distinguished British composer **John Nicolson Ireland** (1879-1962) and first published in *The Public School Hymn Book* (1919). Marnie Barrell says that this tune 'was in my mind before the text had worked itself out very far – usually the case with me.'

> *A reversion to the orthodox text of the Magnificat: Marnie Barrell's original version reads, 'the weak and poor shall teach the strong.'

He came singing love A59, W636
Metre: 5.6.5.6.6.6.7

This widely-known hymn text was written by **Colin Gibson** in 1972 for a national hymn-writing competition organised by Television New Zealand (where it took second place) and was first published in *Servant Songs* (1987), followed by *New Zealand Praise* (1988), the author's first English collection, *Singing Love* (1988), *Alleluia Aotearoa* (1993), his first American collection, *Reading the Signature* (1994), and *He came singing Peace* (2002). It reached an Asian audience in *Sound the*

Bamboo (1990) and has appeared in several American and Canadian hymnals.

The theme and the wording of the first verse were prompted by a reproduction of a poster-text by 'Brother Adrian DM' on the front cover of an American Methodist family magazine of the time. The original text read, 'He came singing love. He died singing love. He rose in silence. If the song is to continue we must do the singing.' The extension of this idea is based on St Paul's famous triad of Christian values, faith, hope and love, with the author's addition of peace (see 1 Corinthians 13:13). While the hymn is intended to stress the need for its singers to take responsibility for the continuation of Jesus' ministry, the words have also been used at funeral services as a tribute to the qualities of the deceased person. One of its more remarkable uses has been for a 2009 Salvation Army celebration in Christchurch, the 125 notes of the melody coinciding with the Army's 125 days of prayer.

SINGING LOVE Composed in 1972 by **Colin Gibson** for this text, this hymn and its setting has been widely used in New Zealand and overseas. Several arrangements of the original unison setting exist, including one by the New Zealand musician Martin Setchell (1993) and arrangements for male quartet (1988) and for TABB choir (1999) by the composer. There are a number of recordings by choirs and soloists. The chief melodic feature of the melody is its climb to a high note on 'he arose' and the indication of a rest after 'silence' to allow for a brief moment of silence itself, an expressive interval seldom observed in practice.

He rongo pai te oranga W634
Metre: 8.6.8.6

Described in *With One Voice* as a traditional Māori hymn, this text was first collected by Christopher Parr in a manuscript now in the National Library dating from 1845-1853. It was published in *He himene whakapai I te Atua* (Auckland: Brett Publishing in 1907 and in *He Himene mo te karakia ki te Atua* in 1910 (London: SPCK), both collections of Anglican hymns in the Māori language. The authorship is unknown as is the date of creation, but given the subject and its development it was probably written by an early Anglican missionary.

The theme of the hymn is the salvation of the world through the sacrificial death of Jesus Christ, and the language is biblical throughout (for instance, Jesus as the Truth, and Jesus as the Lamb of salvation)

LAUGHTON Described as a Māori melody, the tune was recorded with the text as early as 1910. It is more probably Western in origin, possibly an American gospel song. The arrangement in *With One Voice* is by **Guy Jansen**; the tune name was perhaps given as a tribute to Laughton Harris, a music lecturer and choir director at the University of Otago.

Heav'n is ringing (Merry Christmas Rag) C26
Metre: irregular

The birth of Christ is given a joyous communal celebration in this quirky Christmas carol, in which congregation and choir co-operate to make music. It was written in November 1990 for the author/composer **Colin Gibson's** congregation and choir at the Mornington Methodist Church, Dunedin, and was published in his second American collection, *Songs for a Rainbow People* (1998), as well as reaching *Carol our Christmas* (1996).

The text is made up of imagined but natural and informal comments of the kind offered by friends and neighbours on the birth of any new baby – 'Congratulations, Mary, congratulations, Joseph…What a lovely baby, look, I'm sure he's smiling' – with a final touch of religious imagery in 'Heav'n is ringing, angels winging, choirs are singing' (see Luke 2:13-14). But there is also an opportunity for friends and members of the congregation to exchange traditional Christmas greetings: 'Merry Christmas, neighbour…Merry Christmas and a happy New Year!'

MERRY CHRISTMAS RAG The term 'rag' suggests a popular syncopated music form (ragtime) and riotous festivity. The musical form of this carol is a gallimaufry in which choral groups add in succession their own line of sung text to the growing ensemble. As the composer explains, 'The basses lead off, to be joined at the end of their eight-bar line – which they continue to repeat – by the tenors, and so on up the parts until all are ringing out their lines together, with perhaps a final repetition to bring the piece to a close. The congregation enters with the second altos, having previously chosen personal names of relatives and friends they wish to greet (all names will fit the commodious metre).' The 4/4 beat needs to remain steady if the ensemble is not to collapse into actual chaos. At the original performance, each group, including the congregation, stood up as it joined the other singers, and the final group of sopranos, much to the surprise of the composer, appeared wearing Father Christmas hats, with flashing lights attached to their ears!

Here I stand among God's people *H55*
Metre: 8.7.8.7 D

The dedication to 'my godson James Daniell, confirmed 16 May 1999,' gives the date and occasion of this hymn text by **Marnie Barrell**, which was published in *Hope is our Song* (2009) and entered on the Oremus website.

The personal voice of the hymn enables it to be sung in many circumstances, but makes it particularly appropriate as a Confirmation hymn in which the singer claims 'a thread within God's story / that is mine alone to know, / and a vision of God's glory that my life was made to show' (verse 1). The dedicated Christian life set out in the verses is one of corporate worship, prayer and communion, issuing in active work for peace and justice in response to divine direction. The language of the hymn is resonant with familiar words and phrases drawn from church ritual and practice (such as 'God's people, when the bread and wine are blessed, welcome at the table, the Word of God'), but there are some other echoes as well: verse 2, 'when he calls me I'll be there,' from a lyric by the Spinners; verse 3, 'till I see God face to face,' from 1 Corinthians 13:12.

ABBEYFIELD For a note on this hymn tune by **Colin Gibson** see 'Song of faith that sings forever,' F56. A number of other standard tunes have been suggested for these words, among them ABBOT'S LEIGH, AUSTRIA, BLAENWERN and NETTLETON.

Here in the busy city *H56*
Metre: 7.6.7.6 D

'For city-dwellers there are few hymns that echo the pace and activity of modern life,' writes **Shirley Murray**, who created this text in 1986. 'Our parish church is in the capital city [Wellington, New Zealand], across the road from Parliament Buildings and the Treasury, and our "Declaration of Intent" at St Andrew's is to have a special care for those in government.' The text was first published in the author's American collection, *in Every Corner Sing* (1992), set to MERLE'S TUNE by American composer Hal Hopson. It reached its first New Zealand publication in *Hope is our Song* (2009).

As usual, this text, while vividly describing the real life and daily activities of a major city, is highly allusive. The phrase 'where lesser gods are worshipped' may have been prompted by the 1986 release of the American film, *Children of a Lesser God* (referring to demeaning social attitudes towards deaf people). For the message of the gospel as 'Good News,' see Mark 16:15; the popular *Good News Bible* had been published in 1976. 'Living out the Word' as a directive to express Christ's teaching in real life is a common religious expression based on Matthew 4:4. In verse 2, 'moderate' carries the meanings of 'act as moderator between the powerful and the powerless' and 'temper, soften the behaviour of the powerful,' Crisis centres are places offering support and counselling – often for women who have suffered sexual abuse or domestic violence. Verse 3, 'people go to waste'=people are treated like rubbish; their potential is not realized. Lines 5-8 allude to Jesus' teachings about the Kingdom of God resembling yeast working in dough (Matthew 13:33) and the need for his followers to be 'the salt of the earth' (Matthew 5:13). The thought of verse 4, that 'God walks on every street,' is based on Matthew 25:40; in this verse focusing on the commercial aspect of city life, the Church is to freely offer social and moral *good*, by comparison with *goods* (items priced and offered for sale).

CATHEDRAL SQUARE The tune is named after the central square of Christchurch, the hub of the 'busy city' where the composer, **Barry Brinson**, lived. Until September 2010 the square was dominated by the city's Anglican Cathedral, but in the earthquake which struck the town then, followed by a second major quake early in 2011, the cathedral was ruined and is now being restored. The composer writes of his music, 'I decided on a minor key (D minor), as the first half of each verse seemed more pensive and reflective in nature. The second half of each verse is full of hope and assertion of where the church stands in the modern world, and I hope I have reflected this in the more "major key" shift, although ending on a minor cadence – except for the final ending, which *must* be major.' This setting was completed in April, 2009; the composer had previously created a version called BLUE CITY BLUES in jazz style for performance at Christchurch Cathedral in 2006.

Here is a night that's bleak and raw (A Night in Bethlehem) H57
Metre: 8.8.8.8 D

This beautiful Christmas carol by **Willow Macky** existed as an undated, typed manuscript which remained unknown until it was discovered among the author's papers by her Executor Peggy Haworth and brought to the attention of John Thornley, who printed it in 'Willow Macky: Six Poems' (*Music in the Air* 25 (Summer/Autumn 2008), 14-16. It was later included in *Hope is our Song* (2009), with a setting by **Colin Gibson**.

The text precisely imagines an assembly of animals gathered round the infant Jesus; a camel and a mouse join the traditional ox and ass. Verse 1, line 2, 'wittering'=chattering, in this context, squeaking with fear; line 6, 'with hooded eyes'=with eyes partly covered by the eyelids, withdrawn, inward-looking.

Verses 2 and 3 refer to the Christmas star and the angelic chorus mentioned in Luke 2. Verse 3 allegorizes the scene: the wittering mouse represents insignificant humanity with its little fears and panics, the feeding cattle represent human hungers both physical and spiritual, the camel represents disillusioned philosophical knowledge.

ORIANA Invited to set this carol by the chairman of the editorial committee for *Hope is our Song*, **Colin Gibson** named the music after John Thornley's street address in Palmerston North. The prevailing peacefulness of the scene described suggested an equally peaceful setting in E flat major, with a rocking rhythm.

Here is the place, now is the time (Hymn for a Confirmation) A60
Metre: 4.4.4.4.10.4.4

As its author, **Shirley Murray**, explains, this hymn 'was born out of necessity to find something relevant to say at a service of confirmation.' Written in 1988 for a service at the St Andrews Presbyterian Church, Wellington, because the congregation did not know the tune, 'the words were read "voice over" to the quiet accompaniment of the organist.' The hymn first appeared in Murray's American collection *In Every Corner Sing* (1992), then in *Alleluia Aotearoa* (1993). It has since been widely used in communal worship as a general expression of faith: 'I go with all who follow Christ.'

For verse 1, line 2, 'an inner voice' (traditionally the voice of the Holy Spirit) see Mark 13:11. Line 4 alludes to the calling of the disciples; see also Mark 8:34. Verse 2, line 4, echoes Psalm 40:3, 'He has put a new song in my mouth, even praise unto our God.' In this context, 'singleness of heart' (line 3) means 'sincerity, deep conviction'; the phrase is borrowed from Ezekiel 11:19, 'And I will give them singleness of heart and put a new spirit within them.' The final line echoes Numbers 23:12, 'Must I not take care to say what the Lord puts into my mouth?'

GREEN ISLAND The tune name refers to a Dunedin suburb where Murray Wood, a severely handicapped boy, lived with his devoted mother. His regular participation in the services of worship held at the composer **Colin Gibson's** own Mornington Methodist Church, as well as the appropriateness of the words, led to the dedication of this setting to the boy. The principal feature of the melody is the expansive upward movement of the middle phrase accompanying 'here is the company where Christ is known' and the sudden C major chord illuminating the word 'Christ' in a tonal landscape predominantly keyed in D major.

Here to celebrate God's loving H58
Metre: 8.7.8.7 and refrain

In 1990, the Reverend Norman West, a Methodist minister, was appointed to the Dunedin Methodist Parish, and invited **Colin Gibson**, a member of the Mornington Methodist Church, to create a hymn to be sung at his Induction. It was used for this service in 1991 and sung from the Mornington Supplementary Hymn book until its publication in Gibson's American collection *Songs for a Rainbow People* (1998), followed by *Hope is our Song* (2009).

The general themes of the text were suggested by Norman West himself, and constitute his vision for the future life of the parish, a life of loving service shared by members of the community with the larger world. (West himself later became one of the World Council of Churches peace monitors during the 1994 South African elections.) Biblical values of loving service, equality and respect for the divine presence in each soul are endorsed (see for instance, Mark 9:30-50 and Matthew 18 on the discussion among the disciples as to who was the greatest among them). Verse 3, line 2, is effectively the present parish motto, 'Finding good in everyone, finding God in every one.' The refrain offers the image of fluttering banners carrying the words 'Hallelujah' (=praise God) and 'Amen' (so be it). Lines 3-4 allude to John 1:1.

BARR STREET The setting, also by **Colin Gibson**, and written in 1991, takes its name from the Dunedin street where the Wests took up residence. Intentionally cheerful and informal, the music, though set in F major, perversely strays towards C major, the most open and happiest of keys.

Here to the house of God we come
A61
Metre: 8.8.8 D

This hymn was written by **Shirley Murray** in 1987 for the United Nations International Year of Shelter. It was published in her first American collection *In Every Corner Sing* (1992) before reaching *Alleluia Aotearoa* (1993). The author commented in 1992 that this hymn 'written for refugees and the homeless in other places is now much more relevant in my own country. Here, housing has become a huge problem for the disadvantaged, and, sadly, the need for women's refuges is growing.' Just as sadly, as this Companion goes to press more than 30 years later, Shirley Murray's comments and her hymn text remain as relevant to the New Zealand scene as ever.

The hymn identifies Christian communities as 'people of the Way' (see Acts 9:2) with the implication that such a group ought to have an instinctive sympathy for travellers (refugees) of a different kind. Verse 1, line 4, refers to the Lord's Prayer ('give us this day our daily bread'), just as line 6 alludes to Matthew 8:20: 'Foxes have holes and birds of the air have nests, but the Son of Man has nowhere to lay his head.' Verse 2, line 1, may have been suggested by Sydney Carter's 1963 ballad, 'Standing in the rain,' which uses similar images of the homeless knocking on the window of a comfortable home-owner's dwelling. 'The least that is their right,' line 5, refers to the fundamental human right to adequate housing and shelter as recognised in the 1948 United Nations Universal Declaration of Human Rights. Verse 3 presents God-in-Christ as another homeless refugee (for the theological implications of ignoring such human need see Matthew 25:40). The 'borrowed rooms' include both the manger and the room where the Last

Supper was held; for the 'borrowed grave' see Matthew 27:57-60. Ephesians 2:19, 'No longer strangers...but members of the household of God,' is the basis of the final two lines of this verse. Verse 4 develops the idea of the family of God into a vivid picture of a group – all 'tenants of your love' – gathered round a fire, warming themselves 'in company with Christ,' and ends with a plea for a 'heart to feel' (cf. Ezekiel 36:26). 'Bond,' line 5, suggests both the tenant's legal agreement with the landlord and indebtedness, bondage.

KHAO I DANG The name of a huge camp in Thailand (1979-1993) eventually holding over 160,000 refugees from the brutal Pol Pot regime in Cambodia. Repatriation from the camp brought many Cambodian refugees to New Zealand in the 1980s, and it was acquaintance with some of these families that led composer **Colin Gibson** to name his tune after the camp. As Shirley Murray has said, the D minor tune 'evokes the dispirited lines of the homeless shuffling across the world.' It was written in 1988.

Here we bring small or great A62
Metre: 6.7.6.7 and refrain

This offering hymn was written for her St Andrew's on the Terrace, Wellington, congregation by **Shirley Murray** in 1991. She says, 'There seem to be very few hymns on money though the Gospel is full of it. I felt that our congregation might respond to something cheerful and positive while the offering was being taken up to the table, so I worked on this impulse, using Matthew 6:19-21 (in the Good News Bible) as basis.' The hymn was first published in the author's American collection *In Every Corner Sing* (1992), closely followed by *Alleluia Aotearoa* (1993).

As usual, the text is richly allusive. In verse 1, 'Tithe or token' (that is, large amount or small) refers to the biblical injunction (Leviticus 27:30-33) to give one-tenth of all produce and livestock to support the priesthood. 'Bread or stone' recalls Matthew 7:9, 'What man of you, if his son asks for bread will give him a stone.' Verse 3 is a close imitation of Matthew 6:19-20, and the refrain is taken from verse 21 in the same passage. Luke 12:24-28 forms the basis for the final verse: the biblical ravens and lilies of the field become 'wild flowers' and 'birds.'

ASHLEY The tune is named after the Reverend Ashley Petch, a Methodist minister directing national Stewardship (fund-raising) programmes for the Church at the time. The music is by **Colin Gibson** and was also written in 1991. Its tone is a response to Murray's request for something 'cheerful and positive' – and contemporary, as the final repeated phrase with its syncopation and sudden lurch into a flattened 7th chord in C shows. There is an alternative setting by Canadian composer **Ron Klusmeier** (Klusmeier 46).

Hold him tenderly (Cradle Song) H59
Metre: 9.9.7.7.9.7

This Christmas carol is taken from a cantata, *The Animals' Christmas*, written in 2003 for the choir and children of the Mornington Methodist Church by **Colin Gibson**. In the cantata, various animals popularly associated with the manger scene originally devised by **Francis of Assisi**, together with additional creatures including camels, a bantam hen, a rat and the local cat, relate their experience of the Nativity.

This text forms the song of the humans: in the musical Mary (as mother) sings the second verse to her 'precious boy,' while Joseph (as father) sings the third verse to his son, 'our darling little boy,' an arrangement that may be perpetuated by dividing a singing congregation into men and the women. In the final verse, Jesus is described as 'God's message to us all' (cf. John 3: 16). The cantata has received several productions beyond Dunedin, and there are CD and DVD records of live performances.

BRYANT STREET The tune, by the author, is named after the street address of the Reverend Donald Phillipps, who sang in the choir and was soloist for the third verse of this carol.

The simple melodic line, locked into the key of F major and imitated at a bar's distance by an optional instrument such as a flute, flows above a rocking bass line suggesting the hypnotic movement of a cradle.

Holy day, holiday C27
Metre: 6.6.10.11.10

Originally titled 'A Summer Carol,' this carol was written by **Jocelyn Marshall** in 1991 for the choir of St Peter's Cathedral, Hamilton, and was first published both in her collection *A Singing Faith* (1996), and *Carol Our Christmas* (1996), then in her *Hymns for All Seasons* (2007), where it appears twice, once as a plain text, and once with a setting by her son **Christopher Marshall**, written in 1993. In that year it was the winning entry in the Auckland RSCM Carol Competition, and as the author notes 'has subsequently been sung by choirs throughout the country.'*

The first verse of the carol celebrates the New Zealand summer landscape, the holiday time and the Christmas season in this country. Clematis is a native climbing plant with star-shaped white flowers (so, symbolic of the Christmas star), rata is one of the New Zealand equivalents of northern holly berries – pohutukawa is the other – spreading a cloud of red over New Zealand forests in summer. Verses 2-3 describe the life of the mature Christ. Verse 2, line 4 refers to the parable of the lost sheep (Luke 15:1-7) and to Christ's quotation from Isaiah 42:7 (Luke 4:18). Verse 3 honours the Pauline triad of faith, hope and love (1 Corinthians 13). Verse 4 echoes several Christian hymns which worship Christ as 'the new-born king' (for instance, 'Angels from the realms of glory' by James Montgomery (1771-1854)).

[SUMMER CAROL] This setting was written by **Christopher Marshall** in 1993 for his mother's text, and is intended for 4-part choral singing. Set in the celebration key of D major, and with the typical dancing rhythms of this combined song and dance form, the joyous music alternates between 3/8 and 2/4 time in something of a free, medieval manner.

*Jocelyn Marshall adds that 'It was a special moment for me when at an Artist Doctors' Concert in 1994, our youngest son, Dr Andrew Marshall, conducted this carol, with a Waikato Hospital choir he had formed.'

Holy! Holy! Holy! (Responses for Communion) F33
Metre: Irregular

This set of congregational responses for a Communion service was written by Dominican Sister **Cecily Sheehy** and first published in *Faith Forever Singing* (2000).

Originally intended to fit into sections of the Mass, the responses may be used in any service setting and for Protestant as well as Catholic celebrations of the Eucharist. The standard texts are supplied below for purposes of comparison, since the writer's versions contain alterations intended to express her own sense of 'creation spirituality,' which includes the substitution of male titles of supreme power, the displacement of a theology which distinguishes an upper heaven from a lower earth, which attributes to planet earth its own 'glory,' and which insists on salvation and mercy rather than on sinfulness.* The first text is a reworking of the Prayer over the Gifts section of the Mass. The Great Amen text comes from the fourfold Amens sung as congregational responses during the Solemn Blessing directed to be used 'on certain days or occasions.' The text of the Lamb of God section derives from one of the Memorial Acclamations of the People. The final text is a reworking of the congregational response which in the Mass introduces the Breaking of the Bread.

The music, by **Cecily Sheehy** herself, consists of various extensions of the simple 4-bar phrase used for the Great Amen. It is set in F minor to indicate the solemnity of the occasion. It resembles, but is not derived from the opening bars of the hymn tune STUTTGART.

*The following texts are taken from *The Community Mass Book Approved for use in*

New Zealand by the National Conference of Bishops of New Zealand (1975).

> Holy, holy, holy Lord,
> God of power and might.
> Heaven and earth are full of your glory.
> Hosanna in the highest.
> Blessed is he who comes
> In the name of the Lord.
> Hosanna in the highest! (page 28)
> When we eat this bread and drink
> This cup, we proclaim your death,
> Lord Jesus,
> Until you come in glory. (page 38)
> Lamb of God, you take away
> The sins of the world:
> Have mercy on us (x 2)
> Lamb of God, you take away
> The sins of the world:
> Grant us peace. (page 48)

Honour the dead H61
Metre: 10.10.10.10

When this hymn was written by **Shirley Murray** in 2005 it attracted almost immediate public attention and was publicly performed on Anzac Day, 25th of April 2005, at Wanaka (a town in the South Island) by the New Zealand Army Brass Band, using an arrangement of Colin Gibson's piano setting for brass band by Warrant Officer Wayne Bloomfield, and at Paraparaumu (a North Island town) by the Kāpiti Brass Band, using a separate arrangement by their conductor, David Wells. It was also sung over national radio by the boys' choir of Rathkeale College, Masterton, and has since been sung at Australian Anzac Day services and taken to Gallipoli and European memorial services for New Zealand and Australian soldiers. It was first published in the American collection of Shirley Murray's work, *Touch the Earth Lightly* (2008). New Zealand publication followed in 2009 in *Hope is our Song*. It was later published by the New Zealand Hymnbook Trust separately in a special edition (Palmerston North, 2008), with a translation into Māori by **Rangi McGarvey** and **Whirimako Black**, and a front cover reproduction of the famous painting, *Man with a Donkey,** by New Zealand artist Horace Moore-Jones.

Shirley Murray wrote the hymn in memory of her uncles, Norman and Jack, who served at Gallipoli [in Western Turkey, where New Zealand and Australian soldiers known as Anzacs – officially the Australian and New Zealand Army Corps – suffered huge losses fighting the Turkish Army for a narrow foothold on the Gallipoli peninsula], and to honour conscientious objectors, such as the Reverend Ormond Burton, who became a Christian pacifist after his heroic wartime exploits at Gallipoli and on the Western Front in France and Belgium. She says, 'I could not imagine writing a hymn for Anzac Day which did not give an honoured place to those whom other New Zealanders treated very brutally for their sincere beliefs.'

Describing Anzac Day as 'The most solemn day of our year,' Shirley Murray says, 'I wrote this hymn remembering two of my uncles who fought there as young soldiers. The old hymns traditionally sung on this occasion no longer reflect the ethos of successive generations. I felt it was time we had a New Zealand hymn which expresses our respect and gratitude, along with our abhorrence of war, yet honours also those conscientious objectors who were treated very shamefully in our prisons for refusing to fight.' In a Press release she asked, 'whenever you sing this hymn, don't focus on the past – think what you can do for positive peacemaking in your lifetime, and respect those who will never commit themselves to killing another family's son or daughter in warfare.'**

Verse 1, line 3, 'where poppies blow' [=toss in the wind, sometimes misprinted 'grow'] refers to the common wild flowers in the battlefields of France and Belgium; artificial poppies are now worn throughout New Zealand on Anzac Day as a symbol of those theatres of war where thousands of New Zealand soldiers died and were buried 'in a foreign grave.' There may be a memory here of John McCrae's World War I poem 'In Flanders Fields' (dated May 1915): 'In Flanders fields the poppies blow. / Between the crosses, row on row, / That mark our place.' Verse 2, 'buried in the mud,' refers particularly to the early battles in France where atrocious weather turned the fighting ground into a sea of mud. Verse 3, 'answered no bugle, went against the wall,' means 'refused the call to battle, and were lined up to be shot as prisoners of conscience.' This verse honouring conscientious objectors touches on an issue which is still contentious, and the verse is sometimes (unfortunately) omitted when the hymn is sung at Anzac and other public memorial services. The 'dream' (verse 5) refers to the dream of a peaceful world ('peace known in freedom').

ANZAC Named after the acronym for the Australian and New Zealand Army Corps familiar in both countries, the piano setting by **Colin Gibson** was written in 2005 for this text. It has been described as 'the perfect tune for this text, grounded in a C major-A minor tonality and moving at a solemn pace that conveys a sense of *gravitas*. The melody progresses within a limited pitch range, but at mid-point (bar 9) rises to a high C as if in an outburst of grief elsewhere contained within the melodic structure.' As Shirley Murray noted, the tune several times deliberately echoes the beginning of the traditional military bugle call, 'The Last Post,' played at a soldier's funeral. The original score included a descant for the final verse: it is printed with the melody in *Touch the Earth Lightly*. This hymn has been recorded on the CD *Hope is our Song* (2011), and in a fine arrangement for brass band played by the New Zealand Army Brass Band on the CD *Lest We Forget* (1997 and 2007).

*The painting shows a field medic using a donkey to carry a wounded soldier from the Gallipoli battleground. The painting exists in several versions, and was made in 1917 by former sapper Horace Moore-Jones from a photograph taken on the Gallipoli site showing Private Richard Henderson of Waihi (with Murphy the donkey) returning from Shrapnel Gully to Anzac Cove. Australians have claimed the painting as showing their own hero, John Simpson Kirkpatrick: the dispute remains unresolved.

**See further 'On writing a hymn for Anzac Day,' Shirley Murray. Kāpiti Coast: *Kapiti Independent News*, 25 April, 2014.

How happy you who work for peace
A63, HP10
Metre: 8.8.8.8

Described by the author, **Shirley Murray**, as 'an expansion of the beatitude about peacemakers' (Matthew 5:9), this hymn was written in 1985 and first published in Murray's privately issued collection *In Every Corner Sing* (Wellington, 1987). It then appeared in her first American collection *In Every Corner Sing (1992)*, followed by *Alleluia Aotearoa* (1993).

1985 was the occasion of an Ecumenical Service of Commitment to Peace held in Wellington Cathedral, commemorating the 40th anniversary of the nuclear bombing of Hiroshima, and this hymn was sung during the service to the well-known tune GONFALON ROYAL.

Shirley Murray explains to her American readers that '"Aroha" [verse 1] is a Māori word, rich in meaning, combining "love" with "warmth and wellbeing." But if it seems appropriate, the word "harmony" is another concept that would fit.' Elsewhere, the language of the hymn refers plainly to the explosion of the atomic bomb that destroyed Hiroshima on 6 August 1945 – 'destroy, defuse, the scars of earth, blast and bomb, air that radiated death, toys of war' – but such images are counterbalanced by a pastoral vision of tilling the earth, planting and green growth. 'Give life and health, as sun on snow' (verse 2) implicitly contrasts the death-dealing brighter-than-the-sun flash of the bomb with the life-giving radiance of the natural sun. Isaiah 2:4 and Clifford Bax's 1919 hymn 'Turn back O Man, forswear thy foolish ways' can be heard in the background: 'They will beat their swords into plowshares' becomes 'the glint of guns [i.e. gleaming guns] become the tools that till the earth and make it fair.' Verse 4, 'bend the rod' (from the proverb 'Bend the rod while it is still hot') here means 'bring about a change in attitude while it is still possible.'

GOSPEL OF PEACE Its name pointing to the biblical basis for the hymn, this hymn tune was created by **Ian Render** in 1991 to provide a New Zealand setting for Shirley Murray's words. Over a steadily moving bass and with natural modulations from B flat major to E flat major and G minor, a syncopated melody moves in close sympathy with the rhythm and words of the text: the emotional mood is caught up in the word *aroha*. GONFALON ROYAL was written in 1913 by Percy Buck (1871-1947) for the boys of Harrow School, and first published in his *Fourteen Hymn Tunes* (1913).

How is Jesus present? *A64*
Metre: 12.8.12.8

'How is Jesus present' was written by Dominican Sister **Cecily Sheehy** in 1980 as one of a series of such songs for children published in the Catholic magazine *Family Living*. Its first hymnbook appearance was in *New Zealand Praise* (1988), where it is printed in an arrangement for piano by Duncan McLeod, then in *Alleluia Aotearoa* (1993).

The biblical basis for this catechistic song (Matthew 28:20) is presented as a direct quotation in verse 4: 'I am with you always,' he said.' The text develops this as a question and answer dialogue, couched in simple language yet dealing with a serious issue for adults as well as children who fail to detect a 'visible' Jesus and might be worried by the thought of an ever-present ghostly 'presence.' The whole song has a deeper source still in the episode of 'doubting Thomas' (John 20:26-9), who exhibits the need for similar assurances of the risen Christ's reality.

The answers given present, in terms easily accessible to children, articles of Christian faith underpinned by scriptural references: so in the final verse, for 'WORD' see John 1:14; for 'PEOPLE' see Matthew 25:40, for 'BREAD' see Matthew 26:26.

[JESUS PRESENT] The tune by the author is simplicity itself, built out of a single 6-note phrase and ending its first repetition on the dominant chord of A major, but closing on the tonic D with the second repetition. With the exception of the fifth bar, which briefly touches the minor key of B, it remains within the tonality of D major, giving the whole dialogue the impression of a cheerful and confident interchange of voices.

How much am I worth *H63*
Metre: 10.8.10.8 and refrain

This unison hymn for children was written by **Colin Gibson** in 1981 and first published in *Singing Love* (1988) before reaching *Hope is our Song* (2009)

The hymn was occasioned by an incident reported to the author by a young Methodist minister who in the course of teaching a lesson to a Bible in Schools class in a small primary school at Broad Bay on the Otago peninsula discovered that the girls there felt completely overwhelmed by the boys and lacked any self-respect. The resulting text was written to affirm their worth as individuals and enable the singers to declare their own value before God. Although intended for young children, the message of the hymn can be related to many adults who may similarly feel disenfranchised in their own society. See also 'I've never seen an elephant,' *A76*.

Verse 2 refers to Matthew 10:29-31, Luke 12:6-7 ('Fear not; you are of more value than many sparrows); verse 3 to the parable of the lost coin (Luke 15:8-9); verse 4 to the story of the lost sheep (Matthew 12:10-14, Luke 15:3-6). Verse 5 refers to John 15:12-13. The original refrain was entirely personal, the singer was only 'I'; a focus on the community ('you' and 'we') was introduced at the suggestion of Indian Christians when some years later the hymn travelled to Calcutta.

LANGLEY Composed in 1981 by **Colin Gibson** for this text, the tune name refers to Tim Langley, the minister mentioned above. The setting in A flat major is intentionally simple and in the style of American

19th century gospel songs. The rise in pitch in the refrain underlines the insistent message of the whole text.

How small a spark H64
Metre: 10.10.10.10

This hymn was written by **Shirley Murray** in 1988 to mark the 250th anniversary of the conversion experience of John Wesley, founder of Methodism. She notes that 'Colin Gibson [the composer of the ALDERSGATE 88 setting] and I put some heart into this, since we were both Methodists.'

The verses celebrate the major points in Wesley's life. Verse 1 opens with a virtual quotation from a Charles Wesley hymn, 'See how great a flame aspires, / kindled by a spark of grace,' to develop Wesley's own description of his heart being 'strangely warmed' at the Aldersgate Street meeting place, London, where he experienced his religious reawakening on 24 May 1738. 'Warmed a bitter world' (line 2) alludes to the appalling conditions of life for the majority of ordinary people in 18th century England, which Wesley and followers energetically addressed. Line 4 refers to Wesley's practice of open-air preaching when his own Church of England pulpits were closed to him

Verse 2 picks up Wesley's challenge to ecclesiastical authority and restriction. 'The Good News…rides the road' (line 3) alludes to the travels on horseback which took the preacher throughout England – and also to Scotland and Ireland.

Verse 3 articulates the idea of Methodism as being 'born in song,' largely through the astonishing body of hymns created by John's brother Charles – more than 6,500 of them – setting out the doctrines and teachings of the new denomination. Its final two lines weave a semi-quotation from the fourth verse of 'And can it be that I should gain,' one of Charles' most famous (and most Methodist) hymns: 'My chains fell off, my heart was free, / I rose, went forth and followed thee.' The phrase 'loosened tongues' is taken from another Charles Wesley's hymn, celebrating the anniversary of his own conversion, 'O for a thousand tongues to sing': 'Him praise, ye dumb, / Your loosened tongues employ.'

Verse 4 rehearses the theme of the 'warmed heart,' and associates Wesley's conversion experience with similar but earlier encounters with Christ 'on beach, in upper room,' as recorded in the gospels.

ALDERSGATE 88 The musical setting by **Colin Gibson**, also written in 1988, was named after the Aldersgate Street meeting place, London, where Wesley experienced his religious reawakening. Wesley's own practice of riding the length and breadth of England to evangelise (it is estimated that he travelled over 225,000 miles in this way) is imitated in the 'galloping' rhythm of the music, which drives steadily forward in the celebratory key of D, with occasional excursions into the related keys of A minor and B flat major to add to the sense of a triumphant arrival 'home' at the close of each musical phrase.

I am standing waiting F34, HP11
Metre: 11.11.11.11

This hymn was written by **Shirley Murray** in 1990 in circumstances which she describes as follows: '1990 was the year of the United Nations summit meeting on the Rights of Children. St Andrew's on the Terrace hosted a special occasion where people of all faiths or none took part, but it was difficult to find something on the theme for us all to sing. "Au Claire de la lune" served very well with this rather simple text.'

This 'rather simple text' gains much of its emotional force from the dominant image of a small child variously characterized as starving, illiterate, ill, ignored and unloved, waiting at the singer's door for attention. So the Rights of Children are given a human face. Behind this image stands Revelation 3:20, 'Listen! I am standing at the door, knocking; if you hear my voice and open the door, I will come in to you and eat with you, and you with me.'

AU CLAIR DE LA LUNE (French=By the light of the moon). This is a well-known

French folk melody by an unknown composer, probably written in the 18th century. The original sexually suggestive text of the song has now been largely forgotten; it is frequently taught to New Zealand schoolchildren, so served as common ground for the St Andrews congregation. There is another setting by Canadian composer **Ron Klusmeier** (Klusmeier 9).

In the name of Christ H75
Metre: 10.8.10.8 and refrain

This hymn was written in June 2006 by **Colin Gibson**, in response to a commission from the Executive Committee of the Interchurch Council for Hospital Chaplaincy Aotearoa New Zealand to write a chaplaincy hymn for a national Hospital Chaplaincy Week held in September of that year. It was recorded and distributed among hospital chapels before being published in *Hope is our Song* (2009).

A number of the ideas present in the text were developed in the course of conversations between Ron Malpass, the National Executive Officer of the organisation, and the writer about the work of hospital chaplains, following a mandatory decision in 2004 that all hospitals must accommodate and respect their patients' spiritual and cultural beliefs and practices regarding death and dying. It also drew on the writer's appreciation over many years of chaplaincy care offered to his own wife during her time spent in hospital wards.

The concepts of hope, peace and faith referred to in the refrain are, of course, found in Christianity but are common to all the major faiths. Behind the final lines stands St Paul's account of love that never fails (1 Corinthians 13:8).

MALPASS This tune name acknowledges the executive officer responsible for initiating this commissioned work. Ron Malpass became President of the Methodist Church in 2004 and was also active in the New Zealand Association of Lay preachers. The setting was written in 2006 by composer Colin Gibson for his own hymn. Set in B flat major, the tune marches steadily on in a 'walking manner,' working variations on the two complementary phrases which constitute the 5-bar opening of the melody.

I am the light of the world W669
Metre: Irregular

This Epiphany carol was written by American songwriter **Jim Strathdee** and published in 1969 in the Strathdee's album *New Wine*, where it is described as written 'In response to a Christmas poem by Howard Thurman' and given the title it now holds (taken from John 8:12). Since its publication in *With One Voice* (1982) it has been published in several American and Canadian hymnals, including *The Chalice Hymnal* (1995), *The New Century Hymnal* (1995) and *Voices United: The Hymn and Worship Book of the United Church of Canada* (1996), as well as in *Songs: An Eclectic Lyric Collection of more than 580 Songs for Most Occasions* (1978).

Although there is much that is original, the text is based on the words of a Christmas litany by influential American author, philosopher, theologian, educator and civil rights leader Howard Thurman (1899-1981). It was written before 1969 and eventually published in Thurman's *The Mood of Christmas* (1973):

> When the song of the angels is stilled
> When the star in the sky is gone
> When the kings and princes are home
> When the shepherds are back
> with their flock
> The work of Christmas begins:
> To find the lost
> To heal the broken
> To feed the hungry
> To release the prisoner
> To rebuild the nations
> To bring peace among brothers
> To make music in the heart.

The text in *Alleluia Aotearoa* shows further revisions. Verse 2 of the Strathdee lyric reads 'To find the lost and lonely one, / to heal the broken soul with love, / to feed the hungry children with warmth and good food'; verse 3 reads 'To free the prisoner from all chains…To see God's children everywhere'; verse 4 reads 'To make music in an old person's heart.'

LIGHT OF THE WORLD The title of the song gives this carol its tune name. The music, by Jim Strathdee, has been arranged (simplified) by **Jillian Bray** to make it suitable for piano or organ.

I am the vine *F35*
Metre: 10.9.10.10

Shirley Murray, the composer of this hymn, written in 1994, explains that it was created in response to a request from Anglican vicar and composer **Ian Render** for a hymn text with a scriptural metaphor for the Christian Church. It was premièred at the first biennial National Forum of Cooperating Ventures, held in 1995 at Kāpiti (near the writer's Raumati home) under the title 'Growing Together.' This Forum represented five New Zealand denominational churches moving towards union through negotiations which eventually failed, though there remains a body, Uniting Congregations of Aotearoa New Zealand, which in 2010 administered more than 130 union or cooperating parishes, shared by two or more denominations. The hymn was first published in Shirley Murray's American collection *Every Day in Your Spirit* (1996), before appearing in *Faith Forever Singing* (2000).

The text is based on the metaphor of Jesus Christ as the vine and his followers as its branches, found in John 15:1-9. Verse 1 focuses on verse 5 of the biblical text; verse 2 on verses 1-3; verse 3 on verses 8-9. The poet's imaginative additions consist of the image of Jesus' spiritual life-force as coursing 'through stem and leaf, leaping, alive' (Hildegard of Bingen has a similar conception), in Murray's visualisation of 'grapes for the vintage wine [a technical term meaning high quality wine made from fruit harvested in a single year] sweet to the taste' and in the image of tendrils of faith, reaching out and growing strong – suggestive in the context of tentative moves towards church union.

ESKDALE Named after the Hawke's Bay community in Waiapu, the composer, Ian Render's diocese at the time, and written soon after 1994, this setting has been widely sung in New Zealand. It is conceived as a harvest festival dance and the harmonic soundscape – the music is set in D minor with mid-system modulations to G minor and F major – is distinctly Jewish in character. Ian render says the Jewish flavour of the melody was influenced by the well-known 'grapevine' dance steps. In *Every Day in Your Spirit* there is a different, more traditional hymnal setting by **Carlton Young**, named VINEYARD and set in E flat major. There is another setting by Canadian composer **Ron Klusmeier** (Klusmeier 15).

I arise this day *H65*
Metre: 8.6.8.6.9.8

This hymn text, written by **Robyn Allen Goudge** in 1999, was first published in *Hope is our Song* (2009).

Inspired by the opening line of a prayer of St Patrick, 'I arise this day through a mighty strength, the invocation of the Trinity,'* it draws on the Celtic tradition of steeping everyday tasks in prayer. As a poem, it has the simplicity of a Gaelic incantation, each half-line answering the other, with a final summarizing line acting as a refrain. A further Celtic element is the 'invocation of the Trinity,' an address to God, Christ and the Holy Spirit in each verse. Only the verb changes from verse to verse, and as the writer suggests, singers might make up further verses by supplying other verbs.

I ARISE The melody takes its name from the opening of St Patrick's prayer. It was written by the author, who composes to the harp, as is evident from the bass figuration. Like the text, the general musical style is Celtic in its melodic and harmonic construction.

*St Patrick (c.389-461) was the second bishop of Ireland and remains the country's patron saint. Born in Britain into a noble Roman family, he was captured and carried as a slave to Ireland where he learned the native language and became a devout Christian. Escaping after six years, he travelled to Gaul (northern France). He entered the Christian Church and was eventually ordained as a bishop in 432 at the age of 45. He returned to Ireland in 435 as a missionary. After 30 years of successful evangelisation he fixed his seat as a bishop at Armagh, where he was buried, leaving Ireland as a Christian country with a strong and active Celtic church. The prayer attributed to him, and known variously as the Deer's Cry and St Patrick's Breastplate was written c.433. There is an 11th century Irish hymn based on this prayer, translated into English as 'I bind unto myself this day the strong name of the Trinity.'

I cannot dance, O dancing Love
H66
Metre: 11.11.11.11

This hymn, rich in music and dance imagery, is by Canadian-born poet **Jean Wiebe Janzen;** one of a set of three such hymn-poems based on the writings of medieval women mystics. It was commissioned by the Mennonite Church, written in 1991 and first published in *Hymnal: A Worship Book* (1992). It has since appeared in American and Canadian hymn books such as *The Chalice* (1995*)*, *Voices United* (1997) and *Voices Found* (2003), before appearing in *Hope is our Song* (20009).

The poet's original source is a text by **Mechthild of Magdeburg** (1210-1282), a German medieval nun who described her visions of God in a book titled *The Flowing Light of Divinity (Das fließende Light der Gottheit)*, written between 1250 and 1270. A literal translation of the passage runs:

> I cannot dance, O Lord,
> unless thou lead me.
> If Thou wilt that I leap joyfully
> Then must Thou Thyself first dance and sing.
> Then I will leap for love,
> From love to knowledge,
> From knowledge to fruition,
> From fruition to beyond all human sense.
> There will I remain and circle evermore.

The evocative and original imagery of the hymn version of this passage deserves more detailed unpacking than a Companion can provide, but it is in verses 2 and 3 that Janzen develops lines of imagery only hinted at in Mechthild's words. Notable is the bird imagery traditionally associated with the Holy Spirit and frequent in mystical writing, and the image of the Holy Spirit as a woman playing on a golden harp surrounded by singers. An early hymn writer, St Ephrem the Syrian (c. 307-73), was known as 'the Harp of the Holy Spirit.' 'Her hands the currents round us' (verse 2, line 4) suggest that the poet was thinking of the wind harp or Aeolian harp which is played by the passage of the wind over its strings (see Coleridge's poem *The Aeolian Harp*, 1795). The third verse draws on images from round dancing, with '[dance] steps of mercy' leading to fuller knowledge of 'the dances of [Love's] heart.' The composer has added one word in the first line of the hymn, 'dancing,' as an attribute of Love; 'string' (bar 16) is a textual error for 'strings.'

MECHTILDE Named after the source poet for this hymn (Mechtild's name has a number of spelling variants), this setting was composed by **Colin Gibson** in 2005 for his Mornington Methodist choir. It provides a stately 4/4 dance rhythm in the bass over which the melody plays more freely, and introduces in melody and accompaniment a rising five-note motif suggesting harp music. The bass line in the final bars of each verse repeats the motif in reverse, downwards motion.

I come where trust and faith are tried H67
Metre: 8.8.8.8

This hymn was written in 1988 by **Colin Gibson**, who explains its genesis as follows: 'A text written after, as assistant organist [at Wakari Public Hospital chapel] I had noticed how seldom the hymns chosen for chapel services in local public hospitals, Wakari among them, spoke directly to the condition of the patients lying on their beds or seated on their hospital chairs. The hymn attempts to recognize the real test of faith in a hospital ward…or a crucifixion.' It was first published in the writer's first American collection, *Reading the Signature* (1994), before appearing in *Hope is our Song* (2009).

Couched as a personal address to Christ as 'risen Lord,' the first verse places the patient as doubting Thomas, desperately needing to touch Christ's 'wounded side' (John 20:24-25) but holding on to faith in an act of worship to God. In verse 2 the singer comes to identify the experience of 'pain and loneliness' now shared by him or herself with that of the crucified Christ. In verse 4 Christ's presence is invoked to help the singer endure the common hospital experience of helplessness in the face of death. The hymn closes with an expression of gratitude for the skilful care and healing that 'surrounds me here' and praise for Christ's love.

WAKARI The tune, written by author **Colin Gibson** in 1988, is named after Wakari Public Hospital, Dunedin, which represents the many hospitals where the experiences of suffering and courageous acts of faith described in the hymn text are daily witnessed. It was also the hospital where both the distinguished New Zealand poet Charles Brasch and the composer's mother, Ettie Margaret Gibson, died. It is composed for unison singing with piano accompaniment, with pauses between phrases to allow for the infirmity of many of the real singers. The melody is constructed out of a series of gently rising and falling patterns of notes; the underlying harmonies move from E major through B major, C sharp major and F sharp major to return safely to the tonic key.

I didn't hear the angels sing C28
Metre: 14.8.6

This carol was written towards Christmas 1972 by Gisborne hymn writer **Iris McCoy,** at a time when she was leading a Sunday School and writing new words for traditional or popular tunes known to the children. 'I recall that the words just flowed off the end of the biro. Like this one, many of my songs were written while weeding the garden, doing the ironing, or that type of hands-on work where the mind is relaxed.' The text treats the gospel account of the song of the angels, the arrival of the shepherds at the manger (Luke 2:8-16) and the gifts of the Magi (Matthew 2:9-11) from the viewpoint of a modern child or person of faith. The positive faith statements defining Christ as the bringer of joy, the shepherd of all and the gift of God are also biblical in source: see John 16:22, John 10:11 and John 3:16.

[ANGELSONG] This carol was set by **Colin Gibson** in 1984. The melody climbs to give full validity to the affirmation that closes each verse, supported by rising modulations from the tonic key, C major, through F and A flat Major before returning to the tonic key.

I know someone who watches over me (The Children's Saviour) A66
Metre: 14.14.14 and refrain

This children's song was written by evangelical writer and composer **Bonnie Low** in 1982. It reached *Servant Songs* in 1987, *New Zealand Praise* in 1988, *Alleluia Aotearoa* in 1993 and *Together in Song* in 1999.

Despite the informal, 'child-like' language ('He's got to be the nicest friend that I have ever had'), the list of attributes of Jesus which make up the text are biblically-based, and many of the phrases recall earlier hymns for children. The song, like many of its type, fundamentally reaches back to the episode in Luke 18:15-17 (and both Mark and Matthew's gospels) in which Jesus calls children to himself. The first line recalls an old gospel song written in 1905 by Civilla Martin and Charles Gabriel, 'His eye is on the sparrow…I know he watches over me.' Jesus is referred to as Shepherd (as in the 23rd Psalm), Lord and Saviour (cf. Harriet Mckeever's 'Jesus high in glory… Saviour, Lord, we come'), and Friend (cf. 'Jesus, friend of little children,' by Walter Mathams).

[THE CHILDREN'S SAVIOUR] The popularity of this text is undoubtedly due as much to the musical setting with its cheerful, dotted melody and its infectious chorus as it is to the simple phrases that make up the text. It is the work of the writer herself; a joyous world away from the earnest regularity of Victorian writers of children's hymns.

I sing the grace of God within you
H68
Metre: 9.8.10.9

This hymn of blessing was written to celebrate the marriage of the writer **Colin Gibson's** eldest son Marcus, at St Barnabas Church, Christchurch, in 1999, and is dedicated to Marcus and his wife Dorothy. It was incorporated into Gibson's cantata *The Spirit Within* (2000) as a congregational hymn before it was published in *Hope is our Song* (2009) and *New Hymns of Hope* (2010).

The Trinitarian text expresses a mutual recognition of divine grace, love and spiritual life in each other, and the creation of a new grace-filled, loving, spiritual whole in the partnership being formed. It may also be sung as a more general expression of equal self-respect and respect for all other persons. The biblical foundations are Genesis 2:23-4 and Mark 12:31, with its exhortation to love one's neighbour as one's self; but the structure of the hymn derives from a variation on the familiar formula of benediction: 'The grace of our Lord Jesus Christ, the love of God and the fellowship of the Holy Spirit be with us all, now and forever.'

GRACELAND The tune name acknowledges Paul Simon's song 'Graceland' (1986) with its reference to pilgrim travel with a companion, but it also plays on the idea of marriage (or relationship) as a site of grace. The music by **Colin Gibson** is in the style of a solemn spiritual, with the second half of the melody recapitulating the first but at a higher pitch; the single note at the beginning becomes a two-part 'song' in both the upper and lower staves, so miming the coming of two individuals into a new relationship. The hymn is supplied with a descant in his cantata *The Spirit Within*.

I toou arataa tikai W663
Metre: 8.7.11.10.8.7

This text has little obvious connection with the original hymn to which it is related through its tune, though a popular gospel hymn written for seamen and full of nautical imagery must have seemed attractive to those bringing the Christian message to a Pacific Island world. 'Jesus, Saviour, Pilot me,' was the work of pastor Edward Hopper (1816-1888) for the seamen who attended his New York Church of the Sea and Land, and first appeared in *The Sailors' Magazine and Seamen's friend*, April 1871, with a dedication to that magazine. It is not impossible that American Christian sailors were the first to introduce the hymn to the Cook Islands soon after its composition.

The unknown missionary writer of this text – London Missionary Society workers arrived in the Cook Islands as early as 1821 – virtually rewrote the Hopper original, which is a close working of the synoptic gospels' account of Jesus stilling the waves during a storm on the Sea of Galilee (Matthew 8:23-27, Mark 4:35-41, Luke 8:22-25). The extent of the changes can be seen by comparison between the simple instruction to converts given in verse 1 and 4 with verse 1 and verse 6 of Hopper's hymn:

Jesus, Saviour, pilot me
Over life's tempestuous sea;
Unknown waves before me roll,
Hiding rock and treacherous shoal.
Chart and compass come from thee;
Jesus, Saviour, pilot me.

When at last I near the shore,
And the fearful breakers roar
'Twixt me and the peaceful rest,
Then, while leaning on thy breast,
may I hear thee say to me,
'Fear not, I will pilot thee.'

PILOT This melody is adapted from a hymn tune written by **John Edgar Gould** (1821-1875) who first set the popular American gospel hymn, 'Jesus, Saviour, pilot me,' by Edward Hopper. The tune's original title was SAVIOUR, PILOT ME. Gould's music, written so it is said during the onset of an illness from which he later died, first appeared in *The Baptist Praise Book* (1871). The principal adaptation for Cook Islands singers consists of changing the original 3/4 time to 6/8 and smoothing out the original's dotted rhythms and strong march-style beat. The Cook Island version also does not commence as does Gould's melody on an upbeat, but the key remains unchanged in B flat.

I will comfort you A67
Metre: 8.9.8 and refrain

This hymn was written in the early 1980s by **John Weir**, at a time when he was collaborating closely with the hymn's composer, **Gerard Crotty**. Although the text had previously circulated among some Roman Catholic parishes, it was first published in *Alleluia Aotearoa* (1993).

The poet acknowledges Isaiah 66:13 (the basis of the refrain), and Psalm 46 as his sources. The Psalm is treated more freely: there is a rigorous selection of verses and the language is modernized (so 'a very present help' becomes 'so anxious to help'). Verse 1 corresponds to lines 1-2 of the psalm. Verse 2 corresponds to line 5; here the psalmist's 'city of God, the holy habitation of the Most High' becomes 'God is in our city,' probably indicating to the first singers their own city of Wellington rather any remote heavenly place. Verse 3 corresponds to line 9 of the original 11-line psalm. It might be suggested that there is a mismatch between the exultant praise of the power of God found in the psalm text and the personalized voice of the mother-comforter of the refrain; equally it might be argued that the text deliberately displays both masculine and feminine aspects of a personal protective deity and a national deliverer-God.

RUH [Arabic=spirit] The tune name suggests the Hebrew word *ruach*=wind, breath spirit, hence God as the Holy Spirit, the Comforter, and its connection with the text. The setting is by **Gerard Crotty**, in an arrangement for piano by **Jillian Bray**. The original was written for SATB choir, and there is a surviving earlier arrangement for congregational singing by **Douglas Mews**.

The adoption of a 3/4 rhythm allows for a rocking, lullaby-like rhythm, corresponding to the dominant image in the refrain of a mother calming a child. The refrain is made up of three short phrases beginning and ending on a tonic E chord, creating a strong sense of stability and assurance. The verses offer familiar sequentially-descending melodic phrases (cf. 'Kneels at the feet of his friends' by Tom Colvin, c.1965) with echoes of the melodic shape of the refrain. In the verses the harmony shifts to C sharp major, but quickly returns to E major.

I will talk to my heart in the stillness H69
Metre: 10.9.10.9 and refrain

This hymn was written by **Bill Wallace** in 2008 and first published in his American collection *The Mystery Telling: Hymns and Songs for the New Millennium* (2008), followed by *Hope is our Song* (2009).

The structure of the hymn text is unusual. While the verses are presented as personal affirmations ('I will dwell in the space of my oneness'), the refrain offers gnomic generalized wisdom ('trust the Way of inner prayer'). As the repeated phrase 'till compassion is my inner Way' indicates, the words of the hymn were written in the context of the development of Karen Armstrong's Charter for Compassion launched in February 2008. But the whole hymn expresses the writer's distinctive mystical and theological vision of personal wholeness, achieved by following a spiritual path ('my inner Way') that leads towards God by self-surrender to 'stillness' and watchful introspection over mind and soul. There are biblical echoes – cf. verse 1 with Matthew 5:24, and the refrain with Luke 17:21 – but the language of the text is replete with general spiritual concepts such as stillness, talking to one's heart, inner Way, oneness and letting go (of self-divisions).

STILLNESS The tune is named from the first line of the text. The music is by **Barry Brinson** and was written in 2008. Set in F major, it provides a singable melodic line expressing confidence and joy, rather than aiming to replicate the mysterious, numinous aspects of the text.

I'm a fishbowl Christian *F36*
Metre: 12.14.14.12

This hymn text and its setting were written in 1995 by **Colin Gibson**, after encounters with the aggressive convictions of some fundamentalist fellow Christians. The author describes it as 'a song for the people of some faith, who sometimes wish they were as totally committed as more enthusiastic Christians claim to be. The fourth verse is for the certain sure.' It was first published in the writer's second American collection, *Songs for a Rainbow People* (1998), then in *Faith Forever Singing* (2000).

The strategy of the hymn is to place its critique of over-zealous faith in the mouth of an envious but uncertain speaker. The first verse with its figure of a fretting goldfish with large ambitions to swim in the ocean of God's care was prompted by memories of a 1939 song, 'Three Little Fishies (Itty Bittie Pool),' by Saxie Dowell. The second verse changes the metaphor to the world of part-time as against full-time work. Verse 3 addresses the legitimate uncertainties of faith in comic metaphors of a wobbling jelly or the darting flight of a bat. Verse 4 places the 'certain sure' Christian as equally sharing in a troubled yearning – to break free from conventional 'bedrock' beliefs, to become 'flying' fossils. 'Jurassic Park' refers to the 1993 film, in which prehistoric creatures were revived and eventually displaced their human creators. Verse 5 changes again, to metaphors of light (see Matthew 5:15 and John 1:1-5). The 'glowworm' Christian yearns to flare out, to become a 'brilliant' ('intellectually outstanding,' literally 'shining') example of a Christian.

FISHBOWL The tune is named for the bowl of uncertainties which confines the frustrated fishbowl Christian. The musical style is popular, with syncopations, chromatic movement and enriched chords and a fundamentally simple tune over a standard rhythmic bass progression set in D major. The addition of an optional wordless descant completes the imitation of a contemporary secular piece of rock music.

I'm a living stone *H70*
Metre: 7.7.6.6.5.5.5.5 and refrain

Inspired by a sermon given in 2007 by the Reverend Stuart Grant in the Mornington Methodist Church on the text 'like living stones be yourselves built into a spiritual house' (1 Peter 2:5), this hymn, written by **Colin Gibson**, was introduced to the national Methodist Conference in that year and first published in *Hope is our Song* (2009). It carries a dedication to Paul Langston, a recent member of the Mornington Methodist choir directed by the composer.

Paraphrasing the biblical original, the refrain insists on the important place of each individual in a spiritual community, while the verses celebrate manifestations of that individuality, from prayer and praise (verses 1 and 4) to participation in communion (verse 2) and spiritual development (verse 3). A second theme is co-operation with the whole community: 'not a boulder, not a block' (punning on 'block of stone' and 'obstacle'). The singers are invited to consider themselves as neither insignificant (a pebble) nor a crucially important bastion of the faith (a rock), but as living building materials for the house of God, the household of faith.

LANGSTON The tune is named after the choir member to whom it is dedicated and should be sung in a relaxed yet disciplined way. It is conceived of as a set of echoing responses to a lead singer, or as performed by two complementary groups alternating in a psalm-like manner. This is a style imitating much African and gospel church music.

I'm gonna take another step (Treksong) *H72*
Metre: 7.11.7.11 and refrain

The informality of language and music in this song is explained by the fact that it was written in 1994 by **Colin Gibson** for a national Methodist Youth convention held in the South Otago town of Balclutha in 1995. The Convention took as its title, Youthtrek '95, with the sub-title 'Clearing the rubble.' The song was first published with other convention materials in 1995, then in *Hope is our Song* (2009).

The text develops the ancient image of the Way, one of the earliest Christian names for the faith, based on Jesus' description of himself as the Way (John 14:6). The refrain (lines 3-4) alludes to the mix of young men and young women present and to the social dynamics of the group. Verse 1 addresses the theme of the Convention, 'clearing the rubble' [of the past and cramping tradition]; 'thunk' is a coinage suggesting 'what I used to think." Verse 2 takes the singers mountain climbing and into fresh untrodden territory ('making footsteps in the snow'); they are to be sustained by 'gospel fish and chips,' alluding both to the many gospel descriptions of catching and eating fish as well as to the early Christian code sign for Jesus Christ, ICHTHYS. Verse 3 acknowledges the Christian past, Hebrews' 'great cloud of witnesses' (12:1); verse 4 introduces a sandalled, dancing Jesus, the ultimate object of the singers' search.

TREKSONG (Trek *Boer*=migratory journey) The tune, written by the author, takes its name from the title of the Conference. The setting is cast in a popular idiom which allows for relaxed and syncopated rhythms and chromatic melodic movement; radically different from the regular and somewhat staid rhythms of older, more traditional hymns.

I've got knees *A75*
Metre: 8.7.8.7.7 and refrain

'This was a fun song for Elizabeth when she was little,' says the author-composer of this hymn, **Rosemary Russell**, who wrote it in 1981 for her own daughter. 'God did indeed make us and delights when we walk His way with joy and obedience.' It was published in the first update to David Dell's *New Zealand Praise* (1986) before being included in *Servant Songs*, edited by Guy Jansen and Felicia Edgecombe in 1987, and *Alleluia Aotearoa* (1993), and it was later published in *Songs of Life*, by Felicia Edgecombe and Rosemary Russell (Wellington: Festivity Productions, 1996). There are textual variations in the final line of verse 2. The original reading, 'I've got a nose to smell the good things / God has made with me in mind,' becomes in *Servant Songs* and *Songs of Life* 'I've got a nose to smell out trouble, / God is always on my mind.'

Although the text hints at a background of mother-child games (e.g. 'This little piggy'), each named feature is given a religious application, beginning with the refrain: 'I've got a home on earth and heaven' (see John 14:2). Knees are for prayer, feet are for 'walking his way' (cf. John 14:6). Toes tapping 'to the praises / that we sing to him every day' may reflect life in the Russell household or services in the Titahi Bay Community Church, Wellington, of which the Russells have long been members. 'Ears to hear God's message' reflects Matthew 11:15; 'eyes to seek and find,' Matthew 7:7.

[I'VE GOT KNEES] The simple, happy tune, set in F major, its F arpeggio motif repeated six times, but with some lively syncopation, is perfectly suited to its target audience of young children. The version in *Servant Songs* and *Alleluia Aotearoa* begins with a 4-bar piano introduction which does not appear in either of the other two printings. In *Songs of Life* the melody line is detached from the piano accompaniment, which is considerably revised and simplified by the composer.

I've never seen an elephant *A76*
Metre: 8.9.8.9.8.8.8.8 and refrain

This unison hymn for children was written by **Colin Gibson** in 1981 and first published in *Servant Songs* (1987), followed by the author's own collection, *Singing Love* (1988), then in the first update to *New Zealand Praise* (1990) and *Alleluia Aotearoa* (1993).

The hymn was occasioned by an incident reported to the author by a young Methodist minister who in the course of teaching a lesson on the Bible to a class in a small primary school at Broad Bay on the Otago peninsula discovered that the girls there felt completely overwhelmed by the boys and lacked any self-respect. The resulting text was an oblique attempt to affirm their worth as individuals and raise their morale by means of a semi-comical poem recognizing and respecting the abilities and deficiencies of both animals and humans. The refrain enables its singers to plainly declare their own value before God. See also 'How much am I worth,' *H63*.

The mocking-bird is introduced to suggest the teasing that went on in the class, and the spelling 'peli-can' signals a pun on 'can=container' (referring to that bird's huge and capacious beak) and 'is able [to hold].' There have been various substitutions for the named creatures in other singing places where the unknown animals are familiar ones: for instance, 'platypus' for 'crocodile' in Australia. This is a legitimate ploy for any of the animals, fish or birds named in the text.

ALL CREATURES Composed in 1981 by **Colin Gibson** for this text. The tune name intentionally alludes to the older hymn, 'All things bright and beautiful,' written in 1848 by **Cecil Frances Alexander**. The manuscript of the present music gives the instruction 'Jauntily,' and the 4/4 march rhythm in the key of F major, with its simple harmonies, suggests an elephants-on-parade feeling to the setting. There is at least one other (1994) setting, written for the Choristers' Guild by American composer Austin Lovelace.

Ia tatou vivii atu nei A65
Metre: 14.14.14.14 and alleluias

A modern hymn of praise in the Samoan language, written by Deacon **Kelemete Ta'ale**. It was published in *Alleluia Aotearoa* (1993).

While the text is original, it has its basis in the language of the psalms. As a hymn praising God as the creator of 'all things that make us live,' there are close and frequent parallels with Psalm 8. The second verse, 'Make a joyful sound to the Lord God, he is love,' draws on Psalm 100, as well as 1 John 4:8.

IA TATOU VIVII Although it is described in *Alleluia Aotearoa* as a 'traditional' Samoan melody, this four-part choral setting is probably an adaptation of the music of a gospel song brought to Samoa by early missionaries. Its opening phrase recalls George Bennard's 1913 gospel hymn 'The Old Rugged Cross,' but the present writer has been unable to further identify the actual source.

If I take the wings of the morning
A68
Metre: 9.8.10.5.8

This text, drawn from Psalm 139:7-12, was written by **Nigel Eastgate** in 1991. It was first published in 1993 in *Alleluia Aotearoa*. The original manuscript shows some signs of revision: 'take' replaces 'took' (verse 1), and 'from paths of despair' replaces 'journeys to Hell' (verse 4).

This version of the Psalm plainly comes from the hand of a physician interested in the psychology of his patients (or himself). It does not suggest that the singer is fleeing from God's tremendous presence or hiding in the depths of the sea; rather, engaging in adventurous flight over the ocean, accompanied by the reassuring presence of a protective God ('my God'). In verse 2, the writer introduces the image of entrance gateway and portal into unexplored territory (cf. 'If I make my bed in Sheol'), and in the spirit of Bunyan's Pilgrim, declares fearlessness in the present of spirits of evil or death. Similarly, in verse 3, the writer introduces new images of imprisonment in and blindness caused by the dark (cf. 'Let darkness cover me') which are defeated by God as the 'giver of light.' The final verse makes explicit the new slant given the original words: the singer is not escaping from the fearful magnificence of God, as in the Psalm, but from the psychological terrors of despair and death. The life journey begun in verse 1 is completed in full confidence of God's companionship.

[WINGS OF THE MORNING] The tune was unnamed by the composer. Set in F major for four-part choir and in 3/4 time it has the rhythm of a gentle dance, with a lilting effect generated by the four appearances of a dotted note motif. Each section of the melody takes the shape of an arch, gradually declining in height and shortening in length, but altogether suggesting the rising and descent patterns of the flight of the soul described in the opening lines.

If one could speak H73
Metre: 11.10.11.10

The précis of 1 Corinthians 13 which forms the basis of this text was written by **Peter Haskins** in 2001. Verses 1 and 2 correspond with 1 Corinthians 13:1-2; verse 3 draws on 1 Corinthians 13:4-10. The final verse is based on chapter 13:11-12. The occasion of the hymn was a commission for a new School Song, from Gillian Heald,* the retiring Principal of Rangi Ruru Girls' School, Christchurch, one of the top-ranking secondary colleges in New Zealand, a school for young women taking both day and boarding pupils, founded in 1889 and administered by the Presbytery of Christchurch. The school's motto is *Whaia to te Rangi* (Māori=seek the heavenly things), indicating that its educational programme includes a spiritual dimension as well physical, cultural and academic studies.

RANGI RURU (Māori=wide sky shelter). The tune is named after the school. This setting was created in 2002 by **Colin Gibson** as a unison hymn with a descant for the fourth verse. There is both a piano arrangement and an organ score. The composer has attempted to invest the tune with something of the *gravitas* of **Ralph Vaughan Williams'** SINE NOMINE, as befits the School Song of such a distinguished educational institution.

> *Gillian Heald was awarded the MNZM in 2010 for services to education, following a long and successful career in secondary and tertiary education and leadership at a national and international level. As well as heading mathematical education at Christchurch Teachers College, she was Principal of Rangi Ruru for 14 years and co-Principal of Unlimited Paenga Tawhiti, an innovative secondary school which she founded in 2003. She became a prominent consultant in education to the Government and other educational institutions and held a number of Board directorships,

If you shut your eyes (Open your Eyes, open your Ears) H74
Metre: 8.6.8.6 and refrain

A search for a hymn dealing with poverty in New Zealand, to be distributed by the Methodist Church's social agency as a resource for its Lent 2004 theme of 'Poverty – listening, hearing,' prompted the writing of this text by **Colin Gibson** in 2003. It was dedicated to Janet Marsh, the Methodist minister with a strong and active social conscience then working in the ironically named Bay of Plenty, who led the search. The text was first published in *Hope is our Song* (2009) and later made available by Christian World Service.

The words were inspired by too much exposure to public television images safely presenting poverty as a distant domestic spectacle. The hymn takes the form of a dramatic monologue of the kind popularised by Sydney Carter in such hymns as 'When I needed a neighbour' (1965) and 'Standing in the rain' (1964), in which an imaginary character speaks through the singers – a congregation probably including a number of the relatively affluent.

Here the voices of poverty are personified: in verse 1, a representative of many poor, and a mere shadow on the wall – that is, a television image – though the word 'shadow' also suggests an unsettling element of darkness in an otherwise well-lit, comfortable world; in verse 2, a woman begging in the street, unable to pay both for food for her children and adequate lodging; in verse 3, another woman physically abused and driven into prostitution by poverty; and in verse 4, standing with the poor, Christ, begging for a coin, finding the shame of poverty as bitter as any crucifixion. While imaginary, these voices describe the realities of modern poverty in New Zealand as elsewhere. Biblical passages are sourced, too: the refrain alludes both to the Beatitude referring to the poor (Luke 6:20) and the parable of the great banquet (Luke 14:15-24).

SONG OF THE POOR The setting for these words, also written by **Colin Gibson,** is dramatic rather than pious in character. The

D minor melody supporting the verses refers ironically to the early American folk tune 'Bound for the promised land.' The refrain changes to heavy triplets and a limited melodic range to convey a sense of helpless misery, of shuffling feet, of the Christ begging for a spare coin. Not a comfortable melody or a comfortable mood, but neither is the subject.

In the name of Christ H75
Metre: 10.8.10.8 and refrain

This hymn was written in June 2006 by **Colin Gibson**, in response to a commission from the Executive Committee of the Interchurch Council for Hospital Chaplaincy Aotearoa New Zealand to write a chaplaincy hymn for a national Hospital Chaplaincy Week held in September of that year. It was recorded and distributed among hospital chapels before being published in *Hope is our Song* (2009).

A number of the ideas present in the text were developed in the course of conversations between Ron Malpass, the National Executive Officer of the organisation, and the writer about the work of hospital chaplains, following a mandatory decision in 2004 that all hospitals must accommodate and respect their patients' spiritual and cultural beliefs and practices regarding death and dying. It also drew on the writer's appreciation over many years of chaplaincy care offered to his own wife during her time spent in hospital wards.

The concepts of hope, peace and faith referred to in the refrain are, of course, found in Christianity but are common to all the major faiths. Behind the final lines stands St Paul's account of love that never fails (1 Corinthians 13:8).

MALPASS This tune name acknowledges the executive officer responsible for initiating this commissioned work. Ron Malpass became President of the Methodist Church in 2004 and was also active in the New Zealand Association of Lay preachers. The setting was written in 2006 by composer **Colin Gibson** for his own hymn. Set in B flat major, the tune marches steadily on in a 'walking manner,' working variations on the two complementary phrases which constitute the 5-bar opening of the melody.

In the name of Christ we gather
A69
Metre: 8.7.8.7.8

Subtitled 'Hymn for an Ordination,' this text was written in 1988 by **Shirley Murray** to mark the ordination of two women friends, one an Anglican priest, the other a Presbyterian minister, who asked for 'an inclusive language hymn with some contemporary relevance.' It was then used for an even more significant occasion, the installation in 1989 of the world's first woman Anglican (Episcopal) Diocesan Bishop, Dr Penelope (Penny) Ann Bansall Jamieson, in St Paul's Cathedral, Dunedin. The present final verse was added for this event. The author notes that '"servant" could be substituted for 'daughter' if inclusiveness is to be consistent.'

The solemn liturgical occasion for which the hymn was written explains the significant presence of liturgical language, as in the opening line of verse 1 (derived from Matthew 18:20) and verse 2 (derived from 2 Corinthians 6:18). Verse 2, line 3 references the calling of the first disciples (Matthew 4:18-22, Mark 1:16-20); lines 5-6 describe the sacraments of communion and baptism. For the image of the 'commonwealth of Christ' see Ephesians 2:12. 2 Timothy 4:2 is drawn on for verse 3, lines 1-2. Verse 4 describes the solemn ritual of the laying on of hands used in many denominations as part of the ordination ceremony, symbolising the invocation of the Holy Spirit to empower the recipient. Verse 5 draws on Isaiah 42:1 (quoted in Matthew 2:18). Line 3 alludes to John 1:14 and Luke 2:7. Line 8 is compressed: 'also born in each of us who shows Christ-like love to others.'

KNOX COLLEGE The tune is named after the Presbyterian Theological Hall in Dunedin, where one of the woman candidates had been trained. The music is by **Colin Gibson** who wrote it for Murray's text in 1988. Set in G minor, the style is that of measured and confident march. The alternative tune,

WESTMINSTER ABBEY, is by Henry Purcell (1659-95), and was drawn as a separate hymn tune from the 'alleluia' section concluding Purcell's verse anthem 'O God, thou art my God,' preserved in William Boyce's *Cathedral Music, volume 2*, 1760. The tune received its present name in the 1939 edition of Hymns Ancient & Modern, and was made popular by its use during the weddings of Princess Margaret in 1960 and Prince Charles in 1981. Shirley Murray says that 'WESTMINSTER ABBEY is the tune to which I wrote this [hymn], but KNOX COLLEGE…provides a strong, fresh setting.'

In the presence of your people (The Celebration Song) A70
Metre: 8.5.8.5.8.5.8.5

The words of this chorus by **Brent Chambers** were created for a tune he had already constructed in May 1977. According to the author, the words of the second quatrain, 'Let us celebrate your goodness…' were written first, in phrases generally reminiscent of passages in the psalms. The first quatrain, 'In the presence of your people…' was drawn more precisely from Psalm 22:22-25. The song was initially recorded on a 1977 LP and cassette album, *Father, make us One,* and co-published by Scripture in Song in that year in a music book of the same name. The chorus then appeared in *New Harvest* (1979) under the title of 'The Celebration Song,' with a counter melody for verse 2. In 1981, the second volume of *Scripture in Song: Songs of the Kingdom* printed the music without the counter melody and in notes half the value of those in the *New Harvest* version. It is probable that *Songs of the Kingdom*, though published later, offers the original version of the song, while the *New Harvest* version is a later elaboration of the music. It is the *Songs of the Kingdom* version which was the source for the music and text printed in *Alleluia Aotearoa* (1992). *Together in Song* (1999) reprints the *New Harvest* elaborated version.

CELEBRATION SONG This tune name came about from the suggestion of a friend who had heard the melody Brent Chambers composed after attending in 1977 an evening of folk dancing and ethnic music, and when asked what it suggested to her replied that it sounded like a celebration. The music is strongly Hebraic in character, explained by the fact that the composer 'was exploring the Jewish roots of Christianity in those years.' Some of its Jewish features are the strong off-beat start, the clusters of fast quaver (quarter) notes, and the D minor tonality, modulating rapidly through G minor, C major, F major and B flat major before returning to the home key. In *New Harvest*, the composer suggests that the music should go 'With an Israeli feel.'

In the quiet of this day F37
Metre: 7.7.7.7

This hymn was written by **Shirley Murray** in 1997, in response to a tune sent to the author by her friend **Jillian Bray**. Starting in a self-reflective mood of weariness and tension unusual in this writer, this hymn takes its singers from a confession of exhaustion and unresolved strain ('I am tired and out of tune…I am fearful and alone') through to a grateful abandonment to the Holy Presence, 'more than lover, more than friend' and a conclusion in a quiet act of worship, with the repetition of the word *alleluia* (Hebrew='praise to God'). Verse 2 alludes to Jesus' calming of the storm on Galilee (Mark 4:35-40), and verse 3 to the story of the Prodigal Son's return to his home and loving father (Luke 15:11-32).

The text was first published in *Hope Supplement 99* (1999), then in *Faith Forever Singing* (2000) with the setting by Jillian Bray which had sparked its creation. When it was later published in the American collection *Faith Makes the Song* (2003), it was given a different setting, RESPITE, by New Zealand composer **Jenny McLeod**.

TE PIRINGA (Māori=the refuge) Originally named LYDIA by its composer, **Jillian Bray** (who at the time was naming tunes after biblical women she admired), this melody was renamed TE PIRINGA when it was realized that there was a much earlier and well-known hymn tune called LYDIA, attributed to

Thomas Phillips (1844). Shirley Murray was to say of it, 'LYDIA has haunted me since I first heard it. More and more it has become a "first person" rather than a community sort of hymn tune, and finally it has settled into a small meditation.' Lydia was an early convert to Christianity who later supported the apostle Paul and Silas (Acts 16:14-15, 40). Jillian Bray comments that 'her tone colour, purple, suited the mood of the tune' [Lydia was a seller of the hugely expensive Tyrian purple cloth].

Written in 1996, TE PIRINGA has a Celtic sense of tonality, ending in G major but beginning in E minor, and a melodic shape that sinks downwards then turns upwards in a way that might easily suggest a pattern of physical or spiritual exhaustion followed by a gentle recovery. There is a further setting of the text by Canadian composer **Ron Klusmeier** (Klusmeier 35).

In the shaking of God's mantle *A71*
Metre: 8.7.11

While she was studying in 1986 at the Institute of Culture and Creation Spirituality at Oakland, California, **Betty Wendelborn**, composer of this text based on a saying by the 12th century German abbess and mystic **Hildegard of Bingen** (1098-1179), says, she was 'so captivated by the beautiful songs of the mystics that I immediately set to work to translate them into musical settings.' This song, along with 63 others by various authors, was the result, first published in the collection *Sing Green: Songs of the Mystics* (Auckland, 1988).

In the first of three books describing her mystical visions, *Scivias* ('Know the Way'), completed in 1151, Hildegard attributes to God the words, 'In the shaking out of my mantle you are drenched, watered, with thousands of drops of precious dew. Thus is humanity gifted.' This is paraphrased to form the text of the first verse. The second verse is constructed out of other sayings and ideas: 'The Holy Spirit streams through and ties together Eternity and Equality so that they are one' is a saying found in Hildegard's *Letters* (translated Adelgundis Fuhrkotter, Salzburg, 1965, 68-70). Throughout her writings – and in the writings of contemporary mystics like Meister Eckhart – compassion is referred to as the primary characteristic of God.

The highly original image of God shaking drops of dew from his mantle (a long enveloping cloak like the one frequently seen in images of the Virgin Mary, and in a self-portrait of Hildegard illuminating her own writings) has to do both with the biblical belief that dew, like rain, falls from heaven (see Deuteronomy 32:2) and with Hildegard's own distinctive theology of *viriditas*, the 'greening power of God' (cf. 'I am the rain coming from the dew that causes the grasses to laugh with the joy of life').

HILDEGARD The piano setting is by **Betty Wendelborn**; it was written in 1986 and published in 1988. The melody imitates in a rapidly descending four-note scale the fall of dew and rain; the original bass line sweeps upwards to meet it like a chord played on a harp.

In the singing *F38*
Metre: 8.8.8.8.11.11

Originally written at the request of Professor **Peter Godfrey** as a text to be set for his Kāpiti Chamber Choir, of which the author was a member at the time, this hymn by **Shirley Murray** was written in 1994 under the title 'Invocation.'

The text presumes a communion occasion, with the ritual blessing and breaking of bread by the presiding minister or priest, members of the congregation waiting to receive it with their open hands, and the community's belief in the presence of Christ at such a moment. Verse 2, in a way typical of this writer, widens the implications of such a ritual moment. The 'circle of your people' may be the group gathered round the communion table or the wider congregation; the spiritual transaction from question to answer, acceptance, heart's cry and healing is left open to individual singers' interpretation. The refrain, too, puts the writer's characteristic take on the meaning of the ritual of communion. An experience of Christ's 'grace' and 'peace' replaces the older emphasis on a theology of atonement. The concept of 'the bread of peace' probably derives from Proverbs 17:1 ('Better is a dry morsel with quiet than a house full of feasting with strife') as well as from Jesus' teaching on peace.

BREAD OF PEACE Named from a phrase in the refrain, this serene setting in the unusual key of D flat major was written by American composer **Carlton Young**. Murray describes it as 'this simple and beautiful congregational setting,' and notes that the composer supplied it with the comment, 'I've tried to keep it uncomplicated, with the notion that in time those coming to the distribution [of the communion elements] might sing it from memory.'

In this familiar place *A72*
Metre: 6.8 and refrain

The text was written by **Colin Gibson** in 1985 and was first published in *Singing Love* (1988).

The author writes of its circumstances of composition: 'In 1985 I was in England on sabbatical leave from my university (the University of Otago, Dunedin). English friends assisted us in finding accommodation, and in the village of Freeland, a few miles out of Oxford, and as part of a tiny congregation worshipping in the literally 'narrow sphere' of its 180-year-old Methodist chapel, my wife, our daughter and I found all the warmth of friendship and devotion we had known in our much larger church on the other side of the world. The words of "In this familiar place" were written down as I walked down Chapel Lane (as it was then named) to our temporary home after an evening service, and record the awareness that God is to be found in every here and now. The melody came almost immediately after.'

FREELAND Composed by **Colin Gibson** in 1985. The tune name refers to the English village near Oxford, where the hymn and its setting were written down. Grounded in D major, the harmonic shifts in to A minor and G major distinguish the refrain from the simple affirmative tone of the verses, and a melodic descent from a heaven-high D to the earthed tonic note underpins the final phrase, 'I praise and thank you for this here and now.'

In trust we come *H76*
Metre: 8.10.8.9

Marnie Barrell wrote this text in 2007, prompted by the tune WHAKATEITEI, sent to her much earlier by Wellington composer and music teacher **Jillian Bray**. It was first published in *Hope is Our Song* (2009) and is on the SongSelect website. An early draft of the text shows that a number of changes were made before the hymn reached its present form.

Barrell says that the idea behind the first verse came from a line in an old hymn [John Newton's 'Come, my soul, thy suit prepare, / Jesus loves to answer prayer' (*Olney Hymns*, 1779)], 'thou hast come to meet a King, / Large petitions with thee bring.' I think I'd been reading some devotional material about prayer, and the image of God "storing our tears in a bottle" was strong for me. Also something half-remembered from studying at St John's [Theological College, Auckland] – an essay by Beverly Wildung Harrison, *The Power of Anger in the Work of Love* – surfaced as the line about our disappointment, anger and lament containing the power to make positive changes. "Living our Amen through every day" came partly from a sermon I'd heard that urged us to be an active element in the answers to our own prayers.'

The hymn takes some of its language from the Prayer of Humble Access offered before Communion in many Christian traditions ('We do not presume to come…trusting in our own righteousness'). Although the verse opens with a description of the varied experiences brought into the presence of God ('pain… hope'), the emphasis falls on 'our need' as 'our only offering.' Verse two is a prayer for strength to comfort others in their need, alluding in the final line to Galatians 5:22, 'the fruit of the Spirit is love, joy, peace.' Verse 3 opens with a quotation from the 1928 *Book of Common Prayer*, 'Almighty God, to whom all hearts are open, all desires known,' and goes on to stress the necessity to put the powerful emotions of 'disappointment, anger and lament' to positive use or, as the *Book of Common Prayer* puts it, 'to further the work of the Church in the world' (cf. 'to further your work their worth be spent'). Verse 4 focuses on acceptance and obedience, opening with a quotation from the Lord's Prayer, 'Your will be done,' and closing with an echo of the *Book of Common Order*, 'trusting your purposes ('We trust in your good purposes').

WHAKATEITEI (Māori=grow tall, develop your pride of self) This melody was written in 1998 by **Jillian Bray**. The vigorous, march-like opening phrase corresponds well with the text's final resolution to 'go to live our Amen ['so let it be'] through every day.' Beginning in E flat major, the harmony modulates to B flat major, then, as the tune sinks quietly down towards the final tonic note, finds its way back through imperfect resolutions in E flat until it reaches a full cadence, creating what Marnie Barrell responded to as a mood capable of generating the idea of a prayer-hymn dealing with need, suffering, compassion and service to others.

In what strange land H77
Metre: 9.4.9.4.9.9.9.4

Shirley Murray wrote this text in 2005 as a meditation on Psalm 137:4, 'How shall we sing the Lord's song in a strange land?' (King James version). It first appeared in her American collection *Touch the Earth Lightly* (2005), before being taken into *Hope is our Song* (2009).

The original Biblical passage expresses the despair of an exiled people carried into captivity in Babylon after the fall of Jerusalem in 587 CE. Shirley Murray's text addresses a parallel sense of dispossession; she writes, 'The "strange land" here is our contemporary world, if we are still tied to a childish faith and frightened to move into the challenges of [modern] theology, let alone technology. It's about "testing our faith in a different sphere," even to updating the hymns we sing and treasure.'

The language of modern (computer) technology appears, representing the new strangeness of things – 'code, delete, cursor' – and there is reference to the recent astronomical discoveries of an expanding universe, filled with uncounted galaxies dwarfing our own (verse 2, lines 5-8). At the same time, biblical allusions remind us of ancient willingness to change and adapt: verse 3, line 5 references 1 Corinthians 13:11 ('When I was a child, I spoke like a child, I thought like a child, I reasoned like a child; but when I became a man I gave up childish ways'); verse 4, line 1, references Psalm 40:3 ('He put a new song in my mouth'), and line 5 alludes to Matthew 7:9 ('Is there anyone among you who, if your child asks for bread, will give a stone?'). Reassuringly, also, the repeated 'O God, my God' (derived from Psalm 63 ('O God, thou art my God, I seek you…in a dry and thirsty land where no water is') confirms the undaunted faith of the speaker.

MYSTERIUM (Latin=mystery). This setting was written in 2005 by **Colin Gibson**. The tune name refers to the 'strange land' described in the text. Although the dominant key is E minor, into which the melody finally settles, a disturbing alternation of minor and major keys represents in music the experience of strangeness, leaving the singer poised between minor and major tonalities. The final cadence has much the same function, as it leads the singer to expect a resolution in A major, which is denied, and replaced with a confirmed E major close in the final bar of the setting. There is another setting by Canadian composer **Ron Klusmeier** (Klusmeier 44).

Into the hands (A Farewell) H78
Metre: 9.8.9.8

This funeral hymn by **Shirley Murray** was written in 2007 in response to a personal loss. It was first published in her American collection *Touch the Earth Lightly* (2008), closely followed by its appearance in *Hope is* *our Song* (2009). The italicized words make it available for the loss of a person of either sex.

The primary source of the text, as the author confirms, are words by French philosopher and Jesuit priest Pierre Teilhard de Chardin (1851-1955), in his *Hymn of the Universe* (1961):

> Into the hands which broke and quickened the bread, which blessed and caressed little children, which were pierced with the nails, into the hands of which one can never tell what they will do with the object they are holding, whether they will break it or heal it, but which we know will always obey and reveal impulses filled with kindness, and will always clasp us ever more closely, ever more jealously; into the gentle and mighty hands which can reach down into the very depth of the soul, the hands that fashion, which create, hands through which flows out so great a love: into these hands it is comforting to surrender oneself, especially if one is suffering or afraid. And there is both great happiness and great merit in so doing.

However, the first line of the hymn echoes Mark 10:16, 'And he took [the children] in his arms and blessed them, laying his hands upon them.' The final verse echoes phrases from the funeral service of the *Book of Common Prayer* and other similar liturgies: Job 1:21, 'Naked I came from my mother's womb, and naked I will leave this life. The Lord gives, and the Lord takes away'; Genesis 3:19, 'dust you are and to dust you will return.' But the final line makes use of John 3:6: 'What is born of the flesh is flesh, and what is born of the Spirit is spirit.'

ADIEU (French=farewell) The tune takes its name from the title of the poem. It was written for this text in 2007 by American scholar and composer **Carlton (Sam) Young**. Shirley Murray comments, 'The gentle and intuitively tender tune sent me by Sam Young seemed completely right for this text.' Young's melody and at times the underlying harmony is haunted by the Celtic melancholy of the similar Irish tune, 'O Danny Boy.'

Is there no other way? *A73*
Metre: 8.8.8.8

This hymn by **Colin Gibson** was published in the author's 1988 collection *Singing Love* before reaching *Alleluia Aotearoa* (1993).

It was written in Oxford, England, in 1985, following a street encounter with an Iranian collecting money to purchase weapons for forces opposing the Islamic Revolutionary Republic, which had been established in 1979. Gibson says, 'When I refused his request, arguing for more peaceful measures and affirming that was an alternative way to violence to achieve the ends he sought, the Iranian man left, shouting out, "But there is no other way!"'

The three verses develop the argument for a non-violent response to oppression and brutality, drawing on Jesus' rejection of the doctrine of retaliation in Matthew 5:38-39. As contemporary instances of violence, verse 1 alludes to children hurling stones and curses at British tanks in the streets of Belfast during a time of political unrest there (line 2), as well as the brutal methods totalitarian states employ to break down political prisoners. Line 7 quotes the Exodus injunction to violent retaliation, 'Life for life, eye for eye' (21:23). Verse 2 refers to the long history of human violence, culminating in 'the winter bomb'; scientists at the time of writing were predicting a perpetual northern hemisphere winter brought about by the use of atomic weapons. Verse 3 renounces hate and violence as leading to total catastrophe ('loss') and embraces the way of the crucified Jesus ('take up your cross and follow me,' Luke 9:23).

BROAD STREET The tune carries the name of the central Oxford street where the conversation sparking this hymn took place. The relentless C minor totality and the downward pressure of the melody symbolize the destructive force of the violence against which the hymn argues.

Is this the end of the world? A74
Metre: 11.11.11.14

This powerful peace hymn was written by Dominican Sister **Cecily Sheehy** in 1986, and first published in her own collection *Beautiful Blue-Green Planet and other songs of cosmic connection* (c.1987), under the title of 'What in the World!' before reaching *Alleluia Aotearoa* (1993).

Cast as an inner dialogue with one's self, this hymn text heaps question on question, searching for the presence of Christ in a warring world and discovering both conflict and its possible resolution within the divided self.

The first verse announces the four themes of the following text: the contemplation of the possible total destruction of the planet, (see 'Is there no other way?' A73); the senselessness of human conflicts plaguing the world, the incidental destruction done to the planet, and the question, where is God in all this? In verse 2 the question is turned inwards, as the singer recognizes a conflicted self. Verse 3 offers possible solutions: 'Welcome and honour the dark, / look to the light (cf. 'Light of lights beholden,' A89, 'Look towards the light and carry on'), 'Nations and cultures, the rich and the poor, must now unite.' Verse 4 reinforces such solutions and offers a new image of hands holding each other, 'heart bound to heart.'

[WORLD'S END] The melody line is by Cecily Sheehy herself. It is characterised by a powerful upward phrase driving in something like panic towards the tonic note G, then falling back down, a pattern repeated through the first half of the hymn. The second offers a succession of falling phrases, closing on a low B. The arrangement in *Alleluia Aotearoa* is by **Douglas Mews** and **Jillian Bray**, both members of the editorial board at the time.

It all depends on where I'm going F39
Metre: 9.7.9.7 9.7.8.7

The occasion of this hymn by **Colin Gibson** was the news that his brother Ronald Edward Gibson, a Methodist lay preacher and church leader, was suffering from terminal cancer. Written in January 1998, the hymn text elicited Ronald's response: 'You have a real gift for getting the theology right and expressing how I personally feel about the business of coming to terms with a persistent illness. I think that the faith journey is simply an invitation to get on with the business of living out your life to the fullest possible extent – and illness is but an inconvenience to which we are all prone. I can't say that I have ever thought of myself as "suffering": pain is something you live through as a chastening experience. Although we may not have much choice in what we suffer, we can choose our attitude towards it. If anything, suffering provides an extraordinary opportunity to sort yourself out and find meaning in life.' The hymn was dedicated to Gibson's brother (he died in 2011) and was first published in *Faith is our Song* (2000).

An important source is the poem 'Lord, it belongs to not to my care,' written by English clergyman Richard Baxter (1615-91) as a commentary on Philippians 1:21 and dedicated to his own wife, who had died a few years earlier after a lengthy illness. It forms the text of hymn 647 in the 1933 *Methodist Hymn-Book*. Compare verse 2 with Baxter's 'Christ leads me through no darker rooms / Than he went through before; / He that into God's kingdom comes / Must enter by this door.' John 14:15-17 and 16:32 are also sources, as is Philippians 4:11-13.

TE HORO The tune, also by **Colin Gibson**, is named after the area north of Wellington on the Kāpiti coast where Ronald Gibson and his wife Catherine were living at the time. The harmony supporting this simple tune moves steadily from a G minor modality towards an F major close.

Jesus comes to me as a springtime tree A77
Metre: Irregular

The text of this hymn is a psalm-poem by **Joy Cowley**, first published as a hymn text in *Alleluia Aotearoa* (1993), then as a poem in *Psalms Down-Under* (Otane: Pleroma Christian Supplies, 1996), under the title 'Sacrament of the Seasons' (number 40).

The title carries the idea of communion with Christ through the experience of the seasonal cycle of nature ('sacrament' being the long-established Roman Catholic term for Communion or the Eucharist), and this becomes the theme of the hymn, each stanza closing with a link to the following season of the year. This seasonal cycle in the natural world is matched by the suggestion of a parallel human cycle moving from childhood through 'growth' and maturity ('ripeness' – cf. Hamlet's 'Ripeness is all') to freshly-budding old age. In the final stanza the singer/worshipper is finally imaged walking the winter pathway together with the Christ, who has previously come in three manifestations, to be met and 'received' (the word suggests the reception of the elements in Holy Communion.

In this richly poetic text, pictorial and sensual imagery conveys the beauty of the natural world and implies its sacred character, using a Keatsian abundance of sense experiences to do so: fragrance, colour, sound sensations of warmth and coldness. There is a dominant and controlling metaphor used in each stanza, that of the tree, which is both living plant and cross of crucifixion (named in the final stanza, but implied throughout by the refrain ('*Carrying the wood of winter*'). In general, this hymn text is too rich and complex for full discussion in a *Companion*: its symbolism (tree, blossom, sun, fire, torch, path) and its verbal texture deserve both further analysis and quiet meditation.

JOY The tune-name of the melody references both the name of the poet and the delight of the worshipper in the presence of Christ. The original manuscript of the music written for this text by **Ian Render** is undated; and there was some revision for publication in *Alleluia Aotearoa*. Set in F minor and oscillating between that key and E flat major, the tune easily accommodates the metrical freedom of the text and creates a compelling sense of circularity to match Joy Cowley's words. The final cadential F underscores the sense of completion and optimism expressed by the final phrase, 'carrying the buds of spring.'

Jesus, come to our hearts (Song of Southland) A78
Metre: 10.8.6

The composer of this praise song, **William Worley**, first published it in his privately printed collection *Song of Southland: A Collection of Songs of Praise by William Worley* (1992) during his residence as a teacher and Methodist Lay Preacher in Winton, Southland.

The verses are structured round a series of biblical images of falling rain, wind, sun and slain lamb, and conclude with a doxology to the Trinity. The first verse alludes to Psalm 72:6 and Psalm 51:2; the second verse refers to the Pentecost experience of 'rushing wind' and tongues of fire (Acts 2:1-3); the third verse employs the traditional symbolism of Christ as the sun/son of righteousness derived from Malachi 4:2; the fourth verse refers to Revelation 5:12. In the case of this writer (and other New Zealand hymn writers) the combination of the elemental forces of rain, wind and fire with slaughtered lambs is particularly connected with the experiences of farming life in rural areas such as Winton.

SOUTHLAND The tune name reflects the dedication of this song to the people of Southland, to whom it is free of copyright. The melody is by the author; the original simple piano accompaniment was composed by Flora A. Cutler. For *Alleluia Aotearoa* the arrangement of the music is by **David Dell**.

Jesus, I come A79
Metre: 4.5.4.5 D

This hymn was written in 1988 for the congregation of St Andrew's on the Terrace, Wellington, by **Shirley Murray**, who says of it, 'I found the simplicity of this tune [LITTLE VENICE] very engaging, and I felt it might be a good vehicle for words of dedication or a commitment service.' The hymn was first published in Murray's American collection *In Every Corner Sing* (1992), then in *Alleluia Aotearoa* (1993). It has been given fresh choral settings by American composer **Ron Klusmeier** (Klusmeier 16) and by New Zealand composers **Jenny McLeod** in *Godsongs 2: 11 Celtic Godsongs* (2004) and **Colin Gibson**.

The text shows some dependence on biblical sources (for Jesus' kindness, verse 1, see Ephesians 2:7; for 'the truth from the beginning,' in the same stanza, see John 14:6; for 'when I doubt touch me,' verse 2, cf. John 20:24-29, for the cloak of love, also verse 2, cf. Ezekiel 16:2), and its implied portrait of Jesus is richly grounded in the gospel accounts of Jesus' compassionate love and his healing of blindness and physical suffering. The final line recalls the encounter with the rich young man (Matthew 19:21, Mark 10:21, Luke 18:22).

The structure of the poem is liturgical in character. The lines are highly patterned in the Celtic manner, using lists and doublets ('cover, enfold me') as is particularly evident in verses 2 and 3. 'Cloak of your love cover, enfold me' is close to 'The mantle of Christ, my love, be around you' ('Charm of Protection,' from Alexander Carmichael's *Carmina Gaedelica*, 1994, pp. 17 and 246).

LITTLE VENICE The tune, by **Gerald Knight**, is named after an area of London just north of Paddington where the Grand Canal and Regent's Canal meet. It was published in *More Hymns for Today* (1980), where the writer Shirley Murray encountered it and was struck by its potential for a new hymn text.

Jesus, I sing your praise (Song to the Lord Jesus) A80
Metre: 7.5.5.D and refrain

This lyrical song of praise was written by **John Franklin** in 1982 and first published in *Festive Praise Two* (1983), then in *Servant Songs* (1987), *New Zealand Praise* (1988) and *Alleluia Aotearoa* (1993). It is on the SongSelect website.

The writer himself has described the creation of this song: 'It came on a dismal, grey day. Somewhat despondent, I heard myself say, "There is a song here." I paused, I went within, I waited for a spring to bubble [the reference is to Numbers 21:16-17], and when I sensed the "springing up," I went to the piano keyboard and words and music were just waiting to be written down.'

The refrain links the singer with nature 'at praise,' represented by the dawn chorus of birds, the night star-field, the wind and 'flowers in the sun.' This follows the tradition represented by Psalms 19 and 148, and includes the Christian symbolism of wind (the Holy Spirit) and sun (Jesus Christ).

Verse 1 references Isaiah 55:12 (hills), John 1:5 (light), Mark 4:35-40 (peace) and Luke 24:13-15 (fellow traveller). Verse 2 references 1 John 2:20 (the Holy One), John 14:23 (Man of Love) and John 3:16 (Son of God). Verse 3 draws on Revelation 22:1-2 (river of life), Isaiah 35:1 (the wilderness brought to flower) and Galatians 6:10 (household). However, the creative poet is present too, in the image of Christ as 'the song that makes the world sing' or the association of the Holy Spirit with a stream or river rather than the traditional wind and fire, as well as in the variant 'households of love' (rather than 'households of faith,' as in the source passage). Here John Franklin obliquely comments on the problem of domestic violence that still plagues New Zealand society.

[SONG TO THE LORD JESUS] The music composed by the author for his text is in the unusual key of D flat (with guitar figuration). The melody essentially repeats and develops a simple statement and answer phrase, the harmony oscillating on the chords of D flat and G flat.

Jesus, our sun H79
Metre: 11.10.11.10

This Easter hymn was written by **Timothy Hurd** in June 2007 for his All Saints, Dunedin, congregation, and first published in *Hope is our Song* (2009). He describes it as 'An attempt to take our autumnal imagery, particularly striking in Central Otago [the region inland from Dunedin], seriously, and use the metaphors and images that are, for us, "Easter."

Wedded to the liturgical sequence of readings in the Easter season, there is still a place to name emphatically the joy and symbolism we see in autumn's glorious red and gold.'

As verse 1 makes plain, this text is written for an Easter morning celebration and follows closely the gospel narratives of the resurrection. The first verse melds the dawn setting of the resurrection (Luke 24:1) with the ancient play on sun/sunrise/Son of God and introduces Christ as the Good Shepherd (see verse 3). The scattering and regrouping of the disciples following the crucifixion is mentioned in line 4. Verse 2 identifies the singers with the experience of 'doubting' Thomas; its source is John 20:24-29 (cf. 'Christ seeks us out, and peace upon us breathing,' line 3 of the text, with 'The doors were shut but Jesus came and stood among them and said, "Peace be with you"'). Verse 3, line 1, refers to the Emmaus Road and Sea of Galilee meetings with the risen Christ (Luke 24:13-27 and John 21:1-14). Line 2 alludes to John 10:1-6, 'he calls his own sheep by name'). Verse 4 alludes to the disciples' recognition of Jesus at the Emmaus meal (Luke 24:28-31), but its flame-spark imagery derives from Moses' encounter with an angel of God on Mount Horeb (Exodus 3:2). In line 4, the entombment of Christ is made a metaphor for spiritual 'death' in general, and there are echoes here of the sending out of the disciples, Jesus' proclamation of his mission to free those imprisoned and oppressed' (Luke 4:18) and the story of Lazarus. The distinctive New Zealand autumnal setting of Easter is acknowledged in line 3, 'autumn's rich inflection' [=seasonal change], continued into verse 5 with the fall of brightly coloured autumn leaves imaged as a sign of celebration. The coronation of nature as a symbol of 'redeemed creation' is followed in lines 3-4 by the song of the redeemed (see Revelation 5:9-14 and 14:3).

EASTER SUNRISE The setting by **Marnie Barrell**, written in 2008, takes its name from the opening line of the text. The structure of her melody is haunted by the melodic shape of the old 1615 *Scottish Psalter* tune FRENCH ('O God of Bethel by whose hand'), another melody in E flat. But Marnie Barrell gives her modern setting equal weight and greater rhythmic flexibility with freer movement of the inner parts, judicious modulations and off-beat phrase openings.

Jesus, Saviour, Spirit, Sun A81
Metre: 7.7.7.7

Shirley Murray, the author of this hymn written in 1985, describes it as 'my first text on the theme of Christian unity and "the scandal of our divisions."' She continues, 'It has been sung increasingly at ecumenical services in New Zealand, but usually to a mismatching tune.' It first reached print in the author's private publication *In Every Corner Sing* (Wellington, 1987). There Murray's recommended tune is ST BEES, by **John Bacchus Dykes,** 'though a much preferred tune is PSALM 136 (Louez Dieu) [*Genevan Psalter*, 1562].' For its publication in her first American collection, *In Every Corner Sing* (1992), it was matched with the **Orlando Gibbons'** tune SONG 13, 'chosen for its simple beauty.' It next appeared in *Alleluia Aotearoa* (1993) with a new setting by her musician-friend **Jillian Bray**.

Verse 1 opens with the common play on 'sun/Son of God' and the hymn's theme of unity in Christ, drawing on Jesus' prayer 'that they all may be one' (John 17:22). It then introduces the controlling image of melting down, recasting and purifying by fire, which returns in the final verse ('consume our shame in the love which is your flame'). Verse 2 opens up a confessional mood: the divided Christian Church is blind, scattered (a hint of the Tower of Babel story, Genesis 11) and ghetto-minded. Verse 3 introduces a further image of building stone walls of separation between different Christian traditions (the wall dividing the city of Berlin at the time offers a contemporary though secular context). The final verse completes the fiery image and closes formally by repeating the first 2 lines of the hymn.

SHIRLEY The tune is named after Shirley Murray and was written by **Jillian Bray** 'as a tribute to her friend, to replace the Orlando Gibbons tune. 'My second attempt at a [hymn] tune, it was accepted by the [New Zealand Hymnbook] Committee in 1992.' A strongly pulsed rhythm gives the pianistic setting its energy, but, in keeping with the unresolved denominational divisions the text addresses, the key is predominantly A minor, modulating briefly to C major followed by G major, but returning to an A minor close marked by a clashing G/G sharp in the penultimate chord of the tune. There is another setting, by Asian composer **Swee Hong Lim**, SOON EE, published in *Sound the Bamboo (2000),* and a further setting by Canadian composer **Ron Klusmeier** (Klusmeier 17).

Jesus, stand among us W637
Metre: 6.7.6.7 and refrain

This invocation was written by **Graham Kendrick** in 1975, and recorded on his album of the same name in 1979. Kendrick recalls that following the London success of his performing group, 'I began just occasionally to attempt to write worship songs. A song called "Jesus Stand Among Us At The Meeting Of Our Lives" was the first song of mine to become popular to some degree. At that time I remember with the team I was working with we had a whole week where we went away and stayed in someone's house with the simple aim of producing some worship songs. We had many, many hours of worship and praying and out of that quite a number of ideas emerged. If you like we created a stimulating environment. I was the one who was writing the stuff mostly but the other members of the team were creating the stimulating environment. A number of songs came out of that.'

Behind this text stands the older (1873) hymn, 'Jesus, stand among us, in thy risen power,' by William Pennefather; both are based on Luke 24:36 (see also John 20:26), describing the appearance of the risen Christ to his gathered disciples ('we love you, and so we gather here'), who are 'startled and frightened' ('take away all fear').

Alleluia Aotearoa omits a third Communion verse, while the text of the first two verses is so altered from the original that it seems worthwhile to print them as published in *Songs of Fellowship,* Volume 1 (1991) with changes picked out in italic:

Jesus, stand among us
At the meeting of our lives
Be our sweet agreement
At the meeting of our eyes
O Jesus, we love You, so we gather here;
Join our hearts in unity
and take away *our* fear.

So to You we're gathering
Out of each and every land,
Christ the *love* between us
At the joining of our hands
O Jesus, we love You, so we gather here;
Join our hearts in unity
and take away our fear.

YORK Named after the English town where the song was begun, the music is by Graham Kendrick in an arrangement by New Zealand composer **Guy Elwyn Jansen**. In the restrained pitch movement and repeated crochets in the opening bars of YORK there are echoes of CASWALL, the German tune associated with Pennefather's hymn since at least 1905.

Jesus, touch us (Communion Meditation) H80
Metre: 8.7.8.5

This communion prayer-hymn was written in 2001 by Methodist minister **Audrey Dickinson,** who published it in her privately printed collection *Simply Different* (Manurewa, Auckland, 2001). The original poem is lightly punctuated and set out in four, three and five-syllable lines, with the final line (from Psalm 90:14), acting as a refrain.

The text is filled with biblical and liturgical resonances, many of them mediated through phrases echoed from earlier hymns. The 23rd Psalm and the Methodist Communion liturgy contribute to this text, but the strongest presence is that of William Bright's 1874 communion hymn, 'And now, O Father, mindful of the love,' still frequently sung on such occasions.

SACRA [Latin=sacred things] The tune name is appropriate for a sacramental liturgy. The setting for Audrey Dickinson's hymn is by **Trevor Cox**, organist and choir director of Manurewa Methodist Church at the time of composition and her close collaborator ('musician Trevor Cox and I…needed to work in tandem much of the time.'). A simple sequentially-descending melodic line, with some harmonic variation for its repetition, moves steadily from a tonic F through to a serene conclusion on the same note. Some variation in performance is desirable, but singing the long 8-verse text will take most congregations through the ritual of communion, during which it may be sung as a quiet, reflective meditation. Alternative versions are provided for both unison and 4-part choral singing.

Join hands in the Spirit A82
Metre: Irregular

This hymn was written in 1986 by **Radha Wardrop** (later Radha Sahar), and first published in *Alleluia Aotearoa* (1993). Sung by Colla Voce, it was recorded on the matching *Alleluia Aotearoa* CD. It was later recorded on the album *One Earth Chants* (2011) and has been added to the SongSelect archive.

The grand theme of the text is set out at its beginning and its end: 'Join hands'… 'embracing every creed, every race.' The hymn is an impassioned appeal for peace and communality – 'your love is our union,'* The text addresses 'the Spirit' as 'the one holy name,' but many of the attributes given are those traditionally associated with the first person of the Trinity, God – as love (cf. 1 John 4:16), source of life (cf. Genesis 2:7), and primal image (cf. Genesis 1:26). At the same time, and seamlessly, the language suggests the life and teachings of Christ: 'we your children' (cf. Galatians 3:26, 'in Jesus Christ you are all children of God'), 'you call us / to love and forgive,' 'to trust… that in death we may live,' 'your touch our release.' And beyond these the writer creates her own imagery: 'Oh great heart embracing / every creed, every race,' and enriches the text with the conceptual celebratory language of New Testament Christianity, 'joy, peace, grace.'

[JOIN HANDS] The original music for her text, by Radha Wardrop, marked *Andante* and with two preliminary bars, has been arranged by **Ian Render** for *Alleluia Aotearoa*. This process involved a key shift from D minor to F minor and rescoring the work, originally a unison melody with guitar chords, for four-part harmony. At the same time a number of adjustments were made to the melody line. The music remains darkly intense and powerful, partly because the tune is tightly constructed almost entirely from repetitions at different levels of the initial phrase, a six-note (originally eight-note) figure, while its underlying harmonies shift from F minor to E flat major, F (A flat) minor, C minor resolving on F minor with a tierce de Picardy final chord.

*The thinking behind this hymn is well shown by a statement on the writer's Sacred Site website: 'The whole of planet Earth is a sacred site. All people are a chosen people and the purpose of our lives is a spiritual one. May we care for each other and for the Earth, for everything relates to everything else. Feeling this oneness, may we radiate the light of love and kindness that all may live in unity and peace.'

Jumping Jesus H81
Metre: 8.8.8.8.8.8.7.7.7.4

This hymn was written for and dedicated to the children of the Mornington Methodist Sunday School, Dunedin, where its author and composer, **Colin Gibson**, is organist and choir leader. On its initial performance it was illustrated by young children jumping on three trampolines. The hymn was first published in *Hope is our Song* (2009), and later in *Jumping Jesus: Hymns from New Zealand* (Tokyo: Hymn Society in Japan, 2012).

The theme of the text is the spiritual vitality of the resurrected Jesus, seen from a child's perspective. The author says, 'Usually we sing about a Jesus who sits, or kneels in prayer, or walks by the lakeside or stands quietly.

But I wanted to celebrate the huge spiritual vitality of Jesus. So I have a jumping Jesus who leaps, and does cartwheels on the sand, and bounces on the bed – like any other energetic little girl or boy might do.' A major source for the imagery of the text was the story and illustrations of *Jesus' Day Off* by Nicholas Allan (2002). Another was Hayao Miyazaki's 2004 animé film *Howl's Moving Castle*, based on Diana Wynne Jones' 1986 fantasy novel of the same name. 'The film has a delightful character, Prince Pumpkin, with a smiling pumpkin for a head, who bounces along on a pogo stick. All through the story he quietly helps other people – and turns out to be a royal person in disguise. That reminds me of Jesus, the loving Son of God,' says Gibson.

The resurrection is presented as a 'jumping out of a hole in the rocks' (verse 1); Jesus' promise, 'lo, I am with always' (Matthew 28:20) is introduced in verse 2. The Jack-in-the-box (verse 1) and the pogo stick (verse 3) are both children's toys, using springs to propel a figure out of a lidded box or a child bouncing along on a sprung pole.

GALLOWAY STREET This tune name refers to the street in the Dunedin suburb of Mornington where the Mornington Methodist Church is situated. The music, set in a cheerful C major, imitates the 'bounce' in the text, the melody being constructed from a rising 4-note figure incorporating a 'leap' of a third and occasionally taking large octave jumps. The accompaniment uses another bouncing pattern, with the bass line leaping from note to note over an arpeggio range. In the final section (bar 15 onwards) the harmony decides to move upwards too, rising through D minor, E minor and F major before jumping back to the initial bouncing figure.

See also 'Jumping Jesus,' Colin Gibson. *Refresh: A Journal of Contemplative Spirituality*, Encountering Jesus, Volume 7.1 (Winter 2007), 4-5.

Just a cup of water A83
Metre: 10.7.9.9 and refrain

This hymn was written in 1986 by **Felicia Edgecombe,** who explains its origin: 'When a doctor friend of ours left his young family behind to serve in the refugee camps in South East Asia for several months, I felt moved to write this song.' Dedicated to the doctor and his wife, it was first sung in the Titahi Bay, (Wellington), Community Church (formerly the Gospel Chapel), of which the writer-composer has long been a member, then published in *Servant Songs*, edited by Guy Jansen and Felicia Edgecombe in 1987, where it is titled 'Cup of Water,' before appearing in *Alleluia Aotearoa* (1993). It has been reprinted in *Songs of Life*, by Felicia Edgecombe and Rosemary Russell (Wellington: Festivity Productions, 1996) with the melody separated from the piano accompaniment and the accompaniment itself given a new arrangement by Glenys Chiaroni.

In the manner of a modern gospel song, the text is built up from a mosaic of scriptural echoes. The opening line of verse 1 is a quotation from Mark 9:41 and the refrain is built around Mark 12:31, 'love your neighbour as yourself.' Verse 2 echoes Matthew 30:24, 'Jesus had compassion on them and touched their eyes.' Verse 3 starts from Psalm 28:7, 'The Lord is my strength and my shield' and ends with Psalm 27:1, 'The Lord is my light and salvation.'

[CUP OF WATER] The melody of this setting is rhythmical and relaxed, freely using syncopations and a balance of falling and climbing phrases in the style of popular lyric songs. In the verses the A minor tonality moving towards C major carries in musical terms the theme of need meeting 'true charity.' By contrast, the refrain begins in a major tonality, supporting the dominant idea of the song, 'love your neighbour,' then winding back down to E major in preparation for the return to a minor tonality which accompanies the ideas of compassion and powerlessness in the following verses. The work of a talented composer, the harmonic landscape and its shifting moods exactly express the ideas present in the text.

Just a mustard seed of faith will do
H82
Metre: 9.7.7.7.7.7.7.7.7

This hymn was written by **Colin Gibson** in 2004, as a response to a sermon delivered by a lay preacher, Peter Grundy – to whom the song is dedicated – taking his first service, in the Mornington Methodist Church, Dunedin.

The text, like the sermon, is based on the parable of the mustard seed, which appears in three of the canonical gospels, Matthew 13:31-3, Mark 4:30-32 and Luke 13:18-19, and also in the non-canonical gospel of Thomas (20). The full parable text is used in the third verse ('it becomes the greatest of shrubs [a 'tree' in the King James version] and puts forth large branches, so that the birds of the air can make nests in its shade'), but the writer takes the same liberty of imagination in verse 1 and supposes a whole orchard growing up from a single seed planted in the 'salt and bitter sea' (i.e. the Dead Sea of Jesus' time and our own). In verse 2, the extraordinary powers of the tiny seed are referenced to another Jesus saying, 'I tell you, if you have faith so much as a grain of mustard seed you will say to this mountain, "Move from here to there," and it will move' (Matthew 17:20).

ROY CRESCENT The tune name refers to the address of the preacher to whom the song was dedicated (it contains a fortuitous pun on 'crescent'=growing). The music was written by **Colin Gibson** in 2004 to accompany the text. Singers encounter a cheeky pair of high notes placed early on (in bars 2-3) to suggest the remarkable growth of the seed into a large shrub or tree.

Just as a mother sings her baby to sleep (So is the Love of God) *H83*
Metre: 11.8.11.8.8

The genesis of this hymn is recalled by its author, **Shirley Murray**: 'Created from the gift of a tune sent to me by Jillian Bray, PELENISE was the name of the composer's great-grandmother and daughter of a chief on Niue, a tiny Pacific island. The feeling of the tune made me think of the gentleness of those people, and the intimacy of love shared within family and friends.' The hymn was first published in the author's American collection *Touch the Earth Lightly* (2008), closely followed by its appearance in *Hope is our Song* (2009).

The text is constructed out a series of images, many of them intimate and domestic, redefining the nature of the love of God. Verse 1, line 3, hints at Matthew 23:37 (and Luke 13:34), 'How often would I have gathered your children together, as a hen gathers her chicks under her wings.' Verse 2 refers to the way in which sunflowers and other flowers track the passage of the sun (a traditional symbol of the divine) through the day. Verse 3, line 1, the phrase 'the rhythm of life' is at least as old as Alice Meynell's volume of essays, *The Rhythm of Life* (1893). Line 2 refers to Job 38:1-7, 'Where were you…when the morning stars sang together and all the sons of God shouted for joy?' and line 3 alludes to Matthew 28:20, 'Lo, I am with you always even unto the end of the world.'

PELENISE The tune is named after the composer **Jillian Bray's** great-grandmother, a Niuean Islander (see above). Its rhythm is that of a gentle lullaby, sustained throughout its time changes and shifts in modality. There is a further setting by Canadian composer **Ron Klusmeier** (Klusmeier 45).

Ka tirohia te ripeka *W646*
Metre: 8.8.8.8

This hymn is a paraphrase in Māori of the hymn 'When I survey the wondrous cross' by **Isaac Watts**, which Matthew Arnold described as 'the finest hymn in the English language.' Neither the date of the paraphrase nor the name of the translator is known, but it was almost certainly the work of a missionary, as the telltale final 'conversion' verse suggests: 'This is the payment for my sins, all are completely wiped away. My foolish heart will turn to God.'

An early account of a missionary service conducted at the village of Upoko-toto in November 1862 suggests the typical context in which this version was sung, and it may be that the paraphrase was actually written by the unidentified priest who led the service there. 'Now the congregation began to muster, and seating themselves in rows, Clericus [previously described as an unnamed young LMS missionary] gave out the hymn "Ka tirohia te ripeka," which I take to be a version of "When I survey the wondrous cross." Clericus, however, made a mistake I consider in trying to sing the tune "Job" to it, for from the mess they made of it the patience of the Patriarch would have been sorely tried had he heard it. Parnapa [one of the local Māori] was full of his turnshakes and quavers, and the effect was about as harmonious as a good strong rookery' (Thomas Moser, in one of his 'Sketches of New Zealand and its inhabitants' first published in *The Wellington Independent* and later gathered into a book titled *Mahoe Leaves* (1863).

ROCKINGHAM As a complete hymn tune, ROCKINGHAM was first published in *The Psalms of David for the Use of Parish Churches: The Music Selected, Adapted and Composed by Edward Miller, Mus. Doc* (1790), where it is described as 'part of a melody taken from [another] hymn tune.' The source hymn tune in question was TUNBRIDGE, found in Aaron Williams' *A Second Supplement to Psalmody in Miniature* (c.1780). **Edward Miller** named his new tune after his patron and friend the Marquis of Rockingham. It was not associated with Watts' hymn until 1833, when it appeared first in Godding's *The Parochial Psalmist*, then in William Mercer's *The Church Psalter and Hymn Book* (1854). It did not reach *Hymns Ancient & Modern* until 1861, which may explain why the young London Missionary Society priest did not think to use it for his Māori congregation. The harmonisation used in *With One Voice* is by **David Evans** (1874-1948) and first appeared in the Church of Scotland's *Revised Church Hymnary* (1927).

Karakia ki te Wairua Tapu (Prayer to the Holy Spirit) *H84*
Metre: Irregular

This prayer to the Holy Spirit was written in 2000 by Father **John Greally,** and given its Māori form by **Ngapo** and **Pimia Wehi**. It formed part of the text of *Tētē Kura,** a major bi-cultural, multi-lingual, collaborative musical work for choir, Māori performing arts group, kaikaranga [caller onto the *marae*], solo soprano and tenor, composed by **Helen Fisher** with the assistance of Ngapo and Pimia Wehi and Taru mai-i-tawhiti Kerehoma, and performed on 19 August 2000 by more than 120 singers and musicians from Te Waka Huia and Tower New Zealand Youth Choir for the Wellington Youth Arts 2000 Festival. The event was broadcast on Concert FM, Radio New Zealand.

Tētē Kura takes the shape of a *hohou rongo*, a process of reconciliation bringing issues of pain and injustice into the open, in order to restore people's inner dignity and bring about true peace. It opens with an expression of the spiritual values of Māori and Pākehā culture, pairing a *Karanga* with a Gregorian chant invoking the Holy Spirit ('Veni Sancte Spiritus'), then traces the loss of such spiritual values and a journey towards greed and materialism, resulting in experiences of pain, confusion and abuse, out of which come new insights, hope and a sense of self-worth ('Karakia ki te Wairua Tapu'). The work closes by embracing the questions and challenges posed by the new millennium about individuals-in-community and the recovery of social and cultural values based on *aroha*** and the spiritual life (*wairua*).

KARAKIA A TE WAIRUA TAPU The music for this prayer was written by Wellington composer **Helen Fisher** in 2000. The melodic line has the shape of a Western hymn sung in unison and is well within the capability of a prepared congregation; the harmony is Celtic in modality and the steady beating (here on guitar, though other instruments might be used) suggests the rhythm of a chant. The Māori element is particularly present in the sounds of the language (*te reo*). In *Hope is our Song*, the score is arranged by Christchurch composer **Barry Brinson**.

> *The title translates as *Fern Frond*, from the Māori saying, *Mate atu he tētēkura, ara mai he tētēkura*: 'One frond dies; another takes its place at once.'

> **For the rich concept of *aroh*a (Māori=love), see 'Come to this Christmas singing.'

Ke tau fakafeta'i *A84*
Metre: 8.7.7.8 and refrain

This undated Tongan hymn text was written by **Leo Foliaki,** about whom no information has come to light.

As the English translation by an unidentified hand provided in *Alleluia Aotearoa* suggests, the general tenor of the text follows the main ideas of the first four verses of Charles Wesley's famous 1739 hymn for Easter Day, 'Christ the Lord is risen today,' with its repeated alleluias. Verse 1 is a Tongan language version of Wesley's first line. Verse 2 picks up 'Vain the stone, the watch, the seal, / Christ hath burst the gates of hell' and adds 'Where's thy victory, boasting grave?' Verse 3 addresses 'Made like him, like him we rise,' and ends with an echo of 'love's redeeming work is done.'

[HIVA HOSANNA] This setting, by **Douglas Mews**, is unnamed by the composer and undated. But it was written before 1992, the date of its appearance in *Alleluia Aotearoa*. The arrangement for unison singing provides a vigorous, well-breathed melodic line, its rhythm varied by the change in metre from 4/4 for the verses to 6/8 for the alleluia chorus. Harmonic enrichment is provided in the piano accompaniment which shifts the tonality through A major and G major on the way to a rousing close in the tonic key of D major.

Ko tei anoano aere ua mai *W668*
Metre 11.11.11.7 and refrain

An undated and simplified translation into the language of the Cook Islands, probably by a now unknown missionary, of the popular Gospel song, 'Whosoever will may come,' by American evangelist-composer **Philip Bliss**.

The original song was published in *The Prize*, a book of Sunday School songs edited by George F. Root (Cincinatti, Ohio: John Church 1870), and was Bliss's response to a week of preaching by an English evangelist Henry Moorhouse on the text 'For God so loved the world that he gave his only begotten Son' (John 3:16). Revelation 22:17 is the main biblical source of the Bliss hymn, whose full text is given here to demonstrate the work of the translator.

> "Whosoever heareth,"
> shout, shout the sound!
> Spread the blessed tidings
> all the world around;
> Spread the joyful news
> wherever man is found:
> "Whosoever will may come."

> *"Whosoever will, whosoever will,"*
> *Send the proclamation over vale and hill;*
> *'Tis a loving Father calls the wand'rer home:*
> *"Whosoever will may come."*

> Whosoever cometh need not delay,
> Now the door is open,
> enter while you may;
> Jesus is the true, the only Living Way:
> "Whosoever will may come."

> *"Whosoever will," the promise secure,*
> *"Whosoever will," forever must endure;*
> *"Whosoever will," 'tis life forevermore:*
> *"Whosoever will may come."*

KO TEI ANOANO (Cook Islands=whoever is willing) Philip Bliss's distinctive setting of his own Gospel song, published in *The Prize* (1870).

Koutou katoa rā, mea iti nei *W659*
Metre 9.9.9.6 and refrain

This hymn is a translation into the Māori language of the American revival hymn 'Come to the Saviour,' written in 1870 by the poet **George Frederick Root**. The version is anonymous and undated, but it is likely to have been made by a missionary to the Māori people. The parallel texts printed in *With One Voice* fail to show the degree of simplification of the original in the process of translation: the original text of the first verse of Root's hymn reads 'Come to the Saviour, make no delay, / Here in His Word he has shown us the way, / Here in our mid'st He's standing today, / Tenderly saying, 'Come!' / Joyful, joyful will the meeting be, / When from sin our hearts are pure and free, / And we shall gather, Saviour, with Thee, / In our eternal home.' As the Māori text shows, it would have originally been used as a hymn persuading converts to come forward, exactly as Sankey saw it being used in a revival meeting in America in 1879.

Although Isaiah 55:3 is sometimes quoted as Root's biblical source, the likelier source – as is clear from verse 2 – is Mark 10:14, echoed in Matthew 19:14 and Luke 18:16, in which Jesus invites the children to 'come unto me.'

COME TO THE SAVIOUR More properly called INVITATION, this tune was written in 1870 by **George Root** for his own text. The adaptation of the tune printed in *With One Voice* as a 'traditional' Māori version smoothes out the dotted rhythms of the original, losing the energy of what was a lively marching tune. It also changes some of the notes, particularly in the final bars, but its unremitting crochet stress patterns remain.

Learning to Fly *facing F44*

Accompanied by a photograph of a young child's smiling face, these are the first and final verses from a 5-verse prose-psalm by **Joy Cowley**, published in her collection *Psalms Down-under* (Catholic Supplies: Wellington,1996).

The chosen verses hardly do justice to one of the rare visionary poems in New Zealand religious writing. In the full text the poet describes herself as moving from self-ignorance and frustration by the limiting 'walls of birth and death' to an exalted vision 'beyond time' in which she perceives that 'Birth and death were not walls at all / but little ripples coming and going / on an eternal sea that has / neither beginning nor end.' The final verse virtually quotes William Wordsworth's 'Our birth is but a sleep and a forgetting' (*Ode on Intimations of Immortality from Recollections of Childhood*) and the older poet's great Ode (published in his Poems, 1807) also expresses ideas of the flight of the soul and the sea of eternity found in Cowley's poem: 'Our souls have sight of that immortal sea / Which brought us hither.' What distinguishes Joy Cowley's thought from Wordsworth's is her insistence on a loving God: 'Taught by love and held by Love / my heart began to fly a little at a time'; 'the meaning of the eternal sea / which holds everything in its embrace / is Love').

Leftover people in leftover places
H85
Metre: 11.10.11.10 D

In 2007 the Hymn Society in the United States and Canada announced a search for a text on the theme of 'The Least of These' (Matthew 25:40) and author **Shirley Murray** was attracted to 'the idea of trying to capture the essence of God's "upsidedown kingdom" and our places in it.' Her hymn won the award and was first published in her American collection *Touch the Earth Lightly* (2008), closely followed by *Hope is our Song* (2009).

The biblical starting point is Matthew 25:40, 'Truly I say to you, if you did it to one of the least of these my brethren, you did it to me,' but the major source is the parable of the Great Feast, as Luke tells it (Luke 14:12-24). The key metaphor of 'leftover people' derives from 'leftovers,' the remains of a meal (connected with the idea of feasting), but the whole phrase was also current at the time of writing. In 2005, *Leftover People*, a photographic essay on refugees arriving at Sacramento, won the Robert F. Kennedy Award for the Disadvantaged.

Verse 1, line 3, 'scavenging crumbs from society's plenty' alludes to the parable of the rich man and Lazarus (Luke 16:19-31). Verse 3, 'true Easter people'=those whose follow the resurrected Christ, Christians; 'spirited people' is a play on 'lively, energetic people' and 'people filled with the Spirit.' The final line means 'creating more open space,' that is, a more 'open' society, bringing about greater willingness on the part of the rich and the famous to admit the poor and rejected to share in the 'banquet.'

CONNECT The tune name derives from the implicit theme of the hymn, the necessity to reconnect the rich with the poor and the outcasts of society. The music, by **Colin Gibson**, was written almost immediately and spontaneously for this text. The melody carrying the description of the leftover people is set in the 'sad' key of D minor; the second half of the text elevating them as worthy and called to the feast' in God's upsidedown kingdom is set in the 'happy' key of F major, with the melodic line pitched higher and a mirror image of the first section.

Let justice roll down A85
Metre: 8.7.8.7 and refrain

This hymn text was written by **Colin Gibson** in 1989, with a dedication to Dr I-to Loh of Taiwan, who has given his life to recording and publishing indigenous Asian Christian music. It was first published in *Alleluia Aotearoa* (1993), followed by Gibson's first American collection, *Reading the Signature* (1994).

In *Reading the Signature* the author wrote 'Behind the imagery of the text stands the prophet Amos's ringing declaration, "'Let justice roll down like waters, and righteousness like an ever-flowing stream" (Amos 5:24) but I wanted to take it further, to recognize our personal responsibility for the rule of justice on earth, so the images of injustice come from modern tragic experience – famine in Somalia (verse 1), Cambodian refugees in a Thai border camp (verse 2, though the image of 'canyons of greed' was prompted by the view from the pavement of towering bank and other commercial buildings in New Zealand's capital city), street kids in Auckland (or New York), and the oppression silently endured by millions of human beings.' Sadly, it would not be difficult to replace such a list with immediately contemporary images; the theme is still valid and urgent.

WAITAKI This setting, composed in 1989 by **Colin Gibson,** attempts to give a tonal impression of suffering in the falling bass of the verse setting and a strong responsive chorale in the refrain (with trumpet calls to action in bars 4-5 and 12-13). The tune is named after one of the broad rivers that flow from the Southern Alpine range across the Canterbury Plains to the Pacific Ocean. The hymn has also been set by New Zealand composer **Jenny McLeod** (2003).

Let me be kind to you (Kindness, a Children's Song) F40
Metre: 7.7.7.7.7.7 and refrain

This children's hymn on the theme of God's loving kindness was commissioned by Bishop Peter Atkins of Auckland for a book of liturgical resources, *Worship 2000*, published in 1999 to mark the 2000 Millennium year. It was written by **Colin Gibson** in 1998 and first published in the author's American collection *Songs for a Rainbow People* (1998). The original poem, titled 'Kindness,' was marked with indications for the singers to mime the last five lines of the refrain: 'wink, smile, wave, hands outstretched, hands opened out.'

There is little biblical reference in the words, which largely consist of examples of a loving providence in terms of children's own experiences of kindness displayed by adults, their friends and through the goodness of the natural world. Its message is contained in the opening of the refrain, that mutual acts of kindness will create a world 'where it is good to be.' Verse 4, lines 4-6, refer to 1 John 4:7-12. However, the major source of the hymn is contained in words attributed to Teresa of Calcutta: 'Be kind and merciful. Let no one ever come to you without coming away better and happier. Be the living expression of God's kindness. Kindness in your face, kindness in your eyes, kindness in your smile, kindness in your warm greeting. In the slums we are the light of God's kindness to the poor. To children, to the poor, to all who suffer and are lonely, give always a happy smile – Give them not only your care, but also your heart' (quoted in *Worldwide Laws of Life: 200 Eternal Spiritual Principles,* by John Templeton (1998).

KINDNESS The tune name is taken from the theme of the hymn text. The music was written by the author and dedicated to Bishop Atkins. The original was scored for two voices and marked *Vivace*.

Let me turn your light on H86
Metre: Irregular

This song was written in 2006 by **Colin Gibson** for his Dunedin Mornington Methodist Choir. The manuscript carries indications for the verse lines to be shared among sopranos, altos, tenors and basses. It was first published in *Hope is our Song* (2009).

The text focuses on the traditional theme of Jesus Christ, light of the world, but it does so in a modernizing way, in an attempt to give fresh life to an old idea. Verse 1 draws on John 1:5 and John 8:12; verse 2 revisits Matthew 15:11 – in the King James 'bushel' rather than the more modern 'bowl' version. Verse 3 introduces a modern metaphor, the illumination of a room with electric light; verse 4 borrows the Quaker doctrine of the 'Inner Light,' the presence of God dwelling within every human soul. The refrain calls the singers to action, the 'turning on' of the light of Jesus Christ (an electrical metaphor again). The eclectic verbal texture embraces contemporary phrases such as 'right on,' introduces ecstatic shouts of *Hallelujah!* and other exclamations and mixes biblical language with informal modern diction.

POWERPOINT The tune name calls attention to the frequent imagery of modern electric light in the text (when the hymn was written the new sense of the word referring to computer-assisted projection had not yet appeared). The music written by the author for these words is consciously jocular and popular in style with its syncopations, flattened chords and insistent stressing of the beat.

Let my spirit always sing (Hymn on Growing Older) F41
Metre: 7.7.7.7.7.7

The circumstances in which **Shirley Murray** wrote this hymn in 1995 are set out by the author as follows: 'Rusty Edwards sent me this fine tune, REBEKAH, with an open brief as to a theme. I have always wanted a hymn to sing "On growing Older" which is positive and not regretful. This hymn was first sung in a retirement village chapel in Auckland, New Zealand, where the familiar tune LUCERNA LAUDONIAE was used. That Sunday was October 1, United Nations International Day of Older Persons.'

There is no obvious major biblical source for this text, although it engages key religious terms such as spirit, word, soul, wisdom, hope, love, life and death. Verse 2 uses the old English proverb 'the eyes are the window to the soul.' The poet acknowledges that the image 'like a feather on your breath' (verse 4) is borrowed from Hildegard of Bingen (see 'Nothing is lost on the breath of God,' F50). 'Wintering' (verse 1)=growing old, and cold; in verse 2, 'the inner eye'=spiritual insight, and 'becoming whole'=gradually perceived to be a connected whole. Verse 3, 'wit'=good sense, intelligence, 'estrange'=reject, regard as alien.' Verse 4, for 'our hope is not in vain' see 1 Corinthians 15:58.

REBEKAH This tune is named after a personal acquaintance of the composer **Rusty Edwards,** who wrote it in 1995. A lyric melody with something of the shape of older popular melodies, it sits well with the words written for it. The alternative tune, LUCERNA LAUDONIAE (Latin=Lantern of the Lothians, a district in Wales) was written by Welsh musician and composer **David Evans** (1874-1948) and is most closely associated with the Folliott S. Pierpoint (1835-1917) hymn 'For the beauty of the earth.'

Let our earth be peaceful H87
Metre: 6.6.6.5

'I have a liking for "small songs" easily learned and useful to give short bursts within the liturgy, in contrast to heavier hymns,' says **Shirley Murray**, author of this hymn text which she wrote in 2004. It was initially published in her American collection *Touch the Earth Lightly* (2008), then in *Hope is our Song* (2009). It has a sub-title, 'For the Love of God.'

The writer suggests that this hymn 'might be used at the end of worship, or as thanksgiving after an offering, or, separating the stanzas, be used with spoken intercession.' The relationship between the first three lines of each stanza and the refrain, 'for the love of God,' changes from verse to verse. It carries something of the imprecatory force of the expression 'for God's sake!' but it also means 'to express our love of God' and 'because God loves us.' Verse 1, line 1, may recall the 1955 Christmas song 'Let there be peace on earth' by Jill Jackson Miller and Sy Miller, just as line 3, may recall the children's hymn by Margaret Cropper (1886-1980), written about 1926, 'Jesus' hands were kind hands, doing good to all.' Verse 3, line 1, draws on Colossians 1:10; line 2, and reflects the phrase associated with Mother Teresa of Calcutta, 'something beautiful for God.' The final lines echo Psalm 136:1-2.

RANGIMĀRIE (Māori=peace) This hymn tune was written by **Colin Gibson** in 2004. Set in the 'quiet' key of E flat major, the melody and harmony reflect the theme of peacefulness by drifting gently down towards a B flat major chord. Verse 3 modulates briefly to C minor while the melody lifts to reflect the ideas of beauty and playfulness, but the setting soon resumes its quiet E flat major tonality. An alternative setting, FOR THE LOVE OF GOD, by the American composer **Joy Patterson**, is provided in *Touch the Earth Lightly*; Canadian composer Ron Klusmeier has also provided a setting (**Klusmeier** 47).

Let our love shine out H88
Metre: 5.8.5.7.8.8.7.7

Written in 1991 by **Colin Gibson**, this hymn was originally published in the author's first American collection, *Reading the Signature* (1994) and later in *Hope is Our Song* (2009). It was occasioned by a fierce and divisive debate within the writer's local Dunedin Methodist parish over the standing of gay membership of Methodist congregations; a debate reflecting a national social justice issue which was resolved at political level by the passing in 1993 of New Zealand's first Human Rights Act, making discrimination on a number of grounds including sexual orientation illegal.

The text is an appeal for unconditional love and respect for others, which takes its position from the unqualified and unconditional love shown by Christ. Paul's directive to the Corinthian church, equally riven by arguments over sacrifices to idols, 'So whether you eat or drink, or whatever you do, do all to the glory of God (1 Corinthians 10:31) supplies the structural basis for all the verses; a complementary theme is that of the light of the world shining 'through the day and in the darkness' (see John 1:5 and Matthew 5:15). Our love, prayers, deeds and practice of peace are to be carried out 'for the healing of the world' (cf. Revelation 22:2), and they are to be exercised without respect for divisive religious or social labels – saint or sinner, wealthy or needy, same or other, smitten or smiter (language that alludes to Matthew 5:39).

SHINING Although it received this general name in *Hope is our Song*, the original name of the melody was ST KILDA, so named to honour a small Methodist congregation located in the populous St Kilda district of South Dunedin which at a time of fierce debate within the Methodist Church staunchly rejected homophobic arguments and held fast to the principle of inclusive love. The simple, cheerful tune, set in G major, was composed by the writer of the hymn. It gives special emphasis to the thematic core of the text, 'let our love shine out,' by setting these words to crochets among a chatter of quavers.

Let there be light W671
Metre: 4.7.7.6

This hymn, cast in the form of a bidding prayer, was written in 1968 by Canadian poet **Frances Wheeler Davis,** in response to encouragement from Robert and Margaret Fleming (see below), two members of the congregation of St George Anglican Church in St Anne-de-Bellevue, Quebec, where she was a choir member, to write new hymns for use in their church services. It was printed in the same year in a collection of such local-initiative hymns published by the church community. Later it was included in *The Hymn Book of the Anglican Church of Canada and the United Church of Canada* (1971), ironically a joint hymnal produced at a time when both churches were in negotiations for a union which eventually failed. It has since been published in the American *United Methodist Hymnal* (1989), the Unitarian hymnal *Singing the Living Tradition* (1993) and *Voices United: The Hymn and Worship Book of the United Church of Canada* (1997). It appeared in *With One Voice* in 1982.

The original poem was formed as a single sentence, with the first word of each stanza in lower-case, and the stanzas separated by a semi-colon. The original fifth verse has been omitted, it read:

> Your kingdom come,
> (a further quotation from
> the Lord's Prayer)
> your spirit turn to language,
> your people speak together,
> your spirit never fade.

In verse 4, 'Thy' in the final line, a reference to the Lord's Prayer, has been modernised to 'your.'

The text is a powerful mosaic of biblical allusions: it begins with a quotation from Genesis 1:3, line 3 references Isaiah 43:9, line 4 Isaiah 50:8. Verse 2, line 1 references Psalm 51:15, line 2 Luke 24:45, line 3 Revelation 3:20. Verse 3 opens with a reference to Matthew 26:52, line 2 references Matthew 5:22. 'The bombs' in the historical context refers to the arsenal of atomic bombs held by each side during the so-called Cold War. Verse 4, line 4, quotes the second line of the Lord's Prayer. Verse 5 in this tightly constructed text reiterates the repeated opening words of the previous stanzas, creating a powerful cumulative effect.

CONCORD The tune name is derived from the third line of verse 2. The setting was written in 1968 for this text by **Robert Fleming**, a fellow member of the congregation to which the author belonged.

Let there be peace *F42 and HP14*
Metre: Irregular

This original prayer-song was written by **Cecily Sheehy** in 1998 for inclusion in *Faith Forever Singing* (2000) as one of a number of short songs and responses suitable for incorporation into worship wherever fitting (see the Introduction, p. vii). The sharing of the Peace or the Dismissal are two such places, or as a congregational response between the elements of a prayer for peace. The text, with its music, was reprinted in *He Came Singing Peace* (2002).

The text consists principally of the words 'peace' and 'love' repeated in several languages. 'Te rangimārie' is a Māori word meaning 'peace'; 'shalom' and 'aroha' are respectively Hebrew and Māori words of considerable richness of meaning but essentially equivalent to the English word 'love,' in the sense of respectful and affectionate relationships between people and other living beings, but in the largest context the principle of affinity that 'binds the universe together.'

[TE RANGIMĀRIE] The quiet musical setting is by the author and provides a chant-like unison melody sustained by harmonically-coloured, slowly-shifting chords remaining within the framing tonality of E flat major. Such a setting, which already allows for the repetition of the phrase 'te rangimārie,' might be repeated by the congregation several times.

Let there be respect for the earth
F43
Metre: Irregular

This setting of the Millennium Statement prepared in 2000 by the **Churches together in England** is the work of **Colin Gibson** and was written in the same year. The text highlights Christian values of respect for the creation, peace, love, delight in the good and forgiveness. 1 Corinthians 13:6 lies behind it, just as Revelation 21:5 underlies the 'new start.'

MILLENNIUM The tune name records the occasion. The music reflects the sober tone of the statement, moving from an opening in A major through to E major, before dropping to F sharp minor for the words 'forgiveness for past wrongs,' then recovering to A major for 'a new beginning.'

Let us go in your peace (Pāuatahanui Blessing) H89
Metre: 6.6.6.6 D

The gift of a tune from her friend Jillian Bray occasioned this song of dismissal and blessing, written by **Shirley Murray** in 2005. It was published in her fourth American collection, *Touch the Earth Lightly* (2008) before appearing in *Hope is our Song* (2009).

The text is based on 2 Corinthians 13:11-14, 'Agree with one another, live in peace, and the God of love and peace will be with you.' Characteristically, the word 'peace' excites the poet's imagination in a closely rhymed poem which concludes with an imperative to work for peace, a word which incorporates for the writer the ideals of 'kindness, justice and joy.'

PĀUATAHANUI (Māori=place of gathering plentiful shellfish) The name refers to Pāuatahanui Inlet, an arm of the Porirua Harbour north of Wellington where **Jillian Bray**, the composer of the tune which gave rise to this blessing, had her home. Shirley Murray writes, 'As she was about to move house, we decided to commemorate her home in which many meetings of the New Zealand Hymn Book Trust had taken place by naming this short blessing "Pāuatahanui."'

The measured calm of this music, a setting for four voices, is achieved by seven reiterations of the first six-note figure, shifting through modulations into G major, D minor, E minor and F major before returning to the home key of C major. Despite the unusual time signature of 5/4, the equable speed setting of crochet=90 and the close match of each verbal line with a corresponding melodic phrase, makes for easy congregational singing.

Let us talents and tongues employ
W658
Metre: 8.8.8.8. and refrain

This lively hymn, useful among other things as a post-communion celebration, was written by Dutch-born author and Reformed Church minister **Fred Kaan**. It first reached print as one of 20 new hymn texts published by Kaan in *Break Not the Circle* (Hope Publishing, Carol Stream, Illinois, 1975), set to the tune LINSTEAD.

Written at a time when Kaan was Executive Secretary of the Department of Cooperation and Witness of the World Alliance of Reformed Churches, based in Geneva, and co-producer of an ecumenical radio programme broadcast into Europe, it takes as its theme Christ's unifying power ('Christ is able to make us one') and his commission to his disciples to go out into the world as witnesses. Underlying and reinforcing the text are many biblical passages: Matthew 25:15-30 (the account of the *unused* talent), Mark 16:15, Romans 12:6-8, John 6:33, 35, 1 Corinthians 11:23-26, Luke 22:19-20, John 17:11, Galatians 3:28, 1 John 4:11, Matthew 28:19-20, John 15:5, 20-21 and Matthew 1:23 have all been identified as creative sources.

LINSTEAD (or more properly LINSTEAD MARKET) is the melody of a Jamaican folksong referring to a small Jamaican town of that name. The song's first line runs, 'Carry me akee go a Linstead market,' and it describes the sorrow of a mother who cannot sell enough at the market to fee her children. It was collected as early as 1907 and has been reprinted in several anthologies of Jamaican folksong, including *Folk Songs of Jamaica* (London, 1952) and *Beeny Bud: 12 Jamaican Folk-Songs for Children* (London, 1975). In 1980 the original folk song appeared in the World Association song-book of the Girl Guides and the music has been used as a hymn tune with a number of texts in a variety of hymnals, such as *More Hymns for Today* (1980), *Presbyterian*

Hymnal (1990), *With One Voice* (Lutheran, 2000), *Worship and Rejoice* (2001), *Sing! A New Creation* (2002) and *Singing the New Testament* (2008).

Doreen Potter, who received her early education in Jamaica, and later became the wife of Dr Philip Potter, General Secretary of the World Council of Churches, adapted the melody as a hymn tune (set to other words) for the Council's ecumenical hymnbook *Cantate Domino* (1972). She acted as musical editor for *Break Not the Circle*, and it is probable that she introduced Fred Kaan to the song at a time when they were both living in Geneva and were involved in ecumenical activities there. The arrangement of LINSTEAD used in *With One Voice* is by **Guy Jansen**; a calypso-style version by Australian composer Alister Spence with some minor differences in the melodic line and set a tone higher was published in *Together in Song* (1999).

Let's praise the creator *A86*
Metre: 12.11.12.11

This hymn by **Shirley Murray** first appeared in the author's own collection, *In Every Corner Sing* (Wellington, 1987), where it is titled 'Song for a Wedding.' Written for friends, its suggested setting is KREMSER, found at the time in *With One Voice* (1982), though intriguingly an alternative melody is proposed 'to the cowboy tune, "Streets of Laredo." It then reached *Alleluia Aotearoa* (1993) but has not appeared in any of her own American publications. In 2011 it was published in *Worship* (Fourth edition), by GIA, Chicago.

The first verse acknowledges the Genesis story of the creation of man and woman, though Murray replaces the reasons attributed there to God for the creation of Eve with a purpose that gives both partners equal status, 'to celebrate life.' Verse 2 echoes Paul's famous celebration of love in 1 Corinthians 13:8-13, a passage frequently read at a marriage service. But the poet also introduces her own images: 'stronger than storms [marital disturbances?] and more gentle than breath.' Verse 3 carries a typical piece of wordplay: 'compassionate' (line 3) may mean 'equally passionate' or 'sympathetic, deeply pitying.'

KREMSER The tune takes the name of its Austrian arranger **Eduard Kremser**, but the original is by an anonymous 17th century Dutch composer whose work was gathered by the poet Adrian Valerius of Veere (1575-1625). Valerius spent 30 years collecting patriotic poetry and songs written during the war between the Netherlands and Spain but died before his work could be published. Under the title *Netherlands Songs of Remembrance*, the collection was finally issued posthumously by his son François in 1626. The melody later became popular through performances by the Vienna Men's Choir of an arrangement by their conductor Eduard Kremser, who published it with five other such melodies at Leipzig in 1877 as *Six Old Dutch Folk Songs*.

An equally anonymous hymn was set to the tune to celebrate Holland's liberation from Spanish rule in 1697, 'Will heden nu treden voor God den Heere.' It is known to the Dutch as 'A Prayer of Thanksgiving' and to us in Dr Theodore Baker's translation as 'We gather together to ask the Lord's blessing.' Shirley Murray's wedding hymn faithfully follows the metrical structure of Baker's version and shares with it the theme of blessing.

Life into life, the threads are woven *H91*
Metre: 9.4.4.9.4.4.9.9

This hymn by **Shirley Murray**, was written in 2007 because, says the author, 'I could not find a satisfying expression of a deep sense of thanksgiving for life as we know it now.' She goes to say, 'Five stanzas are usually too long for me in a hymn, but I could not decide which of these to omit – so there needs to be some good pace in the singing.' It was published shortly before its appearance in *Hope is our Song* (2009) in Shirley Murray's American collection *Touch the Earth Lightly* (2008).

The theme of the hymn places it alongside the biblical psalms of thanksgiving, such as Psalm 106:1-3, and New Testament expressions of the essential unity of humankind, such as Galatians 3:28. Verse 1 takes as its principal image life as a woven fabric; 'partner' is used as the new generic term for relationships, displacing older terms restricted to legal marriage. Verse 2 glances at the Genesis account of the goodness of the world made by God. Verse 4 concentrates on the image of time as a river (cf. 'Time, like an ever-rolling stream, bears all its sons away,' in Watts' hymn, 'O God, our help in ages past'). The Holy Spirit is imagined as speeding up, enlivening the passage of human life ('quickens,' line 2, means both 'speeds up' and 'gives life to'). 'Charges the flow,' line 6, takes its metaphor from the 'flow' of electric current: 'gives a stimulating electric charge to the flow of life.' In the final verse, the primary meaning of 'spinning' is 'revolving' as the planet does, catching sunlight on its surface as it does so, but there is a sub-allusion to spinning and weaving (cf. verse 1).

STANLEY STREET The name of the tune composed by **Colin Gibson** in 2007 derives from the Dunedin street address where an aging friend of the composer, Pauline Mabon – to whom the music is dedicated – was living at the time. The 'lifting' motif in the opening bars, and repeated elsewhere, echoes the beginning of **Richard Terry**'s famous hymn tune HIGHWOOD.

Life is like a river H60
Metre: Irregular

This meditative poem was written by **Joy Cowley** in 2006 and published in 2008 in *Come and See: Reflections on the life of Jesus among us*. There it is titled 'Flowing Life' (sub-titled 'The River'), and carries as its epigraph a saying from John 7:37-38, 'Let any one who is thirsty come to me and let the one who believes in me drink. As the scripture has said, "Out of the believer's heart shall flow rivers of living water."'

The image of a human lifespan or the passage of the individual soul as a river journey is at least as old as the ancient Egyptians and has been memorably expressed by English poets such as Shelley and Matthew Arnold. In such poetry, the river commonly stands for the time-bound flow of human existence; the sea, its final destination, stands for eternity, dissolution in a greater whole or as in this poem the receptive 'ocean' of God's love. Through this poem for New Zealanders familiar with the oceans that surround their island home and the great rivers flowing from mountain chains to the sea the ancient theme gains an experiential reception.

Joy Cowley has frequently returned to rivers and seas as potent metaphors in both her poetry and her fictional writing for children and adults: see, for instance, *The Silent One* (1981), *Beyond the River* (1994), *The Song of the River* (1994), and 'Living water' and 'The Pool of Siloam' in *Come and See* (2008). In this meditation, shaped like a hymn with a refrain, the presence of an eternal, divine love within the mortal human soul is suggested but left as an unanswered question:

> Already we have knowledge
> of the presence of the sea.
> And I have a question to ask you,
> my friend,
> Where does the sea begin?
> Where does the river end?

Although no music is provided in *Hope is our Song*, the words were set to music in 2006 by Jane Coles, using a folk ballad idiom. This setting in D flat remains unpublished.

Life of ages, richly poured W660
Metre 7.7.7.7

This hymn was the work of American clergyman and author **Samuel Johnson** (1822-82), who first published it in *Hymns of the Spirit* (1864), a compilation by Johnson himself and his friend Samuel Longfellow, the poet, who later published a selection of Johnson's lectures, essays and sermons with a memoir in 1883.

The original hymn consisted of nine stanzas: later hymn book editors usually select verses 1-2 and 7-9, as has been done in the New Zealand Supplement to *With One Voice*. There have been alterations to the original text: 'Yours' for 'Thine' and 'pure' for 'sweet' in verse 2, 'noblest' for 'simplest' in verse 7. In verse 8, 'way' replaces the author's 'track' and the original final two lines, 'Hurling floods of tyrant wrong / From the sacred limits back,' are replaced with 'quelling strife and tyrant wrong, / Widening freedom's sacred way.'

Although Johnson uses a number of familiar religious references, such as 'the prophet's word' or 'the love of God,' the imaginative power of the text is derived from the sustained imagery of water ('poured, flowing, tide, fountain'), culminating in the now-abandoned 'hurling floods of tyrant wrong,' and the active verbal forms, as in verse 3-4: 'breathing, pulsing, nerving, freshening, consecrating, quelling, widening.' Throughout this text there also runs Johnson's profound belief in the liberation of the human spirit (as well the African slaves for whom he spoke out so strongly). It is no accident that the words 'free' and 'liberty' ring out from the beginning of the text to its close.

BRANDENBERG Named after one of the 16 old German states or its capital (Bach named a famous set of concertos after its ruler in his time) the actual source of this tune is unknown. It first appeared in its present form in the *Supplement of Samuel Dyer's Third Edition of Sacred Music*, published in Baltimore in 1826, though there may have been a previous edition in 1823. There it is named GERMAN SET, the only clue to its real source. Samuel Dyer (1785-1835) was an English-born scholar-musician who spent much of his life in the United States and gave much effort to accurately preserving older hymn and psalm tunes.

Lift high the cross A87
Metre: 10.10 and refrain

This popular adaptation by **Shirley Murray** of the hymn 'Lift high the cross' by George William Kitchin (1827-1912) and its further rewritten version by Canon Michael Robert Newbolt (1874-1956) was prepared by the New Zealand hymn writer in 1984. It was initially published in the author's own private collection, *In Every Corner Sing* (1987), followed by her first American collection, of the same name (1992), and *Alleluia Aotearoa* (1993).

Explaining that she had never been able to sing the original words 'because of the military imagery and now inappropriate theology,' Murray says of her own work, 'This adaptation locates the emphasis on the Holy Week story, the cost of conflict and the Gospel imperatives of peace-making.' Kitchin's refrain is retained, apart from the substitution of 'glorious' for 'sacred,' but her five verses completely displace the original six verses of Kitchen's hymn.

Verse 1 draws on Luke's account of Christ's entry into Jerusalem, 'I tell you, if these [the disciples] were silent, the very stones would cry out' (Luke 19:40). Verse 2 draws on the same passage: 'And when he drew near and saw the city he wept over it, saying, "Would that even today you knew the things that make for peace"' (Luke 19:41-42). John 14:27 ('Peace I leave with you; my peace I give to you') and a number of other gospel sources stand behind verse 3, but the metaphor of peace as 'our passport' is both original and typical of this writer's search for contemporary images of the faith. Verse 4 warns of the cost of discipleship (see Matthew 16:24 and cf. Luke 9:57-62) and returns to the Passion theme, 'to follow and suffer with the Song of God.' The final verse recapitulates the sense of the refrain, but its theology is starkly different from the equivalent verse in Kitchen's hymn, 'From farthest regions let them homage bring, / And on his cross adore their Saviour King.'

CRUCIFER (Latin=cross-bearer) The name of the tune is derived from the ceremonial church processions led by a cross carrier with which Dean Kitchin's hymn is still often associated – the original occasion was a Society for the Propagation of the Gospel festival held in 1887 in his own Winchester Cathedral. However, the name may also refer to any person who follows Christ's instruction to 'take up [their] cross and follow [him]' (Matthew 16:24) and this is the sense Shirley Murray's words embrace. The music, a majestic marching tune, was written for Kitchin's text by **Sydney**

Nicholson and has become inseparable from that hymn ever since its first publication in the 1916 *Supplement to Hymns Ancient & Modern*.

Lift up your hearts to the Lord A88
Metre: 7.6.8.6 and refrain

Michael Perry's assemblage of lines from Psalm 98, the basis of the text of this hymn, was first published in 1987 in his *Carol Praise* and again in *Songs from the Psalms* (1990). But the text is a composite one. Line 1 of verse 1 comes from Lamentations 3:41; Psalm 95:6 is the source of verse 2, line 1; verse 3 is constructed from the opening lines of the Magnificat, Luke 1:46-7, 49-50.

LIFT UP YOUR HEARTS The tune name was taken from the first line of the hymn text. This setting was written by **Christopher Norton** and was first published in *Songs from the Psalms* (1990), for which this New Zealand musician had a major role in editing and arranging the music. The chosen tonality is the celebration key of D major. The strong musical shape of the melody, rising to its highest arc with the 'words 'O sing a new song' is supported by a rich pattern of modulations and imitative effects, as in the 'thick' textures of the chords carrying the words 'Harps and horns and trumpets sound.' The style is modern and popular, but the music expresses weight and joyful conviction, without loss of rhythmic vitality.

Light of lights beholden (Indigo II)
A89, C29, HP16
Metre: 6.6.3.5.7.4.8.5 and refrain

This work was created in 1983 by **Jenny McLeod**, its author and composer, as one of a set of choral pieces based on the idea of colour, first performed on the Wellington harbour basin as part of the 1983 Wellington Sun Festival. It is the second of two 'Indigo' songs, this one scored for choir and piano. It was first published in *Alleluia Aotearoa* (1993) and recorded on the accompanying CD; it has remained popular as a Christmas hymn sung by congregations and choirs.

The title 'Indigo,' referring to the rich dark colour midway between blue and violet, carries a wide range of symbolic connotations: its biblical symbolism is heavenly grace (the colour worn by the Virgin Mary in many religious paintings), but in Indian and other thought-systems indigo symbolizes a mystical borderland of wisdom, self-mastery and spiritual realization and the values of devotion, wisdom and justice.

Jenny McLeod simply lists 'Christmas' as an influence on the text. More specifically, verses from John 1 underlie the words: 'In him was life, and the life was the light of men. The light shines in the darkness, and the darkness has not overcome it' (4-5), 'The true light that enlightens every man was coming into the world' (9), '…we have beheld his glory, glory as of the only Son of God' (14). Old Testament promises of peace (Psalm 85:8, Isaiah 2:4, 9:6) underlie verse 1, lines 5-6, and John 14:1 is a possible source for the 'voice of troubled gloom.' Lines 2-3 of verse 1 mean 'we have sung this song since ancient times.'

[LIGHT OF LIGHTS] Despite the irregular line length, the two rhythmic pulses heard in the first bar, one dotted, one not, are repeated throughout the music and frequently in the accompaniment to give the setting a strong forward drive and sense of coherence. Despite some key shifts, the tonality of D major is never lost sight of, sustaining the mood of optimism filling the text.

Little one, born to bring us such love (Hymn for the Funeral of a Small Child) F44
Metre: 9.9.9.9

The words of this funeral hymn were written by **Shirley Murray** in 1996. She describes it as 'not written out of a personal story, but as a reaction to a media report on the mystery of cot deaths at the time…an attempt, in the unutterable grief of losing a child, to offer some comfort. I hope it has few reasons to be used.' It first appeared in *Faith Forever Singing* (2000), then in *Worship and Rejoice* (Hope Publishing, 2001), where it was set to the tune KORU,* by American composer **Joy F. Patterson**.

Addressed to a 'little one,' one of Jesus' own terms for children (cf. Matthew 18:14) it offers the traditional consolation that a life 'given and taken' (Job 1:21) has been returned to the loving care of God. In verses 2-3 the writer then addresses the painful feelings of the mourners, advising against their possible sense of guilt, 'the blame we keep to our cost.' In verse 2, lines 1-2 recall Isaiah 40:11, '[God] will gather the lambs in his arms, he will carry them in his bosom.' In verse 3, lines 3-4 point to the Parable of the Lost Sheep, with its conclusion, 'It is not the will of my Father in heaven that one of these little ones should perish (Matthew 18:12-14). In the final verse, there are echoes of John 14:16 – 'I will pray the Father, and he will give you another Counsellor, to be with you for ever, even the Spirit of truth' – and of the Compline prayer, 'Save us, O God, while waking, and guard us while sleeping, that awake we may watch with Christ and asleep may rest in peace.'

ANGEL was written in 1999 by **Jillian Bray** as a setting for these words and first appeared in *Faith Forever Singing* (2000). The composer writes, 'This tune was pared to its bare essentials, as those attending a child's funeral would have no heart for singing, least of all to an unfamiliar tune. Other uses [than congregational singing] are possible, however, such as a "voice over" [that is, a speaker, supported by quiet background playing of the music].'

> *The American tune name, KORU, chosen by Shirley Murray at the composer's request, is explained by Shirley herself in *Faith Makes the Song* as referring to 'the uncoiling fern leaf, used in New Zealand as a symbol of unfolding life.'

Living Christ, you call us here *H90*
Metre: 7.5.6.4

A hymn for the celebration of communion, this text was written by **Bill Bennett** in 2003 as a response to the Gospel reading John 6:56-59, though the final lines of the first three verses allude to Jesus' declaration in John 14:6, 'I am the way, and the truth, and the life.' The text was first published in *Hope is our Song* (2009), then in the author's *Gradual Praise* (2010).

The theme of the hymn is the living presence of Christ, mediated, as Bill Bennett says, through the Eucharist, 'as the gathering of the servants of God around the Lord's Table, where they are washed spiritually, fed and renewed for service in the community.' Verse 1 draws on John 13:1-15, the account of the washing of the disciples' feet by Jesus, which in Bill Bennett's words, 'remains a powerful image and injunction to all Christians regarding the nature of servanthood and of service to others.' 'Make us one' (line 3) alludes to John 17:21. Verse 2 invokes the presence of Christ as the host of the communion 'supper.' 'Break the Word, shed the light' refers both to the Gospel reading which precedes the act of communion and to John 1:1-5. Verse 3 develops John 6:53-54. Verse 4 has the Emmaus story as its background: the 'friend' who walks with us.

HUARAHI [Māori=way, roadway] **Bill Bennett's** tune is named after the last line of the first verse of his hymn. The setting, which can be sung in four parts, offers a gentle melody composed of short-breathed phrases built on a three-note motif, perfectly suited to a mood of reverence. The harmonic setting is in G major, with mid-section modulations to D major and B minor; the final invocation in each verse is accompanied by a return to the tonic key and an expansive variation on the initial phrase of the melody, completing an intellectually as well as aesthetically pleasing music structure.

Lo matou Tama e *A90*
Metre: 6.7.7.6 and refrain

This offering hymn, written at an unknown date by Deacon **Kelemete Ta'ale** in the Samoan language, was first published with a non-singing translation in *Alleluia Aotearoa* (1993).

Psalm 19:14, 'May the words of my mouth and the meditation of my heart be acceptable in your sight, O Lord,' supplies the framework for the text, and Psalm-derived phrases such as 'the works of our hands' (Psalm 90) and 'the fruit of the earth' (Psalm 105) show the natural affinity between certain traditional Hebrew and Pacific cultural practices.

[LO MATOU TAMA E] The setting is also by Kelemete Ta'ale, in four-part harmony suited to the vigorous Samoan unaccompanied choral singing style.

Look around you H92
Metre: 8.9.8.9.8.8.3.8.9

Titling his carol 'Spring Song,' **Rob Ferguson** wrote this hymn text in 1997 for a Spring Flower service at Beckenham Methodist church, Christchurch, during his ministry there. He describes it as 'a directly contextual piece of writing. The original had the lines "Hear the Heathcote River chuckle" – Beckenham Church is in the loop of the Heathcote River – and "Blossoms blow, flowers grow, Port Hills [the low range of hills to the south of Christchurch] shine." I noted in my notebook that "this hymn is localised and probably won't be sung again."' The phrase 'mountains shine' (verse 1) probably refers to the outline of the Southern Alps, clearly visible from Christchurch on a fine spring day. The text was later revised.

The two verses of the hymn match the outburst of spring growth and the melting of winter snows with the resurrection of Jesus ('our brother Christ who burst his tomb,' verse 2). For the 'Women [who] came there full of mourning' (verse 2), see Matthew 28, Luke 24 and John 20.

SPRING CAROL The author notes that 'the original tune was "Deck the halls," and I noted "I like the tune. Why should Christmas have all the good tunes – or all the carols for that matter! The original title was "Spring Song." It should have been "Spring Carol" really.'

The setting in *Hope is our Song* is by Christchurch composer **Barry Brinson,** and was written in 2006 for this text. It has an appropriate 6/8 carol-like dance rhythm. Those with an ear for musical correspondences will hear echoes of 'The Shepherds' Dance' by English composer Edward German (1862-1936).

Look in wonder H93
Metre: 8.7.8.7 D

This hymn was written by **Shirley Murray** in 2008 and first published in her American collection *Touch the Earth Lightly* (2008), then in *Hope is our Song* (2009). There is an unusual touch of exasperation in the writer's note on the text in *Touch the Earth Lightly*: 'Though I have written several "green" hymns, beginning in the 1980s with "God of the Galaxies" ("Honour the Earth"), followed by "Touch the Earth Lightly," "I am your Mother," "Earth Prayer" and others, it seems the Church needs a critical mass before deciding to catch up with this imperative theology!'

There are two important biblical references: to Genesis 1:1-31 (God's blessing of the creation as 'good') and to Genesis 2:1-25 (the creation of Adam, appointed to 'till and keep' the garden of Eden). 'Unnerve' (verse 3) in this context means 'take away our audacious confidence ('nerve') in our own superiority.' Earth's 'greening' (verse 3) is a scientific term, now in common use, which refers to the effects of global warming.

The highly wrought texture of this poem to earth's beauty – note the echoing of the theme in line 2 by the final line of the poem – deserves attention, with its internal half-rhyming in the first, third, fifth and seventh lines in each verse ('wonder…honour'), the frequent balancing of paired nouns and verbs ('joins the circle, moves the line'), the use of repetition and alliteration to lock words together and reinforce ideas ('ours to cherish, ours to nourish'; 'sense and savour every colour, / every season, sun to star'). Imperatives ('Look, surrender, sense, see') and exclamations (How we plunder, waste and war!) deployed throughout to forcefully express the message of the text and the 'imperative' theology it embodies.

LOOK IN WONDER This melody, by American composer and performer **Jim Strathdee** takes its title from the first line of the hymn; it has the quality of an early

American folksong, with a plaintive sadness in its harmonic shifts into minor keys. Guitar chords are supplied.

Look toward Christmas! *C30 (i) and (ii)*
Metre: 5.4.5.4 D and refrain

As a member of the editorial panel preparing a collection of New Zealand-authored carols, **Shirley Murray** wrote these words because 'I found few on the Advent theme, especially simple texts for young singers.' The carol was written in 1995 and first published in *Carol our Christmas* (1996), followed by Murray's second American collection, *Every Day in Your Spirit* (1997).

The text is marked by almost comic instructions to the traditional figures associated with the Nativity to prepare for their roles: 'Whistle up,* shepherds, / saddle up, kings, / chorus up* angels, / flexing your wings' (verse 1). In the final verse Mary and Joseph are told to 'ready' [=prepare] the donkey, and start on their way. The refrain is likewise introduced with instructions to sing alleluias, then to 'sing out the story,' and finally to 'sing about hope and peace.' In verse 2, unusually, John the Baptist and the whole earth are added to the cast preparing for action; we, the singers, are to hear the Baptist shouting (see Matthew 3:1-6) while the earth is to be aware of the coming of 'Good News' (a play on the secular and religious senses of the phrase). Only in the final verse are orders replaced by the affectionate description of Mary and Joseph as the chosen ones, 'willing to trust' (see the annunciation narratives in Matthew and Luke).

CAMPANE (French=bell) Two members of the editorial board preparing *Carol our Christmas* wrote tunes for Shirley Murray's words in 1995. **Jillian Bray** set the text in C major to a lively 6/8 rhythm, using a dotted figure to give the melody its Advent joyfulness. The refrain introduces a fresh melodic figure for 'Sing, sing alleluia!,' starting on top E then sequencing downwards before a final lift back to high C, the tonic note. The tune name suggests the joyful ringing of church bells on Christmas Day.

MAKORA STREET Named after the Christchurch street address of two Anglican friends, Bill and Lois Ball, and written for Jennifer Murray and her Youth Choir at St Barnabas Anglican Church where they worshipped, this setting of Shirley Murray's carol was written by **Colin Gibson** in 1995. In the key of G major and 4/4 time, it represents the steady advance of the New Year with a melody poised over a regular, rising motif in the bass which reaches B flat major before a new higher-pitched melodic figure releases a joyful and syncopated refrain, finally coming down to earth on the tonic note.

Features of both these settings are found in RAUMATI (Māori=summer, and the name of the beach village where Shirley Murray lives), a lilting tune in 6/8 time by American composer **Carlton Young**, used in *Every Day in Your Spirit*. There is also a setting by Canadian composer **Ron Klusmeier** (Klusmeier 23).

> *Both 'whistle up' and 'chorus up' are neologisms, based on the model of 'saddle up.' The shepherds are imagined in New Zealand terms, whistling to direct their sheepdogs as they drive their flocks.

Lord Jesus, look on this we do *H94*
Metre: 11.8.8.8.8.8.8.8

This text, originally a poem titled 'Lines composed by a patient for the opening of the Chapel of Christ the Saviour,' was written in 1967 by poet and artist **John Paisley**, who was commissioned to do so by Father Cyril Cartwright, the chaplain of the former psychiatric hospital known as Cherry Farm, near Dunedin, now Hawksbury Village. 'It was my only commission,' said the poet, who suffered for most of life from a crippling mental disability. 'I have written about five hymns in all, not very good, and all a long time in the past. He [Father Cartwright] asked me for a poem, but the end product came out more like a hymn, the best I could do, I suppose, under the influence of tranquilizers.

The thought of the second verse is based upon the designs on the four windows of the chapel – the Bread of Life, the Way, the Truth and the Life, the Good Shepherd, and the True Vine. It has been used, I believe, as a hymn at the opening of a church in the North Island somewhere, but I don't know what tune they used.' For the life of Father Cartwright, who 'made a name for himself among the senior staff for his availability, diligence and attention to the patients,' see the obituary in *The Tablet* 126 (October 2007).

The four windows referred to represent biblical texts. John 6:35 ('I am the bread of life'); John 14:6 ('I am the way, the truth, the life'; John 10:11 ('I am the good shepherd'); and John 15:1 ('I am the true vine'). There are Old Testament and New Testament resonances for 'wandering from the way' (verse 2, line 3), but here the way is the path of sanity and mental stability. Verse 3, 'reach out your hand, dispel our doubts,' refers to the episode in which Jesus reassured doubting Thomas (John 20:24-29). The sub-text of the whole verse is the poet's prayer for the healing of his own and his fellow patients' crippling infirmity.

CHERRY FARM Named after the psychiatric hospital where the poem was written, the music was written by **Colin Gibson** in 1993, after he came across the text in *Collected Poems by John Paisley*, edited and published by Dawn Ross, the poet's sister (Dunedin, 1990), and recognized the name of one of his own former students. In keeping with the tone of the poem, the harmonic soundscape of the music starts in uncertainty (D minor) and fluctuates between C, F and G minor before reaching midway the 'secure' key of E flat major, at which point the melody recovers a sense of direction and moves to a confident close in that key.

Lord of all being, throned afar
W626
Metre: 8.8.8.8

Oliver Wendell Holmes (1809-94) wrote this hymn in 1859. It appeared as a poem entitled 'A Sun-day Hymn' in the December issue of the *Atlantic Monthly* at the end of the final installment for the year of Holmes' column, *Professor at the Breakfast Table*. It carried this introduction: 'Peace to all such as may have been vexed by any utterance these pages have repeated. They will doubtless forget for the moment the difference in the hues of truth we look at through our human prisms, and join in singing (inwardly) this hymn to the source of the light we all need to lead us, and the warmth which alone can make us all brothers [see verse 3].'

The text is dominated by images of the sun, light and flames ('kindling hearts that burn for thee'): in a general sense, Psalm 19 is a significant source. In verse 1, Holmes uses the ancient and long-discredited concept of the planets located within concentric crystalline spheres circling the earth: God replaces the planets as 'centre and soul of every sphere.' In verse 2, the sun is matched with the 'star of our hope,' which actually seems to be the moon, with its 'softened light.' 'Quickening' means life-giving.' Longfellow was to repeat the image of the long watches [sentry duties] of the night in his poem *The Cross of Snow* (1879), where he writes of the 'long, sleepless watches of the night'). In verse 3 God is positioned on an ever-blazing throne, an image derived from Revelation 4:3. In verse 4, believers themselves become burning altars (cf. Romans 12:1).

OMBERSLEY This tune, named after a village near Worcester, England, in a constituency which its author **William Henry Gladstone** (1840-91) had represented in the House of Commons, first appeared in Joseph Barnby's *Hymnal* (1872), where it was set to John Keble's 'Sun of my soul' and **Isaac Watts'** 'Jesus shall reign where'er the sun.' It was first set to these words in *Congregational Praise* (1951).

Lord of all love *A91*
Metre: 8.8.8.8

This funeral hymn was written in 1987 by **Colin Gibson**, following the unexpected cot death of Harmony, his second grandchild and the first-born child of his eldest son, Marcus Gibson. At the time the writer was overseas on sabbatical leave; the hymn was written on his return to New Zealand and sent to the bereaved family as a message of solidarity and profound sympathy. The work was first published in the author's English collection *Singing Love* (1988), before appearing in *Alleluia Aotearoa* (1993) and in his American collection *Reading the Signature* (1994). As a representative New Zealand hymn it was reprinted (words only) in *A Panorama of Christian Hymnody*, by Erik Routley and Alan A Richardson (Chicago: GIA, 2005).

The author describes the hymn as 'an attempt to deal honestly with the emotions (not all of them pious) which such an inexplicable loss brought to the surface: emotions, I have since learned, others have felt in similar circumstances.' The text opens with an address to Christ as 'Lord of life,' a phrase taken from Elizabethan poet Edmund Spenser's lines 'Most glorious Lord of life, that on this day / Didst make Thy triumph over death and sin' (Sonnet 68, *Amoretti* (1595), followed by an acknowledgement of Christ's own suffering and death on the cross. Verse 2 faces the crippling sense of sorrow brought about by such death and asks Christ to carry out the act of worship on behalf of the mourners. There is a resonance here from the Roman Catholic prayer addressed to Mary, 'pray for us now and at the hour of our death.' Verse 3 draws on 1 Corinthians 15:51-56, for its description of the mystery of death and the triumph of God in Christ over 'the sting of death' (verse 55). It asks for the turbulent and destructive emotions associated with the experience of death to be replaced by 'faith, trust and consolation.' Verse 4 recalls the words of the burial service, 'Dust to dust, ashes to ashes' (based on *Genesis* 3:19), and closes with the committal of the dead person into the care and good purposes of God.

HARMONY The tune is named after the child whose death occasioned the hymn. The composer is **Colin Gibson**. The shape of the melody suggests a helpless reaching up, which collapses back three times until its final repetition, when it closes on a repeated tonic note. The harmony similarly reaches for a tonal conclusion which is denied until the last two bars. In 1991 the composer added a descant to the hymn.

Lord of the living, in your name assembled W657
Metre: 11.11.11.5

This hymn was written by **Fred Kaan** for his Pilgrim Church, Plymouth, congregation and was first published in his words-only collection *Pilgrim Praise* (1967), where it was titled 'For a Funeral Service.' With the author's permission, the text differs slightly from the original: 'our enrichment' replaces 'the enrichment' (verse 2, line 2) and 'in this day's' replaces 'for the day's' (verse 4, line 3). The hymn has appeared in a number of hymnals, such as *The Hymn Book* (Canada,1971), *Hymns and Psalms* (1983), *Together in Song* (1999), *Worship and Rejoice* (2001) and *Hymns for Today* (2009).

As is usual in a Kaan text, the lines embody a number of scriptural allusions. See Matthew 22:32 (repeated in Luke 20:38) for 'Lord of the living' (verse 1, line 1), Deuteronomy 6:6-9, and Genesis 1:1; John 11:25-26, 1 Peter 1:3 and Matthew 28:7-8 for verse 3; and John 11:44 and Ephesians 2:4-7 for verse 4.

CHRISTE SANCTORUM (Latin=O Christ [the fair glory] of the holy angels). This is the tune selected by **Doreen Potter** for the full music edition of *Pilgrim Praise* published in 1971 (in the 1967 edition of the hymnal DIVA SERVATRIX had been suggested, as used at the Pilgrim Church). It is an old French plainsong melody first found in the Paris *Antiphoner* (1681) and the Cluny *Antiphoner* (1686); its composer is unknown. The name derives from its association with a medieval Catholic office hymn, *Christe sanctorum, decus angelorum*, attributed to Rabanus Maurus (c.776-856), a famous Carolingian poet and theologian who became abbot of the Benedictine monastery at Fulda, then archbishop of Mainz. As well as composing religious poetry, he wrote extensive biblical commentaries, a universal encyclopedia, and other works which circulated widely during the Middle Ages. The melody first reached English congregational singing in the *English Hymnal* (1906) with a setting by its musical editor, **Ralph Vaughan Williams**.

Lord, turn our grieving into grace
F45
Metre: 8.7.8.7.8.8.8

Shirley Murray wrote this funeral hymn in 1999, after what she describes as a spate of funerals at St Andrew's [St Andrew's on the Terrace, Wellington, where her husband was the resident minister], 'among them many good friends of ours.' After its publication in *Faith Forever Singing* (2000), it reached American congregations in her collection *Faith Makes the Song* (2003), where it was set to the tune TRANSFORMATION by composer **Carlton Young**. In that publication Shirley Murray commented, 'Suffering, it seems to me, has a possibility of transforming us if we can bear to turn it into something positive.'

This well describes the theme of the hymn, which calls for 'another way of being…another way of seeing…till, through the anguish of today, hope takes us on another way.' The final line of verse 1 may call to mind Saying 77 in the Gospel of Thomas, 'Raise a stone and you will find me there,' or the stone rolled away from Christ's tomb (Luke 24:2).

SOLOMON'S MEMORY **Ian Render** composed this setting for the text in 1999 and, somewhat unusually, named it for his pet Golden Retriever, Solomon, who had died of cancer aged 10. The composer says of Solomon, 'He had been my companion since being weaned and was much loved for his friendly demeanour.' The melody carrying the final 4 lines of the text literally imitates the lifting of the stone and the movement of hope, then sinks down and settles 'on another way' in the final bars.

Love is your way H95
Metre: 4.5.5.4 D and refrain

The theme for the 9th Assembly of the World Council of Churches held in Brazil in 2006 was 'God, in your grace, transform the world,' and **Shirley Murray** was asked to write an Assembly theme song. The text was written in 2004 and first published in the Assembly's songbook. It was then published in Murray's fourth American collection, *Touch the Earth Lightly* (2008), followed by *Hope is our Song* (2009).

The text is best understood in the light of the writer's own account of the experience of composition: 'The varied ideas for the biblical references for the theme…made it a very wide canvas to cover. I was beset by the feeling that we were becoming dependents on a "deus ex machina" [Latin=deity out of the machine], i.e. the direct intervention of God to solve human problems rather than a pro-active faith community working for transformation. I also needed to keep in mind the cries for justice and human rights in such a country as Brazil.' After consultation, the Assembly accepted the addition of the words 'Turn us to you.'

The refrain versifies the Assembly theme. Verse 1 draws on John 13:34-5, 1 John 4:8, John 8:12. Grace as the miraculous 'chalice that changes / water to wine' is an original metaphor, but there are associations with the Holy Grail and Jesus' miraculous transformation of water into wine at the wedding celebrations at Cana (John 2:1-11). Verse 2, line 3 ('earth as our kingdom') is underpinned by Psalm 8:6. Matthew 24:29 refers to the darkening of the sun, following 'the tribulation of those days.' Verse 3 picks up the theme of contemporary injustice and the abuse of human rights ('hearts without feeling'). 'Grind us to dust,' while it has scriptural resonance, also suggests an industrial society in which the poor are oppressed – cf. the proverb, 'Laws grind the poor, and rich men rule the law.' The final verse acknowledges human responsibility for thwarting God's will, and the urgent need to learn to better care for the environment. (The contemporary destruction of the Amazon rainforest may have prompted this sentiment.) These are thoughts close to those expressed in another Murray hymn, 'God of the Galaxies,' A54: 'Let us care for your garden, and honour the earth.'

GOD, IN YOUR GRACE The music is by **Per Harling**, with whom Shirley Murray worked closely in the creation of this hymn. 'His tune,' she says, 'gave these words a life.' The music, in D minor, has the character of a gracious but somewhat edgy waltz with the universe. A sense of genuine urgency appears in the opening bars of the refrain, where the melodic pattern beginning the verses is inverted and the melody, now in F major, climbs towards G minor before falling from B flat to the tonic note D.

Love to the world A93
Metre: 4.9.5.5.10.10

This song of praise to Jesus was written by **David Dell** in 1990 and first published in the 1990 update to his compilation *New Zealand Praise* (1988). It was then included in *Alleluia Aotearoa* (1993).

The structure of the song seems to owe something to fellow New Zealand composer **Colin Gibson's** 1972 hymn, 'He came singing love,' in that each verse reminds the singers of Christ's death, resurrection and enduring influence, and focuses on one of Christ's gifts to the world: love, peace, hope and joy (cf. Gibson's love, faith, hope and peace). Another possible inspiration is the opening of **Isaac Watts'** famous Christmas hymn, 'Joy to the world,' published in his *Psalms of David* (1719). 2 Corinthians 5:15, 'him who died for them and rose again,' supplies the basis for lines 2-3 of each verse – though 'rose up high' (that is, 'ascended into heaven') in turn echoes John 3:1 – and the repeated fourth and fifth lines of each stanza probably derive from Luke 24:32 in the context of the appearance of the risen Christ to the disciples on the road to Emmaus: 'They said to each other did not our hearts burn within us while he talked to us on the road, while he opened to us the scriptures?' However, the trope of the burning heart has since become a commonplace in both religious and secular writing.

[LOVE TO THE WORLD] The opening falling phrase of the melody written by the author takes the general shape of the opening phrase of the Handel-derived tune ANTIOCH, long associated with Isaac Watts' 'Joy to the world.'* The melodic line is equally imitative of the text, falling with the words 'to the world' and rising sharply with the words 'he rose up high,' and in a general texture of crochets and quavers using a semibreve for the word 'remains' and minims to express 'last for ever.' The rhythm is accentuated by the dotted motif in the tenor line of the accompaniment, and it is given ease and flexibility by a generous use of syncopation.

*See *A Companion to Together in Song*, by Wesley Milgate and D'Arcy Wood (Sydney: Australian Hymn Book Pty Ltd, 2000) for a detailed discussion of the complicated early history of this tune and its uncertain authorship.

Lover of creation H98
Metre: 6.6.5.6.6.5.7.8.6

This hymn was written by **Marnie Barrell** in the 1990s as a then unpublished response to a competition announced by the Hymn Society of America and Canada to fit a new text to the challenging metre of the German chorale by Johann Franck (1618-77) best known in English as 'Jesus, priceless treasure.' It was first published in *Hope is our Song* (2009) and appears on the SongSelect website.

The theme of the hymn is the generosity of God's provision for the created world, and in particular the human creation ('we, your children'). The language is rich and resonant with echoes of scripture, particularly Psalm 109:5, 10-28, and other texts, Robert Bridges' 1898 version of Joachim Neander's 1680 chorale, 'All my hope on God is founded.'* The first verse addresses the Genesis creation (Genesis 1:31), but there are echoes of Walter Chalmer Smith's 1867 hymn 'Immortal, invisible, God only wise' (cf. his 'not wanting, nor wasting' with 'wasting not, nor needing') and the refrain of Jane Montgomery Campbell's translation of Matthias Claudius' harvest hymn 'We plough the fields and scatter' ('all good gifts around us / are sent from heav'n above'). Verse 2 focuses on human praise of

God as 'source of life and health' (cf. 'God of compassion, / source of life and health.' from the *Book of Common Prayer*) and provider of needs (cf. Philippians 4:19). It closes with an allusion to John 8:12, 'I am the light of the world. Whoever follows me will never walk in darkness' (cf. the Quaker doctrine of the Inner Light). Verse 3 celebrates Christian unity and the creative power of love: see Galatians 3:28 and 1 John 4:8.

JESU, MEINE FREUDE (German=Jesus, my brother] This suggested tune for Marnie Barrell's hymn takes its name from the first line of the German chorale to which it was originally set, 'Jesu, meine Freude,' by Johann Franck, a German lawyer, civil servant and hymnist (1618-77), author of more than 100 pietistic hymns, This one, actually modelled on a German love song, 'Flora, meine Freude, meiner Seelen-weid,' was first published at Freiburg in 1655. The translation usually used in English-language hymnbooks is by Catherine Winkworth (1827-78); it was first published in her 1863 *Chorale Book for England*.

The well-known tune, popularized as much by its adaptation and rich choral harmonization by J.S.Bach in several of his cantatas and organ pieces as by its own melodic character, first appeared in **Johann Crüger**'s *Praxis Pietatis Melica* (Frankfurt, 1656), described there as a traditional German melody.

> *Relevant lines from the Neander hymn include 'he doth still my trust renew,' 'God's great goodness aye endureth,' 'Evermore from his store / Newborn worlds rise and adore,' 'Daily doth the almighty giver / bounteous gifts on us bestow,' 'Christ doth call / One and all.'

Loving Spirit, Loving Spirit A94 (i) and (ii)
Metre: 8.7.8.7

'Written as a simple reflection on images of God,' says **Shirley Murray,** the author of this hymn, written in 1986. It was first published in her privately-printed collection *In Every Corner Sing* (Wellington, 1987), then in *Sound the Bamboo* and the first update of *New Zealand Praise* (both in 1990), followed by her first American collection of the same name (1992) and *Alleluia Aotearoa* (1993).

Unusually, the first verse is repeated to frame the three images of God-as-Holy-Spirit presented in verses 2-4. Verse 1 offers three connections between believer and Spirit: choice, attraction and signature. The first reflects both John 15:16, where Jesus says "You did not choose me, but I chose you,' and Ephesians 1:4, 'he chose us in him before the foundation of the world.' The third alludes to the baptismal practice of making the sign of the cross over the child or adult received into the church community.

It is significant that the first God-image is a maternal one, displacing the usual paternal one.* The believer is pictured as a foetus in the God-mother's womb, fed 'with your very body.' Behind this highly original image may stand the ancient symbolism, associated with the Eucharistic feast, of Christ as the mother-pelican, a bird once believed to feed its young with blood drawn from its own breast. The second image is again a variant on the traditional picture of the fatherhood of God. This God protects and teaches the child, and in a completely human way lifts the child up on his shoulder 'to see the world from [on] high.' The third image is even more unconventional: the relationship is conceived of as that between a friend and lover. Line 3 reflects Psalm 119:50, 'This is my comfort in my affliction that your promise gives me life.' Exodus 33:14, 'My presence will go with you, and I will give you rest,' is echoed in the 4th line.

[LOVING SPIRIT] The selection of this text for inclusion in *Alleluia Aotearoa* prompted the composition of two settings by New Zealand writers. The first, by **David Dell**, is set in E flat and displays his characteristic melodic sensitivity and the breathing pauses that create musical spaces between the phrases of the text.

FELICITY The tune name reflects verse 4, line 2, 'I am known and held and blessed.' This setting by **Colin Gibson** positions the third line of each verse as its climax. It is set in D major, but with falling melodic motifs and enriched harmonies to convey the emotion of tenderness. There is a further setting by Canadian composer **Ron Klusmeier** (Klusmeier 48).

> *More than one commentator has remarked on the feminine and motherly perspective found in this writer's work. I-to Loh, in his *Hymnal Companion to Sound the Bamboo: Asian Hymns in their Liturgical and Cultural Contexts* (Chicago: GIA, 2012) also notes that 'Few hymn writers have drawn [such] analogies between one's relationship with the Holy Spirit and the intimate human relationships of the family' (p 373). His own setting of the words, CHHUN-BIN, appears in *Sound the Bamboo* (1990), and was chosen as the theme-song of the Seventh General assembly of the World Council of Churches held at Canberra, Australia, in 1991. 'To my amazement,' writes Loh, 'the first female bishop of Australia chose this hymn to be sung at her consecration.' The tune name honours his two parents, his father Loh Sian-chhun and his mother Ang Bin.

Lullaby, sing lullaby (Lullaby Carol) F46
Metre: 7.8.8.6

This carol, written by **Shirley Murray** in 1998, had its origin in a tune sent to the author by Peter Godfrey, then director of the Kāpiti Chamber Choir in which Shirley Murray was singing, with a note attached: 'Write me a carol with animals and things…for a children's choir to sing.' The resulting text was first published in *Faith Forever Singing* (2000) and later in her third American collection, *Faith Makes the Song* (2003).

The words create a sleepy scene in the manger at Bethlehem at the end of a Christmas Day – St Francis of Assisi's animal-filled manger rather than the barer stall described in Luke 2:1-16. The sentiment is in general tender and protective, with a hint of future danger in the line 'the shadows grow in candleglow,' and the invocation of angels at the close of the text. The shepherds are imagined realistically as counting the sheep they abandoned in the rush to Bethlehem, to make sure none are missing. The final verse, describing Jesus as God's 'little lamb' will carry for adult singers associations with the slain Lamb of God (Revelation 5:12). But the mood is kept light, with assonance assisting: 'oxen snore inside the door,' 'Far away, tall camels sway' and the baby is winningly left to sleep among friendly companions. Shirley Murray's mice 'rustling in the straw' may owe something to **Willow Macky**'s mice, who 'run wittering through the straw' (see 'Here is a night that's bleak and raw,' H57).

[LULLABY CAROL] This unnamed melody was written by **Peter Godfrey** in 1997 for a children's choir. Intentionally or not (the music came before the words in this case) the simple phrases carry quietly down from F major to C major, then, starting one note higher repeat the downward fall to the tonic note, perfectly fitting a lullaby intended to bring sleep: 'Close your eyes, God's little lamb.'

Ma te marie a te Atua W679
Metre: 8.8.8.8 (LM)

This sung blessing is a version in Māori of Philippians 4:7-9 ('The peace of God, which passes all understanding will keep your hearts and your minds in Christ Jesus'), given its usual Trinitarian formulation. The translator and date of translation are unknown, but the translation is likely to have been made by or for an early missionary. The English translation of the Māori text provided in *With One Voice* is a guide to meaning only.

OLD 100TH This setting, in common use among both Māori and pākehā congregations in New Zealand, is the modern form of a hymn tune first published in the second (1551) French edition of the Genevan Psalter (*Pseaumes Octante trois de David*), where it was associated with Psalm 134. (Psalm 100 did not appear in the first edition.) The Old

100th is now one of the best-known melodies in Christian musical tradition; it is usually attributed to the French composer **Louis Bourgeois** (c.1510–60).

> *Although the tune was first associated with Psalm 134 in the Genevan Psalter, it took its current name from its association with Psalm 100 in the Anglo-Genevan Psalter of 1561, and later in the Scottish Psalter of 1564. In both of these Protestant psalm books Psalm 100 was matched to the Bourgeois tune, to which it has been indissolubly joined ever since.

Make me, O Lord, an instrument of thy peace W666
Metre: Irregular

The text of this hymn is a translation by Father **Mark Owen Lee** of a prayer attributed to the 13th century Italian saint **Francis of Assisi**, 'O Signore, fa' di me un instrumento,' though the famous prayer's first traceable appearance was in a 1912 publication in France as a French text in a small Roman Catholic devotional magazine, *La Clochette*, followed in 1916 by an Italian version printed in the Vatican newspaper *L'osservatore Romano* by papal order. Its appearance (unattributed) on the obverse of a card circulated in France during World War I with an image of St Francis on the face has led to its being known as the Peace Prayer of St Francis. Whatever its authenticity as a genuine work by the Italian saint, it has become a much-loved devotional poem, set by a number of musicians.

The version printed in the New Zealand supplement to *With One Voice* omits the second half of the prayer:

> O Divine Master,
> grant that I may not so much seek to be consoled, as to console;
> to be understood, as to understand;
> to be loved, as to love.
> For it is in giving that we receive.
> It is in pardoning that we are pardoned, and it is in dying that we are born to Eternal Life.

ST FRANCIS The setting used for *With One Voice* is by South African songwriter **Sebastian Temple** (1928-1997). Widely known as the Prayer of St Francis, it was composed in 1967 and rapidly became one of the most popular worship songs ever written. It was soon taken up into a number of new British hymnbooks; it became one of the anthems of the Royal British Legion and was sung at the funeral of Diana, Princess of Wales. That it has a chant-like character is unsurprising, since the composer himself became a member of the Franciscan order.

Make spaces for Spirit! (Pentecost Song) H96
Metre: 6.6.6.5 D

The author of this 2001 hymn for Pentecost, **Shirley Murray**, says of it, 'Pentecost Song is taken from a title quoted in Brian Wren's* inaugural lecture at Columbia Theological University (2000). The lively joy of the season is often lost, for me, in rather dreary traditional hymns. This one should be sung with 'wind and fire!' (quoted from *Faith Makes the Song* (2003), where the text was first published, before its appearance in *Hope is our Song* (2009).'

Much of the energy expressed in this joyous hymn is derived from its language, the writer making free play with assonance ('shift and uplift, melding and welding'), alliterative couplings ('a voice and a vision,' 'the flaming of courage, the firing of justice'), repeated imperatives ('Make spaces') and the use of active verbal forms ('changing, opening, flaming, firing').

Verse 1 closely follows the description of Pentecost in Acts 2. 'Spirited people' (verse 2, line 1) carries a play on 'people filled with Holy Spirit' and 'lively people'). Verse 3 alludes to the 'gifts of the Spirit (1 Corinthians 12:1-31) and to the baptismal and communion services ('the water of blessing...the wine poured for sharing'). Verse 4 addresses the social implications of the work of the Holy Spirit.

ERENA The tune name honours the writer, whose second name is Erena (Māori=Helen).

Written in 2001 by **Colin Gibson**, the setting in E flat major attempts to express the liveliness expressed in the text with a syncopated melody line and rising bass ('for energy rising'), punctuated by vigorous scalic scramblings. The second half of the hymn is accompanied by a descending sequence, but this excites the bass into further scalic activity, leading back to the tonic key. In *Faith Makes the Song*, the setting, PENTECOST SONG, is by a long-time friend of the writer, American composer and hymnbook editor **Carlton Young**.

*Writer, preacher, worship and workshop leader, and internationally published hymn-poet, Brian Wren was John and Miriam Conant Professor of Worship at Columbia Theological Seminary, Decatur, Georgia in the United States from 2000-2007.

Maker of mystery *F47*
Metre: 6.6.11 D

Written in 1993 by **Marnie Barrell,** this text was first published in *Faith Forever Singing* (2000) and is on the Oremus website.

The text is constructed on a Trinitarian formula, with verses addressed in succession to God the 'Maker of mystery' (=the mysterious Creator), Christ, 'the strong and living vine' and the Holy ('Wild') Spirit, and a final address to the 'living and loving God.' However, equally important is the structural metaphor of growth and plant life, which runs through the whole poem, starting from God as 'fertile ground of our growing' (verse 1, cf. Protestant theologian Paul Tillich's famous description of God as 'the ground of our being'), including the singers, 'us,' as developing socially-responsible spiritual lives, bearing 'ripe fruit… for the lives of others' (see verse 2).

This is a richly allusive text, repaying close study, with metaphor piled on metaphor, as in the first verse which, without naming God as such, defines the deity as Maker, 'dreamer of what will be,' 'well-spring and fertile ground,' gardener tending 'the buried seed,' fore-seer and the one who draws (=pulls, stretches out) humanity 'into life beyond our knowing.' There are two principal biblical sources, the parable of the Sower (Matthew 13:1-9), as in verse 3, line 6, the 'hundredfold yield,' and Jesus' self-image as the Vine (John15:5). Both are imaginatively developed, as in the description of the 'Wild Spirit' (=natural, undomesticated, untamable), 'coiled in the depths' (as a vine or a serpent), 'springing green… / promise of fruit within the seed maturing.' There are many more biblical echoes, to be traced by those who know the texts well: two instances, are 'dying, you live' (also the title of a 1962 book of Christian testimonies under Nazi rule, *Dying, we live*), and 'new life.' Users of this Companion will also recognise resonances with other New Zealand hymns: see, for instance, **Shirley Murray**'s 'In each of us / God dreams a dream' ('God was in Christ,' H49) and **Cecily Sheehy**'s equally wild Spirit ('O the Spirit she moves on the water,' A109).

[MAKER OF MYSTERY] This setting was written in 1999 by **Colin Gibson** for the inclusion of the text in *Faith Forever Singing*, replacing the original setting to DOWN AMPNEY by **Ralph Vaughan Williams** (for which see 'Come on this wedding day,' A24). Originally set in A major, Gibson's music begins in the darker, more mysterious key of D flat major (suggesting the 'mystery' referred to in the text), then reaches its 'home' key, A flat major, midway, touching on some minor chords to reflect tonal shifts in the text on its way to a confident close in A flat major.

Mary's son, my friend *H97*
Metre: 5.7.5.7

This hymn text, written by **Robyn Allen Goudge** in 2000, was first published in *Hope is our Song* (2009).

It has the simplicity of a Celtic invocation, with its repeated address to 'Mary's son, my friend,' followed by a request for a blessing. Only the nature of the blessings changes from verse to verse, and as the writer suggests, singers might create further verses, using this model to suit other occasions.

MARY'S SON The melody takes its name from the first line. It was written by the author, who is a fine harpist. The general musical style is Celtic in its melodic shape and blend of major and minor chords, which give it a modal feeling.

Matthew was a lonely man H99
Metre: 7.6.7.6.8.8.8.6

This hymn text was written by **Colin Gibson** in 1979 and first published in *Servant Songs* (1987), then in *New Zealand Praise* and *Singing Love* (1988) and *Reading the Signature* (1994) before reaching *Hope is our Song* (2009).

In the author's words, 'In the loneliness, doubt, fear and worry of the four biblical characters in this hymn I found descriptions of common human experience in contemporary society – including the experiences of members of my own congregation. To these, as to all, Christ comes still as friend and saviour.' Each verse refers to an event recorded in the gospels: for lonely Matthew (no tax gatherer could expect to be popular in his community cf. Zacchaeus) see Matthew 9:9, Mark 2:14 and Luke 5:27; for Thomas the doubter see John 20:24-29; for the distracted Martha see Luke 10:38-42; for frightened Peter see Matthew 26:69-75, Mark 14:66-72; Luke 22:54-62 and John 18:15-27.

LONELY MAN Composed in 1979 by the hymn writer's son, **John Gibson**, for this text. At the time theatre-musician and musical director for the Fortune Theatre, Dunedin, John Gibson was immersed in popular music, and wrote this lively, syncopated piano setting which perfectly conveys the jitteriness of the characters mentioned in the text. Not to be played in 'church' style, but with a sense of rhythmic freedom and enjoyment. The music also exists as an arrangement for male voice quartet (TTBB) by the Glory Four of Hamilton, and there is an alternative setting by New Zealand composer Sylvia Jenkins.

May the anger of Christ be mine (A Song of Light) F48
Metre: 8.8.8.9.7.9.7.10

In 1993 New Zealand government health services were being ruthlessly restructured and cut back. A *hui* (regional consultation) protesting the cuts was held by the Baptist Social Services at Holy Cross Church, Mosgiel, on 20 August, with a panel discussion on 'Fighting the Funding.' The hymn 'May the anger of Christ be mine' was commissioned from **Colin Gibson** for the occasion and duly launched there. It was written to express the anger of those working within the health system at what was seen as an assault on the powerless, staff as well as patients. It was first published in the author's American collection, *Reading the Signature* (1994), with a dedication to two friends, Gay and Neil Eaton, descendants of Samuel Eaton, a 17th century Baptist who died in prison in 1639 defending his liberty of conscience.

The text takes its cue from the incident in which an angry Christ overthrew the tables of money-changers in the Temple (Matthew 21:12-13), then generalizes the theme to urging compassionate love for all those marginalized, impoverished and ignored by the well-to-do. The verses move through a cycle of anger, compassion, love and positive action. The refrain alludes to the opening of John's gospel, John 1:5, 'The light shines in the dark and the darkness has not overcome it.'

EATON The tune name memorializes both the dedicatees and their Baptist ancestor. The verses open in D major, but the refrain shifts harmonically into B minor and G to represent the world of restless change referred to in the text. Composer **Colin Gibson's** music relocates its true tonality in D major with a martial-sounding call to action at its close.

May the God of new beginnings F49
Metre: 8.5.10.5.9.5.8.5

In 1999 **John Murray**, then Chairman of the New Zealand Hymn Book Trust and leader of the editorial board working on *Faith Forever Singing*, decided that the hymnbook should contain a number of short texts for liturgical use following the model of those published in *Come all you people: Shorter Songs for Worship*, by John Bell (Glasgow: Wild Goose Resource

Group, 1994). This blessing was one of the texts he created for the purpose.

Though this blessing is an original one, there are biblical resonances. Revelation 21:1-5 describes God as making all things new. Although the combination 'infinite wisdom' is not found in the biblical texts – it has since become a commonplace in Christian expression – Psalm 147:5 refers to God's understanding as 'infinite,' and Colossians 2:2-3 talks of 'God's mystery, in Christ, in whom are hid all the treasures of wisdom and understanding.' The safe homecoming resonates with the welcome given the Prodigal Son (Luke 15).

[GOD OF NEW BEGINNINGS] The setting is by **Colin Gibson**, also a member of the editorial board working on *Faith Forever Singing*, and was written in 1999 for this text.

May the mystery of God enfold us (Arohanui Blessing) *A95*
Metre: 10.9.10.9.9.9.9.9

A blessing in the Celtic style, this text was written by **Joy Cowley** as early as 1990 and first published as number 42 in her collection of psalm-poems, *Psalms Down-Under* (Otane: Pleroma Christian Supplies, 1996). Its title, 'Arohanui Blessing,' carries the usual richness of meaning of Māori words: literally, 'much love,' but also 'enfolding love, love binding a community together, love that creates bonds of mutual trust and loyalty.'* Joy Cowley explains that 'Aroha Nui blessing was written for our little retreat house in the Marlborough Sounds, which was called Aroha Nui. We called it that because we both felt a great loving presence in the bay, one that healed tired and fragmented people. The words of Aroha Nui Blessing came when I was sorting through some of Terry's photos of the Sounds, deep water, misted hills, palpable peace.' Terry is Joy Cowley's photographer-husband, whose images accompany the psalms published in a series of such books.

The rhyming couplet verses list a number of traditional biblical attributes of the divine, energized and made vivid by potent verbs of action. For God as mystery see Job 11:7, as wisdom see Job 12:12, as brightness see 1 John 1:5, as love see 1 John 4:8, as peace see Philippians 4:7. God's 'moving' in the final line of the blessing suggests the moving of the Spirit of God over the waters at Creation (Genesis 1:2). The phrase 'fragrance of God' may have been suggested by 2 Corinthians 2:15, though Paul writes of the lives of believers as the 'fragrance' of Christ rising up to God.

MARLBOROUGH SOUNDS The setting by **Ian Render** was written in 1990, with the tune name COWLEY. The present tune name refers to the idyllic coastal setting in the South Island where Joy Cowley and her husband Terry lived and ran their retreat house Aroha Nui for a number of years. The original score was a four-part setting of the blessing, in D minor. It was transposed to F minor, renamed and revised for its appearance in *Alleluia Aotearoa* (1993). The tonality powerfully suggests the mysterious nature of God; the melody has the character of an ancient Hebrew chant. Catholic musician Michael McConnell has also given this text a four-part choral setting, which he has named MIRABILIS (2002).

*See further, 'Come to this Christmas singing.'

More than we know *H100*
Metre: 9.8.10.7 and refrain

The Christian Conference of Asia commissioned this hymn by **Shirley Murray** on the theme of their Assembly in 2000, 'Life in all its fullness.' The hymn was written in that year. The theme and the refrain of the text derive from John 10:10, 'I came that they may have life, and have it abundantly.' The hymn was first published in the author's American collection *Faith Makes the Song* (2003), then in *Hope is our Song* (2009).

After verse 1, which uses an allusion to the parable of the mustard seed (Mark 4:30-42, also found in the other synoptic gospels) the words form a poetic litany of praise to Christ. The expression is frequently compressed and allusive. 'He is God's eye, changing our focus' (verse 2) means 'those who follow Christ will look with a new and profound love on humanity as did Christ, the embodiment of God's loving and omniscient providence (see Psalm 33:18 and Proverbs 15:3). The remaining lines of this verse connect John 8:12, 'I am the light of the world,' with modern floodlighting and spiritual enlightenment. For 'fire, Spirit' see Acts 2:1-4. Verse 3 associates Christ with the smiling face of God and the rainbow (see Genesis 9:8-17). The rainbow has become the symbol in New Zealand and elsewhere of the peace movement and of the movement for gay rights, so 'peace, and blending us all in' (line 2). The imagery of coin and a new economy has its origin in Jesus' actions and stories (see Mark 12:16-17 and 12:41-44), but the writer is also thinking of conservative and liberal social and economic policies among governments. The final verse uses images of the heart of God and air (by implication the uplifting wind of the Holy Spirit); lines 3-4 refer to the crucifixion of Christ ('arms stretched out') and Jesus' inspiring courage (see Luke 9:51).

BROAD BAY The tune, by composer **Colin Gibson**, is named after a small and courageously liberal Christian community located on the Otago Peninsula at Broad Bay. The setting was written for this text in 2000, and communicates the key ideas of energy and joy present in Shirley Murray's text with a driving rhythmic pulse and a syncopated melodic line in the festival key of A major. By contrast, in *Faith Makes the Song* the setting by Swedish composer **Per Harling** is more sober, in a sedate 3/4 time signature and the key of A minor, though closing on an A major chord to underline the word 'joy.'

My heart is leaping (Mary's Song)
H101
Metre: 5.4.7.5.4.8

This poetic version of the exalted speech attributed to Mary, Jesus' mother-to-be, was written in 2001 by **Marion Kitchingman.** After being sung in several Dunedin churches it was first published in the local Supplementary Hymnbook before appearing in *Hope is our Song* (2009).

Marion Kitchingman's text closely follows the original song of praise in Luke 1:47-55. Known as the *Magnificat* from the first word of the Latin version of the text or the *Song* or *Canticle of Mary*, it is one of the eight most ancient Christian hymns and the earliest Marian hymn. Luke's words are a virtual compilation from several Old Testament biblical passages, but the principal source is the *Song of Hannah* (1 Samuel 2:1-10), spoken in the knowledge of her conception of a child, who would become the great prophet Samuel.

MARY'S SONG The tune name is taken from the author's title for this hymn. This setting is by **Barry Brinson** and was written for this text in 2008. Its 6/8 dance time and melodic line captures the rising emotional excitement of the words. An earlier setting was composed by Dunedin musician Malcolm Gould.

My soul sings in gratitude (Magnificat) *facing H62*
Metre: free

A modern version of the Magnificat, the song attributed to Mary, the mother-to-be of Jesus (Luke 1:46-55), and originally titled 'A Modern Magnificat,' this poem was written for Christmas 2006 by **Joy Cowley** in response to a request from Glynn Cardy, then vicar of St Matthew-in-the-City, Auckland. After appearing on Bishop John Spong's website in 2007, it was first published in a hymnbook in *Hope is our Song* (2009).

Detailed comparison with the original biblical text is the work of a literary critic rather than the editor of a Companion such as this, but there are several obvious changes in this modern interpretation of an ancient song.

The self-characterisation of Mary as the 'handmaiden of the Lord' and as a celebrant of the history of her people (see Luke 1:54-55) is replaced by a more objectified speaker ('I'), who becomes a representative of her people ('us') only in the final stanza of Joy Cowley's poem. This is in keeping with turning a 1st century CE gendered, exclusively Jewish monologue into a modern inclusive religious poem.

Another major change is the introduction of a new master-theme: that of divine love. Luke's strong and majestic deity shows mercy only to those who fear him (verse 50); love as an attribute of God is not mentioned. Joy Cowley's speaker is filled not with fear but with awe at the nature of divine Love and has no need of mercy; she (or he) is free to dance in the 'mystery of God.' This poet's theology of God is radically different and modern.

A new secondary theme of fullness and emptiness is introduced: in Luke's song the rich are sent empty (=empty-handed) away, the hungry are filled with good things. In Joy Cowley's poem the proud have 'no room' for love, but those who 'know their emptiness / can rejoice in Love's fullness.' Such a love 'fills our heart space.' Wealth and hunger as signs of social status are replaced by fullness and emptiness as spiritual conditions.

Mary's Magnificat ends with Abraham and his posterity for ever; Joy Cowley's with the symbolic rebirth of the Holy One in the individual believer. (See her poem 'Virgin Birth,' facing C52, for a fuller development of this theme.)

Nativity *facing C28*

This poem by distinguished New Zealand poet, novelist, children's writer and Catholic Christian commentator **Joy Cowley** heads her 1996 collection, *Psalms Down-under*, first published by Catholic Supplies, Wellington.

It reinterprets the traditional elements of the gospel accounts of Jesus' nativity – star, angel song, the magi, the shepherds – as 'part of ourselves': the locus of her nativity is 'in the small rough stable of our lives.' But this reduction to individual personal terms is played out against a background of mega-values – 'Love,' 'truth,' 'the harmony of the universe,' 'wonder,' 'miracle.' And poet that she is, we are commanded to look at her vivid images: 'a high spring tide / …swelling to fullness and overflowing / the banks; 'the white flame of truth / blazing the way for us / through a desert; 'the impulsive, reckless shepherd / [running] helter skelter with arms outstretched.' There are is an allusion to the Old Testament Exodus from Egypt (Exodus 13:20-22 re-imagined as an escape from a desert of dead words), and to the classical idea of the marvellous music supposed to be created by the circling of the planets. Within this action-filled, dramatic presentation of Christ's nativity the speaker finds herself speechless, aching with awe, trembling with miracle (cf. 'Praise,' facing C135).

Nativity *facing C42*

This is a shortened and somewhat bowdlerised version of a ballad-poem by **Peter Cape,** folk-singer and Anglican priest. It was written before 1968, when Cape recorded it for broadcast by Television One. The original title was 'Epiphany,' but it has since acquired the name of 'New Zealand Christmas' and 'Backblocks Nativity.' In 1989 it was printed in the *Manawatu Standard* newspaper under the heading 'A New Zealand Christmas.' In 2000 the original full text emerged from Arthur Toms, Cape's close friend and fellow musician, with the comment that the Rev. Peter Cape 'obviously intended this version of the song as a church hymn, although the reference to an old joker with a billygoat beard would have disconcerted his congregation.'* With Cape's own setting, the song has been recorded on at least two CDs: *I'm an ordinary Joker: The Songs of Peter Cape* (2001) and *Sled: A Kiwi Sings* (2014). For a fuller account of what is now as iconic poem, see *An Ordinary Joker: The Life and Songs of Peter Cape*, ed. Steele Roberts (Wellington: Steele Roberts, 2001). The text printed in *Carol our Christmas* was taken from an anthology of New Zealand poetry for secondary school students, *Nowhere far from the Sea* (Christchurch: Whitcombe and Tombs, 1971).

The poet places the ancient Nativity story in the ordinary world of country life he himself knew well. His strategy is to emphasize the remarkable by presenting it as completely ordinary and unremarkable. His unexcited narrator has the authentic accents of a backblocks farmer-observer, and the world he describes has nothing of the miraculous about it (cf. Joy Cowley's 'Nativity'). Rain pelts down, a horse goes lame, a homeless couple ('Joe' for 'Joseph') find a roadman's shack** for shelter and the baby is born on a bed of fern leaves. Three riders appear out of the night, presumably wandering miners, for they leave a single 'river nugget' in the child's hand. The unnamed mother watches, 'but she didn't understand,' as low cloud breaks to reveal a single star.

Although the poem was printed in *Carol our Christmas* without a musical setting, according to Arthur Toms, Peter Cape set and sang it to his adaptation of 'an old Anglican hymn tune.' The score is published and a CD recording of the song supplied in *An Ordinary Joker: The Life and Songs of Peter Cape*, ed. Steele Roberts Wellington: Steele Roberts (2001).

* The original text of the poem:

Epiphany

They were set for home, but the horse went lame
And the rain came belting out of the sky
Joe saw the hut and he went to look
And he said, "She's old, but she'll keep you dry"

So her kid was born in that
roadman's shack
By the light of a lamp that'd hardly burn
She wrapped him up in her hubby's coat
And put him down on a bed of fern

Then *they* came riding out of the night
And this is the thing
that she'll always swear
As they took off their coats
and came into the light
They knew they were going to
find her there

Three old jokers in oilskin coats
Stood by the bunk in that leaking shack
One had a beard like a billygoat's
One was frail, and one was black

She sat on the foot of the fernstalk bed
And she watched,
but she didn't understand

When they put those bundles
at the baby's head
And this river nugget into his hand.

Gold is the power of a man with a man
And incense the power of a man with God
But myrrh is the bitter taste of death
And the sour-sweet smell
of the upturned sod

Then they went,
while she watched through the open door
Weary as men who had ridden too far
And the rain eased off
and the low cloud broke
And through a gap shone a single star.

**A 1904 photograph of a road builder's 'shack,' actually a canvas-roofed building, is reproduced with several online printings of this poem.

New child of God, come to be blest
A 96
Metre: 8.8.8.8

This text was written by **Shirley Murray** in March 1987 for the occasion of an infant baptism in her own church of St Andrew's on the Terrace, Wellington. She says of it, 'This hymn for a child's baptism links the church and the world in which a new life must grow. The child inherits our faith story but has to live in the society we have created.' With the title 'Hymn for a Child's Baptism,' the text was first published in Shirley Murray's own collection *In Every Corner Sing* (1987), before reaching her 1992 American collection of the same name and *Alleluia Aotearoa* (1993).

The text takes the form of a congregational address to the baby. Galatians 3:26-7 is one of the many scriptural sources for the expression 'child of God,' the child who has come to be blessed (see Matthew 19:13-14). 'Signed' refers to the baptismal practice of making a sign of the cross on the child's forehead with fingers dipped in the baptismal font. Verse 2 calls in other scriptural expressions: 'lamb' (see John 1:29) and 'house of faith' (see Galatians 6:10). Verse 3 describes an ideal society in terms much like those Shirley

Murray later uses in her Waitangi Day hymn 'Where mountains rise,' A155: see especially verse 4. The author supplies a note on her use of the Māori word *aroha*, allowing the words 'warmth of heart' as an alternative, 'if the Māori word *aroha* is inappropriate.' Verse 4 draws on 1 John 4:8, but it is the poet who imagines the future development of the child as a bird stretching and feeling its wings and finally taking flight.

WATER'S EDGE This tune, named for the Jordan waters of Jesus' baptism (see Mark 1:9-10), is by **Ian Render**. The music, set in G major with modulations to D and E minor, has the voicing and harmonic structure of an American spiritual; a gentle cradling of the child in congregational sound. The suggested alternative tune, HERONGATE, is an English folk melody associated with the folksong 'In Jesse's city' collected in 1903 by **Ralph Vaughan Williams** near Herongate, Essex. He arranged it for his *English Hymnal* (1906), and Methodists came to know it from the 1933 *Methodist Hymnbook*, where it is set to 'It is a thing most wonderful.' HERONGATE (found in the 1982 edition of *With One Voice*) was the tune used for the original baptism ceremony. In the American edition of *In Every Corner Sing* Shirley Murray's hymn was given a new setting, GIDEON, by American composer T.B. Southgate. Another setting, by New Zealand composer **Nigel Eastgate**, exists in manuscript.

No te aroa maata noou A97
Metre: Irregular with refrain

The text and setting of this Cook Islands Māori hymn were written by **Taria Kingstone** before 1993, when it was published in *Alleluia Aotearoa*. The occasion of the song is unknown.

The text weaves together echoes of the Psalms to create a song of praise and trust in God. For verse 1 see Psalm 122:1, for verse 2 see Psalm 91:14-16, for verse 3 see Psalm 23:3, 5 and for verse 4 see Psalm 40:4 and Psalm 30:12.

TANGI-TUAKANA (Cook Islands Māori=funeral song for an older person). The music, by the author, is arranged for traditional Cook Island four-part unaccompanied congregational singing, with prominent lead singing by the women (see the 1st and 5th bars of the chorus (*koreti*). The setting is in F major but the use of dropping inner parts and a brief shift into D minor in the chorus gives the whole setting a gentle melancholy.

No, I've never seen an angel H103
Metre: 14.14.14.14.9.6.11.7.7.11

Rob Ferguson created this hymn in Palmerston North in 1994. He describes it as 'written in response to fundamentalist publicity in the newspaper of the time. It has within it my theology of life as church. It relies for effect on a reasonable knowledge of Gospel stories, and I hope has a lightness that brings a smile as it's being sung.' Elsewhere he writes of it as being 'a serious piece of whimsy.'

The text contrasts 'the old, old stories' of miraculous events which lie outside the singers' experience with the 'real live miracles' of modern life, and concludes that 'the ancient stories come to life, if I've eyes to see, in the people all around me every day' (verse 3).

The biblical stories and popular myths alluded to include, in verse 1, the song of the angels at the Nativity of Christ (Luke 2:13-14), Mary's conversation with the Angel Gabriel (Luke 1:26-38), the star of the Nativity (Matthew 2:1-10), Peter and the keys of heaven (Matthew 15:16-19); in verse 2, Jesus walking on the sea of Galilee (John 6:16-21), stilling the storm (Mark 4:35-40), turning water into wine (John 2:1-11), exorcising the Gadarene madman (Mark 5:2-20), feeding the 5,000 (Mark 6:30-44), healing the sick (as in Mark 2:6-12); in verse 3, the calling of the disciples (Mark 1:16-20, Matthew 4:18-22) and 'the justice river' (Amos 5:24).

MALCOLM AVENUE Named after the Christchurch address of the hymn writer at the time, this setting was written for Rob Ferguson's words by **Colin Gibson** in 1998 after several others had attempted to create melodies for it. 'Unfortunately the words came to me without the benefit of an existing metre,' says the author. 'I had a folk-music feel in mind...which Colin has captured very well.'

Nothing is lost on the breath of God F50
Metre: 9.7.10.7.9.9.11.9

In 1994 **Colin Gibson**, then Head of the English Department at the University of Otago, learned that his secretary had taken compassionate leave to fly to Auckland to deal with the imminent death from cystic fibrosis of her son, aged 19. The young man died at Greenlane Hospital, Auckland; with him were his mother and his English fiancée, who married him shortly before the end. 'Nothing is lost on the breath of God' was written to address the profound sense of loss following such a traumatic experience for the two women who had to travel back to Dunedin and take up their lives again. It first appeared in the Mornington Methodist Church supplementary hymnal and was sung on several occasions, including a service at Dunedin Public Hospital for nursing staff and parents who had lost babies prematurely. In 1996 it reached American publisher Hope's *Supplement 96*, followed by Gibson's second American collection, *Songs for a Rainbow People* (1998), and *Faith Forever Singing* (2000). It has since appeared in a number of international hymnals and is included in *A Panorama of Christian Hymnody* (expanded edition, 2005).

The starting point for the text is Benedictine abbess **Hildegard of Bingen's** unforgettable image of human life floating like a feather on the breath of God; its theme is the brevity of human life and the infinite preciousness of each and every individual, held forever in the loving providence of God. Verse 1 draws on biblical and secular images of small, frail but infinitely valued things: Hildegard's feather, a single hair (cf. Luke 12:7, 'the very hairs of your head are all numbered'), a flower (cf. Psalm 103:15, 'As for man, his days are as grass: as a flower of the field, so he flourishes'), a water drop, dust (cf. Genesis 3:19, 'you are dust, and to dust you shall return'). Verse 2 draws images of difficult journeys from the real experience of the two women, from Psalm 23:4, 'though I walk through the valley of the shadow of death,' and the Parable of the Lost Sheep (Luke 15:1-7). The imagery of the final verse is drawn from the devoted love given by the mother to her son throughout his life, her constant 'offices of care.' Despite its personal beginning, the hymn has been found useful in many contexts of loss and grief, with its assurance that 'nothing is lost' within the eternal presence of the universal soul. 'All that we value most about ourselves is loved by God, made part of God, taken into the life of God and preserved safe in God for ever (David Bromell, 'Processing toward death,' *Creative Transformation*, volume 7.2 (Winter 1997) 6-9.

GREENLANE The setting, written in 1994 by **Colin Gibson**, is named for the Auckland public hospital where the young man died. The melodic pattern is intentionally simple and repetitive, the harmonic structure – G, D, G major – equally so. The treble voices constitute a soprano-alto duet over a third bass voice line, while emotional emphasis is given by the frequent use of appoggiaturas. The text has been set for male voice choir by American composer J. Lloyd Kauffman.

Not on a snowy night A98, C31
Metre: 6.6.6.6.5.5.5.6

This first and most famous of New Zealand's early indigenous carols was written by New Zealand poet **Willow Macky**, but ironically first published in London by the English firm of Chappell and given its first performance two years later in New Zealand by an Australian choir. 'Te Harinui' (Māori=tidings of great joy), the title by which it is best known and the poet's preferred title, was written in 1957 and published in the same year; since then it has been arranged many times and given fresh settings by New Zealand composers such as **David Hamilton**. Its New Zealand popularity began with its inclusion in a Girl Guide songbook, and it has now achieved the status of a New Zealand classic.

The text contrasts the biblical account of the birth of Jesus (Luke 2) with historical accounts of the first Christian service held in New Zealand on 25 December 1814. Verse 1 lists the winter night setting, the star of Bethlehem and the song of the angels found in Luke's account of the nativity. Verses 2-4 contrast this with the summer day, the quietness of Oihi Bay, Bay of Islands, the sermon delivered by the Reverend Samuel Marsden on the text, 'Behold, I bring you tidings of great joy' (Luke 2:10) and the gathering of the Māori people of Rangihoua who formed the greater part of his congregation. For a detailed illustrated account drawing on contemporary reports see 'Te Harinui: the song about New Zealand's first Christmas service,' by Patricia Bawden and John Thornley, *Music in the Air* 24 (Winter/Spring 2007), 28-33. The refrain repeats the Māori version of Marsden's text and its English original.

[TE HARINUI] The music for this carol was written by its author. It remains rooted in a comfortable E flat major tonality with some natural modulations to related keys, and has a regular 3/4 folk-dance time setting. Some resemblance between the refrain and the popular early Italian aria, 'Caro mio ben,' attributed to Giuseppi Giordani, has been noted.

Nothing, nothing in all creation
H102
Metre: 4.5.5.4 D and refrain

Shirley Murray is the author of this text, written in 2005. It was first published in her fourth American collection, *Touch the Earth Lightly* (2008), which carries a dedication to her husband **John Stewart Murray**, 'without whom these hymns might never have been written, and to mark a life-long passion for singing the faith, with my love and gratitude.' When the text was next published, in *Hope is our Song* (2009), the refrain was repeated, to fit the musical setting by New Zealand composer **Barry Brinson**.

Although the refrain is based on Romans 8:36-39, Murray acknowledges a 'marvellous passage' by Hesychios of Sinai* as its principal source, describing her own work as a paraphrase of his ideas. She quotes from a collection of maxims attributed to Hesychios, 'When we are in trouble or despair or have lost hope, we should do what David did: pour out our hearts to God and tell him of our needs and troubles, just as they are.'

In verse 1 Shirley Murray adds 'grief' and 'sickness' to the tribulations listed in the passage from Romans, suggesting that a personal experience may lie behind the writing of this hymn. Lines 7-8 echo Matthew 6:8, 'Your Father knows the things you need before you ask him.' Verse 2, 'powers of our day, / angel and devil, / danger and evil, / make their own play' rewords Romans 8:38, 'nor angels, nor principalities nor things present, nor things to come, nor powers.' 'God's love is sure' is picked up from Romans 8:39, 'For I am sure...' The opening lines of verse 3 constitute a further updating of the tribulations listed in the Romans passage, notably introducing 'human' error by way of contrast to the metaphysical threats catalogued in Romans. Line 5 of this verse gave the title to the New Zealand hymnbook in which this song was published.

REASSURANCE This 2008 setting of Shirley Murray's text by **Barry Brinson** takes its name from the general theme of the hymn. Although the music, with its 3/4 time signature, has something of the character of a dance, the emphatic double notes ('nothing, nothing') at the beginning of each repetition of the refrain gain additional stress by contrast with the easier, more regular rhythm of what follows. The harmonic shifts in the verse passages through E minor, A major, G major and F sharp major, perhaps suggest the kaleidoscope of troubles to be defied by a resolute faith in God. Both **Jillian Bray** and **Colin Gibson** have written other settings for the hymn. In *Touch the Earth Lightly* a new setting by American composer **Jane Marshall** is used.

*Hesychios of Sinai was a Byzantine hieromonk or priest-monk, a monk who was also a priest in the Orthodox Church and Eastern Catholicism. He is associated with Batos [Greek=thorn-bush] Monastery on Mount Sinai. Nothing definite is known about his career or the exact time at which he lived. Only fragments of his writings have been preserved, and they have still to be given full scholarly attention. In several manuscripts he is given the honorary title of 'Our Holy Father.' He is the attributed author of a collection of some 300 maxims or wise sayings gathered under the title of *On the Subject of Temperance and Courage*.

Now as we go *A99*
Metre: 9.9.9.9

This benediction was written by **Shirley Murray** in 1989. In her first American collection, *In Every Corner Sing* (1992), she writes, 'In New Zealand there is a favourite song used at the end of worship which reminds me strongly of "The Last Waltz" [A 1967 waltz-time pop song by British singer Engelbert Humperdink]. In reaction to the sentimentality of it I wrote this, only to realise that it fits a 3/4 [waltz] time (and may have a dash of sentimentality!).' The text was first published in New Zealand in *Alleluia Aotearoa* (1993). In keeping with Murray's strong support for gender equality, the singers address each other as 'sister and brother.'

BENEDICTION This simple unison melody over a rocking bass line was written in 1989 by **Colin Gibson** for this text, and printed in both *Alleluia Aotearoa* and *In Every Corner Sing*. The original version was composed as a four-part setting for SATB choir.

Now Jesus came among us *A101*
Metre: 14.8.15.9 and refrain

An experimental text which mixes actions (clapping and waving) and words, 'Now Jesus came among us' was written by Dominican Sister **Cecily Sheehy** as one of a series of such songs for children published in the Catholic magazine *Family Living* in 1985. Its first hymnbook appearance was in *New Zealand Praise* (1988), followed by *Alleluia Aotearoa* (1993).

The theme of the song, Christ's loving acceptance of others as the model for Christian behaviour – in the words concluding each verse, 'I love you and welcome you today' – is presented as an action song for young children. The first verse dramatizes the singers as an applauding, waving crowd greeting the arrival of Jesus. In the refrain, they are to join hands as a symbolic gesture of community, reaching out for contact and healing (the laying on of hands). The final line of the refrain associates this with the celebration of the Eucharist as an experience – in Catholic theology – of the actual presence of Christ (Luke 22:19). The second verse adds another symbolic action: 'we turn and look at everyone and say a little prayer.' The third verse acknowledges the physical departure (ascension) of Jesus – see Luke 24:51 and Acts 1:9 – and encourages the singers to think of their own loving actions towards others as a means of realising the presence of the risen Christ 'with us.'

[JESUS AMONG US] The tune, by the author, closely follows the movement of the text, with running quavers to convey the narrative and a repeated motif in the refrain to reinforce the instructions to 'join hands, 'join hearts, reach out.' Throughout the song the modality remains securely in F major, with repeated returns to the tonic chord.

Now the silence *H104*
Metre: Irregular

The best-known of the more than 200 hymns written by American Lutheran pastor **Jaroslav Vajda**, this text was written in 1968 while Vajda was editing a church magazine, *This Day*. Finding that he needed to fill a blank page before the copy went to the printer three days later, he decided to fill it himself. Vajda writes, 'The hymn text originated while I was shaving one morning (a time when I get a lot of original ideas)… Somewhere in the back of my mind, during my previous 18 years in fulltime parish ministry, I was accumulating reasons and benefits in worship. I have felt that we often get so little out of worship because we anticipate so little, and we seldom come with a bucket large enough to catch all the shower of grace that comes to us in that setting. Suddenly the hymn began to form in my mind as a list of awesome and exciting things that one should expect in worship, culminating in the Eucharist and benediction. The introit or entrance hymn resulted.

Subconsciously I was producing a hymn without rhyme and without worn clichés, depending entirely on rhythm and repetition to make it singable. The reversal of the Trinitarian order in the benediction was made not only to make the conclusion memorable, but to indicate the order in which the Trinity approaches us in worship: The Spirit brings us the Gospel, by which God's blessing is released in our lives.' He wrote the first draft of 'Now the Silence' in the next 30 minutes.

The lines of the hymn roughly follow the order of the regular liturgy of the Lutheran Church, centred on Holy Communion ('Now the Body, now the Blood'). 'Wedding,' line 9, suggests the union of Christ with his 'bride' the church (Ephesians 5:25). 'Epiphany,' line 12, means the revelation or appearance of a divine being: here Jesus Christ, as the son of God.

GALLOWAY The setting printed in *Hope is our Song* was written by **Colin Gibson** in 1986 for the Mornington (Dunedin) Methodist Choir. It carries a dedication to John Gerry, a communion steward for many years, who lived across the road from the church, in Galloway Street. The original setting, popular in the United States, is by Carl Schalk (1969).

Now the star of Christmas (Three Faiths Carol) H105
Metre: 6.5.6.5 D

This important carol was written in October 2008 for the season of Epiphany by **Shirley Murray**, and received its initial publication in *Hope is our Song* (2009). The typescript carried the title 'The Three Faiths Epiphany Carol.' Reflecting the difficulties of writing into a new and problematic field of religious thought, there was editorial debate over the original version of the third verse. As Shirley Murray records, 'The New Zealand Hymn Book Trust editors did not at first warm to the third verse without some theological debate, and this [the text printed in *Hope is our Song*] is the accepted version I agreed to.' The problematic words were 'Christ within the Christian, / Jesus in the Jew, / Prophet for the Muslim, / each tradition true.'

The first New Zealand carol to deal with this inter-faith theme, which has come to the forefront of religious attention in recent years, in the author's own words, 'It is a hymn about kindred spirits and common hopes in a world which seems to forget how much we have always shared with these other faiths [the Judaic and Muslim faiths].' She speaks of '[hijacking] the three magi to point to the three great faith traditions represented by Christian, Muslim and Jew, and to indicate the wisdom treasures within each of these.'

The first verse, with its key reference to the Christmas star followed by the magi (Matthew 2), describes the modern 'new-born spirit' of inter-faith respect and co-operation as 'broadening our view.' Verse 2 obliquely refers to contemporary outbreaks of inter-religious hostilities, 'the clouded vision / hurting humankind,' and implicitly compares modern 'kindred spirits drawn towards the light' with the ancient magi of the Nativity story. Verse 3 directly acknowledges the 'wisdom' found in the three Abrahamic faiths of Christianity, Judaism and Islam, and Jesus' status within each of them. Verse 4 completes the quiet insistence throughout the text on the image of light as enlightenment, which begins with the star '[shining] into our day' (verse 1, line 1).

KUPE According to Māori tribal traditions, Kupe was the first Polynesian to discover the islands of New Zealand; his name accordingly fits this setting by **Colin Gibson** for a carol which celebrates 'another landscape to be travelled through.' The music was written in 2008; it ventures into several other keys – D, A, E minor – before returning to the home key G. An optional descant for paired (or single) instruments is provided; flutes or recorders would be appropriate. The original tune suggested 'for immediate singing' was the traditional French carol melody NOEL NOUVELET (French=new Nativity Song). A New Year's carol rather than a Christmas one, and written in the Dorian mode, it dates from the 15th century. Its first five notes echo the beginning of an ancient Latin hymn in honour of Mary, 'Ave Maris Stella' (Hail, Star of the Sea).

Now to your table spread A100
Metre: 12.12.8.8

Titled 'Hymn of Approach to Communion' in her first collection of her own work as a hymn writer, *In Every Corner Sing* (Wellington, 1987), this hymn text was written by **Shirley Murray** in 1986, with a World Communion Sunday* gathering in mind, "as though all humankind around one table stood."' 'But,' adds the writer, 'It is also, for me, about the search for meaning in our individual and community life.' The hymn was later published in both her first American collection, *In Every Corner Sing* (1992) and *Alleluia Aotearoa* (1993).

Verse 1 draws on John 6:48-58: 'life and death' (line 2) are to be understood as meaning spiritual life and death. In verse 2, the 'hands of the world' are literally those of congregations worldwide as they reach out to receive the communion elements of bread and wine, but the poet imagines them as symbolizing deeper spiritual yearnings, an idea that may be based on the story of the woman healed of a long illness by reaching out to touch Jesus (Mark 5:24-34). The 'mystery' of line 2 is the mysterious presence of the living Christ, thought to be experienced in the sharing of the elements during the Eucharist (actual, in Roman Catholic belief; symbolic in Protestant belief). Verse 3 stresses the unity of Christians, and potentially of all humanity, – line 1 alludes to the way in which early Christian communities shared their resources (Acts 2:44) – and concludes with an allusion to Christ's prayer 'that all of them may be one' (John 17:22).

LOVE UNKNOWN This tune by **John Ireland** is named after the first line of the 1664 hymn 'My song is love unknown' by Dean Samuel Crossman (1624-84), for which it was composed by the distinguished English songwriter and composer at the request of Geoffrey Shaw, co-editor of *The Public School Hymn Book* (1919). A correspondent to *The Daily Telegraph* of 5 April 1950 claimed that the music was immediately written down within a quarter of an hour of receipt of Shaw's request. One striking feature of the melody is the combination of short and long sweeping phrases which creates a perfectly natural rhythmic sequence, difficult to reduce to a time signature but easy to sing and perfectly matched to the lines of verse. Another is the abrupt shift into F minor followed by C minor resolving on the tonic key of E flat major which occupies the final 4 bars of the hymn.

*World Communion Day, held on the first Sunday in October in Christian churches worldwide, is a celebration begun in 1933 that promotes Christian unity and ecumenical cooperation.

Now unto him A102
Metre: Irregular

This scripture-based praise song was written by New Zealand composer **Olive Wood** in 1970 and later published in a collection of 25 such songs collected by her husband's second wife Norma Wood, under the title '*My Glorious Redeemer*': *Songs by Olive Wood*. It is usually employed as a benediction and is so titled in the original manuscript. The text was printed from the 1972 collection in the words-only edition of *Songs of Praise* (Scripture in Song, 1976); in the Combined Music Edition of that publication (1979) part of the melody is preserved but much of it, together with the accompaniment, has been altered by an unknown arranger.

The text is taken without change from Jude 1:24-25 (King James version).

[NOW UNTO HIM] The music is a straightforward setting of the biblical text, one of several settings of one of the more famous benedictions in the New Testament. The music has been transposed down to G major from the original B flat major key, and although the essential chord structure is retained an arranger has been at work on the time signature (6/4 replaces 3/4), the melody (introducing dotted notes, for instance) and the left-hand accompaniment, relaxing the original regular, vertical chordal arrangement. In the 1979 *Songs of Praise* version a similar time and key change has been made, but the arrangement has gone further, extending to substantial alterations in the melodic line.

The *Scripture in Song* version of the work is recorded on the 1972 album *Prepare Ye the Way*.

O be joyful in God *A103*
Metre: 6.6.6.4 and refrain

Psalm 100 has been set many times by composers in every age; here New Zealand composer and hymn writer **Nigel Eastgate**, writing in 1989, makes another joyful version, using his own paraphrase of the text and setting it for unison choir (or congregation) and piano. The work was first published in *Alleluia Aotearoa* (1993).

The text follows the structure of the original four verses of the psalm, but the language is modernized, the verse form is considerably altered (for instance by the triple repetition of 'serve the Lord with gladness') and there are both significant additions and omissions. Selective comparison illustrates such alterations: verse 1, line 1, of the standard English translation of the psalm, 'Make a joyful noise to the Lord, all the lands,' becomes 'O be joyful in God, all you people of earth,' while verse 4, line 2, 'and [enter] his courts with praise' becomes 'O come into his courts from far abroad' (a concealed, even humorous reference to the distance between ancient Palestine and modern New Zealand). Similarly, in verse 4, the goodness and 'steadfast love' of God praised in the Psalm are replaced by 'mercy' and 'grace,' and there is no mention of 'his faithfulness to all generations.'

[O BE JOYFUL] The melody, by **Nigel Eastgate** himself, aims for a maximum of off-beat rhythm to mime extreme happiness, and although the tonality remains anchored in G, from the introductory bar the harmony playfully engages with C, D and A major until the last possible moment. The joyfully leaping bass line takes on the character of 3+3+2 quavers in a bar, rather than the 4-crochet beating indicated by the 4/4 time signature. This music shows a talented composer engaging fully with his subject, joy and gladness in the presence of God.

O beauty ever ancient *H107*
Metre: 7.6.7.6 and refrain

This hymn of praise was written by **Shirley Murray** in September 2000, and first published in her American collection *Faith Makes the Song* (2003) before appearing in *Hope is our Song* (2009). The author explains that the text was the outcome of her being given access to a quotation from the *Confessions* of St Augustine, later Bishop of Hippo (354-430).* 'I set off on my own thoughts from the opening phrase. It caught me in a moment of reflecting on the paradoxes of beauty, expressed in the different senses and also in the seeming negatives (darkness, silence, stillness) as much as in sound, sight and movement. I have not often written in this mildly ecstatic mode, but something propelled me into it.'

The theme of the hymn is praise of the manifestation of the presence of God apprehended through the senses in human artistic creations in the physical 'world of sound and sight.' Verse 1, as the author acknowledges, begins with an allusion to St Augustine, 'Beauty so ancient and so new, too late I came to love you,' But there is a larger indebtedness in the structure of the verses and in some of the details: cf. 'O Beauty that is stillness / in lovely form or face' (verse 3, lines 3-4), with St Augustine, 'I drove against the beautiful things and beings you made.' However, the delight expressed in the beauty afforded by silence and darkness (verse 2) and in 'the liquid line of grace' (verse 3) – 'line' is a technical term used both for a type of dance and the posture of an individual dancer – is wholly original.

MANOR PLACE The name of a street in Dunedin where Shirley and John Murray were staying for a time. The music, written by composer **Colin Gibson** in 2000, takes the character of a graceful swaying dance in 6/4 time, modulating immediately from D major to G, then through A major before finding its way back to the tonic key note. The impression sought is of a 'liquid' musical line.

*The full quotation from the *Confessions*. Book 10, written c.398 AD, is now one of the official readings in the Roman Office of the Catholic Church, set down for Wednesday of the 8th week in Ordinary Time:

'I came to love you too late, O Beauty, so ancient and so new. Yes, I came to love you too late. You were inside me and I was outside my body and mind looking for you. Like an ugly madman I drove against the beautiful things and beings you made. You were inside me, but I was not inside you. You called, shouted, broke the bowl of my deafness; you flared, blazed, banished my blindness. You lavished your fragrance; I gasped, and now I pant for you. I tasted you, and now I want you as I want food and water. You touched me, and I have been burning ever since to have your peace.'

O Bread of joy *A104*
Metre: 9.9.10.10

This devotional poem, addressing Christ as the bread broken and shared during the Eucharist, was written by Sister **Mary Veronica Daley**, a New Zealand Sister of Mercy, some time before 1993, when it was included in *Alleluia Aotearoa*.

The text has its origin both in the gospel accounts of the Last Supper and in the description in Acts 2:46 of the behaviour of the first Christian communities: 'breaking bread in their homes they partook of food with glad and generous hearts.' The phrase repeated in the final line of each verse, 'heart of my heart,' echoes a line from the ancient Irish hymn translated by Mary Elizabeth Byrne (1905) and versified by Eleanor Henrietta Hull (1912), 'Be thou my vision': 'heart of my own heart, whatever befall.' Verse 1, line 2, 'Body of Christ' is the liturgical phrase signalling the presence of Christ (symbolic or actual) in the bread used in the celebration of the Eucharist. Verse 2 references Psalm 80:5, 'You fed them with the bread of tears.' Verse 3 again draws on 'Be thou my vision,' whose final verse describes Christ 'after victory won' as 'bright heaven's sun,' though there is an ancient scriptural tradition regarding the 'radiance' of the body of the resurrected Christ, which has given rise to much Christian iconography and art (see, for instance, Revelation 1:12-16).

[BREAD OF JOY] This setting by **Douglas Mews** is derived from an arrangement for unison singers and piano. The melody climbs gradually upwards to a top E flat before falling quietly back to the tonic. The rhythm is that of a stately dance in 3/4 time; harmonic sequences take the singers up through G minor and B flat major to reach E flat, then return to the tonic key via A flat major. This is one of the finest of the many compositions created by Douglas Mews for *Alleluia Aotearoa*.

O Christ who by a cross *A105*
Metre: 10.10.10,10

This hymn was written by **Shirley Murray** in 1985 and first appeared in her privately published collection *In every Corner Sing* (Wellington, 1987) under the title 'Hymn for Peace.' The author comments that the last line is a quotation from A.J. Muste, 'which I saw on a Peace Movement poster. As with almost all my peace hymns, this was premièred at St Andrew's on the Terrace [Wellington], which in 1983 declared itself a Peace Church.' The hymn was later published in her first American collection of the same name (1992), and *Alleluia Aotearoa* (1993).

The Reverend Abraham Johannes Muste (1885-1967) was a Dutch-born American clergyman and political activist, remembered for his involvement in the American trade union movement, the peace movement and the United States civil rights movement. Unable to subscribe to the fundamentalist position of the Dutch Reformed Church, Muste left for a position as an independent Congregational minister and finally joined the Quakers. A committed pacifist, he became a member of the Fellowship of Reconciliation soon after its founding in 1916. The saying quoted in the hymn appeared in the New York Times, 6 November 1967; it has also been attributed to Mahatma Gandhi.

'Shalom,' (verse 1, line 7), is a Hebrew word meaning 'complete peace.'** 'The blinding bomb' (verse 3, line 3) and 'the arsenal of hatred' (verse 4, line 3) both refer to the stock piling of atomic bombs that went on during the so-called Cold War between Russia and the United States. One of the known effects of such bombs was blinding from the intense nuclear flash that occurred when they were detonated.

SURSUM CORDA (Latin=lift up your hearts). The author identified this hymn tune as her preferred setting, finding it in *With One Voice* (1982). The tune was written by **Alfred Morton Smith** in 1941 as a setting for 'Lift up your hearts! We lift them, Lord, to thee,' by Henry Montague Butler. It was first published in the American Episcopal hymn book *The Hymnal 1940*, then achieved wider recognition, reaching the *BBC Hymn Book* (1951), *The Hymn Book* (Canada, 1971), the Scottish Presbyterian *Church Hymnary* (3rd edition, 1973) and *The Australian Hymn Book* (1977). The melody is constructed as a set of four nearly identical phrases, its pyramid structure and stepwise melodic movement giving it the measured, unexcitable character of ancient plainsong.

> *'Peace is not merely the cessation of hostilities, but Shalom, an environment of mutual good-will, co-operation and shared prosperity' (Carl Daw).
>
> **'Shalom means wholeness and health, welfare, harmony with God, with nature, life and others: Shalom is the meaning and the context of life itself' (Bishop Mortimer Arias of Bolivia).

O Christ, you hang upon a cross
H108
Metre: 8.6.8.6 and Kyries

This powerful Good Friday confessional hymn was written by **Shirley Murray** in April 2006. The author says of it, 'I wrote this in the hope that, with some imagination, it might be integrated into a Good Friday liturgy. I don't often resort to the Greek imprecation [prayer, invocation], but there is a universality which these words carry that I find poignant and fitting for such a day.' The hymn was first published in the author's American collection *Touch the Earth Lightly* (2008), then in *Hope is our Song* (2009). The original title of the poem, 'Hymn for Good Friday,' does not appear in either of these publications.

The text follows the events of the crucifixion of Jesus Christ which the singer is invited to imagine ('O Christ, you hang upon a cross'), while suggesting that the modern world with its battlefield brutality, financial market manipulation and dubious public and private ethical and moral behaviour re-enacts a similar crucifixion of the innocent, another kind of war against the Word of God (verse 3). The biblical sources are Matthew 27:45ff and Luke 23:26ff., but John 1 and Genesis 1 are also drawn upon. The ancient Greek phrases *Kyrie eleison* and *Christe, eleison* mean 'Lord, have mercy on us, Christ, have mercy on us.'

GOOD FRIDAY The tune name was taken from the original title of the poem and reflects the occasion for which this text was written. The music is by **Colin Gibson** and was written in immediate response to the author's communication of the text. The somber character of the words suggested music set in the key of C minor conveying the idea of a slow, funeral-like march to the cross, while the Greek text called for a plainsong-like melodic phrase, falling through an octave range, caught up and echoed in the accompaniment – an effect that could be carried out vocally if a choir was available.

O God we bear the imprint of your face A106
Metre: 10.10.10.10.10.10.10

Originally entitled 'A Hymn about Racism,' this text was written by **Shirley Murray** in 1981 and first published in her privately printed collection, *In Every Corner Sing* (Wellington, 1987). It was then printed in her first American collection of the same name (1992), followed by *Alleluia Aotearoa* (1993). As a representative New Zealand hymn it was reprinted (words only) in *A Panorama of Christian Hymnody*, by Erik Routley and Alan A. Richardson (Chicago: GIA, 2005).

The writer has described the circumstances of its composition: 'In that year [1981] I was just beginning to learn the cost of racism. The anti-apartheid movement in New Zealand protested against the Springbok rugby team coming to play on our soil, and our family's involvement meant police arrest for our son, David, and public denunciation of my husband, John, who was placed under a banning order from entering the House of Parliament.'

The text draws on Genesis 1:20, 'God said, "Let us make man in our image, after our likeness,"' the implication being that all human beings of whatever colour or race bear the divine likeness, and passionately denounces state-sponsored or cultural racism, which [dishonours] 'your living face on earth.'

In a way typical of this poet, the human body as a divine creation is equated with the embroidery practice of stretching fabric on a frame (verse 1, line 5). 'Victims made because we own our name' (verse 2, line 4) refers to the prosecution of those behaving in a Christian way – by resisting the apartheid regime and its perceived support by the New Zealand government of the day. Verse 3, line 4, alludes to Galatians 3:26-28, 'In Jesus Christ you are all sons of God…There is neither Jew nor Greek, there is neither slave nor free, there is neither male nor female, because you are all one in Christ Jesus.'*

SONG 1 The first setting chosen for this powerful text was the familiar hymn tune by the Elizabethan composer **Orlando Gibbons**, known simply as 'Song 1' from its first appearance in George Wither's *Hymns and Songs of the Church*, 1623. The harmonization is by **Ralph Vaughan Williams**, prepared for the 1906 *The English Hymnal*, for which he was the music editor.

*For further textual analysis see *Hymns for Today* by Brian Wren, Louisville: Westminster John Knox Press (2009) 52-3.

O God, beyond our knowledge H71
Metre: 10.10.10.10

This hymn was written by **Lois Henderson** of Pauanui, on the Coromandel Peninsula, and first published in *Hope is our Song* (2009).

The hymn begins by celebrating God's transcendence, imminence and providential love. Verse 2 acknowledges God's 'lavish love' as displayed in the astonishing variety of the natural world. Verse 3 praises God's compassionate love, 'which you transform to creative deeds,' and celebrates God's renovative influence in the crumbling of 'long-held rigid creeds,' and their replacement by new and 'unimaginable' seeds of thought (cf. Revelation 21:5. 'Behold, I make all things new'). Verse 4 alludes to three manifestations of God's presence: Elijah's experience on Mount Horeb (1 Kings 19:11-18), Pentecost (Acts 2:1-4*) and the ministry of Jesus. Line 2 alludes to Luke 6:20 and Isaiah 35:6. God escapes human filing systems; as manifested in Jesus who is both King of Kings (Revelation 17:14) and a helpless human baby. The final verse abandons the attempt to 'comprehend' God, leaving the singers to trust in the divine purpose and calling them to action, 'that everything in earth may truly live.'

CHILTON FOLIAT Named after a village on the River Kennet in Wiltshire, England, the recommended tune for this text was written by George Currie Martin (1865-1937), a Scottish-born Congregational minister who worked in Scotland and England before becoming Professor of New Testament Language and Patristics at Bradford United College and Lancashire College, Manchester. He wrote a number of hymns and hymn tunes, published in *Hymn Tunes and Carols* (1923), and a book on *The Church and the Hymn Writers* (1928). CHILTON FOLIAT was contributed to *The Westminster Abbey Hymn Book*, edited by Sir Frederick Bridge and published in 1897.

> *The reading 'ice and fire' in verse 4 may be an authorial error for wind and fire, the elements associated with the Pentecost experience. However, Job 37:10 says that 'By the breath of God, ice is given, and the broad waters are frozen fast,' so the writer may have had in mind real experiences of winters in earlier years experienced in Hawkes Bay.

O God, our God, disabled God
H112
Metre: 8.8.8.8

This hymn was written in 2000. **Shirley Murray**, its author, explains the circumstances of its creation: 'An Anglican friend asked for a hymn to a familiar metre for Disability Sunday, and the theme that year was "Holy, Wholly Accessible." My disabled friend sent these words to help focus: "Disability is gift and struggle. There is joy and pain. It is part of creation. It is both and…rather than all positive or negative." The text was first published in Murray's American collection *Faith Makes the Song* (2003) without a musical setting, as it was in *Hope is our Song* (2009).

The text uses every prompt offered in the friend's words. Verse 1 addresses God first in general ('O God'), then on behalf of the disabled ('our God'). God – in Christ – is then described as having a body broken by crucifixion, with the resurrected body as its 'truth and grace' (cf. 'O Bread of light and resurrection / Body of Christ in all perfection,' lines from the hymn 'O Bread of joy' (A104). Verse 2 takes up the idea of disability as a 'gift,' honed by endurance, 'unique and blessed.' In remarkably direct language, verse 3 admits 'the secret hell' often hidden by the body language of the disabled, 'the selves we do not choose to show.' Verse 4 works with the theme 'Holy, wholly accessible' and introduces the biblical image of Christ as the open door (John 10:9). The final verse focuses on the sentence 'There is joy and pain. It is part of creation.' For the writer this recalls Romans 8:22, 'For we know that all the rest of creation has been groaning with the pains of childbirth.'

The tunes suggested are WALY WALY or ANGELUS. WALY WALY is a traditional English folk melody collected by Cecil Sharp and published in his *Folk Songs from Somerset* (1906). It has been traced back to the early 1700s, and has become a popular hymn tune, used in nearly 70 North American hymnals. The melody ANGELUS was named after the *nom de plume*, Angelus Silesius, of Johann Scheffler, German author of a hymn text to which this anonymous melody was set in a collection of Scheffler's poems, *Heilege Seelenlust* (Breslau, 1657). The melody was later altered and finally appeared in its received modern form in the second edition of *Hymns Ancient & Modern* (1875).

O God, to you I cry in pain *H106*
Metre: 8.6.8.6

Written in 2006 **by Shirley Murray**, this hymn directly expresses the author's own experience of illness and pain. She writes, 'I have found very few hymns that do not become unreal and even pietistic about this theme. Many forms of suffering are accompanied by fear, despite the traditional allusions to healing miracles. And the effect of human touch and concern is sometimes a miracle in itself. I have tried to express my own experience in this, while blessing the health professionals who show dedication and genuine concern for all aspects of our body and soul. I like the words of Henri de Tourville, [1842-1903] French priest and spiritual writer: "God eliminates illness through the growth of knowledge and of human wisdom."' The text was first published in *Touch the Earth Lightly* (2008), then in *Hope is our Song* (2009).

The writer's acknowledged sources of the text are Psalm 103:1-5 and Mark 5:1-20, the story of the miraculous healing of a man with an 'unclean spirit' in the country of the Gadarenes.

But these are not so much verbal prompts as expressions of the positive attitude to suffering and its accompanying fears that informs the whole text. The model is Psalm 130 ('Out of the depths I cry to thee') which also names a desperate situation but affirms belief in the restorative nature of God. Note the structural use of implorative verbs: '*Give* me strength to face my ill,' '*Remind* me I am not alone,' '*Restore* in me a larger sense of what it is to live,' '*Allow* my mind to rest in you.'

AFFLICTION The tune name is self-explanatory. This music, by a personal friend, **Jillian Bray**, was also written in 2006. Set in the 'sorrowful' key of A minor, it has the appropriate character of a Passion chorale, and is harmonised in the manner of Bach. It is the tune used in both the American and New Zealand hymnals which print this hymn. There is an independent setting by Canadian composer **Ron Klusmeier** (Klusmeier 49).

O he is born *A107, C32*
Metre: 7.6.7.6 and refrain

Written in 1981 by **Felicia Edgecombe**, a long-time member of the Titahi Bay Community Church, this carol celebrates the birth of Jesus, drawing on the narratives of the Nativity according to Matthew and Luke. It was first published in *New Zealand Praise (1988)*, followed by *Alleluia Aotearoa* (1993) and *Carol our Christmas* (1996). It is on the SongSearch website and has been reprinted in *Songs of Life*, by Felicia Edgecombe and Rosemary Russell (Wellington: Festivity Productions, 1996).

Felicia Edgecombe describes the occasion which prompted the writing of the carol: 'Still feeling the euphoria from the birth of our* third son, Robert, I decided to write a Christmas carol for the Festival Singers' [1981] Christmas concert, which attempted to highlight the intense joy that Mary must have felt at the birth of Jesus.' The carol is dedicated to their baby Robert Edgecombe.

The text, titled 'Christ is Born' in *New Zealand Praise and Songs of Life*, closely follows the two biblical accounts of Jesus' birth, working selectively between both of them.

Verse 1 opens with a phrase adapted from Matthew 26:10 referring to Mary of Bethany's gesture of anointing Christ's feet, 'she has done a beautiful thing to me.' It then quotes Luke 1:31, 'And the angel said to her, "The Holy Spirit will come upon you,"' though it is Gabriel and not the Holy Spirit who promises Mary a child. Verse 2 turns to Matthew 1:18-21 as a source for the characterisation of Joseph as 'a righteous man.' Verse 3, draws from Matthew 1:23, though John 3:16 provides line 2, 'the only Son of God.' Verse 4 reverts to Luke for the wise men and shepherds who come and worship.

[CHRIST IS BORN] This intensely rhythmical and joyful musical setting is the work of the author. It remains securely within the tonality of A flat major with an off-beat beginning and pronounced syncopation a compelling feature of the melodic line. The carol has been recorded on CD by the Festival Singers, *Tell my People: Twenty years of Festival Singers* (Wellington: Festivity Productions, 2000).

*Kenneth and Felicia Edgecombe were married in 1971.

O little love who comes again (Peace Carol) *A108 (i) and (ii), C33 (i) and (ii)*
Metre: 8.8.8.8

This carol was written by **Shirley Murray** in 1986, and first printed privately by the author in her collection *In Every Corner Sing* (Wellington, 1987), followed by her first American collection, *In Every Corner Sing* (1992) and *Carol our Christmas* (1996).

Shirley Murray described the conception of the carol in *In Every Corner Sing* (1992). 'Peace Carol was written when a great deal of my energy was going into "Christians for Peace" and New Zealand was struggling with the implications of declaring itself "Nuclear-Free." I was playing with the double entendre of "disarm" [= 'charm' and 'free the world of its weapons'] when this carol first took shape.'

As usual, the text frequently alludes to biblical ideas and expressions. For verse 1 see John 1:1-

5, while there is a play on 'little darling' and 'the expression of ultimate love in a tiny baby' in the first line. 'Comes again' refers to the annual celebration of the Nativity by the singers as well as alluding to the Second Coming, as in the wording of the Nicene Creed, 'He [Jesus] will come again in glory to judge the living and the dead, and his kingdom will have no end.' For Herod's ruthless exercise of power and 'Mary's home' in verse 2 see Matthew 2:16-18 and Luke 2:31. The Magi's search (Matthew 2:1-2) is referred to in verse 3, as is Jesus' declaration, 'I am the light of the world' (John 8:12). The compressed opening lines of verse 2 mean 'There is no nature so brutal (unyielding) that it cannot be stirred by your love, nor is there any hatred so deep that it can resist your defenceless / undisguised love.'

ST AIDAN'S This unison setting in G major was written by the writer's friend **Jillian Bray** in 1987. The tune name refers to the composer's home church in Porirua, Wellington.

PEACE CAROL Shirley Murray wrote of this setting in F major composed by **Nigel Eastgate** in 1987, '[The Peace Carol] was first sung to EISENACH, but is much more suited to the sensitivity of Nigel Eastgate's writing.' She chose this setting for the carol's appearance in her first American collection, *In Every Corner Sing*. Although in different keys, the melodic germ in both cases is a triad, rising in Nigel Eastgate's setting and falling in Jillian Bray's setting.

O living Word *H109*

Metre: 4.8.8.7.4

Setting herself to write in an unusual metre, **Marnie Barrell** created this reflection on the first 18 lines of the gospel of John 1:1-18 in 1997, intending it as a hymn for the Advent-Christmas season. It was first published in *Hope is our Song* (2009).

The text is best understood as a paraphrase of the acknowledged biblical source, freely combining and selecting phrases and sentences. So, the opening line is made up of John 1, verses 1 and 4; line 2 is a compressed version of John's line 3. Verse 2, line 3, 'you came home and few received you' is made out of John's verse 11, 'He came to his own home and his own people received him not': here the writer's work is shown in the personal address to Christ as 'you' and in the replacement of 'his own people' (that is, the Jewish nation) by 'few received you' (that is, the small group of Jesus' closest family members and his early disciples and other followers). There are supplementary sources, importantly 1 John 4 and Psalm 80:3. But the final positioning of the singers as freed to become 'the bearers of your story' is the addition of the hymn writer.

LIVING WORD Named after the first line of the text, this setting by fellow Christchurch composer **Barry Brinson** was written in 2007. Challenged to match both the subject and the unusual metre of the text, the composer chose a D minor tonality to emphasize the serious and thoughtful nature of the hymn as it ponders the mysteries evoked by John's words. There are significant modulations to A major and C major, and the conclusion first hints at then finishes on a D major chord. The rocking bass might half-suggest a nativity lullaby, but the melodic structure – which carefully allows for the strongest emphasis to fall on the final phrase of each verse – also recalls the 17th-century English folk tune, GREENSLEEVES, often matched with the carol 'What child is this?'

O Lord my God, I stand and gaze in wonder *W628*

Metre: 11.10.11.10.10.8.10.8

This now world-famous hymn is the product of a succession of translations and adaptations of an original nine-verse poem written in 1885 by Swedish pastor **Carl Boberg**. According to the writer's own account it was inspired by the experience of walking home from church and being caught in a violent thunderstorm, followed by the appearance of a rainbow and a deep calm in which the song of a thrush and church bells could be heard. Boberg published the poem in his home town's newspaper in 1886, and in 1891, after he had heard it sung to an old Swedish folk tune, printed the full text together with its acquired musical setting (arranged in 3/4 time for piano and guitar) in his weekly journal *Sanningsvittnet* (Witness for the Truth).

A German translation made in 1907 was itself translated into Russian in 1912. In 1931, English evangelist, Stuart K. Hine, working with his wife in the western Ukraine near the Polish border, heard the Russian version being sung and began using it in his own services. Hine later made an English paraphrase of the first two stanzas of the hymn. He added a third, reportedly after witnessing an evangelical act of repentance in a Ukrainian village, and a fourth, in England, after hearing Polish refugees from Nazi Germany speak of their longing for a heavenly reunion with lost relatives. However, the ideas in those verses are already present in the Swedish original, as literally translated by American Professor E. Gustav Johnson as early as 1925.

Hine's version, completed in 1948 (though he published 2 more verses in 1953) and circulated through his own Russian gospel magazine *Grace and Peace*, was popularized by its use as the signature tune for the Billy Graham crusades, which reached New Zealand in 1959. There are a number of other translations and paraphrases, including a Māori version, 'Whakaaria Mai,' sung during a Royal Command Performance for Queen Elizabeth II on the occasion of her visit to New Zealand in 1981, and popularized by Howard Morrison, who released it as a single in 1982.

The Committee of the New Zealand Supplement to *With One* Voice chose a version of Boberg's poem by Welsh hymnist **Eluned Harrison** (b. 1934), as being closest to the Swedish original. There is an even more recent (and more accurate) version of the Swedish original written by Auckland poet Allen Bell and published as 'How great you are, Creator God: New words for a popular hymn,' in *Music in the Air*, 25 Summer/Autumn 2008, 23.

O STORE GUD (Swedish=O mighty God). This is a genuine old Swedish folk melody, resembling many other Scandinavian and Baltic folk songs in circulation before the first World War. Dr Carlton Brown describes it as 'delightful…in its original subtle dancing triple-time setting' (*Companion to the United Methodist Hymnal* (Nashville: Abingdon, 1993, 410). It has gone through a number of transformations at the hands of later musicians, with different harmonies and changes in key and time signature. The *With One Voice* arrangement is by **Philip Begbie Watson** (1936), also used in *Together in Song: The Australian Hymnbook II* (1999), but with the Stuart Hine text.

O mai i lenei vaipuna W632
Metre: 8.7.8.7.11.11.7.7

Described in *With One Voice* (1982) as an 'old traditional Samoan hymn,' this text is undoubtedly based on a still older English or American gospel song translated and introduced into Samoan culture in the 1860s or later, most probably by missionaries of the London Missionary Society. It remains one of the most popular of the 'old' hymns, frequently recorded by modern solo artists and singing groups; a modern Samoan, born and raised in America, says of it, 'I can still recall the elders solemnly singing this song while the communion was being passed out.'

The text, with its powerful insistence on coming (forward) as a declaration of faith or in response to the invitation to share in the Eucharist, has as its dominant image 'the spring of life opened up by Jesus.' There are resonances with the story of Jesus' encounter with the woman of Samaria reported in John 4:7-15, (cf. 'who drinks of the water that I will give him will never thirst' with 'If you drink this water you will be satisfied'), but the basic source is Revelation 22:17, 'The Spirit and the Bride say "Come." And let him who hears say "Come." And let him who is thirsty come, let him who desires take the water of life without price.' The 'spring of life' (verse 1) morphs into the redeeming blood of the Lamb (Revelation 7:13-14, cf. verse 3, 'Wipe away whatever is bad in you. In the blood of Jesus you will find peace.') There are additional biblical sources: the invitation in verse 3 to the blind, the sick and the weak derives from Matthew 15:30, and the final verse is a paraphrase of Psalm 100:5, 'The Lord is good, his steadfast love endures forever, and his faithfulness to all generations.'

O LE VAIPUNA The tune has not been identified, but it has the hallmarks of an early gospel melody adapted to the Samoan choral style of vigorous four-part unaccompanied singing, as demonstrated in the classic performance by the choir of Western Samoa Teachers' Training College, Apia, recorded on *Samoan Songs of Worship* (Hibiscus Kiwi records, Wellington, 1973) and accessible on YouTube.

O mai, Iesu, tai meitaki W638
Metre: 8.7.8.6 and refrain

Described in *With One Voice* as a 'traditional' Cook Islands hymn, and now part of the well-loved body of Cook Islands hymns, this text is probably the work of an early missionary (London Missionary Society workers arrived in the Cook Islands as early as 1821).

In early printings the original text is associated variously and vaguely with Jeremiah 17:7 and Isaiah 26:4, but the paraphrase reduces that text to simpler matters. Verse 2 refers to the parable of the Sower found in the three synoptic gospels and the non-canonical gospel of Thomas, though the 'good seed' (line 2) is strictly seed that fell upon good ground. Verse 3 refers to the worship of the Lamb in heaven as described in Revelation 22:3. The reiteration of 'Tai mei taki / No matou ka aere ei' (=bless us as we go) suggests that this text was intended to be used as a hymn of dismissal at the end of a service.

I AM TRUSTING The tune name comes from the first line of **Francis Ridley Havergal**'s hymn 'I am trusting thee, Lord Jesus'. The music is adapted from a setting of her text by American evangelist, singer and musician **James H. Burke,** written in 1891. Burke visited England, Scotland, Australia and New Zealand with preacher James McNeill on evangelical missions, and it is possible that the missionaries who followed John Williams to the Cook Islands (he died in the New Hebrides in 1839) first heard the tune sung by its composer at such a meeting.

O spring in the desert (Prayer for the Presence) F51
Metre: 6.5.6.5 D

The text of this invocation was written by **David Adam**, then Vicar of Lindisfarne, and published in his collection of modern prayers in the Celtic tradition, *Tides and Seasons* (Triangle, 1989). It first appeared with this setting in Colin Gibson's American collection *Songs for a Rainbow People* (1998) then in *Faith Forever Singing* (2000).

The text is a prayer for the presence of the divine in the life of the believer, a concept that is both deeply Christian and found in many other faiths as well. It is made up of a list of titles of that manifestation – finally defined in this prayer as Christ – consisting of images, many of them drawn from the world of nature in the Celtic manner; all of them biblical in origin, and focusing on refreshment, protection, guidance and deliverance from sadness or weakness. Matthew 28:18-20 is the foundation bible text; for individual images see Isaiah 43:19 (spring), Isaiah 4:6 (shelter), John 1:5 (light), Psalm 199:105 (guide), John 16:20 (joy), Isaiah 40:29 (strength).

PRESENCE The tune name is taken from the key term in the text. The music was written by **Colin Gibson** in 1995 as a four-part choral setting in the shape of a lyric song – more a solemn dance than a chorale.

O the Spirit she moves on the water A109
Metre: 10.9.12.6.12.3 and refrain

One of the many hymns written by **Cecily Sheehy** for the Family Programme magazine produced by the Auckland Catholic Religious Education Centre in the early 1980s, this passionate hymn about the Holy Spirit reached book publication in 1993 in *Alleluia Aotearoa*. Written originally as a unison melody with guitar chording, the tune was given a piano accompaniment by **Jenny Bennett**.

Dominating the text is an image of the Holy Spirit as a woman – mother and lover (verse 1, 'and she sweeps us all up in the flame of her love') – wild, moody, unpredictable, tremendous: the ultimate personification of the life-force and vital energy (verse 3, 'living energy, given to all'). The text is interactive – 'Do you see, do you hear?' – and as if speaking in tongues, ends in rapturous, wordless vocalization, 'La, la, la.' However, for all its celebration of unlimited, even abandoned surrender to the presence of the Spirit, it consistently and authentically draws on scriptural sources. Genesis 1:1 forms the basis of verse 1 'And the Spirit of God was moving over the face of the waters.' The Hebrew noun for Spirit, *ruach*, with its senses of 'breath' or 'wind' and its feminine gender, gives rise to many of the ideas in verses 1 and 2 ('her breathing is felt far and near,' 'she can roar with the power of a hurricane wind'). The concept of the Spirit as life-giver (verse 1, line 3) draws on both Genesis 2:7 and John 3:3-8; the traditional Spirit-fire imagery derives from Acts 2:3. Verse 2 returns to Genesis 1 for its images of darkness and brooding* (line 1); to John 3:8 for the Spirit's unpredictability. Lines 5-6 may be indebted to the Roman Catholic practice of the Rosary of Divine Union (the author is a Dominican nun): cf. 'When emotional turmoil seems to abate, or in the middle of such turmoil, we find a silence. In this silence, the Holy Spirit draws us deeper than our emotions, and invites us to dwell in the place where the warmth of the Spirit leads us to still waters, to the stillness of the Presence of God' (*Rosaries of the Divine Union*). Verse 3 begins with an allusion to Romans 8:1-2, 'the law of the Spirit of life in Christ Jesus has set me free from the law of sin and death.' Lines 3-4 draw on 1 Corinthians 13:12.

[SPIRIT SONG] Unusually, this religious song takes the musical form of a habanera, as the bass line shows, with much syncopation and triplets throughout the melodic line. The key signature suggests A minor but the harmony is fluid, modulating immediately to D major and moving sequentially through a number of keys until it reaches a final open cadence in E major, never resolved on A and suggesting the unpredictable, open-ended movement of the Holy Spirit herself. This is not a hymn for staid Christians; it is a wild celebration that will delight those willing to accept and be swept up into its dance rhythms. In that sense, it perfectly imitates the text, which celebrates 'being one with creation and life / and the Spirit.'

> *The Hebrew word used in Genesis 1:1 for the action of the Spirit of God may mean moving (stirring), hovering protectively or brooding over, as a hen might its eggs or its chickens. English adds the idea of 'thinking profoundly.' All of these senses are available in this text.

O threefold God of tender unity
A110
Metre: 10.10.10.10

In 1988 the Hymn Society of America announced a search for 'New Hymns with a New Vision of the Living God.' This hymn, written by **Bill Wallace** in 1979 and revised in 1990, won the competition. It was published in 1990 in Book 2 of the author's three-volume collection *Singing the Circle: Darkness and Light*, before appearing in *Alleluia Aotearoa* (1993). In 1997 it reached American publication in *Wonder, Love and Praise: A Supplement to the Hymnal 1982*, and has since been published in *Church Hymnary 4* (2005) and *A Panorama of Christian Hymnody* (2005).

Bill Wallace describes the hymn as 'an attempt to hold together the intangible and incarnate dimensions of the Trinity, while at the same time avoiding paternalistic concepts of power.' The traditional figures of the Trinity, Father, Son and Holy Spirit, are replaced by 'Parent, Spirit, Child' (verse 4, line 4) in 'tender' unity (the word here means 'gentle, loving'). Verse 1 celebrates the mysterious nature of God, using antithesis – 'binds and sets us free,' 'sought... found' – to express it. Verse 2 addresses God in classical terms as 'blinding light, blaze of radiance, fiery splendour.' The metaphor 'living well' derives from John 4:1-26 (Jesus' encounter with the Samaritan woman) and John 7:38, 'Whoever believes in me, as the

Scripture has said, "Out of his heart will flow rivers of living water."' Verse 3 develops the idea that God may be encountered in other human beings and the beauty of nature. 'Blood' may carry the meanings of 'living creatures' and 'sexual passion.' Verse 4 discovers the life of God in 'every making [artistic work], each creative dream' as well as in love and reconciliation. The final verse recapitulates the first verse to constitute a unified verbal structure.

UNITY The tune name is taken from the first line of the hymn; its composer is **Jillian Bray**, who wrote this setting in 1992 for *Alleluia Aotearoa*. The melody is constructed from three sweeping phrases that carry the harmony into related keys before returning to the unifying key of D major. The hymn has attracted other settings. The author's own choice was ST AGNES by James Langran (1835-1909); the Gaelic melody AZAIR was used in *Church Hymnary 4*, while in *Wonder, Love and Praise* the preferred setting was FLENTGE by contemporary American composer and hymn writer Carl Flentge Schalk.

On a cool and autumn dawn *H110*
Metre: 7.9.9.7.7

This hymn for Good Friday was written by **Bill Bennett** in 2006. It was first published in *Hope is our Song* (2009), then in the author's collection of hymns and songs intended to be sung as Graduals based on the Gospel readings of the three-year revised Common Lectionary, *Gradual Praise* (2010). In verse 4 in *Hope is our Song* the final line reads 'autumn day'; in *Gradual Praise* 'autumn eve.'

The writer explains that 'Lent and Holy Week occur during the autumn or fall in the southern hemisphere, so Easter Day does not come at a time when creation is bursting into life. Rather, it is the time when the leaves of deciduous trees are falling, the nights grow longer and colder, and everyone is preparing for the chill of winter. Hence the first line of each verse – "On a cool and autumn morn."'

The verses trace the progress of the day of Jesus' crucifixion and death. Verse 1 presents the dawn trial and judicial sentencing of Jesus (John 18:28, 'It was early'). '…you were such a risk,' refers to John 18:12-14 and Caiaphas' infamous dictum that 'it was expedient that one man should die for the people.' Verse 2 presents the crucifixion of Jesus ('about the sixth hour,' John 19:14). In keeping with the southern context of this hymn, Jesus is nailed to a beam of kauri (the most splendid and largest of the native trees of New Zealand). Verse 3 addresses the words of forgiveness from the cross (Luke 23:34). Verse 4 presents Jesus' cry of completion, 'It is finished' (John 19:30) as a cry of hope and foreknowledge of the resurrection to come. Luke places this at 'the ninth hour' (Luke 23:44). The final verse presents the burial of the dead Christ (Luke 23:50-53), 'waiting for God's Pentecost,' here applied to the moment of resurrection (see Acts 2 for the later Pentecost and the gift of the Holy Spirit).

TE RIPEKA (Māori=the cross). **Bill Bennett**, the composer as well as writer of this hymn, notes that this name is sometimes given at baptism within a Māori community of faith. The setting is written in D minor, in something of the style of a Lutheran chorale, with falling chromatic shifts in the bass line to express the emotion of grief.

One small child *F52*
Metre: 6.11.6.8

This hymn treatment of a gospel episode was written by **Shirley Murray** in 2000 and first published in *Faith Forever Singing* (2000), then in her American collection, *Faith makes the Song* (2003).

The biblical passage which underlies the words is Mark 9:33-37 which is virtually paraphrased in verse 1 and 3 in language of great simplicity. The scriptural context is Jesus' response to a private conversation among his disciples as to which of them was the greatest. 'And he took a child and put him in the midst of them; and taking him in his arms, he said to them, "Whoever welcomes one such child in my name receives me; and whoever receives me receives not me but him who sent me."' Verse 2 offers the thematic context and an invented dramatised speech drawing on John 5:24. The final line of this verse has the sense, 'trust my word as readily as does this small child.'

LITTLE ONE The setting in *Faith Forever Singing* is by **Colin Gibson** and was written for these words in 2000. An alternative setting, by another New Zealand composer, **Jenny Mcleod**, was written in 2002 and chosen for *Faith makes the Song*. Both composers deliberately aim for simplicity of melody and harmony and select a dance-like 4/4 rhythm. Gibson's chosen key is D minor, though the melody closes on a major chord (*Tierce de Picardy*); McLeod chooses D major as the tonality throughout.

One, two, three, alleluia! A111
Metre: 5.5.5.5 with alleluias and refrain

This energetic, intensely rhythmic action song was written in 1980 by Dominican Sister **Cecily Sheehy** as one of a series of such songs for children published in the Catholic magazine *Family Living*. Its first hymnbook appearance was in *New Zealand Praise* (1988) – where, under the title '1 2 3 (clap clap) alleluia,' it is arranged for piano and voice by **David Dell**, followed by *Alleluia Aotearoa* (1993).

The verses lightly draw on scriptural texts. For verse 1 see Matthew 1:23, ('Immanuel, which means "God is with us"') and Revelation 21:5, 'behold I make all things new.' Galatians 5:22-23 provides the list of God's gifts in verses 2 and 3. The repeated final line of each verse and the refrain, 'Praise to you, our God,' personalizes Psalm 59:17.

[BOOM, BOOM] The unison tune, written by the author in imitation of playground clapping games, has been arranged for *Alleluia Aotearoa* by **Douglas Mews**. It easily accommodates clapping, cries of *alleluia* and vocal imitations of a rising bass line played by a plucked double bass.

Open, open, open the stable door
C34
Metre: 11.11 and refrain

This carol was written by **Colin Gibson** in 1993 and first published in his American collection *Reading the Signature* (1994) where it is titled 'Welcome, welcome,' before reaching New Zealand publication in *Carol our Christmas* (1996).

The author/composer has this to say about its inception: 'This cheerful contemplation of a Christmas manger capable of welcoming to the birth of Christ not only the traditional crowd of shepherds, kings and assorted animals but those on the fringe of respectable modern society as well, had its origin in my astonished reading of a so-called 'Christian' polemic [published in a local newspaper at the height of the national controversy over the legal and religious status of gay people] which attacked those its writer disapproved of as "some of the most insanitary walking pieces of human debris ever to fall out of a skip (a large rubbish container)," an expression of virulent intolerance which the carol attempts to counter.' It is dedicated to the writer's friends, Euan Thompson and Malcolm Gould, a gay couple of 43 years standing, before Mr Gould's death in 2012. The shepherds are imagined as 'puffing' because they have run all the way (see Luke 2:16) and the wise men are suffering the effects of long-distance riding on lurching camels (see Matthew 2:1). Among the 'crowd of folk come to see the baby' are an alcoholic, a mentally disabled person, by implication gay people, a desperately poor solo mother and a lone and lonely person.

The text was later adapted for Gibson's musical, *The Animals' Christmas* (2003), though its message remains essentially the same:

> Here's the local rat
> and his friend the bantam,
> She lays all the eggs
> while he plays the Phantom.
> Here's a patient ox and a weary donkey,
> Here's a cat who dances the honky-tonky.
> Here's a flock of sheep – yes,
> I think there's forty,

And a camel train,
looking proud and haughty.
Here's a new-born child,
and his parents sleeping,
Here's a gift from God
put into our keeping.

MORNINGTON is both the name of the Dunedin suburb where at the time one of the dedicatees ran an excellent delicatessen, and of the musical Irish aristocrat, Garrett Colley Wellesley (1735-81), First Earl of Mornington. A friend of John and Charles Wesley, he attended and later taught at Dublin University, and from his *Chant in E* a hymn tune also named MORNINGTON was derived in 1805. The setting by **Colin Gibson** uses syncopation and a driving rhythm to reinforce the key concept of openness in the text, and a burst of Gilbertian chatter style for the verses to keep the tone light.

Our Father in heaven *W676, A112*
Metre: Irregular

The text of this version of the Lord's Prayer (following the Matthew 6:9-13 version plus the usual doxology) was provided in 1970 as a new common translation of the prayer for all churches by the International Consultation on English texts, an ecumenical association of liturgists in the English-speaking world formed in 1969 which worked to develop and promote English versions of common liturgical texts. After publishing early drafts from 1970 onwards, it completed its work with a booklet, *Prayers We Have in Common* (1975), including this agreed version of the Lord's Prayer.

OUR FATHER This setting is by **Richard Gillard** and **John Smith**; it has been arranged by **Guy Jansen**. The melody was developed when Gillard and Smith were both members of the St Paul's Singers, a group of young musicians modelling themselves on the American Fisherfolk and working in the creative environment fostered at the St Paul's Anglican Church, Auckland. It first appeared in the 1974 words-only edition of *New Harvest* published by the St Paul's Outreach Trust of the St Paul's Anglican Church, Auckland. In the 1979 full-music edition of *New Harvest* it was printed in an arrangement for voice and piano by the book's editor, Christine Allan.

Among hundreds of such musical settings this music has now established itself among many New Zealand congregations. The melody retains a chant-like quality while using variations in pitch to match the emotional character of the words, dropping to an almost inaudible murmur at 'do not put us to the test' and rising triumphantly for 'the kingdom and the power and the glory are yours.' Guy Jensen's fresh arrangement preserves the dominance of the original B flat key, while shifting through a rainbow of related minor as well as major chords, many of them with added sevenths.

Our life has its seasons (There's a Time) *A113*
Metre: 12.10.12.10 and refrain

Written in 1989 as a theme song for a national Stewardship (finance-raising) campaign run jointly by the Methodist and Presbyterian Churches, this hymn is the work of **Shirley Murray**, who describes it as 'based on Ecclesiastes 3:1-6, with a refrain which echoes 1 Corinthians 13:13.' She goes on to say, 'I considered this song a "throw-away" until I heard it being sung with great zest by a congregation not noted for its singing abilities. Since then it has "taken off" and been recorded for religious radio.' The words, with their setting to the tune KŌTUKU, were first published3eans pulling up a plant. Similarly, 'breaking' refers to an original sense of breaking down, wrecking, in contrast to building up. In verse 3, the ambiguous 'a time to be hurting' (feeling pain, or harming someone else) replaces the original 'a time to kill.'

KŌTUKU As Murray notes, this is the Māori name of the rare New Zealand white heron, 'seen to fly perhaps only once in a lifetime.' It was chosen by the composer, **Colin Gibson**, who wrote this setting in 1989, to suggest that this hymn might also be an occasion for congregational 'lift-off,' like the magnificent spreading of the wings of the kōtuku as it launches elegantly from a branch into the air. The music has a driving 5-5-2 quaver rhythm, to be sustained throughout. Neither the editors of *In Every Corner Sing* (1992), or *Alleluia Aotearoa* (1993) were comfortable with the composer's raw beat-style introductory bar (repeated quavers descending from bass G to D), and have rewritten it (or written it out); the editors of *Alleluia Aotearoa* somewhat tediously stretched out the final bars of each verse to avoid it.

Out of such sun and air *A114*
Metre: 6.4.8.7.8.8.6.8

This hymn was written in 1987 by **Colin Gibson**, following a visit to Northland, New Zealand, and the Waipoua forest of giant kauri trees on the western coast north of Dargaville. The experience prompted the thought that 'in such an astonishing world as New Zealand, Christianity must surely find a different expression from its northern hemisphere manifestation. What that might be we are yet to discover, but we must be open to the possibility of a radical transformation of the traditions imported from the other side of the world and another age.' The hymn was first published in the author's English collection *Singing Love* (1988), followed by *Alleluia Aotearoa* (1993). It is now on the American Hope Publishing website.

Although the repeated invocation in this hymn text, 'come, Christ, however you will come,' has its origins in ancient scriptural and liturgical traditions (cf. Revelation 22:20), the invitation is not a call for the return of Christ in glory (often associated with thoughts of the Last Judgement) but for the transformation and revitalising of the spiritual life of contemporary Christians, described variously as dim, shrouded, sleepy, settled, calm and peaceful. The atmospheric conditions described in each verse are all typical of the changeable weather of these islands, but they are also serve as metaphors for states of life from the fine and calm to the uncertain and stormy.

Those keen to find scriptural bases for the text may consult 1 Kings 18:44 and Acts 2:17 for verse 1, 1 Corinthians 13:13 for verse 2, and – with alteration – the storm passages in Psalm 107:29 and the synoptic gospels (e.g. Matthew 8:23-27) for verse 3. 'Winds of change' echoes British Prime Minister Harold Macmillan's phrase spoken to the South African apartheid parliament in 1960.

NORTHLAND The tune is named after the northernmost province of New Zealand (see above). The music, by the author, is set in C major, but modulations are introduced at points where the text speaks of change: so a shift to G major accompanies the word 'new' in bar 4, and there is an abrupt shift to E flat major marking the words 'stirring our sleepiness.' A further shift into G major underlines 'out of this sun and air' and the melody closes with a return to the tonic key of C.

Out of the storms *F53*
Metre: 9.8.9.8.9.8

In 1998 the province of Otago celebrated its 150th anniversary, and Denzil Brown, minister of First Church, one of the two principal Presbyterian churches of the city of Dunedin, commissioned a hymn to honour that occasion. The hymn and setting was completed by **Colin Gibson** in 1997, premièred in 1998 and first published in *Faith Forever Singing* (2000).

The first verse celebrates the arrival in 1848 of the first two ships bringing immigrant families from Scotland, the 'islands of their birth' (though the phrase 'voyagers all' allows for the inclusion of the earlier Māori migrations to New Zealand). The Otago Settlement, as it was known, was an outgrowth of the Free Church of Scotland, and brought families hoping for religious freedom and a better life. Verse 2 sets out their vision of 'freedom, justice and true equality.' Verse 3 lists the civilized and religious values to be hoped for in the developing communities of Otago; they include freedom from religious dogmatism, care for the natural world (there is an echo of Psalm 8:6-8 here), wise and compassionate social behaviour and the fostering of the arts. The final verse recognises the presence in the modern Otago community of many faiths and cultures, but affirms Christ as 'the mark [goal] of all we strive for, / measure of our humanity.'

OTAGO Named after the province whose anniversary the hymn celebrates, the music was originally written for four-part choral singing with organ accompaniment. In *Faith Forever Singing* it is presented as a unison melody with piano accompaniment. The melodic line is formed from variations on the initial 2-bar phrase with its distinctive triplet motif. The idea of change and exploration is carried through in harmonic shifts away from the tonic key D major as far as F sharp minor before the return to the tonic key.

Peace be with you *H111*
Metre: 9.9.10.9

The original version of this text, written in 2003 by **Shirley Murray,** contains 4 verses and was first published in full in *Sing for Peace: The Hymns of Shirley Erena Murray set to the Tunes of Jane Marshall and Carlton R. Young* (Nashville: Abingdon, 2004). It was later published in a shortened 3-verse form in both her American collection *Touch the Earth Lightly* (2008) and *Hope is our Song* (2009). The omitted third verse runs:

> Peace be with us in the face of war,
> peace that blesses neither bomb nor gun:
> peace delivers bread,
> saves where blood is shed,
> works with justice until war is done.

John's gospel (20:19-23) records this blessing spoken by the risen Jesus to his fearful disciples, and Shirley Murray indicates that John 14:27, 'peace I leave with you, my peace I give to you,' was also a source for the text, though its elaboration is her own. 'Determine' (verse 1, line 3) means here, 'set limits to, shape our behaviour,' but also 'lend us determination.' The 'sting' (verse 2, line 3) is probably the sting of death, or sin (see 1 Corinthians 15:56), leading on to 'the hour of death' in the following verse.

PAX VOBISCUM (Latin=peace be with you] The tune name is taken from the formula of salutation and blessing in the Latin Catholic and Lutheran liturgies, derived from Luke 10:5. (The phrase is actually much older still: it is recorded in Genesis 43:23 and Judges 6:23.) **Barry Brinson** is the composer of this setting, which is marked on the score 'slowly, with devotion.' The melodic line falls quietly towards the tonic and there is an effective modulation sequence in bars 5-6 through G and E minor, before the return to the tonic D major. **Carlton Young** wrote an earlier setting for the words, published in *Sing for Peace*, and described by its composer as 'a gentle, graceful dance.' It adopts an A minor, Israeli-sounding tonality.

Peace Child *C35*
Metre: 2.6.6.2.6.6.4

This carol was written by **Shirley Murray**, who says she began thinking of it over the 1990 Christmas season. 'In the event, the Gulf War had just begun as I finished it.' It was first printed as a poem in her American collection, *In Every Corner Sing* (1992). In 1996 it was published in New Zealand in *Carol our Christmas* with a setting by **Colin Gibson**, and in America, in *Every Day in your Spirit* (also 1996) with a setting by **Amanda Husberg**. It has attracted other choral settings as well, among them one by Canadian composer **Ron Klusmeier** (Klusmeier 12).

It is typical of Shirley Murray's poetic imagination that Christ's association with peace and peace-making in the gospel accounts of his birth and teaching – for instance, the birth song of the angels (Luke 2:14) – is translated into a striking new title, 'Peace Child' (cf. Isaiah 9:6, 'his name will be called...Prince of Peace'), and he is imagined as coming 'in the dark before light' (verse 1) to a world of 'hunger and dirt' (verse 2), poised for the outbreak of violence and war. Verse 1 alludes to John 1:5 (The light shines in the darkness') and Luke 2:11 ('Unto you is born this day...a saviour, who is Christ the Lord'). Verse 2 alludes to the codename of the 1991 Gulf War land offensive, 'desert storm.' In the final verse, a modern world's 'darkness' and 'sleep' replaces the sleeping world of Christ's nativity (verse 1, line 2), and a new nativity of the dream-child of peace, 'held in hope, wrapped in love' – cf. Luke 2:7, 'she gave birth to her first-born son and wrapped him in swaddling clothes' – is invoked. Finally, the Peace Child is renamed 'God's true Shalom,' meaning the blessing of complete peace and wholeness.

KINGSLAND The lullaby-like tune was written by **Colin Gibson** in 1992 and named for the Auckland district where his son John and his wife Shona were celebrating the birth of their first son, Arlo. It was published in an arrangement for unison voice, obbligato flute and piano, in *Let the Peoples Sing, Volume 3: An International Christmas*, edited by Marian Dolan (Minneapolis: Augsburg Fortress 2005).

Peace is not fighting (The Peace Hat Song) H113
Metre: 5.6.6.6.5.5.9

Written on commission for use at an Auckland beach mission for young people, this text and its setting was written in 2002 by **Colin Gibson**. It was distributed as a pamphlet, then formally published in *Hope is our Song* (2009).

The first verse ('walking the Peaceful Way') nods in the direction of John 14:6; for the 'Peaceful Tree' see Micah 4:4 and Revelation 22:1-2. The words express in a simple way the nature and appropriate behaviour of people (or children) of peace, at both personal and national levels.

CHAPEAU DE PAIX (French=Peace Hat) The original manuscript of this text was garnished with an image of the Cat in the Hat, from Dr Seuss's children's book of that name, hence the name given to the melody. The musical setting by Gibson for piano imitates a jaunty American song style, and the original instruction, 'Cheerily,' indicates its light-hearted character.

Peace to the world H114
Metre: 5.6.5.6.8.8.8.6.8.6

'Peace, peace to the world' was written by **Willow Macky** and published in 1985. It was one of the texts and poems advocating world peace she wrote following her time in America during the Vietnam War. She seized on its popularity by initiating a 'Bells around the World' campaign for Armistice Day, 11 November 1986, with this song being played on carillons in four different countries for the United Nations International Year of Peace. In 1988 she initiated another 'Bells for Peace' campaign, supported this time by the New Zealand Guild of Artists. Its first phrase derives from the song of the angels in Luke 2:14, 'On earth, peace to those whom he favours'; the second phrase was probably suggested by the popular traditional English carol 'I saw three ships come sailing in': 'And all the bells on earth shall ring / On Christmas Day in the morning.'

PEACE SONG The tune is by the author, its name derived from the reiterated word 'peace' in the text. The pealing of bells is suggested in the second half of the tune. The arrangement in *Hope is our Song* is by **Joan Stevens**, who has introduced the ding-dong sound of bells in the bass part of her setting for voice and piano.

Peace to you, sisters, brothers F54
Metre: 7.6.7.6.8.6

Written in 1998 by **Shirley Murray**, this is a paraphrase of Philippians 4:7-8, which the author describes as a passage she has always loved 'for its nobility of language and thought.' It was brought forward to the editorial committee preparing *Faith Forever Singing* as 'Paul's Farewell,' and was published in that collection in 2000 and again in Murray's American collection, *Faith Makes the Song* (2003). The full passage reads, 'The peace of God, which passes all understanding will keep your hearts and your minds in Christ Jesus' (verses 1 and 4). 'Finally brethren, whatever is true, whatever is honourable, whatever is just '(verse 2), 'whatever is pure, whatever is lovely, whatever is gracious, if there is any excellence, if there is anything worthy of praise' (verse 3), think about these things (refrain). The poetic gloss on the Pauline passage is particularly evident in lines like 'Christ Jesus in you shine' (Verse 1), 'all that stands tall and steadfast' (verse 2) and 'luminous things and lovely' (verse 3) where the writer indulges her delight in alliteration.

ILLUMINATION The tune takes its name from the third line of the third verse. It was written by **Jillian Bray** and drafted four times before reaching its final state in 1999. Set predominantly in G minor, it passes through B flat major on its way to a close in the minor key. The minor tone suggests, perhaps, the sadness of a final message from the great apostle.

Piko nei te matenga W655
Metre: 7.7.8.8.8.7

Described simply as a 'traditional' Māori hymn in *With One Voice*, this famous Māori hymn of lament (*waiata tangi*) is actually a translation into te reo of the hymn 'When our heads are bound with woe' by Henry Hart Milman (1791-1868), Professor of Poetry at Oxford University (1821-31) and from 1849 Dean of St Paul's Cathedral, London. Milman's text was first published in Bishop Reginald Heber's posthumous *Hymns Written and Adapted to the Services of the Church Year* (1827) and did not appear in his own *Selected Psalms and Hymns* (1837); it is not known who the New Zealand translator was or the date of the translation and its first publication, probably in the early 19th century.

Milman's text is paraphrased and simplified; as in many other versions and for theological reasons the refrain is changed – here, from 'Jesus, Son of Mary' to 'Jesus, Son of God.' The full original English text follows:

> When our heads are bowed with woe,
> when our bitter tears o'erflow,
> when we mourn the lost, the dear,
> Jesus, Son of Mary, hear!
> When the solemn death bell tolls,
> for our own departing souls,
> when our final doom is near,
> Jesus, Son of Mary, hear!
> When the heart is sad within
> with the thought of all its sin,
> when the spirit shrinks with fear,
> Jesus, Son of Mary, hear!
> Thou our throbbing flesh hast worn,
> thou our mortal griefs hast borne,
> thou hast shed the mortal tear,
> Jesus, Son of Mary, hear!
> Thou hast bowed the dying head,
> thou the blood of life hast shed,
> thou hast filled a mortal bier,
> Jesus, Son of Mary, hear!
> Thou the shame, the grief hast known,
> Though the sins were not thine own,
> thou hast deigned their load to bear;
> Jesus, Son of Mary, hear!

Both Māori and English versions of the hymn were in common use in New Zealand in the 1800s, when it was sometimes sung in Māori at European funerals: see *The Daily Telegraph*, 27 November 1900: 'A portion of the service was read in Māori and responded to by the pupils of Te Aute College. The pupils sang very harmoniously in Māori "Piko te matenga," a translation of "When our hearts are bound with woe."' But the Māori version became iconic when it was sung by the Māori battalion at funeral services for their dead in World War II. It is still sung at the Anzac Day Dawn memorial services held at Hyde Park Corner, London, and was sung at the burial of the Māori King Koroki and the state funeral service for Governor-General Sir Paul Reeves.

PIKO NEI (Māori=bowed) The tune name is taken from the first line of the hymn in the Māori language. But while the music printed in *With One Voice* is an exact transcript of what is still sung on the marae and elsewhere, this tune is not an authentic Māori melody, and the setting is one of more than 300 existing hymn tunes in this metre. The original Anglican Church tune which came into use among Māori, along with the name of its composer, remains unidentified. The standard tune for this hymn in Victorian English hymnals was ST PRISCA by Richard Redhead, published as number 57 in his *Church Hymn Tunes, Ancient and Modern* (1853) and known by a variety of names, such as REDHEAD 27 and ST DUNSTAN.

Praise *facing A135*

This is a poem originally published in *Zealandia*, a tabloid newspaper brought out by the Catholic Bishop of Auckland, and later included in the collection known as *Aotearoa Psalms: Prayers of a New People*, published by Pleroma Christian Supplies, Otane: 2004. It was written by the distinguished New Zealand novelist, children's writer, poet and Catholic commentator **Joy Cowley.**

Patterning her own writing on such grandiose biblical tropes of praise as are found in Psalm 68:34 and Psalm 98:7, the poet searches for New Zealand equivalents and finds them in bellbirds (renowned for their beautiful fluting song), jumping spring lambs (a frequent sight in a land filled with sheep), mountain streams and the oceanic waves that crash against New Zealand's extensive coastline. Her final term of praise, 'Yippee!' chosen to displace the Hebrew term 'Hallelujah' and the classical Church terms 'Gloria' and Hosanna,' is a shout expressing jubilation, but is not unique to New Zealand speech; its point is rather its informal register, by contrast with the ancient formal words used in liturgical speech and song.

Praise God, from whom all blessings flow *W678*
Metre: 8.8.8.8

The text of this doxology is taken from the final verse of one of the morning, evening and midnight hymns (Awake, my soul and with the sun,' 'Glory to Thee, my God this night,' 'All praise to thee, in light arrayed') by **Thomas Ken,** who used the lines at the close of each hymn. It must therefore have been written shortly before 1674, the date of publication of Ken's *Manual of Prayers for the use of the Scholars of Winchester College* in which all three hymns first appeared, though the texts were probably printed for the students before this time.

STRATHDEE Named after its composer, **Jim Strathdee,** this modern setting of Ken's words by the American religious folk-singer and composer, first appeared on his album *The New Wine Sound* recorded with the Celebration Singers in 1970 as a companion to his songbook *New Wine (Songs of Celebration)*. Older settings are THE OLD HUNDREDTH and TALLIS' CANON.

Praise God, I am welcome at the table *H115*
Metre: 10.9.10.9

The author of this approach-to-communion song, **Colin Gibson**, says, 'I wrote this in 2003 after listening to some praise songs and thinking I should experiment in writing one of those myself. This text was the result, and when it was tried out with its tune the congregational response was so affirmative I thought I should submit it to the editors of *Hope is our Song*, which I did do.' The hymn was first published in *Hope is our Song* (2009).

In the first verse, 'Praise God' is used in its popular sense of an expression of relief and gratitude, in this case for unqualified acceptance 'at the table of the Lord' (for the Methodist tradition behind this phrase and its possible meanings see **This table is the Lord's,** F64). The second verse places the singers among 'the family of God,' meaning both the local congregation and the larger community of the Christian faith (cf. Ephesians 2:19). The final verse uses an ambiguous 'you,' which in its context may mean God, or Christ or both; there is a similar expression with different connotations in the Sara Groves song, 'Going home' (2000).

WELCOME The music, by the author, is in praise song style, rooted in its tonic key throughout; its melody consists of a single 4-bar phrase with one answering replication.

Praise the all-sustaining Word *H116*
Metre: 7.7.7.7.7.7

This text was written by **Colin Gibson** in 1993 and dedicated to two friends and members of St Ninian's Presbyterian Church, Christchurch, Tom and Jessie Dodd. Its first print appearance was in a supplementary songbook of the

Mornington Methodist Church, Dunedin, followed by *Hope is our Song* (2009).

This hymn of praise has a Trinitarian construction and subject: the three verses focus on God, Christ and the Holy Spirit. Its theology presents a God of never-failing love, 'drawing endless good from ill,' rather than the Old Testament vision of a retaliatory Judge. Verse 1, lines 1-4 offer a paraphrase of John 1:1-5. Verse 2 draws on the Genesis story of Noah (Genesis 7-8). The rainbow and dove are singled out for their modern significance of inclusive love and the search for universal peace. Verse 3 displaces the older understanding of God as severe Father to a 'chosen' people with a 'parent-God of all,' and alludes to the continuing presence of the Holy Spirit (John 14:26). The language of the hymn is solemn and formal: the line-filling phrase 'inextinguishable flame' is a borrowing from Charles Wesley's hymn, 'O Thou who camest from above' ('kindle a flame of sacred love upon the mean altar of my heart…There let it for thy glory burn with inextinguishable blaze').

CLONBERN PLACE The musical setting is named after the address of the dedicatees, and was written by **Colin Gibson** in 1993 as an experiment in constructing a chorale in the style of J.S. Bach. While the printed version in *Hope is our Song* provides a four-part setting for voice only, the original manuscript supplies an independent piano setting, which was orchestrated for the later appearance of this chorale in Gibson's cantata, *The Spirit Within* (2000). The simple chording and celebratory D major key are intended to reflect the grandeur of the subject.

Praise to God, whose Holy Spirit
C36
Metre: 8.7.8.7 D

Written in 1995, this Christmas hymn by **Marnie Barrell** praises the Holy Family in whose nurture Jesus grew up from childhood. The text was first published in *Carol Our Christmas* (1996) with a setting by **Colin Gibson**. It is on both the Oremus and SongSelect websites.

The hymn closely follows the accounts of Jesus' birth and family in the gospels of Matthew and Luke. Verse 1, line 1, draws on Luke 1:35; line 2, on Matthew 19:21-22. The theme of the whole hymn is fully stated in the following lines from the first verse: 'praise to God for Jesus' home. / We give thanks for those who loved him, / fed his body, shaped his mind.' Verse 2 extrapolates from the same sources the character of the family of Jesus. 'Humble' refers both to their social status as a tradesman's family in a small rural village and to Mary's quiet acceptance of the divine will (Luke 1:38). 'Gentle' used as an adjective for Joseph (line 3) links the kindly behaviour of the father towards his mysteriously pregnant wife with the gentleness later displayed by this son. Line 6 refers to the devout lives of Jesus' parents and alludes to Jesus' famous prayer, seen here as a reflection of that pious life (Matthew 6:10). Line 8 draws on Matthew 3:17 (echoed in Luke 9:35). Verse 3 acknowledges the family's Jewish heritage ('chosen from the chosen race' – see Deuteronomy 14:2), and draws on Matthew's genealogy of Joseph as a descendent of Abraham, to whom Marnie Barrell adds mention of his wife Sarah (Matthew 1:1-16). 'Faithful Israel' (line 1) distinguishes this family's behaviour from the many instances of the nation and its leaders' faithlessness recorded in the pages of the First Testament. Line 4, 'first to see God's human face,' resonates with both John 1:14 and Colossians 1:15-19. See Deuteronomy 28:2-8 for an ancient list of divine blessings promised, though this writer extends them beyond the Jewish race to 'all the families of earth.'

REBECCA The tune is named after the mother of a loving and active church family belonging to the composer's own Mornington Methodist congregation, Rebecca, and Alistair Neaves, and their children Jake and Vincent, to whom the music is dedicated. Set in F major, the hymn setting has an A-B-A structure, with a gentle descending scale passage (A) answered by a rising pattern of notes (B). The parallel shape of the first and last sections is intended to suggest a connection between the descent of the Holy Spirit on Mary with the general blessings descending through Christ to 'all humankind.'

Prayer for Discernment *facing F73*

Placed deliberately immediately after Shirley Murray's 'When I was a child' in *Faith Forever Singing* (2000) – with which it may be compared – this meditation is taken from **Joy Cowley's** *Psalms Down-Under* (Catholic Supplies, Wellington, 1996). Both texts start from St Paul's 'When I was a child (1 Corinthians 13:11-13), but where Murray closely follows Paul's line of thought and closes as she began with 'now I am grown, / the child's way is gone, / is weathered by thoughts of a different season,' Joy Cowley insists on an adult awareness of the difficulties of making wise choices when 'it sometimes seems / that good and evil aren't separate at all, / but mixed in every action.' Her final prayer is for courage to 'step past the ignorance and fear / which make me self-protective…[and] always lean towards the common good.'

Purea nei e te hau *A115*
Metre: Irregular

This text is believed to have had its origin in a Nga Pui proverb, *Hoki kia purea koe e nga hau o ou maunga, kia horoia koe e te ua* ('Return to your ancestral mountains to be cleansed by the winds of Tāwhirimatea'), which was developed into a song by Henare Mahanga of Ngati Hine, a teacher at Hillary College, Otara, in the 1980s. It was further modified by **Hirini Melbourne** for one of his students at Waikato University, Kiwi Tuteo. Tuteo, a blind student, was going through a period of great adversity at the time and the song was written as a gesture of support; it is not known when the song was composed. A translation reads,

> Scattered by the wind, washed by the rain and transformed by the sun, all doubts are swept away and all restraints cast down. Fly, O free spirit, fly to the clouds in the heavens, transformed by the sun, with all doubts swept away, and all restraints cast down, yes, all restraints cast down.

The original song is thought to be about Ueoneone, a chief from Whangape, who travelled to the Waikato, where he proposed marriage to two sisters, Reitu and Reipae, famous in Māori tradition. He sent a great bird to the Waikato to carry them northward to Whangape, but when the bird landed near present-day Whangārei Reipae fell in love with a chief named Otahuhupotiki and married him instead. Reitu carried on alone, and married Ueoneone at Whangape. Their twin daughters married Tupoto, from whom every tribe north of Auckland traces its descent.

So the text becomes an example of a dramatic song arising out of a Māori tribal genealogical narrative, first adapted for group singing for cultural reasons, then for a psychological purpose, and finally as a spiritual song invoking the Holy Spirit. An authentic performance by Māori singers can be found on www.Māorilanguage.net as well as on YouTube.

[PUREA NEI] This unison melody is substantially the work of **Hirini Melbourne**; the date of composition is unknown.

Rejoice, be glad (One Day…Right Now) *A116*
Metre: Irregular

This song was written by Dominican Sister **Cecily Sheehy** as one of a series of such songs published in the Catholic magazine *Family Living* between 1980 and 1985. Its first hymnbook appearance was in *Alleluia Aotearoa* (1993).

The text is constructed to give maximum weight to the switch from future blessings to the call for immediate action to protect the environment – one of this writer's frequent themes. Implicitly, the 'suffering' of the earth and its peoples is to be seen as another form of crucifixion or 'cup of suffering' (an image drawn from Luke 22:42).

The refrain takes its cue from Luke 6:20, 'Blessed are the poor, for yours is the kingdom of heaven' and the description of the 'new heaven' in Revelation 22:3-4. The verses have a twofold scriptural source in the list of blessings known as the Beatitudes (Matthew 5:1-12) and the words of Jesus on the cross to one of the criminals beside him: 'Today you will be with me in Paradise' (see Luke 23:42-43).

[RIGHT NOW] The composer of the melody is Cecily Sheehy who has chosen a folk dance style, beginning the refrain in A minor but modulating through a falling sequential pattern towards a happier close in C major. The arranger of the tune, **Jenny Bennett**, has chosen to emphasize the dance element with a dotted bass line figure.

Relentless lover, God in Christ (Can You Drink the Cup I Drink?)
F55
Metre: 8.6.8.6 D

Written in 1999 by **Marnie Barrell**, this Eucharistic hymn was first published in *Faith Forever Singing* (2000). It is also on the Oremus website.

The text can be seen as a challenge to commitment and an intensity matching Christ's own to a congregation placidly gathering to celebrate the Eucharist, for it translates into modern terms the episode recorded in Matthew 20:17-23 (and Mark 10:35-38) when two of Christ's disciples ask to be placed on either side of him 'in your glory.' To which Jesus replies, 'You do not know what you are saying. Are you able to drink the cup that I drink?' This source passage is supplemented from the gospel accounts of the Crucifixion.

Unusual adjectives – 'relentless, unswerving, courageous, fierce' – are piled up to impress on the singers the extraordinary nature of the love it celebrates. Similarly, the standard invitation to come forward to the communion table is given a number of transformations; the word 'life' (in several senses) appears no fewer than six times. This rhetorical aspect of the hymn is supplemented by the frequent use of liturgical and biblical phrases: among them, 'God in Christ,' 'died to set us free,' 'walk with Christ through death to life,' 'drink his cup, the blood he shed,' 'broken body,' 'he lives, and sends us out.' 'Bitter cup' (verse 1, line 8) refers to the drink of vinegar offered to Jesus on the cross (John 19:29); verse 3, line 6, 'thousandfold increase,' is an allusion to Deuteronomy 1:11. Luke 10:1-6, which describes the sending out of the disciples with a blessing of peace, is the source for the final two lines of the hymn.

WALLIS HOUSE The name of this tune refers to Frederick Wallis House, a retreat and conference centre in Lower Hutt, Wellington, where the editorial board met to select hymns for inclusion in *Faith Forever Singing*. Written by **Colin Gibson** in 1999, the melody has touches of **Parry**'s tune REPTON but is necessarily much longer and modulates through F and E minor before returning to its main key, A major. The hymn was originally written to fit the tune KINGSFOLD (known in Ireland as THE STAR OF THE COUNTY DOWN); a folk melody perhaps as old as the Middle Ages, but collected as an English country song in 1893, and later still collected by **Ralph Vaughan Williams** near the Sussex village of Kingsfold. The composer introduced his own arrangement of the tune in the 1906 *English Hymnal* and also used it as the basis for *Dives and Lazarus*, a fantasia for strings and harp.

Rockin' the boat *H117*
Metre: 9.11.9.11 and refrain

Written in 1995 by **Bill Bennett**, this hymn was originally intended as a children's song. It was first published in *Hope is our Song* (2009), then in the author's *Gradual Praise* (2010).

Bill Bennett says, 'The scripture behind the hymn is of course the calling of the first four disciples' (Mark 1:14-20 and the synoptic parallels). In 1955, says the author, he was vicar of a seaside parish near Napier, on the east coast of New Zealand. '[I] would walk along the beach each day and see the fishing boats and trawlers heading out into the wide Pacific. Of course, the real 'captain' is Jesus, the challenger, the disturber of our preconceptions.'

Though written for children, the theme of the text is an adult one, the vision of a challenging Christ 'rocking the boat'; the phrase, repeated in the refrain, means upsetting the status quo, disturbing long-established preconceptions. 'Luke 5:1-11 portrays a frustrated Peter unable to understand why this land-based teacher should suggest another location to fish and then find the nets are breaking,' says Bill Bennett. The second verse suggests that we are the fishermen, and that our 'ocean' or 'sea' is the community, school or street where we live. A secondary theme is the unexpected, overwhelming generosity of God: line 2 of verse 1, 'then the catch overwhelms,' is followed up by 'Kaimoana* everywhere abound.' The final line may be read as meaning fishing on behalf of the Lord, or fishing to 'catch' the Lord.

TE WAKA (Māori=the boat, or canoe, though the word can mean whatever is used as a means of transport). Bill Bennett, who composed the melody, says that the 'slightly off-beat rhythm' was intended to appeal to an original audience of younger people. 'The changes between 3/4 and 4/4 time help catch the unsteadiness of the boat as the fishermen haul on the nets.'

> *'Kaimoana is an inclusive Māori word meaning the food/fish we gather from the sea so that we are fed and sustained. Māori have traditionally claimed traditional customary fishing rights over sections of the coastline where fishing has been their source of livelihood and sustenance. The harvest of the Spirit, however, is overwhelming' (author's note).

Safe in the hands of God *A117*
Metre: 9.8.9.8

This hymn text, based on Psalm 27 and written by **Michael Perry,** was first published by the English Jubilate Group in their *Psalm Praise* (1973), in a successful attempt to revitalise the singing of psalms by using modern English language versions, matched with musical settings in a contemporary popular style. It was republished by Jubilate in *Sing Glory: Hymns, Psalms and Songs for a New Century* (1989) and *Songs from the Psalms* (1990) before reaching *Alleluia Aotearoa* (1993).

The text is more a revisioning than paraphrase of the original, the language is simplified and the content much compressed: for instance, lines 11-14 of the original,

> Teach me thy way, O lord, and lead me on a level path because of my enemies, Give me not up to the will of my adversaries; for false witnesses have risen against me, and they breathe out violence. I believe that I shall see the goodness of the Lord in the land of the living! Wait for the Lord, be strong, and let your heart take courage; yea, wait for the Lord!

become:

> Teach me your way, and lead me onwards, Save me from those who do me wrong, Give me the grace to wait with patience, help me to trust, hold firm, be strong.

SAFE IN THE HANDS The tune name is taken from the first line of the hymn text. The setting is by New Zealand composer **Christopher Norton** and was written for *Songs from the Psalms* (1990), in which he had a key role in editing and arranging the music. The theme of security ('safe in the hands of God') which predominates in the hymn text is recognized by the musician. The choice of C major (modulating to E major before returning to C major) suggests a fundamental stability – freshened by the key change, as does the throbbing dotted rhythm of the phrase, consisting of three repeated notes, which dominates the bass line.

Set the sun dancing (A Song for Epiphany) *C37*
Metre: 10.10.10.10.12.10.10.9

This joyful carol for Epiphany was written in 1995 by **Shirley Murray** in response to a commission by the Presbyterian Association of Musicians for their Montreat Conference in 1996. In the event the theme of the conference was changed, but the carol was published in 1996 in both *Carol Our Christmas* and in the American collection *Every Day in your Spirit*.

The author says that the text was 'designed as a lively song' and remarks that the refrain is 'based around Matthew 5:16,' but the fuller passage (verses 14-16) is relevant. The verses, with their references to the star (verse 1), the Wise Men (2) and the Holy Family (verse 4), recall familiar elements of the Christmas story as it is recounted in the gospels of Matthew and Luke. But Shirley Murray places her own emphases on the biblical texts. The dancing sun / Son of God is matched with our need to 'move on' (verse 1); the Wise men become kingly representatives of 'power and right'; modern Christians are presented as 'foolish and wise,' dedicated to 'crossing the borders of culture and race' (verse 3, cf. Murray's 'Wise men came journeying,' C51); and verse 4 iterates the author's constant theme of peace and non-violence. 'Epiphany wrapped in a shawl' is a particularly striking image for the child Jesus, typical of Shirley Murray's imaginative vision.

BUSHBURN **Shona Murray** wrote this setting in 1992, naming it after her home in Takapu Valley near Tawa. Bushburn means forest stream (from Scottish 'burn=small stream'). In the American publication the carol was set to the tune SUNDANCE, composed by Daniel Charles Damon. Shona Murray's music is syncopated and rhythmically varied: a delightful dance, but not to be taken too quickly for congregational singing. There is a further setting by Canadian composer **Ron Klusmeier** (Klusmeier 26).

Simply to be *H118*
Metre: 9.8.9.4.4

'A meditative piece, written to help focus and slow myself down,' is how the writer, **Shirley Murray**, describes this simple but profound hymn. It was written in 2006 and first published in her American collection *Touch the Earth Lightly* (2008), anticipating its appearance in *Hope is our Song* (2009).

The author gives Psalm 139:1-18 as a biblical source, but the connection is not so much verbal as similar in mood, with the psalmist recounting the history of Israel under God's guidance, with an insistent refrain, 'for his steadfast love endures for ever.' The first phrase of the hymn text, 'Simply to be,' means 'just to be alive'; the following lines paraphrase Psalm 46:10, 'Be still and know that I am God.' The final line of the hymn uses the image of a blanket, cloak or mantle, 'enfolded, wrapped up in peace.'

KĀPITI The tune name identifies the part of the coast north of Wellington where Shirley Murray and her husband John had their Raumati Beach home, from which they could see Kāpiti Island just off-shore. The setting was written by **Colin Gibson** in 2006 in response to the reception of this immediately compelling text. In its key choice (E flat), slow pace, repetitive and severely restricted melodic line, as well as its gentle arc of modulations, it attempts to capture the mood of peaceful reflection. Another setting, by American composer **Jane Marshall**, was chosen for *Touch the Earth Lightly*, and Canadian composer **Ron Klusmeier** has also composed a setting (Klusmeier 52).

Sing a carol for summer *C38*
Metre: 7.7.8.9.9 and refrain

New Zealand Christmas carols are usually written with an over-the-shoulder awareness of the immense heritage of Northern Hemisphere winter-time carols. This summer-time carol, written by **Shirley Murray** in 1995, was prompted by the gift from a composer friend, **Jillian Bray**, of 'a quirky, accented tune with the suggestion that I write a "down to earth" song about the New Zealand Christmas summer season.' Shirley Murray went on to comment, 'We still lack carols which depict our own way of celebrating in the Southern Hemisphere.' This text, with its setting by Jillian Bray was published simultaneously in 1996 in the author's American collection *Every Day in Your Spirit* and in the New Zealand collection *Carol our Christmas*.

The text is set in the pre-Christmas period and lists the usual countryside and holiday activities as well as describing preparations for the religious celebration of the Nativity of Christ. In verse 1, 'Aotearoa' is the Māori name for New Zealand, with its deep lakes ('island waters') and high alpine region (cf. Shirley Murray's 'Where mountains rise,' A155). The final line of this verse glancingly alludes to the famous medieval English folksong 'Sumer is icumen in.' Verse 2 describes seasonal farming activities and the gathering of the cherry crop – always a keenly anticipated mark of the Christmas season. 'Hoisting pack' refers to the tramper's backpack (cf. Shirley Murray's 'When we lift our pack and go,' A153). Verse 3 attends to the close of the educational and business year for the long two-month Christmas 'break.' Verse 4 surveys the icons of the biblical nativity story, including the usual end-of-year nativity play presented at primary schools. And the refrain changes at this point to declare forcefully, 'Jesus Christ is the reason to sing.'

SMILE The tune name alludes to the general happiness associated with the pre-Christmas season. Perhaps wisely, the composer did not mark time signatures, because the shift from 6/4 to 8/4 at bar 8, reverting to 6/4 then 7/4 for the refrain, hardly captures the cheerfully eccentric rhythmic progression of the melody. However, the melodic line is less daunting than it appears, since much of the movement is stepwise. A carol to be introduced carefully to congregations used to unsurprising religious songs, but one that well captures the fling-about, head-bobbing progression of a happy person without a care in the world.

Sing a happy alleluia! *A118*
Metre: 8.7.8.7 and refrain

The author, **Shirley Murray,** says of this hymn, 'Dedicated to our son, Alistair, this was given a world première and sung with much joie de vivre [at the 1989 World Council of Churches Assembly held in Canberra, Australia] during the sing-a-long night for public visitants and participants. Despite all, I know God must have a sense of humour.' The hymn was first published in Shirley Murray's American collection *In Every Corner Sing* (1992), then in *Alleluia Aotearoa* (1993).

'Alleluia,' the word used in several verses and the refrain of the hymn is a form of 'hallelujah' and literally means 'praise God Jah [Jehovah], you people.' For humans as made in the image of God (verse 1, line 4) see Genesis 1:27, which the author extends to the concept of a humorous, benevolent deity. Verse 2, line 2, plays on the word 'twinkle,' meaning both 'sparkle with merriment,' and 'flicker' or 'glimmer' with light (as in 'twinkle, twinkle little star'). Verse 3 accumulates biblical instances of human expressions of happiness: for Sarah see Genesis 18:12-15; for the song of Mary (also known as the Magnificat) see Luke 1:46-55; David's dancing before the Ark of the Covenant is recorded in 2 Samuel 8:14; Jesus' welcome of children (Murray imagines him as actually smiling and hugging them) is described in Matthew 19:13-15.

All the adjectives for humanity in verse 4 carry serious implications. Philosophers like Sartre argue that human absurdity arises from the search for meaning in life where none is to be found, 'human' implies 'faulty, imperfect' – as in 'only human.' For 'foolish' see 1 Corinthians 1:25, and 'chosen people' is a term applied to the Christian community in both 1 Peter 2:9 and Colossians 3:19. 'God still takes us at our word' alludes to the promises made at baptism by parents or sponsors.

STANSFIELD The name of the tune, written by **Colin Gibson** in 1989, records the Dunedin street address of two particularly cheerful Christian friends of the composer and members of his own congregation, Joy King and Mabel Chandler. The music is modelled on West Indian calypso tunes to convey a sense of lively merriment, with much syncopation and a modulation from C major to F major and back again to spice the general sense of jollity.

Sing green A119, HP19
Metre: Irregular

The author **Shirley Murray's** concern for the protection of the natural world was the springboard for this hymn text, written in 1990. She comments that 'This came alive when first sung by young people [in her Wellington Presbyterian church] and seems specially useful for schools and colleges. It was offered to Greenpeace NZ for their publicity, but was politely deemed irrelevant!' It was first published in her American collection *In Every Corner Sing* (1992), then in *Alleluia Aotearoa* (1993).

The repeated references to 'green' refer both to the symbolic colour of a healthy natural world and to the Greenpeace organisation, formed in the early 1970s to protect the environment from commercial and military exploitation and destruction by taking direct action. In New Zealand, the main focus of Greenpeace was on resistance to nuclear weaponry, especially after French government agents blew up its flagship, the *Rainbow Warrior*, in Auckland harbour in 1985, when the vessel was preparing to sail to Mururoa Atoll to protest against nuclear testing in the Pacific Ocean.

There are biblical elements in the text – God's creation of the world, as described in Genesis 1-2 (see verses 1 and 5), and the Covenant made between 'God and every living creature of all flesh that is upon the earth' symbolised by the rainbow (compare Genesis 9 and both refrains) – but the focus is on human destruction of the environment and the need for urgent political action to restore planetary life (verse 3). Acid rain (verse 2) is rain made dangerously acidic by air pollution, a phenomenon that came to urgent attention in the 1980s; 'driftnet death' refers to the practice of deploying fishing nets of enormous length and depth (so-called 'walls of death') that catch and kill every form of marine life indiscriminately, a technique eventually banned by the United Nations in 1992. Verse 4, 'returning spring,' alludes to the work of Rachel Carson (1907-64), whose book *Silent Spring* (1951) called attention to the massive destruction of wild life caused by the use of synthetic pesticides.

NEW FERN The tune name alludes to the *koru*, or uncoiling new fern leaf, which in New Zealand symbolises the vital life of nature and its renewal. The music is by **Colin Gibson,** who with the intended audience described by the author in mind, provided a cheerful and energetic melody in a popular-style setting for unison verse and 4-part harmony chorus, accompanied by piano and optional paired flutes, published as a full score in *In Every Corner Sing* (1987*)*. A simplified unison version was provided in *Alleluia Aotearoa* (1993*)*.

Sing no sad songs today (Hymn to Celebrate a Long Life) F56
Metre: 6.7.6.7.6.6.6.6

Described by the writer, **Shirley Murray**, as 'a celebratory hymn for a long life,' this text was written in 1999 for a funeral occasion. It was first published in *Faith Forever Singing* (2000), then in Murray's American collection, *Faith Makes the Song* (2003). The only textual difference is that the optional pronoun is *her* in the New Zealand hymnal; *his* in the American collection.

The hymn was originally sung to **Johann Crüger's** NUN DANKET, which leaves its trace in the final line of the first verse (cf. Crüger's 'all praise and thanks to God' with Murray's 'We give God thanks and praise'). Verse 1, 'dear,' means 'precious, loved.' Verse 2, line 3, may allude to **Colin Gibson's** 1994 hymn. 'Nothing is lost on the breath of God.' Line 8, 'memory's bequest,' is a beautiful and original image which means 'what is passed on to us through our memories of the dead person.' Verse 3 draws on Genesis 2:7, 'Then the Lord God formed man of dust from the ground and breathed into his nostrils the breath of life,' and 3:19, 'You were made from dust and to dust you will return.' T.S. Eliot's famous line, 'In my beginning is my end' (*Four Quartets*. Part 2, 'East Coker'), lies behind the second line of this verse. The picture of the soul of the deceased person, rising 'on wings of hope and trust,' is an ancient image of the winged soul's release from the body at death, at least as old as the Homeric poems of Classical Greece.

NUN DANKET (German=Now let us give thanks). This famous melody is named after the first line of the text best known in English as 'Now thank we all our God,' originally intended as a sung grace before meals and written by the German Lutheran pastor Martin Rinkard (1586-1649), with which it has been associated since text and melody were first combined in Johann Crüger's *Praxis Pietatis Melica* [The sweet Practice of Piety] (1647). Crüger identifies himself as its composer in his 1653 *Gesang Buch* [Song Book].

There is a natural carryover from the hymn 'Now thank we all our God,' with its expression of profound gratitude to an ever-present God 'who from our mothers' arms / hath blessed us on our way,' to Shirley Murray's hymn of gratitude for a long gifted life which has enriched the lives and memories of those who now mourn.

Sing of the saints *A120*
Metre: 12.10.12.10

This hymn was written towards 1990 by **Marnie Barrell** for the festival of All Saints. It was first published in *Alleluia Aotearoa* (1993). At about the same time, the author prepared an amended version of William Walsham Howe's famous 1864 hymn, 'For the all the saints who from their labours rest,' which she later revised in 2011.*

It is probable that this text was written as a counter to the gentrified prettiness of Lesbia Scott's long-popular hymn, 'I sing a song of the saints of God' (1929). Where the earlier hymn was commendably written for the poet's own children to help them understand that saints were people who not only lived in the distant past but could be found and imitated in modern, everyday life, Marnie Barrell's hymn underlines the extraordinary variety and vitality of the saints. They are presented as faulty but inspiring figures whose love for God 'raised them up from confusion and vanity'** as well as 'addiction to sin,' to become icons of humanity, capable of filling modern Christians with hope because of both their 'failings and powers,' 'pointing the way to the heart of the mystery' of 'their God and ours.' The marvellous – the word is used in both the sense of 'entrancing' and full of miracles and wonders – stories of the saints are acknowledged as important to Christian history and exemplary and inspirational in effect.

[SAINT SONG] This energetic setting of Marnie Barrell's hymn was written by **Colin Gibson** in 1990. Composed in a dactylic crochet metre (3/4) to match the long dactylic lines of the hymn, it uses the heavily stressed rhythm to suggest the idea of the saints 'setting the pace' (verse 1, line 4). Beneath the long descending then rising melodic line the harmony modulates from B flat major through F major and G minor before crossing the finishing line with the galloping saints in B flat major once more.

*For the revised text see the website: https://re-worship.blogspot.com/2011/10/hymn-for-all-saints-day.html

**That is, ennobled them, lifted them out of a life characterized by confusion, pride and sin. St Augustine comes to mind, among many others.

Sing out a song (The Heart will Sing) *H119*
Metre: 11.10.12.5 and refrain

This inspirational song was written by **Sylvia Purdie** in 2006 while she was engaged in a ministry internship at St Heliers Presbyterian Church, Auckland. She says of it, 'It expressed my emerging convictions about ministry, and my own sense of calling. I agree with Bill Hybels* that the local church is "the hope of the world" and I am passionate about building dynamic all-age communities around Jesus Christ.' The song was first published in *Hope is our Song* (2009). It might be used as a Eucharistic hymn ('taste…touch…live').

In this text the writer puts her own construction on a popular religious and secular trope, the singing heart.** The argument is that a universal and profound sense of joy will result from commitment to faith in God and Jesus, the respectful treatment of others, and a life lived to the full with courage and honesty.

There are biblical sources for some of the imagery. Verse 1 follows Revelation 3:20, 'Behold I stand at the door and knock; if anyone hears my voice and opens the door, I will come in to him and will dine with him, and he with me.' Line 3 recalls the more than sufficient feast for the 5,000 (John 6:1-14). The connection with the Holy Spirit as the source of all energy derives ultimately from the Genesis account of God breathing life into the primal human beings (Genesis 2:7). The refrain is a modern version of Acts 2:17 (derived from Joel 2:28-29), a vision of rejuvenation and celebration, with more than a hint of Ezekiel's vision of the restoration to life of the 'dead' people of Israel, 'I prophesied as he commanded me, and breath entered them; *they came to life and stood up on their feet* – a vast army' (37:10).

ST HELIERS The tune is named after the suburb of the New Zealand city of Auckland where the author was studying at the time. The original melody composed by the author has been arranged by Christchurch composer **Barry Brinson** for *Hope is our Song*. It has the structure and heavily syncopated character of a contemporary praise song melody.

> *Bill Hybels was the founding and senior pastor of Willow Creek Community Church in South Barrington, Illinois, one of the most popular churches in North America, with an average attendance of nearly 24,000.
>
> **This is a very ancient as well as a popular modern metaphor: there are 'singing heart' songs from the Hillsong and New Wine groups and many others. It is at least as old as Isaiah, 'My servants shall sing for joy of heart' (65:14) and cf. Psalm 30:11-12, 'Thou hast turned my mourning into dancing…and girded me with gladness, that my heart may sing your praises and not be silent.'

Sing to celebrate the city *A122*
Metre: 8.7.8.7 D

'With accent on the positives of city life, and the place of a Christian presence there, this offers an alternative to "sin city," says the author, **Shirley Murray,** who wrote this text in 1988. At the time, Murray was the wife of the Presbyterian minister of St Andrew's on the Terrace, an inner-city church, having been born in Invercargill and studied in Dunedin, both South Island cities, before moving to Wellington.

The hymn presents an alternative vision of big city life to the not uncommon perception among religious people of urban living as comparatively corrupt and 'sinful' (fostered by some biblical passages such as Revelation 17-18). 'In the dictates of the dollar' (verse 1, line 5) means 'in a world subject to commercial imperatives, a world driven by profit-making and the effects of poverty.' Verse 2 alludes to Mark 12:28-31 (echoed in Matthew 22:34-39); the 'human face' is that of Jesus, as the Son of God. In the final line of verse 3, 'table' plays on the idea of the domestic meal-time table and the communion table, both to be prepared for the presence of Christ.

WELLINGTON Named after Shirley Murray's 'adopted city,' this setting was composed by **Colin Gibson** in 1988. It is written for piano in a popular style, with a driving rhythm imitating the frenetic traffic of city life and a certain kind of big-band city music. It modulates from D minor to B flat major and D major before returning to its minor modality, and employs melodic syncopation to suggest the disjunctions of urban existence. This is not conventional religious music, as the text is not a conventional religious poem isolating faith from its context in lively daily life.

Sing we a song of high revolt (Magnificat Now) W643
Metre: 8.8.8.8

This modern version of the Magnificat (Luke 1:46-55) was written by **Fred Kaan** for his Plymouth, England, congregation. When it was published in his first collection of hymns 'to fill the gaps,' *Pilgrim Praise* (1968), it rapidly became one of the ringing declarations of the 1960s, first reaching the supplementary English Anglican hymnal *100 Hymns for Today* (1969), followed by the *Hymnbook of the Anglican Church of Canada and the United States* (1971) and the American Roman Catholic hymnal *We Celebrate with Song* (1976). Eric Routley pronounced it to be 'blemished' (probably because of the possible and unfortunate play on the final word 'flat' – by which Kaan meant the crowded and often slum-like tenements built by city councils – but it reached the New Zealand Supplement in *With One Voice* (1982) and the new revised standard version of *Hymns Ancient & Modern* (1983) and for a time was frequently sung by socially-aware congregations.

Given the metrical and verbal likeness of the opening line of Kaan's hymn with a translation by Benjamin Webb of the Venerable Bede's 11th-century Latin hymn, *Hymnum canamus gloriae*, 'Sing we triumphant hymns of praise,' it is probable that the modern text was in part prompted by the older one. 'High revolt' (line 1) has a suitably Miltonic ring and suggests rebellion against the highest authorities responsible for 'human wrong' (line 4). Verse 2 calls in Psalm 68:19, as well as Galatians 6:2. But much of the remaining material draws directly on the Magnificat, except for the final line which devastatingly grounds Mary's protest in the realities of modern city life.

AGINCOURT The tune name is drawn from the subject of the famous English 15th century song commemorating the victory of Henry V's much smaller army over huge French forces at Agincourt in Normandy in 1415. The melody was brought back to attention in modern times through its use by composer William Walton as music for the 1944 film of Shakespeare's *Henry V*. No information has surfaced about the English arranger, **John Hind**, other than his birth date of 1916. In Kaan's *Pilgrim Praise* (1968) this text is set to both the German folksong tune TANNENBAUM and Nicholas Gatty's TUGWOOD, associated in the 1906 *English Hymnal* with Webbe's translation of Bede's *Hymnum canamus gloriae*, 'Sing we triumphant hymns of praise.' I have not discovered which of these tunes (if either of them) was used by the Pilgrim Church congregation when Kaan's hymn was first introduced there, but TUGWOOD seems the likelier of the two.

Sing with the angels, Gloria! C39
Metre: 8.8.9.10

This acclamation was written by **Shirley Murray** as a response to a challenge from the Chairman of the New Zealand Hymnbook Committee to its editorial board to create carols or acclamations on the Gloria theme for *Carol our Christmas* (1996). In the first verse the poet imagines the sun bowing in worship and the earth shouting 'Gloria!'; in verse 2 her thoughts dwell on the coming of peace and a world united (see the Song of the Angels, Luke 2:14).

NGAKURU (Māori=orchard) Named after a relative who died at an early age from cancer and whose farm was at Ngakuru, near Rotorua, this two-part setting was written by **Shona Murray,** then Head of Music at Tawa College, Wellington and a member of the editorial committee for *Faith Forever Singing*. An assured choral musician, Shona Murray has created a piece that may be performed as a congregational carol or as a more elaborate work for choir, women or children, with a vocal or instrumental descant.

Sisters and brothers, gather around (Carol for a Hard Winter) H120
Metre: 9.9.9.9

This Christmas carol was written by **Colin Gibson** in 1998, and dedicated to his Mornington Methodist Choir, who first performed it as part of their Christmas music programme. It was inspired by a *Life* magazine photograph of a United States soldier tenderly holding a baby found abandoned in a bunker during the Vietnam War. At the time, there was war in the Congo, Vietnam, Eritrea and Ethiopia, Abkhazia, Guinea-Bissau, Chad, and Albania!

The carol sets the familiar and traditional characters and events associated with the Nativity of Christ as described by Matthew and Luke and celebrated in religious art beside the realities of childbirth in a time of war, with a view to bringing a note of reality into a genre now dominated by pious sentiment. The first verse was prompted by Renaissance paintings like that of Hugo van der Goes of the Holy Child lying on the ground, surrounded by his worshipping family and adoring shepherds. The final verse identifies the infant Christ (actually born in an occupied country) with modern children beginning their lives in a war zone: its theological underpinning is found in Matthew 25:31-46 and John 3:16.

HADLEY CLOSE The tune name refers to the Dunedin address of friends of the composer, Colin Gibson. The setting for 4-part choir or unison singing is written as a lullaby and set in the 'mild' key of F major. This text has also been set by New Zealand composer **David Hamilton**, whose entry came second in a worldwide choral competition and was performed and broadcast from York Minster, England, in 2008.

Small things count *A123*
Metre: 7.7.7.7

Shirley Murray says of this hymn, written in 1990, 'The challenge of two small grandchildren – Fergus and Alexander – has meant a first attempt for me at hymn-writing for children.' 'Small things count' was the result, published in 1993 in *Alleluia Aotearoa* and previously in *In Every Corner Sing* (1992), where it was associated with the Orlando Gibbons melody, Song 2, though the author, concerned by the possibility of it being sung at the usual sedate speed, directed that it be taken at a 'lively, positive pace.'

The text incorporates several biblical elements that give substance to its reassurance to young singers that 'small things count' and that God loves us 'from top to toes.' Verse 1 refers to Matthew 10:42 ('Who ever gives to one of these little ones even a cup of cold water... shall not lose his reward') and to the healing of the Syro-Phoenician's daughter described in Mark 7:25-30 ('Even the dogs under the table eat the children's crumbs'). Verse 2 alludes to Matthew 13:33, the parable of the yeast. Verse 3 refers to Matthew 10:29-31 ('Are not two sparrows sold for a penny? And not one of them will fall to the ground without your Father's will. But even the hairs of your head are all counted').

[SMALL THINGS] **Jillian Bray** wrote this attractively simple and happy tune for Shirley Murray's words in 1992. Following its appearance in *Alleluia Aotearoa*, in 1997 it reached *Voices United: The Hymn and Worship Book of the United Churches of Canada* (Etobicoke, Ontario: United Church Publishing House), where it was suggested that a leader might sing each line, repeated by the remaining singers, and it was noted that 'the keyboard setting can easily be played by students, and guitar accompaniment is also an option.'

Snap us out of it, Lord (The Ho-hum Hymn) *H121*
Metre: 6.6.9.6.6.9 and refrain

The origin of this hymn, written by **Colin Gibson,** is described by the author: 'The satirical title of a theological work popular in the 1960's, *God's Frozen People*, [by Mark Gibbs and T. Ralph Morton (London: Fontana, 1964)] provoked this 1995 hymn, which considers with dismay, but also with some hope, the alarming ability of Christians to lapse into deep spiritual hibernation.'

It was first published in the American hymnbook publishing company Hope's *Supplement 96* (1996), where it appeared with a setting by **Carlton R Young,** followed by its appearance in the author's collection, *Songs for a Rainbow People* (1998), with the original setting.

The verses address various aspects of contemporary spiritual inertia, starting with mindless hymn singing, moving on to the lack of passionate engagement with the world (which is the subject of the Gibbs and Morton book), followed by the practice of comfortable and listless rote prayers – a verse which glances at Psalm 79:13: 'Then we, your people, the sheep of your pasture, will praise you always.' The hymn concludes with an appeal to join the 'dance of the riotous Spirit of God,' an image suggested by Sydney Carter's 1963 carol 'I danced in the morning.' The refrain suitably expresses rejection of such a state of spiritual boredom entailed in the expression 'ho-hum' and a craving for 'new life every day' (see John 3:7).

HO HUM The tune name picks up the theme of religious inertia, The music, set in G major, was written by **Colin Gibson** in 1995 in the manner of a jerky, half-asleep dance; the refrain imitates a yawning 'ho-hum,' then regains some final momentum and closes with a musical snap. An alternative setting, in D major and quite independently entitled HO HUM, was created by American composer **Carlton Young**. It allows for preliminary vamping 'until bored,' and closes with a startling additional 'Hey! Hey!' It appeared in *Supplement 96*.

Some hae meat (Selkirk Grace)
A124
Metre: 7.7.8.7

This old Scottish grace is popularly attributed to **Robert Burns**, but an earlier 17th century version known as the Galloway Grace or the Covenanters' Grace is known to have existed. The association with Scotland's national poet is said to have come about when Burns gave an extempore version of the grace (in standard English) at a dinner given by the Earl of Selkirk. The original grace was in Lallans, a Lowland Scots dialect, and it is this version that is printed in *Alleluia Aotearoa*.

Traditional Burns Suppers, held in honour of the poet, always begin with this expression of thanksgiving.

An English version of the grace follows:

> Some have meat [food] and cannot eat,
> And some have no meat [food],
> who want [lack] it,
> But we have meat and we can eat,
> And so the Lord be thankèd.

There is a textual error in *Alleluia Aotearoa*: the second line of the poem should read, 'And some hae nae that want it.'

[SELKIRK GRACE] The melody used here is by Auckland composer **Ronald Dellow**. It was written as part of a setting for SATB choir, with the direction that its tune might be sung as a round, which is the version printed in *Alleluia Aotearoa*.

Something beautiful for God *H122*
Metre: 7.4.4.7.7

'A hymn of personal dedication, echoing words attributed to Mother Teresa,' is how the author of this hymn, **Shirley Murray** describes her text, written in 2000. It was first published in her American collection *Faith Makes the Song* (2003), before its publication in *Hope is our Song* (2009).

The key source for the words is the title of a book, *Something Beautiful for God*, written by the English author Malcolm Muggeridge and first published in 1971, which describes the life of an Albanian nun, Agnes Gonxha Bojaxhiu (1910-1997), who became known to the West as Mother Teresa for her selfless work on behalf of the poor and destitute in the slums of Kolkata (formerly Calcutta). The context of the saying is Mother Teresa's prayer for blessing on those taking part in the fourth United Nations-sponsored World Conference on Women, held in Beijing in 1995: 'My prayer for all of the delegates, and for every woman whom the Beijing Conference is trying to help, is that each one may be humble and pure like Mary, so as to live in love and peace with one another and make our families and our world something beautiful for God.' Shirley Murray turns this traditional Catholic vision of womanhood as humble and pure into something much more personal and self-determining, although there is an echo of the Magnificat (Luke 1:38) in the last lines of verses 1-2. The simplicity and plainness of language of this prayer-text gives it the quality of high poetry.

BARRINGTON The tune name refers to the composer, **Barry (Barrington) Brinson's** own name. Written in a popular and richly harmonized style, the music is intensely sensitive to the rhythm and mood of the words (as in the treatment of the phrase 'beautiful for God'); a lilting lyrical song almost better suited to a single voice than to group congregational singing. In *Faith Makes the Song*, another setting written in 2000 by American composer **Carlton Young** is used; it is titled DEDICATIO MEA (Latin=my personal dedication). Canadian composer **Ron Klusmeier** has also set this text (Klusmeier 28).

Something's dead inside me (God Dancing in the rain) *facing F24*, H123 (i) and (ii)
Metre: 6.6.8.6.7.6.8.6.6

This text, written by **Joy Cowley**, was originally published in 1996 in her collection of psalm-poems, *Psalms Down-Under*, under the title 'Loss' (number 24). It appeared in *Faith Forever Singing* (text only) in 2000 and *Hope is our Song* in 2009.

The theme of the poem is suffering, death and resurrection, making this an appropriate hymn for Easter, but it also focuses on the inner grief caused by loss and affirms 'a hope I can't explain.' The singer's experience is imaged as a kind of crucifixion and may relate to a personal tragedy ('this time of grief'). However, against this is set a vision of God forever dancing in the rain (symbolic of a time of tears), and the words of Jesus, paraphrased by the poet, 'Unless a grain of wheat falls into the ground and dies, it remains alone: but if it dies, it bears much fruit' (John 12:24). The picture of God dancing in the rain may recall both Sydney Carter's 'I danced in the morning' and the famous scene of Gene Kelly dancing in the rain in the 1952 American musical '*Singin' in the Rain.*' The 'mystery of loss that turns to gain' (verse 2) alludes to another saying of Jesus, 'whoever loses his life for my sake will save it. For what will it profit a man if he gains the whole world and forfeits his life?' (Matthew 16:25-26).

RAIN DANCE was composed by **Colin Gibson** for this text in 2006. The dotted rhythm of its opening phrase suggests a graceful slow dance and is repeated throughout the setting, being taken up in the bass in the final repetitions of the words 'God dancing in the rain,' at which point the predominant minor key is displaced by a major key. The tune name alludes to the ritual practice in many early cultures of engaging in a religious dance to summon rain and bring fertility to the crops.

NIMBUS, the meteorological name for a rain cloud, was composed by **Marnie Barrell** for this text in 2006. It too responds to the idea of dance. But the melody has the character of a vigorous folkdance, shifting between minor and major modes.

Sometimes the boundless beauty
II124
Metre: 10.10.10.10

This text was written by Wanganui poet and short story writer **Kathleen Mayson** in 1988. As a hymn text it was first published in Colin Gibson's second American collection *Songs for a Rainbow People* (1998) followed by *Hope is our Song* (2009). As a representative New Zealand hymn it was reprinted (words only) in *A Panorama of Christian Hymnody*, by Erik Routley and Alan A. Richardson (Chicago: GIA, 2005).

The theme of the poem is the relationship of human arts and artists to the 'craft of God' as displayed in the beauties of the natural world. The argument begins with an admission of defeat: "try though we will…we cannot match the glory God has made.' However, the poet claims that 'in us all the urge to beauty [that is, the urge to create beautiful works of art] moves' (verse 3) and the poem concludes with a plea for the hallowing of the work of artists and the gifted ability to make their representations 'more real,' 'worthy your grace and seal of provenance,' the divine stamp of quality and authenticity. The text incorporates a remarkable list of human arts – sculpture, painting, literature, textile art, engraving, woodcarving, pottery, weaving and music – and is itself a further example of the work of the poet. There is a biblical resonance in the references to God's 'craft' and 'all-creating' nature (see Genesis 1-2), but Platonic ideas of human existence as a 'shadow' of ultimate reality, and of earthly beauty as a shadowy imitation of an ultimate and quintessential beauty are also present.

MITCHELL The tune takes its name from that of two talented friends, both ordained ministers of religion, Rod and Sarah Mitchell, one of whom found it hard to choose between his religious calling and his creative impulse as a sculptor and wood carver. The composer, **Colin Gibson,** wrote this setting in 1994. The musical setting in F major moving quietly upwards to a point of climax in G minor, then equally quietly returns to the tonic key, suggesting a rapt meditation on the beauties described in the text.

Song *facing F21*

James K. Baxter, the most famous of New Zealand's 'folk-poets,' wrote this striking religious poem in 1969. Although it circulated among Catholic and other groups before its first formal publication, in the first edition of the *Collected Poems of James K. Baxter,* ed. John Weir, Oxford University Press, 1979.

It takes the form of a ballad briefly narrating the life, death and resurrection of Jesus, as told by a loving follower who has left his 'books and his bed and his house' (cf. Luke 5:11). The narrative offers snapshots based on gospel events, but arranged in a non-historical order for greater dramatic effect. There has been later criticism of the poem for its unhistorical portrait of Jesus as a working class European rather like the poet himself,* as well as the discrepancy between Baxter's own treatment of the women in his life and the gentleness and kindness he attributes to Jesus.** However, there is no denying the eloquence of the poet's simple, direct language, and the occasional heightening by myth, as in verse 2 (a universal stillness previously attributed to the moment of Christ's birth) or verse 5 (where the sun's darkness, as recorded in Luke 23:44, is attributed to creation's 'lack of his company'). For a representative fuller treatment of this poem see the *Collected Poems of James K. Baxter,* ed. John Weir, Oxford University Press, 2004.

*At the time of writing this poem, Baxter was living as a *guru* with the Jerusalem community he founded on the banks of the Wanganui river. 'Flowers and candles' (verse 7) typify the 'hippy' life-style of his followers there.

**As late as July 2020 a quotation from this poem ('Truth' – he said, and 'Love' – he said / But his purest word was 'Mercy'), was removed from long-standing display in St Patrick's Basilica, Dunedin, on the grounds that 'In recent times there has been a growing restlessness in society in recognition of the suffering caused to women, people of colour and children by those in power.'

Song of faith that sings forever *F57*
Metre: 8.7.8.7 D

The writer, **Shirley Murray,** says of this hymn, created in January 1999, 'I wrote this to give myself courage, a reminder in times when the Church seems to stagger along, of the people who have never stopped singing.' Before its first publication in *Faith Forever Singing* (2000), followed by her American publication *Faith makes the Song* (2003), the text was slightly modified after consultations between the author and composer **Colin Gibson** with a view to better match verbal and musical stressing. Verse 1, line 8, originally read 'hope has given us the key'; verse 2, line 4, originally read 'offered in the open air.' The words were dedicated to the writer's 'life-long friend, Faith Christine Williamson.'

There is a biblical precedent for endless song in the unceasing song of the four living creatures in John's vision of heaven (Revelation 4:8), but this text concentrates on the circumstances which militate against the survival of the 'song of faith' raised on earth. The poet deploys a remarkable number of musical terms – song (the word is repeated 7 times), sing(s), sounding, counterpoint, key, tune, descant, voice – and the force of feeling behind the text is revealed by the frequency of repetition (always, all, endless). Verse 1, line 3, is taken from Colossians 1:17, where it refers to Jesus Christ (cf. verse 3, line 5). Lines 7-8: All experiences of despair are equally matched by signs of hope, and it is that which establishes the dominant 'tone' of life as a whole. Verse 2, 'vaults of prayer' means 'arches of heaven to which we lift our prayers.' Line 4 refers to open-air worship in general, but that the writer is thinking of early Methodist gatherings is suggested by the following reference to 'chapel and cathedral' (cf. the common English expression, 'church and chapel,' for the disjunction between the Anglican and Methodist denominations in that country). Line 6 refers to the song of faith as a high-voiced accompanying melody to the standard soundscape of our daily life. Verse 3, 'constant,' puns on 'uninterrupted' and 'bravely loyal.'

ABBEYFIELD Like the dedication of the text, the tune is named to honour Faith and her husband Bill Williamson, who at the time of writing were closely associated with the Nelson branch of the world-wide Abbeyfield organization, which raises funds and builds lodgings for people otherwise unable to obtain adequate housing. In 1999 the Nelson society had recently built such a residence, named Abbeyfield, at Stoke, near the city of Nelson. This hymn was later sung at a Service of Thanksgiving held by Abbeyfield International in Glasgow Anglican Cathedral. The music, by **Colin Gibson**, seldom strays from G major and is given a powerful swinging rhythm to express the determined optimism of the text.

The composer has said of the genesis of the music, 'Shirley Murray and I have worked together over many years now, and when her text was sent to me [in 1999] for setting it immediately struck me as inspired, the kind of text that lifted the spirits and demanded corporate singing to a lilting tune. I hope that my setting works in the same way, too; it seems to have done so for many congregations.' A descant was added later for a performance of the hymn by the Auckland Choral Society, broadcast over the Sunday national radio hymn programme *Hymns for Sunday Morning*. There are alternative tunes, among them SONG OF FAITH, written in 2001 by distinguished American composer Hal Hopson.

Speaking up for those who cannot speak (Putting people first) *H126*
Metre: Irregular

This song was written in 1995 by **Colin Gibson** to mark the 50th jubilee of the Christian World Service organization (CWS). It was recorded in an arrangement by **Martin Setchell**, and received wide distribution among New Zealand churches; it was also recorded and distributed by the national Correspondence School.

The refrain is based on promotional material prepared by CWS for its Jubilee.

PEOPLE FIRST The musical setting was written by the author and directed at the schools and public choirs as well as the congregations which might perform it. A strongly rhythmic pedal bass supports the refrain, and the simple harmonic shape (A major to D major) changes only to highlight the motto of the Jubilee event, 'Putting people first.' The song was launched in a performance by the choirs of St Barnabas Church, Fendalton, Christchurch, directed by Dr Martin Setchell, their director as well as Associate Professor of Music at the University of Canterbury.

Spirit of love *H125*
Metre: 7.7.7.5.5.7

'My deeply held belief is that God is a spirit, the spirit of love – not an entity, person, creator or any of the other extraordinary notions that man has invented. So eventually I tried to write a hymn that embodied that,' says **Ian Harvey**, the creator of this hymn, which he wrote shortly before its publication in *Hope is our Song* (2009).

This invocational text takes as its theological starting point John 4:24, 'God is spirit,' then draws selectively on the gifts of the Spirit as they are articulated in Romans 12:6-18 (compassion, love, peace), 1 Corinthians 12:4-11 (wisdom) and Galatians 5:22-23. Luke's account of the child Jesus who 'grew in wisdom and in years' stands behind verse 2, lines 4-5, and there is an echo of the Lord's Prayer in verse 3, lines 4-5, 'Freed from temptation / to yield to ill-will.' The writer's personal belief that 'Heaven can exist only on earth, as Jesus maintained,' is expressed in the final verse.

Structurally, the four verses focus on four different aspects of the activity of the Spirit, but the reiterated imperative verbs, 'infuse, inspire, enfold' surround,' are enriched with many others, and the 'me' of the hymn is gradually defined as one seeking a 'Jesus' life of spiritual energy ('enthuse, fire me') and self-giving social action ('help me to love all around me').

STANMORE The tune name refers to the suburb of Stanmore Bay on the Whangaparaoa Peninsula near Auckland, where the composer and his wife Valerie were living at the time and attended their local Presbyterian church. The setting shows the work of an accomplished musician. The melodic pattern established in the first two bars is carried throughout the setting (inverted in bars 5-6 and repeated in the final bars). The music is set in the key of F major, but modulates towards the related key of D major / minor in the middle section, before returning to close in the home key. It conveys a sense of earnest request rather than the imperative mood suggested by the verbal text.

Spirit of love (Weaver Spirit) A125
Metre: 11.10.11.10

This text was written by **Shirley Murray** in 1988 for one of the sub-themes of the 1991 World Council of Churches Assembly held at Canberra, Australia, 'Come, Holy Spirit, reconcile your people.' It was first offered at a World Council Pacific Workshop on Liturgy and Music held in 1989. The author comments that the hymn did not surface until the last day of the Australian Assembly, when it was published in the final edition of the Conference newsletter, *Assembly Line*. In 1992 the hymn and its setting were published in the first American collection of Murray's work, *In Every Corner Sing*, followed by its appearance in *Alleluia Aotearoa* (1993).

It is possible that one source for the text was the poem 'The Master Weaver's Plan' by Benjamin Malachi Franklin (1882-1965), circulated by the Dutch Christian and post-World War II reconciler Corrie ten Boom (1892-83), but Shirley Murray's own craft interests and biblical knowledge are equally evident.

The opening invocation to the Holy Spirit addresses the theme of the Assembly, and verse 1 draws on Genesis 1:2 before establishing the weaving metaphor used throughout the text (no fewer than 12 weaving and cloth terms are introduced, with 'weave' repeated in the refrain). The argument is made that under the impulse of the Spirit the creation of loving relationships between human beings will be humanity's real salvation (see Galatians 5:22 and 2 Timothy 1:7). Verse 2 memorably acknowledges the human failure to love each other: 'we have frayed the fabric of your making, / tearing [ourselves] away from all that you intend.' In verse 3, in a strikingly original image with roots in both Christian and ancient Greek mythology,* God becomes the divine weaver, working on the loom of history itself, and providing Christ as the pattern (controlling design, ideal model) for humanity (see John 3:16).

WEAVER The tune is named after the title of the text. It was written by **Colin Gibson** in 1989 at the editorial meeting held at the church of St Andrew's on the Terrace, Wellington, where the hymn was selected for inclusion in *Alleluia Aotearoa*. Set in E minor to reflect the profound nature of the operation of the Holy Spirit described in the text, the music moves through A, B and D major before closing in a *Tierce de Picardy* on an E major chord. The slow dropping bass at the beginning and end of the setting suggests a descent into mystery, while contrary motion between the melody and the tenor line in the final 2 bars illustrates the weaving into one mentioned in the text.

> *In Greek mythology, the Parcae are three female deities, crones who spin, weave and cut short the individual fate of human beings.

Spirit of peace *F58 (i) and (ii), HP20 (i) and (ii)*
Metre: 4.4.4.4.5.4.5.4

Written by **John Murray** in 1999, this is one of a number of short responsive verses published in *Faith Forever Singing* (2000) on the model of similar material created by the Taizé community (see the Introduction to *Faith Forever Singing*, page vii). This text was reprinted in *He Came Singing Peace* (2002) with the first of its two settings. In *Faith Forever Singing* the lines are laid out in units of four or five syllables; in *He Came Singing Peace* as units of eight or nine syllables.

The biblical model for the text is the list of the fruits of the Holy Spirit given in Galatians 5:22-23, to which the writer adds truth (John 16:13), life (John 6:63) and earth (see Psalm 24:1). The final line is derived from Ephesians 4:4, 'There is one body and one Spirit.'

[SPIRIT OF PEACE (i)] This setting is by **Colin Gibson**. Also written in 1999, the melody is developed from its initial 2-bar phrase and moves sequentially through D minor and E flat major before returning to its home key in B flat major.

[SPIRIT OF PEACE (ii)] The second setting is by **Cecily Sheehy**. Written in 1999, and set in E minor over what is effectively a ground bass, it may be sung as a round for four voices, closing on an open B major chord. In both these settings the short-breathed musical phrases respond to the short-lined version of the text.

Spirit of springtime (Spring Song) *F59*
Metre: 11.5.4.11.5.4

Another example of the creative partnership between Shirley Murray and Jillian Bray, this springtime carol was written by **Shirley Murray** in 1999. It was first published in *Faith Forever Singing* (2000), then in *Faith Makes the Song* (2003), where the author explains to her American audience that her poem 'celebrates the new hope of the season – August till November, where I live – but universally the explosion of new life.'

The text shows a poet at play with language, using showers of adjectives ('fresh...keen... bright... bold'), alliterative couplings ('seen in the sunlight') and energetic participle chains ('tingling...tickling...rising... sleeping') to con-vey a mood of excitement and delight. Verse 1, 'creation's garden,' offers a glancing allusion to the Garden of Eden (Genesis 2:8-14), and an impudent pun on 'push for'=promote, strive for / 'push' as in the muscular contractions of childbirth. Verse 2, 'God in the promise,' recalls Galatians 3:16; the 'rush of a mighty wind' experience of the disciples at Pentecost (Acts 2:2) figures in verse 3.

VERDURE The tune name given to her melody by the composer, **Jillian Bray**, refers to the greenness and prolific growth associated with spring. Bray writes, 'Imagine my delight in receiving this text so full of vitality to my tune "Verdure" sent to SEM [Shirley Erena Murray] in 1999.' In fact this melody communicates vitality with its spiky 7/8, 4/4 time shifts, its high tessitura, leaping intervals and C major setting, spiced with shifts into G and F major. There is another, quieter setting, by Canadian composer **Ron Klusmeier** (Klusmeier 53).

Spirit who broods A126
Metre: 4.4.4.4 and refrain

Shirley Murray wrote this text in 1988, the first of her hymns for a World Council of Churches workshop on Liturgy and Music held at Melbourne, Australia, in advance of the major 1991 World Council of Churches Assembly at Canberra, the country's capital. It was published in her first American collection, *In Every Corner Sing* (1992), then in *Alleluia Aotearoa* (1993).

The sessions of the Assembly were focused on the theme 'Come, Holy Spirit: renew the whole creation.' This theme becomes the second line of the refrain; the first line is derived from Christ's prayer 'that they may all be one' (John 17:21). The verses develop from biblical prompts, concentrating them into a few words. Verse 1 draws on Genesis 1:2 for lines 1 and 3, 1 Corinthians 14:15, 'I will sing with the Spirit' (line 2), and Luke 3:22, 'the Holy Spirit descended on him like a dove' (line 4). Verse 2 begins from John 14:17, 'the Holy Spirit, who leads into all truth,' though this original poet introduces fresh modern images of laser beam and torch light. Verse 3 starts from Romans 5:5, 'the love of God has been poured out in our hearts through the holy Spirit' then draws on 1 Corinthians 13:5-6 (New English Bible translation). The final verse draws on Romans 15:13, 'You will overflow with hope through the power of the Holy Spirit,' and 2 Corinthians 3:17, 'the Lord is the Spirit,' then plays briefly with the terms 'God' and 'Good.'

SONG TO THE SPIRIT This setting was written by Dunedin composer **Nigel Eastgate** in 1988. The melody is built out of the initial 4-note phrase, and the harmonic soundscape is made interesting by a shift from flat keys for the verses (E flat and C minor) to sharp keys (G major, E minor, G major) for the refrain. As Shirley Murray acknowledges, there are other settings by **Colin Gibson** (New Zealand) and **I-to Loh** (Taiwan). In *Singing the Faith* (UK, 2011) the hymn is matched with the tune KENNICK by Colin Avery.

Star-Child, earth-Child C40 (i) and (ii)
Metre: 4.5.4.5 and refrain

This carol was written by **Shirley Murray** in 1993, and first published in 1996 in both *Carol our Christmas* and her American collection, *Every Day in Your Spirit*.

Shirley Murray writes, 'A carol which grew out of increasing concern at the market values dictating our welfare system, now creating more and more "social rejects."' This carol is marked by fresh and adventurous imagery, as in verse 1, 'go-between of God' (usually in the context of an intermediate in a secret human love affair), 'love Child' (a common term for the illegitimate child of human lovers' and possibly intended to refer to the circumstances of Jesus' conception and birth) and 'heaven's lightning rod' (the first instance of this powerful and poetic metaphor in hymn literature)*. In verses 3-5 the Star-Child is contrasted with other children abandoned and neglected (the 'social rejects'), with children who will grow up happily – or sadly, with spoiled children 'having, wanting more,' and children who will acquire wisdom and faith. Verse 5 returns to the Star-Child and plays with the idea of 'star' as both of divine origin and famous celebrity. There is some word play of the kind frequent in Shirley Murray's texts: 'beat child'=beaten child and a child of the 'beat' generation; 'down-to-earth-child'=realistic child and child who came down to earth (from heaven). Verse 4, 'Spared child, spoiled child,' perhaps unconsciously, alludes to the proverb, 'Spare the rod and spoil the child.'

STAR-CHILD (i) Written by **Colin Gibson** in 1994 and named independently in response to the same Christmas card which caught the attention of Carlton Young (see below). Interestingly, although Gibson's setting is in 4/4 time and Young's in 3/4 time, the melodic shape of both settings is very similar.

[STAR-CHILD (ii)] Written by the American composer **Carlton Young** in 1994, named after the first line of the carol, and described by Shirley Murray as a 'simple, lilting tune [that] was an immediate response by Carlton Young to our Christmas card on which the words were printed.' There is yet another setting by Canadian composer **Ron Klusmeier** (Klusmeier 11).

> *Shirley Murray herself said that she had found this image in Teilhard de Chardin's writings.

Stranger, standing at my door *F60*
Metre: 7.7.7.7.7.7.7.7

This hymn was written by **Shirley Murray** in 1997 for the Ecumenical Year for Churches in Solidarity with the Uprooted marked by the World Council of Churches, as well as for Amnesty's International Campaign for Refugees. It was first published in *Faith Forever Singing* (2000), then in *Faith Makes the Song* (2003), where only the words were given and the long verses printed in the New Zealand publication were broken into four-line stanzas with a one-line refrain.

The World Council definition of 'uprooted' was, 'those forced to leave their homelands for political, environmental or economic causes,' and this is reflected in the compelling central image of an unknown stranger or strangers standing at the speaker's door at night.* The primary reference in Murray's hymn text is to Revelation 3: 'Behold I stand at the door and knock; if anyone hears my voice and opens the door I will come in to him and eat with him and he with me.' The 'screen' (verse 2) is a television screen offering pictures of 'worlds away'; the 'angel come to stay' (verse 3) alludes to the angelic visitors welcomed in by Abraham and Sarah (Genesis 18:1-8); but the final revelation that the troubling stranger is Christ is drawn from Matthew 25:31-46 ('I was a stranger and you welcomed me'), with its implied warning of ultimate consequences for the rejection of this 'stranger.'

STRANGER This setting, written by **Jillian Bray** in 1997, went through several arrangements before the composer settled on a version for solo rather than group singing. She says, 'The words "you my own compassion's test" [marked] it out for solo treatment rather than a hymn.' Canadian composer **Ron Klusmeier** offers a four-part choral setting (Klusmeier 36).

Sydney Carter's 1965 carol, 'No use knocking on the window,' printed in the *Australian Hymn Book* (1977) offers an earlier and similar image.

Summer's a time to discover (Real Christmas) *C41*
Metre: Irregular

This cheerful carol was written by **Jackie Wise**. She explains that 'Some years ago, towards Christmas, I was teaching a Christmas song to a class of young children, and one of them asked, "What's a Bethlehem?" As I explained to her that it was a place, a real place, the place Jesus was born, I realized she had no concept that the story of the birth of Jesus was any different from any of the fictional stories she read at school every day. And so the idea behind the song (whose actual title is 'Real Christmas') was born, as I pondered what *is* real to New Zealand children at Christmas time? School breaks up, they go on holiday out into the New Zealand summer countryside, they take out their Christmas decorations and go through the whole gift-giving and gift-receiving process. So I wanted, with my song, to acknowledge the children's reality and to put before them also the thought that the birth of Jesus was just as real as any of their summer experiences in our beautiful country.' [Christmas falls in the summer season in New Zealand, and marks the beginning of the long summer school holiday.]

The carol was first published in *Carol our Christmas* (1996). The text elaborates the pleasures of activities during the summer holiday season. The 'mantelpiece' (verse 3) is a ledge over a fireplace where a Nativity scene or an Advent calendar might be set up; Christmas trees (often real pine trees or branches of pine are set up in New Zealand homes and decorated with lights and hangings, following northern hemisphere custom).

REAL CHRISTMAS The tune name is taken from the actual title of the poem by Jackie Wise. The music was written by the author herself for piano accompaniment, and pilots the singers easily through some natural modulations before returning to the prevailing key of F major.

Take a grape (The fruits of the Spirit) *H127*
Metre: 14.14.12.12.12.11.11

This text was written in 2007 by **Colin Gibson** as a contribution to a youth service which focused on the fruits grown and eaten in biblical times compared with the fruits of the Spirit, as described in Galatians 5:22. It was published for the first time in *Hope is our Song* (2009).

Along with a virtually complete listing of the fruits and grains mentioned in the Bible and a free rendering of the full text of the Pauline passage, the words of the song draw out the theme of the abundance of nature, based on a prayer used in the service which began, 'We bless you for this world which is like a banquet of good things.' In the contemporary context, fruit salad and nourishing soup become appropriate metaphors for such banqueting food. In the refrain the stress falls on human responsibility for the good care of the earth.

YAMSONG This song is dedicated to the Yam group of the Mornington Methodist Church, Dunedin, Yam being an acronym for Youth at Mornington. It was composed by the author in 2007. Floating behind the music is a memory of Sydney Carter's song in praise of George Fox, 'There's a light that is shining in the heart of a man,' Carter's reworking of an even older Shaker melody.

Take my gifts *A127*
Metre: 8.7.8.7 D

'Take my gifts' was written by **Shirley Murray** in 1988 in response to a request for a hymn for her Presbyterian Church's Stewardship programme, Response. [Such programmes typically invited members of congregations to offer their particular talents and skills as gifts in the service of the church, as well as increasing their contributions to its finances.] After appearing on a Stewardship pamphlet, the text was published in her American collection *In Every Corner Sing* (1992), then in *Alleluia Aotearoa* (1993).

The theme of the hymn, the glad offering of self in a loving response to the providential love of God reaches beyond the specific occasion which brought it into being, and it is now sung frequently in church services of every kind. There are scriptural allusions: verse 1 draws on the parable of the talents (Matthew 25:14-30, also Luke 19:12-8), 1 John 4:10-12 and 1:5, and Matthew 13:33, the parable of the woman and the leaven. Verse 2 draws on the image of the fruits of the Holy Spirit (Galatians 5:22-23) and the story of Jesus turning water into wine at the Marriage in Cana (John 2:1-11) – though the spicing and lacing of the 'wine of God' with humour and laughter is the writer's highly original addition to the gospel account, as is the accumulation of contemporary commercial terms relating to vivid flavour, 'tang,' 'taste,' 'zest.'

TALAVERA TERRACE The tune was named after the Wellington street on a steep hill where the author and her family were then living in the St Andrew's on the Terrace Presbyterian Church manse. It was written by **Colin Gibson**, 'almost instantaneously,' says Shirley Murray, in a breakaway from the then staid and formal style of religious music, taking its cue from American popular and commercial music, with a trio of talented backing singers crooning behind a charismatic star soloist of undoubted charisma but unexceptional singing ability. Until the final two lines, the emphatic music slowly descends in two sets of sequences, but for the two final lines the rising 'bread of love' is imitated in a rising series of four notes to close out the music in an exuberant, 'zesty' way.

Take our bread, we ask you *W656*
Metre: 10.11.10.6 and refrain

This communion hymn was written by composer/author **Joseph Wise** and was first published in his *Gonna Sing, My Lord* album (1966). It was widely used by Roman Catholic Americans in the 1970s, who sang it at the offertory and during the serving of Holy Communion. It was included in the United Methodist *Supplement to the Book of Hymns* (1982), then in the *United Methodist Hymnal* (1993) as well as in the Disciples of Christ *Chalice Hymnal* (1995) as well as entering the New Zealand supplement to *With One Voice* (1982).

The second verse, as printed in *With One Voice*, was written by **Colin Gibson**, and displaces Wise's original text:

> Your holy people standing
> washed in your blood,
> Spirit-filled yet hungry we await your food.
> We are poor, but we've brought ourselves
> the best that we could,
> We are yours, we are yours.

The text neatly reverses the gospel account of the Last Supper (Matthew 26:17-30 and the other three gospels) in which Jesus offers to those at the table bread and wine, symbolizing his body and blood to be broken and shed on the cross. Here the participants offer Christ their own bread, hearts and lives in an act of total dedication. Verse 1, line 3, alludes to John 14:20, 'On that day you will know that I am in my Father, and you in me and I in you.' Original verse 2, line 1, references Revelation 7:14; line 3 alludes to the poor widow's gift at the Temple, Mark 12:41-44 and Luke 21:1-4.

TAKE OUR BREAD The tune name is derived from the first line of the refrain of this folk-pop hymn; the original music was composed by the author. *For the United Methodist Hymnal* the music was supplied in an arrangement by **Carlton Young** published in *Songbook for Saints and Sinners* (1971). The arrangement in *With One Voice* is by New Zealand musician **Guy Jansen**.

Tama ngākau mārie (Son of a peaceful heart) *W633, A128*
Metre: 7.6.6.5

Neither the author nor the composer of this Māori hymn has been traced, though the text is a free paraphrase of 'Jesus, meek and gentle,' by George Rundle Prynne (1818-1903) and probably dates from the late 19th century. Among Māori it is often sung at a funeral or commemorative service, and it was adopted as a troop song by the Māori Battalion serving with the New Zealand forces in the Second World War, sung as they buried their dead on the battlefields of North Africa and Italy.

A hymn common to both Māori and Pākehā culture it is often performed on ceremonial and ritual occasions. It has been frequently recorded as a classic example of Māori religious music, performed by school and other choirs and given orchestral and solo arrangements. It entered Pākehā (non-Māori) congregational singing in the 1960s, where unusually it has continued to be sung in the original language. It has also been taken into liturgical use, appearing, for instance, in *A New Zealand Prayer Book of the Anglican Province of New Zealand* (1989). To some singers its ethnicity is its key feature, to others its theme of peace.

The hymn has been published in most Māori-language hymnals but also in many English-language national and international hymn books such as *The New Zealand Radio Hymn Book* (1962), *The EACC Hymnal* (1964) – with a paraphrase in English by B.T. Niles, *With One Voice* (1977), *Sing Praise* (1981), *Servant Songs* (1987), *New Zealand Praise* (1988), *Alleluia Aotearoa* (1993), as well as a number of Asian hymnals including *Sound the Bamboo* (1990 and 2000) and such ecumenical hymn books as *Drawn to the Wonder: Hymns and Songs from Churches Worldwide* and *Thuma Mina* (both 1995). It is likely to remain an iconic Māori hymn in its own country and internationally.

[TAMA NGĀKAU MĀRIE] In an early Māori hymnal, *He Himene mo te Karakia ki te Atua* (1890) this hymn text is set to **William Henry Monk's** ST CONSTANTINE, with Matthew 14:30, 'Lord, save me,' as an epigraph. The composer of the now familiar tune which has displaced it, TAMA NGĀKAU MĀRIE, is unknown, but unusually among so-called 'traditional' ethnic hymns its slow-paced, simple melodic line and its setting in a G major/modal key has the ring of authentic indigenous composition.

Te Atua mou o Betela A129
Metre: Irregular

This hymn in Cook Island Māori was written by **Taria Kingstone** at an unknown date. It was first published in *Alleluia Aotearoa* (1993) after circulating among Cook Island congregations in an oral tradition.

The text is an adaptation of the hymn 'O God of Bethel' by Philip Doddridge (1702-51), published posthumously in *Hymns Founded on Various texts from the Holy Scriptures by the Reverend Philip Doddridge D.D. Edited from the Author's manuscript by Job Orton* (Salop, 1755). A manuscript copy in Doddridge's own hand exists, dated 16 January 1736/7, with the first line as we have it now. The 1755 text gives the same line as 'O God of Jacob,' and there are a number of other variations from the modern received text.*

According to the 1755 edition, Doddridge's text was based on 'Jacob's Vow,' Genesis 28:20-22, and there are other scriptural sources, including 1 Kings 8:57, Psalm 17:8 and Psalm 91:4.

The choice of this text for adaptation and use by Pacific Island congregations is significant since its theme is the guidance and protection of God's people, as desert wanderers seeking a promised land – much as Pasifika have roamed the Pacific ocean to reach New Zealand. Verse 1 equates to the first two lines in verse 1 of the original hymn, though the providential attribute of God stressed there ('by whose hand your people still are fed') is replaced by a statement of the unchanging nature of God. Verse 2 draws on the third and fourth lines of Doddridge's first verse ('[God] who through this earthly pilgrimage / hath all our fathers led'). Verse 3 takes its theme of God's leadership and provision from verses 1 and 3 of 'O God of Bethel.' The adapter adds new lines about a loving and righteous heart. The refrain is drawn from the first two lines of Doddridge's verse 4, 'O spread your covering wings / till all our wanderings cease.'

[TE ATUA MOU O BETELA] This original setting by **Taria Kingstone** is written with Cook Island unaccompanied four-part choral singing in mind. There is a characteristic freedom of rhythm and strong fundamental chording, allowing for male strength of sound and female keenness of melody.

> *For a fuller account of the complicated establishment and transmission of the text, see *A Companion to Together in Song: Australian Hymn Book II*, ed. Wesley Milgate and D'Arcy Wood. Sydney: The Australian Hymn Book Pty Ltd (2006), 407-8.

Teach us, O loving heart of Christ A130
Metre: 8.6.8.6

This text was written in 1987 by **Shirley Murray** to provide a hymn of community confession during Holy Week for her congregation at St Andrew's on the Terrace Presbyterian Church, Wellington. It was published in 1992 in her American collection, *In Every Corner Sing*, followed by *Alleluia Aotearoa* (1993).

Murray says of the text, 'It has since been used for themes of peace and justice. I wanted to say that the world is being crucified, and the Church has not yet identified enough with its pain [see verse 2, lines 3-4].' The dominant image of the poem is that of the crucified Christ. For verses 1 and 5, see Luke 23:34; for verse 2 see John 19:34. Verse 3 acknowledges Christ's commandment to love one's neighbour as oneself (John 13:34-35). The final lines of verse 5 echo the words of the General Confession in the Book of Common Prayer, 'We have left undone those things which we ought to have done.'

KHANDALLAH The hymn was originally sung to the tune WIGTOWN from the Scottish Psalter, but new music was written in 1988 by **Jillian Bray,** who named her tune after the Presbyterian church in the suburb of Wellington where the composer grew up. She writes, 'It was suggested that I remove the bass D notes from the setting, but they represented the tolling of a bell, which I thought added to the solemnity of the words.' Shirley Murray has commented that her text 'now gains a depth and solemnity from Jillian Bray's setting.'

Tell my people I love them *A132*
Metre: 7.7.8.7.8.6.6.6

This is a hymn of composite authorship. The refrain began life as a gospel chorus written by **Leonard Bartlotti** (*Alleluia Aotearoa* misspells the name) in the early 1970s, published by the Assemblies of God Gospel Publishing House, Springfield, Missouri, in 1972. Two additional lines, 'Last night Jesus came to me, wiped the tears from my eyes, / And he said not to worry, I'll be there by your side,' have since vanished from successive versions. Additional verses were written by an American conductor and music arranger **Jan Harrington**: they appear in *Alleluia Aotearoa* as the first two verses, though with considerable editorial changes. The original text of these verses, as published in *Complete Mission Praise* (London: Marshall Pickering 1999) reads:

> Tell My people I came and died
> To give them liberty,
> And to abide in me
> is to be really free.
> Tell My people where e'er they go
> My comfort they can know,
> My peace and joy and love
> I freely will bestow.

Verses 3-5 in *Alleluia Aotearoa* were added by **Guy Jansen,** and reflect contemporary social issues, the fair distribution of wealth, the plight of refuges and the poor, and the search for peace.

[TELL MY PEOPLE] The music for this hymn is attributed to the American gospel writer **Leonard Bartlotti** (in *Complete Mission* Praise a descant by Jan Harrington is added), but it appears in *Alleluia Aotearoa* in an arrangement of the original melody by **Guy Jansen**, at the time one of the members of the editorial board for *Alleluia Aotearoa*.

Thank you for the night *H128*
Metre: 5.6.10

This hymn of ecstatic thanks and praise was written by **Jenny McLeod** and first published in *Hope is our Song* (2009). Although the text richly alludes to biblical and creedal material, its expressed delight in the natural world may be a reflection of the writer's physical circumstances. A visitor describes the location of her home as 'set high above the Kāpiti Coast between Pukerua Bay and Paekakariki [north of Wellington on the west coast of the North Island]. On a clear day she would see the Sounds and Farewell Spit at the top of the South Island, and Mt Taranaki as the furthest western point of her view along the coastline of the North Island. She looks out to Kāpiti Island, always a brooding presence at the meeting of sky and sea. Her house is exposed to the full blast of the westerly winds. The sea and landscapes are dominated by the ever-changing weather patterns around the two land masses bordering Cook Strait. All these natural elements are inspirational to the writing of this hymn' (John Thornley, communication 28 August 2013).

Each verse of the hymn associates the writer's experience of a particular natural phenomenon with praise of God, Christ or the Holy Spirit. Verse 1 refers to the resurrection of Christ (Luke 24:1-5, with its dawn setting and the presence of 'men in dazzling clothes'). But Jenny McLeod has also spoken of her 'whole-hearted identification with the night,' stemming from early experiences at her Kāpiti home when she would 'sit for hours at my front bay window in darkness at night-time, veritably bathing in the starlight' and simultaneously 'hearing the waves on the beach at the bottom of the cliff.' Verse 2 associates the clarification brought by daylight with the presence of the Holy Spirit as Comforter (John 14:26); 'kindly' is perhaps an echo of John Henry Newman's 1833 hymn,

'Lead kindly light.' Job 4:9 and 37:10 refer to the breath of God as a corrective and natural force, but verse 3 more probably celebrates the effect of the winds for which the Wellington coastal area is famous. Verse 4 recalls Kate Chopin's 'The voice of the sea speaks to the soul. The touch of the sea is sensuous, enfolding the body in its soft, close embrace' (*The Awakening*, 1899), but Psalm 46:1, 'God is our refuge and strength,' is also in play here. Verse 5 alludes to Philippians 2:9, 'Therefore God highly exalted him [the resurrected Jesus]. Psalm 54:4, 'God is my helper; The Lord is the sustainer of my soul' (KJ version), underlies verse 6.

FERNER Mcleod describes this as 'just a name I quite liked that came to hand more or less at random.' It carries the implication of 'ferns' or 'fernery,' one of the most prolific and characteristic native plants of New Zealand. The work of an experienced and professional composer, the melodic line quickly rises to its tonic note B flat, then gracefully falls in a sequence based on a three-note phrase repeated four times, while the harmonic landscape moves from B flat major through G minor, F major, E flat major and C minor to a point of return. As the score printed in Hope is our Song shows, the individual chords are richly harmonized throughout. There exists a further arrangement of the hymn by **Guy Jansen** for choir and piano accompaniment.

Thank you God (Alive to God)
A133
Metre: 7.8.8.8

This hymn for children was written by **Jillian Bray** shortly before the publication of *Alleluia Aotearoa* (1993), when the editors, of whom she was one, realised there were few hymns for children in the collection. 'It was not written with a particular group of children in mind,' says the author-composer.

The theme is clearly announced in the final verse, 'May children value their senses five, / and thank you, God, for being alive.' Each verse deals with one or more of the five senses; implicit in each stanza is the idea of God's loving presence in the world made apprehensible through our senses. Verse 1 introduces sight. The objects seen all carry symbolic associations: for the 'hills' see Psalm 121:1, for 'night creeps up on day' see Genesis 8:22. Jesus as friend (Matthew 19:14) and Lamb of God (John 1:29), and the sight of a church spire complete these religious associations. Verse 2 addresses the faculty of hearing: bird song and the sounds of wind, rain and river are framed within the idea of the music of God's world and the praise of nature. Verse 3 takes in two senses, smell and taste, with references to the scent of flowers and the taste of nourishing fruit. That flowers 'refresh the air' is not a poetic fancy; although leaves are the major natural means of replenishing the air with oxygen, some flowers, among them orchids, succulents and bromeliads, do refresh the atmosphere. Verse 4 describes pleasant touch experiences, including 'loving hugs.' Verse 5 draws out the lessons already passed on, though there is an odd switch from implied child voice to adult voice in the third line. Here the teacher briefly steps forward.

[ALIVE TO GOD] The easy rhythmic flow of the melody and its dance-like movement in 6/8 time make this music well suited to young voices, as does the setting in F major. There are modulations to A, C and D major to enrich the harmonies until reaching the point of final cadence in F major once more.

Thanks be to God *A134*
Metre: 11.7 with repetitions

This grace was written by Dominican Sister **Cecily Sheehy** as one of a series of songs published in the Catholic magazine *Family Living* between 1980 and 1985. Its first hymnbook appearance was in *Alleluia Aotearoa* (1993).

The text both expresses gratitude for refreshment and a meal and praises the goodness and plenitude of the earth, so exhibiting the creation spirituality which is fundamental to this writer's theology.

[THANKS BE TO GOD] The music, written by the author and set in the comfortable key of G major, allows for two alternating groups of singers with a slight overlap between their voices. The sentences may be passed backwards and forwards as many times as the hunger of the singers requires. The melody has an African praise song feeling, derived from both the driving down G-D opening phrase and the syncopated fourth bar.

The Blessing of water and light and air *H130*
Metre: 10.9.11.8

Shirley Murray wrote this hymn in 2007, as 'my Christmas greeting to friends.' It was published in both her American collection *Touch the Earth Lightly: New Hymns written between 2003 and 2008* and New Zealand's *Hope is our Song* in 2008.

She recalls that 'I once saw a blessing on the wall of a home in the Philippines which has stayed with me, mostly because it sharpens the element of transience, and time slipping away.' This blessing, which she quotes in *Touch the Earth Lightly*, runs: 'Bless our home, Father, / That we cherish the bread before there is none, / Discover each other before we leave / And enjoy each for what we are / While we have time.' While it has given her a metrical form and leaves its trace in the repeated phrase 'the time to discover,' she takes a larger and characteristic view of 'home' as 'the earth and its beauty' (verse 1), and ranges through the elements of the natural world as well as the human experiences of joy, friendship, music and laughter, closing in the final blessing of 'life's own breath.' It is interesting that, given the Christmas festival with which it is associated, this text mentions Jesus only as 'our teacher.' Perhaps, in verse 2, there is a glancing reference to John 3:16, 'God so loved the world that he gave his only begotten son.'

TE MOANA (Māori=the ocean) This gentle, lullaby-like musical setting in F sharp minor was provided by Shirley Murray's close friend **Jillian Bray**. The melody, constructed on an F sharp major triad, gradually rises to a climax with the words 'and give us time to discover' before it settles back to the tonic note, remaining in a dreamlike minor mode.

The bread is blessed, the wine is poured (Invitation to Communion) *H131*
Metre: 8.8.9.8

Shirley Murray, the writer of this pre-communion hymn, created in 2004, explains that 'In this text, which is an invitation to communion, I have interwoven the lines of the familiar psalm [Psalm 23] with a short-lined poem (originally four stanzas of a 4.4.4.4 metre) and used the resonance of the traditional introductory words, while expanding the meaning of the elements – bread and wine – to be used to satisfy hunger and to create justice and health for humanity.' The hymn was first published in her American collection *Touch the Earth Lightly* (2008), then in *Hope is our Song* (2009).

The 'traditional introductory words' (as spoken at St Andrew's on the Terrace Presbyterian Church, Wellington, where Shirley Murray then worshipped) are repeated in verses 1 and 5. Verse 3 alludes to Matthew 18:14 ('It is not the will of your Father...that one of these little ones should be lost'). The following line refers to the Easter events of the crucifixion and the resurrection.

CARDRONA The tune, written for this text in 2007, is named after a small Central Otago town associated with two English friends of the composer, **Colin Gibson**, made memorable when a swarm of sand flies made it impossible for one of them to paint the scenery there. The music establishes a mood of quiet solemnity. Each verse is set to a normal pitched melody with a shifting modality from A minor to A major; the refrain, setting the words of Psalm 23, is set off by being chanted on a single note with supporting harmonies moving in fifths beneath to suggest ancient plainsong.

The Gamble *facing F79*

This unusually bitter text was written by **Shirley Murray** shortly before its publication in *Faith Forever Singing* (2000), followed by American publication in *Faith Makes the Song*

(2002 and her collection *Life into Life* (2019). It has not yet found a musical setting.

Drawing on John 19:23-24, with brutal directness the poet compares the indifference of the soldiers playing dice at the foot of the cross to the suffering of their victim to what she perceives as the equal indifference of contemporary humanity to its responsibility for the slow 'death' of the earth by planetary degradation/desecration.

There is serious punning in lines 7-8, 'who gave a toss / for the man on the cross?' (cf. the slang phrase 'I don't give a toss'=I really don't care), as there is in lines 9-10, 'now we throw the dice, / the earth is slowly dying,' suggesting both that humanity is risking the destruction of the planet and making a crucial choice about its future. There is another pun on 'crying' (line 12), which means both 'crying out for help' and 'weeping.' By implication, humans have taken over a god-like domination of their own environment and are now recklessly risking their own survival with that of their own planet.

The God of heaven thunders *A135*
Metre: 7.7.7.5.6

This selection of verses from Psalm 29 is by **Michael Perry** and was first published by the English Jubilate Group in *Psalm Praise* (1973), then in *Sing Glory: Hymns, Psalms and Songs for a New Century (1989)* and *Songs from the Psalms* (1990).

Verse 1 is constructed from verse 3 of the Psalm, 'The voice of the Lord is upon the waters; the God of glory thunders,' to which is added verse 9, 'and in his temple all cry "glory!"' Verse 2 is assembled from verses 7-8, 'The voice of the Lord flashes forth flames of fire; the voice of the Lord shakes the wilderness' together with verses 5-6, 'the Lord breaks the cedars of Lebanon. He makes Lebanon skip like a calf.' Verse 3 is drawn from verses 10-11, 'the Lord sits enthroned as king forever; may the Lord give strength to his people,' with a repetition of verse 9.

[THUNDER] This setting – unnamed in *Alleluia Aotearoa* – was originally written by **Christopher Norton** for SATB choir and piano and first published in *Songs from the Psalms* (1990) in which this New Zealand musician had a major role in editing and arranging the music. The music has much in common with the setting by this composer of the psalm-hymn 'The majesty of mountains,' A139, also by Michael Perry, including its melodic structure and rhythmic patterns, although the key is shifted from E minor to E flat major and crochets replace quavers to match the more exalted and excited mood of the text.

The grace of God has appeared *F61*
Metre: 7.7.7

This short responsive song was written by **Cecily Sheehy** in 1998 as a contribution to a group of such brief sung responses introduced into *Faith Forever Singing* (2000). See the Introduction to the collection, page vii.

The text is a modernized version of Titus 2:11, 'For the grace of God has appeared for the salvation of all men.' By 'grace of God' the author of the letter – earlier attributed to Paul, though this is questioned by modern scholars who prefer to attribute this pastoral epistle to an unnamed member of one of the later Pauline church communities – means Jesus Christ, as God's loving and undeserved gift to humanity and the means of salvation for all human beings (cf. John 3:16).

[TITUS] The music, by **Cecily Sheehy** herself, is a choral setting for four voices which allows for some inner voice independence. It can be performed as a unison melody.

The grace of our Lord Jesus Christ *A136*
Metre: Irregular

This setting of the traditional words of the Grace was written by **Ian Render** for a local congregation, before its publication in *Alleluia Aotearoa* (1993).

The text is taken from 2 Corinthians 13:14, with the usual addition of an Amen.

[THE GRACE] This is a setting by Render himself for two voices, which may be assigned to priest or cantor, with a response by congregation or choir (see the final chord). The musical accompaniment, set in C major, is relaxed and rhythmical, with considerable syncopation.

The heavens are telling the glory of the Lord W625
Metre: 12.12.11.11.12.11

This hymn text was written by **Colin Gibson** in 1974 for the choir and congregation of Mornington Methodist Church, Dunedin, and was first published in the 1975 edition of the songbook of that church. It is a paraphrase based on Psalm 19:1-6, with the last two lines of verse 1 repeated as a refrain in verses 2-3.

The whole hymn is an adaptation for congregational singing of a famous chorus, 'The heavens are telling' from **Franz Joseph Haydn's** oratorio *The Creation*, written over two years (1796-8) and first performed in Vienna in 1798. The idea for such a hymn was the result of the writer's personal involvement in an inspiring performance of the oratorio in Dunedin by the City of Dunedin choir of which he was a member; it was originally titled 'The Psalm of the Heavens.'

In verse 1, the psalmist, in a way typical of Hebrew poetry, turns the abstract idea of awe at the spectacle of the night sky into the concrete image of a paradoxically soundless yet continuous verbal proclamation of 'the glory of God.' In verse 2, the paraphrase word 'music' displaces the original 'voice' (there was an ancient belief that the movement of the stars and planets created a divine music, the music of the spheres), and 'dwelling' replaces the more particularly eastern image of a tent set in the firmament. In verse 3 the sun is successively compared to a newly-married man emerging from his bedroom glowing with satisfaction and pleasure (Psalm 19:5, 'as a bridegroom coming out his chamber'), and with an athlete delighting in his own physical condition for running a race, the psalmist's image for the sun's transit. The paraphrase omits the final description of the sun, again characteristic of an Eastern culture, 'and there is nothing hid from its heat.' In Christian symbolism, the sun is commonly identified with Christ as the risen sun/Son of God.

CREATION The tune takes its name from the oratorio by Haydn, and the music is a simplified version of Haydn's more elaborate choral score for soloists and choir. In the original Mornington version this hymn was directed to be sung by both choir and congregation, with the congregation repeating after the choir the first two lines of each verse.

The jersey cow came mooing C42
Metre: 11.12.11.12.11.12.11.12. 5.10.11

This gleeful Christmas carol for children was written by **Joy Cowley** in the mid 1990s, and published in *Carol our Christmas* in 1996. Under the title *Cowshed Christmas* it later became a best-selling full-colour Christmas book, illustrated by Gavin Bishop and published by Random House New Zealand in 2009. It was listed as a finalist in the New Zealand Post Children's Book Awards for 2010. However, there the text was radically revised with the original 'old shed' replaced by a cowshed, and collie dogs, ginger cats, kune kune pigs, and bantam hens joining or displacing the original farmyard animals and the shepherds.

This is a very Kiwi take on the shepherds and animals usually present in the Italian nativity scenes originated by St Francis (**Giovanni Francesco Di Bernadone**). The traditional manger becomes an old shed, the cow is described as a Jersey, a breed famed for its milk, lambs mingle with sheep (possible in an Antipodean early summer), and cattle-dogs and ducks are added to the standard list. The shepherds come running to the birthplace, as they do in Luke 2:16, but the poet adds a noisy chorus of mooing, barking, quacking and baaing to the traditional song of the angels. The carol comes to a sudden quiet, even devotional close, in the repeated answer to the question, 'Guess what they saw? / Little baby Jesus, Jesus, Jesus, / little baby Jesus by the old shed door.'

[OLD SHED DOOR] This setting, by **Colin Gibson,** written in 1995, mimics the actions of the characters. The quacking of ducks is imitated in the discordant bass of verse 3, the melody of the nursery rhyme 'Baa baa black sheep' briefly appears in the bass of verse 4; the scurrying shepherds are matched by divergent scalic passages in verse 5. The abrupt key shift and pause which accompanies the question, 'Guess what they saw?' allows for a quiet, slower take-up in the final verse.

The journey of life may be easy, may be hard *W670*

Metre: Irregular

This children's hymn was written by **Valerie Collison,** author of 'Come and join the celebration.' It achieved wide popularity when it was included in the BBC's 'Together' radio programmes in the 1980s and was published in their *Come and Praise,* Book 1 (1978), reprinted in *The Complete Come and Praise* (1990). It has also been published in *Sing for Joy* (1999) and *Someone's Singing Lord: Hymns and Songs for Children* (2002). Its modern currency is suggested by the fact that in 2008 a blogger suggested it would be an appropriate song for Reepicheep, the mouse hero of C. S. Lewis's *Prince Caspian, The Voyage of the Dawn Treader,* and *The Last Battle.*

The text has been altered for its use in *With One Voice*: In verse 1, 'I'll take courage as I ride' replaces 'I'll do battle as I ride'; the weak original third verse of the song has been omitted:

> When doubts arise,
> and when tears are in my eyes,
> When all seems lost to me,
> With Christ as my guide I can smile whate'er betide,
> For he my strength will be.

The theme as well as the metre of the song has much in common with an earlier English school hymn, 'Forth rode the knights of old,' by Vera Evelyn Walker, but there are also hints of Sydney Carter's 'One more step along the road.' Scriptural echoes occur in verses 1 and 3, (Matthew 28:20) and the chorus is based on the gospel writers' account of the Entry into Jerusalem (see Mark 11:7-10). Both titles, 'King of Kings' and 'Son of God,' are biblical in origin (1 Timothy 6:15 and Luke 1:35). Verse 3 recalls Matthew 11:30 and Psalm 40:3; verse 4 begins with a reference to the children's game of Follow the Leader, and recalls both Walter Mathams' 1882 hymn 'Jesus, friend of little children' and John 14:1-3.

FOLLOW MY LEADER The tune name is taken from the fourth verse; the catchy, rhythmic music was written by the author, **Valerie Collison.**

The Kingdom is within you *A137*

Metre: Irregular

This song was written in 1982 by Dominican Sister **Cecily Sheehy** as one of a series published in the Catholic magazine *Family Living*. Its first hymnbook appearance was in *New Zealand Praise* (1988), followed by *Alleluia Aotearoa* (1993).

The biblical basis for this text is threefold. The refrain draws on Luke 17:20-21, though the writer significantly shifts Jesus' original saying, 'the Kingdom of God is in the midst of you [that is, among you]' into 'the Kingdom is *within* you.' This saying is linked through the line 'like a little seed planted in the ground let it grow' to the Parable of the Mustard Seed, which appears in all three synoptic gospels, though only Matthew and Mark stress the smallness of the seed (see Matthew 13:31-32, Mark 4:30-32).

The verses explicate the planting and growing of the 'seed' of the kingdom, drawing on further gospel passages. The first verse provides a differentiated version of the Parable of the Sower (found in the three synoptic gospels and the Gospel of Thomas). In this writer's version the person broadcasting the seed is imagined as tossing it into the face of the prevailing wind (against the forces of secular society?), rather than using the forward assistance of the wind – in ancient times the normal practice in spreading seed by hand. In this verse, the stress falls on the courage required to 'keep on facing the wind.'

Verse 2 draws on another saying of Jesus, 'No man, having put his hand to the plough, and looking back, is fit for the kingdom of God' (Luke 9:62). A number of biblical passages imply that 'the fullness of the kingdom' is 'not quite yet' (line 3), among them Matthew 25:34 and 2 Timothy 4:1). But here the singers/sowers are enjoined to patiently persist, and not 'split the seed': that is, they are to stay united as Christians (cf. 'that they may all be one,' John 17:21).

[KINGDOM WITHIN] The setting is by **Cecily Sheehy**, who uses the driving dotted rhythms and chromatic melodic movement of 1980s secular rock music. The tonality steadily shifts back and forth between E major and A major, the narrow harmonic range increasing the powerful emotional emphasis on the key idea that 'the kingdom is within you.'

The light, the Christmas light H132
Metre: 6.7.7.6.6.6.6.6

This Christmas carol was written in 2003 by **Shirley Murray**, who describes it as a kind of 'seekers'* carol, using the simple imagery of the story, especially the elements of light, and leading on to the ministry of Jesus yet to happen. In some sense, and with reference to the New Year, this is more an Epiphany carol than a Christmas one.' The carol was first published in 2008 in her American collection *Touch the Earth Lightly*, then in *Hope is our Song* (2009).

The text draws on John 1:1-9, Matthew 2 and Luke 2 for its references to the light shining out in darkness, the stable birthplace of Jesus and the star leading the Wise Men, but each of these ideas is developed in this writer's own distinctive way. Verse 1 looks forward to the coming of the Holy Spirit which will ignite the glimmering spark of the Jesus-light; the stable door becomes a symbol of openness and inclusiveness (cf. John 10:9); in verse 2 the star is redefined as the 'cosmic star,' with a possible allusion to Matthew Fox's influential book, *The Coming of the Cosmic Christ: The Healing of Mother Earth and the Birth of a Global Renaissance* (1988). The 'pointer flying solo' (line 2) is the significant single star which in the southern hemisphere night sky points to the constellation of the Southern Cross. The striking phrase in verse 4, 'a shining thread,' may have been suggested by the title of a history of black women in America, *A Shining Thread of Hope*, by Darlene Clark Hine and Kathleen Thompson (1999).

SHINING THREAD The tune name is drawn from the final lines of the carol, which use the imagery of thread and stitchwork frequent in this author's poetry. The composer, **Colin Gibson,** wrote the music in 2003, dedicating the setting to church friends, the Hughson family. By a happy accident the setting written by American composer **Jane Marshall** in 2005 for Shirley's hymn was also named SHINING THREAD, although the music differs considerably: Gibson's setting is in D, with a 4/4 signature (with a 3, 3, 2 quaver pulse); Marshall's more stately setting is in G, with a 5/8 signature. The New Zealand composer delivers an altogether more exuberant version of the carol, with an optional flute or recorder descant and an extended flourish on the last word of each verse, inviting finger-snapping to the jazzy off-beat rhythm established in the accompaniment.

> *In clarification of the term, Shirley Murray writes, 'In simple terms, it's about being a seeker of light and enlightenment, drawn on by a shining star/light/thread and therefore an Epiphany carol. Hence the reference to the wise who seek new horizons. Verse two is the clue to my thought: "the searching and the hopeful who look and long for more," and, in the last verse, "the faith we lodge our hope in will seek a door to open."

The Lord bless you and keep you A138
Metre: Irregular

This scriptural song, which draws its text from Numbers 6:24-26, was written by **Dale Garratt** in 1976. It was first recorded on a 1977 LP and cassette tape album, *Father, make* us One, and published by Scripture in Song in the accompanying booklet of the same name. It then appeared in *Scripture in Song: Book One: Songs of Praise* (1979), followed by *New Harvest* (also 1979). In both of these 1979 editions the song is titled 'The Blessing Song.'

Following the practice in such songs, the text closely follows its biblical source, known as the Aaronic Blessing. The context is God's instruction to Moses to direct Aaron and his sons to bless the people of Israel with the words here set to music by Dale Garratt. The blessing has become part of many Christian liturgies, ancient and modern, and has been set by many composers. A popular contemporary version is by English composer John Rutter, and the Australian hymnbook *Together in Song* prints two settings, one adapted from plainsong, the other by Donald Britton.

[BLESSING SONG] The original Dale Garratt composition (used in *Alleluia Aotearoa*) was for paired voices set over a running bass piano accompaniment in D minor, repeated with a closure in D major. *New Harvest* published an arrangement by Christopher Allan which reduces the original two-voice melody to a unison line and simplifies the bass accompaniment.

The Lord God walked in Paradise
F62
Metre: 8.6.8.6 D

This hymn was written in 1995 by **Colin Gibson** to meet a request from Craufurd Murray, Vicar of St Barnabas Anglican Church, Christchurch, to whom the hymn is dedicated for a text to match the theme 'Consider your Call,' brought to the parish by a visiting group of Franciscan friars. It was first published in the writer's second American collection, *Songs for a Rainbow People* (1998), then in *Faith Forever Singing* (2000).

The four verses take as their subject matter four biblical 'calls,' relating each of them to modern life. Verse 1, drawing on Genesis 3:8-13, questions what humanity has done with the knowledge acquired in the post-Edenic world. While the Genesis story focuses on the penalty of banishment from Eden, the second half of the verse prefers to stress God's eternal invitation to return to the harmony originally known as Paradise. Verse 2, drawing on Exodus 3:1-12 presents the divine call to Moses for social action and the liberation of his own oppressed people. 'Bricks and straw' alludes to the episode in Exodus 5:1-9 in which the appeal for liberty is met by even harsher conditions of slavery. The second half of the verse extends the theme of liberation to all modern forms of oppression and slavery, using Jesus' statement of his own mission to 'free the captives' (see Luke 4:16-21). Verse 3 draws on John 21:1-14 and Matthew 11:28 to personalise Christ's call to faith in himself. John 17:20-23 is the basis for verse 4, using new images of profound union to create a call to community, and relationships that are enriching, inclusive and affirmative, rather than damaging and destructive. 'Blossom on the tree' is an image drawn from William Butler Yeats' 1928 poem 'Among Schoolchildren,' suggesting the deepest unity of things:

> O chestnut-tree, great-rooted blossomer,
> Are you the leaf, the blossom or the bole?

The final line draws on 1 Corinthians 13:13.

TEESDALE STREET The tune name acknowledges the Christchurch address of two close friends and members of the St Barnabas Anglican church. Written by **Colin Gibson**, the setting provides a simple lyrical melodic line for the text, rooted in E flat major, in keeping with the stress on gentle and loving callings (rather than heated evangelical exhortations) present in the text.

The love of God is broad like beach and mountain *W667*
Metre: 11.10.11.10 and refrain

Swedish hymn writer **Anders Frostenson** wrote his hymn 'Guds kärlek är som stranden' in or shortly before 1968, when it was published with a Lars Lundberg tune in Stockholm. It was then published in *Psalmer och* [Eight psalms] in 1971 and had become popular among Swedish congregations before it was translated by **Fred Kaan** for the fourth edition of *Cantate Domino* (1974), where it appeared under the title 'The love of God,' together with the Swedish text and only the melody line of Lundberg's setting. In 1976, Frostenson included it with Kaan's translation in a collection of hymns published in England as *Songs and Hymns from Sweden* (1976), and the English words were also printed in Kaan's own *Hymn Texts* (1985).

When the hymn was published in the American *United Methodist Hymnal* (1989), with Kaan's approval inclusive language was introduced, 'you' and 'your' replacing 'he,' 'him' and 'his'. This text begins with 'Your love, O God.' The New Zealand editors have replaced meadows with mountains, 'can grow' with the more cautious 'may grow'; they have retained the original male terms for God.

The theme of the hymn is God's limitless, compassionate and all-embracing love, contrasted with the imprisoning fear-built structures of hatred, mistrust and pride that lead to hatred and war in human society. Its dominant image is that of prison walls and prison costumes set in opposition to the freedom of the natural world where 'our truest being is given hope and courage to unfold.' There is no obvious reliance on scriptural texts – the hymn is remarkable for that alone – but in the text there are biblical concepts, of a divine – but liberating – judgement (verse 4) and the unconfined wind of the Spirit (see John 3:8).

GUDS KÄLEK (Swedish=God's love) This tune is also known as SOM STRANDEN. The composer is **Lars Lundberg** (see above), whose full setting did not reach English and American congregations until the 1980s when the musical score with its delicate and subtle rhythms was published in the 1980 edition of *Cantate Domino*. It was arranged by **Carlton Young** for the 1989 *United Methodist Hymnal*, and further arranged by **Guy Jansen** for the New Zealand Supplement to *With One Voice*.

The majesty of mountains *A139*
Metre: 7.6.8.6.8.6

This considerably lightened and cut-back version of Psalm 104 (the original runs to 35 long verses) is by **Michael Perry** and was first published by the English Jubilate Group in *Come Rejoice* (1989), then in *Psalms for Today* (1990) and *Songs from the Psalms* (1990).

The specifically Christian content of this text – particularly obvious in the Trinitarian third verse – is imported into the Old Testament psalm, as is the idea of God as 'the Lord of love' and 'Saviour.' So too is much of the detail: the 'regal rocks' arching above 'veils of vapour,' the 'surging seas' (which are put to flight in the original) and the 'fruiting trees' (suggested by 'the earth is satisfied with the fruit of thy work') are all this writer's inventions. In fact, in general the text is closer in sentiment to the old German harvest hymn 'We plough the fields and scatter' (by Matthias Claudius, 1740-1815) than it is to the colossal God celebrated in Psalm 104, who 'looks upon the earth and it trembles, who touches the mountains and they smoke' (verse 32).

[MISTERIOSO] (Italian=with a sense of mystery, though the word is usually spelled 'mysterioso,' and its spelling here may be an allusion to the waterfall image of 'veils of vapour' in verse 1). The tune name – not given in *Alleluia Aotearoa* – suggests the mood of mystery and awe expressed in the original Psalm on which this text is based. This setting was written by **Christopher Norton** and was first published in *Songs from the Psalms* (1990), in which this New Zealand musician had a major role editing and arranging the music. The key choice is E minor which sufficiently suggests a mood of awestruck wonder, but this is soon lightened with harmonic sequences taking the music into G major before a final return to the more ominous and mysterious E minor tonality.

The spring has come *A140*
Metre: 12.12.4.8.4.12

Author **Shirley Murray** writes of this springtime hymn, '"The springtime of the

Church" is a phrase associated, for me, with the Taizé community. The text was written on one spring morning in August [1990], and grew from a line in a prayer, "God is at the heart of it." The text was first published in her American collection *In Every Corner Sing* (1992), then in *Alleluia Aotearoa* (1993).

The association of the Taizé community in France with springtime stems from Pope John XXIII's comment to Brother Roger, founder and leader of the community, 'Ah, Taizé, that little springtime of the church,' a comment repeated by the reforming Pope John Paul II in 1986 on a visit to Taizé and again in a speech to pilgrims gathered in Rome for Pentecost 1988.

The writer uses the renewal of nature at springtime as her principal metaphor for the spiritual renewal of the Christian Church; for instance, in verse 2 the pushing through the earth of bulbs images a new 'thrust' or driving force in the life of the Church. Verse 3 introduces additional, scriptural images: for 'new people' see John 3:1-8; for 'the Spirit's fruit' see Galatians 5:22-23.

VERVACITY This tune name is a play on 'Vivacity' plus the Latin word for Spring, *Ver*. The music by **Colin Gibson**, written in 1991 for this text, uses changing stresses and rhythms (the time signatures include 2/4, 5/4 and 4/4) and syncopations as well as a harmonic setting in the celebration key of D major, to suggest the riotous drive and joyful energy referred to in the text. Cautious congregations and staid musicians had best refrain from attempting this exuberant Spring carol.

The stars danced, the angels sang
C43
Metre: 6.5.6.5 and refrain

The words and music of this popular Christmas carol were written in 1975 by **Barbara Gillard** for the congregation of St Paul's Anglican Church, Auckland. The St Paul's Outreach Trust first published the text in *New Glory: Songs of Renewal* (1976). The words and music (arranged by **Val Fleetwood**) were published in *New Harvest* (1979) by the same group. The carol appeared in *Carol our Christmas* in 1996, with the music in a different arrangement by **David Dell**, whose version had been published in 1988 in his *New Zealand Praise*.

The text follows the traditional sequence of the events of the Nativity taken from Luke 2, and Matthew 2: verse 1, the song of the angels, verse 2, the arrival of the shepherds, verse 3, the gifts of the Wise Men, while in verse 4 all are invited to join in praising the Child. The author's own pleasure in dancing emerges in the repeated references to the dance of the stars, imitated in the refrain by the dance of rejoicing worshippers. The 'vault of heaven' (verse 1) refers to the ancient belief that the sky, or the heavens (the firmament) consisted of a huge overarching vault or dome, which the writer imagines ringing, reverberating, with the sound of angelic music. 'Forlorn,' verse 3, means 'neglected, abandoned.' Of the gifts of the Magi, or 'Wise men' (verse 4), frankincense and myrrh were costly resinous gums, the first used in priestly worship, the second for the burial of the dead (see Isaiah 60:6 and John 19:39). Philippians 4:4 is the source of the phrase 'rejoice in him always' (verse 4).

[STAR DANCE] The unnamed lilting tune is by **Barbara Gillard** herself. The original arrangement of the music by **Val Fleetwood** is closely followed by **David Dell**; both composers set the carol in G major and maximize the strong dance rhythms established in the tune with rhythmic figures in the bass accompaniment. This is a fine New Zealand instance of the carol as a dance form, its original character in religious folk music.

The Tenth Leper *facing F37*

Accompanied by a photograph of a white flower, this is one of the modern prose-psalms created by distinguished New Zealand writer **Joy Cowley**, and published in *Psalms Down-Under* (Catholic Supplies: Wellington, 1996).

In the form of a dramatic monologue, the poem focuses on the gospel story of the one leper out of ten healed who returned to thank Jesus for his cure, as told in Luke 17:11-19. But the poet positions herself as that one grateful leper and translates his physical cure and return home into her own spiritual recovery from a moment of 'careless enthusiasm' to a retreat to 'the inner stillness where you waited / to share in my rejoicing.' There the grateful speaker receives 'yet another healing,' being gifted a heart overflowing with divine love or love for God (the word 'your' is ambiguous). The image of 'my heart / like a bowl' recalls the leper's begging bowl, not mentioned in the gospel story but the defining equipment of indigent people in every age.

The wind blew keen (Carol of Cold Comfort) A141, C44
Metre: 8.8.8.8 and refrain

This Christmas carol was written in 1986 by **Colin Gibson** and first published in his collection *Singing Love* (1988).

The verses of the text recapitulate the major events of the Christmas story, as they are described in Matthew 2 and Luke 2, focusing on the winter conditions in which, according to tradition, the Nativity took place. They set the scene for a refrain in the form of a prayer making universal the imperative to relieve suffering in similar conditions in the present world. For the concept of Christ as the God hidden in the stranger in need, see Matthew 25:31-46. For Christ as the 'child of light' see John 1:1-5, 9-11. 'Fire and bread' represent warm lodgings and adequate food ('give us this day our daily bread'). The final line of the refrain embodies a concept given fuller articulation in Joy Cowley's poem *Virgin Birth* (C52*).

SOUTHERLY The name of the tune refers to the cold wind blowing up from Antarctica, bringing wintery conditions to the South Island of New Zealand. The music for the verses, written by the author, imitates the swirl of wind and is set in the 'cold' key of A minor, modulating into C major only with the final invitation to the 'child of light' to be 'born within my heart this night.'

There is no child so small (Carol of the Least Child) H133 (i) and (ii)
Metre: 6.7.7.6

Author **Shirley Murray** wrote this carol for Advent 2006 and describes it as 'An attempt, yet one more, to address the need of the world and specially the plight of children. This [carol] was used by Christian World Service in New Zealand for their annual Christmas appeal. Because it had wide circulation, and also because it was included on a card for friends, I received an unprecedented number of settings.' The text was first published in her American collection *Touch the Earth Lightly* (2008), set to NO CHILD, by American composer **Amanda Husberg**; then in *Hope is our Song* (2009) with settings by **Jillian Bray** and **Colin Gibson**.

The crying, starving, lost, nameless, insignificant children who figure in the first four verses signify 'the least of these my brethren' in the parable of the sheep and the goats (Matthew 25:31-46), which forms the theological basis of the whole text. As in the parable, though without administering the penalty of eternal punishment, God is presented as the One who demands justice and holds us accountable for indifference to suffering that makes even the Creator weep.

JEWEL The tune name alludes to the precious nature of the children who are the subject of the song; the music was written by **Jillian Bray** in 2006. The composer chooses a D minor setting which closes in D major to match the exhortation in the final verse. A chromatic descending figure carries much of the tone of sadness which characterises this setting.

ROTORUA The name of a New Zealand tourist town, famous for its natural hot springs, but also associated with an infamous case of abuse within a family, leading to a child's death. The composer, **Colin Gibson**, dedicated his melody 'to Nia and all the others,' the others being the many instances of violent domestic child abuse in New Zealand society. The musical concept is of a gentle lullaby, with some of the soundscape of a lyric song from Carl Orff's *Carmina Burana*. The setting, written in 2006, is for the most part in C major: the pulsing two chord figure in the right hand of the accompaniment expresses discordant grief resolved.

This carol has caught the attention of a number of composers: there are three other settings by American musicians **Jim Strathdee** (LEAST CHILD), **Jane Marshall** (SHERIDAN) and **Joy Patterson**, a setting by Canadian **Ron Klusmeier** (Klusmeier 56) and a further New Zealand setting by **Suzanne Stewart** written in 2007 (these last three unnamed).

There shall be life and love H134
Metre: 6.6.6.6.7.7.7.6

Written in the mid-1980s, when the author, **Bill Wallace**, was leading courses on Creation Spirituality and Liberation Theology, this text was first published in Book 1 of his trilogy, *Singing the Circle: Sacred Earth, Holy Darkness* (1990), before appearing in *Hope is our Song* (2009).

The thinking behind this declarative, prophetic hymn is set out by the writer himself: 'Because the Gospel in context is the Gospel in creation and in liberation, it is primarily an experience of nurture, new birth and ecstasy rather than an intellectual exercise.' The formula 'There shall be' in verse 1 derives from God's Creation declaration, 'let there be light' (Genesis 1:3). The ideas that follow concisely spell out Wallace's statement, 'Let us all determine to build a just, sustainable and celebrating society' (Preface, *Sacred Earth, Holy Darkness*). In the second half of the verse, refrain-like lines connect the resurrection of Christ with the 'new life' of the believer (see John 3:1-21) and the mortal-immortal existence 'that links us all to Earth.' In verse 2 the coded words 'rainbow' and 'rest from toil' call attention to biblical thought (see Genesis 3:17-19 and 9:8-17), but 'rainbow' also carries the modern association with peace-making (cf. the infamous 1985 sinking by French agents of the Greenpeace vessel, the *Rainbow Warrior*, in Auckland harbour). The importance given to compassion as the moral agent which will release restorative concern for the environment and lead to the greening of the face of Earth* antedates the contemporary interest in this core value (as shown in the Charter for Compassion launched in 2009 by Karen Armstrong). Verse 4 uses symbolic images of the circle of love and the rising of sap in plants and trees as Spring approaches to articulate the ideas of spiritual and planetary renewal.

TARANAKI The tune is named after the district on the east coast of the North Island of New Zealand where Bill Wallace was teaching at the time of writing the hymn text. The melody and its piano accompaniment were written by Christchurch musician **Judith Thornley**. The melodic line is skillfully derived from the shape of the opening 2-bar phrase. On its original publication it was set in E flat major; for *Hope is our Song* that has been changed to D major to bring down the high tessitura in the second half of the tune.

> *The use of the term 'greening' (as in 'make green the face of Earth') as an ecological slogan dates from Ian McHarg's advocacy of human co-operation with nature rather than domination (see his pioneering book, *Design with Nature* (1968), as well as the modern scientific controversy over the effects of global warming).

There's a wideness in God's mercy H135
Metre: 8.7.8.7 D

This hymn is a reconstruction of selected verses from the original text by **William Frederick Faber**, which first appeared in the third collection of his own hymns written for services in the Brompton Oratory, *Oratory Hymns* (1854). It began as an eight stanza poem, but was expanded to 13 stanzas and titled 'Come to Jesus' by the time it appeared in his fourth collection, *Hymns* (1862). The hymn quickly became widely popular and has been frequently reprinted in both Roman Catholic and Protestant hymnals, but editors have made many different selections from the 13 verses and often changed their original order. In a number of hymnbooks the hymn begins with verse 9, 'Souls of men, why will you scatter like a crowd of frightened sheep?' Faber was a distinguished scholar and theologian: among the biblical sources for the text identified by previous editors are Psalm 103:11-12, 86:5, 89:14, John 3:34 and 10:11, Romans 10:1-4, Ephesians 5:8, Colossians 1:18-20 and 1 Peter 2:9.

The version in *Hope is our Song* was made in 1993 by **Colin Gibson,** who dedicated it to the Reverend Paul and Judy Tregurtha as they began their first ministry at the Milton United Church. At a time when the New Zealand Methodist Church was being racked by ferocious arguments over the place of gay and lesbian Christians in its ranks, Gibson was struck by 'the humanity and generosity shown everywhere in the hymn' as well as by the daring idea of 'fresh creations in that upper home of bliss' (original verse 4). His reconstruction makes one verse of Faber's first two, a second stanza from Faber's verses 5 and 11, and a third from Faber's verses 4 and 8. There are a number of verbal alterations: 'God's justice' for 'His justice,' 'human sorrows' for 'earth's sorrows,' 'deeply felt than heaven' for 'more felt than up in Heaven,' and 'There's no place where human failings' for 'There is no place where earth's failings' (new verse 1); 'the limits of our own' for 'false limits of our own,' 'God's strictness' for 'his strictness' and 'Love' for 'He' (new verse 2); 'endless realm of bliss' for 'upper home of bliss,' 'we would trust the living Word' for 'we should take Him at His word,' 'fill with gladness' for 'be all sunshine' and 'joy of Christ our Lord' for 'sweetness of our Lord' (new verse 3).

TREGURTHA The tune was named after the couple to whom it was dedicated at the time of composition (1993) by the reviser. This new setting joins at least 61 other settings of the Faber hymn, and was first printed with the new text in *Hope is our Song* (2009). In that year it was used by the World Council of Churches as part of its commemoration of the United Nations year of Reconciliation.

There's straw in the manger C45
Metre: 6.6.11.6.6.11 D

This carol celebrating the 'madness' of pre-Christmas behaviour in New Zealand was written by **Colin Gibson** in 1995 and dedicated to 'the merry Mornington Methodist choir' [the writer's choir at the Mornington Methodist Church, Dunedin]. It was first published in *Carol our Christmas* (1996), then in the author's American collection *Songs for a Rainbow People* (1998). It has since been incorporated as a 'Christmas Party' sequence in Colin Gibson's cantata *The Spirit Within* (2000).

Gibson says the carol 'contemplates the commercial mayhem and summer holiday-taking which is as much part of a South Pacific Christmas as manger scenes and the Holy Family. The "fellows in flannels" [verse 3] are playing the traditional summer game of cricket, as foolish and mysterious a pastime to all but the players and its followers as is the notion of God sending a helpless baby to redeem a cruel and indifferent world.' Paul's first letter to the Corinthians 1:23-5 provides the theological heart of the carol, but there are also allusions to Luke 2:7-16 and Matthew 2:16-18 (verse 1, 'babies in danger'). The 'fathers caught napping' (verse 1) have eaten too much Christmas dinner and fallen asleep in the hot afternoon; the 'children awake' are unable to sleep for excitement on Christmas Eve. Verse 2 celebrates summer holidays on the beach; the plum pudding for Christmas dinner notes the survival in New Zealand of an English custom, faintly absurd in a southern summer. The 'old aunties gone vocal' refers to the author's elderly relatives bursting into song during Christmas festivities. Verse 3 mixes the Magi (Matthew 2:1-12) with modern Christmas-time long distance phone or computer-assisted calls to overseas relatives, Christmas cards displaying religious paintings of Mary as the Madonna, the omnipresent Father Christmas and decorated Christmas trees both public and domestic with the song of the angels and 'God come to earth' in the person of the infant Jesus (John 1:14).

FOLLY OF LOVE The tune takes its name from the third line of the text; the music was written by the author. If its tessitura is too challenging, a transposition to E major would prove more comfortable. The tune has a 3/4 dance-like rhythm and each section of the melody ends in a stamping or clapping double crochet figure. This carol has been incorporated into Gibson's cantata *The Spirit Within* (2000) in an arrangement for choir and congregation, supported by piano, organ and chamber orchestra; the instruments introduce three other traditional Christmas songs, 'The first Nowell,' 'The Holly and the Ivy' and 'Silent Night.'

These hills where the hawk flies lonely F63
Metre: 8.7.8.4 D

In 1996 the Conference of Churches in Aotearoa New Zealand asked **Colin Gibson** for a hymn on a Conference theme, 'Living Theology in Aotearoa New Zealand.' 'These hills where the hawk flies lonely' was the result: the hymn was premièred at Holy Name Catholic Church, Dunedin, at a Conference Forum held in August, 1996, recorded for Radio New Zealand in 1997, first published in the writer's second American collection, *Songs for a Rainbow People* (1998) and sung on Te Mata peak near Havelock North by members of the New Zealand Choral Federation in March 2000, shortly before its publication in *Faith Forever Singing* (2000). The hymn was later arranged for choir and orchestra and incorporated in Gibson's cantata *The Spirit Within* (2000), recorded in its entirety by the Festival Singers on their CD *Spirited People* (2000).

A visit to Kaikōura and the experience of whale-watching there generated the musical theme and some of the content of this hymn, which takes as its theme the care of New Zealand's natural world and its people as an expression of indigenous theology in action. Verse 1 particularly describes rural areas like Central Otago where lone hawks patrolling the skies are a common sight, and New Zealand's long and relatively empty shoreline, and its spectacularly high mountain ranges. Human care for such an environment is traced in the work of farmers, orchardists – and domestic gardeners creating their own small version of Eden. Verse 2 identifies the country's magnificent rain forests, rivers, and oceans 'where the great whales wander' unthreatened, as 'our care,' matching these physical elements with social ideals such as racial equality, justice for past wrongs (in particular the land grievances of the indigenous population, which are now being settled by arbitration and agreement) and respect for each individual, as 'our prayer.' Verse 3 identifies urban social problems and the claims of the 'homeless and powerless' as the nation's pressing concerns, while celebrating worship and 'serving love' among the 'faiths of our many cultures' as a corporate act of prayer. Verse 4 honours the heritage of the past and the many gifts contributed to New Zealand society by successive waves of immigrants as being now our concern, and prays for a world in which people find 'joy and value' in their lives, religious faith is open-minded and truth-seeking, and there is a general sense of the spiritual 'in all things.'

KAIKŌURA The tune is named after the spectacular east coast South Island mountain range directly fronting the Pacific Ocean, where whalers once slaughtered the magnificent migratory creatures which now quietly accept their peaceful visitors. The music, by the author, attempts to imitate the huge oceanic swells drawing towards the coastline. The melody traces the wave patterns while the bass line surges up and down; underneath, the harmonies move in sequential patterns from A minor through to a triumphal conclusion in C major.

This is our faith H136
Metre: 4.6.7.7.7 D

This powerful hymn text was written by **Marnie Barrell** in 2007 and first published in *Hope is our Song* (2009). It is on the SongSelect website.

The author says, 'I remember being struck by something I heard at a funeral…which likened death to birth into a new dimension of being. I liked the image…and after a while it germinated into this text. I always wanted to say something about heaven which is credible for thoughtful contemporary Christians, but at the same time makes sense in traditional terms and doesn't just sound watered-down and equivocal.' The hymn carries a dedication to the daughter of two friends of the writer, Catherine Mary Peters, who died in a tragic accident shortly after beginning her university studies. 'I wanted to offer [the hymn]…as a token of my admiration for their faith and strength through their unbearable grief.'

The three stanzas of the text are built from out of Paul's famous triad of Faith, Hope and Love (1 Corinthians 13:13), but the development of thought is highly original and independent of the Pauline passage. Verse 1 brings together the beginnings of human life and the Christian hope of life after death in a single, detailed image of birth from the 'safe confinement' of the womb into the 'bright and open day.' The first wailing cry of a human baby, 'protesting, fearful,' is the prelude to a second birth (cf. John 3:3-6) from the 'narrow' coffined confinement of death into the 'burst of glory where God is all and always, / and our tears are wiped away' (Revelation 21:4). Verse 2 pursues the thought that 'all we have become' in this life 'will be found to have a place' (cf. John 14:2). In an echo of the Prodigal Son story (Luke 15:11-32), 'We will come home, / forgiven, understood' to 'the soaring dance of Heaven.'* Line 10, 'to the intimate embrace,' is a further echo of the Prodigal Son story (cf. Luke 15:20, 'his father… ran and embraced him and kissed him'). Verse 3 expresses the idea of the hidden providential love of God (see Job 10:12-13). Most of the images in this verse are scriptural in origin – 1 John 4:19 (God's love), Psalm 63:8 (God's hand), 1 John 4:8 (God's name) – but their expression is the poet's, as is the affirmation that the elements of 'chance and choice' are woven together 'with wise creating purpose.' The stanza concludes with a quotation from the 14th century English anchoress **Julian of Norwich**'s *Revelations of Divine Love*, 'All shall be well, and all manner of thing shall be well.'**

CREDO (Latin=I believe) The tune name is derived from the creedal nature of the text. The setting was written by **Colin Gibson** in 2008. The key chosen is the celebratory key of D major, and the melody moves steadily down sequentially until it reaches a strong and stabilising cadence in bars 4-5, then comes to a quieter close to reflect the tender and ultimately assuring tone of the final lines of the verses. Another setting, BRIGHT DAY, has been written by the American composer Paul Mack Somers.

*Psalm 149:3 seems to be the biblical source of Renaissance and medieval pictorial images of angels dancing around the throne of God, though they may also derive from the figure of Kerubiel (the flames which dance round the throne of God), an angelic spirit mentioned in the Apocryphal *Book of Enoch*. 'Soaring' is a term frequently used in modern dance schools and performances, referring to the high leaps and lifts used in the art form; the word also carries the normal sense of upward flight (towards the heavens). The hymn writer found the image in C. S. Lewis' science fiction novel, *Out of the Silent Planet* (1938).

**For a further discussion of this hymn text see 'This is our faith,' Marnie Barrell, *Word & Worship*, 7.2 (Autumn 2009) 23-6.

This is the day W653
Metre: 11.10.11.10

This hymn, by **Fred Kaan,** was written for his congregation at the Pilgrim Church, Plymouth, England, and first published in his printed collection of such hymns, *Pilgrim Praise* (revised edition, 1968).

The text, a celebration of the Sabbath, does not claim a calendar match between Sunday and the Christian festivals listed in the text; it rather recalls for the singing congregation the theological significance of each act of worship.

Verse 1 begins with an echo of Psalm 118:24 ('This is the day which the Lord hath made'), then recalls Genesis 1:3-5, together with John 3:16 ('God so loved the world'). Verse 2 addresses the Easter event, using Mark 16, which stresses the astonishment of the women at the tomb. The imagery of love's uprising 'against the rule of hell and death and grief' may have been suggested by Kaan's childhood experience of living in a Dutch resistance family. Verse 3 is informed with the writer's ecumenical spirit as well as by Acts 2:1-11, a theme continued in verse 4. Pentecost is often considered to be the birthday of the Christian Church. Verse 5 returns to the Genesis myth and the seventh day as God's day of rest (Genesis 2:3). 'Lay a good foundation' recalls 1 Timothy 6:19, 'laying up for themselves a good foundation for the future.'

NORTHBROOK The tune was named after the residence of Frank Fletcher, headmaster of the English school Charterhouse where its composer **Reginald Thatcher** was director of music from 1919 to 1928. Fletcher wrote a hymn for the boys at Charterhouse, 'O son of Man, our hero strong and tender,' for which the tune was originally composed, and the text with Thatcher's setting was used there in manuscript copies until its first publication in *The Clarendon Hymn Book* (1936), which was essentially the hymnal used at Charterhouse. The melody is expertly crafted (Thatcher was a fine musician who later became the President of the Royal Academy of Music); the initial 13-note phrase is reworked four times, modulating first to A and then to F sharp major before returning to its celebratory D major home key.

The suggested alternative tune, HIGHWOOD, by **Richard Terry** is one of his finest, used for another Fred Kaan hymn text in *With One Voice*, number 665.

This table is the Lord's F64
Metre: 6.6.8.6

In 1992 **Colin Gibson** and his wife were visiting an old friend, Anne Mai Dudgeon, in the Swedish city of Gothenburg. Their conversation turned to the controversy then raging in the New Zealand Methodist Church over the status of gay congregational members and gay ministers. The wise and tolerant attitude of Anne Mai, herself a Swedish Lutheran, sparked the writing of this communion hymn, which carries a dedication to the Reverend David Bromell and the congregation of his small Dunedin Methodist church, which was and is a model of the loving acceptance and inclusiveness of which the hymn speaks. It was published in the author's first American collection, *Reading the Signature* (1994) before reaching *Faith Forever Singing* (2000).

The hymn begins with the traditional words of open invitation to communion used in the Methodist Church tradition, though it also places the 'ownership' of the communion table with Christ rather than any human agency of control. The last line alludes to the common formula used in the Eucharistic liturgy, 'the gifts of God for the people of God.' The second verse affirms the Christian values which underlie this invitation: see Matthew 11:25-30. The following two verses acknowledge the presence of both those who bring 'a troubled secret world' to the communion table and those who bring to it an experience of joy and gratitude for 'comfort on the way' ('way' carries its usual connotations of 'the Way,' the spiritual life-long journey following the values of Jesus Christ. The final verse affirms the Eucharist as the place of gathering for 'the world,' leaving no one outside the group assembled to share 'love's feast' (cf. the Parable of the Wedding feast (Matthew 22:1-14)).

GOTHENBURG The tune is named after the Swedish city where the author/composer found the inspiration for this hymn. The original key of E flat major has been changed to D major to avoid the original high tessitura of the opening phrase.

This thread I weave F65
Metre: 8.8.8.8

What **Shirley Murray**, its author, calls 'This rather spare text – never conceived as a hymn' was written in 1987, as 'an attempt to refine the idea that every small, positive action is a move toward universal Peace.' The poem first appeared in Shirley Murray's earliest American collection, *In Every Corner Sing* (1992), where it was set to the melody JACOB by American composer **Jane Marshall** – possibly named after the many-coloured coat worn by the biblical character, later famous as the protector of the migrant Hebrew tribes in Egypt. The text then reached *Alleluia Aotearoa* (1993), with a setting by another American composer, **Jim Strathdee**. Set to Strathdee's tune the hymn has also been published in the American hymnals *The Faith We Sing* (United Methodist Church, 2000*) and Sing the Faith: New Hymns for Presbyterians* (2003).

The text consists of lists of constructive activities, not randomly selected, although sometimes their order is determined by the rhyme scheme. The arts are honoured, as are political forms of protest; so too are activities for the 'public good' like building (verse 1), nursing and gardening (verse 2). In a number of instances, symbolic values are suggested, as with lighting fires, leaping fences, mending rifts.

[THREAD] Shirley Murray's words have been set by several composers, including American composer **Jane Marshall** and Canadian musician **Ron Klusmeier** (Klusmeier 19). The setting in *Alleluia Aotearoa*, left unnamed by the composer, **Jim Strathdee**, was later published in his collection *Pieces of our Lives* (1998). The style is American folk, with a typical middle section modulation from major to minor before a return to the original D major key by means of a plagal cadence.

Thou art the peace H137
Metre: 8.8.8.8

The text of this hymn was written by **David Adam**, former Vicar of Holy Island, Lindisfarne, and author of a number of books on Celtic spirituality. It was first published in *The Edge of Glory: Prayers in the Celtic tradition* (London: Triangle/SPCK) 1985, and reprinted in *Landscapes of Light: An Illustrated Anthology of Prayers* (London: SPCK) 2001.

The poem is a revoicing in Celtic style of a number of biblical passages referring to Jesus Christ. The original title, 'Thou art God,' suggests that it was conceived as a modern response to the question posed to Peter by Jesus, 'Who do you say I am?' (Mark 8:29, Matthew 16:15 and Luke 9:20). It is constructed as a patterned set of rhymed answers or declarations. Some of the sayings are interconnected by theme: three of them have to do with light and another three with a house and its door. Some are connected by virtue of their previous use as titles for Jesus such as 'Lord' and 'Saviour.' Verse 1, line 1, draws on Christ's stilling of a storm on the Sea of Galilee (Mark 4:35-41, Matthew 8:23-27); line 3 is a quotation from John 1:4-5. 'The heart's eternal spark' (line 4) means the undying presence of Christ prompting compassion and love. The word 'spark' itself carries connotations of the soul, the Holy Spirit and the lighting of a hearth fire. For verse 2, line 1, see John 10:9 (Christ as the door); lines 2-3 allude to Matthew 25:35, 43. Luke 14:13, 'when you give a feast invite the poor,' is the basis of line 4. Verse 3, line 1, matches Matthew 16:15 with Matthew 28:20 'Lo, I am with you always.' Line 2, 'my love' means 'the one whom I love' and draws on John 21:15-17. John 8:12 and 14:6 are combined in line 3. Luke 2:11 is the probable source of the final line.

BURNSIDE (Scottish=beside a stream or 'burn') This is the name of the gracious Victorian house near Oamaru, North Otago, where **Colin Gibson** was staying when he composed this setting for David Adam's words. The music is dedicated to his hosts, Bruce and Alison Albiston. Set in G major, it deliberately imitates the harmonies and typical vocal style of a Scottish folk song.

Through winter cold H139
Metre: 8.8.8.8

Shirley Murray wrote this hymn on 28 June 2006 (mid-winter in New Zealand). It was first published in 2008 in her American collection *Touch the Earth Lightly*, then in *Hope is our Song* (2009).

The author describes her work as 'a hymn about the warmth and comfort of being befriended, of speaking up for the poor and of giving hope when hope seems buried. Though we do not expect harsh winters where I live, there is always poverty and loneliness in every community. This hymn is also about the wintering of faith, and the need to shed old skins for change to come about.' The writer adds, 'I may have been reacting to a theology which leaves it all to God and God's whims to inflict cold, and then keep us warm in his (sic) love.'

Shirley Murray thinks that the hymn may have been prompted by memories of a Victorian hymn sung at assemblies at the school she attended in Invercargill, Southland Girls' High School. The hymn was Samuel Longfellow's "Tis winter now: the fallen snow,' written in 1864 and sung at Southland Girls' High School to DANBY, an English traditional melody arranged by **Ralph Vaughan Williams** for *The English Hymnal* (1906).

In this text, winter becomes a central metaphor – for spiritual despair (verse 1), for the period of apparent dormancy before change and re-growth (verse 2), for poverty and oppressive social conditions (verse 3) and for the numbness of grief and consequent loss of faith (verse 4). Against it is set spring as a matching metaphor for revival and growth, from the silent sprouting of seeds to full-grown tree,* the recovery of warmth and the melting of the snows. All this is set reassuringly 'Within God's world' and the natural pattern of seasonal change. Compassion expressed in action emerges as a principal value (Karen Armstrong launched her Charter of Compassion in 2008), and despite the prevalence of 'freezing' conditions, the text celebrates survival, change and revival accompanied by the inevitable spring 'melt.'

CHILCOMBE (Anglo-Saxon=cold valley) The tune name is that of a Christchurch street, itself named after a small English hamlet near Bridport, Sussex. The name carries a play on the etymological meaning, suggesting 'chilly' conditions. The Christchurch-based composer, **Barry Brinson**, has created a carol-like setting whose harmonies allow for a symbolic blending of minor and major modes and whose melody twice turns – in bar 5 suddenly and surprisingly – from a minor to a major key. The composer says of his setting, 'This has a major / minor feel – from the cold of Winter, to the new life of Spring.' In *Touch the Earth Lightly*, Murray's text is set to the tune ERIKSSON, by the American composer **Amanda Husberg**, and there is a further setting by Canadian composer **Ron Klusmeier** (Klusmeier 42).

*As well as using such plant, winter and spring imagery, Shirley Murray draws on the Bible – the Parable of the Mustard Tree (Matthew 13:31-32, Mark 4:30-32 and Luke 13:18-19) is alluded to in verse 2 – and (also in verse 2) refers to the biological phenomenon of snakes shedding their skins in spring to allow for their bodily growth. The phrase 'silent seeds of spring' may have been prompted by the title of Rachel Carson's influential book on environmental damage caused by pesticides, *Silent Spring* (1962); 'shed old concepts' picks up a common thematic image in Murray's writing, the metaphor of not putting new wine into old wineskins, found in all three synoptic gospels, Matthew 9:17, Mark 2:22 and Luke 5:39.

To compassion and to justice F66
Metre: 7.5.9.5.9.5

One of a set of original short texts created in 1999 by **John Murray**, leader of the editorial board preparing *Faith Forever Singing* (2000).

The text is a profession of commitment to compassionate action and the redress of past and present wrongs, to care for the natural environment and to the expression of divine love and intention. There are echoes here of the 1894 hymn 'God is working his purpose out' by **Arthur Campbell Ainger** (W652), and the positioning of compassion as a key value for social action interestingly antedates the emergence in 2008 of Karen Armstrong's Charter for Compassion.

[TO COMPASSION] This vigorous two-part setting of Murray's text was composed by **Colin Gibson** in 1999.

To God the process H140
Metre: 8.6.8.6 D and glorias

An ecstatic hymn of praise by **Bill Wallace**, marked by opening and closing *glorias*, this hymn was written in 2005 and first published in the author's second American collection, *The Mystery Telling II* (2008), then in *Hope is our Song* (2009). It is also used as the finale of his *Sacred Energy: Mass of the Universe* (2005).

The text is constructed as a litany of praise containing both traditional and original ascriptions. The term 'process' indicates that God is conceived of as ever-moving, fully implicated in the evolving universe – 'God in everything' – the originator and embodiment of its 'sacred energy.'* Verse 1, line 2, 'spring' means 'source' as of a stream. Line 6 refers to the mystical presence of Christ as God in the elements of the Eucharist. Line 8, 'thread' carries the meanings of both 'constituent element' and 'clue to meaning'; cf. Shirley Murray's management of this metaphor in her hymn 'Spirit of love,' A125. Verse 2, line 2, refers to a concept with roots in ancient classical mythology, the Song of the Universe, which meant to Greek thinkers the actual harmonies given out by the movement of the planets. As defined in *Sacred Energy*, this song is 'a song of oneness, a song of unity with all that is… O Universe / You are filled with the Cosmic praise of God.' Line 5 draws on Psalm 149:4, 'The Lord delights in his people.' The final image of a burning heart suggests the presence of the Holy Spirit; it is also a Methodist symbol used here by a Methodist minister and poet. Verse 3 breaks into liturgical language, alluding to Revelation 22:20 and to Psalm 30:12, as well as to the Hebrew greeting *Shalom* ('peace be with you'). But it closes with this writer's original thought and vision of the universe within our lives dancing God's liturgy (cf. *Sacred Energy*: 'Deep within us is our I AM, / our true self, 'that of God' / the WAY of God, the WISDOM and the TRUTH, / the SONG, the DANCE, the JOY.')

EDITH The hymn tune is named after Edith Wallace, the writer's mother. The three volumes of **Bill Wallace's** *Singing the Circle* (1990) were earlier dedicated, among a group of close relatives, 'to the memory of my mother Edith, whose song of love nurtured me.'

The melody was written by Bill Wallace and given a four-part choral setting by Christchurch musician **Graham Hollobon**. The muted *glorias* at the beginning and end of the text and the setting in G minor suggest reverence in the presence of a mystery, and this tone is sustained throughout. Even when the harmony modulates to B flat major (as it does in bar 11) it quickly reverts to the minor mode which characterizes the whole hymn tune. The effect is spacious and majestic, the summarizing chorale at the conclusion of a cantata or mass.

> *In his *Sacred Energy: Mass of the Universe*, Wallace writes, 'Earth is God the presence adorned in nature's flesh, / The shadow of the mystery who is both host and guest.' And later, describing the moment of creation: 'And the energy was in process / the process of the ever-moving / ever-constant One, / the All in All.'

To matou Metua A142
Metre: irregular

This text is a version of the Lord's Prayer in Cook Islands Māori, by an unknown translator, probably dating from the middle of the 19th century, since missionary activity in the Cook Islands only began in 1834, under the auspices of the London Missionary Society, and a Cook Islands London Missionary Society Church was established by 1852.

[TO MATOU METUA] The choral setting for four voices is by **Ta Upu Pere**, a distinguished Pacific Islands leader and choirmaster. It was probably created in the 1950s or 60s, and is laid out for Cook Islands congregational unaccompanied singing, in long, clearly defined phrases, with a strong rhythmical sense in the music.

Toku wairua, oho mai W664
Metre: 7.7.7.7

This is a popular translation into Māori – better understood as a précis rather than a literal translation – of the English hymn, 'Hark my soul, it is the Lord,' written by **William Cowper** in 1761 and later published as one of his Olney hymns (1779). It was often taught by early missionaries, in Africa as well as Australasia. The name of the translator is unknown, as is the date of first publication. This version omits Cowper's third verse, 'Can a woman's tender care / cease towards the child she bear? / Yes, she may forgetful be, / yet will I remember thee.' It also turns an ardent and intensely personal poem into a much simpler form of catechism-like question and answer. The English translation of the Māori text provided in *With One Voice* is a guide to meaning only.

The original hymn was written at Huntingdon, England, at a time when Cowper, in the care of Morley Unwin, a retired Church of England clergyman, and his wife, was recovering from a period of mental instability which had led to three attempts at suicide. Its biblical starting point, acknowledged in the motto to the hymn when it was printed in the Olney hymnal, is John 21:16, 'Lovest thou me?' Cowper's poem, set in the unusual form of a dialogue between Jesus and the believer, acknowledges the saving love of Christ and in answer to Christ's question, 'Say, poor sinner, lov'st thou me?' modestly expresses the singer's love and adoration: 'my love is weak and faint, / Yet I love Thee and adore. / O for grace to love Thee more.'

ST BEES The tune was written by **John Bacchus Dykes**, and was originally composed for a different hymn, William Walsham How's 'Jesus, name of wondrous love.' It first appeared in *The Congregational Hymn and Tune Book* (1862) and only became wedded to 'Hark my soul, it is the Lord' after it was associated with Cowper's hymn in the 1875 revised edition of *Hymns Ancient & Modern*. The tune name recalls the small Cumbrian village of St Bees on the Irish Sea coast of northern England where Dykes often holidayed.

Touch the earth lightly A143
Metre: 5.5.10 D

Shirley Murray wrote this hymn in 1991, and it was first published in her American collection *In Every Corner Sing* (1992), closely followed *by Alleluia Aotearoa* (1993). It has since been published in a number of international hymnbooks.

The theme of the hymn* is concern for planet earth as a sacred creation held in trust for the God who brought it into being (there are several echoes of Genesis 1-2, as in 'God's garden'). The text takes its beginning from an ancient Australian Aboriginal saying (which has elsewhere been applied to an architectural style and even to tourist programmes). 'Surrender' means here 'let go our controlling hold': there is a scriptural resonance behind the words (Matthew 16:25); 'trust' means '[the earth] held in trust to be passed on.' Verse 2, line 2, implies that if food supplies were distributed equally there would be no instances of famine; lines 4-5 referred at the time of writing to the nuclear weapon testing being conducted in the Pacific by France in defiance of New Zealand and other protesters. 'Forestall' (line 6) means here 'prevent before we go too far.' Verse 3, line 2, is an agricultural image relating to the burning-off of old crop residues to stimulate fresh growth. 'God's children' is a phrase from 1 John 3:2. Verse 4, line 7, 'deflect' means change, throw off direction our present destructive course of action. The final line, 'Using us gently,' asks that Christ will not condemn humanity for its destructive use of the earth; the phrase also deliberately recalls the opening of the poem, 'use the earth gently.'** 'Making us one' alludes to Christ's prayer for the unity of his followers with God and himself (John 17:21) but in this context it becomes an all-inclusive phrase, incorporating humanity and the whole life of the natural world with the divine.

TENDERNESS The name of the tune is drawn from the opening of the hymn, suggesting physical sensitivity to any rough handling, but also gentle affection. The music is by **Colin Gibson** and was written in 1991 for this text. It was dedicated to Paul and Phyllis Every, two friends and devoted conservationists. It has a simple A-B-A-B form; the last two notes of its initial five-note motif were intended to suggest a delicate touching of the earth. The change from a B flat major key to minor in verse 2 is intended to underline the dark change in subject, a litany of lament describing the destructive impact of human activity on the earth. It is not difficult for congregational singing, but is ignored in a number of modern reprintings of the hymn. Rhetorically, the recovery of a major tonality in the following verses allows for an enhanced sense of the change and optimism expressed in the words of the hymn. Canadian composer **Ron Klusmeier** has created another setting (Klusmeier 57).

> *For a detailed metrical and verbal analysis see *Praying Twice: The Music and Words of Congregational Song*, by Brian Wren, Louisville: Westminster John Knox Press (2000) 293-5, and *Hymns for Today*, by Brian Wren, Louisville: Westminster John Knox Press (2009) 59-61.

> **Paul Westermeyer, in his *Hymnal Companion to Evangelical Lutheran Worship* (Minneapolis: Augsburg Fortress, 2010, p 602), reports a conversation between his daughter and Shirley Murray, in which Murray's use of the word 'use' was challenged as having connotations of 'abuse' and the suggestion made that it be replaced with 'treat'. The author replied, 'I prefer to keep "use" for the reason that it's hands-on activity where I live and do the garden, and is the positive side of "abuse" in some sense. I realize it can be interpreted otherwise, [but] "treating" the earth has other connotations for me when the agricultural industry uses poisonous pesticides [sic] to "treat" under-nourished soil. Words can be so duplicitous.'

Tree of Eve and Adam's blame (The Sevenfold Passion Mysteries) *H138*
Metre: 7.7.7.5

This Easter hymn was written by **Timothy Hurd** in March 2002 for his congregation at All Saints Anglican church, Dunedin. It was first published in *Hope is our Song* (2009). The writer describes it as 'A meditation on the Cross, with reference to the Old Testament prefiguring of these seven "marks" of the passion.'

As the title suggests, the hymn is written in an ancient devotional tradition in which each of the physical objects associated with the crucifixion of Christ becomes the subject of intense contemplation. Seven was regarded as a 'sacred' number, and 'mysteries' is used in its special sense of a spiritually profound event, here, the suffering of Christ on the cross. However, the insistent theme of the hymn is that Christ suffered 'that we might know life,' a theological reflection taken from 1 John 5:13, 'These things I have written to you who believe in the name of the Son of God, so that you may know that you have eternal life.'

Playing on the centuries-old associations between tree and wooden cross (as in the eighth-century or older Anglo-Saxon poem *The Dream of the Rood*), verse 1 connects the Tree of the Knowledge of Good and Evil (Genesis 2:16-17) with the deciduous trees that brilliantly colour a New Zealand autumn Easter and the cross-tree on which Jesus died (for 'a people's shame': see Matthew 27:15-26). Verse 2 contrasts the nails used to build Noah's ark (Genesis 6) with those used to crucify Christ – note the play on 'anchored' (line 2). Verse 3 connects the spear thrust into Christ's dead body, 'to mark all pain's release' (see John 19:33-34) with the spear hurled at David by King Saul, so breaking the peace between them (1 Samuel 18:10-11), in turn symbolizing all weapons of war. Verse 4 lines 1-2, link the blood shed at the crucifixion with the primal murder of Abel (Genesis 4:8-10), and the association of bloodlines with social status and behaviour (as in 'bad blood'). Verse 5 links the water flowing from Christ's side with 'creation's seas' (Genesis 1:6-7), the Hebrew escape through the Red Sea (Exodus 14) and water used a symbol of purification as in the ritual of baptism. In verse 6, breath, as wind, is linked with the Holy Spirit moving over the waters (Genesis 1:2); as the failure of human breathing with Christ's death, and as speech with Jesus' word of forgiveness from the cross (Luke 23:34). Verse 7 opposes death with life redeemed. 2 Samuel 14:14, 'We all must die, we are like water spilled on the ground which cannot be gathered up,' is the likely source here, since it suggests the image of the 'bitter' waters of death (see Exodus 15:25 and Sumerian and Classical mythologies in which death is represented as the crossing of a river or sea).

Although no hymn tune is suggested, VENANTIUS (*With One Voice*, 397), by Australian composer Richard Connolly, fits this unusual metre.

Twelve disciples Jesus had H141
Metre: 7.7.7.7.7

Written on request for the Reverend Craig Forbes, a Methodist minister, and the children of his Waiwhetū Uniting Church, Wellington, this song was created by **Colin Gibson** in 2002 to teach the children the names of the original twelve male disciples* of Jesus. It was first published in *Hope is our Song* (2009).

Although the song is intended to assist young memories it also carries a theme: the singers are to see themselves as 'the new disciples.' The chosen biblical textual basis is Mark 3:16-19, though Matthew 10:2-4, Luke 6:12-19 and Acts 1:13 were also consulted. James, 'the other one' (verse 2), is also known as James the Younger or James the Less. For John (verse 3) traditionally 'the beloved disciple,' see John 20:2; Philip was the disciple who asked Jesus to show the group the Father (John 14:8-11). For Peter 'named the Rock' (verse 4) see Matthew 18:18; Thaddeus is also known as Judas, brother of James. For 'doubting Thomas,' see John 20:24-29.

WAIWHETŪ (Māori=star-reflecting water) The tune is named after the suburb of Lower Hutt, Wellington, where the church and Sunday school for whom this song was written is located. The music by the author, set in the cheerful key of D major, offers a simple melodic phrase repeated sequentially four times, closed off with a six-note refrain, ending on the tonic note.

> *Confusingly, the biblical lists of Jesus' inner group of male disciples (or apostles) follow no agreed practice in naming them. They may be referred to by their first name only (Philip), their father's name (James, son of Zebedee) or their appellate name (Simon the Zealot, also known as Simon the Canaanite). There are also minor disagreements between the biblical lists: Thaddaeus is named Judas, son of James in Luke's gospel and Lebbaeus in Matthew's gospel. None of these lists mention women, though it is not in dispute that Jesus had a close and loyal following of women.

Two tired people asked for rest (No Room! No Room!) C46
Metre: 7.6.8.6 and refrain

This simple retelling of the Nativity story was written by poet and musician **Joye Taylor** in the 1940s, probably for her own school children (see her biography). An additional verse has been created by **Cecily Sheehy** for its publication in *Carol our Christmas* (1996).

The biblical source for the poem is Luke 2:1-18. The writer gives some tension to the retelling of Luke's narrative by creating two voices: that of the narrator used in the verses, and that of the innkeeper and his wife (effectively including the singers) who reject Joseph and Mary, the 'two tired people,' and consign them to a straw bed in the manger. The original conclusion (verse 4) makes Jesus one of us – 'The baby Jesus sometimes cried / as other babies do, / went laughing to his mother's arms / and lived like me and you' – and other than an implicit criticism of the landlord's action there is no commentary on the story; certainly no theological reading of this very human child. The additional verse by Cecily Sheehy contrasts the storied past with the present plight of children around the world, and replaces the original refrain with a new voice of welcome and concern: 'Let all the children have a home, and not a bed of straw.' The pictured star-field in the third stanza owes something to both the nursery rhyme 'Twinkle, twinkle, little star' and to the ancient practice of representing stars as golden (cf. Shakespeare's *The Merchant of Venice*, V.i.58, 'Look how the floor of heaven is thick inlaid / with patines of bright gold.') Young singers might be reminded of the common award of a golden star for good work.

[NO ROOM] The melody of this hymn was written by the author; it has been arranged by **Jillian Bray** for *Carol our Christmas*. Two different melodic ideas keep the voices of verse and refrain distinct from each other. Each musical idea is effectively repeated, making the song easy to learn.

Ua soona olioli nei *W630*
Metre: 8.6.8.6.and refrain

This is a paraphrase into the Samoan language of a 19th century American gospel hymn by Eliza Edmunds Hewitt (1859-1920, words) and **John Robson Sweney** (1837-99, music), published in *Sing Joyfully* (1887) and therefore dating to the turn of the century. The writer was probably an early missionary to Samoa (for which see 'A'ou manatu ifo nei,' W647).

The original text is considerably changed to fit its new context; the extent of the adaptation may be judged by a comparison with the final verse and refrain of this version (which paraphrases Mark 10:29-30) with Mrs Hewitt's hymn:

> There is gladness in my soul today,
> And hope and praise and love,
> For blessings which he gives me now,
> For joys "laid up" above.
>
> *O there's sunshine, blessed sunshine,*
> *When the peaceful happy moments roll;*
> *When Jesus shows his smiling face,*
> *There is sunshine in the soul.*

The second and third verses show the adapter at his most creative and original; they introduce the biblical image of the tree of life (Revelation 22:2) but in terms of a Pacific island palm tree with Jesus as its stem. The refrain is equally independent, introducing an *alleluia* and the idea of Jesus as Saviour.

SUNSHINE The name of the tune is drawn from the original refrain, 'There is sunshine in my soul.' The music was written by **John Robson Sweney** and first published in *Sing Joyfully* (1887). The score in *With One Voice* is an exact match with its original, which has continued in print in more than 15 hymnals, most of them American, the latest being the *Baptist Hymnal* (2008).

Virgin Birth *facing C52*
Metre: Irregular

This remarkable poem by **Joy Cowley** was first published in *Carol our Christmas* (1996), before it appeared in her 2004 *Psalms Down-Under* collection.

The title suggests a focus on the disputed doctrine of Christ's miraculous conception (that is, one not 'spoiled' by ordinary human fertilisation) and birth by a virgin mother (see Matthew 1:18-25 and Luke 1:26-38), but this text ignores the arguments to appropriate and turn the idea of virgin birth into a metaphor for the spiritual potential within every human being – the term used, 'us' (line 1), excludes nobody.

As the second verse makes plain, the dominant image of the poem is that of a spiritual womb, parallel in every way to a physical womb. In verse 2 the language of the act of conception is close to Luke 2:35, but Matthew 1:23 supplies the title of the 'Emmanuel [that is, 'God with us'] space' (verse 2, line 5). Even more audacious is the poetic idea that 'we…day by day give birth to Christ in the world.' The metaphysical poets of the English 17th century would have applauded such a 'conceit.' But it places full responsibility on the believer to daily bring into the world the spirit of Christ.

This text was set as an anthem for choral singing by **Colin Gibson** in 2005 and recorded in 2007 on their CD *Spirited People* (FPCD2008) by the Festival Singers of Wellington under the direction of Rosemary Russell.

Wake up! (Wake up! You're special!) *A144*
Metre: 9.8.4.4.5.12 and refrain

This cheerful song was written by Dominican Sister **Cecily Sheehy** as one of a series of such songs published in the Catholic magazine *Family Living* between 1980 and 1985. Its first hymnbook appearance was in *Alleluia Aotearoa* (1993).

This text centres on the concept of the preciousness of every member of the family of God (or of any ordinary human family). As such, it has its roots in Christ's teaching and actions towards individuals as recorded in the gospels.

The refrain puts a young person's spin on the respectable (and biblical) adult idea of being called awake: cf. Philip Nicolai's famous 1599 chorale 'Wachet auf' (Wake, oh wake). The image of a garden of friendship, used in the verse, is as ancient as the Greek philosopher Epicurus' teachings about friendship, and there are numerous actual public gardens of friendship in Asian cultures. This poet adds the image of a family tree, to suggest the naturalness of a world in which each person's uniqueness is respected as much as the value of social cohesion is acknowledged.

[WAKE UP] The composer, **Cecily Sheehy**, has created an A-B-A structured melody, which is suitably light-hearted, rhythmically interesting and harmonically varied, with a mid-sectional modulation to A minor. The original unison melody with chord indications has been arranged for voice and piano by **Douglas Mews**.

We are a wheel *A145*
Metre: 9.9.9.8

While she was studying in 1986 at the Institute of Culture and Creation Spirituality at Oakland, California, **Betty Wendelborn**, composer of this text based on a saying by the 12th-century German abbess and mystic **Hildegard of Bingen** (1098-1179), was, she says, 'so captivated by the beautiful songs of the mystics that I immediately set to work to translate them into musical settings.' This round, along with 63 other songs by various authors, was the result, first published in the collection *Sing Green: Songs of the Mystics* (Auckland, 1988).

This text is based on a saying from the second vision in Hildegard's *De Operatione Dei* (*On the Work of God,* or *Concerning The Activity of God*) accompanied by an illumination created by Hildegard herself, in which the universe is pictured as a fiery cosmic wheel (reproduced in *Illuminations of Hildegard of Bingen* by Matthew Fox, Santa Fe, NM: Bear & Co, 2003): 'A wheel was shone to me, wonderful to behold. Divinity is in its omniscience and omnipotence like a wheel, a circle, a whole, that can neither be understood nor divided nor begun nor ended.'

In March 2019 this round was used as part of the ritual celebrating national Women's History Month.

[HILDEGARD'S WHEEL] The melody is by **Betty Wendelborn**; it was composed in 1986 and published in 1988. The musical form of a round perfectly illustrates in musical terms the concept of the circle in the text. The round may be repeated as often as the occasion of its use requires. It can also be danced as it is sung.

We are an Easter people *A146*
Metre: 7.6.8.6 and refrain

This hymn for the Easter season was written by **Bill Wallace** in 1986, 'in reaction to the rather gloomy faces of some members of a congregation on Easter Day 1986.' It was first published in *Darkness and Light,* the second book of the series *Singing the Circle,* privately published by the author at Christchurch, 1990, and made its first appearance in a public hymnbook in *Alleluia Aotearoa* (1993).

The hymn opens with a famous quotation from one of the early Church fathers, St Augustine of Hippo (354-430), 'We are an Easter people, and Alleluia is our song' (*Discourse on the*

Psalms [Psalm 148]). Verse 1 then draws on the imagery of yeast (see Matthew 13:33 and Luke 13:18-21) and vintage wine (alluding to the celebration of the Lord's Supper; see Matthew 26:27-29). The refrain imitates the traditional Christian Easter acclamation, 'Christ has died, Christ is risen, Christ will come again!' which itself is founded on Matthew 28:6.

ALIVE This A major setting of the hymn is by **Alison Carey**, the writer's daughter. The tune name attempts to capture the impulse behind the text, as well as its resurrection theme, while the syncopated rhythms express something of the vitality of the life force itself. In *Darkness and Light*, Bill Wallace prints his own musical setting in C major, named NEW LIFE, his melody harmonized by Suzanne Lennon.

We are children of God H142
Metre: 10.10.10.10

The six verses of this song for children, written by **Cecily Sheehy** in the 1980s for the Catholic *Family Living* magazine, reiterate its theme of working for peace, following the example set by Jesus. It was first given hymnal publication in *Hope is our Song* (2009). The text was originally sub-titled 'Advent Song for Children,' which explains why the children are watching and waiting for 'Jesus who will not delay' – as a baby soon to be born, not the Jesus of the Apocalypse.

There are biblical sources unobtrusively worked into the text. Galatians 3:26, 'In Christ Jesus you are all children of God' (King James version), introduces the song, and Thomas' question to Jesus, 'How can we know the way?' and the answer, 'I am the way' (John 14:4-7), backgrounds the last line of each verse. At a deeper level, the life of Jesus as a model of non-violence, as well as such passages as John 14:27, 'Peace I leave with you, my peace I give to you' form the context for the association of Christ's way with peace-making. A sub-theme of great importance to this writer is introduced in verse 5, 'We will care for our earth' (cf. her collection of creation songs, *Songs for a Blue-Green Planet*). Verse 6, 'we are walking with love,' means 'we are following Christ's way, with love in our hearts.' Some of the vitality of this text comes from the constant use of 'action' words (present participles), like 'watching, waiting, walking': the singers are themselves energetically 'at work.'

CHILDREN OF GOD **Cecily Sheehy's** tune takes its name from the first line of the song. The melody is made easy by its construction from the triad of the tonic chord F, though harmonic shifts to D minor and C major add some musical spice. It becomes a chant by virtue of its many repetitions, to the delight of younger singers. Several of the lines (e.g. verse 2, 'We are joining our hands') suggest that it could become an action song as well.

We are heirs of the Father W673
Metre: Irregular

This scripture-based song was written by **Jimmy and Carol Owens**, an American husband and wife Christian songwriting team.*

The text, based on Romans 8:17, was first published in *Praise the Lord* (1974), followed by *Songs of Praise* (1979). Its arranger for the New Zealand Supplement to *With One Voice* (1982), **Guy Jansen**, has selected and in part rewritten four verses from a longer religious song which included verses beginning 'We are washed, we are sanctified, / We are cleansed by the blood' and 'We are longing for his coming, / We are looking to the skies.' Some textual changes such as 'Let God's people shout and sing' for 'Men and angels, shout and sing!' (verse 4) make the hymn more inclusive than it was in its original form.

INHERITANCE The tune name is derived from the first line of the hymn. The music was written by Jimmy and Carol Owens and appeared in their album *Praise the Lord* (1974). It has been arranged for the New Zealand Supplement to *With One Voice* by **Guy Jansen.**

*For fuller details, see the biographical entry for Jimmy Owens.

We are many, we are one F67
Metre: 7.7.11.7.7.11.7.7.11

In 1998 the incoming President of the Methodist Church of New Zealand, the Reverend Margaret Hamilton, asked **Colin Gibson** for a new hymn as a worship resource for the national Conference to be held in November of that year. Aware that there was likely to be a strenuous debate over the status of gay people in the Church, and that a reactionary breakaway group was threatening to form what it called the New Wesleyan Church, the writer created this hymn, which was sung several times at the Conference before its publication in *Faith Forever Singing* (2000). It is on the LicenSing and SongSelect websites.

The theme of the essential unity of Christians as the body of Christ is announced in the first three lines of the text. Although there are biblical sources in Christ's prayer 'that they may be one' (John 17:21-22) and his own image of the grapevine (John 15:1-5), which is repeatedly referred to in the text of the hymn, the energizing inspiration for the words of the hymn was the scientific fact that every snowflake that has ever fallen has a unique crystalline structure (see verse 3, line 7). Similar images are accumulated to reinforce the theme that 'we are many, we are one.' The author comments that 'I have mostly used metaphors for the community of the church drawn from the natural and creative world because that is how I understand the character of a living church: as an organic whole, in process, vibrant with activity, complete in itself and yet consisting of individuals (a flock of birds in flight, a whole field of flowers, thousands of snowflakes), a unity comprehending great diversity – as indeed this universe in which we exist comprehends diversity and individuality on a scale we can scarcely conceive, yet all of it a coherent whole, a creation held together within itself and by the loving providence of God. Or, to use the metaphor Jesus himself used, as the clustered grapes (our separate and individual existences in Christ) on the vine plant, which is the unifying life-bearing Spirit of God.' Verse 2, line 3, refers to Matthew 25:40-46; verse 3, line 1, to Psalm 96:1. 'Flames within a fire' (verse 3, line 5) references the international Methodist symbol of a flame; 'the colours of a bow' refer to the rainbow as an ancient symbol of reconciliation (see Genesis 9:8-17) and as a modern symbol of peace and inclusiveness.

HAMILTON The tune name honours the Reverend Margaret Hamilton who as incoming President of the New Zealand Methodist Church commissioned this hymn. The setting is the work of the author, **Colin Gibson**. To combat the tensions underlying the original circumstances of its singing, the composer wrote music with a driving rhythm and sequential melodic patterns to carry the singers irresistibly along. The setting is in the voice-easy key of C, shifting up through G and A major before a return to G; the refrain reverses the process, bringing the singers down from A minor through to a full close in C.

We are the singers who celebrate Jesus F68
Metre: 11.10.11.10 and refrain

This text was written in 1995 by **Shirley Murray** in response to a revised commission* from the American Presbyterian Association of Musicians to write a hymn to be used for six worship sessions at their 1996 Conference held at Montreat, North Carolina. The result of that commission, 'We are the singers who celebrate Jesus,' was first published in *Every Day in Your Spirit* (1996), then in *Faith Forever Singing* (2000) and *Faith Makes the Song* (2003).

The writer was required to include in the text six Biblical images – one for each day of the week's worship – earthen vessel, light, ship, kingdom, vine, household. 'I found this a useful discipline!' says Shirley Murray modestly; what she eventually provides is an astonishing range of images, most of them biblical. Verse 1 immediately offers an additional (and unbiblical) image, 'we are the cast of a play to unfold' and includes no fewer than five terms from the theatre ('cast, play, part, action, story'). Verse 2 begins with a near-quotation from 1 Peter 2:9, then draws on

2 Timothy 2:20-1 for the image of earthenware vessels to describe 'ordinary' Christians and Matthew 13:44 for 'the great treasure' hidden (as the writer imagines, in a pot). In 'clay in a mold' there are also hints of Jeremiah 18:6, 'as the clay in the potter's hand, so are you in my hand.' The reference to 'light of more power than sunburst [corona] or star' references Matthew 5:14, 'you are the light of the world.' Verse 4 develops a ship image possibly with the story of Jonah as its background, but the writer imposes her own 'dream of [a] regime of acceptance' on the metaphor: her ship is not a ship of fools but a vessel carrying 'in loving accord' 'whoever will board': an extension of the major theme repeated in the refrain of unconditional acceptance as a mark of the Church, 'one open circle / round Jesus Christ.' Verse 4 begins with the image of Jesus as the vine (John 15:5), but it rapidly modulates into further images: 'each rainbow' here seems to mean 'every colour in the rainbow' (pursuing the theme of unlimited acceptance from the previous stanza; 'household of faith' recalls Galatians 6:10, 'let us do good to all, and especially to the household of faith [i.e. fellow Christians]' and 'pledge of new wine' alludes to Matthew 9:17. This is altogether a virtuoso display that far exceeds the terms of its commission; and this is without mention of the poetic skill displayed in inner rhymes ('part at the heart') and alliterative couplings like 'singers who celebrate,' 'sunburst or star,' 'greening and growing.'

KEY UP The *Faith Forever Singing* tune name refers to the rising sequence of keys in the refrain, with a possible play on 'Gee up,' used to urge on a horse. The music by **Jillian Bray**, set in the jovial key of D major, is happy and relaxed, built out of syncopated scalic runs above a bass that now jog-trots along, now imitates or reflects the lively melody. An alternative setting, in a jazz/blues style, is provided by fellow New Zealand composer **Jenny Mcleod** in *Faith Makes the Song*; yet a third setting, by American composer **Jane Marshall,** in *Every Day in Your Spirit*, uses shifting from minor to major keys and switches time signatures (6/4, 4/4) between verse and refrain. Canadian composer **Ron Klusmeier** offers another lively musical version of the text (Klusmeier 18). This hymn has clearly challenged the musicians' skills, and is capable of several different musical interpretations.

> *The original commission had been to write an Epiphany hymn, the outcome being the Epiphany carol 'Set the Sun Dancing,' C37.

We could not love you more (St Joseph) facing *C8*
Metre: 11.10.11.6

This poem by **Eileen Duggan** was written as an expression of devotion to Joseph, the father of Jesus Christ, celebrated as a saint at least as early as the 8th century.

Although she was a devout Roman Catholic, her own Church regarding her as something of a poet laureate, the writer rejects the popular pious fiction, immortalized in hundreds of religious paintings, that Joseph was an old man incapable of siring a child, a belief which protects the idea of a virginal Mary (see Matthew 1:18-25 and Luke 1:26-38), but leaves unexplained gospel references to Jesus' brothers and sisters (Mark 6:3, Matthew 13:55-56).

Eileen Duggan's St Joseph is re-imagined as a New Zealander, 'a tall, grave, country workman,' in a North Island New Zealand setting. A 'quarter acre' is the classic description of a smallholding of land in the country; 'piecework' is work paid by the job and not by the time taken to complete it; 'Caesar bade you forth' refers to the Roman census which brought the holy family to Bethlehem, mentioned in Luke 2:1-5. Tokomaru (verse 2, line 1) is a small town between Palmerston North and Shannon on the southwestern side of the North Island. The 'hot, dust-deep December road' refers to a New Zealand midsummer Christmas time and the then unsealed dirt roads in the district. The Roman census is mentioned again in verse 2, 'the counting.' Although modern Karori (verse 4) is a suburb on the western edge of Wellington (the poet's home) and therefore well beyond reach from Tokomaru for such a couple, it was in Duggan's day still mostly rural dairy farm land. The image of father Joseph singing lullabies to his son is made delightfully realistic: Joseph's voice is characterised as 'droning,' that is as being dull and monotonous.

We do not hope to ease our minds (We stand with Christ) A147 (i) and (ii)
Metre: 8.8.8.8 D

This Passion-tide hymn was written by **Marnie Barrell** in 1989 and first published in *Alleluia Aotearoa* (1993). Since then it has appeared in *Church Hymnary 4*, (2005) and *Singing the Faith* (2011). As a representative New Zealand hymn it was reprinted (words only) in *A Panorama of Christian Hymnody*, by Erik Routley and Alan A. Richardson (Chicago: GIA, 2005).

The theme of this powerful and uncompromising hymn is a declared willingness to 'stand with Christ' and work to reform the modern circumstances paralleling his life among the poor, his trial and crucifixion. It begins with disclaimers – 'We do not hope,' 'we cannot ask,' 'we will not pray' – and moves through to dedication and commitment – 'disturb us still,' 'give us no peace,' 'we stand with Christ.' The sources were, in the writer's words, 'partly Scriptural story and partly contemporary events. "We do not hope" was an echo of T. S. Eliot's *Ash Wednesday* (1930), a poem I loved at the time, with its implication of choosing not to turn back to familiar ways' ['Because I do not hope to turn again'].

The first verse contrasts the well-off condition of most Christian congregations with the homelessness, hunger and poverty of those around them, a contrast which has dramatically increased since 1989 with an ever-widening gap between rich and poor in New Zealand's previously much more egalitarian society. Verse 2 uses Jesus' trial before Pilate and his walk to Calvary as powerful metaphors to address the contrast between a comfortable national sense of peace and security beside the facts of national and international political, religious and social oppression. The writer says, 'In my mind Christ's trial was connected with the rigged trials and political prisoners publicised by Amnesty International. I remember being shocked at the stories of corrupt government and ruthless suppression of protest, hence "hatred stifles truth / and freedom is betrayed by fear," which to me works equally well as a reference to Jesus' own arrest and contemporary ones.' Verse 3 uses Christ's agonized cry from the cross (Matthew 27:46) and the flight of his disciples to represent modern despair and hopelessness, against which believers with 'hope to share' must stand. Marnie Barrell says, 'the idea of "we stand with Christ all through the night" came from a modern illustration…of the women at the tomb, weighty figures with windblown hair standing immobile with grief, still faithfully present though hope was gone. It connected for me with South American mothers whose adult children had been murdered or imprisoned by the regime, grimly standing in silent vigil, holding up their photos.' She explains that the last four lines in each verse, 'signify that we always do have something to contribute, even if only solidarity.'

GABBATHA (Aramaic=elevated place) The name given in John's Gospel (19:13) to the place where Pilate delivered judgement on Jesus – see verse 2 of the hymn. Archaeologists have discovered an elevated paved platform on the site of the Antonia Fortress in Jerusalem which they believe to be the location of the actual judicial seat from which Pilate delivered his sentence. The setting, named and written by **Ian Render,** was composed in 1990. It is a strong march-like tune set in E minor moving to a positive close in E major.

[BARRELL] This setting by **Colin Gibson**, named after the hymn writer, was composed in 1990. The music, written in imitation of a Passion chorale, begins in the key of G minor to reflect the pain and fear-filled worlds described in each stanza. However, as the verses reach their bold declaration 'we stand with Christ' the melody rises to its highest peak and the harmony modulates to close in B flat major.

There are alternative settings by New Zealand composer **Douglas Mews** (for SATB choir) and Iona's **John Bell** (an arrangement of the Scottish folk tune MARY MORRISON). In *Singing the Faith*, the hymn is set to Vikki Cook's BEFORE THE THRONE OF GOD ABOVE.

We praise our country's saints of old (Pilgrimage Song) H143
Metre: 8.8.8.8.7.8.8.8

This hymn, written by **Bill Bennett** in 2004, arose out a suggestion by the then Bishop of the eastern North Island Anglican diocese of Waiapu, the Right Reverend John Bluck, that a pilgrimage hymn be written to mark the first 150 years of the existence of the diocese. It was first used to accompany pilgrimage walks to various remote places associated with its founding. Copyrighted in 2005, the hymn was then published in *Hope is our Song* (2009), followed by the author's own collection, *Gradual Praise* (2010), where it is titled 'Diocese of Waiapu Pilgrimage Song' and begins with the line 'We praise the Waiapu saints of old.'

Bill Bennett notes that it was on the Waiapu River that the gospel was first preached in this area, 'not by European missionaries, but by local Māori who had come under Christian influence when enslaved and taken away by marauding tribal enemies some years before. When they were able to return, they brought a gospel of hope and peace. Church Missionary Society missionaries first came to the diocese in the 1830s, their mission primarily to the Māori population. They travelled by foot, horse or ship. There were no roads.'

The second verse deliberately includes a number of Māori phrases, suggesting the history of the diocese. *Te rongopai* is the Good News of the Gospel, *te ara hau* is the new way (of Christ); *te aroha* means in this context Christian love, while *te mamae roa* [literally, the long, hard suffering] refers to the hardship and suffering that the early missionaries, both Māori and Pākehā, had to endure (author's note). The reference to sowing the seeds of faith stems from the Parable of the Sower (Matthew 13). The third verse, in the author's words, 'enjoins present-day Christians to also follow the pilgrimage way of faith.' 'We are the bearers of good news' derives from Isaiah 40:9, echoed in Luke 2:10.

WAIAPU (Māori=fresh, sweet water) The tune, written by **Bill Bennett**, is named after the diocese for which it was composed and a principal river which threads the district on the extreme north-east coast. Written for easy singing and memory, the melody is securely rooted in F major, though it has an A-B-A structure which allows for mid-section modulation to D minor and C major. It provides an engaging and memorable syncopated setting of the *alleluias*, and invites simple two-part singing.

We thank you for the gift of life A148
Metre: 8.6.8.6.7.6.8.6

This hymn was written in 1988 by **Marnie Barrell** to the tune ST LOUIS ('O little town of Bethlehem') and first published in *Alleluia Aotearoa* (1993). It was among the first hymns this author wrote, and she says of its creation: 'At the time I was casting around for ideas of what was conspicuously lacking in our hymn repertoire. I wrote it for the general use of our parish, since we seemed to get a lot of baptisms of people without much church background who didn't know our hymn tunes and would make even less sense of the inherited Victorian texts than the parishioners did.' In the event, as well as coming into general use in her own Anglican parish of St Mary the Virgin, the hymn was sung at the baptism of the author's own daughter, Gen, in 1991.

The text is richly worked, drawing on both the earlier hymn and other scriptural passages. The subject of verse 1, 'the gift of life, / the miracle of birth,' naturally arises out of the nativity hymn and its associated tune, 'O little town of Bethlehem,' written in 1868 by American pastor Phillip Brooks: cf. lines

1-2 with 'how silently / The wondrous gift is given.' Romans 6:5-11 stands behind lines 5-8. Verse 2 draws on the Exodus story of liberation from bondage in Egypt and escape through the waters of the Red Sea, here made analogous to the water used in baptism as a symbol of cleansing and renewal: cf. 'Cast out our sin and enter in, / Be born in us today' with 'you cleanse and remake our lives.' Verse 3 addresses the Holy Spirit as the active spirit of Christ alive now: cf. 'Your Holy Spirit comes to live / in all who will receive' with 'Where meek souls will receive him, still / The dear Christ enters in.' But it is Ephesians 4:3-15 which generates most of the language and ideas in this stanza. Verse 4 summarizes the thought of the preceding verses, but Philippians 4:19 ('my God will supply every need of yours') generates lines 1-2, and John 3:5 ('unless one is born of water and the Spirit he cannot enter into the kingdom of God') backs lines 5-8, with the concept of God's family displacing the idea of a divine kingdom.

ST LOUIS The tune, selected by Marnie Barrell 'as being one that everyone vaguely knows, but in New Zealand is not strongly associated with the Christmas carol,' was not named by its composer, **Lewis Henry Redner** (1831-1908), who described it as 'too humble a child to name,' but by William R. Huntingdon, the compiler of an 1884 hymnal titled *Church Porch*, in which it later appeared. LOUIS is a homonym (similar-sounding word) of the composer's first name, Lewis (duly sainted). Redner, who spent 19 years as organist at the Church of the Holy Trinity, Philadelphia, by his own account set to music on Christmas Eve, 1868, 'O Little town of Bethlehem,' a poem by his pastor Phillip Brooks, drawing on Brooks' memories of a recent pilgrimage to Bethlehem. The hymn and its now famous tune was first sung at Holy Trinity the next day.

We thank you for the heritage (Heritage of Faith) H144
Metre: 14.14.14 D

In September 2001 the Mornington Methodist Church, Dunedin, celebrated its 125th Anniversary and commissioned this hymn, written by **Colin Gibson**, its organist and choirmaster, to mark the occasion. It was first published in *Hope is our Song* (2009).

Isaac Watts' 1719 hymn 'O God, our help in ages past,' a paraphrase of a section of Psalm 90, underlies this new text, in which the achievements of the past are recognized, the ethos of the modern community celebrated and the future addressed with confidence. Verse 1, line 3, identifies the characteristic Methodist theological emphasis on God's grace. Verse 2 focuses on the community's long tradition of liberal preaching and thought; line 5 quotes as evidence of its ministers' open exploration of the scriptures from the 1853 hymn 'We limit not the truth of God / To our poor reach of mind' by George Rawson (1807-89), 'The Lord hath yet more light and truth / To break forth from his Word.' Verse 3 honours the 'open table' tradition of Methodism kept at the celebration of the Eucharist at this church, a tradition which on occasion has extended beyond fellow Christian denominations to members of other faiths. 'Outcasts and strangers' alludes both to Isaiah 56 and to Matthew 25:35-36, and refers to those marginalized by society, in particular because of their sexual orientation. Verse 4 addresses the special place given to children in the community: the opening lines draw on scriptural images of Christians as the light of the world (Matthew 5:14) and Christ as the Way (John 14:6). Verse 5 incorporates in its description of the present community its strong tradition of music and creativity in song.

WHITBY STREET The tune is named after the street in the suburb of Mornington, Dunedin, where three generations of the Methodist church building have stood. The setting, by **Colin Gibson**, is in the metre of ST ANNE, the tune attributed to William Croft (1678-1727), now inseparably matched with Watts' words. The melody is built out of the opening 2-bar phrase, and although it briefly modulates to E minor remains securely within a G major tonality. The original score was arranged for congregation, choir, descant, violin, cello, two pianos and organ.

We thank you, God, for this beginning (A Hymn for a New Ministry) H145
Metre: 9.8.9.8 D

This hymn was written by Christchurch hymn-writer **Marnie Barrell** in 2007 to mark the induction of two friends, Lawrence and Elizabeth Kimberley, as leaders for an amalgamating pair of Anglican parishes in Opawa-St Albans, Christchurch. It was first published in *Hope is our Song* (2009). Her 1993 hymn, 'Maker of Mystery' (F47), was written for the same couple on the occasion of an earlier appointment.

Its theme is a prayer for a co-operative, shared ministry, expressed through repeated phrases referring to a single, united community. Here the word 'us' carries its full weight. There are occasional echoes of biblical language, as in 'walking your way' or 'intending that your will be done' (verse 1), as there are traces of Anglican ritual, 'with all your church on earth united / we'll praise you, Holy Trinity' (verse 2), but the text also stresses the acceptance of diversity and shared strength in harmony.

POULTNEY The tune name refers to the happy coincidence that at the time of co-operating on this hymn and its setting the composer, fellow Dunedin hymn-writer Colin Gibson, was acknowledging the installation into a new parish of a Methodist minister, the Reverend David Poultney. Rather than suggest the solemnity of the occasion, the music attempts to convey the joy and celebratory nature of the moment, with a syncopated rising phrase. A shift from D major into G major gives some variety the second half of each, but the final exuberant phrase brings the singers safely back to the original key.

We turn to you, O God of every nation W665
Metre: 11.10.11.10

This notable hymn was written in 1965 by **Fred Kaan** for the congregation at his Plymouth Church, Devon, to use on United Nations Sunday (the Sunday nearest to 24 October). Consequently, it is sometimes titled 'The Family of Nations.' Its first publication was in the author's collection of his hymns, *Pilgrim Praise* (1968). The first denominational hymnbook to include it was *Hymns & Songs* (Methodist, 1969), but the fourth verse was omitted there. The full text was printed in the Anglican hymnbook *More Hymns for Today* (1980) and it appeared in the Methodist hymnal *Hymns & Psalms* (1983) in its original form after permission to make some alterations had been refused. These alterations do appear in the New Zealand Supplement to *With One Voice*: they consist of the replacement of 'love the other man' by 'love our brother man' (verse 2), 'On men who fight' by 'On those who strive' (verse 4) and 'we are born as brothers' by 'we are sisters, brothers' (verse 5). 'Brotherhood' (verse 1) remains unchanged in all texts, perhaps because it is an irreplaceable rhyming word.

Verse 1 draws on Genesis 2:7 and John 1:4-8; verse 2 on the gospel accounts of the Crucifixion as well as on Mark 12:31; verse 3 addresses Proverbs 11:14; verse 4, Romans 12:8 ('he that ruleth, with carefulness' (Rheims-Douay version). 'To give and not to count the cost' (verse 5) is a line taken from a famous prayer by St Ignatius Loyola (1491-1566). The memorable final line of the hymn contrasts the Tower of Babel story of the destruction of the tower and the scattering of the nations (Genesis 11) with the unifying event of Pentecost (Acts 2:5-6, 'Now there were dwelling in Jerusalem Jews, devout men from every nation under heaven. And at this sound the multitude came together'). The recent scientific discovery of the single-cell origin of the human species makes the original triple repetition in this hymn of the word 'brother' even more resonant today.

HIGHWOOD This tune name refers to a wood on the estate of Lord Runciman, **Richard Terry's** uncle, at Doxford, Northumberland. Widely regarded as the composer's finest hymn tune, the broad flowing melody was written at the suggestion of his uncle to accompany Dorothy Gurney's hymn 'O perfect love, all human loves transcending' on the occasion of a wedding. It was first published in the *Methodist Hymn Book* of 1933 as a setting for Frederick Myers' 'Hark, what a sound, and too divine for hearing.' The tune used by Fred Kaan's congregation in 1965 was INTERCESSOR, by **Charles Hubert Hastings Parry** (1848-1918), which has remained a popular alternative to HIGHWOOD for these words.

We wait for you *A149*
Metre: 10.10.10.10

'This is not an Advent hymn – rather a call to action,' writes **Shirley Murray**, who created this hymn in 1991. 'There is a passivity in many Church people who know the Gospel story, yet wait for someone else (God?) to take all the initiative and meet the cost.' The text first appeared in Murray's American collection *In Every Corner Sing* (1992), then in *Alleluia Aotearoa* (1993).

The hymn centres on the two great festivals of the Christian Church, Advent and the Nativity of Jesus, and his Passion and Resurrection. Much of its effect stems from its powerful rhetorical structure. Throughout the text there runs as a structural element the reiterated word, 'wait.' Also in each of the first three verses the final emphasis comes down on the 'cost' in physical pain and suffering implicit in the gospel narratives – the dark side generally avoided or ignored by celebrants and their congregations. There are surprises along the way, too. Verse 2 unexpectedly exchanges the usual sequence of Last Supper and condemnation by Pilate. Verse 4 effectively reverses the pattern established by the previous three verses, as Jesus becomes the one who now waits for action from the singers. 'We' is suddenly replaced by 'you.' That verse changes other patterns, too, as it builds a list of new and old symbols of fresh creative energy: a birthing place, a justice 'tree' (with a play on 'living plant' and 'cross'), a flag, a fragrance, fresh bread, new wine (the familiar communion elements, but also the well-known sensual experience of freshly-baked bread and the new wine not to be put into old wineskins, referred to by Jesus in Matthew 9:17).

EXPECTATION The tune name addresses the theme of the hymn, the comfortable expectations of too comfortable Christians. Written by **Colin Gibson** in 1991, with the intention of unsettling the usual harmonious aural experience of the singers, the melody rises and falls over deliberately unresolved harmonies and the beating of slightly discordant chords, only completely cleared and resolved in the final bar of each verse.

Welcome the child *F69 (i) and (ii)*
Metre: 9.9.9.9

A baptismal hymn, written by **Shirley Murray** in 1993 for use by her own congregation at St Andrew's on the Terrace, Wellington, this text was first published in 1996 in her second American collection, *Every Day in Your Spirit* (1966). It then appeared in *Faith Forever Singing* (2000). The hymn was originally titled 'Baptismal Hymn for a New Daughter' and refers to 'her' throughout; the author explains that 'I feel the importance of removing an historical imbalance by printing the feminine gender as the standard one.' The word 'koru' (verse 3) was replaced by 'fernleaf' in the American publication.

Verse 1 alludes to Jesus' welcome to the children brought to him (Matthew 19:14), 'Let the children come to me, and do not hinder them,' modernizing and making it specific to a baby daughter. Verse 2 expresses hopes for the future life of the child. Verse 3 deals with the unfolding spiritual life of the baby, using an image familiar to New Zealanders, that of the *koru*, a Māori word for the unfolding of a young curled-up fern leaf. Line 1 refers to the rite of baptism; line 2 to participating in the Eucharist. Verse 4 invokes a church community that has a real 'family' character and is not merely Christian in name but in ethos, too. Finally, the baby is invested with hoped-for religious and social values as a bringer of light, joy and grace (undeserved blessing).

HUSH-A-BYE BABY The tune and its name refers to the nursery lullaby rhyme, and the text was deliberately written to fit this tune. Shirley

Murray explains that 'Fewer and fewer families coming to a baptism in our congregations now know the traditional hymn tunes. So I set this "Baptismal Hymn for a New Daughter" to fit the nursery rhyme tune…(hoping the baby would co-operate).' The melody was arranged by the writer's friend, composer and music teacher **Jillian Bray**.

HIGHFIELD A second setting of the hymn, by Christchurch composer **Barry Brinson**, is named after a new residential complex built on the north side of the city, intended to uphold traditional community values, but reflecting new design and energy standards – an architectural parallel to the future envisaged for the new daughter. Although the key differs (D rather than F major) and the harmonies are richer, with modulations to A and G major, the melody is still haunted by the nursery rhyme tune. For *Every Day in Your Spirit* the American composer **Joy Patterson** created yet another setting, naming it KORU from a line in the text, 'draw her like frond of koru uncurled.' Even this setting pays homage to the nursery rhyme with its dotted rhythms.

Whakarongo ki te kupu W648
Metre: 8.7.8.7 D

Now known as a traditional Māori hymn, this text is by an unknown writer and is undated. It appears to be a greatly simplified version of the gospel hymn by **Philip Paul Bliss**, 'Man of sorrows! What a name.' Written in 1875, Bliss's hymn, which became popular among evangelical missionaries, first appeared in the *International Lessons Monthly*, entitled 'Redemption' and was later included in *Gospel Hymns No 2* (1876), compiled jointly by Bliss and Ira D. Sankey. The words were matched to Bliss's own tune GETHSEMANE, which first appeared in England in the first of the long series of Sankey's *Sacred Songs and Solos* (1883). The text draws on Isaiah 53:3-6 and John 19:30.

The Māori version refers to the earthquake following Jesus' death as described by Matthew (27:51-54), but concentrates on Jesus' words from the cross. 'It is finished' (John 19:30).

CONVERSE The tune name is that of its composer, **Charles Converse**, who wrote the music as a setting for Joseph Scriven's famous hymn, 'What a friend we have in Jesus.' It was first published in Ira D. Sankey and Philip Bliss's *Gospel Songs Number 1* (1876). Here is the unusual case of a translation of one popular gospel hymn matched to the equally popular tune of another such gospel hymn. To fit the text to the tune the fifth line and the last two lines of each verse are repeated.

Whakatau mai te Atua A150
Metre: Irregular

This text, which dates from the 1980s, is the work of a group of senior Māori; its origins are unknown. The authors' names are **Mona Riini, Hoki Tawa, Kitty Temara** and **Reg Wharekura**, about whom no information has come to light.

The words are curiously addressed, making a plea to God on behalf of 'these young people bogged down in this world of confusion.' The text begins with a liturgical phrase suggestive of the opening of the Te Deum but it soon focuses on a world ignoring the offer of divine love, with only one way out – looking to the cross for salvation. In fact, it has much of the character of a sermon rather than an act of praise.

[WHAKATAU MAI TE ATUA] The tune published with this text is similarly a cooperative work composed by an unnamed group led by **Mona Riini**. It is a melody of the utmost simplicity, with a range of three notes barely straying from the tonic note D, given an A-B-A-B structure.

What does our God require of us H146
Metre: 8.5.3.6

This hymn was written by Christchurch hymn writer and Methodist minister **Bill Wallace**, and was first published in 1990 in his collection *Sacred Earth, Holy Darkness*, Book 1 of his 3-volume collection of hymns, poems and reflections, *Singing the Circle* (1990). It reached an American audience in *The Mystery Telling:*

Hymns and Songs for the New Millennium by William L. Wallace (New York: Selah, 2012), and appeared in *Hope is our Song* in 2009.

The words on which the pattern of the hymn is formed are taken from Micah 6:8, 'What does the Lord require of you but to do justice, and to love kindness, and to walk humbly with your God.' The writer interprets this as meaning for modern Christians, 'What does our God require of us: Justice, Peace and [respect for] the Integrity of Creation.' Correspondingly, the verses emphasise the demands of God, the planet and its peoples, with a summary in the final verse and an invitation to 'seek justice, find stillness, and treasure Earth with God.' The ambiguity of 'with' (=as well as, on a par with) is intentional.

The writer offers two illuminating glosses on his own text: (1) 'The word humility comes from humus, the earth. To walk humbly is to know one's value as a part of the interwoven fabric of nature created by God'; (2) 'The supreme act of showing mercy to oneself is allowing oneself to move through the darkness of guilt, fear, destruction and loneliness to the deep point of stillness within. This stillness, combined with the pursuit of justice is the source of all peace, and allows us to pursue Justice, Peace, and the Integrity of Creation.'

The phrase 'reverence all of life' (verse 2) alludes to the ethical philosophy developed by the German theologian, musician and medical doctor Albert Schweitzer (1875-1965). Schweitzer's own words, 'ehrfurcht vor dem Lebe,' more accurately translated as 'to be in awe of the mystery of life,' were said to have come to him on a boat trip in French Equatorial Africa (now Gabon), while he was searching for a universal concept of ethics for his own times.

MICAH The tune name refers to the prophet whose words form the basis of the hymn. The melody is by Bill Wallace himself, harmonized by his daughter **Alison Carey**. On the CD accompanying *The Mystery Telling* the hymn is sung by the choir of Napier Anglican Cathedral.

What have we done to you? (Good Friday Lament) F70
Metre: 6.6.6.9.6.9.8

'A lament centered on the Cross, and with echoes of Psalm 130. It has been used as a response in a Good Friday liturgy where Scripture is read between its stanzas and at the conclusion.' This is **Shirley Murray's** description of her Good Friday Lament. Written in 1999, it was first printed in her American publisher's *Supplement 99* (Hope Publishing, 1999), then in *Faith Forever Singing* (2000), followed by her third American collection, *Faith Makes the Song* (2003).

This text, more an impassioned cry for forgiveness than a lament, positions the singers at the foot of the cross and implicates modern Christians together with Jesus' own Jewish race ('your people') in his agonised death. Some details are taken from Luke's passion narrative. Verse 1 draws on Luke 23:44-45, 'there was darkness over the whole land.' Verse 2 refers directly to modern social violence, equated with the physical brutality of the crucifixion. 'Save our destructive fall' means 'save us from our sinful destructiveness.' Verse 3 draws on Psalm 130 verbally ('Out of the depths I cry to you, O Lord'), but the Psalm has suggested the structure of the whole text, based as it is on desperate appeals – not to God, as in the psalm, but to the crucified Jesus. 'Our passionless passing by' alludes to Luke 23:35.

HOANI (Māori=John) The tune name refers to **John Murray**, then chairman of the New Zealand Hymn Book Trust and the driving force behind all its work. The melody, written by **Jillian Bray** in 1999, is set in the 'sorrowful' key of D minor. The varying length of text line is smoothly accommodated by the 3/2, 2/2 interchanges of time signature, and the whole melody is consistently developed from the first 1-bar phrase. A deep sense of sorrow is dramatically conveyed by the dropping bass line and the harmonies above it, replete with discords and emotive appoggiaturas. Another setting, LAMENT, by American composer **Carlton Young**, given an E minor tonality, is provided in the American publications of this hymn.

Whatever is true and honest and good F71
Metre: 10.9.9.8

Drawing on Philippians 4:8,* these words were written by **John Murray** in 1999 for inclusion in *Faith Forever Singing* (2000) as one of a number of short responsive texts of the kind popularised by the Taizé Community (see the Introduction to *Faith Forever Singing*, page vii).

[PHILIPPIANS 4] Scored for piano, this setting, also written in 1999, is by **Cecily Sheehy**. It provides a simple lyric tune, with some echoes of Fanny Crosby's 'Blessed assurance' (1873). The melodic line rises to a peak as the text speaks of 'whatever reveals the face of God,' and there the harmonic landscape, centred on C major, equally effectively shifts upwards to G major, modulating back down through F major to return to a C.

> *Finally brethren, whatever is true, whatever is honourable, whatever is just, whatever is pure, whatever is lovely, whatever is gracious, if there is anything of excellence, if there is anything worthy of praise, think about these things.

Whatever this life has been (A Parting Blessing) F72
Metre: 14.14.14.14.13.13

This hymn of blessing, intended to be sung at a funeral, was written in 1995 by **Shirley Murray**, who says of it, 'First used as a spoken prayer at a funeral in St Andrew's on the Terrace, Wellington [the author's own church], my hope was that the words would gather up those aspects of a life which are known only to God.' The hymn was first published in the author's American collection *Every Day in Your Spirit* (1996), followed by *Faith Forever Singing* (2000). The reading 'where love prepared a room' (line 11) is doubtful: 'where love has prepared' or 'where love prepares a room' better satisfies sense and grammar.

This text is an instance of sheer poetic skill, using language of great simplicity, and perfectly imitating in the repeated clauses beginning with 'Whatever' followed by the imperative 'now let her spirit go,' the act on the part of the mourners of releasing the soul of the deceased into the loving presence of God. The 'inner eye' (line 7) is the visionary 'eye' of the soul, capable of seeing whatever of God's self has been opened to the person's spiritual perception. Line 11 refers to Jesus' assurance in John 14:1-3, 'I go to prepare a place for you'; line 12 echoes Isaiah 32:18, 'My people will abide in a peaceful habitation, in secure dwellings, and in quiet resting places.'

BENISON (a blessing) The setting is by **Colin Gibson**, who wrote it in 1996 and dedicated it to his own mother, Ettie Margaret Gibson (1907-58). The composer has used a repeated chant-like motif suspended over shifting chords which begin indeterminately on an E flat bass (the key signature is 4 flats) then modulate through C major and F minor before reaching at the point of final assurance (lines 9-12) an A flat major resolution which then closes Amen-like on a final F major chord.

When at this table (Hymn of Approach to Communion) H148
Metre: 11.10.11.10

This hymn was written by **Shirley Murray** in 2004, and published in her American collection *Touch the Earth Lightly* (2008), then in *Hope is our Song* (2009). Murray says of the text, 'I am trying to evoke the reasons why we come to the table, and a feeling of more than our personal needs, so that the table opens up to the needs of the world about us.'

The first verse of the text recapitulates the liturgical practices used in many churches, the blessing of the elements, the sharing of the peace of God, and the priestly words used in the distribution of the elements, 'the broken bread, the wine of life for you.' This is the pattern repeating Mark's account of the Last Supper 14:22-24. Verse 2 pursues and personalises the injunction in Matthew 5:23-24 to seek reconciliation before approaching the altar. 'Unbidden grief' may mean 'an unsought cause of grievance' or 'spontaneous sorrow.' Verse 3 addresses indifference to hunger, homelessness and war: there is a biblical sub-text in the Parable of the Sheep and the Goats, Matthew 25:31-46. Verse 4 offers dedication and submission to the will of God of the kind expressed by Jesus in his Gethsemane prayer, Luke 22:42. The final verse echoes Revelation 21:5, 'see I [God] am making all things new.'

AHIMELECH The tune name refers to the barrier-breaking story told in 1 Samuel 21:1-9 of Ahimelech, the 12th High Priest of Israel, who sheltered and fed David and his starving followers on sacramental bread, and was later cruelly executed on the orders of King Saul. It is the subject of a stained-glass window in the Mornington Methodist Church where the composer **Colin Gibson** worships, and seemed to offer a model of the kind of compassionate action commended in the text. The setting, written in 2004, is given the 3/4 rhythm and D minor tonality of an Israeli folk dance. It should not be sung too quickly. In *Touch the Earth Lightly* the setting is by American composer **Jane Marshall**, who gives the words an E flat major tonality in a more measured 4/4 rhythm. Canadian composer **Ron Klusmeier** provides a further setting (Klusmeier 59).

When evenings shorten H147
Metre: 8.8.8.8

This 'Hymn for a Southern Easter,' as she called it, was written by **Shirley Smith** as an entry for a 1998 Hymn Competition associated with the Presbyterian Synod of Otago and Southland's 150th Jubilee. It was eventually sung at her funeral at Knox Church, Dunedin, to the tune KILLIBEG.

The text affirms the meaning of Easter in a southern hemisphere setting. Its imagery reflects her love of gardening and her encyclopedic knowledge of plants. It also reflects her poet's eye for precise natural detail, and her awareness of indigenous religious symbolism ('When grapes turn purple on the vine'). The memorable line 'As rowans fade along the hill' (verse 2) refers to the deciduous European rowan trees planted by many New Zealand settlers; their bright red berries provide welcome autumn fruit for native birds as well as our acclimatised northern hemisphere birds.

CAVELL STREET The tune name refers to the Dunedin street where the writer and her husband were living in 1998. It was composed for this text by **Colin Gibson** at Easter 2009, and was dedicated to Robin Smith and the memory of Shirley Smith.

When human voices cannot sing
A151
Metre: 8.7.8.7

This funeral hymn, written by **Shirley Murray** in 1989, was, in the author's words, 'first sung at the funeral of my longtime friend, the Rev. Warren Schrader, who saw and approved the words before he died.' It was first published in Shirley Murray's American collection *In Every Corner Sing* (Hope Publications, 1992), followed by *Alleluia Aotearoa* (1993).

The structure of this funeral hymn leads the singers gradually from grief and silence to the surrender of the loved one and acceptance of death as our common destiny; in a masterful final phrase, 'to make an end to sorrow.' The hymn begins with an acknowledgement of the paralysing effects of grief; verse 2 recognises the fear and sense of the darkness of death. Murray's phrase, 'the cloud of dark unknowing' (line 2) is a direct allusion to a late 14th century mystical work by an unknown English author, *The Cloud of Unknowing*, which argues that God can only be glimpsed by a surrender of self into the realm of 'unknowingness.' Verse 3 recalls the events of the resurrection, 'the hope of Easter morning' (John 20:1).

For a sympathetic and detailing reading of this text, see ' "When human voices cannot sing": a hymn for a funeral liturgy,' by Bernadette Gasslein and Gordon Johnston, *The Hymn*, 50, 2 (April 1999), 43-4.

ST COLUMBA This familiar tune was the one used on the first occasion of the hymn's use. It is a traditional and anonymous Irish melody preserved in the Petrie Collection (1855) edited by C.V. Stanford in 1902, where it is described as 'An Irish hymn sung on the dedication of a chapel, County of Londonderry.' The tune is named after the Celtic saint who is credited with bringing the Christian faith to Scotland from Ireland by way of Iona. **Jillian Bray** later composed a setting, LAMENT, which was printed with the hymn in *In Every Corner Sing* and is described by Murray as 'opening the text to other possibilities.'

When I was a child *F73*
Metre: 5.5.5.6 D

Paraphrases of scriptural passages are rare in this writer's *oeuvre*, but **Shirley Murray** says of this text, written in 1994, 'The final verses of 1 Corinthians 13 evoke more meanings for me as time passes. They resonate with Bonhoeffer's "world come of age," and the need for us Christians to grow up from a childish dependence on God, to learn to live in the world, not by doctrinal certainties, but by those "things that remain."' The hymn was first published in *Every Day in Your Spirit* (1996), then in *Faith Forever Singing* (2000).

The source passage is 1 Corinthians 13:11-13; 'those "things that remain" are faith, hope and love (verse 13). In letters sent from one of the Nazi prison camps in which he was to die German Lutheran pastor and theologian Dietrich Bonhoeffer (1906-45) developed the idea that the modern world was one which had 'come of age.' Freed from the necessity to believe in divine oversight, humans have entered the 'adulthood of the world,' having achieved autonomy from 'the working hypothesis which is God.'*

HAVELOCK The name records the Havelock Street, Dunedin address of Blanche Jensen, an independently-minded elderly Christian friend of the composer to whom the music, written in 1994, is dedicated by the composer, **Colin Gibson**. The striding bass line suggests the more adult understanding towards which the text aspires; the lighter melodic line, broken into phrases, represents the 'childish' side of the text and is gradually subsumed into the 'adult' chordal world of the middle section of the music. In *Every Day in Your Spirit* the words are set to a charmingly simple melody named JUDIT, by Swedish composer **Per Harling**, who gives it what Shirley Murray calls the 'disarming' sub-title, 'Lullaby for Aging people.'

*Man has learnt to deal with himself in all questions of importance without recourse to the "working hypothesis" called "God." In questions of science, art, and ethics this has become an understood thing at which one now hardly dares to tilt. But for the last hundred years or so it has also become increasingly true of religious questions; it is becoming evident that everything gets along without "God" – and, in fact, just as well as before. As in the scientific field, so in human affairs generally, "God" is being pushed more and more out of life, losing more and more ground.

...Christian apologetics has taken the most varied forms of opposition to this self-assurance. Efforts are made to prove to a world thus come of age that it cannot live without the tutelage of "God." Even though there has been surrender of all secular problems, there still remain the so-called "ultimate questions" – death, guilt – to which only "God" can give an answer, and because of which we need God and the church and the pastor. So we live, in some degree, on these so-called ultimate questions of humanity. But what if one day they no longer exist as such, if they too can be answered "without God"?...The attack by Christian apologetics on the adulthood of the world I consider to be in the first place pointless, in the second place ignoble, and in the third place unchristian (*Letters and Papers from Prison*, 8 June, 1944).

When Joseph and Mary were turned from the inn *C47*
Metre: 11.7.10.8.10.8.10.8

Written in 1984 by author/composer **Colin Gibson** for a Christmas service in which his

Mornington Methodist choir took part, this carol first appeared in his English collection *Singing Love* (1988) before its publication in *Carol our Christmas* (1996).

Framed as a dramatised scene in which the animals gathered round the manger comment on the new arrivals in their stable, Joseph, Mary and her baby, the text illustrates some of the attitudes of contemporary society to immigrant families and the houseless poor. The biblical starting point is Luke 2:7, but Jesus' own remark about his homelessness, 'Foxes have holes and birds of the air have nests; but the Son of Man has nowhere to lay his head' (Luke 9:58), is also a source. The singers, themselves, are implicated in the situation in the final verse: ' "Not now," we say; yes, they will go away / If we shut the indifferent door.'

SHELTER The tune name acknowledges both the needs recorded in the text and the right to adequate housing and shelter enshrined in Article 25 of the United Nations Universal Declaration of Human Rights. This point is made by the ass in verse 3. Modulations beneath the cheerful chatter of the melodic line move the soundscape from F major through several other keys before leaving the tune stranded in C major, which is where the transient visitors at the heart of the text in real life find themselves.

When our lives know sudden shadow *F74 (i) and (ii)*
Metre: 8.7.8.7.8.7

This hymn was written by **Shirley Murray** in 1995 at the suggestion of George Shorney, head of Murray's American publishers, Hope Publishing, to provide an appropriate hymn for an AIDS [Auto Immune Deficiency Syndrome] service or an AIDS awareness workshop. At the time, the pandemic, which had begun to manifest in the United States as early as 1969, was reaching its peak of mortality (with over 41,000 deaths in 1995). The hymn was almost immediately taken up by the World Council of Churches which had held an AIDS consultation at Geneva. The text was first published in the Hope collection *Every Day in Your Spirit* (1996), followed in New Zealand by *Faith Forever Singing* (2000).

There is considerable biblical underpinning of the text. For 'God, our God,' verse 1, line 5, see Psalm 63:1, and for 'the stones rejected,' verse 3: line 5, referring to the further marginalising of members of the gay community under the mistaken belief that AIDS was a specific 'gay'-related disease, see Psalm 118:22, quoted in Acts 4:11. The 'friend, befriending the afflicted' (verse 3, line 1) refers to the many gospel stories of healing by Christ. In verse 4, line 5, there is an allusion to the parable of the Prodigal Son (Luke 15:11-32); the final line of the text alludes to Isaiah 30:18, 'the Lord waits to be gracious to you,' and Isaiah 43:1, 'fear not, for…I have called you by your name'; see also the description of the Good Shepherd, who 'calls his own sheep by name' (John 10:3).

However, for the most part the text directly addresses the effects of AIDS and calls for compassionate care on the part of the whole community for those suffering from the disease. Verse 2 refers to the patchwork quilts made as a way of commemorating victims of AIDS and frequently displayed at memorial services.

LLANGWYM (i) The name of a parish near Usk in the county of Monmouth, Wales. This setting is by **Ian Render** and was written in 1995, when it was decided to include this hymn and members of the editorial committee for *Faith Forever Singing* were asked to put forward tunes.

QUILTINGS (ii) This tune by **Colin Gibson**, also written in 1995, takes its name from the second verse of the text. In *Every Day in Your Spirit* the chosen setting is American composer Carl Daw's FORTUNATUS NEW. All of these settings are cast in minor keys: D for Render's and Daw's settings, G for Colin Gibson's.

When the child is at the centre *H149*
Metre: 8.7.8.7 D

Bill Wallace wrote this Christmas hymn in 2006 and it was first published in *Hope is our*

Song (2009). It has since been incorporated into his *Boundless Life* collection on the Progressive Christianity website.

The springboard for this hymn is a poetic vision of the baby Jesus lying in the Bethlehem manger surrounded by the familiar cast of angels, wise ones, and shepherds. But the text attempts more than a rerun of the familiar Christmas stories and carries its learning lightly (see John 2:1-11 and Luke 13:20-21 for the glancing gospel allusions in the second line of verse 3). Perhaps influenced by the episode in Matthew 18:2 when Jesus places a child before the group of disciples and declares that the greatest in the kingdom of heaven will be whoever becomes like such a little child, the writer advocates for a Christmas repeated in the birth of every child (see verse 1, 'the vision shines…in each daughter and each son'), and an encounter with the divine lived out daily in every perception of God's grace, in every moment of discovering Christ within another's face (verse 2). The third verse invites the singers to a joyous celebration of 'the Child's great feast' (an allusion to the parable of the Great feast, Matthew 22:1-14 and Luke 14: 15-24), endorses 'the Christmas wisdom' and calls for a dancing following of 'the Way that Jesus taught' (see John 14:6).

WANDERING Arranged by Christchurch musician **Barry Brinson**, and based on a traditional Yorkshire carol, 'We've been a-while a-wandering,' also known as the Yorkshire Wassail Song, this melody was first brought to attention by **Ralph Vaughan Williams** as one of his *Eight Traditional English Carols* (1919). The link with Wallace's hymn was probably suggested by its child-focused theme and the imagined performers of the English carol, 'We are not daily beggars / That beg from door to door; / We are your neighbours' children, / For we've been here before.' In Brinson's setting it retains its folk character and modal harmonies; beginning in D minor it closes affirmatively in D major.

When the storm winds blow (In the Shelter of My Hand) A152
Metre: 7.5.7.5 and refrain

The acknowledged source of this hymn is Isaiah 51:16. It was written by **John Weir**, working with the musician **Gerard Crotty** sometime between 1981 and 1984,* and was first published in *Alleluia Aotearoa* (1993).

The text offers the image of a protective God, a vision of nature and humanity proclaiming God's splendour, and a picture of the redeemed as 'pilgrims of the dawn,' joyfully travelling 'home.' The refrain projects the words of God, drawing on Isaiah 51:16 for line 3, but line 1 probably derives from the previous verse in Isaiah ('I am the Lord your God, who stirs up the sea so that its waves roar') and line 2 alludes to the 'dark' time of the crucifixion (Mark 15:33 and the other synoptic gospels). Verse 1 draws its picture of a revived nature from Isaiah 35:1-2, 'The wilderness and the dry land will shall be glad, the desert shall rejoice and blossom.' Verse 2 draws on John 3:17 (though the phrase 'his own' refers to John 1:11) and Matthew 11:5. 'Travel home,' in this context means 'journey on towards their heavenly home'; for the concept of heaven as final home see for instance 1 Kings 8:30 and Philippians 3:20. The source of the final verse is Isaiah 35:10, 'And the ransomed of the Lord shall return, and come to Zion with singing; they shall obtain joy and gladness, and sorrow and sighing shall flee away,' but the striking phrase, 'pilgrims of the dawn,' with its reference to the dawning of Easter Day, is the creation of the modern poet.

[STORM WINDS] This setting is by John Weir's frequent collaborator Gerard Crotty. The music was written between 1981-4, with the score later given a final arrangement by **Guy Jansen**, then a member of the editorial board for *Alleluia Aotearoa*. The melody closely matches the natural speech rhythms of the text, and the harmonies effectively oscillate between major and modal forms of the E tonality, so that a mood of confidence in the protective and energising power of God is sustained throughout, despite the reiterated references to storm and darkness in the refrain.

> *See the entry under the authors' names for fuller information about the circumstances of composition of this and other hymn texts by John Weir and Gerard Crotty.

When we go into the night (Song of the Wilderness) *H150*
Metre: 7.7.11 D

Written for a choir member who was experiencing prolonged difficulties in a marital relationship, this hymn was created by **Colin Gibson** in 1984. It was first published in his English collection *Singing Love* (1988), then in *Hope is our Song* (2009).

Taking the desert wilderness as both a geographic feature and a metaphor for human experiences of spiritual exhaustion and emotional barrenness, the text draws on two desert experiences recorded in the Bible: Exodus 13:18-22, which describes God's leadership of the Hebrews fleeing Egypt in the form of a pillar of cloud by day and a pillar of fire by night, and Christ's 40-day period in the Judean desert (also known as the temptation in the wilderness) as it is described in Matthew 4:1-11. Mark 1:12-13 and Luke 4:1-13. Verse 2 is based on the Exodus passage; verse 3 on the synoptic gospels. Verse 4 invokes the three persons of the Trinity as mighty saviour, companion and peace-bringer. For the Holy Spirit as a 'heavenly dove' see Luke 3:22.

GLENROSS The tune name refers to the Dunedin street address of the person to whom the hymn is dedicated. The music, set for four-part choral singing in F major with a brief modulation to G minor, was written by the author and is cast as a slow-paced march matching both the struggling forward movement through the desert of the biblical characters referred to in the text and the equally difficult spiritual journey of a single human soul.

When we lift our pack and go (Song for Travellers) *A153*
Metre: 7.8.7.7 and refrain

Shirley Murray, who wrote this hymn in 1988, says it was intended 'to fill a gap in the hymnal, and came to me because I find myself often at airports, watching family and friends saying goodbye. It seems an important part of our faith that we will find God wherever we go, in other people.' It was published in her American collection *In Every Corner Sing* (1992), then in *Alleluia Aotearoa* (1993).

Prior to the onset of the Covid pandemic, this hymn took an increasingly significant place in the vocabulary of New Zealand congregations as travel within the country and beyond its borders became more frequent and easier. But the open language of the hymn has also allowed for deeper readings of the words, for not all travel is physical and the term 'journey' has many connotations, religious and secular.

Verse 1 refers to the common badge of a travelling New Zealander (especially a younger person), the bulging backpack as a piece of traveller's luggage. Verse 2 alludes to Matthew 10:29, 'Not one of them [sparrows] will fall to the ground without your Father's will.' For 'The open door of strangers' (verse 4, line 2), in addition to the literal sense, see Revelation 3:20.

LEONARD This setting was written by **Ian Render** in 1989; it commemorated the return of his own parents to England after a visit to their son. The tune name refers to Leonard Render, the composer's father. The music is built around a rapid four note rising scalic passage followed by three minims, giving a sense of swelling emotion. For the first 9 bars carrying the verses describing departure and travel of various kinds, full harmonic resolution is denied, conveying a sense of openness, or, in the words of the text, journeying 'free.' In the refrain affirming the welcoming presence of God, the harmony twice cadences decisively on D major, then on G major, the tonic chord of the whole piece. The text has also been set for unison choir by **Jenny McLeod** as one of her *School Godsongs* (*Godsongs* 9, 2004).

Where are the voices for the earth?
F75
Metre: 8.8.8.8

'This is one of several "green" hymns I have written to contribute to the World Council of Churches programme for Justice, Peace and the Integrity of Creation,' says the writer of this 1999 hymn text, **Shirley Murray.**

The hymn is described by Murray as 'an increasingly persistent cry for respecting the health and protection of the earth.' The passion that underlies her words is indicated as much by their rhetorical formation as by their meaning; this text conveys a message that is intended to move its receivers into action. The personification of the planet (Gaia) as a woman weeping in pain, emphatic repetitions ('sacred, sacred, sacred'), rhetorical questions ('Where are?' is repeated 4 times), alliteration ('wasted, weeping'; 'cherish her beauty, clear her breath'), emotive imagery (cf. 'soil that hugs the seed' with 'tears of poisoned rain,' 'ruined gifts') and stark oppositions ('live that our planet may not die') work insistently on mind and emotion. And deeper still is the theological basis for the hymn, the belief that, as the creation of God, the earth is a sacred being, not to be subjected to the sacrilege of unbridled consumption or careless destruction (cf. 'the world that God decreed' with Genesis 1).

In verse 1 'consuming path' as a metaphor for the unchecked consumption of the world's resources suggests the driving of roads and swathes of clearance though forests, as well as a destructive secular alternative to 'the Way' of Christ; 'tears of poisoned rain' refers to industrial pollution of the atmosphere and the acid-laden rainfall already experienced in Europe, America and elsewhere. Verse 2 derives much of its emotional power from the image of mother and child (line 1) and the symbolic association of white with snowfall (line 2). Verse 3, 'break this code' means 'contravene these laws of nature.' Verse 4, 'cry,' means both 'weep sorrowfully' and 'cry out against'; 'her breath' refers to the atmosphere surrounding and protecting the planet and its life forms.

PORTENT here means a sign foretelling the imminence of a calamity. The tune, written and named in 1999 by **Jillian Bray,** seeks to convey an appreciation of the beauty and sacredness of the earth as well as the threat to its survival by providing a simple melody in E flat major 'clouded' by darker chords in the accompaniment (see the final 3 bars). In *Faith Makes the Song*, Swedish composer **Per Harling** sets the text in A minor to suggest a mood of grief for the present condition of the earth. Canadian **Ron Klusmeier** has also set these words (Klusmeier 60), but, in this writer's view, none of these settings, manages to convey the sheer intensity of Shirley Murray's text.

Where is the room? *A154, C48*
Metre: 4.7.7.6

Its author, **Shirley Murray**, explains that this text was written in 1990 for a Christmas card for the national [Presbyterian] Church when her husband, the Very Reverend John Murray, was its Moderator. The first publication was in Shirley Murray's American collection *In Every Corner Sing* (1992), followed by *Alleluia Aotearoa* (1993).

This is one of several question and answer hymns and carols by this author, springing from the gospel accounts of the overcrowded inn at Nazareth (Luke 2:7). Another possible source is the poem by G. K. Chesterton, 'The House of Christmas,' a phrase echoed in verse 1, line 2. The poem concludes, as does the hymn, with a modern home in which the example of God's love shown in the Christmas stable is being lived out: 'To an open house in the evening / Home shall men come.'

Verse 1 reiterates the title question of Jesus' lodging in our time. Verse 2 declares his centrality 'at the heart of living…cradle for hope and peace.' Punning on 'room' (=room in a house, sufficiency of space) verses 3-4 stress the need for inclusiveness ('Room for whoever come') and a continuation of the divine love demonstrated by the nativity of Christ 'to be shared all year.'

This Christmas hymn was associated with the tune CONCORD by Robert J. B. Fleming in the American collection which preceded *Alleluia Aotearoa*, but Shirley Murray was uncomfortable with the choice of setting. 'CONCORD was suggested as a known tune, but I respect its matching with "Let there be Light" too much to appropriate it. Hopefully another tune will appear.'

MICHAELA New Zealand composer **David Dell** provided just such a tune for *Alleluia Aotearoa* (1993) and the words have become firmly associated with this setting among New Zealand congregations. The tune's name, given in *Carol our Christmas*, is a personal dedication. The question and answer format of the text is beautifully matched by the rise and fall of Dell's melody, supported by the gentle modulations through D and G minor and the suspensions in the bass line that suggest questions posed and finally answered in the return to the tonic key of F major. There is another setting by Canadian composer **Ron Klusmeier** (Klusmeier 14).

Where mountains rise to open skies (Hymn for Waitangi Day)
A155
Metre: 8.8.8.8

This magnificent hymn by **Shirley Murray** was written in 1990 to celebrate the 150th anniversary of New Zealand's founding document, the Treaty of Waitangi, signed between Queen Victoria and the Māori people. She says, 'It was originally titled "Hymn for Waitangi Day" in the hope that it would serve as a national hymn for the many state and community commemorations of the Treaty held on February 6 of each year.' She also says, 'I approached the possible themes cautiously, conscious that I was writing not only for a Christian community, but also for citizens of every faith and none.' In this respect it has more than met the writer's expectations, becoming both a general congregational hymn and an official hymn, chosen for Queen Elizabeth's state visit to New Zealand in 1995, and sung at Westminster Abbey in 2003 to commemorate Anzac Day. It was first published in *Alleluia Aotearoa* (1993), then appeared in the author's American collection *Every Day in your Spirit* in 1996.

The author describes the broad theme of the hymn as an attempt to express the bicultural life of Europeans (*pākehā*) and Māori in 'a stunningly beautiful' natural environment. This element of the hymn is partly articulated through the introduction of significant Māori-language terms, such as *aroha* (=warm, all-embracing love) and *mana* (=dignity, prestige, self-respect).

The hymn is also a bidding prayer for the endowment of the spiritual values required to create a true sense of community. 'The first two verses express the wonder of God's creation in the landscape, then concern not only for New Zealanders' stewardship of the environment but also everywhere else for feelings of mutual respect and friendship.' 'Open skies' (verse 1) refers both to the vast skyscapes of this oceanic country and to the concept of freedom from restriction, openness to all. Kauri are the giant, ancient and iconic trees of the North Island. Verse 3 'refers to the bitter Land Wars of the 19th century' as well as the continuing grievances over land issues played out into the 21st century, and expresses 'the hope for a creative way to plan the future.' Verse 4, the last verse prays for God's way of peace, in a committed spirit of covenant [a religious agreement between God and humanity] bringing the whole world into harmony. 'Distil'=clear, purify.

DUNEDIN This noble hymn tune by **Vernon Griffiths** (1894-1985), is named after the southern city where the composer taught at the King Edward Technical College from 1933-1942. It was written about 1935 and used for many years afterwards for unison singing at the College assemblies of a hymn by the American Unitarian pastor Octavius Brooks Frothingham, 'Soldiers of the Cross.' The tune may be regarded as a principal source since, in the author's words, 'For years, I had been nudged by the idea of addressing a tune which was, in its very essence, a New Zealand one.'

Carlton Young, editor of the *Companion to the United Methodist Hymnal* (USA,1993) writes of it, 'Composed in the unison voice style reminiscent of C.H.H. Parry, it is one of the finest of 20th century Long Metre tunes, with stanzas designed to be sung in alternation between choir and congregation.'

It was first published in England in the *New Catholic Hymnal* (1971) – Griffiths was himself a Roman Catholic – and has since been matched with a variety of texts in many international hymnals. It has also figured in collections of original hymn preludes; see, for instance, *Four Preludes on English Hymn Tunes*, by William H. Bates, (Concordia: 2008), where it is included with SINE NOMINE, DOWN AMPNEY and THAXTED.

See further 'Where mountains rise to open skies,' by Shirley Murray, *The Hymn*, Winter 2007, pages 51-3.

Where shall be found (Tree of Peace) H151
Metre: 8.8.8.6

Written in 2005, this peace hymn by **Colin Gibson** was first published in *Hope is our Song* (2009), and later included in the songbook of the International Ecumenical Peace Convocation held at Kingston, Jamaica, in May 2011.

The inspiration behind the central image of a tree of peace is biblical in origin (the Iroquois of North America have a similar symbol), drawing on 1 Kings 4:24-25, '[Solomon] had peace all around him. And Judah and Israel dwelt safely, every man under his vine and under his fig tree,' as well as on the tree of the water of life, 'whose leaves shall be for the healing of the nations' (Revelation 22:2). The modern practice of planting trees symbolising peace also contributed, though the transferred image of Jesus as 'that young and greening tree / growing for you and me' (verse 3) is original.

In verse 1, 'fire' and 'storm' represent the destructive force of the elements, but also suggest 'fire-storm,' the horrific conflagration caused by nuclear weapons. Verse 2 draws on both the vision of peaceful living in 1 Kings 4:24-5 and Jesus' picture of the mustard tree as 'shelter for everyone' (Matthew 13:31-32). Verse 3 identifies Christ as being – for Christians – the primary apostle of peace (cf. Matthew 5:9). Verse 4 answers the question posed in verse 1 by declaring that 'Here is the place where… / we in our time must plant Christ's peace.'

PEACE TREE The original name given the tune was PAX VOBISCUM (Latin=peace be with you], after the traditional words of greeting still used in worship liturgies among members of the congregation, but the new name refers more directly to the central image of the text. The music is by the author, and its melody features a steady rise from C to D octave, suggesting in musical terms the growth of the tree. The key is A flat, chosen to suggest the numinous world of the 'holy ground' where the tree of peace may be grown.

Where the light of Easter Day H153
Metre: 7.8.4.4.7.6

Both the text and tune of this post-Easter hymn were written in 2007, the one prompted by the other. Hymn writer **Shirley Murray** says, 'This sturdy, uplifting tune seemed to suit a post-Easter mood of "action with intent" to make real the blessings of Easter in a positive spirit and live out the signs of "God's good kingdom."' The hymn and its setting first appeared in Shirley Murray's fourth American collection, *Touch the Earth Lightly* (2009), closely followed by *Hope is our Song* (2009). It is on the SongSelect website.

The patterned stanzas of the hymn ('Where… here') work out the theme that the resurrection of Christ is to be seen in the changes brought about in the world by faith in action. Familiar images in this writer's work – light, yeast, colour, flame – provide an imaginative focus for thought. As usual in Shirley Murray's writing biblical allusions underpin the text.

The key phrase, 'God's good kingdom,' derives from Jesus' first recorded words in Mark 1:15, 'the kingdom of God is at hand; repent and believe in the gospel.' Verse 1 draws on the association of the light of dawn with Easter Day Luke 24:1. The reference to the yeast of love and its association with the kingdom of God derives from the Parable of the Yeast (or leaven) in Matthew 13:33 and Luke 13:21. Verse 3 focuses on the abuse of power in political and social life, constant themes in Shirley Murray's writing. 'Grow in trust' means 'grow up trusting in the affection and good care of parents and other adults.' Verse 4 may draw its image of ripening harvests from Jesus' Kingdom picture in Mark 4:26-22, but there is also a hint of Isaiah 2:4. Verse 5 alludes to the Pentecost event (Acts 2:3), but John 6:13 is also in play, together with Matthew 5:15, 'Neither do men light a candle, and put it under a bushel, but on a candlestick; and it gives light to all that are in the house.'

CRUSADER The tune name responds to the implicit call to action in the text (though without the usual military associations of the word). The music is by **Jillian Bray**, and takes the form of a vigorous march in G major. The melody steadily climbs upwards, miming aspiration as is seen in both the introductory and final flourish. The sequence of harmonic shifts in bars 9-13 serves the same idea of confident faith in Christ, alive and moving ahead, the music taking the singers to a top D, only outdone by the final chord with its top G.

Where the love of God is guiding
F76, HP25
Metre: 8.7.8.6.8.5.8.5

As the author, **Shirley Murray**, explains, her friend and musician **Jillian Bray** sent her a tune [in 1999], 'as a spur to provide something visionary for the new millennium.' Her response, 'Where the love of God is guiding,' was first published in *Faith Forever Singing* (2000), the New Zealand Hymn Book Trust's publication to mark the millennial year, then in *He Came Singing Peace* (2002). It reached American congregations in *Faith Makes the Song* (2003).

In this hymn the writer identifies key values* which will bring about the reformation of human society: compassion – Karen Armstrong's Charter for Compassion was to emerge 10 years later – love for others, a concern for truth and respect for different faith traditions, concern for the environment, and a recovery of the sense of the sacredness of all life.

Although it can hardly be considered a source, the opening line of this text suggests a memory of Mary Bowley Peters' 1847 hymn 'Through the love of God our Saviour, all will be well.' Biblical thought underpins some of these lines: for verse 1 see 2 Corinthians 5:17, 19; for verse 2 see Romans 1:25 and John 14:6, which also underlies the repeated references to 'another way.' There is some remarkable imagery. The crosses raised and lowered in verse 2 refer to the use of the symbol of the cross as a badge of Christian armies (cf. 'Cross and Crescent') as well as the centre of theological disputes which have led to denominational and sectarian conflict. In verse 4 Shirley Murray introduces the wholly contemporary imagery of rockets sent on missions into outer space, with God as the 'flight-path' and the power,' 'lifting all who grasp the vision into understanding.'

RECONCILIATION **Jillian Bray's** tune name identifies one of the elements in this values-packed text. Beginning in E flat major, with a forceful march-like tune that recalls the Welsh traditional melody RHUDDLAN associated with Henry Scott Holland's 1902 visionary text, 'Judge eternal, throned in splendour,' modulations steadily raise the singers up to a climax reaching top E flat, so allowing for a powerful octave descent to the tonic note.

*The thought behind this text is usefully exposed in a paragraph from her husband John Murray's introduction to *He Came Singing Peace:*

'We live in a violent world...the violence of war and fighting, the abuse of people, especially women and children, the arrogance of the rich and powerful, the destructiveness of hunger and poverty, of injustice and indifference, the desecration of earth, sea and air... What songs shall we sing to overcome violence?'

Where the road runs out W672, A156
Metre:10.9.9.7 and refrain

This text and its setting were created in 1976 by **Colin Gibson,** in response to a request for a hymn about 'facing the future,' to suit the theme selected that year for the national Conference of the Methodist Church of Aotearoa/New Zealand. After its appearance as a Conference broadsheet and in the supplementary hymn collection of the Mornington Methodist Church (see below), it was published in the New Zealand Supplement to *With One Voice* (1982) and the author's English collection *Singing Love* (1988), before reaching *Alleluia Aotearoa* (1993).

The dominant image of the lyric is that of a journey into the unknown, a version of the Way. The known way, the road with its defined course and road signs, is left behind and the singers voyage out onto the unknown and uncharted oceanic waters of the future.

Each verse addresses a different member of the Trinity: the God of Abraham (see Genesis 12:10); the dolphin Christ (an image derived both from the Orphic soul-journey on the back of a dolphin and from the many dolphin legends that haunt our coastlines – Tuhirangi, who guided Kupe the legendary Māori explorer who first reached New Zealand, Opo, Moko and Pelorus Jack among them); and finally the Holy Spirit, the Comforter and Helper (John 14:16), imaged as 'the spirit bird hovering overhead,' in the composer's mind the giant Northern Royal Albatross – sacred to Māori – which circles the planet and uniquely nests on Taiaroa Head at the tip of the Otago Peninsula, Dunedin, the only colony of these birds in the world which nest on the mainland. The refrain honours God as the alpha and omega* beginning and end (see Revelation 1:8), and 'our hope for heaven and earth' (see Psalm 62:5).

COLUMBUS The name celebrates the Italian explorer Christopher Columbus (1451-1506) who by sailing the uncharted waters of the Atlantic Ocean reached the Americas in 1492. For a time the tune was named COLUMBUS 100 to mark the fact that 1976 was both the year of the Conference theme which led to its composition and the 100th anniversary year of the Mornington Methodist Church, to which the composer belonged. The music, set in G minor in four-part harmony, has a strong march-like character expressing a sense of sturdy determination, and the rise and fall of the melody and the supporting inner and bass voices imitates the movement of a ship cresting ocean waves.

*Alpha (A) and omega (Ω) are the Greek letters beginning and ending the Greek alphabet.

Whispering gently (Blue Sky, Lord of Creation) F77
Metre: 11.10.11.10 and refrain

'The Heretaunga Plains of Hawke's Bay have the largest pip and stone fruit orchard area in Aotearoa New Zealand. Springtime there is a season of dazzling colour, especially the whites and pinks of the apple, pear and plum trees. This song tries to evoke the splendour of that season, and that it is a time when winter is past and all the hopes of spring hold promise for the future' (Bill Bennett). The hymn and its melody was written by **Bill Bennett** shortly before its publication in *Faith Forever Singing* (2000).

'If the northern hemisphere spring which occurs during Lent looks forward to the renewal of hope at Easter, then the southern hemisphere spring is also a reminder of our need for repentance and renewal within our own lives, warmed by the love that God brings to all creation. The Pentateuch stories of creation, of the land flowing with milk and honey, and such Psalms as 147 and 148 all evoke a caring, creating, loving God.'

Verse 1, line 1, 'the mountain' may be a generic term, but the Kaweka Ranges of Hawke's Bay may particularly be remembered here. Line 4, 'kereru,' the native pigeon, described by the writer as 'a large, colourful bird which feeds on the edible berries of the forest and when disturbed flies noisily off.' Refrain, line 3, 'blossom'=bring into blossom or flower: an unusual transitive form of the verb. Verse 2, line 3, 'kowhai,' described by the writer as 'a native tree of the bush, whose yellow blossoms are usually the earliest to be seen in spring. The native bird, the *tui*, is a common gross feeder on its nectar.' Verse 3, line 1, draws on John 3:1-7. Line 3, Bennett remarks that 'A drive through the countryside in spring gives us opportunity to see thousands of newly born lambs and calves.'

[WHISPERING GENTLY] The cheerful, skipping music by the author, set in C major, has been freshly arranged by **Jillian Bray** for *Faith Forever Singing*.

Who are these strangers F78, HP26
Metre: 4.4.8 D and refrain

In 1984, civil war between the Hutu and Tutsi populations of the Republic of Rwanda, Central Africa, led to tragic scenes of thousands of refugees fleeing to the lakeside town of town of Goma, whose overcrowded refugee camps were soon devastated by a cholera epidemic.* Television images of the horrors of war and 'ethnic cleansing' provoked the writing of this hymn by **Colin Gibson** in 1994. The original text is sub-titled 'A communion hymn for a suffering world.' The hymn was first published in *Faith Forever Singing* 2000 and reprinted in *He Came Singing Peace: Songs to Overcome Violence* (2002).

In the hymn the writer imagines a New Zealand congregation taking part in a communion service which is silently invaded by the presence of such refugees. What can be done for such appalling, yet impossibly distant human suffering, asks the hymn, and answers the question with the thought that they can at least be made part of our compassionate prayers in 'this holy place.' 'Grace,' an unmerited act of (divine) love and compassion, becomes a key term in the shifting final lines of the refrain.

Verse 1 associates the violence and the suffering of the refugees with an earlier act of violence, the crucifixion of Christ, memorialized in the Eucharist. Verse 2 includes among the haunters of the communion space those who are responsible for such violence, and alludes to the massacre at Bethlehem: 'A voice was heard in Ramah, wailing and loud lamentation, Rachel weeping for her children...because they are no more' (Matthew 2:16-18). Verses 3 and 4 picture the long lines of refugees, with the unburied dead lying on the roadside, 'passed by a thousand dusty feet.' That such suffering should be acknowledged, 'heard,' is presented as a wordless act of grace, a helpless gesture of compassion – all that is possible for those made aware of such human catastrophes.

GOMA The tune, by **Colin Gibson**, is named after the Congolese town which became in 1994 the centre of this humanitarian crisis, and has figured in even more recent fighting (2013) in the area. The tonality chosen is the 'sorrowful' key of G minor (which happens to be the first letter of the name Goma). Plangent musical effects like a sustained ground bass and chromatic falls in the inner parts are used to express the compassionate mood of the text, until a partial recovery is signaled in the bass line movement upwards towards the tonic note of G.

*The hell fires are burning in Goma. As cholera and starvation spread, the dead cannot be buried because the ground is too hard and inhospitable. The horrors confronting the Hutu refugees are beyond comprehension even to the aid workers on the spot – and the TV cameras zooming in on this haze of human debris can only convey a flicker of the full suffering. But, if the images now flooding the small screen in Europe and the US are enough to galvanise the rich world into providing emergency aid, then at least they achieve what none of the agonised appeals from the United Nations High Commissioner for Refugees have contrived. (*The Guardian* 23 July 1994).

Who are these who ride by starlight
C49
Metre: 8.7.8.7 D

This hymn for Epiphany (so named on the Oremus website) was written by **Marnie Barrell** in 1996 and first published in the same year in *Carol Our Christmas*. It was included in **David Hamilton**'s Christmas cycle, *Angels and Shepherds and Wise Men All* (2012), has been set by American composer Paul Mack Somers (to his tune STARLIGHT RIDE), and is on both the Oremus and SongSelect websites.

Each verse of the text deals with an episode in the Nativity story as related in Chapter 2 of Matthew's gospel, the arrival of the three Magi, Herod and the massacre at Bethlehem and the Flight to Egypt. Each is universalized and brought into relationship with the present singers: 'we will read the signs,' 'we will mourn the murdered children' and 'we will know you when we meet you / by the shadow of your cross.' Verse 1, line 2, 'from the corners of the earth,' draws on the Armenian tradition that the Magi came from Arabia, Persia and India, though there is no evidence concerning either their number or their country of origin – Matthew says simply 'from the rising of the sun' – and many other countries including Russia and China have claimed them. Verse 2 addresses Herod, seen as personifying all those who 'crush what cannot be controlled.' The murdered children are those mourned at Bethlehem following the massacre there (Matthew 2:16-18), but their deaths are associated with more modern examples of violence perpetrated against children (including by implication New Zealand children). Verse 3 links Jesus' childhood experience as 'a homeless exile' (in Egypt – see Matthew 2:13-14) with his 'destined' life of 'rejection, conflict, danger' and eventual crucifixion, presented as a demonstration of God's glory 'shining through despair and loss' (see John 1:4-5).

ESTHER The name given by the composer **Jillian Bray** to her 1996 setting of the text references the biblical heroine Esther (at the time the composer had adopted the practice of naming her tunes after strong women mentioned in the scriptures). But it also honours Esther McKenzie, a family friend who had recently celebrated her 100th birthday, the mother of Jillian's own bridesmaid Judith McKinley, who became a noted biblical scholar and made a specialist study of biblical women. The first half of each verse is set to a tune in D minor, creating an eastern-sounding tonality, with a figure suggesting riding prominent in the accompaniment. For the second half of this long text, there is a shift to a D major modality before the music ends with a return to D minor, responding to the darker images of blood and crucifixion in the final lines of the last two stanzas of the text.

Who is moving through the silence? (Father, I have seen Your Kingdom) A157
Metre: 8.7.8.7

This poetic and visionary text was written by Father **John Weir** sometime between 1981 and 1984,* and was first published in *Alleluia Aotearoa* (1993).

The allusion to Revelation 3:20, in lines 3-4 of verse 1, 'Behold, I stand at the door and knock; If anyone hears my voice and opens the door, I will come in to him,' and the term 'gentle' in line 2 (cf. Charles Wesley's famous 1742 children's hymn, 'gentle Jesus, meek and mild') suggest that the answer to both questions posed in the first and final verses of this hymn is Jesus Christ. However, 'moving through the silence' also suggests an allusion to Genesis 1 and the Spirit of God, and verse 2 confirms such a reading. That verse consists of two biblical paraphrases, one referring to the Holy Spirit (cf. John 14:26), the other to Jesus (cf. John 3:16 and the Parable of the Lost Sheep, Luke 15:3-4). Verses 3 and 4 identify the present existence of the Kingdom of God wherever God is worshipped and in the practice of compassionate love and mercy (cf. Micah 6:8, 'what doth the Lord require of thee, but to do justly, and to love mercy, and to walk humbly with thy God'). Verse 4, 'little towns' hints at the Nativity town of Bethlehem, as well as the smaller towns of New Zealand (cf. the hymn 'O little town of Bethlehem'); 'shadows of the city' may be taken literally as referring to the shadows cast by tall buildings, but it may also suggest 'dark places' where social evils thrive. But such sourcing does not do justice to the highly original strategy of the hymn: its voicing, in enigmatic questioning and confident perception of the Kingdom through an unidentified 'I,' lending a sense of both mystery and prophetic proclamation (cf. 1 John 1:3) to the text.

MOVING THROUGH THE SILENCE The tune name is taken from the first line of the text; the melody was written in 1992 by **Ian Render** and arranged by **Guy Jansen**, both at the time members of the editorial board preparing *Alleluia Aotearoa*. In keeping with the adventurous nature of the text, this is one of their freest musical creations for voice and piano accompaniment, as the changing but natural and unconfusing time signatures and harmonic shifting around a secure D major central tonality show. The melody is flexible in time but logically patterned on the opening phrase throughout through its length; rich chords arise out of a bass line falling, then rising steadily. It has the hallmarks of two confident and accomplished musicians at work, unafraid of departing from conventional hymn melodies and time signatures. The original tune for this text composed by **Gerard Crotty** is now lost.

> *See the entry under the author's name for fuller information about the circumstances of composition of this and other hymn texts by John Weir.

Who is my mother *A158*

Metre: 10.9.10.9

Shirley Murray, who wrote this hymn in 1991, says that it rose out of her experience at the World Council of Churches Assembly [held at Canberra, Australia, in the same year], 'where meeting people of many orientations, including the differently abled, evoked the words of Jesus from Mark 3:31.' The hymn was initially published in her first American collection *In Every Corner Sing* (1992), and *100 Hymns of Hope* (1992), followed by *Alleluia Aotearoa* (1993). It has since figured in several American hymnbooks, including *The Chalice Hymnal* (1995), *Supplement 96, Every Day in Your Spirit* (1996) and *Worship and Rejoice* (2001). As a representative New Zealand hymn it was reprinted (words only) in *A Panorama of Christian Hymnody*, by Erik Routley and Alan A. Richardson (Chicago: GIA, 2005).

The text sets the scene described in Mark 3:33-35*, with Jesus at the centre of a pressing crowd in his own home, then develops it as symbolic of the gathering of a modern multitude of people of faith, the new inclusive family of Jesus Christ. Among them are the 'differently abled,' a term described in at least one dictionary as 'a politically correct 1990s euphemism for "disabled,"' and others stigmatized and segregated by their difference from social norms. They have become 'kindred' with each other and with all people of faith, in the spirit of Christ.

Verse 1, line 4, 'Spirit-blown,' here means 'driven on the winds of the Holy Spirit'; line 5, 'born from the Gospel,' alludes to John 3:1-8 and Jesus' night encounter with Nicodemus, the source for both these lines. Line 6, 'Sit at the table,' suggests a modern gathering at the communion table – a table is not mentioned in Mark. Verse 2 is effectively a plea to 'widen the circle,' that is to include within the Church both those physically disabled ('crutches') and people of problematic sexual orientation ('stigmas'), whose status is even now subject to dissension and fierce debate within the Christian Church. Verse 3 modernizes Galatians 3:28, including those rejected by their own families or considered to be failures because of their 'deviation' (the writer's metaphoric word is 'derailments') from social norms. Verse 4 focuses on the new unity and singleness of purpose of an all-inclusive family of God reaching beyond the blood-ties of a narrowly-defined nuclear family. The writer has in mind Jesus' so-called Great Commission (Matthew 28:16-20).**

BRONWEN (Welsh=white breast) Named after his own mother, this hymn tune was written by **Ian Render** in 1992. Set in a simple F major tonal landscape (though the increasingly urgent sequences in bars 9-12 allow for modulation to B flat major), and given a graceful 3/4 rhythmic movement, the melody is finely crafted to match its text. Two short musical phrases, one rising, one falling, correspond to the two initial questions and are answered by a longer sweeping phrase built from the rising figure of the first bar. The second half of the melody reflects this shape, except that the long sweeping phrase now falls in answer, rather than rises. There are other settings by American composers **Jack Schrader** (KINDRED) and **Jane Marshall** (HELEN), but they lack the sympathetic and expressive qualities of this one.

> *This episode is also recorded in Matthew 12:46-50 and Luke 8:19-21.

> **See further, '"Who is my mother?": Origins and Biblical Sources of a Hymn,' Shirley Erena Murray. *Music in the Air: Song and Spirituality*, Summer 2007, 7-9.

Who is the child that is to be born
C50, A159
Metre: 9.4.10.10.4

This carol was written by **Shirley Murray** in 1990 and first published in her first American collection, *In Every Corner Sing: The Hymns of Shirley Erena Murray* (Carol Stream, Illinois: Hope Publishing, 1992).

Shirley Murray described the carol as one which 'looks through Christmas, into the future as far as ourselves.' In a series of questions and replies the text first describes the paradoxical nature of the child to be born, 'less than a wisp of straw' yet 'brighter than sun' (verse 1). Then, in a set of metaphors drawn from music, dance and pregnancy, it describes the people who will best carry the message of the Christ child into the world of the future: those 'rearranged' by love, those who will 'hold the world in a welcome' (that is, are inclusive in attitude) and those who will bring compassion and peace into being. In verse 3 the line 'limbs that are leased a life into freedom' compresses the idea of dancers (Limbs was the name of a famous New Zealand contemporary dance group at the time) who are allowed (released) to dance freely, and those who are given the right to a new life of freedom (using 'leased' in its legal sense of a life-long lease). In verse 4, 'bearers' puns on the ideas of giving birth and carrying something.

LIAM This carol was set as a unison song by **Colin Gibson** in 1991 using a 3/4 dance rhythm, picking up on the textual reference to dancing. The setting is named after the composer's grandson, Liam Shanahan, who was at the time of writing about to be born to his daughter, Philippa, in England.

Who sweeps the stable? (Another Servant Song) *H154 (i) and (ii)*
Metre: 11.10.11.10

This hymn was written in 2003 by **Shirley Murray** and first published in her American collection, *Touch the Earth Lightly* (2009). Shirley Murray says of it, 'I entitled this Another Servant Song [the reference is to 'Servant Song' by Richard Gillard, A8] when I sent it to a friend, Dr. Austin Lovelace, and he approved the idea when he set it as an anthem. He gave the first stanza to women's voices since, as he said, "They are usually the ones who do it!" (i.e. the dirty work, exemplified in sweeping the stable).'

The author continues: 'There are few hymns I can find which express gratitude to the "hands-on" people who deal with crisis and catastrophe, tidy up the pieces of a situation, do the necessary and menial tasks with a dedicated and caring spirit. This hymn was used for an ecumenical service in St. Joseph's Catholic Church, Wellington, in recognition of !volunteers of all kinds and their service to the community. This included police, fire service people, counsellors, ambulance drivers, Red Cross workers and many more.'

The theological theme of the hymn text (serving love) is drawn from James 2:14-17 and Luke 22:24-47. Verse 1, line 4, references John 13:2-17 ('he poured water into a basin and began to wash the disciples' feet'); verse 4, lines 1-2, allude to the parable of the Good Samaritan (Luke 10:29-37). The tasks of those for whom this hymn was written will be recognized by its singers (for instance, those who 'drive the road when the crisis is there.')

BATH STREET The setting, by **Colin Gibson,** was written in 2003 and was dedicated to the staff of the Dunedin Methodist Mission, a social service organization which at the time of writing was located in Bath Street, Dunedin. Set in D major, but with modulations to B and F minor, it provides a running tune made up of small 'brushing' gestures (the 3-note motif in bar 1 is the first of them).

SERVANT LIFE This setting by **Jane Marshall** was named with reference to the theme of the hymn and was also written in 2003. It was first published in the 2009 American collection of Shirley Murray's hymns referred to above. Set in F major it, too, is constructed from a single motif, appearing in bar 3.

There are further unnamed settings by American composer Carol Schurr and Canadian **Ron Klusmeier** (Klusmeier 62).

Who will carry the cross with me?
F79
Metre: 8.7.8.5

The words and music of this hymn were composed by **Bill Bennett** shortly before 2000 (though Bennett himself dates it to 2003). It was first published in *Faith Forever Singing* (2000), then in the author's compilation *Gradual Praise* (2010).

The hymn is based on the episode reported in Matthew 16:21-28, Mark 8:34-9:1 and Luke 9:22-27 in which Christ declares: 'If any man would come after me, let him deny himself and take up his cross and follow me,' and develops the theme of sacrificial service and obedience to the call of love. Successive verses explain that carrying the cross with Christ involves walking the way of love, responding to his call, sharing the broken bread, showing the fruits of grace (see Galatians 5:22-23), surrendering one's life fully for his sake and living out the resurrection. Verse 2 draws on the call to the first disciples (Matthew 4:18-22 and the other synoptic gospels), verse 3 recalls the Last Supper (Matthew 26:26 and the other synoptic gospels). In the final verse questions are abandoned for the divine promise of resurrection within the believer's life, and the solemnity of the previous verses is replaced by a dance 'for hope restored' (a possible borrowing from Sydney Carter's 'I danced in the morning').

[QUI CRUCIFER] (Latin=who will be a cross-bearer?) Given its serious theme, the music composed by **Bill Bennett** is appropriately set in E minor and the melody is tightly constructed from the initial 2-bar phrase.

Who would walk cheerfully (Song for Quaker Friends) *H129*
Metre: 6.5.6.5.6.6.6.5

Shirley Murray, author of this text, describes it as growing from a visit to the 1999 exhibition of Quaker tapestries travelling around New Zealand which depicted some of the deeply-held precepts of the Friends, and their history. It was written in 2009 and published in that year in the New Zealand Society of Friends Newsletter (with the substitution of 'Quakers' for 'Christians') before reaching *Hope is our Song* (2009).

She says, 'I have always felt close to the Society of Friends because they are peace people. Woven into these tapestries were the stories and principles they treasure, and my song tries to reflect the staunchness of Quaker faith, "walking cheerfully across the world," attending to "the inner light" and immense practical goodness.' Singers familiar with John Bunyan's song 'Who would true valour see,' from *The Pilgrim's Progress* Part 2 (1684), where it is sung by Mr Valiant-for-Truth to Mr Greatheart as the pair approach the Enchanted Ground, will also recognize its formative part in the generation of Murray's text.

'Wise to the rainbow' (verse 1, line 4) suggests the staunch Quaker support for gay and lesbian people (for whom the rainbow is a common symbol of both inclusiveness and 'gayness'), and in general for inclusiveness in society and religion – cf. 'to see all colours blend' (verse 4, line 6). The 'Inner Light' (verse 1, line 7) refers to a central Quaker principle, that implanted in every human soul is an element of God's own spirit and divine energy, known as the 'Inner Light,' or 'the Seed' (cf. verse 3, line 3), the equivalent of 'the true light that enlightens every man [person]' (John 1:9). Verse 2 expands on the Quaker principle of 'walking cheerfully across the world' (cf. verse 4, line 1). 'Freedom's sounding bell' (verse 3, line 5) suggests the iconic symbol of American independence, the Liberty Bell, hung in Philadelphia ('city of brotherly love'), the city founded by the Quaker leader William Penn, as well as to Quaker adherence to the principle of religious freedom. Quakers have a long tradition of visiting and supporting prisoners, recognized in verse 3, line 6. 'Friend' (verse 4, line 7) plays on the usual Quaker salutation, 'friend' (cf. Society of Friends), as well as the common meaning of the word.

MONKS GATE The suggested tune is an English traditional melody collected by **Ralph Vaughan Williams** at Horsham, West Sussex, in 1904 from a Mrs Harriet Verrall of the nearby village of Monks Gate (hence the name). His arrangement was originally associated with Percy Dearmer's imitation in *The English Hymnal* (1906) of John Bunyan's song 'Who would true valour see,' but Bunyan's own words have displaced Dearmer's in most later hymn books.

Will you offer me compassion? (The Mercy Tree) *A160*
Metre: 8.7.8.7

This hymn was written by Father **John Weir** during a creative period between 1981 and 1984, and was first published in *Alleluia Aotearoa* (1993).

The hymn takes the form of a dramatized conversation between 'I' and 'you,' personages left for the singer to define. Behind it lies the Parable of the Talents (Matthew 25:14-30) and the Beatitude 'Blessed are the merciful, for they will be shown mercy' (Matthew 5:7). The theme is the human need for compassion, divine or human.

'The notion of compassion resonates with me,' says John Weir, 'it is a "feeling together with" another… a reminder of our humanity, our condition of being human, being vulnerable. Christ showed that vulnerability when he was crucified on the mercy tree, the cross which is the source of mercy for us and for our world.'

The author also speaks about the source of the major image in the text, the Mercy Tree: 'There are old pictures of the cross like a flowering tree, and from its roots flow the waters of grace and baptism. I knew those pictures and they helped supply the image. The fathers of the Church thought of the cross of Christ as being the tree of life from the centre of the Garden of Eden. I knew that, too. There are other dimensions to the image of the mercy tree. For me, it calls up the marvellous tree of Revelation 22: 2, with its leaves for the healing of the nations. And the ripe fruit could well be the gifts of the Spirit, evoking kindness, friendship and peace.'

MISERICORDIA (Latin=pity, mercy, compassion) The tune is named after the theme of the hymn. The music, quiet and gentle, was written by **Douglas Mews** for these words and is one his most successful collaborations. The setting in F makes the range of the melody comfortable for singers, and the double time signature of 3/2 2/2 allows for a close match with the changing length of poetic line. The shift to B flat major at bar 6, and longer descending phrase lengths from that point onwards create a perfectly judged A-B structure, in keeping with the tone of the words throughout.

See further "Will you offer me Compassion," Shirley Erena Murray, *The Hymn*, 58. 3 (Summer 2007), 46-7.

Wind on the water H155
Metre: 11.8.9.7

This sea hymn was written by **Shirley Murray** in 1999, and first published in her American collection *Faith Makes the Song: New Hymns Written between 1997 and 2002* (Carol Stream, Illinois: Hope Publishing, 2003). It reached New Zealand attention in *Hope is our Song* (2009).

At the time of its writing, Shirley and John Murray were living on the Kāpiti coastline, and regular beach-walking contributed to the formation of the text. Although there is a strong biblical basis to the association of the Holy Spirit with wind (cf. John 3:8, 'The wind blows where it wishes and you hear the sound of it, but do not know where it comes from and where it is going; so is everyone who is born of the Spirit') the development of the metaphor in this hymn owes almost everything to personal observation, from the movement of sand-blown wind to the exceptionally high shore reach of storm waves. Only in verse 3 is there a further biblical allusion, to the remarkable description of the life of sailors in Psalm 107:30, 'They were glad when it grew calm, and he guided them to their desired haven.' But equally remarkable is the choice of the word 'the groundswell of goodness' in verse 4, line 3, which brings the sustained sea imagery of this hymn to a landed conclusion.

SEASTRANDS Literally, sea beaches, using the Irish word for a sandy shore. This setting, by Shirley Murray's close friend **Jillian Bray**, is almost as striking as the text it serves. It brings the unusual line lengths into a visual pattern which replicates the rise and fall of waves, and the underlying harmonic movement, couched in G minor, constructs a huge downwards 'wave' curve which only crashes down onto the tonic note mid-way through, to lose its energy in smaller repetitions of the same pattern, working through F major, E flat major and C minor to allow a return to the unsettled first note A.

Wisdom be our Guide (Ordinary People) H156
Metre: 5.6.6.5 D and refrain

Written in 2007 by **Shirley Murray** and published unusually only in *Hope is our Song* (2009), this hymn text is only loosely related to the Apocryphal book, *The Wisdom of Solomon*, which the author names as her source. The identified lines, verses 22-30, constitute a famous passage describing the nature of Wisdom. Too long for quotation here, its relationship to the Murray text can be illustrated by verse 26, 'For she is the brightness of the everlasting light, the unspotted mirror of the power of God, and the image of his goodness,' which becomes in the hymn, 'Wisdom be our light: lead us and illumine / all that's fully human, / simple, sane and right.'

The motto-refrain of the hymn – *'with God's help, / ordinary people / ... will turn the world around'* – is original, as are the topics canvassed in the verses: war and terrorism (the War in Iraq was being conducted in 2007), human greed and the destruction of the environment ('earth's appalling hunger'). Jesus is claimed as the exemplar of true wisdom, and wisdom is redefined as 'common sense with vision.'

SERENAM The name of the setting by **Colin Gibson** plays on the idea of calmness and peace. A simple four-bar phrase grounded in D minor begins the melody and takes new forms, imitating the lifting of wings in bars 9-10, and the refrain shifts into F major to reflect the optimism of the text.

Wisdom far beyond our knowledge H157
Metre: 8.7.8.7 D

This hymn was written by **Colin Gibson** in 2002 in response to a request from the incoming President of the Methodist Church of Aotearoa New Zealand for a new hymn on his chosen theme for the national Conference that year. It carries a dedication to the President, the Reverend Norman West and his Vice-President, Heather Watts. It was first published in *Will You Come and Follow Me?* (Birmingham, Alabama: Samford University Press, 2005), after it was submitted to a competition organised by Samford University on the theme of 'Vocation, faith and Learning,' where it was awarded second place. Its first New Zealand publication was in *Hope is our Song* (2009).

Although the hymn takes its initial inspiration from the frequent biblical praise of the Wisdom of God, especially in the Old Testament (see, for instance, Proverbs 1:20-33), the text soon focuses on the nature of God as Word and Creator, perceived more from a New Testament than an Old Testament perspective (see John 1:1). The first verse stresses God's gift of free will; humanity is described as 'set free to wander, world on world' yet is 'haunted by the hope of heaven' and 'nurtured by [God's] constant grace.' The second verse stresses the unfailing love of God for all creation; the third verse focuses on the unity of all things in God, and the divine vision of ultimate harmony. In the final verse God is perceived as the ultimate truth behind 'our perplexity,' the 'magnet of our questing mind.' The verb 'haunted' (verse 1) troubled American sensitivities, but it is used here in the good English sense of 'habitually visited by [hope].'

CORONATION ROAD This tune, written by **Colin Gibson** for his own text, took its name from the street in Takapuna, Auckland where The Reverend West was living at the time. The metronome speed indicates a stately dance movement in 6/4 time rather than a joyful jig. As prepared for the 2002 Conference the unison setting was accompanied with a descant for the final verse.

Wise men came journeying (Song for Epiphany) *C51*

Metre: 10.10.10.10

A carol written by **Shirley Erena Murray** in 1992, and published in 1996 both in *Carol our Christmas* and the American publication *Every Day in your Spirit*.

In Shirley Murray's words, 'This song for Epiphany echoes, for me, words quoted by the Reverend Lois Wilson, a former President of the World Council of Churches, "Wise men (sic) are those who cross boundaries."' The first verse recreates the biblical winter journey of the Wise Men carrying their gifts, as recorded in Matthew 2:1-12. But the male reference immediately gives way to more inclusive phrases such as 'Wise ones' (verse 4). In verse 2 the search for the child marked out by a star (Matthew 2:2) is extended to all who follow 'signs where the Christ light has shone' and cross 'the lines' (defined boundary or battle lines, cultural or otherwise). In verse 3, wisdom is defined in terms of openness to change, respect for the 'strange' (the alien or outsider, a constant Murray theme), openness to fresh information ('light'), and concentration on reality and what is morally right. 'Stargazer people' is an unusual coinage, referring to the science of astrology used by the Magi or astronomy used by modern scientists looking out into the star worlds of the universe. The final verse urges the continuing journey of modern 'wise ones' in search of God's peace, linking it with that of the Magi (lines 1-2) and Abraham (Genesis 12:1-3, echoed in Matthew 28:18-20).

WINGATE WAY This setting, written by **Colin Gibson** in 1992, is named after the street in Trumpington, Cambridgeshire, England, where the composer was living at the time. There is an intentional oriental modality to the melody, which moves through G minor to a close in C major, while the bass suggests the lurching progress of camels.

The carol was originally written with the Scottish folk tune 'Bonnie George Campbell' in mind. Shirley Murray writes, 'The strong swinging metre [of the Scottish tune] contributes to the journeying image,' and the carol was published with this tune in her American collection, *Every Day in your Spirit*.

With a hoot and a toot (Psalm 151) *A161*

Metre: 6.6.8 D and refrain

Inspired by the final psalm in the biblical *Book of Psalms*, Psalm 150,* in which the poet exhorts everything that breathes to praise the Lord, employing trumpets, lutes, harps, timbrel and dance, strings and pipe for the purpose, this modern extension of the corpus of Hebrew psalms, was written by **Colin Gibson** in 1986 and first published in his collection *Singing Love* as well as in *New Zealand Praise* (both 1988), before reaching *Alleluia Aotearoa* in 1993.

The text incorporates the biblical instruments named in Psalm 150 but adds a variety of modern orchestral instruments (cello, bassoon, trombone), popular musical instruments (like the paper and comb), together with bands (brass or otherwise), choirs, bells and human vocal sound effects from hooting (with laughter), humming and clapping to cheering and exuberant yells. Altogether, 'a joyful noise' indeed (a phrase used in both Psalm 98 and Psalm 100:1, 'Make a joyful noise unto the Lord'). The tone is intentionally light-hearted, but the theme is that of Psalm 118:24, 'This is the day which the Lord has made; we will rejoice and be glad in it' (cf. the final line of the refrain).

TOOTING The name of the tune, also the work of **Colin Gibson**, refers to line 1, 'With a hoot and a toot.' The melody carrying the verses is simple enough, but the refrain introduces imitations of some of the instruments named, with a rising trumpet call, a double horn passage and a relatively deep open fifth chord imitating the throaty sound of a bassoon. An optional form of the second verse introduces the named flats and sharps into the musical texture but soon recovers its normal equilibrium and speed. The composer's instruction to add sound effects wherever possible has been carried out literally on at least one occasion, when choir director and organist **Roy Tankersley** led a Palmerston North choir and orchestra in a memorable performance. The psalm has been recorded on the *Alleluia Aotearoa* CD issued in 1993.

> *It seems necessary to add that this modern psalm was not inspired by the title of India's hugely popular children's magazine, or by the names of two railway engines in an equally popular British television series for younger viewers.

With grateful hearts our faith professing W654
Metre: 9.8.9.8

This baptismal hymn text was written in 1968 by **Fred Kaan** for a baptism among his congregation at the Pilgrim Church, Plymouth, Devon. It was later altered to allow for its use by denominations that practised infant baptism and to protect tender sensibilities from Kaan's realistic assessment of the possible threats to young children's health and wellbeing. The original first verse reads:

> With grateful hearts our faith professing,
> We ask you, Lord, come to our aid. ('God,' in other versions)
> That we, our common faith professing,
> May keep the vows that we have made.

The third verse read:

> Give to all parents love and patience,
> Each home with Christian graces fill,
> Protect all children in temptations,
> And keep them safe in every ill.

The hymn was first printed in the original edition of *Pilgrim Praise*, published by the Pilgrim Church, then in the New Zealand Supplement to *With One Voice* (1982) and subsequently in Kaan's *Hymn Texts* (1985); still later in *The Only Earth We Know* (1999).

This is no standard baptismal hymn; it rather addresses the parents of the child being baptized, focusing on the relationships between parents and their children and between all adults and children in a church or the wider community. There are few specific biblical allusions, though the Christian graces of love and patience mentioned in the third verse derive from St Paul's classic description of the nature of love (1 Corinthians 13). The phrase in the last line, 'a faith for life,' was derived from the title of a series of epilogues broadcast by Westward Television, Plymouth, in which Kaan had taken part.

SPIRITUS VITAE (Latin=breath of life). The tune name is taken from the hymn text with which it was originally associated, 'O breath of life,' by Bessie Porter Head (1850-1936). SPIRITUS VITAE was written by **Mary Jane Hammond**, and first appeared in *Hymns for the Living Church* (1974). At the Pilgrim Church Fred Kaan's hymn was sung to the ancient tune LES COMMANDEMENTS DE DIEU.

Wounded world *F80*
Metre: 8.7.8.7 D

Shirley Murray, the writer of this 1992 hymn, describes it as 'An overtly political hymn, written for an ecumenical occasion called "Healing the Health System." There was outrage when, in 1992, our government made drastic cuts to health and welfare benefits. This was first sung at St Peter's Anglican Church, Wellington, as a hymn of protest and resolve.'* It was initially published in her American collection *Every Day in Your Spirit* (1996), and went on to reach American Methodist and Presbyterian congregations in *The Faith we Sing* (2000) and *Sing the Faith: New Hymns for Presbyterians* (2003). In 2000 it was published in New Zealand in *Faith Forever Singing*.

The text imaginatively explores the central image of a wounded or diseased body in need of care and cure, standing at times for the general body of society ('wounded world'), at times for the New Zealand public health system and those within it as healers or patients ('wounded systems, bruised and bleeding'). New Zealand is described a nation of pent (pent-up)** frustration at the changes being made. Even the physical buildings which house hospital and social services have become 'corridors of stress.' Compassionate figures, divine and human – 'Jesus of the healing Spirit,' [those nurses and doctors] 'whose loving spirit nurses hope, restores and heals' – are contrasted in their 'kindlier wisdom' with the unnamed powers whose economic policies are rationing out compassion and making 'hard' (with a play on 'difficult' as well as 'unfeeling') decisions.

There is a good deal of impassioned punning: 'in the tending, in the mending' (verse 3) refers both to hospital services and to the work of those reforming state social services; in the same way the final two lines speak of 'wholeness' in both the senses of restoration of physical health and a unified community, while 'care' suggests both care for each other in the medical and social senses of the word, and carefulness – considerate action – on the part of the reformers. The ideal presented is that of Jesus in his role as healer and as the humble servant of others (see John 13:2-15).

JUSTICE VOICE This hymn was published in *Every Day in Your Spirit* with a setting by the American composer Hal Hopson, named HEALING SPIRIT. The New Zealand composer and friend of the writer, **Jillian Bray,** wrote the setting in *Faith Forever Singing* in 1992. The name identifies the social and political protest which is the theme of the hymn. Cast as a determined march but set in the 'sorrowful' mode of D minor, it takes the singers into A and F major before returning to D minor through G minor. There is another setting by Canadian composer **Ron Klusmeier** (Klusmeier 20).

*Colin Gibson's 'May the anger of Christ be mine' (F48) is a response to the same situation.

**In the American publication *Every Day in Your Spirit,* there is a misprint, 'spent' for 'pent.'

Yahweh, breathe the breath of God *H158*
Metre: 9.9.10.9

This hymn was written in 1994 by **Colin Gibson**, following his attendance at a workshop given by Karen Morrison-Hume* (to whom it is dedicated). In the course of the workshop, participants were invited to take part in a breathing exercise using the word 'Yahweh,' and the words of the hymn text were developed from that beginning into a meditation on breath as the life-giving characteristic of God (see Genesis 2:7). Its first publication was in *New Hymns of Hope* (2005) followed by *Hope is our Song* (2009), though it had earlier been used in the Mornington Methodist church community, to which the writer belongs.

The word chanted in the hymn, 'Yahweh,' is one English form (the other is 'Jehovah') of an ancient Hebrew name for God, and is so used in the New Jerusalem Bible.** In Gibson's text the name is associated with the divine attributes of life-force and supreme love. 'Fill me, empty me' suggests the process of human and spiritual breathing (breath of the Spirit), but also the believer's complete acceptance of the will of God. Compare John Wesley's formulation in the 1780 Methodist Covenant Prayer:

> I am no longer my own, but thine.
> Put me to what thou wilt,
> rank me with whom thou wilt.
> Put me to doing, put me to suffering
> Let me be employed for thee
> or laid aside for thee,
> exalted for thee or brought low for thee.
> Let me be full, let me be empty.

Another text which invokes the image of the breath of God is Sister Miriam Winter's 1965 song 'Spirit of God in the clear running water': "Blow, blow, blow till I be / But breath of the Spirit blowing in me."

TE RAHUI (Māori=act of protection) This tune name was chosen to honour the social work of the dedicatee. However, TE MAURI might have been a more appropriate name, using the Māori word for the essential spirit of life. The 3/4 time of the music allows for both a sense of the calm rhythm of breathing and the pulse of God mentioned in the text. The melodic line in its rising and falling also reflects the thought of the text, presenting itself as a slow (rising) intake of breath reaching a peak at bar 16, followed by a gradual (falling) expulsion of breath. The harmony remains grounded in E flat.

*Karen Morrison-Hume was the Director of Anglican Action (previously Anglican Social Services). As a proponent of 'justice through service,' she has championed a wide range of social initiatives, including the creation of Te Ara Hou social services village for women and children in Hamilton, residential support for ex-prisoners returning to ordinary social life and youth mentoring. In 2012 her work was honoured with a Distinguished Alumni Award from the University of Waikato.

**Modern archaeological research has found that before becoming the name of the national god of Israel and Judah Yahweh was probably a name for El, supreme god of the Canaanite peoples.

The Jahwist strand of the Hebrew scriptures, initiated by southern scribes, refers to God as YHWH. The Elohist strand of scripture, the work of a more northern culture, names God as El.

In biblical Hebrew script only the consonants making up a word were written, leading to different pronunciations of the word (YHWH) as Yahweh or Jehovah. It was not until the 6th century BC, among the Jews of the Babylonian Exile, that Yahweh was first worshipped as the creator of the cosmos and the only true god. In early post-biblical Judaism the name came to be regarded as too holy to be pronounced and was eventually replaced by Adonai (Merciful Lord). Jesus is not recorded as having used the name Yahweh (or Jehovah); as an Aramaic speaker he probably used the Semitic word closest to the Muslim Allah (cf. Eloi, 'My God,' in Mark 15:34).

Yes, as the clay *A162*
Metre: Irregular

This is one of the songs created by Dominican Sister **Cecily Sheehy** in a series first published in the Catholic magazine *Family Living* between 1980 and 1985. Its first hymnbook appearance was in *Alleluia Aotearoa* (1993).

It is unusual for a modern hymn to be voiced as if spoken by God or by Christ, as happens in this text written by an inventive poet and musician, but there are plenty of biblical precedents. The refrain quotes Jeremiah 18:6, 'Like the clay in the potter's hand, so are you in my hand.' Verse 1 draws on the words of Jesus in Matthew 10:31 as well as Luke 12:37. Verse 2 quotes God's voice from Isaiah 43:1, 'Fear not, I have redeemed you, I have called you by name, you are mine,' and Paul's voice from Colossians 1:12, 'I thank God the father, who made us worthy.' Isaiah 41:10 is the source for verse 3: 'Have no fear, for I am with you,' followed by a second quotation from Isaiah 43:1, 'you are mine' – though the poet adds, 'and I am yours.' Verse 4 takes up Isaiah 43:4, 'You are precious in my sight,' followed a quotation from John 13:35, '[Your love for one another will prove to the world that] you are my disciples.' And the verse is closed off with an allusion to Psalm 19:14, 'O Lord, my strength and my redeemer.'

[POTTER'S HAND] This text, essentially a pastiche of biblical phrases, is given essential unity and a degree of solemnity by the low-pitched tune, descending stepwise and moving in 3/4 time as if in a sacred dance. The work of the author, **Cecily Sheehy**, it has been arranged for piano by **Jenny Bennett,** who gives it a modal flavour, with the melody carried beneath in sixths and supported by shifting descending harmonies.

You are born in us again C52
Metre: 7.10.14.14.10.10

This text was written in 1995 by visually-challenged poet and musician **Mark Wilson** as a contribution to *Carol our Christmas,* the first book of New Zealand carols published by the New Zealand Hymnbook Trust. It was premièred at St Michael's Anglican Church, Clyde on 30 July 1995. It was first published in *Carol our Christmas* (1996) and was included on the accompanying CD and tape in a performance by the Wellington Youth Choir. It was later published in the Author's *Seeds of Faith Hymnbook* (Queenstown: Rendall Music, 2014) in a musical arrangement by **Timothy Hurd**.

Mark Wilson has described how 'On one particularly wintry July morning, my mind began to focus on Christmas in the midst of a Central Otago summer. For me, there are three striking aspects to summer in Central Otago: first, the warmth of the summer wind, that irresistible caress of the warmth on the face, like a gentle breath. Second, the scent of the summer rain. After a period of prolonged dry weather, the parched ground seems to jump for joy when the first longed-for raindrops descend, bringing out the fragrance of plant life, and bringing out a special scent which happens when water hits concrete. Third, the light of the summer sun. As for light, though I am blind, I can see sunlight, so I know its beauty, and light, after all, is the sign of the hope which the newborn Christ-Child represents... I remain proud of this hymn as I think it manages to be simple and profound at the same time.'

Natural images drawn from the extreme climate of Central Otago (wind, dust, heat, light, icicles) combine with sub-textual references to John 3:3-8 (the rebirth of the believer, and the unknowable passage of the wind), Matthew 5:6 ('Blessed are those who hunger and thirst after righteousness for they shall be filled'), John 16:69 ('We know and believe you are the holy One of God'), Isaiah 9:2 ('Those who walked in darkness have seen a great light') and John 8:12 ('I am the light of the world') There is also the common play on Son of God/sun in verse 3.

DUNSTAN The melody for this carol was written in 1995 by **Mark Wilson** for his own text. His tune name refers to the Dunstan Anglican Parish in Central Otago, where at the time of writing the author's father, Boyd Wilson, who prompted the writing of the carol, was the Vicar. **Shona Murray**, the arranger, says of her work, 'I wanted to feature one of our lovely voices at Tawa College at the time... I think it gave the treatment of the song a personal and intimate reflective nature.' As printed in *Carol Our* Christmas the third verse of the carol is given a descant by **Colin Gibson**. There is also an unpublished two-part setting by **Nigel Eastgate**, written in 1995.

You hold us with a tender parent's hand (Living Creatively) H152
Metre: 10.10.10 D

This hymn text was written in 1994 by **Jocelyn Marshall** for the congregation of St Peter's Cathedral Church, Hamilton, and published in her collection *A Singing Faith* (1996) and in her later *Hymns for All Seasons* (2007), before its inclusion in *Hope is our Song* (2009).

The first verse uses a series of strong verbs ('hold,' 'empower,' 'uplift') to describe God's loving dealing with humanity. The second verse develops this thought by listing 'special moments' of joy or pleasure given by God, whose 'presence in them all we, seeking, find.' The third verse shifts ground to uncover the declared theme of the text, 'released to live creatively,' comparing such transformations to natural and human events – a butterfly's emergence from its chrysalis, the unfolding of a flower-bud and the miner's discovery of 'a seam of gold' within a fractured rock. So the singers are led from a conventional beginning through to an unexpected but still affirmative conclusion. It is a happy accident that this text, with its encouragement to further creativity, concludes the *Hope is our Song* collection.

SONG 1 For the settings of her hymns, Jocelyn Marshall's intentional practice was to revive 'much excellent music that has fallen into disuse because the words that accompany it are no longer acceptable.' For this text she has chosen from the Anglican standard hymnbook, *Hymns Ancient & Modern*, a melody by the great Elizabethan/Jacobean composer **Orlando Gibbons** (1583-1625). It was published in a collection by George Wither titled *Hymnes and Songs for the Church* (1623) where it appears as the first of several such melodies and with no other title than 'Song 1.'

The People

David Adam

David Adam was born in Alnwick, Northumberland, on 18 October 1936. He left school at 15 and worked underground as a coal miner for three years before training for the Anglican priesthood at Kelham Theological College (1954-59). He was ordained in 1959, and after serving parishes in Auckland (England) and West Hartlepool became vicar of the parish of Danby in North Yorkshire, where he ministered for over 20 years (1967-90). There he began writing reflections and prayers in the style of early Celtic Christian writing. In 1990 he became vicar of Holy Island, Lindisfarne, where he ministered to thousands of pilgrims and other visitors. He was made a canon of York Minster in 1989, and retired from his Lindisfarne ministry in 2003. He died on 24 January 2020.

Adam published many collections of art, reflections, prayers, and meditations based on the Celtic tradition, including *Tides and Seasons: Modern Prayers in the Celtic Tradition* (1989) and *Landscapes of Light* (2001), an anthology of prayers illustrated with photographs of Holy Island. His first book of prayers in the Celtic style, *Edge of Glory* (1985), achieved immediate popularity and his books have been translated into several languages. He said of his work, 'A love for the mystery and wonder of creation inspires most of my writing, along with the Celtic saints and peoples with their poetry, prayers and songs.' He also wrote in his autobiographical volume, *The Wonder of the Beyond* (2011), 'I lived in a land of open fields, moorland and beaches: a land of castles, of history, of heroes, saints and story ... a radiant world ... full of the mystery of existence.' — F51, H137

Arthur Campbell Ainger

Arthur Campbell Ainger, an English hymn writer, was born at Blackheath, London, on 4 July 1841. Following an education at Eton and Trinity College, Cambridge, in 1864 he became a schoolmaster at Eton College where he taught until 1901. During his time there he wrote the Eton School Song and a number of hymns, many of them intended for singing on school occasions, including his best-known hymn, 'God is working his purpose out.' Ainger retired from Eton in 1901, and died at Buckinghamshire on 26 October 1919. — W652

Geoffrey Jackson Ainger

Ainger was born on 28 October 1925 at Mistley, near Manningtree in Essex, England. He was educated at Richmond College, London, and Union Theological Seminary, New York City. A British Methodist minister, he held various posts as a minister and lecturer, including four years at Loughton, Essex (1958-1962), and nine years as a member of the ministry team at Notting Hill, London (1962-1971). He finished his ministry in the Methodist circuit of South East London before eventually retiring to Lichfield. Beginning in the 1950s and strongly influenced by the hymns and songs of Sydney Carter, he worked to connect the Christian gospel and the poverty of the people to whom he ministered, expressing his vision of the radical mission of Jesus which he set out in *Jesus our Contemporary* (1967). He created a small group of now famous carols and hymns written in plain language and set to his own equally simple melodies. These were gathered in *Songs from Notting Hill* (1974). He died on 4 January 2013. — W 642

Robyn Dianne Allen Goudge (née Goudge)

Robyn Goudge was born at Huntly on 26 August 1961, the daughter of a Methodist clergyman and a singing teacher. She was educated at Lynfield College and Trinity Methodist Theological College, and holds a BSc from Auckland University and a BD from Otago University. She was ordained in 1987 as a minister of the New Zealand Methodist Church and has served in many different parishes. In 1998 she recorded a CD of 12 original songs that arose out of working with people in parish life, entitled *The Love I'm In*. She was for a time choir mistress at Takapuna Grammar School, and wrote music for the poem 'In Flanders Fields' which was given an award winning performance in the Big Sing Auckland championships in 2009. She married Geoffrey Allen, a professional actor and teacher, in 1991, and has a family of four sons. She has often collaborated with her husband, Geoff in providing incidental music for his drama productions, and in 2008 they co-wrote a kidult pantomime entitled *Fairytale – The Musical*.

Robyn has been involved in music from an early age, learning the piano and violin as a school girl, performing in orchestras and choirs, and becoming a pupil of the world-famous singing teacher Dame Sister Mary Leo. She now has a parallel career as a singer and folk harpist, noting that St. Clement of Alexandria (c.150-c.215) urged Christians of his time to choose the harp as a Christian emblem. In 2000 she commissioned Wellington harp maker, Keith Harrison, to make a 36-string Celtic harp, which she uses to sing and play a wide repertoire of religious and secular music at church and community events, schools, rest homes, women's groups and private functions. She sings in a variety of styles from folk music to popular, both secular and religious, arranging and composing her own songs as well as those of others. In 2013 she wrote a song for Girls' Brigade New Zealand's 85th anniversary celebration, *Give a Girl a Hope*. — **H65, 97**

Richard Kinsey Avery

Richard Avery was born on 26 August 1934 in Visalia, in California's central valley, and educated at the University of Redlands, California, and Union Theological Seminary, New York. He spent 40 years as pastor of First Presbyterian Church, Port Jervis, a small city near New York, eventually retiring to Santa Fe, New Mexico. With his colleague **Donald Marsh** he conducted workshops in creative worship and music, travelling throughout the United States and Europe. With Marsh he also wrote more than 120 religious songs, carols and hymns and founded Proclamation Productions to publish them in 10 songbooks such as *Hymns Hot and Carols Cool* and *Songs for the Search*. This body of material with additional songs is collected in *The Marsh and Avery Songbook* and *The Second Marsh and Avery Songbook* (1973).

Avery's collaboration with Marsh is characterised by their use of simple language, the direct treatment of real-life experiences, sympathy for the disabled and underprivileged, catchy tunes, uncomplicated harmonies and compelling modern rhythms. Avery says, 'We were known for a long time as being terribly joyful, fast and loud,' but this is unfair to their wide range of tones and themes. These writers' notes on their own work and their suggestions for performance (found in their second Songbook) are a revelation for staid singers and conservative choir directors and often constitute a sermon in themselves. — **W 675**

Dorothy Mary Neal White Ballantyne (née Neal)

Dorothy White was born at Christchurch on 22 December 1915, and educated at Avonside Girls' High School and Canterbury College. In 1933 she became a library Assistant at the Canterbury Public Library and in 1936 was one of only two young New Zealand women selected to train as librarians in the United States at the Pittsburgh Carnegie Institute of Technology Library School.

On her return to New Zealand she became the Children's Librarian at the Dunedin Public Library, a position she held from 1937-1942. There followed two years as Acting Deputy Librarian, and a further two years as Librarian of the Dunedin Training College. In 1939 she had married a noted Dunedin second-hand bookseller, Richard (Dick) White, and from 1946 to 1956 she retired from professional work to raise her two daughters. In 1957 she returned to the Dunedin Public Library as Head of Children's Services and held that position until her retirement in 1974. Widowed in 1967, in 1968 she married Dunedin doctor, Robert Ballantyne. His death in 1991 preceded hers on 12 February 1995.

Author of two now classic books in her field, *About Books for Children* (1946) and *Books before Five* (1954), she made the cramped quarters of the Dunedin Children's Library the finest in New Zealand and the promotion of good quality books for children became her life-long work. For her significant development of professional librarianship especially for children see the entry in the *Dictionary of New Zealand Biography, volume 5, 1941-1960* (Auckland: University Press, 2000), 555. She wrote a few poems of a private nature, among them 'Carol for a New Zealand Child,' which was first published in 1947 in *The Horn Book*, an American journal of books and reading for children and young people, then reprinted in *Told Under the Christmas tree: An Umbrella Book,* published jointly in 1948 by Macmillan and the American Association for Childhood Education. A devoted Anglican churchwoman, she served on the diocesan committee of the Association of Anglican Women, and in 1987 she was made an honorary life member of the New Zealand Historic Places Trust. She was awarded the Queen's Service Order in 1994. — C11

Reginald Barrett-Ayres

See 'Come teach us, Spirit of God (**F11**) for information about this Scottish composer.

Leonard (Lenny) Bartlotti

Alleluia Aotearoa misspells this American gospel song writer's name as Barlotti; American records confirm the correct spelling as Bartlotti. He was born on 19 July 1920 in Falerna, Italy and died in Sewickley, Pennsylvania, on 10 September 2002. He was a 1939 graduate of Quaker Valley High School, and survived as a veteran of World War II. After the war he worked in at least three engineering companies. At the time of his death he was a member of the St James Catholic Church, Sewickley. There is no record of him as a priest or pastor; he seems to have been simply a talented lay member of the Church. — **A132**

Margaret (Marnie) Louise Barrell

Marnie Barrell was born on 30 December 1952 in Ashburton. She was educated at Timaru Girls' High School and Christchurch Girls' High School, and the University of Canterbury, where she completed a BA in Psychology (1973), then worked as a science technician at Lincoln University. From 1991-5 she studied at the University of Auckland, where she completed a Bachelor of Theology degree, and for a time served as a lay preacher and music director at St Barnabas Anglican Church, Mount Eden. Marnie Barrell holds an LTCL, an AMusTCL and a Diploma of Teaching and has taught the piano since 1990. In 2004 she shifted from Auckland to Christchurch and taught at the Christchurch School of Music. She was brought up in an Anglican family, and after a period of disconnection followed by a period with the Open Brethren returned to the Anglican Church, 'where I remain to this day.' She is now a lay preacher, music leader and People's Warden at the Opawa-St Martin's Anglican Church, and a much-valued member of the editorial board of the New Zealand Hymnbook Trust.

Encouraged in 1986 by **Shirley Murray** to attempt hymn writing, Marnie Barrell has since created a considerable number of hymns and liturgical texts, many of which have been published in *Alleluia Aotearoa* (1993), *Carol our Christmas* (1996), *Faith Forever Singing* (2000), *Hope is our Song* (2009), the *Church Hymnary 4* (2005), *Singing the Faith* (2011) and posted on the British *Oremus Hymnal* and SongSelect websites.

She says of her hymns and hymn writing, 'I like to write new texts for the well-loved hymn tunes, so that people can use them without learning lots of new music, though I love the fine new tunes that have been supplied for my work. If a scriptural theme or story doesn't suggest a still-singable hymn, I write something I'd like to sing in response to that subject…I don't generally just paraphrase scripture to set it to music. Often I call on several passages to illustrate one main idea I'm writing about, using a phrase here, an image there. I also make use of non-scriptural material, such as the baptismal and eucharistic liturgies, traditional prayers and devotions, sermons I've heard or books I've read. Completing a degree in theology has given me a lifetime's worth of ideas for writing. I particularly appreciate the insights of feminist theology. I don't consciously try to be a New Zealand writer, but when I read hymns from elsewhere I'm increasingly aware of a certain characteristic New Zealandish slant about my way of seeing things.'

A number of Marnie Barrell's hymn texts have been set by New Zealand musicians, including **Jillian Bray**, **Barry Brinson**, **Colin Gibson**, **Ian Render**, and Leonie Holmes, and she has composed some of her own hymn settings. — A27, 48, 55, 58, 120, 147, 148; C4, 15, 36, 49; F47, 55; H2, 3, 14, 31, 35, 38, 50, 52, 55, 76, 79, 98, 109, 123, 136, 145

James Keir Baxter

James Baxter was born in Dunedin on 29 June 1926, In 1944 he began his education at the University of Otago, though he failed to complete a course there, Wellington Teachers' College (1951-2) and Victoria University of Wellington (BA 1953-6). He became an assistant master at Epuni School, Lower Hutt, in 1954 but left the position in 1956 to edit school bulletins for the Department of Education. In 1958 on a Unesco stipend he travelled throughout Asia and particularly India; in 1966 he took up a Robert Burns Fellowship at the University of Otago.

Claiming that he had been instructed in a vision to do so, in 1968 he left a University position and a job writing catechetical material for the Catholic Education Board to found a commune at the small Māori settlement of Hiruharama (Jerusalem) on the bank of the Whanganui River. Baxter also spent some time in Grafton, Auckland, where he set up a centre for drug addicts. In 1969 he moved to Jerusalem where he lived the life of a hermit, making frequent trips to the nearby cities where he worked with the poor and spoke out against what he perceived as a social order that sanctioned poverty. By 1972 he was too ill to continue living at Jerusalem and moved to a commune near Auckland, where he died on 22 October 1972.

Baxter's life was marked by an intermittent but strong interest in the Roman Catholic faith, renewed in 1957, and some of his poetry, notably *Fires of No Return* (1958) and *Jerusalem Sonnets* (1970) reflects that interest, but he is now remembered more broadly as a major literary figure in New Zealand writing. He claimed to have begun writing poetry at the age of 7 and he left 34 books of poetry, literary criticism and plays. His *Collected Poems* were published in 1979, the *Collected Plays* in 1982, and in 1996 there appeared a further collection of unpublished early work. His religious poetry included ballads, carols and hymns; his carol, 'How small the Lord of Angels there,' was published in the New Zealand Catholic hymnal *Sing Praise* (1981). — **F 21***

John Lamberton Bell

John Bell was born at Kilmarnock, Ayrshire, Scotland, on 20 November 1949. He was educated at Kilmarnock Academy and Glasgow University (where he was elected Rector while still a student), graduating with an MA and a Bachelor of Divinity. He was ordained as a minister of the Church of Scotland in 1978, worked as a youth adviser, then joined the Iona Community first as a youth co-ordinator then as a worship resource worker, becoming a charismatic world-wide traveler, lecturing, preaching and conducting workshops with the aim of renewing congregational singing. His many publications include *The Singing Thing: A Case for Congregational Song* (2000) and *The Singing Thing Two: Enabling Congregations To Sing* (2007). He is a frequent broadcaster on the BBC, and regularly contributes to 'Thought for the Day' on Radio 4's Today programme. In the words of D'Arcy Wood, 'Thousands of people, not only musicians, have benefitted from his unique ability to communicate and enthuse' (*A Companion to Together in Song*, Wesley Milgate and D'Arcy Wood, Sydney: The Australian Hymnbook, 2006, 542).

A principal member of the Wild Goose Resource Group, and working in collaboration with the late Graham Maule and others, he has produced no fewer than 15 collections of hymns and songs, many of them with a strong peace and social justice emphasis. He is the author of five books of anthems, and has written sermons, prayers and liturgical material for the Iona Community. He composes much original music, but sets many of his hymn texts to Scottish folk tunes. He also takes a keen interest in world Christian religious music, which he collects and publishes, and his own work has been translated into a number of European languages and Japanese. A past convenor of the Church of Scotland's Panel on Worship, he was the convenor and music editor of the committee which drafted the ground-breaking hymn and liturgical collection *Common Ground* (1998), followed by the fourth edition of the Church of Scotland's *Hymnary* (2005). In 1999 he became a Fellow of the Royal School of Church Music, and in 2002 was awarded an honorary doctorate from the University of Glasgow. — **A147; F10(i)**

Charles William (Bill) Bennett

Bill Bennett was born in Dannevirke on 19 April 1938. His father was at the time manager of a large sheep and beef farm east of Dannevirke. Bill was educated at Mangatoro Primary School (1943-44), Mahora Primary School (Hastings) (1945-49), Havelock North Primary School (1950-51) and Hastings High School (1952-51). He studied at Canterbury University (1958-60), where he took papers in music, and St John's Theological College, Auckland (1961-63). After ordination in 1963 as an Anglican deacon, then priest, he served in a number of parishes: Tauranga, Clive, Napier Cathedral, Waerenga-a-hika (rural Gisborne), Norwich Diocese (UK), Te Puke, Dannevirke, and Westshore. The latter years of his working life were as a Ministry Enabler in the Diocese of Waiapu, and incorporated a period in the Diocese of Lichfield (England). Married to Wendy Barnett in 1964, they have three children, all now adult and working.

Although now retired he has been employed as priest in charge of several Hawke's Bay parishes, has spent four years as rural parish visitor for Waipawa Parish, and been Interim Bishop's Chaplain for Hawke's Bay, which he describes as a sort of Archdeacon.

Coming from farming stock, he was drawn towards developing rural ministry as a theological discipline, and wrote three books on the subject. Two of them, *Listen to the Shepherd: Whakarongo ki te kupu* (1999) and *Seasons of the Land: People's Prayers for Town and Country* (2001) provided contemporary prayers for rural New Zealand congregations; *God of the Whenua: Rural Ministry in Aotearoa New Zealand* (2005) explored Māori and Pākehā views of land and ministry. He has also contributed a number of articles to periodicals such as *Rural News Network, Ruminations, Rural Theology, Waiapu News* and *Music in the Air*. In 2013 he published *The Shepherd's Call*, a collection of liturgies and prayers for rural congregations.

Bill Bennett began writing hymns and religious songs in a rural setting: 'I realised there were very few New Zealand hymns, so while being vicar of Te Puke parish I began to write hymns and songs that had a New Zealand flavour.' He has always written both lyrics and melody, for working among small rural congregations he realised that 'both words and music exist in a symbiotic relationship – not only do the words need to be authentic and real for them, but the melody has to enhance the words yet be sufficiently melodic to be easily remembered and enjoyed.' The introduction of contemporary rural terms and images and the use of the Māori language as well as English ('so that people get accustomed to using both languages, especially in hymn and song singing') are features of his writing.

Bill Bennett's hymns have been published in *Carol our Christmas* (1996), *Faith Forever Singing (2000)* and *Hope is our Song* (2009). In 2010 he published *Gradual Praise: Nga Waiata Whakapono,** a collection of 116 of his own hymns and songs related to the Gospel readings in the revised Common Lectionary. There are also setting for congregation and/or choir of liturgies from the *New Zealand Prayer Book*, a *St Matthew's Passiontide* cantata, *Starlight Taonga*, a musical presentation of the St Matthew nativity story for children, a *Christmas of Luke* cantata and a musical version of the story of *Balaam and his Donkey*.

— C6; F2, 6, 77, 79; H18, 24, 45, 90, 110, 117, 143

*See further, 'Gradual Praise by Bill Bennett,' a review by Colin Gibson. *Music in the Air*, Winter/Spring 2011, 619-20.

Jennifer (Jenny) Bennett

No information about this musician has been found other than that she was responsible for piano arrangements of three of **Cecily Sheehy's** hymns. — A109, 116, 162

Giovanni Francesco Di Bernadone

See under *Francis of Assisi*

Barbara Whirimako Black

Whirimako Black was born at Whakatane in 1961, of Ngāti Tūhoe, Ngāti Tūwharetoa, Ngāti Ranginui, Kahungunu, Te Whakatohea, Te-Whanau-a-Apanui, Te Arawa and Ngāti Awa descent. In 1983 she studied music theory at the Sydney School of Music and completed a BA at the Auckland Institute of Technology in 1997. She has also studied classical piano, guitar theory and Mataatua Waiata. In 1991, she formed the female Māori band Tuahine Whakairo but left the group in 1993 to start a solo career. Between 2000 and 2011 she has released eight albums. In 2009 she performed at the Wellington Jazz festival and in 2010 she made a national tour, *Soul Talk*, with fellow artist Nigel Gavin.

She is now a successful recording artist with several albums to her credit, singing mostly in the Māori language, using traditional Māori musical forms and collaborating with players using traditional musical instruments. She has performed in Greece, Korea, Taiwan and at Gallipoli, and collaborated with numerous world music celebrities; her 'Te Moko' track featured on the internationally successful *One Giant Leap* album, and she has worked with a number of New Zealand's leading performers, including Richard Nunns, Don McGlashan, Neill and Tim Finn and Dave Dobbyn.

Whirimako Black has also worked to foster young Māori musical talent. For five years she served as a judge on Māori Television's *Māori Oke* talent show, and she has conducted workshops at Auckland University of Technology, Auckland School of Music and Otago University as well as all of the major Māori universities and institutions of learning.

Her musical achievements include composing and singing the title songs for the Television New Zealand series *The New Zealand Wars*, as well as composing with Hori Tait the initial title music for the Māori news programme *Te Karere*. She has also recorded hymns for services at Gallipoli. She has received a number of awards, including best Māori Album, Best Jazz Album and Best Māori Composition in the New Zealand Music Awards. For her services to Māori music she was made a Member of the New Zealand Order of Merit in the 2006 New Year Honours. In 2011 she received an Arts Foundation Laureate Award. — H61

Philip Paul Bliss

Philip Bliss was born on 9 July 1838 in Clearfield County, Pennsylvania, the son of a music-loving Methodist family. After working as a farm boy, then in timber camps and sawmills, he became a schoolteacher at Hartsville, New York. There his musical talent was recognized. He had a fine bass voice and received some formal voice training from composer-editors J.G. Towner and W.B. Bradbury. At the age of 22, he studied at New York's Normal Academy of Music, and was urged to become a music teacher, which he did in 1858. The following year he married Lucy Young, the daughter of a musical Presbyterian family, and joined her Church. His first songs date from this period.

After a period as an itinerant teacher, riding from community to community with a melodeon as his musical instrument, Bliss and his family moved to Chicago where he became known as a singer, teacher and writer of gospel songs. He joined the First Congregational Church of Chicago, where he was a choir member and Sunday Superintendent. He worked with a Chicago firm of music publishers from 1865 to 1873, leading revival gatherings, singing schools and concerts for his employers, while continuing to compose hymns which were often printed in his employers' books. In 1869 he joined the famous evangelist Dwight L. Moody and became a fulltime evangelist himself. In the 1870s he assisted with the compilation of at least five gospel song collections, including two edited by Ira D. Sankey.

On 29 December 1876 he and his wife died in a tragic accident when a trestle collapsed under the Pacific Express train in which they were travelling. He left over 100 hymns, choir pieces and gospel songs, which remained popular in America and Britain long after his death, and travelled with missionaries working in the Pacific. — **W648, 668**

Carl Gustaf Boberg

Boberg was born at Monsteras, on the southeast coast of Sweden, on 16 August 1859. He began life as a sailor, then, after his conversion at the age of 19, studied at Kristinehamn Bible School and returned to minister at Monsteras where he became one of the evangelical leaders of his generation. From 1890 to 1916 he edited a weekly journal, *Sanningsvittnet* (Witness to the Truth), published several books of verse and wrote many hymns, including the now-famous 'O Store Gud' ('How great thou art'). He also assisted in the compilation of the first two hymnbooks published by the Swedish Covenant. He was a gifted writer and speaker, and from 1912 to 1931 served as a member of the Swedish Parliament. He died at Kalmar on 7 January 1941. — **W628**

Margaret Helen Bond (née Wilkinson)

Margaret Bond was born in Hobart, Australia, on 9 January 1934, the third child of the Reverend Leo and Mrs Gwen Wilkinson, both of whom were themselves children of a Methodist minister's family. She was the middle child of a family of five, and when her father was appointed to parishes in Victoria they lived in three Victorian country towns—Benalla, Warragul and Horsham. Margaret received her primary education at schools in those three towns; her secondary education was at Methodist Ladies College, Melbourne. She describes herself as always active in whichever church she attended, both in choir singing, reading and in conversations with adults and young people like herself.

After training as a primary school teacher, she taught in classrooms and later in a School Camp situation (a pre-cursor to Outdoor Education). There she led group singing and learned to play the piano-accordion for the campfires. She says, 'Writing words to familiar tunes was part of that, and I guess it was here that the thought of writing hymns was born. I became particularly interested in exploring where and how the stories of our tradition melded with the everyday experience of living in the world as we were coming to understand it. I met Pierre Teilhard de Chardin's writing in the late 1950s and 60s and then the work of Thomas Berry and Brian Swimme in the 1990s, and as part of that exploration realized that the words of hymns I was singing were not only gender exclusive but came from a world view I could no longer relate to, deriving mostly from a theology of Fall and Redemption which no longer made sense to me.'

By the 1990s she was worshipping in the Anglican parish of St Peter in Mornington, Melbourne, where creativity in music, art, and poetry was celebrated, and there she wrote several hymns, inspired by what she was reading and sometimes for a particular church programme. These hymns were sung in St Peter's, but because the composer of the music – another member of the same congregation – did not want it to be published, when she moved to New Zealand in 2000, the hymn words 'came with me and sat in a folder until a friend encouraged me to send them to the New Zealand Hymnbook Trust. I was deeply grateful when Colin Gibson wrote tunes to two of them.' She now worships in St Stephen's Anglican Church, Tamahere. Margaret says of her writing, 'The flow of writing hymn words has not been re-kindled since those creative years in Mornington, but may still burst into life again.' — **H17, 40**

Thomas Bracken

Thomas Bracken,* author of one of New Zealand's two national anthems, was born into a Protestant family at Cloinee, County Meath, Ireland on 21 December 1843. He lost both of his parents while still a child and was sent to the care of an uncle on a farm near Melbourne, Victoria, Australia. He published his first volume of verse there in 1867. Two years later he travelled to Dunedin, New Zealand, and began a career in newspaper journalism. A strong concern for the underprivileged led to his entry into politics, and he held the parliamentary seat for Central Dunedin for a term of three years (1881-3). He continued to write verse prolifically and published in New Zealand, Australia and occasionally England. His last major verse collection was a selection from earlier volumes, *Lays and Lyrics: God's Own Country and other Poems* (1893).

Bracken also edited a short-lived literary periodical, and wrote much other prose, including a set of essay sketches of Dunedin clergymen, reminiscences of his life in Australia, and other pamphlets and literary compilations. Robert Stout, twice Premier of the country, was to say of him, 'he is helping, and has helped, to create a national literature.' Bracken's single most important literary work was the poem **God Defend New Zealand**, written in the 1870s. In later life he fell into financial difficulties, was offered a government post as reader and record clerk of the House of Parliament which he was forced to leave due to ill-health (1894-5), and died at Dunedin on 16 February 1898. — **W677, A51**

*For a full account of his active life see the entry in *The Dictionary of New Zealand Biography, Volume Two: 1870-1900*, (Wellington, 1993).

Jillian Margaret Bray (née Ballinger)

Jillian Bray was born in Wellington on 14 February 1939. She was educated at Queen Margaret College and studied for a music degree at Victoria University College, completing her BMus in 1962. She gained a Licentiate from the Royal Schools of Music in 1960, became a Registered Music Teacher in 1961 and taught piano privately and school music at Samuel Marsden School and the Correspondence School.

Active at Khandallah Presbyterian Church throughout her youth, as Bible class leader, choir member and organist, she was married there in 1963, then joined Tawa Union Parish and later Titahi Bay Gospel Chapel before returning to her roots at Waikanae Presbyterian Church, assisting with the music at each location.

In 1998 she became a music editor for the New Zealand Hymnbook Trust on which she served for 18 years. There she formed a creative partnership with **Shirley Murray**, she was to write about 60 published hymn tunes by authors including **Joy Dine**, **Joy Cowley**, **Marnie Barrell**, and Americans Brian Wren and **Rusty Edwards**. The Hope Publishing website lists 28 of her tunes on line, and there are nine of her arrangements and settings in the Australian-New Zealand publication *Servant Songs* (1987).

From an early age she began composing music for school, church and community, writing vocal, piano, organ and chamber music pieces. She has also written a number of piano pieces for her music pupils. She directed two community choirs and sang in several others, resulting in the composition of a number of choral arrangements, including hymns for **Peter Godfrey**'s Kāpiti choirs, and other extended choral works including *Anno Domine* (2001), written for the Porirua City Choir and performed at St Andrew's on the Terrace and the national museum, Te Papa, *Centennial Anthem* (2002), written for the Khandallah Presbyterian Choir, and *Jubilee* (2006). *Sing with me friends* was written to words by Shirley Murray for the V8 Vocal Ensemble, who performed it in Hamilton, Tauranga and Auckland in 2006. *Island* and *The Bay* (words by Denis Glover) and *Homage to Bach* (words by Shirley Murray) were written for the Kāpiti

Chamber Choir and sung locally in 2007 and 2008 respectively.

As well as continuing to compose hymns until her death at Wellington on 27 March 2018, Jillian wrote music for family and friends as the occasion arose, ranging from solo songs, piano and organ pieces, to chamber works and pieces to mark a friend's passing, weddings and farewells. — **W650, 669, 674(ii); A13, 15, 19, 25, 29, 44, 67, 74, 81, 108, 110, 123, 130, 133; C3, 4(ii), 5, 7, 10, 11, 13(i), 15, 16, 17, 19, 22, 23, 26, 28, 30, 34, 35, 36, 41(i), 42, 44, 45, 47, 50, 51, 52; F1, 5, 8, 10(ii), 11, 16, 19, 22, 32, 37, 44, 54, 59, 60, 68, 69(i), 70, 75, 76, 77, 80; H76, 83, 89, 106, 130, 133, 153, 155**

Barrington (Barry) Gordon Michael Brinson

Christchurch musician Barry Brinson was born in Hastings in 1939 and educated at Napier Boys' High School. While still at school he learned the pipe organ in Napier, playing at St Peter's Anglican Church, Waipawa, his first church organist appointment. Later he moved to Wellington to study accountancy and continued organ tuition with Stanley Jackson, becoming assistant organist at St James' Church, Lower Hutt. Moving to Christchurch in 1966, he became for a time organist and choir director at St Michael and All Angels Church.

Barry Brinson has since become one of New Zealand's most versatile musicians, with interests ranging from classical organ and jazz piano, to composing and arranging, and directing choral and instrumental ensembles. He is a member of the Christchurch Baroque Trio formed in 2010, playing continuo organ and harpsichord. In 2010 he became a part-time lecturer and *repetiteur* at the Christchurch-based National Academy of Singing and Dramatic Arts. He has had a long association with the prize-winning Addington Brass band as conductor and arranger, and was appointed its Artist-in-Residence in 2012. Since 1981 he has played as a backing musician for Christchurch Jenny Blackadder's banjo recordings; in 2003 he released a jazz piano trio CD, *Pick Yourself Up*, and a CD of organ music, *Barry Brinson: More than you know*.

In many years of involvement with the music of the Christchurch Anglican Cathedral since joining its choir in 1971 as a lay clerk, he has been its sub-organist and from 1996-9 was director of the Cathedral Singers, the Cathedral's auxiliary adult choir. In 1992 he was instrumental in introducing jazz services and these remained regular events until 2005. In 1992 he composed music for a Jazz Eucharist which has been presented in cathedrals in New Zealand, Australia and the United Kingdom. It was rewritten in 2011 as a full Jazz Mass with a Latin text and received its first performance in St Paul's Cathedral, Dunedin, in 2012. Prior to the earthquakes which ravaged Christchurch in 2010 and 2011 and destroyed most of the city's principal church buildings he was organist and choir director at the Oxford Terrace Baptist Church. He presently sings with the Christchurch Jubilate Singers and works as an independent musical professional from his Christchurch base.

He joined the editorial board of the New Zealand Hymn Book Trust in 2006 and contributed a number of original musical settings to their hymnals *Faith Forever Singing* (2000) and *Hope is our Song* (2009). He has composed settings for texts by **Shirley Murray** as well as for Christchurch hymn writers **Marnie Barrell**, Jane Simpson and **Bill Wallace**. — **F69(ii); H8, 9, 14, 15, 31, 37, 52, 56, 69, 84, 92, 101, 102, 109, 111, 122, 139, 149**

Robert Burns

The son of a poor farmer, Scotland's national poet, was born at Alloway near Ayr in 1759. His literary education was begun at Alloway Mill school and continued by a tutor John Murdoch, but he also learned the folk tales and ballads of old Scotland from an elderly woman, Betty Davidson, who lived in the family home. Acquaintance with sailors and smugglers broadened his education, as did his numerous affairs with local young women.

Following the death of his father in 1784, a failed attempt at farming and a love affair with Jean Armour (whom he eventually married in 1788), his poetry came to national attention when he published the Kilmarnock edition (1786) of his verse, and its close connection with old Scottish melodies and words emerged with the publication in 1787 of the *Scots Musical Museum*. He died at Dumfries in 1796. — **A124**

James H. Burke

There is little information available about this once popular 19th century American evangelist, hymn writer and singer. One standard site gives his birth dates (improbably) as 1800-1900! He was actually born in 1858 and died in 1901, and from 1889-91 was Minister of Music at the New York Gospel Tabernacle. He is known to have been associated with several of the evangelical crusade tours led by such famous teams as Moody and Sankey and Alexander and Chapman, as well as Scottish evangelist James McNeill (1854-1933). Burke generally featured as a soloist, sometimes singing with large choirs of up to 200 members. He toured in America, England and Scotland, and even reached 'the Southern colonies,' as a Brisbane newspaper report of his visit there describes Australia and New Zealand. (Burke actually spent two months travelling New Zealand with McNeill.) He wrote a number of religious songs and hymn tunes for texts such as 'Alive for evermore,' 'Many crowd the Saviour's kingdom,' 'I am trusting thee, Lord Jesus,' 'Take the step, my brother,' 'Hear me, blessed Jesus,' 'On Zion's rock I stand' and 'Spread the temperance banner out.' — **W638**

Elisabeth Havens Burrowes (née Havens)

Elisabeth Havens was born on 13 January 1885 at Detroit, Wayne, Michigan. She married Paul deNyse Burrowes in 1901 and raised five children, living for a time in Englewood, New Jersey, before moving to Berkeley, California. She published two books and wrote a number of poems, including several hymn texts. A committed churchwoman, she became an ordained Elder of St John's Presbyterian Church in Berkeley. She died on 27 March, 1975, at Stockton, San Joaquin County, California, at the age of 90.

Her hymn 'God of the ages, by whose hand' (not to be confused with Daniel C. Roberts' 1876 patriotic hymn 'God of the ages, by whose almighty hand') was copyrighted by the Hymn Society of America in 1958, and collected in their anthology *Hymns published for Special Occasions and On Special Subjects, 1942-1979* (1978). It also appeared in the American *Methodist Hymnal* (1966) and the Presbyterian *Worshipbook, Services and Hymns* (1972). Her children's hymn 'Our Father, who dost lead us' was published by the Hymn Society of America in *Twelve New Hymns for Children* (1965). With composer Margaret Nikoloric, Elisabeth Havens Burrowes also wrote the lyrics for *a Pageant of the Nine Doors, with Mexican Folk Music* (1936). — **W662**

Geoffrey Butcher

Rev Dr Geoffrey Butcher was born on 18 April 1941 in Orange, New Jersey. He has a distinguished history as a priest and musician in the American Episcopal [Anglican] Church and beyond.

Ordained a deacon in 1965 and a priest in 1966, he holds a doctorate in Ministry from McCormick Theological Seminary, Chicago, an MA from New Mexico Highlands University, Las Vegas, and an MD from the General Theological Seminary, New York. He took his undergraduate degree from Hobart College, New York. His ministry has included positions at three universities, Christ Church Cathedral, Nashville (1992-2010), the Cathedral Church of St John, Albuquerque, New Mexico, where he was organist and choirmaster from 1968-1980, and briefly at St Paul's, Nicosia, Cyprus. He is presently priest-in-charge of Trinity Episcopal Church, Russellville, Kentucky.

He is known nationally in America for his work with various music-related conferences, the Evergreen Music Conference (1984, 1988), the Mississippi Conference on Church Music and Liturgy (1987, 1981) and the Sewanee

Province Church Music Conference (1985, 1987). From 1980-1986 he was a member of the Tune Sub-Committee of the Episcopal Church's Standing Commission on Church Music, which produced that Church's *Hymnal 1982* (1985). — **W639**

Peter Irwin Cape

Peter Cape, described by Steele Roberts as 'an anguished Anglican priest, a prolific writer and a poet, an editor, broadcaster, arts commentator, photographer and film director *An Ordinary Joker: the Life and Songs of Peter Cape* (2001) was born at Helensville, near Auckland, on 17 January 1926. His family were peripatetic merchants, living in caravans, and his early education was largely conducted through Correspondence School lessons. He completed a BA at Auckland University (1947-9) then pursued post-graduate studies in philosophy at Canterbury University (MA, 1950). There he met and married Barbara Henderson in 1951. The following year, he studied at Selwyn College, Dunedin, and completed a LTheol degree. In 1953 he was ordained into the Anglican Church at Kalgoorlie, Western Australia, but he abandoned a full-time career in the church in 1954 and from 1955 worked for the New Zealand Broadcasting Service, becoming head of religious programming from 1958 to 1962. In 1962 he trained with the BBC as a television producer and on his return to New Zealand produced religious and arts programmes as well as documentaries and current affairs programmes for television. 'Nativity' was written and broadcast by NZBC TV in 1968. In 1973 Cape moved to the vicarage at Maungaraki in the Hutt Valley hills, working part-time as a priest, but focusing on his writing. He briefly worked as Director of Volunteer Service Abroad before moving in 1974 to Richmond, Nelson, where he took up a farming life with Gladwen McIntyre. Peter Cape died at Richmond on 30 May 1979.

His writing career had begun with contributions to *Craccum*, the Auckland University student newspaper. From 1968 he built a reputation as an independent broadcaster and writer for journals such as the *Listener, Church & People*, the *Sunday News*, and *Arts and Community*. He also became a university extension lecturer on New Zealand painting. From his time in Wellington Peter Cape intermittently wrote, performed and recorded his own folk songs, the first of them 'Taumarunui on the Main Trunk Line'; by 1975 he was able to release a full album titled *Peter Cape's Kiwi Ballads*. His legacy consists of 9 books, mostly on art topics, 2 films, more than 30 songs, as well as a large number of radio and television broadcast scripts and numerous articles for journals and newspapers. — **C42***

> *For more information and a CD of some of Cape's songs, including 'Nativity,' see *An Ordinary Joker: the Life and Songs of Peter Cape,* by Steele Roberts, Wellington: Steele Roberts (2001).

Alison Rosemary Carey (née Hall)

Alison Carey was born in Lower Hutt in 1936. As a child she learned the piano and studied musical theory. Her understanding of classical harmony and melody was extended by weekly acquaintance with the 1933 *Methodist Hymnbook*. Her secondary schooling began at Queen Margaret College, Wellington; while still at school she started organ lessons at St Paul's Pro-Cathedral, Christchurch. These were continued at St Alban's Methodist Church, Christchurch, while she studied with **Vernon Griffiths** and John Ritchie at Canterbury University College. She majored in music and graduated BA from the University of New Zealand in 1958.

Since her student days she has played the organ intermittently for church services and sung in a number of church choirs, including Durham Street Methodist in Christchurch, and St James' Anglican in Lower Hutt. In Lower Hutt she taught music theory both privately and in association with other teachers at the Chilton School of Music, located at Chilton Saint James School.

Compositions for community groups and churches followed, including anthems and hymn tunes. She wrote a number of settings for hymn writer **Bill Wallace's** words, several of which have been published in New Zealand and international hymn books and heard on New Zealand radio and television programmes. In 1982 she wrote a cantata for the St James' Choir, *A Disciple's Journey*, which has been given repeat performances. In recent years she has enjoyed membership of the Wellington Organists' Association and has written three books of organ voluntaries. She has also played monthly for services at St Mark's Uniting Congregation, Lower Hutt, and sang for several years in a madrigal group. She married, and had four children, one of whom is now a composer and pianist, and another a teacher of the cello and violin.

Ten of Alison's hymn tunes and arrangements of hymn melodies or folk tunes were published in Bill Wallace's *Singing the Circle*, Books 1-3 (1990), and eight of them in *The Mystery Telling: Hymns and Songs for the New Millennium* (New York, 2001). Three more appeared in *Alleluia Aotearoa* (1993) and *Hope is our Song* (2009). — **A146; H4,146**

Sydney Bertram Carter

English folk and religious songwriter, performance poet and occasional satirist **Sydney Carter** was born in Camden Town, London on 6 May 1915, and educated at Montrem Street School, Islington, where he first met and enjoyed old English folk songs, and Christ's Hospital, Horsham, West Sussex, where he enjoyed singing hymns at chapel services. He completed an MA at Balliol College, Oxford, after which he became a schoolteacher at the famed liberal and independent Frensham Heights School, Farnham, Surrey, until the outbreak of World War 2. From 1940-5 he served with a Quaker ambulance unit in the Middle East and Greece – another pacifist, Donald Swann, was also a member of the unit – where he discovered the inspiration of Greek folk music. After the war had ended, he lectured for the British Council in Norway, Spain, Poland and Germany, and went on to write radio and television scripts for the BBC which sometimes included his own songs. His work on ABC's TV series *Hallelujah* gave further scope for his (irr)religious song writing.

At the age of 13 Carter underwent what he called a conversion experience, followed by confirmation within the Anglican Church, but he became disillusioned with formal Christianity and went through a long period of doubt. However, his desire to 'belong to the Christian gang' persisted and he eventually became one of England's most notable (and independent) religious songwriters. Beginning to compose and perform his songs wherever he could find an audience, he took a leading role in the folk music revival of the 60s and 70s. Championed by Donald Swann and Stainer & Bell (under its Galliard Imprint) he went on to publish his work in several collections, including *Nine Songs or Ballads* (1964), *Ten New Songs*, *Nothing Fixed or Final* (a collection of his poems), and *Sydney Carter in the Present Tense* (1969), and *Green Print for Song* (1974). In two books, *The Rock Of Doubt* (1978) and *Dance In The Dark* (1980) he set out the stages of his faith journey as a folk poet and musician, a holy sceptic and an iconoclastic theologian. Carter died on 13 March, 2004, after a long battle with Alzheimer's disease.

A number of his songs, such as 'Lord of the Dance' (now regarded as an iconic modern hymn), and 'One more step,' were eventually taken into regular church hymnals: *With One Voice* includes 3 of them; the New Zealand supplement adds another. — **W640; F32**

Valerie (Val) June Carter Cash (née Carter)

Valerie (Val) Carter was born on June 23 1939 in Maces Spring, Virginia. She was born into a country music performing family and toured, sang and recorded with her parents and two sisters from the age of ten. In 1943 she became part of an enlarged country music group, Mother Maybelle and the Carter Sisters. She had a natural comic talent: a highlight of the family roadshows was her 'Aunt Polly' routine. In 1950, together with her group, she became part of the legendary Nashville Tennessee Grand Ole Opry company. She went on to develop a double career as a songwriter and solo singer, and a paired act with her third husband, Johnny Cash (whom she married in 1968). Encouraged by director Elia Kazan, she studied acting and took several roles in Hollywood films and television shows, including *Gunsmoke* (1957), *The Apostle* (1998) and *Dr Quinn, Medicine Woman* (1993-7). She died on 15 May 2003, at Nashville, followed by her husband only four months later, and the pair were buried together near their home in Hendersonville, Tennessee.

Val Cash with her husband won Grammy awards in 1968 and 1971, and her solo album, *Press On*, won the 2000 Grammy award for best traditional folk album. Her song 'Keep on the sunny side' won the 2004 Grammy award for best female country performance. Her posthumous album, *Wildwood Flower* (2003), won two further Grammy awards. In 2009 she was inducted into the Christian Music Hall of Fame. She published her autobiography in 1979 and a later memoir, *From the Heart*, in 1988. A movie for television based on her life, *The June Carter Cash Story*, was released in 2012. — **A29**

Brent Sinclair Chambers

Brent Chambers was born at Napier in 1948, educated at Colenso High School in that city, then at the Bible College of New Zealand (where he completed a LTh degree in 1974) and the University of Auckland. From 1990 to 1994 he worked with Youth with a Mission Family Ministries, and taught courses on worship and song writing at the Elkanah School of Music Ministry as well as contributing to the Kiwisong Music Ministry organisation.

He began writing gospel and scripture-based songs in the 1970s, describing himself as 'mad on music' from his earliest years, and as 'a full-time songwriter who repaints houses for a living.' He has now been active in the New Zealand and international Christian music scene for more than 40 years, for some 20 of them involved with Scripture in Song and travelling widely with David and Dale Garratt performing and teaching in charismatic and evangelical circles. He describes his work as 'teaching worship life-skills, songwriting, mainly in Singapore and India in recent years, and in churches around NZ.'

He has recorded and/or published more than 80 songs and recorded and self-published three albums, *To Know God and to make Him Known* (1994), New Zealand Gospel Album of the Year *Living Sacrifices* (1995) and *Towards Intimacy* (2003). His song 'Be Exalted, O God' has been performed or published in over 20 languages world-wide and 68 of his songs are on the Songselect website. Composer or co-writer of over 500 religious songs, he is on record as saying 'my life's calling is to love God, love my family, write songs that honour God and bless God's people, in that order.' — **A70**

Frank Von Christierson

Frank von Christierson, pastor and hymn writer, was born near the Swedish town of Helsinki on 25 December 1900. He moved with his family to America and was educated at San Jose High School, California, Stanford University (BA in Psychology, 1923) and San Francisco Theological Seminary (BD, 1929). He was ordained into the Presbyterian Church of America in 1929 and served as youth director at the First Presbyterian Church, San Luis Obispo, California, then as pastor for 14 years at Calvary Presbyterian Church, Citrus Heights, California, and at Trinity Presbyterian Church, North Hollywood, California. In 1983 he was made a Fellow of the Hymn Society of America and Canada. He died in Roseville, California, on 29 April 1966.

As well as becoming known as a religious presenter on American radio and television, Christierson wrote a number of hymns and prayers, most of them published in his collection *Make a Joyful Noise: Hymns and Verses by Frank von Christierson* (1982); some of them were translated into other languages and several have appeared in North American hymnals such as *The [Presbyterian] Hymnal II* (1982), [Mennonite] *Hymnal* (1992), *Voices United* (1997), *Common Praise* (Anglican

Church of Canada, 1998), and *Worship and Rejoice* (2001). — **A33**

Churches Together In England

Churches Together in England is an ecumenical organization formed in 1990 as the national instrument for the different Christian churches in England. It helps them to work together instead of separately so that they can be more effective and credible. It operates through a network of Intermediate bodies, each covering an English county or metropolitan area and co-ordinating groups which bring together the Churches' officers in various areas of work. The Presidents of Churches Together in England are the Anglican Archbishop of Canterbury, the Roman Catholic Archbishop of Westminster, the Moderator of the Free Churches and a fourth President chosen from one of the other member Churches. In 2000 they issued a Millennium Statement of agreed social and ecological values. — **F43; HP15**

David John Clark

David Clark born in Wellington on 20 July 1947 and was educated at Ngaio Primary School, Onslow College and Victoria University, Wellington, gaining a BA in History and Asian Studies from Victoria University, before studying at the Presbyterian Theological Hall, Knox College, Dunedin (1970-2) where he completed an LTheol. In his student days he was active in the nuclear disarmament and anti-Vietnam War movements as well as student politics. Ordained in 1973 at Knox Church, Dannevirke, he served in Presbyterian parishes in southern Hawkes Bay, southern Taranaki, and Christchurch, before becoming the minister of St Luke's, Auckland, in 1988. In 1994 he gained a Master of Theology degree from Oxford University, having completed a distance learning Masters programme in practical theology from Westminster College, Oxford. For ten years as a minister he was the editor of Forum, a monthly magazine for Presbyterian ministers. David Clark died in Auckland on Tuesday 13 March 2012.

A progressive thinker, while in Christchurch he was active in the homosexual law reform campaign and after moving to St Luke's was one of the organisers of the first New Zealand Gay Christian conference (1991), which was held at St Luke's. For some years he was active as a Christian minister within the Auckland gay community, featuring in a number of TV documentaries and print media articles. He contributed to the Interfaith AIDS Ministry Network and the New Zealand Association of Counsellors; he also developed close supportive links with refugees from Laos, Thailand and Cambodia. — **H21**

Elizabeth Cecilia Douglas Clephane

Born on 18 June 1830, the third daughter of a Scottish advocate and county sheriff, Elizabeth lived most of her short life near Edinburgh. A frail child, she was always fond of reading and writing poetry, and when about 15 years old began to confide to a younger sister what she had written. When the editor of a children's magazine, *The Children's Hour*, invited contributions, she submitted several hymns. They were copied into a Christian newspaper, *The Christian Age*, and later still, between 1872 and 1874, eight hymns were published posthumously in a Presbyterian magazine, *The Family Treasury*, under the title 'Breathings near the Border.' They included 'Beneath the Cross of Jesus' and 'The Ninety and Nine.' Both of these hymns were promoted by the American evangelist Ira D. Sankey (1840-1908), who published them in his *Sacred Songs and Solos* (1873). According to Clephane's sister, Sankey, when touring Scotland, had accidentally come across them in a copy of *The Christian Age* left behind by a previous passenger in the train. In her lifetime, Elizabeth and her sister became well-known in Melrose for their generosity and charitable work; she was known in the town as 'the sunbeam.' Elizabeth Clephane died on 16 February 1869 near Melrose, Scotland. — **F27**

Helen Diana Clyde

Helen Clyde was born in Dunedin in 1889. In 1905 she won a free place at her secondary school, Otago Girls' High School, and came to

Wellington in 1907, where she worked for the Department of Education until her retirement in 1944. She was described later as 'probably the most colourful feminine character who has graced the staff of the Department.' In 1907 she joined the Presbyterian congregation of St John's in the City, Wellington, and during her 75 years of continuous membership there took leading roles in the Young Women's Bible Class, the Choir, the Board of Managers and the Women's Association.

She joined the New Zealand Women Writers and Artists' Society, becoming a Life Member after serving in many roles on the Executive, and some of her verse was published in the Association's anthology *Poems: An Anthology by New Zealand Women Writers* (Invercargill, 1953). She wrote and illustrated two books of poetry for children published by the Epworth Press, London, *A Pocketful of Rhymes: A Book of Children's Verse* (1950) and *Up the Stairs: A Book of Children's Verse* (1958). Her writing included material for radio, newspaper articles, poetry and hymns. She was a member of PEN (NZ), the Founders' League and the Poetry Society of London; one of her poems was accepted by Queen Elizabeth II. As well as her children's Christmas carol 'And did you see him, little star,' which was published in two New Zealand Hymnbook Trust's publications, one of her hymns for adults written in 1966, 'Go ye into all the world, tell of Christ,' was published in the Hymn Society of America's collection, *Hymns Published for Special Occasions and on Special Subjects 1942-79* (New York, 1978). She died on 25 November 1983. — **W644; A4; C5**

Ronald Stephen Cole-Turner

Ronald Cole-Turner was born at Logansport, Indiana, on 22 December 1948. He was educated at Wheaton College (BA in Literature) and Princeton Theological Seminary (M.Div and PhD in Systematic Theology). He became an ordained minister of the United Church of Christ in 1974. His wife, Rebecca is a spiritual director and retreat leader; they have two daughters, Sarah and Rachel. In 1995 he became Associate Professor of Theology at Memphis Theological Seminary, and he currently holds the position of H. Parker Sharp Professor of Theology and Ethics at Pittsburg Theological Seminary (1996-), a position concerned with relating theology and ethics to developments in science and technology. He is also Vice-President of the International Society for Science and Religion.

He has taken a special interest in children, that is, in contemporary science and its impact on human conception and genetic understanding. Among his many books are *The New Genesis: Theology and the Genetic Revolution* (1993), and with Brent Waters as co-author, *Pastoral Genetics: Theology and Care at the Beginning of Life* (1996) and *God and the Embryo: Religious Voices on Stem Cells and Cloning* (2003). He is not known to have written other hymns than the popular baptismal text 'Child of blessing, child of promise.' — **A11**

Valerie Collison (née Tagg)

Valerie Collison was born at Bromley, Kent, on 23 March 1933. She was educated at Bromley Grammar School for Girls and then at a secretarial college. She worked as a medical secretary at Bromley, Salisbury and Exeter, before retiring to Devon. In 1972 she entered a Southern Television contest seeking new carols for children and won the competition with her now highly popular 'Come and join the celebration,' which was published in *Carols for Children* (1972) and a number of hymnals including *Praise for Today* (1974), *Songs of Worship* (1980), *Complete Mission Praise* (1999), *Church Hymnal* (2000) and *Church Hymnary* (2005). Several of her other hymns and songs – among them 'The journey of Life,' have been published in the Scripture Union's *Praise God Together* (1985). — **W670**

Charles Crozat Converse

Charles Converse was born on 7 October 1832. After attending Elmira Academy, New York, he studied music in Berlin and Leipzig, where he enjoyed the friendship of Franz Liszt and Louis Spohr. Returning to the United States in 1857, he pursued a career in law, graduating at the Albany Law School in 1861, completing an LLD at Rutherford College and becoming an attorney. He worked in Eric, Pennsylvania, at the same time continuing his professional interest in music and composing a number of musical pieces, some of which were performed by the leading American orchestras of his day. He wrote a now forgotten cantata based on Psalm 26 (1855) and two oratorios, as well as editing a hymnal and collections of church music such as *The Church Singer* (1863) and *The Voice of Praise* (1872). He became the friend of gospel singer Ira D. Sankey, who included his setting of Joseph Scriven's 'What a friend we have in Jesus' in the first of his evangelistic hymnals, *Gospel Hymns Number 1* (1876). He died at Highwood, New Jersey, on October 18, 1918. **W648**

Cassia Joy Cowley (née Summers)

Joy Cowley was born at Levin on 7 August 1936, daughter of Peter and Cassia Summers and grew up in Foxton. She was educated at Palmerston North Girls' High School and took papers in Pharmacy from the New Zealand College of Pharmacists. Following two earlier marriages (to Ted Cowley, by whom she had four children (1956-67), and Malcolm Mason (1970-85), in 1989 she married Terry Coles, a photographer whose work often illustrates her religious writing.

Cowley began her serious writing career in 1958. Following the success in the United States of her first novel for adults, *Nest in a Falling Tree* (1967), she wrote several more adult novels, collections of short stories, and numerous books, picture books and basic readers for children. These include *The Silent One* (1981, filmed in 1985) and the anti-war story *The Duck in the Gun* (1969). Creator of Greedy Cat, Mrs Wishy-Washy and the Meanies, she now enjoys an international reputation, especially for her writing for the Story Box series and Storylines, a Children's Literature Foundation.

Joy Cowley was brought up in a Plymouth Brethren-Presbyterian family; she later explored other non-Christian faith traditions, but found that 'my culture was Christian and my religious connection was with the teacher Jesus Christ whom I saw as the great fire of God.' In 1982 she joined the Roman Catholic Church and has since written hymns, religious poetry and meditative pieces and conducted many retreats and workshops for Catholic and more broadly ecumenical groups. Her series of modern psalm-poems, *Aotearoa Psalms* (1989), *Psalms Down-Under* (1996), *Psalms for the Road* (2002), and *Come and See* (2008), are modern liturgical classics.

Joy Cowley has been awarded the New Zealand 1990 Medal, an OBE for services to children's literature (1992), the Margaret Mahy Lecture Award (1993) and an honorary DLitt (Massey University 1993). She has twice won New Zealand Post Children's Awards for junior fiction. In 2002 the Joy Cowley Award was established in her honour and in 2005 she became a Distinguished Companion of the New Zealand Order of Merit. She published *Navigation: A Memoir* in 2010. In that year she received the Prime Minister's Award for Literary Achievement. In 2018 she was admitted to membership of the Order of New Zealand and in 2020 she was made an Icon of the New Zealand Arts Foundation. — **A**25*, 77, 95, 135*; **C**28*, 42, 52*; **F**4(ii)*, 12(i)*, 24*, 37*, 44*, 46*, 61ˣ,73ˣ; **H**9, 33, 60, 62, 123

William Cowper

William Cooper was born at great Berkhamstead. Hertfordshire, England, on 15 November 1731, the sensitive son of a rural rector. He was educated at Westminster School, London and prepared for a career in law, but a nervous breakdown – he suffered for the rest of his life from depression – ended such hopes. He was befriended by Morley and Mary Unwin, and later by John Newton, the reformed slave-trader, who encouraged him to write more of the hymns he had begun following his conversion in 1764. Together they collaborated on what became known as the Olney hymns (from the village where Newton was curate). Three volumes were published in 1779, including most of the now famous hymns by each of them.

However, Cowper's deep depression returned on the death of his brother, and although he wrote much poetry at the urging of sympathetic friends (including the humorous ballad *John Gilpin*), he was unable to recover, and died at East Dereham, Suffolk, on 25 April 1800. Both Coleridge and Wordsworth greatly admired his poetry, and he was described by Erik Routley as 'the only great classical English poet who was a great hymn writer.' — **W664**

Trevor Cox

See under **Audrey Dickinson** *and* 'Jesus touch us' **(H80)**

Gerard Malcolm Crotty

Gerard Crotty was a Marist priest and composer who was born at Te Awamutu, North Island, on 6 June 1958 and died at Auckland on 26 August 1988. He was educated at Korakonui Primary School, Sacred Heart College, Auckland (1972-5), Loretto Hall Catholic Training College (1978-80) and Victoria University, Wellington, where he completed a MusB in composition in 1986. He also gained an ATCL. He served as a Marist Brother in Miramar, Wellington, and Auckland, teaching in intermediate and secondary schools. An excellent pianist, for a time he was Head of School Music at Sacred Heart College, Auckland, and he played as a church organist from 1974 to 1982. In 1983 he served as assistant to Father **John Weir**, and in that year took his final vows. He also held the position of composer-in-residence with the Wellington Youth Orchestra in 1983. In 1985 he became Director of Music at the Wellington Catholic Cathedral and was Director of Youth Liturgy for the Papal Visit of 1986. He won Wellington City Music Awards in 1984 and 1985. In addition to liturgical pieces such as 'Song from Amos' (1982) and 'To Our Lady in Winter' (1987) he wrote a wide range of songs, chamber music, choral and orchestral works. His manuscripts are now deposited in the National Library, Wellington.

John Weir gives an account of his collaboration with Crotty at a time when he himself was Rector of St Patrick's College, Wellington, and Gerard Crotty was teaching at the Marist brothers' intermediate school at Miramar; a collaboration which led to the creation of about 60 congregational hymns: 'We both recognized that…what was most needed was plain-English, fairly strictly metrical pieces with recognizable tunes which congregations could pick up after hearing the melody once or twice. After that I would write a lyric – sometimes from a scripture text – sometimes from a notion that popped into my head. He would place it on the rest of his piano, ask me a question or two clarifying some point of rhythm, and then after fingering the keys and playing a few notes softly, the melody would begin to emerge. Usually the basic melody would emerge in about sixty seconds. When I expressed my astonishment at this he would say that the melody was already there in the rhythm and expression of the words and that his only task was to discover it. Between 1981 and 1984 we wrote about 60 songs in this manner.' — **A67, 152**

See further, the article on Crotty in John Mansfield Thomson's *Biographical Dictionary of New Zealand Composers*. Wellington: Victoria University Press (1990) 48-9, and 'Gerard Crotty: An Introduction to his Life and Work,' Noel Sanders, *Music in New Zealand*, 10 (Spring 1990) 8-20.

Johann Crüger

Crüger was born at Gross-Briesen, Brandenburg, Germany, on 9 April 1598. He was educated at local schools, then at the Jesuit College at Olmütz and the Poets' School at Regensburg. In 1615 he became tutor to the children of a captain of the guard of the Elector Friedrich Wilhelm I. He went on to study theology at the famous University of Wittenburg, after which his fine voice and growing reputation as a composer led to his appointment as Cantor of the Lutheran Cathedral of St Nicholas in Berlin, a position which he held from 1622 to 1667. He founded the famous cathedral choir there and began collecting chorales and magnificats into printed volumes. He wrote on the theory and practice of music and composed a number of concertos, motets and chorale tunes himself. His most important collection of German chorales, *Praxis Pietatis Melica* (1644) went through 40 editions and became the principal source for later Lutheran hymnals. He died at Berlin on 23 February 1662. — **F56**

Colin John Daley

Colin Daley was born in Temuka in 1955 into a Salvation Army family. He was educated at Kings High School, Dunedin (1969), and Cashmere High School, Christchurch (1970-3). He completed a BA degree in Music at the University of Canterbury (1974-6) and a postgraduate qualification in teaching at Auckland Teachers College (1977). This was followed by BSc papers taken from Massey University, Palmerston North. He also gained an LMusTCL in 1984. He is a long-time member of the Salvation Army in Wellington and has been involved in performing and conducting brass bands and vocal groups. Through this he has been able to share in musical ministry throughout New Zealand as well as overseas (Australia 1987, Japan 2007, and Japan/Hong Kong 2013). He is also featured on numerous CDs and TV recordings.

He taught at Te Awamutu College (1978-1981), before taking up a position with the New Zealand Correspondence School, Wellington, where he eventually became the Head of its Music Department (1981-2007), followed by a post as National Assessment Moderator in Music for the New Zealand Qualifications Authority, Wellington (2008-10). Presently he is self-employed as a foreign exchange trader and educational consultant. He continues to assist with a range of musical and educational activities for the Salvation Army, and co-moderates an informal Salvation Army Facebook website, 'Salvos for an inclusive church.'

As a Christian, he is passionate about prayer, studying the Word and living out Micah 6:8, 'What does the LORD require of you but to do justice, and to love kindness, and to walk humbly with your God?' His personal ministry in recent years has focused on working with Christian churches and groups to create an inclusive gospel that welcomes all, regardless of age, race, gender, orientation, and ability. He regularly visited the United States to attend Christian conferences, and in January 2014 he was awarded the prestigious Brian Eckstein award in Chicago for service to GCN (the Gay Christian Network).

Colin Daley's computer skills led to his employment as the music typesetter for all the New Zealand Hymnbook Trust publications to date, from *Alleluia Aotearoa* (1993) to *Hope is our Song* (2009). He is also an internationally published composer himself, with his vocal setting of the gospel song 'Jesus Saves' printed in *The Musical Salvationist* (London, 1987). — **A92; C21**

Mary Veronica Delany

Mary Veronica Delany was born at Ngaruawahia on 10 August 1915. She was educated at St Mary's Primary School, Avondale, and St Mary's College, Ponsonby, Auckland. A brilliant scholar, she studied at the University of Auckland, where she gained an MA in English (1936), then at Linacre College of Oxford University, England, where she graduated MA in 1979. In 1936 she entered the Catholic order of the Sisters of Mercy at St Mary's Convent, Ponsonby, remaining a member of the Auckland Congregation until her death on 29 July 1998. She taught for many years at St Mary's College, eventually becoming its Principal, and was also greatly in demand as a speaker to various groups on a wide variety of Scripture and literary topics. The school's new library, opened in 2006, was named after her.

In 1978 Oxford University Press published her edition of the works of the 17th century English Catholic poet Patrick Cary, and she contributed the biography of Mary Cecilia Maher, founder of the order of the Sisters of Mercy in New Zealand, to the *Dictionary of New Zealand Biography*. In 1952 she published

Gracious is the Time, commemorating the centenary of the arrival of the Sisters of Mercy in New Zealand in 1850. She is the author of the hymn 'O Bread of Joy,' composed the St Mary's school song, and wrote poetry all her life. — **A104**

David Raymond Scott Dell

David Dell, hymn-writer, composer, archivist and historian, was born on 13 October 1959 at Upper Hutt, Wellington. He was educated at Fraser Crescent School, Maidstone Intermediate and Upper Hutt College. He received training in singing, piano, guitar, violin and the pipe organ. After working for five years as a sound engineer for Radio New Zealand, he trained for the Presbyterian ministry at the University of Otago, where he studied music, drama, playwriting and theology, he graduated BTheol from the Presbyterian Theological Hall in Dunedin. In 1985 he married Brenda Philip, daughter of the New Zealand executive director of Music for Youth and later herself a Presbyterian youth worker. In 1987 he was ordained as a part-time assistant minister at Napier West Presbyterian Church, and in the same year became associate minister of St Andrew's, Hastings. In 1992 he was appointed pastor and choir organiser of Rimutaka Baptist Church, returning in 2001 to the Wellington Presbytery as Minister within the Bounds. In 2002 he formed in Upper Hutt and led until 2007 the Take Note Singers; this leisure singing group later expanded to Kāpiti, Porirua, and Wellington City. From 2002 he served as a chaplain for the New Zealand Police in the Hutt Valley and later at their Porirua College. In 2012 he became National Co-ordinating Chaplain for the New Zealand Police Force.

David Dell has written over a hundred Christian songs, hymns and choruses, and much other music. He has also led worship and music workshops throughout New Zealand. He published an important early collection of contemporary New Zealand Christian hymns and songs in *New Zealand Praise* (1988), including several of his own hymns and arrangements. This was followed by two supplements published in 1990 and 1993. His songs also appear in *Alleluia Aotearoa* (1993) and *Carol our Christmas* (1996).

In 1987 he began collecting printed Christian music, gathering New Zealand's largest private library of such material, consisting of some 8,000 hymnals and songbooks and 5,000 pieces of sheet music. In 1996 he shifted focus and founded the Sheet Music Archive of New Zealand, gathering historic sheet music, musical memorabilia and old musical instruments. It is now the largest such collection in the world. — **A10, 21, 78, 93, 94. 154; C43, 48**

Ronald Graeme Dellow

Ronald Dellow was born in Auckland on 29 September 1924. He became an Auckland choirmaster, composer, organist, harpsichordist, teacher and administrator. He was one of New Zealand's first professionally trained church musicians, and his skill as choirmaster and organist enriched many Auckland churches. He studied music at Auckland University College in 1942 and 1946-7 and he later travelled to Britain to study at the Royal School of Church Music (1957-8). From 1950 to 1990 he lectured and organized music courses at the University of Auckland's Centre for Continuing education.

For 21 years he was one of the driving forces behind the famous Cambridge Music School, and he established the Hamilton Music School. He was co-founder in 1954 of the New Zealand Recorder Society, he formed the choral group the Community Arts Singers, and in the 1970s he headed the Auckland Bach Cantata Society, which later became the city's Bach Musica society.

Of his more than 100 compositions, many are organ pieces and choral music written for the church. They include anthems, psalm settings, carols, liturgical music, five Magnificats and a Missa Brevis, versicles and responses, graces and doxologies. It has been said of him that 'Ron had a particular skill in writing for the ability, the sound and the type of group that [a request for a composition] came from. I remember going to his church to hear a piece he had written, and there were only seven singers in the choir. Yet it was beautiful. If someone else had tried to do that with such a small group it could have been disastrous. Ron had a real knack.'

In 1980 he was awarded an MBE for services to music. He died on 12 April 2004, and many of his papers were deposited in the Alexander Turnbull Library, Wellington. — **A124**

See further, the article on Dellow in John Mansfield Thomson's *Biographical Dictionary of New Zealand Composers*. Wellington: Victoria University Press (1990) 53, which lists many of his compositions.

Audrey Nina Dickinson (née Daysch)

Audrey Dickinson was born on 14 January 1930 in Masterton. She worked in a law office and as a hostess/coordinator at friendship House, a social service centre in Manukau City, Auckland, where she developed an innovative ministry, before completing a LTh degree at Trinity College, Auckland, and entering the ordained Methodist ministry in 1983. She served in the parishes of Remuera, Mangere and Manurewa (on two occasions), and on several Church committees, and became a member of the Wesley Historical Society. She married James William Dickinson in 1950, and brought up a family of five. She wrote a number of children's stories, and became a prolific hymn writer, publishing 40 of her hymns and songs in two volumes, *Simply Different Hymns* and *More Simply Different Hymns* (both 2001). She retired in 1995 and died at Nelson on 19 December 2009.

Audrey Dickinson has described her hymn writing as the result of a single burst of creative energy late in her life: the outcome of an invitation to write words to a piece of music for church use. 'So began a process of sometimes the words coming first and sometimes the music. Music writer **Trevor Cox** and I needed to work in tandem much of the time. What happened from then on was little short of miraculous. It was like a drug. I simply could not stop. Almost every day there were words to be recorded. Within 12 weeks 20 hymns (which we think are something different) were written. Some were set to music by organist Trevor [Cox] who provided the first pieces, some seemed to fit better to ancient tunes and another to one of my simple airs…Don't think it stops here. There is already another book almost written. The drug has not released its hold nor the dramatic outpouring of ideas slowed its force' (*Something Different Hymns*, 'From poetry to hymns'). — **H80**

Eleanor Joy Dine (née Tibble)

Joy Dine was born in Papakura on 20 November 1937, the daughter of Methodist and Anglican parents. She was educated at Auckland Girls' Grammar School and the University of Auckland, where she graduated BA in 1958. In 1995, after a teaching career and marriage to the Reverend Mervyn Dine in 1959, she began study at Trinity/St John's College for a BTheol degree and was capped in 2000. Before her marriage she was very much involved in the worshipping life of the Mt Albert Methodist Church, including its choir, and participated in the Student Christian Movement at University. In 1970 she was made a member of the Faith and Order Committee of the Methodist Church, a position she held with some interruption due to illness (she suffered from severe rheumatoid arthritis from her 20s until her death on 9 August 2001).

Joy's association with the Faith and Order Committee brought participation in creating public orders of service, and from the 1980s she began writing liturgies, prayers and meditations for both formal and informal occasions; of particular significance was the preparation of worship material for the 2001 Christmas Appeal of Christian World Service. When the Methodist Writers' Guild was formed in the early 1990s she became a member and editor. Her earliest hymn was written for the Centennial of the Takapuna Methodist Church in 1983, and she continued to write hymn texts, including 'God who sets us on a journey' (1993) out of her strong interest in the Methodist Church's journey and her personal commitment to regular Sunday worship. — **F32**

A fuller account of her life and writing is given by her husband Mervyn Dine in 'God who sets us on a journey: the life, liturgy and hymns of Joy Dine,' *Music in the Air* 16 (Winter 2003), 8-13.

Philip Doddridge

Philip Doddridge was born in London on 26 June 1702, the last of the 20 children of Daniel Doddridge, a dealer in oil and pickles. Before he could read, his mother taught him using the tiles on the chimney place in their sitting room as a visual aid. But he was orphaned and left destitute before he was taken into the care of a Presbyterian minister Samuel Clark of St Albans who later encouraged his call to ministry. He rejected an opportunity offered by a wealthy patron to enter the Anglican priesthood, choosing instead to lead a dissenting Academy at Kilworth in Leicestershire.

Over the following years, through extensive visits and correspondence he developed close relations with many religious revivalists and independents. In this way he helped establish and maintain a circle of influential independent religious thinkers and writers, including Isaac Watts. He also became a prolific author and hymn writer. His *The Rise and Progress of Religion in the Soul* (1745, dedicated to Isaac Watts) was translated into seven languages. His six-volume *Family Expositor* (1739-56) was drawn on by John Wesley for his Notes on The New Testament. Of his four hundred hymns, several have become classics. The Universities of Aberdeen awarded him the degree of Doctor of Divinity in 1736. However, when his health broke down under his enormous academic and pastoral load, he sailed for Lisbon, hoping for a cure, but he died there on 26 October 1751. — **W662; A129**

Eileen May Duggan

Eileen Duggan was born at Tuamarina near Blenheim, Marlborough, on 21 May 1894, the daughter of an Irish Roman Catholic family. She attended Tuamarina School from 1901 to 1910 and Marlborough High School. She then taught as a trainee teacher at Tuamarina School (1912-13) and attended Wellington Teachers Training College (1914-15). She studied at Victoria University College, Wellington, where she completed a BA (1916) and an MA with first class honours in History (1918). She taught for a time at Dannevirke and Marlborough High Schools, as well as St Patrick's College, Wellington, and briefly held the position of Assistant Lecturer at Victoria University College. Ill health forced her to give up teaching and she took up journalism, supporting herself from 1927 by writing for the Catholic newspaper *The New Zealand Tablet*.

Her first poems were published in *The Tablet* in 1917, and she continued writing and publishing poetry until about 1951. She published individual poems in various New Zealand and overseas journals, and by the 1930s was perhaps the best-known poet in New Zealand, with an Eileen Duggan Society formed in America. She was awarded an OBE in 1937 for services to the Dominion (as New Zealand then was), one of the first New Zealand writers to be honoured in this way. In 1942, Prime Minister Peter Fraser, who was a personal friend, arranged for her to receive a small state pension. She died at Wellington on 10 December 1972.

She published five volumes of poetry, much of it religious: *Poems* (1921), *New Zealand Bird Songs* (1929), *Poems* (1937), *New Zealand Poems* (1940) and *More Poems* (1951). — **C8***

Alex J. Duncan

This New Zealand musician/composer collaborated with **Bing Lucas**, a fellow member of the Tawa-Linden Baptist Church, Wellington, in the writing of several hymns and the rock musical *Saultalk* (1974).

Three of his hymn settings appear in *Servant Songs* (1987), including the popular Christmas carol 'From pastures green, when sheep come in for shearing' (also included in *Carol our Christmas*, 1996). — **C18**

Samuel Dyer

Born in Hampshire, England, on 4 November 1785, Samuel Dyer was instructed in music by the singing-master Thomas Walker. In 1811 he emigrated to America where he taught music and directed choirs in New York City and Philadelphia, Pennsylvania. He later moved to Baltimore, Maryland, leading singing schools in the south and north of the country and conducting New York Sacred Music Society concerts. He published collections of religious music including *A New Selection of Sacred Music* (1817, with supplements in 1823 and 1826) *and The Philadelphia Collection of Sacred Music* (1828), and a number of his own anthems appeared in *Anthems* (1822 and 1834). A reformer, he condemned the then common practice of altering and mutilating existing tunes and tried to improve the physical quality of American music publishing. He died at Hoboken, New Jersey, on 20 July 1835. — **W660**

John Bacchus Dykes

John Bacchus Dykes (his second name that of his maternal ancestors, not the Roman god of wine) was born at Kingston-upon-Hull on 10 March 1823. He attended Kingston College, and the age of ten began playing the organ at St John's, Hull, where his grandfather was the minister. His earliest hymn tunes, now lost, were written for Sunday School anniversaries there. When the family moved to Wakefield in 1841 he completed his education and frequently played the organ at Holy Trinity Church. He became a student at St Catherine's Hall, Cambridge, in October 1843, and joined the University Madrigal Society; he was co-founder of the Cambridge University Musical Society and became its President. He took a BA in 1847, read for holy orders, and was ordained in York Minster by the Archbishop of York (1848). After a brief curacy at Malton, he became a minor canon and then precentor of Durham Cathedral, assisting at the organ. From 1853 he was made librarian, master of the choristers and organist. He received an honorary DMus from the University of Durham in 1861, and following a dispute with the Bishop (Dykes was an Anglo-Catholic churchman, the Bishop was not) left the Cathedral to became vicar of St Oswald's, Durham (1862-67). He moved from Durham to Sussex, and died on 22 January 1876 at Ticehurst, Sussex.

Dykes published many sermons, wrote articles on religious subjects, and composed some anthems and other music. But he is remembered chiefly for his more than 300 hymn tunes, which appeared in hymnals beginning with John Grey's *Hymnal* 1857) and *Hymns Ancient & Modern* (1861) and have continued into modern use. — **W664**

Nigel Onslow Eastgate

Nigel Eastgate was born in Dunedin on 2 November 1930. He received his secondary education at Christ's College, Christchurch, and graduated MB ChB from the University of Otago in 1956. He showed something of his many talents while at the university; there he edited the Capping Book and began nearly 40 years of writing witty lyrics for the Otago University Capping Sextette and Capping Concert farces. While studying medicine, he completed most of the units of a music degree and trained the University choir for concerts and performance with the New Zealand Symphony Orchestra.

In 1959 he joined New Zealand's first group practice in South Dunedin and worked there until his retirement in 1997. He took a special interest in neurology, psychiatry and medical ethics, chaired the Ethics Committee of the Otago branch of the New Zealand Medical Association for many years and was a member of the national executive council during the difficult period of abortion law reform. He also served a term as President of the Otago branch of the NZMA. He used hypnosis in his work and was a member of the Australasian Hypnosis Society, as well as a practising acupuncturist. Even while working as a busy medical practitioner, he tutored in the University of Otago's Music Department, particularly in counterpoint and fugue, and at one time performed a series of harpsichord recitals for television.

After the death of his first wife Lindsey Harrington he married again. Nigel Eastgate died in Dunedin on 7 September 2001 at the age of 71: his second wife, Coreen, his five children and nine grandchildren survive him. He left behind a one-act comic operetta, *Bridge to Somewhere*, with music by Professor John Drummond, performed in Dunedin in 2001 as part of the Otago Festival of the Arts, and a number of pieces of religious music, not all of them published. They include five carols and hymns published by the New Zealand Hymn Book Trust and two choral works, *Estas in Exilium*, and *O be joyful in God*. *Estas in Exilium* was recorded by the University of Auckland Festival Choir in 1972. — **A8, 96, 103, 108, 126; C33(ii); F12**

Felicia Rosemary Elizabeth Edgecombe (née Auld)

Felicia Edgecombe was born at Napier on 6 December 1945, and educated at Tauranga Girls' College, then at Auckland University, where she studied English and Music for a BA degree, completed in 1967. She went on to teach at Lynfield College, Auckland (1968-9), Newlands College, Wellington (1972-3) and Porirua College, Wellington (1988-93). For 10 years she served as Head of Music at Queen Margaret College, the largest independent girls' school in Wellington (1994-2003), then at Samuel Marsden Collegiate School, Whitby (2006-11). In 1992 she attended a world conference of the Scripture Union held in the Netherlands, then in 2001 directed the music at the next world conference held at Nottingham, England. She has since written a number of hymns and songs for that organisation.

Like her close friend **Rosemary Russell**, she is a long-time member of the Titahi Bay Community Church (formerly known as the Titahi Bay Gospel Chapel) in Porirua City, north of Wellington. There she directed the recording of 2 CDs of Titahi Bay Gospel Chapel music, *Transmission* (1998) and *Sounds of Grace* (2004). She also recorded 10 songs for the national radio programme Praise Be in 2000. Much involved with choirs and church music in the larger musical scene in Wellington, she has written choral music ranging from contemporary church songs to children's songs and four-part choral works for the choirs in which she has sung or directed: Festival Singers (with **Guy Jansen**, 1977-89), The Queen's Singers (1997-2003) and Capital Choir, Wellington (2004-), the singers she currently directs. Many of her songs have been recorded and performed on television; she has also been involved in recordings of school groups, community groups and churches. In 2014, with Rosemary Russell, she produced for Scripture Union's Supakidz programme for primary schools a CD of 12 original children's songs, called *Godsongz for Kids*, featuring children from the Titahi Bay Gospel Chapel.

In the preface to their joint publication *Songs of Life* (1996) she and Rosemary Russell write, 'Celebrating life's special moments, grappling with life's challenges and moderating it all with our knowledge and understanding of God has helped produce the songs in this collection. The songs have been born out of the experiences of two New Zealand women, their families, friends and their communities. They represent moments of passion – birth, death, disaster, love, gratitude for special provision and concern for suffering. Things like the death of a friend, the birth of a baby, the joy at seeing love develop between friends, a devastating fire at the school, new understanding of some spiritual truth, all require expression, and in that expression become a dialogue with the Almighty, assisting us to make sense of it all. God is there in all our struggles, sadness and joy, and often a passage of Scripture takes on a new meaning and gives rise to a new song.'

She describes herself as 'passionate about the beauty of New Zealand, the love of God, of family and the importance of community music-making.' She married Ken Edgecombe in 1970, has four adult sons, Mark, James, Robert and Philip, and now lives in Paremata, Wellington.

Her choral and worship songs and arrangements appear in *Servant Songs*, which she co-edited with Guy Jansen (1987), *New Zealand Praise* (1988) and its 1993 update, *Alleluia Aotearoa* (1993), *Songs of Life: Songs to celebrate the Special Moments of Life*, by Felicia Edgecombe and Rosemary Russell (Wellington: Festivity Productions, 1996) and *Sounds of Grace: Music of Seven original Songs from Titahi Bay Gospel Chapel* (2004). Other works include *The Last Word*, a musical co-written with Rosemary Russell (1998), and a number of choral settings held at the SOUNZ centre: 'Nation Prayer,' 'Consider the Flowers,' 'Pied Beauty' by Gerard Manley Hopkins, 'Place' by Brian Turner and 'World' by Rachel McAlpine. She is currently working on 'Shaky Places,' a song-cycle commissioned by Rachel McAlpine, using a number of New Zealand poems. — **A46, 83, 107; C32**

Howard (Rusty) Milton III Edwards

Known as Rusty Edwards, this American Lutheran pastor and hymn writer was born in Dixon, Illinois on 22 January 1955. He graduated from Interlochen Arts Academy, the University of Nebraska and Lutheran Northwestern Seminary, and has a doctorate in creative ministry from Notre Dame, Indiana. He was ordained in 1985 and became senior pastor of Gloria Dei Lutheran Church, Rockville, Illinois (1991-8) before he went on to become senior pastor of Christ Lutheran Church in Marietta, Georgia (a suburb of Atlanta), where he still serves.

His hymns have been published in 70 books used by 36 denominations in Australia, Canada, China, England, Japan, New Zealand, Scotland, and America. As well as anthems and CDs of his work, five collections of his hymns have appeared: *The Yes of the Heart* (1993), *Grateful Praise* (1998), *As Sunshine to a Garden* (1999), *Each breath, Every Heartbeat* (2007), and *Bidden, Unbidden* (2004). His sixth book, *Come, My Chosen*, involved co-writers from several countries. He has worked with a number of writers and composers, including Dave Brubeck, Hal Hopson, Pablo Sosa and Shirley Murray. He is an honorary citizen of Austin, Texas and a Kentucky Colonel. He was 2009 Visiting Fellow at Yale University Institute of Sacred Music and 2012 Visiting Fellow of Africa University in Zimbabwe. He is a member of the Blues Hall of Fame. — **F29, 41**

Janet Elspeth Sim Elder (née Sim)

Janet Elder was born on a farm near Tuatapere, South Otago, on 3 March 1948. A member of a staunchly Presbyterian family, she recalls singing and playing hymns and Scottish songs with grandparents, aunts, uncles, cousins and friends around the piano on Sunday evenings. She was educated at Pukemaori primary school (1953-59), then attended Columba College, Dunedin (1960-65) where she accompanied the school choir. She completed a BA Hons with first class honours in music at the University of Otago (1966-69), singing with the University A Capella Choir led by Professor Peter Platt, then completed a Diploma in Teaching with Distinction at Christchurch Teachers College (1970). She taught as a Music Specialist at Cashmere High School, Christchurch, singing with the Royal Christchurch Musical Society Choir and working with **Guy Jansen** as one of his assistant conductors for the Christchurch based Celebration Singers. She then undertook relief and part-time teaching at Central Southland College, Winton (1974-79). This included conducting its award-winning orchestra in the Bank of New South Wales Schools Chamber Music contest in Wellington. She formed a 60-strong youth choir attached to the Winton Presbyterian Church, which drew young people from all over Western and Central Southland and also founded an adult chamber choir, the Ionian Singers. Both of these choirs performed throughout Southland for a number of years and 'introduced country people to composers they would not normally have heard in live performance, such as Schütz, Josquin Desprez and Vivaldi.'

She took up a position teaching music at South Otago High School, where she established yet another youth choir. In 1984 she returned to Dunedin to teach the piano at Columba College and carried out some relief teaching at John McGlashan College, as well as offering University Extension tutoring. She also joined the Southern Consort of Voices, led by Professor Jack Spiers, a former teacher and friend. She returned to tertiary studies at Otago University from 1997 to 1999, completing a Dip Grad in Theology, and in 2003 was a Sabbatical Visitor at the United Reformed Church's Westminster College, Cambridge, England. She is an Elder of Knox Church, Dunedin, and occasionally sings with the church Choir. She describes herself now as 'happily retired.'

Janet Elder has been involved in choral singing throughout her life and has written arrangements for several of these choirs, including the Celebration Singers (Christchurch) and the Southern Consort of Voices (Dunedin). — **W635**

George Job Elvey

Born into a family with a long history of musical activity at Canterbury, England on 27 March 1817, Elvey began his musical career as a chorister at Canterbury Cathedral. He studied at New College, Oxford, and at the Royal Academy of Music, taking a B.Mus in 1938 and a D.Mus in 1840. At the age of only 19 he was appointed organist and master of the boys' choir of St George's Chapel, Windsor and held the position for 47 years until his retirement in 1882.

There he was required to compose music for royal ceremonies and other state occasions, including the wedding of Queen Victoria's daughter Princess Louise (after which he was knighted). He also composed hymn tunes, anthems, oratorios and much service music. He died at Windelsham, Surrey, on 9 December 1893. — **H19**

David Evans

David Evans was born on 6 February 1874 at Resolven, Glamorgan. At 13 years of age he started work in the coalfield, where he remained for five years. He spent his free time studying music and by the age of 15 had his own choir. He won a three-year Summer School College Scholarship, and attended a two-year course at Cardiff University College, under the tutorship of Dr Joseph Parry. In 1895 he became the youngest Oxford Mus. Bac. in Wales. From 1899 to 1903 he was organist and choirmaster at Jewin Calvinistic Methodist Church, London. In 1903 he succeeded Parry as lecturer in the Music Department at University College, Cardiff, and in 1908 became the first Professor of Music there. Throughout his lifetime Dr Evans was well known in Wales as an adjudicator and conductor; he also arranged a number of hymns and published much religious and other music, including *Llyfr Emynau ac Thomas* (1929) and the *Revised Church Hymnary* (1927). He retired in 1939 and died 17 May 1948 at Rhosllanerchrugog, Wrecsam, Denbighshire. — **W646**

Frederick William Faber

Faber was born at Calverley, Yorkshire, on 28 June 1814, the son of strict Calvinist parents. He was educated at Shrewsbury and Harrow, then completed a BA at Balliol College, Oxford (1836). He became a scholar, then a Fellow of University College, Oxford, in 1837. In 1839 he was ordained a priest in the Church of England and in 1843 became Rector of Elton in Huntingdonshire, where he gained a reputation as a preacher and a Romanist. In 1838 he had published an attack on the Roman Catholic Church, but soon afterwards came under the influence of Cardinal Newman and his Oxford Movement. Faber had journeyed to Rome in 1843; following a further visit to Rome and Florence in 1845 he converted to Roman Catholicism. At Cottam Hall near Cheadle, Staffordshire, he founded a community called the Brothers of the Will of God. When in 1847 Faber was ordained a Roman Catholic priest, with his community of 40 members he set about converting the entire parish, which he succeeded in doing, with the exception of 'the parson, the pew-opener and two drunken men.' In 1848, when Newman set up his congregation of the Oratory of St Philip

Neri at Birmingham, he joined him there, taking his followers with him.

In 1849 he was sent to London, to establish a branch of the Oratory, first in a former tavern in the Strand, and from 1854 at Brompton in South Kensington. As well as conducting regular services, preaching, and concerning himself with the lives of the many poor Londoners who lived in the area, he published a number of theological works, pamphlets, poems and translations and edited the *Forty-nine Oratorian Lives of the Modern Saints*. Inspired by the example of William Cowper and Charles Wesley, and keen to promote congregational singing at his services, he wrote some 150 hymns, published in four collections. Faber's piety and unswerving loyalty to the Holy See was rewarded by the Pope with a Doctorate in Divinity (1854). He died at the Brompton Oratory 26 September 1863. — **H135**

Alfred Victor Fedak

Leading American church musician and composer, Alfred Fedak was born on July 4 1953 in Elizabeth, New Jersey. He graduated from Hope College in 1975 with degrees in Organ Performance and Music History and subsequently earned a Masters' degree in Organ Performance from Montclair State University. A Fellow of the American Guild of Organists and a Life member of the Hymn Society of America, Fedak has performed and lectured widely throughout the United States. He is also a widely-published composer of church music with over 200 choral and organ works in print, and his hymn tunes appear in hymnals and collections in the United States, Canada, England, Scotland, New Zealand, China and Japan. Four anthologies of his hymns have been published: *The Alfred V. Fedak Hymnary* (1990), *Sing to the Lord No Threadbare Song* (2001), *God of the Future* (2009), and *Stones Unthrown* (2014). In addition, he has written articles and reviews for *The American Organist, The Hymn, Reformed Worship*, and *Music and Worship*. Fedak has served as organist and choir director for many churches and synagogues in eastern and midwest America, and currently serves as Minister of Music and Arts at Westminster Presbyterian Church on Capitol Hill in Albany, New York. — **A55; F73**

Robert (Rob) Ferguson

Rob Ferguson was born in Dunedin, on 4 October 1949. He was educated at King's High School (1963-1967) and the University of Otago (1969-1971) where he graduated with a BA in English; then at Massey University (1988-9), graduating with an MA in English and a thesis on contextual hymnology, *How Shall We Sing the Lord's Song in a Strange Land?* An overview of this thesis and the substance of the fourth chapter, 'The Dilemma of the Modern,' is published in the Winter issue of *Music in the Air: Song and Spirituality* (1997), 25-34.

From 1972 to 1976 Ferguson was employed as a secondary school teacher; in 1977 he entered St John's Theological College and trained for the Methodist ministry, graduating LTheol in 1980. He was ordained and married his second wife Dawn in 1979, then worked as a parish minister in Taranaki, at Palmerston North and in Christchurch, at Beckenham Methodist Church, St Albans Uniting Parish and at St Ninian's Presbyterian Church. After the Christchurch earthquakes, he was associated with the Durham Street Methodist Church for two years (2016-18) as a 'walking pastor.' Now living in Whanganui, he serves as the Co-Superintendent of the Lower North Island Synod of the Methodist Church. His time at Palmerston North included an exchange year at Trinity United Church, Port Coquitiam, Canada. He has worked as an educational consultant for the national Methodist Church, and as a clinician for the Stop Trust, dealing with adult sexual abusers.

Although he claims no musical skill, he has written a number of hymn texts, four of which are published as 'New Wine: Old Bottles' in the Summer issue of *Music in the Air: Song and Spirituality* (1997), 25-28. He says of himself, 'I have always been a scribbler. Degrees in English gave me a sense of what works when written. Leading worship, trying to choose relevant hymns each week, has given me a practical take on the craft of public worship. It has also raised my awareness of the paucity of relevant modern material I believe strongly that New Zealand hymns give us a valuable sense of ourselves as we struggle with issues of faith in a communal context. My hymns, such as they are, are not about individual piety but about a community focus. No "Just as I am" in my small body of work.'

'My hymn writing has usually been sparked by either a request for words, or a specific service, or something that is happening around me I am musically illiterate, but have a good sense of the rhythm of words, and understand church tune metres well. So most often I have written words which are coupled with known and possibly hackneyed church tunes. I am grateful that the New Zealand Hymnbook trust has encouraged musicians to make tunes for my words.' — **H20, 51, 92, 103**

Donald Fishel

Born on 1 November 1950, in Hart, Michigan, United States hymn writer Donald Fisher began studying the flute in 1960 and after completing his high school studies attended the University of Michigan School of Music at Ann Arbor, where in 1972 he graduated with a BMus in Music Education (Instrumental). He then embarked on a career in music publishing for Word of God Music. He had already in 1969 joined the Word of God community in Ann Arbor, where he became a music leader, conducted the orchestra and was part of the music ministry planning team. His earliest Christian music composition was **Alleluia No 1**, written in 1971, but he went on to become a writer of several popular religious songs, some of which he edited for his publishers.

In 1981, he returned to college and completed a degree in Computer Science, beginning a new career in 1983 as a Systems Programmer. He has continued to exercise his skill as a flautist, becoming principal flautist for the Ann Arbor Civic Band (2001-6), and playing in several musical theatre productions and as a soloist.

In 2004 he created and performed a new work for two readers, flute and organ, *The Breath of the Spirit*, which he has performed in New York, Paris and Lisbon, as well as Ann Arbor and Sarasota, Florida. He has continued to teach the flute, and now works as an instructor and freelance performer based in Antioch, Tennessee. — **W674(ii)**

Helen Wynfreda Fisher

Helen Fisher was born at Mapua, Nelson, on 4 February 1942, and grew up there before attending secondary school in Wellington. In 1964 she completed a BA in English at Canterbury University, then taught English, Music and French in New Zealand and Canadian secondary schools. While raising her family of three daughters, she studied music at Victoria University. In 1986 she began composition studies with Ross Harris, David Farquhar and Jack Body and in 1987 her *Woodwind Trio* won first prize in Victoria University's Composers' Competition; in 1989 her choral work *Pounamu* [Greenstone] won second prize. She graduated BMus (Hons) in composition in 1991.

In 1990 and 1991, she held an Arts Council residency as Composer-in-Schools in the Wellington region. In 1993, she initiated the first New Zealand Composing Women's Festival. Since 1992 she has been working in Wellington as a free-lance composer, receiving commissions to compose for a variety of vocal and instrumental ensembles and also for dance theatre. Her 1994 Christmas choral work, *Te Whakaaro pai ki Nga Tangata* (revised 1997), based on texts from Isaiah and St Luke, was performed by two choirs in 1994 and at the Big Sing choral festival held at Dunedin in 2009. Two CDs of her chamber music have received critical acclaim, and her compositions have been performed in Europe, the United Kingdom, Asia, the United States, Australia and regularly in New Zealand.

Beginning with her first large-scale work, *Te Tangi A Te Matui* [The Call of the Matui] (1986), many of Helen Fisher's compositions have explored the interface of Western classical and Māori musical styles. She has collaborated extensively with Māori communities and performing artists; her *Tētē Kura*, was premièred by Te Waka Huia and the New Zealand Youth Choir in 2000. She sees her inspiration as resulting from a fusion of own Celtic heritage with that of the *tangata whenua* (people of the land) and the land itself. *Music for a New Millennium* (Auckland: Millennium Music Publications, 2003), included her 'Te Miha Tuituia Mass' [Mass that weaves people together with God], written in 1999. — **H84**

Valerie (Val) Fleetwood

This member of the congregation of St Paul's Anglican Church, Auckland, in the 1970s, was the musician responsible for nearly 40 piano arrangements of songs in the music edition of *New Harvest* (1979). — **A8**

Robert James Berkeley Fleming

Robert Fleming, composer, pianist, organist, choirmaster and teacher, was born in Prince Albert, Saskatchewan, on 12 November 1921. His family settled in Saskatoon where he first studied with his mother. Between 1937 and 1939 he studied at the Royal College of Music, London, under Arthur Benjamin and Herbert Howells. On his return to Saskatoon he taught piano before launching a career as a concert pianist and touring Saskatchewan giving recitals.

While studying piano in 1941-2 he became the assistant organist at the Church of St Alban the Martyr in Saskatoon. In 1941 and 1945 he attended the Toronto Royal Conservatory of Music, studying composition, piano, conducting and the organ. Between 1945 and 1946 he taught at Upper Canada College, Toronto, a private school for boys, before joining the Canadian National Film Board. He worked in Ottawa and Montreal as a staff composer for the Board between 1946 and 1958, before becoming music director between 1958 and 1970.

He was music director for the Ottawa Ballet Festival in 1953 and organist-choirmaster at Glebe United Church in 1954 and at St George's Anglican Church in Sainte-Anne-de-Bellevue, Quebec. In 1970 he and his family moved back to Ottawa where he taught 20th century music and Canadian composers at Carleton University. In 1972 he was appointed organist-choirmaster at St Matthias' Anglican Church in Ottawa (Westboro). He died on 28 November 1976. — **W671**

Leo Foliaki

A Tongan hymn writer about whom no information has emerged. See 'Ke tau fakafeta'I' (A84). It is possible that he is the person whose full name is Leopino Foliaki (1924-2000). — **A84**

Guthrie Hubert Foote

Guthrie Foote was born at Tunbridge Wells, Kent, England, on 15 January 1897, and educated at Skinner's School, Tunbridge Wells, where his father had founded a local choir. He went on to train as a violinist at the Royal Academy of Music, London, before engaging in War service. After the war he entered the Royal College of Music, London, and from 1916 studied conducting under Sir Henry Wood. This led to a position as conductor for the Carla Rosa Opera Company; he then founded and led the Tunbridge Wells Symphony orchestra and the Wells choir. In 1944 he joined the music department of the Oxford University Press, where he eventually took charge of the hymnals and religious services book department. He retired in 1962, but continued to act as an adviser to the Press until his death on 11 January 1972 at Bolney, Hayward's Heath, Sussex.

He wrote a number of hymns and hymn tunes (sometimes under the pseudonym of Hubert Grierson) which appeared in *The English Hymnal Service Book* (1962), *The Surrey Hymn Book* (1964), *Gathered Together* (1971) and the third edition of *Church Hymnary* (1973). He also published a collection of Christmas hymns and carols, *Merrily on High* (1959) and carols for young singers in *Merry Christmas* (1962), as well as editing *Infant Praise* (1964). — **A50**

Francis of Assisi

Born Giovanni Francesco di Bernadone at Assisi, Italy, in 1182, the son of a wealthy Italian cloth merchant and his French wife, Francis abandoned a military career and luxurious lifestyle following a vision in 1204 and adopted a life of poverty, consorting with beggars and lepers. Although he chose never to be ordained as a priest, he began preaching to ordinary people and gathered a small likeminded community of 'friars' around himself. In 1210 Pope Innocent III licensed this community as a new Order of Franciscans. In 1211 Francis constituted a similar order for women, known as the Poor Clares after their leader Clare of Assisi. Determined to bring the gospel to all, Francis attempted to reach Jerusalem and Morocco and in 1219 sailed to Egypt and succeeded in preaching to the Saracen Sultan there. Subsequently, the Franciscan order has been present in the Holy Land without interruption since 1217, when brother Elias arrived at Acre.

In later life Francis was occupied with regulating his own Order, which had spread rapidly beyond Italy to Germany, Hungary, Spain and the East, calling its members to a way of poverty, chastity and the apostolic life. Around 1220, Francis, whose love and respect for nature and its wild creatures was legendary, set up the first Christmas manger. Becoming blind and weakened by illness, in 1224 he withdrew from the leadership of the Franciscans and retired to a hermitage; he died in 1226. He was pronounced a saint by Pope Gregory IX in 1228. He is now known as the patron saint of animals, the environment and (with Catherine of Siena) of Italy. The prayer associated with his name, 'Make me an instrument of thy peace,' together with his own reputation for gentleness, has led to his being honoured. — **W 666**

Bernard John Franklin

John Franklin was born in January 1947 at Auckland, and educated at Henderson High School. He completed a BA degree at the University of Auckland, and went on to study at Knox Theological Hall. He was ordained to Presbyterian ministry at St David's, Auckland, in 1973. A few years later, after living and working in parish ministry in the United States at Toledo, Ohio, he gained a ThM degree from Princeton Theological Seminary. After parish ministries in Maumee, Ohio, Gisborne and Palmerston North, in 1999 he gained a Doctor of Ministry degree from McCormick Theological Seminary, Chicago. In 1989, at Ann Arbor University, Michigan, he completed a qualification as a Myers Briggs Type Indicator practitioner, and in 2002 at Palmerston North, he obtained the Trinity College, London, Certificate in TESOL. From 1999-2007 he was a part-time teaching assistant and senior researcher with Massey University, Palmerston North; he has also studied supervision, at Waikato University. In 1985 he married Trish (Patricia Dow-Hammonds). They have four children.

In 1981, following what he calls 'a very formative retreat at the Church of the Saviour in Washington, DC,' and at the invitation of the Presbyterian Church of New Zealand, he established a ministry of spiritual formation which grew into the ecumenical organisation Spiritual Growth Ministries. At Auckland, John eventually became a fulltime worker in this field; he is presently a member of the New Zealand Association of Christian Spiritual Directors and Spiritual Directors International, and regularly contributes to the New Zealand journal of Christian spirituality, *Refresh*.

After working for many years in Anglican networks, he was ordained into the Anglican priesthood in 2004. Now based in Dunedin, he serves as Chaplain to the Bishop of the Diocese of Dunedin, responsible for prayer and encouragement in the spiritual life. He also operates as a spiritual director, a professional supervisor, and Myers Briggs Type Indicator consultant. He describes himself as 'a priest, a pray-er, a spiritual director, ministry supervisor, preacher, eucharistic celebrant, husband, father, friend, gardener and musician.'

He has written a number of occasional hymns and has explained his own method of writing and composing as a period of waiting for the 'springing up' of inspiration: 'When I am prompted to make music, I pause, I go within, I wait for the spring to bubble, and when I sense the "springing up" I am ready. What follows is often a surprise to me. And it is a delight, as I sense the Spirit within me giving voice' ('Sounding the Song: Creativity and Music,' Refresh 6.2 (2006-7) 8-9). Some of his hymns have been published in *Festive Praise Two* (1983), Servant Songs (1987), *New Zealand Praise* (1988) and *Alleluia Aotearoa* (1993). — **A80**

Anders Frostensen

This Swedish pastor and hymn writer was born at Loshult, Kristianst Island, on 23 April 1906. He studied theology at Lund University and was ordained as a Lutheran clergyman. Frostensen served as pastor on the Isle Lovi beyond Stockholm, leading worship at the royal castle of Drottningholm, where he was preacher to three Swedish kings.

He became a leading figure in the movement to revive Swedish hymnody, beginning in 1935 and writing until 1955. He resumed hymn writing in 1960 and eventually completed some 70 hymns. His hymns, known for their poetic imagery, liberal theology and 'luminous simplicity,' became known beyond Sweden when his text 'Many are the shinings from the one light' was translated into German, English and Spanish for the Worship Book used at the Sixth Assembly of the World Council of Churches held at Vancouver in 1983. His hymns in translation have appeared in *Cantate Domino* (1974) and numerous English and American hymnals. In 1976 he edited a collection titled *Songs and Hymns from Sweden*, translated by **Fred Kaan**, and containing a number of Frostenson's own hymns. He died on 4 February 2006. — **W667**

Dale Garratt

Born in Auckland, New Zealand, in 1939, and, with her husband David Garratt (born in Wellington in 1938), one of the originators of the worldwide 'worship music' phenomenon that had its roots in the 1960s in New Zealand, Dale Garratt first worked with David, whom she met in 1962 through the Youth for Christ movement, as a musical evangelist singing at youth conventions and gospel meetings. In 1963 the pair withdrew to refocus their ministry on incorporating scripture into contemporary worship music. They married in 1964, and in 1968 published their first album, *Scripture put to Song*, commonly recognized as the initiator of the modern Praise and Worship movement. Scripture In Song became the name under which the Garratts compiled and released their music in the form of LP and tape cassette albums, songbooks and 3 *Scripture in Song* hymnals, *Songs of Praise* (words only, 1971, words and music, 1975), *Songs of the Kingdom* (1981) and *Songs of the Nations* (1988), almost all of their original work written in the 1980s. They went on to release 18 albums. Dale Garratt has said of herself, 'neither of us were musicians; we were congregational singers rather than performers…[but] a song is a tremendous way of communicating and learning God's word.'

She has since continued to exercise a national and international ministry of music, travelling widely with her husband and **Brent Chambers** as a team of evangelistic worship leaders, while continuing to compose scripture-based songs and choruses. In 1974, she and her husband held huge outdoor meetings at racetracks in Palmerston North and Tauranga, with the Garratts leading the singing of devotional songs.

In the early 1990s the pair entered a new phase of musical evangelism, inspired by the vision in *Revelation* of every nation on earth praising God in their own language. They travelled widely, visiting indigenous peoples and assisting them to express traditional Christian doctrine in their own musical forms and idioms, as described in their documentary film, *Let My People Go: A Journey to Worship*. In 1993 they sold Scripture in Song to form a new company, New Sound Publishing, with the goal of publishing indigenous expressions of worship: a recent collection under this company name is *Coming Home* (2006). In 2020, following the Christchurch earthquakes, they wrote 'We will prevail,' a song dedicated to the people of Otautahi. — **A138**

Germanus of Constantinople

Germanus was born in Constantinople (the modern Istanbul) about 645, the son of a prominent nobleman who was involved in imperial politics and executed by the then Emperor Constantine IV. Germanus himself was castrated and sent to a monastery. He entered the service of the Greek Orthodox Church and became bishop of Cyzicus, where he defended the Orthodox faith against the Iconoclastic heresy (a refusal to venerate sacred icons). In 715 Germanus was elected Patriarch or head of the Greek Orthodox Church, but only two years later a new iconoclastic Emperor, Leo III, took the throne and in 730 forced Germanus to resign and go into exile in a monastery where he remained until his death in 740. Germanus wrote a famous treatise *On the Divine Liturgy*, several commentaries on scripture and the feasts of the Church, as well as several hymns, including the original version of 'A great and mighty wonder.' — **W639**

Orlando Gibbons

Orlando Gibbons, one of the greatest of the 17th century English keyboard players and composers, was baptised at St Martin's Church, Oxford on 25 December 1583, the son of William Gibbons, a member of a band of town musicians, or waits, as they were known, William Gibbons was an Oxford man, who belonged to both the Oxford and later the Cambridge Waits. Orlando was the fourth of William's musical sons. At the age of 12 he became a chorister at King's College, Cambridge, even then a famous singing school, and went on to enrol as a Cambridge University student, completing his MusB in 1606. In 1603 he became a Gentleman of the Chapel Royal attached to the royal court at St James Palace, London, and one of the two organists there. In 1616 he was appointed player on the virginals [an early keyboard instrument] to the court of James I, and in 1622 was given a DMus by the University of Oxford. In 1623 he became joint organist (with Thomas Tomkins) and Master of the Choristers at Westminster Abbey; two years later he conducted the funeral music in the Abbey for the death of James I. He went with the royal party of the new king, Charles I, on their way to greet Charles' bride, Henrietta Maria, but he fell ill and died at Canterbury on 5 or 6 June 1625.

Gibbons began composing while still a student at Cambridge; he went on to write numerous anthems and motets, madrigals, two church services, three *in nominees* and much polyphonic vocal and instrumental music of the highest quality. Virtually all his church music was written for the services of the Anglican Church or state occasions, but he did write 17 hymn tunes, of which all but one were published in George Wither's *Hymns and Songs of the Church* (1623). In modern times they were recognised as masterpieces and revived in their authentic forms in *The English Hymnal* edited by **Ralph Vaughan Williams** (1906). — **A106**

Colin Alexander Gibson

Colin Gibson was born into a musical Methodist family, on 26 March 1933 at Dunedin. He was educated at Mornington Primary School, Macandrew Intermediate and Otago Boys' High School before attending the University of Otago, where he studied English, classics and music, completing an MA in Latin (University of New Zealand, 1955) and a DipHons in English (University of New Zealand, 1956). In 1956 he married Jeanette Jones and the couple raised a family of three children, one of whom, **John Gibson**, has become a professional composer and performer. He then studied at Christchurch Teachers' College and the University of Canterbury, before joining the staff of the English Department at Otago University (1947), where he completed a PhD (1963). He went on to teach at Otago for 42 years, becoming Professor of English in 1979 and Donald Collie Professor of English in 1984. After retiring he has continued to teach, broadcast and lecture widely on literary and musical topics.

He studied the piano and completed an LTCL in that instrument in 1951; he became organist of Mornington Methodist Church in 1955 and has directed the church choir since 1958. He was a founding member of the New Zealand Hymn Book Trust, and in 1981 established at the Dunedin Public Library a collection of hymnology now known under his name. In addition to leading workshops and giving lectures on hymn-related topics throughout New Zealand and in Australia, America, England, the Philippines and Japan he has published essays, reviews and articles on hymnology and New Zealand hymn-writing in academic and specialist music journals published in New Zealand and overseas. For some years he led an Ecumenical Institute for Distance Theological Studies course on Music and Worship, and as the dictionary's Australasian Editor has contributed all the entries on Australian and New Zealand hymn writers and their hymns to the massive online Canterbury Dictionary of Hymnology (2013). He is the author of the present Companion. In 2002 he was awarded the New Zealand Order of Merit for services to literature and music.

In 1972, stimulated by the visit to New Zealand of a group of Taizé brothers, he began writing psalm paraphrases, setting them to folk and classical melodies. This led to the writing of his own hymn texts and tunes as well as settings for many other writers' hymns, including New Zealanders **Marnie Barrell**, **Shirley Murray** and **Bill Wallace**, as well as overseas writers like Brian Wren and Adam Tice. Some of these hymns are gathered in *Singing Love* (1988), *Reading the Signature* (1994) and *Songs for a Rainbow People* (1998), but many more appear in the publications of the New Zealand Hymn Book Trust, *Alleluia Aotearoa* (1993), *Carol Our Christmas* (1996), *Faith forever Singing* (2000), *He Came Singing Peace* (2003) and *Hope is our Song* (2009). His work is well represented in hymnals published in Australia, Canada and the United States, Asia and England. His hymns have been translated into several languages, including Chinese and Japanese. In addition to hymn texts and melodies, Gibson has composed longer choral works, such as *The Spirit Within* and *The Animals' Christmas* and cantatas such as *The Saint up the Pole* [Simeon Stylites] and *Balam and Balak*. His liturgical works and arrangements as well as his children's songs lie outside the scope of this Companion, but they are numerous.* — **W625, 635, 636, 639, 644, 656. 672, 674(iii); A4, 9, 11, 17, 18, 20, 26, 33, 34, 36, 40, 42, 43, 47, 52, 53, 55, 57, 59, 60, 61, 62, 69,72, 73, 76, 79, 85, 91, 94, 99, 113, 114, 118, 119, 120, 122, 125, 127, 140, 147, 143, 147, 149, 156, 159, 161; C2, 4(ii), 5, 7,10, 11, 13(i), 15, 16, 17, 19, 22, 23, 26,28, 30, 34, 35, 36, 40(i), 42, 44, 45 47, 50, 51, 52; F4, 7, 9, 14, 15, 17, 18, 20, 21, 24, 25, 27, 28, 31, 36, 39, 40, 43, 47, 48, 49, 50, 51, 52, 53, 55, 57, 58, 62, 63, 64, 66, 67, 72, 73, 74, 78; HP12, 13, 15, 17, 20, 23, 26; H1, 2, 6, 10, 11, 12, 13, 17, 20, 22, 25, 26, 278, 28, 30, 33, 35, 36, 40, 44, 46, 49, 51, 53, 54, 55, 57, 58, 59, 61, 63, 64, 66, 67, 68, 70, 72, 73, 74, 75, 77, 81, 82, 85, 86, 87, 88, 91, 94, 96, 99, 100, 103, 104, 105, 107, 108, 113, 115, 116, 118, 120, 121, 123, 124, 126, 127, 131, 133, 135, 136, 137, 141, 144, 145, 147, 148, 150, 151, 154, 156, 157, 158**

*More complete listings of this writer and composer's work are to be found in the FINDING LIST.

John Wallace Gibson

John Gibson, second son of the hymn writer **Colin Gibson**, was born in Dunedin on 24 January 1959. He experienced choral and instrumental religious music from an early age at his parents' church, Mornington Methodist. He was educated at Kaikorai Valley High School, then at Otago University. He learned the piano, oboe and double bass while still at High School, and there with another pupil, Ian Landreth, at the age of 16 he co-authored his first rock opera *Tittivulus* (1975), which was recorded and performed both at the school and in the Regent Theatre. He became Musical Director for the Fortune Theatre, where with co-author Michael Gilchrist he wrote, produced and performed in another musical show *Life with the Lions* (1981) and directed and performed the music for Stephen Sondheim's *Pacific Overtures;* he also played for ballet classes and began to write film music scores, working with the Dunedin Natural History Unit on several documentaries, including *Wild South, Bandits of the Beech Forest, Journeys across Latitude 45* and *The World at your feet: Milford Track.*

In 1983 he moved to Auckland and became Resident Musical Director at Theatre Corporate. He has continued writing scores for such television documentaries as *Epitaph, Party Animals* and *Shackleton* (2011); television series and dramas (*The Boy from Andromeda, Donuts for Breakfast, Red Scream*); theatre plays and shows such as *A Midsummer Night's Dream, The Duchess of Malfi, Equus, The Angel and the Beloved* (settings of Rilke songs) and T.S. Eliot's *The Waste Land*; and contemporary dance – working in collaboration particularly with Douglas Wright, Shona McCullagh and Anna Dewey as well as the Hungarian group Artus. His feature film credits include *Children* (2007). He has acted in television series such as *Heroes* and provided commissioned music, dance, theatre and carillon pieces for Wellington's International Festival of the Arts and the 2007 Auckland Festival. His work for theatre now numbers 80 original scores and over 150 songs and he has performed at the Edinburgh Festival. He won a GOFTA award in 1984 for his music for *Heroes*, and a Qantas Film and Television award in 2008 for his music for *Rain of the Children*. — **H99**

Barbara Maysel Gillard (née Williams)

Barbara Gillard was born on 22 January 1930 in Enfield, Middlesex, England. She was educated in Enfield, but during the Second World War her father brought his family to New Zealand to escape the privations and dangers of the war, and from 1944-5 she was educated at Takapuna Grammar School, Auckland. On her return to England she trained as a school teacher and taught at Luckington Primary School in Wiltshire. She married Charles Edwin Gillard of Hankerton, Wiltshire, on 25 July 1952.

In 1956, with the help of her father, who with her mother and siblings was by then a permanent resident of New Zealand, Barbara and Charles emigrated to New Zealand with their two young sons, **Richard** and Robert. She had four further children, Elizabeth, Rachael, Peter and Rebekah. Life in New Zealand began, for the Gillard family, in Cockle Bay, not far from her parents who lived in Howick, Auckland. A series of moves eventually brought them to the Whangarei district, to which Barbara later returned.

Although from a Presbyterian family, Barbara Gillard attended both the Anglican and Assembly of God churches, and in later life became a Roman Catholic. She spent time as a member of St. Paul's Anglican Church, Auckland. There she enjoyed singing, worship, dancing, writing poetry and reading. She wrote several religious songs, including the carol 'The stars danced' (C43), but the others have been lost. Her love of music can be traced to her mother, Maysel Williams, who was a very talented pianist and chorister, serving the Presbyterian parishes of Howick and Kohimarama.

Barbara Gillard took up teaching again in various New Zealand schools, mainly in the Whangarei area, working for the most part with five and six year olds. She was a member of St Francis Xavier Roman Catholic parish in Whangarei for the last 17 years of her life, and when she died on 16 March 2007 in Whangarei her ashes were scattered in the flower gardens there. However, a small remnant of those ashes was later surreptitiously deposited in a Vatican flower bed by one of her daughters. She would have been delighted. — **C43**

Richard Arthur Moss Gillard

Richard Gillard was born on 22 May 1953 at Malmesbury, Wiltshire, England. With his family, he migrated to New Zealand in 1956 and spent his early years in Auckland, later moving with his family to Northland, where he attended Whangarei Boys High

School, before returning to Auckland and completing his secondary education at Takapuna Grammar School, Auckland. He trained to be a primary school teacher at the North Shore Teachers College but left teaching early in 1975 and eventually took up work as a warehouseman. He has since retired and now lives in Whangarei.

He grew up in a family belonging to a local Assemblies of God congregation; in the early 1970s with his wife Sue he became a long-time member of the Auckland St Paul's Anglican Church congregation, which he describes as 'an anglo-catholic parish caught up in the first flush of the charismatic movement.'

He had no formal musical education, but at St Paul's he found a creative environment and was encouraged to write a number of songs and hymns, including his best-known hymn, 'Brother, Sister, let me serve you.'* He participated in the production of several LP records and song books, and traveled to other parishes and denominations with the St Paul's Singers, a group of musicians modelled on The Fisherfolk, teaching new songs and worship styles.

He is well represented as a hymn writer and composer in the publications of the St Paul's Outreach Trust associated with that church, *Harvest of Praise* (1975), and *New Harvest* (1979). The second collection contains 8 of his songs, including The Servant Song and a version of the Lord's Prayer written in collaboration with his brother-in-law **John Smith**, which was later published in *Alleluia Aotearoa* (1993). Other Australasian collections containing his work include the Scripture in Song volumes *Songs of Praise* (1976) and *Scripture in Song* (1979), the Australian Presbyterian hymnal *Rejoice!* (1987), *Servant Songs* and *Sing Alleluia* (1987) and the *New Journeys Songbook* (1991). The Servant Song has gained a wide international audience; 'Lift high the banners of love' is another successful song which gained considerable popularity among American charismatic Roman Catholic congregations.

Richard Gillard's hymns and praise songs have a strong scriptural underlay and his themes are traditional charismatic ones: praise of Christ, defiance of evil, spiritual warfare and the Christian's pilgrimage towards heaven. But they are written as a means of expressing his personal love of God and of life in the family of God, as well as his own understandings of faith and theology. He says of his own work, 'I wanted to be somehow musically different, even experimental, and to bring an individual and poetic quality to my lyrics rather than echo Scripture or recycle the current clichés.' His lyrics contain many moments of poetry – 'Between the singing mountains and the dancing trees there runs an age-old song' – and his melodies display a variety of styles within the folksong vocabulary. — **W676, A8, 112**

William Henry Gladstone

William Henry Gladstone, born at Hawarden, Flintshire, on 3 June 1840 and composer of the hymn tune OMBERSLEY, was the oldest son of William Ewart Gladstone, the British statesman and Prime Minister. He was educated at Eton and read Greek and Latin at Oxford University, where he joined the Musical Society. He became a Liberal Party member of Parliament for 20 years, representing in turn Chester, Whitby and East Worcestershire.

Gladstone was a good amateur musician, a competent organist, a good singer and a member of the London Bach Choir. Knowledgeable about Anglican church music, he wrote a number of articles on musical topics, once expressing the view that choral church services were to be deplored because choirs often discouraged congregations from singing. He wrote several anthems, hymn tunes and chants, some of which were long in use at St Paul's Cathedral, also introits and organ voluntaries. In 1882 he compiled a hymnal entitled *A Selection of Hymns and Tunes, made and arranged by W.H. Gladstone,* of which one contemporary musical authority said, 'It is the only one I know in which there are no bad tunes.' It included OMBERSLEY among nine other tunes by Gladstone himself.

In 1870 Gladstone was one of two MPs to play for Scotland in the first unofficial soccer match between England and Scotland. He was a Lord of the Treasury (1869-74) and High Sheriff of Flintshire (1888-9). He died at London on 4 July 1891. **W636**

Stanley Glasser

Stanley Glasser, born at Johannesburg on 28 February 1926, the son of Lithuanian Jewish immigrants, was a South African composer and academic who studied under Matyas Sebier at Cambridge University. On his return to his native country he became a lecturer at the South African College of Music at the University of Cape Town and quickly established himself at the forefront of the nation's musical life. He contributed to the first South African musical and created the country's first full-length ballet score. However, he was forced to leave South Africa to escape its notorious Apartheid regime and eventually became Head of the Music Department of Goldsmiths College, University of London (1979), where he pioneered the exploration of electronic music. An ethnomusicologist, he researched native African music, including the Zulu music he heard on the streets of Johannesburg, and brought together a collection of *Street Songs* (1977), among them his version of the Zulu lullaby 'Lala Mntwana' (Sleep, child). His most popular compositions from that collection were recorded by the King's Singers, with Evelyn Glennie as percussionist and Glasser himself as a whistler. He is the author of *The A-Z of Classical Music* (London, 1994) which he later turned into a 52-part radio series broadcast on Classic FM. In 1975 he became chairman of the Composers' Guild of Great Britain, and was an adviser to the Higher Education Funding Council of England. His religious compositions include an eight-part setting of the Magnificat and Nunc Dimittis for the choir of St. George's Chapel, Windsor.
— **W645**

Peter David Hensman Godfrey

Peter Godfrey* was born at Bluntisham, Huntingdonshire on 3 April 1922. He was educated at Bluntisham Church of England School, King's College Choir School, Cambridge, Denstone College, Staffordshire (1937-40), and King's College, Cambridge University, where he completed a MusB (1942), BA (1946) and an MA (1951). He went on to study at the Royal College of Music, London (ARCM, ARCO 1948, FRCO 1951 and FRSCM 1973). From 1942-5 he served in the British Army, finishing the war as a Captain in the King's East African Rifles. He then held various positions as an organist and music teacher, including five years as Director of Music at Marlborough College (1954-8).

In 1958 he and his family emigrated to New Zealand where he took up a lectureship at Auckland University and became Director of Music at Holy Trinity Anglican Cathedral (1958-74). From 1959 to 1968 he became conductor of the Auckland String Players, which he developed into the Auckland Sinfonia. From 1961 to 1982 he took over the leadership of the Auckland Dorian Singers turning that choir into one of New Zealand's finest. In 1969 he founded the Auckland University Festival Choir (later the Auckland University Singers). In 1974 he became Professor of Music at Auckland University, a position from which he retired in 1982 to become organist and Director of Music at Wellington Cathedral (1982-89). During this period he briefly returned to England to direct the choir of King's College, Cambridge, and conduct the Cambridge Musical Society chorus and orchestra.

In 1979 he joined **Guy Jansen** as co-conductor of the newly-formed New Zealand National Choir and became their Director from 1983 to 1988; from 1984-1981 he conducted the Wellington Orpheus Choir. In 1985 he founded the New Zealand Choral Federation and became its first President. In 1989 he took up an invitation to help form a choral foundation at Trinity College, University of Melbourne, after which in 1991 he returned to live at Waikanae, on the Kāpiti Coast, north of Wellington. This led to his formation in 1992 of the Kāpiti Chamber Choir (to which both **John and Shirley Murray** belonged) and the larger Kāpiti Chorale (1994). On retiring from his professional activities in 2004 he took over the church choir of St Michael's, Waikanae, where he continued to play the organ for morning services.

Peter Godfrey began writing religious choral music at King's Choir School. His more than 20 choral compositions include several carols, and many liturgical settings. Among these is a setting of the Communion Service used at St Michael's, Waikanae, based on Māori tunes.

In recognition of his remarkable services to music, Peter Godfrey received a Citation for Services to New Zealand Music in 1977, an MBE in 1978, a CBE in 1988 and an Arts Foundation Icon Award in 2005. He was made Emeritus Director of Music by Wellington Cathedral in 2002 He died at Porirua, Wellington, on 28 September 2017. — **F46**

> *See further, *Peter Godfrey, Father of New Zealand Choral Music*. Elizabeth Salmon. Wellington: Makaro Press (2015).

John Edgar Gould

Composer, conductor, publisher and merchant, Gould was born on 9 April 1821 at Bangor, Maine. He ran a music store in New York City and later a piano dealership under the name Gould and Fischer in Philadelphia, and there with Edward L. White compiled and published 8 books of secular songs and gospel music for Sunday Schools and congregations, including *The Modern Harp* (1846), *The Wreath of School Songs* (1847), *The Tyrolian Lyre* (1847) and *The Sunday School Lute* (1848), as well as his own *Harmonia Sacra* (1851) and *Songs of Gladness for the Sabbath School* (1869). He was best known as the composer of the tune PILOT for the hymn 'Jesus, Saviour, pilot me' by Edward Hopper. He fell ill and travelled to Africa for his health, but died at Algiers, Morocco, on 4 March 1875. — **W663**

John Greally

John Greally was born in Belfast, Northern Ireland, on 14 May 1934. He studied there, intending to enter the Jesuit order, and completed a Graduate Diploma of Theology at the Irish Institute of Liturgy, but before ordination decided to follow a career in journalism. He emigrated to New Zealand and studied at the University of Otago, where he graduated BTheol. He later entered the Compagnat Marist Order, and became the chaplain and a member of staff of St Patrick's School, Silverstream, Upper Hutt, as well as Spiritual Director to the Wellington Eucharistic Convention. He was involved in liturgy training within the Archdiocese for many years as an associate staff member of the Catholic Institute of Aotearoa New Zealand.

As well as creating the English text for Helen Fisher's *Tete Kura* (see 'Karakia ki te Wairua Tapu,' H84), Father Greally wrote a number of hymns on liturgical themes. One of them, 'See us, Lord, about your altar,' appeared in several English, American and other Australian hymnals as well as in the Catholic Supplement to The *Australian Hymn Book* (1977) and *Together in Song* (1999). A self-taught composer of instrumental and choral music, his piano sonata has been aired several times by the BBC, and his violin concerto drew praise from violinist and conductor, Yehudi Menuhin. His music for the church includes Latin anthems and Christmas carols. Now described as a musician, artist and writer, he currently resides in Wales with his wife. — **H84**

Ian Douglas (Doug) Grierson

On 9 November 1934 Ian Douglas Grierson was born into a family of Scottish Presbyterian descent living at the central Taranaki town of Stratford. He received his early education there and went on to obtain a BA degree from the University of Auckland in 1960 followed by study at Knox Theological Hall, Dunedin (1961-3). In 1963 he made the first of two marriages. He was licensed by the Presbytery of Waikato in 1964 and briefly exercised an associate ministry at the coastal town of Ord Point, England, in 1966. In 1971 he took up an appointment at Te Aroha, a rural town in the Waikato, from which he resigned in 1977 to become Chaplain of St Andrew's College, Christchurch (1977-1983). He then went to rural or semi-rural appointments at Twizel in the Mackenzie Basin, Oxford, North Canterbury, Mayfield, Mid Canterbury, the Waitaki District, and Greymouth on the West Coast of the South Island. He became Moderator of the Presbytery of Nelson-Marlborough in 2000 and has since retired. — F31

Thomas Vernon Griffiths

Vernon Griffiths* was born at West Kirby, Cheshire, England, on 22 June 1894. He was the son of an Anglican priest, and was educated at Norwich Grammar School where he began his musical studies. After war service during World War I in Europe, from which he was invalided home, he won an organ scholarship to the University of Cambridge where he became the Pembroke College organist and choirmaster from 1919 to 1922 and completed a BA in History (1921) and a MusB (1922). He converted to Catholicism, and after holding senior music master appointments at schools in Somerset and Canterbury, emigrated in 1926 to New Zealand to take up a post as Lecturer in Music at the Christchurch Teachers' Training College, with responsibility for the development of music in the region's schools. There he founded Saturday morning classes for children which were later the inspiration for the Christchurch School of Music and edited the national periodical *Music in New Zealand* (1931-7), to which he contributed many articles and commentaries.

In 1933 he became a music master at the large Technical College in Dunedin and set up a programme of music education for all of its pupils which gained an international reputation. During this time he graduated MusD in the University of New Zealand (1937). In 1942 he returned to Christchurch as Professor of Music at Canterbury University College, a position he held until 1961, but he maintained his interest in school and community music-making, writing a wide range of music for schools, churches and community groups. In 1957 he was awarded the Order of the British Empire for services to education and music. In 1975 he was awarded an honorary doctorate in music by the University of Canterbury and received the CANZ Citation for Services to Music in 1980. He died in Christchurch on 23 November 1985.

Throughout his career, he composed and arranged liturgical music and hymn tunes for the Catholic Church and for school and college classes. His arrangements include *Twelve Well-known Songs, Sacred and Secular, for Four-part Choir, Twelve Well-known Hymns* and *Twenty Well-known Hymns* in an undated series of *Dominion Song Books* for schools and amateur choirs, and he contributed to the *Catholic Hymn Book: Melodies Harmonised*, 1947. His original hymn tunes CAUSA LAETITIAE, DUNEDIN, and EDLINGHAM, appeared in the Roman Catholic hymnal *Sing Praise* and its music supplement (1978). His best-known tune, DUNEDIN, written in 1935, and intended for unison singing at school assemblies, has been used as a setting for many hymn texts in national and international hymnals. — A55

*For further information see the articles on Griffiths by Rachael M. Hawkey in *The Dictionary of New Zealand Biography, Volume Four: 1921-1940*, Auckland and Wellington: Auckland University Press and the Department of Internal Affairs (1998) 207, and by John Mansfield Thomson, *Biographical Dictionary of New Zealand Composers*. Wellington: Victoria University Press (1990) 71-2.

David Blair Hamilton

David Hamilton,* composer, choral conductor, music educator and adjudicator, was born at Napier on 21 December 1955. After completing his secondary schooling at Taupo he attended Auckland University (1974-9), majoring in music composition and gaining a Master of

Music and a BA degree. In 1980 he attended Auckland Teachers College after which he began a long teaching association with Epsom Girls Grammar School (1981-2001), becoming Head of Music there in 1986 and conducting the school's award-winning choir Opus. He was a foundation member of the National Youth Choir, touring overseas with them in 1982 when they performed his *Stabat Mater* and *Lux Eterna*. From 1996 to 2011 he was Deputy Music Director of Auckland Choral and has been active as a choral conductor with community choirs in Auckland, Tauranga and Napier. He has been extensively involved in the development of national music education, and from 1999 to 2003 was a member of the Music panel of experts guiding the implementation of the National Certificate in Educational Achievement (NCEA).

Since 1978, as a composer he has won a number of national awards, and international awards in England, Italy, Israel and the United States. His prize-winning compositions include *Veni Sancte Spiritus* (2000), *Deus, Deus Meus* (2005) and *Carol of Cold Comfort* (2008). He has a particular affinity with choral music and has composed well over a hundred works of this kind. He has received commissions from most major New Zealand musical institutions, including Radio New Zealand, the New Zealand Symphony orchestra, Auckland Choral Society, Chamber Music New Zealand and the New Zealand Youth Choir, and his music is increasingly performed, recorded and published internationally. Recent major works include *Missa Semplice* (2007) and *Missa Pacifica* (2005); his smaller scale choral writing is particularly popular with school choirs. He is now a full-time composer; his work was featured in the 2013 national choral event Sing Aotearoa. He has published four volumes of works for treble voices, and two volumes for mixed voice choirs: all of them contain settings of religious texts. — **C31, 49; H21**

*See further the article on Hamilton in John Mansfield Thomson's *Biographical Dictionary of New Zealand Composers*. Wellington: Victoria University Press (1990) 73-4.

Mary Jane Hammond

Little is known about this English composer, other than that she was born in Liverpool in 1878, lived in Harpenden, Hertfordshire, and in the later part of her life at St Albans in the same county. She died at St Albans on 23 January 1964. Her tune SPIRITUS VITAE first appeared in *Hymns for the Living Church* (1974), *The Australian Hymn Book* (1977) and *With One Voice* (1982), and reached the United States in the *Presbyterian Hymnal: Hymns, Psalms and Spiritual Songs* (1990). — **W664**

Per Gunnar Harling

Per Harling, clergyman, writer, translator and composer, was born in Sweden on 20 June 1948. He says of his earliest work, 'The first time as a young teenager I was asked to sing something in church, I had nothing to sing, since my instrument was the guitar and the guitar is not the most useful instrument for Lutheran hymns. I wrote my first song using what I had and what I knew, the guitar, and I have not given up composing since.'

In 1974 he was ordained by the Lutheran Church of Sweden and worked for some years on worship renewal programmes, writing several books on worship, including *Our Beloved Hymns* (2007). From 1986-88 he was secretary to the group that produced a supplement to the 1986 *Hymnal* of the Church of Sweden. In the late 1980s and early 1990s he hosted a television series on the Psalms and in the early 2000s a television documentary, 'The Whole World Sings,' which led to the editing of an associated songbook, *The Whole World Sings*. During the years 2007–2012, Harling worked as a pastor of the Church of Sweden in Switzerland with a placement in Lausanne.

For much of his time he has been a freelance composer, a guitar-playing performer and writer, working on occasion with **Shirley Murray**. Many of his hymns and songs have been published in Swedish hymnals such as *Verbums* (2003) and *Hymns of the 2000s*, and been included in more than 14 international hymnals; he has written several musicals and has issued nearly 20 CDs. More recent publications include *In every heartbeat breathe heaven: 48 songs for worship and devotions* (2002) and *Our Beloved Hymns* (2007) and *Everything Is Related: 50 songs for worship and devotions* (2007).

He has served the World Council of Churches as consultant on several occasions, and in 1991 he was *animateur* for the Canberra Assembly. Since 1994 he has been a member of the Global Praise project of the United Methodist Church of America. From 2007-12 Harling served as pastor of the Swedish Church in Switzerland, based in Lausanne; he has also been Pearson Distinguished Professor at Bethany College, USA (2010-11). Since 1991 he has won several awards for his contribution to Swedish musical culture and in 2011 he was awarded the Royal Medal of Sweden.

He says, 'For me the challenge is – within my composing – always to remain a bridge-builder between the contextual reality (that is, in constant flux) and the inherited theology. The hymn writer Fred Kaan said about his writing that he always tried to be earth-bound, people-focused and Christ-centred. I agree.' — **H95**

Jan Donald Harrington

Jan Harrington, American conductor, arranger and educator, was born in Goodland, Kansas in 1943. He was educated at Southern Methodist University (BM, 1965) and Indiana University (MM, 1967), then took up positions directing choral activities at the State University of New York at Fredonia (1969-71) and the University of Oklahoma (1971-3). He has worked with the London Philharmonic orchestra and the London Symphony orchestra. From 1979-82 he was on the staff of the Aspen Choral Institute and has regularly conducted at the Aspen Choral Festival as he has done at the Dartmouth Conducting Institute. In 1973 he joined the staff of the Indiana University School of Music, completing his DM there in 1980. He held the position of Chancellor Professor and Chair of the Choral Conducting Department (1988-2009). For 10 years he was conductor of the Indiana University Contemporary Vocal Ensemble, a group devoted to the performance of avant-garde vocal music; he directed the University Singers and regularly conducted orchestral concerts, operas and oratorios. In 2010 he became the Director of the choral activities of DePauw University School of Music, a liberal arts school in Greencastle, Indiana. Harrington is Artistic Director of Apollo's Voice, a professional chamber chorus based in Bloomington, Indiana, which performs and records with Raymond Leppard and the Indianapolis Symphony Orchestra. He regularly leads master classes in conducting and score analysis. He has recorded for Spectrum Records and was a member of the editorial team for the second edition of *Choral Conducting: A Symposium* published by Prentice-Hall (1987). — **A132**

Eluned Harrison (née Cornish)

Eluned Harrison, the chosen translator of **Carl Boberg's** famous hymn 'O store Gud' known in English as 'O Lord my God I stand and gaze in wonder' (W628), was born at Cardiff, Wales on 19 December 1934. Following her graduation from University College, London, she taught physics at the Oxford College of Technology (now Brooks University) and various comprehensive schools in the Newport area, ending her teaching career as a lecturer at Gwent College. She married Graham Stuart Harrison, who became minister of Emmanuel Evangelical Church, Newport, Gwent, Wales (1962-2010).

She has written a number of hymn texts, all of them first printed in *Christian Hymns*, published in 1977 by the Evangelical Movement of Wales. Her husband, also a hymn writer, was joint editor of this hymnbook, which went into a second edition in 2004.

The circumstances under which Eluned Harrison wrote her version of the text are described by her husband: 'I was preparing the original edition of *Christian Hymns*, and having contacted the author of "How great

Thou art" for permission to use that very popular hymn...frightened by the fees that would be required, I asked my wife to do something "useful" while she was laid aside in sickness, and gave her an English translation of Carl Boberg's Swedish text. This translation, which as I remember ran to over thirty verses, appeared in a couple of issues of the journal of the American Hymn Society in about 1972-3....Boberg's poem is much more theological than "How great Thou art," and in my opinion my wife's version is much to be preferred to the latter.' Mrs Harrison's text was also preferred by the editorial committee responsible for the New Zealand supplement to *With One Voice*, although it underwent some further minor revision. — **W628**

Ian Le Clerc Harvey

Ian Harvey was born in Dunedin on 21 July 1929, and grew up in that city. Taught the piano by Hazel Larsen, he passed the practical and theory exams of Trinity College with honours in all eight grades. At the age of 17 he became organist and choirmaster at the Opoho Presbyterian Church, then under the ministry of (Sir) Lloyd Geering, whom he acknowledges as one the most formative influences on his life and thinking he went on to Dunedin Teachers College and the University of Otago, completing his studies with a Mus B degree, Dip Tchg, and ATCL and LTCL (teaching) Diplomas. Further study with pianist Maurice Till led to an LRSM (performers) Diploma, and he was awarded an Associated Board scholarship to attend the Royal Academy of Music in London. There, from 1951 to 1953, he studied piano under Professor Frederic Jackson. His teacher was also chorus master of the London Philharmonic Choir, which Ian joined, singing for two years under conductors such as Thomas Beecham, Adrian Boult, Malcolm Sargent, William Walton and **Ralph Vaughan Williams**. At the Academy he also took classes in singing, conducting, composition and musicianship, leaving with an LRAM in piano teaching.

Encouraged by Jackson to return to New Zealand, he taught 60 piano pupils a week at Waitaki Boys High School for two years before transferring to Otago Boys High to take every class for music, the whole school for singing, and choirs, orchestra and brass band – in addition to coaching the First Soccer XI. Four years later, Ian moved to Horowhenua College, Levin. Over these years of Secondary teaching he began adjudicating competitions throughout New Zealand and had his first experiences of stage musical direction. He continued teaching a few private pupils, including such subsequently leading musicians as William Southgate, Jenny McLeod and Gillian Bibby. In Levin he chaired the Arts Society and conducted performances by the combined churches choir.

In 1963 he became the foundation Head of Music Education at the new North Shore Teachers College. Ian also held positions in numerous music organisations: Government Nominee on the Music Teachers Registration Board, founding and first President of the Institute of Registered Music Teachers under a new Act of Parliament; inaugural Chairman of a first New Zealand Society for Music Education in Auckland; member of the Ritchie Committee to Study the Needs of Music Teaching in New Zealand. When no action followed the report of this body, Ian set up a Diploma Course through the Institute. This continues to provide a New Zealand qualification for performance teachers.

To maintain his own performance skills he formed the Northcote Chamber Orchestra from the group that accompanied his direction of a Gilbert and Sullivan production for the North Shore Operatic Society. This orchestra gave concerts on a regular basis and accompanied musical productions for the Operatic Society and North Shore Teachers College. Ian conducted about 20 of these over the years. In 1970 he conducted the Auckland Festival production of Jenny McLeod's *Earth and Sky*. One of the 12 performances was attended by the Queen and Duke of Edinburgh with Prince Charles and Princess Ann. A recording of this production was made from a compilation of three of the performances.

In more general educational organisations he was for three years President of the New Zealand Teachers' Colleges Association. Later he was appointed to the National Advisory Council on Teacher Training. In Auckland he was elected to the Board of Governors of Northcote College. In his second term he was elected to the Chair and held this role for ten years. He retired from the position of Dean of the Auckland College of Education in 1988 and later chaired the to Orewa College Board for nine years. He has been a Rotarian for the last 40 years, and is a lifelong member of the Presbyterian Church. Since retiring, Ian has played the organ every few weeks at his local church, but considers himself a Progressive Christian rather than a Presbyterian. Unhappy with 'the constant repetition of hymns from earlier times which reinforce old beliefs and concepts modern scientific knowledge refutes,' he has taken up hymn writing himself, 'to help people grasp and fix in their minds what Jesus really taught.' His personal view is that '[hymn] tunes reinforce the memory and the words stick. So I thought we should try to get people to sing, and by that means establish in their minds religious ideas that accord with reality in the 21st century.'

Ian Harvey was awarded an MNZM in 1989 for his services to music. He died at Auckland on 1 May 2018. — **H125**

Peter Mervyn Haskins

Peter Haskins was born at Wantage, Oxfordshire, England, on 26 October 1948. He was educated at Faringdon Secondary Modern School and King Alfred's Sixth Form, Wantage, before completing a BEd in Physics and Educational Philosophy and later certificates and diplomas in Christian Studies at Westminster College, Oxford. His studies in science and education at Brookes University, Oxford, and Cranfield University (MSc, 1996) led to a career as a laboratory technician and later a lectureship in electronics. He is a member of Christians in Science and the Science and Religion Forum.

He became a Lay Preacher in the Witney and Faringdon Methodist Circuit, Oxfordshire, and for 16 years was a youth leader in the church. He has written a number of hymns arising from his own experiences as a church leader. One of his hymns, 'There's a song throughout creation,' was published in *Songs for the New Millennium* (2000), and in 2004 he published a booklet of 25 of his own hymns, *There's a Song throughout Creation*. Several of his hymns are on the Hope Publishing (USA) website. — **H73**

Frances Ridley Havergal

Frances Ridley Havergal was born at Astley, Worcestershire, on 14 December 1836, the youngest daughter of a vicar who was himself a musician and hymn tune writer. Chronic ill health resulted in her living with her parents for the next 24 years. However, she had a gift for languages, eventually learning French, German, Italian, Latin, Greek and Hebrew, and she began writing verse at the age of seven. She was also a fine singer and pianist. At the age of 14 she underwent a spiritual experience which she described as 'a deep and lasting sense of consecration,' and she spent the rest of her life in study, writing much religious verse including hymn and hymn tunes, material for children and religious tracts, as well as carrying out philanthropic work. Between 1869 and 1883 she published six volumes of hymns, which were gathered by her sister as her *Poetical Works* in 1883. She died at Caswell Bay, Wales, on 3 June 1879. — **W638; A6; C13**

Franz Joseph Haydn

Haydn was born at Rohrau in Lower Austria on 31 March 1732, the son of a wheelwright. His fine tenor voice attracted the attention of the Roman Catholic Church authorities and he was given an education at the choir school of the Cathedral of St Stefan, Vienna (1740-49). However, when his voice broke he was expelled and forced into supporting himself by playing in street bands, writing some music, and teaching. For a time he worked as accompanist and servant for the Italian composer and teacher Porpora. He composed his first mass in 1750, and published a set of string quartets in 1755.

He came to the attention of aristocratic families in Vienna, and in the 1750s he worked for two aristocratic patrons before he became director of music for Prince Anton Paul Esterházy, head of one of the wealthiest families in the Austro-Hungarian empire (1761). Haydn was made responsible for all musical entertainments at Eisenstadt as well as services in the Esterházy chapel, and began a 30-year long period of directing and composing music. On Prince Anton's death, his music-loving son Nicholas succeeded to the estates and until his own death in 1790 retained Haydn. The new Esterházy prince dismissed most of the musicians, and Haydn was at last free to travel beyond Europe. He spent two hugely successful years in England where he was awarded the DMus by the University of Oxford (1791). He returned to Vienna, and after another equally successful visit to England (1794-5) lived in that city for the rest of his life.

His output as a composer was prodigious, including 107 symphonies, 77 string quartets and much other chamber music, 47 piano sonatas, 22 operas as well as incidental music for plays, 14 masses and 6 cantatas and oratorios – among them *The Creation* (1798) and *The Seasons* (1801). Known as 'Papa Haydn,' he was the friend and supporter of many famous European musicians, among them Mozart and Beethoven. He was a devout Roman Catholic, who prefaced his scores with *In nomine Domini* (In the name of God) and closed them with *Laus Deo* (Praise be to God). 'When I think of God,' he said, 'my heart dances within me, and my music has to dance, too.' He wrote one famous hymn tune, AUSTRIA, as the melody for the Austrian National Anthem, having been impressed by the respect shown in England for their national anthem. — **W625**

Lois Ruby Henderson (née Whitehead)

The daughter of Baptist schoolteacher parents, Lois Henderson was born in Fielding on 10 November 1936. Her father died when she was aged 4 and the family shifted to Rotorua, where she did all her schooling, attending the Rotorua High School (now a boys' school, but then a co-educational institution). She was taught to play the piano and organ, and it was as an organist that she met her future husband, Malcolm Paul Henderson, then a young Salvation Army officer and an accomplished brass band player. After their marriage in 1956, Paul attended a Bible Training Institute while his wife worked in a hostel in Auckland. When a hoped-for call to missionary work failed to eventuate they involved themselves with the Baptist Church in Dannevirke, where Lois became church organist and choir leader. She also led a high school age choir.

When the Baptist Church closed, they joined the Dannevirke Anglican Church, where Lois again played the church organ and sang or led the choir. 1979 saw a shift to Thames for 7 years; there Paul became an Anglican priest. From Thames, the couple returned to Dannevirke, where Lois taught mathematics, remedial reading and assisted with the local Māori cultural group at Dannevirke High School. She particularly enjoyed working with children, and produced at least one work for children, *Psalty, the Singing Songbook*. Appointments to Woodville and Waipukurau followed, but on the death of her husband in 2003 Lois retired to Pauanui, on the Coromandel Peninsula.

Inspired with a deep love for words and writing, she went on to compose several hymn texts, including her own version of 'Jerusalem' and 'O God beyond our knowledge' (H71). She died at Thames Hospital on 11 August 2010. The family relate that having played for many funerals over the years she insisted that she didn't want her coffin at her own service. 'She felt coffins were a depressing focus and she wanted a joyful service of thanksgiving.' Accordingly the family sat around her coffin at the Hamilton crematorium and shared stories, and on the following day held a thanksgiving service without a coffin at St George's church in Thames. — **H71**

John Hind

For this music arranger, see 'Sing we a song of high revolt,' W643.

Graham Howie Hollobon

Graham Hollobon was born on 29 August 1938 in Christchurch. He was educated at Christchurch West High School (now Hagley High School) and is a graduate of the University of Canterbury, where he completed a BSc (1961) and a MusB (1962); he went on to complete his music studies at Yale University (MMus, 1966). He married Kathleen Bennett in 1963. His professional career as an organist, recitalist, accompanist and teacher stretches back to 1954. He taught music at the St Louis Institute of Music from 1966 to 1972, and from 1973 until his retirement in 1993 he lectured at the School of Music of the University of Canterbury, where he was Head of Department from 1989 to 1993.

Hollobon studied the piano with Esther Brown and the organ with William Hawkey and Charles Krigbaum; since 1954 he has held positions as organist in a number of Presbyterian, Methodist, Anglican and Congregational churches. His return to Christchurch in 1973 eventually led to his playing in almost every church in the city, and well beyond, as an organist, occasional choir director and recitalist (he is a member of the Apollo musical group). His lifelong interest in and dedication to church music has involved the transcription and harmonization of some of the original melodies by William (Bill) Wallace. Now retired, he continues to play the organ and piano at various churches in his home town of Christchurch. — **H140**

Oliver Wendell Holmes

Oliver Wendell Holmes was born in Cambridge Massachusetts, on August 29, 1809, the son of a Congregational minister. He was educated at Phillips Academy, New Hampshire, and at Harvard College, where he graduated in Arts and Medicine. He also studied medicine in the finest medical schools of Paris. In 1836 he was granted his M.D. from Harvard Medical School and was appointed Professor of Anatomy and Physiology in Dartmouth College. In 1847 he took the chair of Anatomy at Harvard, where he taught until 1882. There he was recognized as an important medical reformer.

Holmes began writing poetry at an early age and continued to do so until his death. A constant contributor to periodical literature, he founded the *Atlantic Monthly* and brought it to international attention with his own articles. Becoming known as an essayist, novelist, poet wit, humourist, and conversationalist he developed an international reputation. For his literary achievements and other accomplishments, he was awarded numerous honorary degrees from universities around the world. He rejected the strict orthodoxy of his parents' church, developed a broadly humanist position and joined the Unitarians. After his retirement from Harvard in 1882 he continued writing poetry, novels and essays until his death on 7 October 1894. — **W626**

John Hughes

The composer of the tune CWM RHONDDA was born at Dowlais, Glamorgan on 22 November 1873. Soon afterwards, his family moved to nearby Llantwit Fadre where, at the age of 12, he began work at Glynn Colliery. He moved on to the traffic department of the Great Western Railway where he worked for the remainder of his life. Alan Luff, in *Welsh Hymns and their Tunes* (1990) says of him, he was 'like so many musicians, a product of the South Wales coal fields, with their harsh conditions alleviated by a vigorous chapel life that in turn supported a strong musical, above all choral, movement.' Hughes was a life-long member of the Salem Baptist Church in his hometown where he succeeded his father as deacon and precentor. He composed a number of anthems and marches as well as hymn tunes, including CWM RHONDDA. He died at Llantwit Fadre, Pontypridd, Glamorgan, on 14 May 1932. — **W661**

Timothy (Tim) Charles Hurd

Timothy Hurd was born on 27 February 1973 at Invercargill, and grew up in Nelson, where most of his schooling was done. He attended Nelson College and became a chorister at Nelson Cathedral. He then studied History and Music (composition and musicology) at the University of Otago, graduating with a BA in History and a BMus (Hons) in 1997. He was accepted as a candidate for ordination by the Anglican Church of Aotearoa New Zealand and sent for theological study to the ecumenical Pacific Theological College at Suva, Fiji, where he graduated in 2000 with a BD (Hons). He was deaconed in 2000 and priested in 2001 and was appointed to a curacy at St Paul's Cathedral, Dunedin (2000-2), before becoming Vicar of All Saints Church in Dunedin's University precinct (2002-9). In 2010 he became Vicar of the Oamaru-Maheno parish, continuing to write hymns of both a general and occasional nature.

He says of his writing that it began with his ministry 'and probably with parish ministry, often out of "need" or a gap that required filling. Or sometimes the sheer joy of being. Perhaps one of those things that seems possible only when one feels oneself to be a legitimate "grown-up."' — **H3, 41, 79**

Amanda Husberg

Amanda Husberg was born in Chicago on 7 December 1940. She studied education, and organ performance at Concordia Teachers College, Seward, Nebraska (B.S. in Education, 1962), and completed her studies in early childhood education at Hunter College, New York (M.S., 1971). After two years teaching at a Lutheran school in New Jersey, she worked for 36 years as the director of several daycare centres in Brooklyn and Queens, New York. Concurrently, from 1964 to 2006 she held the position of Director of Music at the Lutheran Church of St John the Evangelist in Williamsburg, Brooklyn, a large inner-city, multi-cultural faith community.

She has written almost 400 hymn tunes as well as some texts of her own, published in the United States, Canada, Brazil, the United Kingdom and China. There are also three books of Psalm settings (2012, 2013, 2014), two liturgical masses and a requiem mass. On 10 June 2000, she was presented with the Servant of Christ award from the Atlantic District of the Lutheran Church–Missouri Synod for her contribution to the greater church in the field of music, specifically in the area of hymns and congregational song. She was made a life member of the Hymn Society in the United States and Canada. She died on 15 February, 2021 — **F19(ii); C35; H10, 133, 139**

Witi Tame Ihimaera-Smiler

Known generally as Witi Ihimaera, this distinguished writer was born on 7 February 1944 near Gisborne, on the East coast of the North Island, and is of Māori descent (his tribal affiliations are with Te Aitanga a Māhaki, Rongowhakaata, Tāmanuhiri, Tūhoe and Kahungunu) through his mother, and Anglo-Saxon descent through his father. He was educated at Te Karaka District High School, the Mormon Church College of New Zealand Hamilton, and Gisborne Boys High School before studying at Auckland University and Victoria University, Wellington, where he graduated with a BA (1970). After working as a journalist and Post Office official, he joined the Ministry of Foreign Affairs for whom he worked from 1972-89, serving in various diplomatic posts in Canberra, New York and Washington D.C. This time was interrupted by his holding of literary Fellowships at the University of Otago (1975) and Victoria University of Wellington (1982). In 1990, he took up a position at the University of Auckland, where he became Professor and Distinguished Creative Fellow in Māori Literature. He retired from this position in 2010.

He was the first Māori writer to publish both a novel and a book of short stories: he is known for such works as *Pounamu, Pounamu* (1972), *The New Net goes Fishing* (1975), *The Matriarch* (1986) and *The Whale Rider* (1987)—later made into a successful film. He also co-edited

Into the World of Light (1982), an important anthology of Māori writing (1982). His autobiographical work *Māori Boy: A Memoir of Childhood* (2014) was among the winners of the 2016 Ockham New Zealand Book Awards. He has served on literary committees for the Queen Elizabeth II Council, the Katherine Mansfield Menton Trust and Te Ha Māori Writers.

He was awarded the Queen's Service Medal in 1987 for services to the Māori community and was made a Distinguished Companion of the New Zealand Order of Merit in 2004 for services to literature. In 2017 he was awarded the Prime Minister's Award for Literary Achievement. — **H21**

John Nicholson Ireland

John Ireland was born at Bowdon, Cheshire, on 13 August 1879. He was educated at Leeds Grammar School and from the age of 14 at the Royal College of Music. He became a Fellow of the Royal College of Organists in 1895, and completed a BMus at Durham University in 1905. He was for a time assistant organist at Holy Trinity Church, Sloane Square, London, organist and choirmaster at St Luke's, Chelsea, for 22 years (1904-26) and Professor of Composition at the Royal College of Music from 1923-39.

However, most of his time was given to composition, and by the age of 40 he had established a considerable reputation with his chamber music, particularly the second sonata for violin and piano. He was a fastidious composer, and in 1908 withdrew everything he had previously written, as immature work. He wrote much piano music and some works for organ, about 90 solo songs, some motets and part-songs and a number of major works for orchestra, including *The London Overture*, a piano concerto, and orchestral choral works such as *These Things Shall Be*, written for the coronation of George VI, *Greater Love hath No Man*, written for the choristers at St Paul's Cathedral, London, *The Holy Boy: A Carol of the Nativity*, and a setting of Fortunatus' *Vexilla Regis*, composed in 1898, when he was still a student at the Royal College of Music studying under Stanford. He also composed a number of excellent hymn tunes, among them LOVE UNKNOWN.

His church affiliations were ambivalent, despite his long connection with mostly Anglican congregations. He wrote to his Irish mentor, Father Thompson, 'I am a bad sort of (Anglo) Catholic – not a constantly practising one, though it is ever in my heart and mind. It is the only thing which represents and prevents what is permanent, and age-long….I am a Pagan, a Pagan I was born and a Pagan I shall remain. That is the foundation of religion. The deepest religious emotions I have ever felt have been at the ceremonies on the Thursday and Friday before Easter – and what we cannot have – the ceremonies on the Saturday before Easter as practised by the Roman Church – something absolutely agelong and everlasting – the kindling of Fire.'

In 1932 he was awarded an honorary DMus by Durham University, and was made an Honorary Fellow of the Royal College of Music and the Royal Academy of Music. He died at Washington, Sussex, on 12 June 1962. — **A100**

Guy Elwyn Jansen

Guy Jansen, one of New Zealand's most outstanding composers, choral conductors and music educators, was born at Carterton on 27 May 1935. He was educated at Horowhenua College, Levin, and completed a Diploma of Education at Wellington Teachers' College in 1963. He then studied at Victoria University, Wellington (MA, 1967, BMus, 1969) and the University of Southern California (DMA in Choral Music, 1984.) He was a Licentiate of the Royal Schools of Music (1968) and a Fellow of Trinity College, London (1969). He was a founding member of the editorial committee of the New Zealand Hymn Book Trust, and in the forefront of the international movement to broaden the repertoire of church music to include the new 'folk-hymn' genre, which he promoted with five recordings, concerts, national and international tours, and the publication of *Festive Sounds: Choral*

Arrangements of Contemporary Folk-Hymns (1979), *Festive Praise One and Two* (1983) and *Servant Songs* (co-edited with Felicia Edgecombe, 1987). *Sing New Zealand: The story of choral music in Aotearoa.* Guy Jansen's richly-informed historical survey, was published posthumously by Massey University Press (2019).

Jansen became a senior lecturer in music at the Christchurch Teachers' College (1968-74) and National Curriculum Officer for Music in the Department of Education. He went on to become senior lecturer in music at the University of Queensland, and subsequently taught and conducted at the Wheaton Conservatory of Music, Illinois. He is a former President/Secretary of the New Zealand School Music Association and founder of the Secondary Schools Choral Festival (now the Big Sing). He established the Wellington Society for Music Education, and founded the National Youth Choir of New Zealand (1979) – the first such choir in the world, which he directed for its first three years, the Celebration Singers of Christchurch, the Festival Singers of Wellington, the Wellington Bel Canto Vocal Ensemble, the New Zealand Secondary Students' Choir (1986) and the University of Queensland Chamber Singers. In 1986 he pioneered training in choral conducting through the establishment of the International Summer Schools in Choral Conducting, now held throughout New Zealand and Australia.

He gave papers at International Society for Music Education conferences in Montreux, Perth and Canberra, and at the Royal Schools of Church Music Conference in Adelaide (2010). In 1990 he was awarded the New Zealand Medal and in 2011 was made a member of the New Zealand Order of Merit for his services to music. He was Chairman of the New Zealand Choral Federation (2010-12), director of the St Johns-in-the City [Wellington] church choir, and the Kāpiti Chamber choir (2007-11). He was made a Life Member of the New Zealand Choral Federation in 2013.

In 1960 he married Judy Mary Rolls; of his three children, Nicola (b. 1964), Michael (b. 1969) and Gregory (b. 1970), Nicola is named as a fellow arranger of A31. Guy Jansen died on 27 May 2019. — **W634, 637, 639, 649, 656, 658, 667, 673, 674(iii), 676, 677; A31, 39, 98, 112, 12l, 132, 152**

Nicola Marie Jansen

See under **Guy Elwyn Jansen**. Some of Nicola Jansen's arrangements appear in *Servant Songs* (1987).

Jean Wiebe Janzen (Wiebe)

Jean Janzen was born on 5 December 1933 in Delmeny, Saskatchewan, Canada, the seventh of her parents' eight children. Her Evangelical Mennonite Brethren father was a schoolteacher and pastor and the family moved with him to Mountain Lake, Minnesota, in 1938, and a year later to Kansas. She attended Meade Bible Academy, Tabor College and Grace College. As a child she had little exposure to literature except for hymns and the Bible, but at college she majored in English literature; the work of American poet Emily Dickinson became a particular enthusiasm.

She married Louis Janzen, a medical student, and the couple moved to Chicago, where she worked as a medical secretary while studying at Northwestern University. In 1961 they moved to Fresno, California, and raised four children there. When her youngest child was at school Janzen joined a writers' group and she later returned to college, graduating with a BA in English from Fresno Pacific College (1968) and an MA in creative writing from the Fresno campus of California State University (1982). She taught the writing of poetry at Fresno Pacific University (1989-2001) and Eastern Mennonite University, West Virginia. She also served as a worship leader at the College Community Mennonite Brethren Church in Fresno. In 1995 she received a National Endowment for the Arts Creative Writing Fellowship in Poetry.

Jean Janzen published over 100 poems in six poetry collections, beginning with *Words for the Silence* (1984), and a book of essays on writing. In 1991 she wrote eight hymn texts commissioned by the Mennonite Church, three of them based on the writings of medieval women mystics Hildegard of Bingen, Mechtild of Magdeburg and Julian of Norwich. They were published in the *Hymnal: A Worship Book of the Mennonite Church* (1992). Several of them have been set to music and appear in other American and Canadian hymnals. In 2012 she published a memoir, *Essays on Faith and Writing*. Jean Janzen died in 2013. — **H66**

Samuel Johnson

This remarkable American clergyman and author was born 10 October 1822 at Salem, Massachusetts (the location of the infamous witch trials in 1692), and died at North Andover, Massachusetts, on 19 February 1882. He was educated at Harvard University from which he graduated AB in 1842. He took a degree in Theology from the Harvard Divinity School in 1846 but did not join any religious denomination and was never formally ordained. He spent one year (1851) with a Unitarian Church in Dorchester, Massachusetts, where he tirelessly lectured and preached against slavery to the displeasure of the congregation. In 1853 he established an independent religious society in Lynn, Massachusetts, and served as its minister until his retirement in 1870. He withdrew to pursue other studies, notably of non-Christian religions, publishing three volumes of exemplary scholarship on the faiths of India (1872), China (1877) and Persia (1885). He wrote an acclaimed critical study, *The Worship of Jesus* in 1868, and published important essays on religion and social reform in *The Radical* and other journals. In these he strongly expressed his liberal social views, and his transcendentalist belief in a universal religion.

Johnson was a friend and associate of the poet Samuel Longfellow, and collaborated with him to compile *A Book of Hymns* (1846, enlarged edition 1848) and *Hymns of the Spirit* (1864), both of which contained a number of his own hymns. A volume of hymns and other poems was published after his death in 1899, but the best of his hymns, notably 'Life of Ages richly poured' and 'City of God, how broad and far,' have become part of the world heritage of Christian hymnology. — **W660**

Beverley Jones (née Cooper)

Beverley Jones was born on 13 March 1934 at Wellington. She was educated at Wellington Girls' College (1955-8) and completed a Primary Teacher's certificate at Wellington Teachers' College in 1968. She went on to a career in New Zealand as a teacher and administrator. She married in 1967 and brought up two children. Her husband died in 1987 and she married again in 1992, moving with her husband to Clitheroe, Lancashire, England, where he became a town councillor, then Mayor of Clitheroe and Ribble Valley over the period 1984-95. In 2003, Beverley entered politics herself and gained a ward seat which she held for eight years, before becoming Mayor of Ribble Valley from 2009 to 2010.

A Methodist by upbringing and personal choice, she was engaged in ecumenical and educational activities both in New Zealand and in England. There she has held office in the Methodist Church at local, district and national level. She is a pianist and organist and led a church children's choir in New Zealand (1978-85). She has a keen interest in literature, including writing poetry and hymn texts. — **F27**

William Herbert Jude

William Herbert Jude was an English composer and organist born in Westleton, Suffolk, in September 1851. He was a precocious child, composing incidental music for school plays by the age of eight. He attended Liverpool Organ School and Liverpool College of Music, after which became organist for Stretford Town Hall near Manchester, with a growing reputation as a lecturer and music teacher. Frequently referred to as the most brilliant organ recitalist of his day, he was asked to 'open' new organs across the United Kingdom, Ireland and Australia, and between 1890 and 1894 he toured Australia and New Zealand as an organ recitalist.

From 1904 he served as the editor of several music periodicals and compiled a number of hymnbooks, including *Music and the Higher Life* (1900), *Mission Hymns* (1911) and *Festival Hymns* (1916). Some of his anthems and hymn compositions, like 'Consecration' and 'Galilee,' were sung by choirs and congregations through the British Empire. He died in London on 8 August 1922. — **A6**

Julian of Norwich

Julian of Norwich (1342-c.1416) is the adopted name of a famous medieval Christian woman mystic, venerated in the Anglican and Lutheran Churches, but never canonized by the Roman Catholic Church, probably because so little is known of her life apart from her writings – including her birth name. She is associated with the northern English city of Norwich, which at the time was a large and important centre with its own cathedral. In Norwich, Julian became an anchoress, living out a life of prayer and contemplation in a totally enclosed room or 'cell' attached to the wall of a local church dedicated to St Julian the Hospitaler. The building was restored after its virtual destruction during World War II and has now become a shrine to Julian and Norwich.

At the age of 31, while still living at home (whether as a married or unmarried woman is not known) Julian suffered an illness which brought her near to death and gave her a series of intense visions of Jesus Christ which she described as *Sixteen Revelations of Divine Love*. Some 20 years later she wrote a longer theological treatise known as the *The Showings of Love*, exploring the meaning of these visions. This is thought to be the first book and the first autobiography written in English by a woman. She is now well known, partly because the poet T.S. Eliot quoted her most famous saying, 'Sin is behovely [necessary], but all shall be well, and all manner of thing shall be well,' in his famous religious poem 'Little Gidding,' the last of his *Four Quartets*, published in 1943.

Julian held that God was perfect in love and utterly without wrath; that sin was the result of ignorance, not of original evil, and was a necessary means to self-knowledge. Her insistence on the feminine, motherly nature of God and Christ has greatly influenced modern feminist theology. **Betty Wendelborn**, in *Sing Green: Songs of the Mystics* (Auckland, 1988) says of her, '[She] sings of the Divine love of God, in which evil has no reality, only in so far as it brings the errant human will more in touch with the Divine Mercy. She, more than all the great mystics, paints us a picture of the Motherhood of God, the compassionate, ever tender, ever wise caring of the Divine.' — **A2, H4**

Frederik Hermanus Kaan

Fred Kaan, as he was universally known, was one of the writers who revitalized English hymnody in the 1960s. Born in Haarlem, the Netherlands, on 27 July 1929, his childhood was passed under German occupation. His father was a member of the Dutch resistance and the family sheltered a Jewish woman and later a political prisoner who had escaped from Belsen. He studied theology at the University of Utrecht (1949-52), then in England at Western College, Bristol. He graduated BA from the University of Bristol in 1954. He was ordained by the Congregational Union in England and Wales in 1955 and served Windsor Road Congregational Church at Barry, South Wales (1955-63), and the Pilgrim Church, Plymouth (1963-68), where like Shirley Murray, he first began to write hymns out of frustration at what was available in contemporary hymnals and the practical demands of worship. His first collection of hymns 'to fill the gaps' was titled *Pilgrim Praise* and printed in 1968; it grew to include 70 hymns with music (1972,1975).

He was an executive member of the Congregational Union (1957-63), on the board of the London Missionary Society (1957-64) and joint secretary of the Plymouth Council of Churches (1964-8). In 1968 he was called to the office of Minister-Secretary of the Geneva-based International Congregational Council (1968-78), becoming an executive secretary of the World Alliance of Reformed Churches with which it merged in 1970. From

1970-8 he was editor of the Reformed Press Service and co-produced an ecumenical radio programme; in 1975 he published 20 new texts with music by Doreen Potter, in *Break Not the Circle*. In 1976 he brought out a collection of his Swedish translations set by Scandinavian composers, *Songs and Hymns from Sweden*. During his time in Geneva he was also involved as a staff member of the World Council of Churches translating 20 texts from French, German, Spanish, Portuguese and Swedish for the ecumenical hymnal *Cantate Domino*.

In 1978 he returned to England as Moderator of the West Midlands Province of the United Reformed Church, and from 1985 to 1989 was a member of the ministerial team at Central (Ecumenical) Church, Swindon, and pastor of Penhill Reformed Church. From 1993-7 he combined a busy life of travel and public speaking with the role of Secretary of the Churches' Human Rights Forum of Britain and Ireland.

He was awarded an honorary Doctorate of Theology by the Reformed Seminary, Debrecen, Hungary (1978) and gained a PhD from Geneva Theological College in 1984 for his dissertation on 'Emerging Language in Hymnody.' He wrote more than 200 hymns, which demonstrate his commitment to the ecumenical movement, his pacifism and his passionate concern for the poor and powerless. They appeared in *The Hymn Texts of Fred Kaan* (1985) and *Planting Trees and Sowing Seeds* (1989), and were revised and gathered with his lyrical poems in *The Only Earth We Know* (1999). He died on 4 October 2009. — **W643, 653, 654, 657, 658, 665, 667**

Thomas Ken

Thomas Ken was born at Little Berkhampstead, Hertfordshire, England, in July 1637; he died at Longleat, Wiltshire, England, 19 March 1710. Orphaned at the age of nine, he grew up under the guardianship of Izaak Walton, who was married to Ken's sister, Ann. He was educated at Winchester College and Hart Hall, Oxford, and became a Fellow of New College, Oxford, in 1657, where he took the degrees of B.A. and M.A. Following his ordination in 1662, he was made rector of Little Easton (1663-5) and a Fellow of Winchester College (1666). After holding rectorships on the Isle of Wight and at Brixton, he returned to Winchester (1669) as prebendary to the cathedral and chaplain to Winchester College and to his friend Bishop Morley. It was during this time that he wrote his famous morning, evening and midnight hymns. In 1679 he was appointed chaplain to Princess Mary at the Hague; after being dismissed for protesting against immorality at her court he was appointed bishop of Bath and Wells in 1865 by Charles II, who declared he would go to church to hear Ken 'tell him of his faults.' He ministered to the King on his deathbed, as he did to the prisoners taken at the Battle of Sedgemoor (1685). He also attended the Duke of Monmouth at his execution. Because he refused to subscribe to James II's Declaration of Indulgence, he was sent to the Tower in 1688. He was acquitted, but under the reign of William III was forced to resign his bishopric. Left destitute, he was given hospitality for the rest of his life by Lord Weymouth at Longleat House. His most well known hymns are found in *A Manual of Prayers for use of the Scholars at Winchester College*, 1674. He wrote a book on the catechism, *The Practice of Divine Love* (1685), and after his death his poems were published in four volumes (1721), including *Hymns for All the Festivals of the Year*. — **W678**

Graham Andrew Kendrick

Graham Kendrick, the son of a Baptist pastor, was born on 2 August 1950 at Blisworth, Northamptonshire. He moved with his family to Laindon, Essex, and then Putney, London. He began composing songs as a 15-year old, teaching himself to play the piano before learning to read music. He studied at Avery Hill College before joining an evangelical team in 1972, touring schools and colleges with his music group. From 1976-80 he was Music Director of British Youth for Christ, and joined the church leadership team of the South London Ichthus Fellowship (1984-2004). In 1986 he founded the global March for Jesus movement, which began in Soho, London and now involves more than 60 million people annually. He and his wife run the successful Make Way Music company.

Kendrick launched a career as a religious singer/songwriter in 1972 and began producing albums such as *Footsteps on the Water* and *Paid on the Nail*. In 2001 his *What Grace* was the year's best-selling album of worship and praise music in the United Kingdom. Initially writing mostly for worship services, he was later commissioned by groups such as the Tear Fund, the Church Army and Care for the Family to write songs dealing with wider social issues. From the 1990s his songs began to appear in mainstream British hymnals; *The Source* (2007) for which he was consultant editor, included most of his significant compositions to that date. He has now written over 300 religious songs, including such hits as 'Majesty,' 'Shine, Jesus, shine' and 'Let the flame burn brighter.' His many albums include *The Prayer Song Collection* and *The Psalm Collection* (both 2002).

In 1995 Kendrick was given a Dove Award for his international work and in 2000 received honorary doctorates from the London School of Theology and Brunel University in recognition of his contribution to Christian worship. A further honorary DD was awarded by Wycliffe College in 2008. — **W637**

Taria Kingstone

'I find my identity in the people who came before me.' Taria Kingstone was an outstanding Pacific leader, the grandson of the Reverend Taipu Pere, one of the first Cook Island Presbyterian ministers in New Zealand. Born on 28 December 1961 in Raupunga, Hawkes Bay, he became a Sunday School teacher, musician, and education liaison officer associated with the St Luke's Pacific Island Presbyterian Church at Tokoroa. He went on to become a lecturer in Cook Islands Māori at the University of Waikato, then at the Centre for Pacific Studies, University of Auckland, from 2003 until his death in 2006. Fluent in 14 languages, including Cook Island Māori, English, French and Chinese, he was a founding member of the Lu'l Ola Group and a member of the Churches' Youth Ministry Association. Taria Kingstone died on 3 August 2006 and is buried at Tokoroa.

He wrote a book on Cook Islands culture in New Zealand (including an account of his own wheelchair disability) *Ko E Vemepaea I Uapou* (1991), *Pacific Way: The Cook Islands* (2001) and *Te Pepe Kuki Airani: A Beginner's Guide to the Māori Languages of the Cook Islands* (1994, revised and published posthumously in 2009 by the Faculty of Arts, University of Auckland), together with some nine books for children and other educational resources in Cook Islands Māori. He also published an annotated collection of Cook Islands songs, *'E au 'imene Kuka Arani no tatou / Aotearoa nei: Cook Island Songs* (2002). — **A5, 97, 129**

Marion Agnes Kitchingman (née Johnston)

Marion Kitchingman was born on 20 April 1939 at Auckland into the family of a Methodist minister, Andrew and Doris Johnston. She was educated at Wellington East Girls' College and the Wellington Teachers' College, training as a kindergarten teacher. She taught in Wellington and Dunedin before marrying Methodist minister David Kitchingman in 1961. Following an initial ministry at Māori Hill Methodist Church, Dunedin, the couple spent five years as missionaries in the Papua New Guinea Highlands. On their return to Dunedin they raised a family of three children, Ginny, Colin and Simon. Marion is a talented stage performer and has written several one-woman shows, including *Letters Home*, *Annie Schnackenberg* and *Susannah*, a dramatised life of Susannah Wesley which she later toured nationally.* She is a long-time member of the choir and congregation of Mornington Methodist Church and has written 4 hymn texts between 1996 and 2001. — **H101**

*Published in the Summer/Autumn 2011 issue of *Music in the Air*.

Ronald (Ron) Klusmeier

Ron Klusmeier was born at Sheboygan, Wisconsin, Canada, on 26 June 1947. He was educated at Lakeland College, Sheboygan, and at the University of Wisconsin-Milwaukee. As a composer, editor, arranger and music resource consultant he has worked in music and arts since 1971, leading workshops, seminars, concerts and worship celebrations in churches throughout Canada and in almost every American state. In the 1970s he acted as the National Music Ambassador for the United Church of Canada, whose hymnbook, *Voices United*, and its supplement *More Voices* contain more tunes by this composer than by any other contributor. His settings are also found in Canadian Anglican, Presbyterian, Lutheran and Roman Catholic hymn books, as well as in many American denominational hymnals.

Early in his career he collaborated with Walter Farquharson and **Fred Kaan** in two collections, *Praise to the Lord* (1974) and *Worship the Lord* (1977); he went on to write the music for a cantata, *God's Gentle Gift* (1993), a musical, *For Nineveh's Sake* (1994) and an Easter cantata, *Stay with Us* (1999) all with librettos by Farquharson, and it was with Farquharson that he created the theme hymn 'Walls that Divide' for the 1995 Assembly of the World Council of Churches. In 2002 he was awarded an honorary Doctorate of Divinity by St Andrew's College, Saskatoon, for his contribution to the worship life of the church.

As well as setting texts by leading hymn leading hymn writers in England, America and Canada, he developed a special friendship with **Shirley Murray**, and has composed settings for most of her hymns. — **A19, 22, 36, 41, 62, 79, 94, 143, 148, 154; C3, 37, 40, 48; F9, 11,12, 15, 20, 21, 22, 25, 34. 59, 60, 65, 80; HP2, 4, 6, 11; H6, 7, 35, 77, 83, 87, 90, 122, 118, 139**

Gerald Hocken Knight

Gerald Knight was born on 27 July 1908 in Par, Cornwall. He was educated at Truro Cathedral School, where he studied and played the organ, and at Peterhouse, Cambridge (BA, 1928). He became organist of St Augustine of Canterbury Church, Queens Gate, London (1931-7), then organist and Master of the Choristers at Canterbury Cathedral (1937-53). He was Director of the Royal School of Church Music and the College of St Nicholas from 1954-73, and was made a Fellow of the School in 1964. As overseas Commissioner for the School he visited Nigeria and Australia. He died in 1974. The Gerald H Knight Memorial Prize for the highest marks in the RCO Choir Training Diploma examinations was established in his honour.

Knight published several of his own compositions and books on musical topics, including *Incidental Music to The Zeal of Thy House* by Dorothy Sayers (1938), *The Treasury of English Church Music*, vol 1 (1100-1545) (1965), *The Coventry Mass: Adapted from medieval sources and with accompaniments by G.H. Knight* (1966), *Accompaniments for unison Hymn-Singing* (1971) and *A History of the Royal School of Church Music: The First Forty Years* (1968). As music editor of the 1950 edition of *Hymns Ancient and Modern*, he also served on the committees that compiled its two supplements, *100 Hymns for Today* (1969) and *More Hymns for Today* (1980). Several of his hymn tunes or harmonisations of earlier melodies appear in international hymnals such as *Hymns Ancient & Modern* (revised edition, 1950), the Church of Scotland's *Church Hymnary* (4th edition, 2005) and the American *Presbyterian Hymnal* (1990). Among them are LITTLE VENICE, THE ASH GROVE, DEUS TUORUM MILITUM and VALLEY. — **A79**

Eduard Kremser

Kremser was born in Vienna on 10 April 1838 and became renowned as a conductor of choral societies and choral concerts in that city, leading the Vienna Men's Choir from 1869 to 1899. He wrote several operettas, four cantatas for male voice choir and orchestra, several symphonic sketches for orchestra, and many piano pieces and songs. In 1877 he published a set of 17th century Dutch patriotic songs drawn from *Netherlands Songs of Remembrance* (1626), Adrian Valerius of Veere's posthumous collection of poems and songs associated with the War against Spain (1555-1625), which he arranged for his choir as *Six Old Dutch Folksongs*. The melodies became popular through the choir's performances of them and were taken into many hymnals. He died in Vienna on 27 November 1914. — **A86**

Karen Lafferty

The composer of 'Seek ye first the kingdom of God' ('First set your mind on the kingdom of God') was born on 29 February 1948 at Alamagordo, New Mexico, where she was brought up in a Baptist church. She was educated at Eastern New Mexico University, where she completed a BA in Music Education with a focus on choral directing and the oboe. She then worked for a time as a nightclub entertainer and guitar teacher without much success. In 1970, a Christian friend 'helped me understand the glorious truth of walking daily with Jesus.' With the support of a scholarship she undertook a course of Bible study in Costa Mesa, California, then began a music ministry with Maranatha! Music, an offshoot of the Costa Mesa Calvary Chapel of which she was a congregational member.

The success of her praise song 'Seek ye first the kingdom of God' led to an international career as an evangelical musician/performer. After missionary training in Holland with Youth with a Mission, in 1980 she founded the Musicians for Missions International organization there. In 1995 she returned to the United States and relocated with her organization to Santa Fe, New Mexico, where she developed the organization Sangre de Cristo Arts and Culture. She continues to tour internationally.

She has recorded several albums of her music for Maranatha! Music, including *Bird in a Golden Sky*, *Sweet Communion*, *Life Pages*, *Country to Country*, *Land of No Goodbyes*, *Heart Cry* and *Multitudes: The Sound of Many Nations*. She continues to compose songs, both religious and secular, though she has never repeated the success of 'Seek ye first.' Her 2020 autobiography was titled *Seek Ye First: The Story of Karen Lafferty*. — **W635**

Mark Owen Lee

Owen Lee, also known as Father Owen Lee, was born in Detroit on 28 May 1930. He was educated at the University of Toronto and the University of British Columbia. In 1947 he became a Roman Catholic priest and entered the order of the Congregation of St Basil. He went on to hold academic positions at the University of St Thomas, Houston, Texas, Loyola University, Chicago, and the University of Toronto, where he was Professor of Classics for 30 years (1975-95).

He became Emeritus Professor of Classics at St Michael's College, University of Toronto, the holder of four honorary degrees and the author of 20 books and numerous academic articles, principally in the fields of Greek and Roman studies (Virgil and Horace) and grand opera (Wagner). He was the translator of the Prayer of St Francis published in *The New St Basil's Hymnal* (Cincinatti: Ralph Jusko, 1958) and used in *With One Voice*. He was active as a popular commentator on musical topics and over a period of 23 years be became especially well-known for his contributions as an intermission commentator, pianist, and quiz panelist on the regular Metropolitan Opera radio broadcasts. Father Lee died at Toronto on 26 July 2019. — **W666**

Michael Leunig

Michael Leunig, Australian cartoonist, painter, poet, philosopher, cultural and political commentator, was born in East Melbourne on 2 June 1945. He was educated at Maribyrnong High School and began a degree at Monash University, where his first cartoons appeared in the student newspaper *Lot's Wife*. In the early 1970s his self-taught art appeared in various newspapers and satirical magazines. Since that time his work has regularly appeared in two major Australian newspapers, Melbourne's *The Age* and *The Sydney Morning Herald*. In

1989, asked to produce a weekly cartoon for the *Sunday* Age, he wondered 'if newspapers might carry some small spiritual message of consolation as a tiny reparation for the enormous anxiety and distress they can create.' Out of that have come three books of prayers and drawings, *A Common Prayer* (1990), *The Prayer Tree* (1991) and *When I talk to You: A Cartoonist talks to God* (2006), but all of his work incorporates spiritual and philosophical themes as their titles, such as *Everyday Devils and Angels* (1992), suggest. Other titles include *Short Notes from the Long History of Happiness, Ducks for Dark Times, The Curly Pyjama Letters, The Travelling Leunig* and *The Lot: In Words*.

Leunig speaks of living by 'the personal things in which you believe, your sense of conscience, your sense of right action in the world' as a religious act. 'These are the delightful parts of life, this wonderful meandering of the soul through the mystery of life. It's not about getting it right – it's about being there and loving it, expressing, coming into relationship with each other and the mystery of life.' However, his vision of life includes an understanding of the fragility of human nature and its relationship to the wider natural world.

Michael Leunig has published more than 30 books of cartoons, and expressed his quirky, compassionate, hopeful view of humanity and its foibles in a variety of other mediums. In 1999 he was named one of Australia's Living Treasures by the National Trust of that country, and has been awarded honorary degrees by La Trobe and Griffiths University. He now lives on a farm in northern Victoria. — **F28**

Swee Hong Lim

Swee Hong Lim was born on 11 June 1963 in Singapore and educated in the Philippines and the United States. He holds degrees from the Asian Institute for Liturgy and Music, Manila (BChurch Music), Southern Methodist University, Dallas, Texas (MSacred Music), and Drew University (PhD in Liturgical Studies). He has taught at Trinity Theological College, Singapore, in the areas of worship, liturgy and music, and at Baylor University, Waco, Texas. In 2012 he was appointed Deer Park Assistant Professor of Sacred Music at Emmanuel College, Toronto, where he directs the Master of Sacred Music programme and is the Director of the college chapel.

From 2008-2010, he chaired the Board of Worship and Music for the Trinity Annual Conference of the Methodist Church in Singapore, 2008, and was a member of the Worship Planning Committee for the 2011 Ecumenical Peace Convocation sponsored by the World Council held in Jamaica He served as Co-Moderator of the Worship Committee for the 10th General Assembly of the World Council of Churches at Busan, South Korea (2013). He is currently Director of research for the Hymn Society in the United States and Canada. A strong advocate for the contextualisation of Christian worship and music practice, he is the author of *Giving Voice to Asian Christians* (Berlin: Verlag Dr Muller, 2008) and has written a number of new tunes for Charles Wesley hymns, as well as other hymns and liturgical music. Several of his settings of Shirley Murray hymn texts are on the Songselect website, and he is well published in the *Chalice Hymnal*, the *New Century Hymnal*, *The Faith We Sing* (a United Methodist hymnal supplement), *Sound the Bamboo, Let the Asian Church Rejoice*, and the *Global Praise* series. — **H7**

I-to Loh

I-to Loh has been described as Asia's foremost musician and ethnomusicologist. Born in Taipei, Taiwan on 28 September 1936, the son of a Presbyterian minister and scholar, he was educated at the Tainan Theological College and Seminary, the Union Theological Seminary, New York, and the University of California in Los Angeles (PhD, 1974-82). From 1982 to 1994 he taught at the Asian Institute for Liturgy and Music in Manila. He now holds the position of Adjunct Professor of Worship, Church Music, and Ethnomusicology at Tainan Theological College and Seminary, Taiwan Theological College and Seminary, and the Southeast Asia Graduate School of Theology. Since the early 1960s he has passionately promoted the use of indigenous Asian music for Asian hymns, gathering regional folk melodies, writing hymn settings himself, adapting Western-authored hymns to Asian harmonies, publishing scholarly articles on Asian hymnology in Mandarin and editing major Asian hymnals. These include *New Songs for Asian Cities* (1972), *Hymns from the Four Winds* (1983), *Sound the Bamboo* (1990, revised 2000), and *Let the Asian Church Rejoice* (2015), as well as a massive hymnal companion to *Sound the Bamboo*, with its sub-title *Asian Hymns in their Cultural and Liturgical Contexts*. Australian, New Zealand and Papuan New Guinean hymnwriting is considered as part of the Asian context. He now serves as an adviser in liturgy to both the World Council of Christian Churches and the Council of Churches of Asia. 'There is no greater voice throughout Asia for developing indigenous congregational singing than I-to Loh,' wrote Michael Hawn in his survey of Christian World Music, *Gather into One: Praying and Singing Globally* (2003). — **A12; C8; F58; HP20**

Bronwyn (Bonnie) Low

Bonnie Low was born at Picton on 18 October 1948. Placed in a Salvation Army children's home in Hamilton, she was adopted by a Tauranga couple with whom she moved to Gisborne. When she was five her adopted father died and she spent time with a Māori family on the East Coast, learning Māori songs and aspects of the culture and life style. At the age of eight her widowed mother married a Scottish Presbyterian lay preacher, and mother and child moved into his Gisborne home and a church environment. She says, 'Life evolved around music, school and sport, with a weekly dose of Glaswegian sermons.' Following her secondary education at Gisborne Girls' High School, and on the death of her stepfather, whom she remembers gratefully as a powerful influence on her life, she moved to Auckland, married and raised a family. She became involved in the Pentecostal movement of the 1970s, writing worship songs published by Scripture in Song and Queen Street Music, the latter releasing them on records such as 'Promise of things to come' (1977) and the popular children's album 'Rejoice Young One' (1979, re-released in 2013), which included 'The Children's Saviour.' Another New Zealand publisher, Parachute, released her songs 'Hungry for You' and 'We seek your face' on their album *You Alone* (1999).

In 1980 she began working for advertising agencies as a freelance jingle writer and producer, 'which is how I learned recording production.' She also composed documentary and film tracks and co-wrote the music for the 1990 Commonwealth games. Another Christian music album followed, co-written with a friend Tony Walker for a missions project and titled *Lord of the Breakthrough*. A move back to Gisborne led to the establishment of a worship school called Eastgate Ministries, where she was associated with a group of Christian musicians, artists, poets and dancers; she also became a Performing Arts tutor in songwriting and vocals at Tairāwhiti Polytechnic College. It was then that she wrote the songs for the album released in 1999 as *Fragile Warriors*, containing Christian songs blending Māori and *pākehā* materials. She has said of it, 'These songs capture something of the prophetic heart of New Zealand, with her unique blending of spirit and blood, ancient and new, culture and sound, so that to *tahi hau ora* – with one breath, we can touch the heart of God together.'

Since then she has developed an international career as a Christian performing artist, composer, writer and workshop leader. In 2000 Bonnie Low moved back to Auckland where she has continued writing and helping other songwriters develop and record their work. Four of Bonnie Low's praise and worship songs were published in *Scripture in Song*, volume 2 (1981), three in *Servant Songs* (1987) and a further 14 appeared in *New Zealand Praise* and its supplements (1988-93). *Servant Songs* (1987), *Alleluia Aotearoa* (1993), and *Together in Song* (1999) all include her popular song 'The Children's Saviour,' and she has a substantial list of religious songs registered with the United States Manna Music organisation. A number of her songs are listed on the Songselect site. — **A66**

Percy Hylton Craig (Bing) Lucas

Bing Lucas,* one of New Zealand and the world's most distinguished conservationists, was born at Christchurch on 9 June 1925. Educated at St Albans Primary School, Christchurch Boys' High School, Canterbury University College (1944-8), he went on to further education at the New Zealand Staff College (1966) and the University of Michigan (1969). He had a distinguished career in the Department of Lands and Survey, becoming Director of National Parks and Reserves (1969-75) and Director-General of Lands (1980-6). He chaired the New Zealand Walkways Commission (1976-86) and was a long-serving member of the Council of the New Zealand Historic Places Trust (1969-75). He worked with a number of international institutions involved with the protection of land and seascapes around the world, becoming a consultant for both UNESCO World heritage sites and the International Union for the Conservation of Nature.

He was much honoured for this work: he was awarded the New Zealand Queen's Service Order in 1986 and received the 1990 Medal for services to conservation. International awards included Fellow of the East-West Centre (Hawaii, 1990) and membership of the Order of the Golden Ark (Netherlands, 1994). After his death on 17 December 2000, several national and international publications were dedicated to his memory, expressing great affection and deep respect for his work on protected natural areas around the world.

A member of the Tawa-Linden Baptist Church for many years, Bing Lucas wrote hymns and lyrics for Christian musicals, the most famous of them *Saultalk* (1974), a rock musical on the life of St Paul, which ran (exceptionally) for three years.** Three of his hymns texts were published in *Servant Songs* (1987). — **C18**

*See further the entry on Lucas in *New Zealand Who's Who in Aotearoa* (2001). He has a long list of conservation-related publications to his name, several of them seminal in his field

**See *Caught in the Acts: The Story of Saultalk, Tawa's Christian Rock Musical of the Life of Paul, and the Seasons it Played Between 1974 and 1976*. Ken Edgecombe, Wellington: Saultalk Incorporated, 1999.

Lars Åke Alfons Lundberg

On 28 August 1935 Swedish priest, composer, writer and singer Lars Lundberg was born into a musical family living in northern Sweden. He studied theology at the University of Uppsala and in 1960 was ordained a pastor of the Swedish Lutheran Church. He soon became aware that 'many people, especially young people, could not join in the singing of the traditional hymns to the accompaniment of [an] organ. Their music and that of the church were miles apart. I therefore started setting texts by Anders Frostensen [and others, including in particular Margareta Melin].' He went on to compose and write about providing spiritual resources for children, creating a *Children's Prayer Book* in 1991.

From 1979 to 1987 he was the publishing editor for Verbum, a Swedish publishing house specialising in non-biblical Christian books. He served both as a priest and prison chaplain. During his time as a prison chaplain in Österåker (1993–2001), he was involved in developing 'Peace of Mind' services in All Saints church there. He had a strong commitment to vulnerable groups in society and was an important link between the Swedish churches and the Twelve-Steps (AA) organisation. He also frequently toured as a religious singer, and recorded a number of albums, the most famous of which was *We put ourselves in the ring*. For his many years of service in the Church's spiritual and social work he was awarded the King of Sweden's Medal in 2009. He died on 22 May 2020.

He is represented in the 1986 Swedish *Psalter* by two translations as well as by nine hymn settings; in the Norwegian *Psalter* by two translations and a melody, and in *The Young Church's Hymnal* (Helsinki, 1994). He is the author or co-author of several books, among them *Jesus Christ the World's Hope* (1984), and he has written some 15 hymns as well as hymn settings. — **W667**

Iris Elizabeth McCoy

Iris McCoy was born at Gisborne on 22 September 1920. She was educated at the Waerenga-o-Kuri and Waipaoa primary schools and Gisborne Girls' High School. She worked in a solicitor's office and the State Advances Corporation before marrying Harry McCoy in 1944 and raising 6 children. She became a Sunday School teacher at the Bright Street Methodist Church, Gisborne, in 1940, later at the Atkinson Methodist Church, where as its Superintendent she began writing songs and hymns for the children, set to popular tunes, and, later, adult hymns – some 50 in all. She trained as a Lay Preacher and completed both Methodist and Presbyterian Lay Preacher Certificates; she eventually received a 40 years Long Service Award from the New Zealand Lay Preachers' Association. She became a member of the Mangapapa Union Parish in 1967 and wrote the history of the union in *Our Story. Mangapapa Union Parish 1913-2007* (2007). Some of her hymns reached print in *Songs for Worship* (1968), *Sing a New Song* (1970) and *New Zealand Praise* (1988). She also contributed texts to Contemporary Hymns (NZ). At an advanced age and living in a retirement home, she still attended her church and led weekly bible studies. She died at Gisborne on 10 November 2017. — **C28**

Rangi Karaitiana McGarvey

Rangi McGarvey was born at Ruatoki in 1958, of Ngāti Tūhoe and Ngāti Whakaue descent. After studying at Tawera Native School (Ruatoki North) and Waikato University he became a professional Māori language consultant and translator, registered on the national Te Reo Māori translators panel. He became a senior manager in the Ministry for Culture and Heritage, and from 1998 worked at Parliament as a highly-regarded translator and interpreter. He contributed significantly to *Te Ara Encyclopedia*, the official online New Zealand information source, as Māori co-editor for its biographical section and author of the major article on Ngāti Tūhoe. He also played a role in the development of the national website on the history of the 28th Māori Battalion, an infantry battalion which distinguished itself in action in World War II. He died on 12 October 2017 and was buried at the Tauarau marae in the Ruatoki Valley. — **H61**

James McGranahan

James McGranahan was a 19th century American singing evangelist and composer, best known for his hymns and musical settings. He was born on 4 July 1840, in West Fallowfield or Adamsville, Pennsylvania. His father was a farmer who sent his son to singing school where by the age of 19 he had organized his first singing class and soon became a recognized teacher. He later attended the Normal Music School founded by evangelist William Bradbury at Geneseo, New York, and eventually became a director and teacher at George Root's Normal Musical Institute. During this time he gained a reputation with his writing for glee, chorus and Sunday school groups. He was a fine tenor, and for a time seemed destined for a career in opera, but on the sudden death of his close friend **Philip Bliss** he decided on a life as a singing evangelist and teamed up with Major Daniel Webster Whittle (1840-1901). For 11 years the pair travelled the United States and made two successful visits to Great Britain and Ireland – the second (in 1883) with Moody and Sankey.

McGranahan composed some 25 hymns. He edited some 15 gospel hymn collections, including *The Choice*, *The Gospel Choir* (with Sankey), *Gospel Hymns 3-6* (with Stebbins and Sankey) and *Harvest of Song. Songs of the Gospel* and *The Male Chorus Book* – he pioneered the use of a male choir and male quartet at evangelical meetings – were published in England. Ill health eventually compelled his retirement to Kinsman, Ohio, but he continued to write gospel hymns and songs there. He died on 9 July 1907 at Kinsman, Ohio. — W631

Jennifer (Jenny) Helen Mcleod

Jenny McLeod* was born in Wellington on 12 November 1941, and grew up in Timaru and Levin. 'I learned to read music aged five, this came almost as naturally as a mother tongue.' Throughout her childhood and adolescence she was involved in music as a school pianist and church organist. With her brothers she formed a band and played for local occasions and accompanied singers, violinists and choirs. She was educated at Timaru Girls' High School, Horowhenua College, Levin, and (on an American Field Scholarship) at Stephen Decatur High School, Illinois, before studying extramurally at Massey University for a year and Victoria University, Wellington (1962-4), where she was taught by Frederick Page, David Farquhar and Douglas Lilburn and completed a BMus degree with first-class honours. A New Zealand Government Overseas Bursary enabled her to continue her studies at the Paris Conservatoire under Olivier Messiaen (a powerful influence on her style), and Luciano Berio, and at the Rheinisch Musikschule, Cologne, where she studied with Stockhausen.

She returned to New Zealand in 1966, and in 1967 took up the position of Lecturer in Music at Victoria University, later becoming Professor and Head of the Music Department, a position she held from 1971 to 1976. A growing interest in Hindu and Buddhist philosophy led to her involvement from 1975 to 1981 in the Divine Light Mission, which brought about her retirement from the University and took her to Australia and the United States as a volunteer missionary.

Over the course of her career as a composer, dating from 1964, she became one of New Zealand's foremost musicians, receiving numerous commissions from the Queen Elizabeth II Arts Council and the New Zealand Composers' Foundation. She achieved particular fame for her large-scale theatrical-musical events performed in smaller communities such as Masterton and Palmerston North, involving orchestral sound and several choirs, including large groups of children. *Earth and Sky* (1968) recounts the Māori Creation myth; *Under the Sun* (1971) involved 1000 performers and artwork contributed by the children of 16 local schools. The 1983 Wellington Sun Festival featured eight of her 'colour' pieces performed on the Wellington harbour.

In 1983 she began a close association with the annual choral festival held at Easter in Wanganui, He Iwi Kotahi Tatou, becoming a member of Ngāti Rangi and writing many hymns and religious songs in Māori for the competing choirs. In 1988, when she retired to Pukerua Bay, north of Wellington, she became the local organist, and following a conversion to Roman Catholicism continued writing hymns and religious songs. Her work includes sets of Christmas carols, a long series of 'Godsongs' – hymns and songs for nominated groups, and religious choral works – many of them with texts in Māori. In 2012 her opera *Hōhepa* was premièred at the New Zealand International Festival of the Arts. In 1997 Jenny McLeod was awarded the New Zealand Order of Merit for services to music. In 2008 she was awarded the CANZ (Composers' Association of New Zealand) KBB Citation, for services to New Zealand music. — **A89, 153; C29; F37, 68; HP16; H128**

> *Much further information can be found in John Mansfield Thomson's *Biographical Dictionary of New Zealand Composers*, Wellington: Victoria University Press (1990) 97-101, the *New Zealand Who's Who in Aotearoa 2001*, Auckland: Alister Taylor Publishers, 2001, and on the SOUNZ website. Jenny McLeod's colour carols have been recorded by the Wanganui Schola Sacra Choir in their compilation *Pohutukawa Carols*, 2000.

Willow Katherine Faith Macky

Willow Macky, who has been described as one of this country's great but largely unheralded composers of New Zealand songs, was born in Auckland on 25 June 1921. She began writing poetry at the age of 3, before entering Auckland Normal primary and intermediate School, followed by 5 years' education at Iona College and St Cuthbert's College. In the 1940s she studied piano, guitar (with a Māori teacher, Walter Smith) and voice, and began to collect and sing folksongs from around the world. In 1955 she composed her first New Zealand songs, and visited the United States. 1956 saw the publication of her *Song of Zion*, a dramatic history of the Jewish people; in the following year her carol 'Te Harinui' was published in London.*

Then American balladeer William Clauson brought her songs to public attention by his performances and recordings. From 1961-3 she was based in England, where she met the distinguished Māori bass Inia Te Wiata, who recorded the composer's 'The Māori Flute' with the BBC Light Orchestra. He was later to praise her as 'the only New Zealand composer besides Alfred Hill who can capture the authentic Māori atmosphere.' In 1968 and again in 1973 she visited the United States. That country's engagement in the Vietnam War inspired a body of poetry, and she engaged in active correspondence with leading figures in the arts and media on environmental and peace issues. In 1986 she organized a 'Bells around the World' campaign for Armistice Day, with her own song 'Peace to the World' playing on carillons in four different countries. 1989 saw the publication of her 'Waitangi Anthem' and in 1993 she brought out 'The Treaty Tree,' describing it as 'a song for the children of Aotearoa.'

Willow Macky eventually wrote over 200 songs and lyrics, most of them folk songs – she said that the reason she started writing songs was because while she had collected many folksongs from around the world, she couldn't find any about her hometown of Auckland – but she also wrote a number of religious poems and songs and an unpublished folk opera called *The Māori Flute*. There are several volumes of her verse, amounting to 300 poems.

She was a strong exponent of writing about local experiences, history, people and places, especially Māori legend and tradition. She said of herself, 'I've been guided, you know, all the way, even though I haven't always seen it very clearly. Some kind of Divine Guidance, although I don't think of myself as being very faithful in that line. But I do believe in the Holy Spirit – and I hope it comes through a little in some of my songs, especially the peace ones.' Her song 'Land of the Fern' has been claimed by the Girl Guides; 'Te Harinui' has been sung at countless end-of-year school assemblies and Christmas services in New Zealand.

In 2004 Willow Macky received a Good Citizen Award from the Mayor of Auckland; in her 95th year she received the Queen's Service Medal for community service, and she died in that year on 10 December 2006. — **A98, C31, F46; H57, 114**

*The story behind the writing of 'Te Harinui' is told by Patricia Bawden in the Winter/Spring 2007 issue of *Music in the Air*. Six of Macky's anti-war poems are discussed in the Summer/Autumn 2008 issue of the same magazine, and an introduction to *The Spirit and the Bride*, a sequence of over 80 poems covering a journey from the Garden of Eden to the New Jerusalem is given in the Winter/Spring 2013 issue.

Richard Donald Madden

Richard Madden was born in Dunedin on 21 March 1953. He was educated at Otago Boys' High School (1966-71) and the University of Otago (1971-6). There he studied cathedral music with Donald Byars, composition with Byars and Edwin Carr and singing with Honor McKellar, graduating BMus (hons) and completing the LRSM Diploma in Singing in 1977. He became a chorister of St Paul's Cathedral Choir, Dunedin, and in 1974 held the position of acting choirmaster. All of his religious music has been written with this choir in mind. Since 1979, Madden has been Music Master at St Hilda's Collegiate School in Dunedin; he has also held the position of assistant choirmaster of the St. Paul's Cathedral Choir, co-conductor of the City of Dunedin Youth Choir and conductor of the Dunedin Royal Male Choir (2000-2019). Until recently he was Head of Music at Columba College, and Director of the Choral Scholars at Knox College Dunedin.

Richard Madden has composed a range of church music which includes a communion service, prayers and responses, chants, anthems, carols and hymn tunes.* In 1982 he composed a set of *Preces and Responses*, and in 1983 set the words of the New Zealand Liturgy for a Communion Service to honour the Archbishop of Canterbury's visit to New Zealand. Some of this choral music has been published in *Three Christmas Carols* (1992), written for the boys of St Paul's choir, and his setting of the medieval English carol, 'I sing of a maiden,' (matched in the Trust's publications with Shirley Murray's carol 'Child of Christmas story,' A12) has attracted international attention. His work is always harmonically rich and eminently tuneful, informed by the classical English cathedral choral tradition. In 2017 he was awarded a Queen's Service Medal for his services to music. — **A12, C8**

> *There is a detailed list in *Joy in the Singing: The Choral Commitment of St Paul's Cathedral Choir, Dunedin, 1859-1959*, by the former Director of Music at the cathedral, Dr Raymond White (Dunedin: Musick Fyne [1989], 100-101). See also the entry on Madden in John Mansfield Thomson's *Biographical Dictionary of New Zealand Composers*, Wellington: Victoria University Press (1990) 103-4, and 'Richard Madden: A Voice from the South,' Raymond White, *Music in New Zealand*, 18 (Spring 1992), 41.

John Marriott

See 'Ave lou ola,' erroneously associated in *Alleluia Aotearoa* with John Marriott, an English clergyman (1780-1825) and author of 'Thou whose almighty word'). — **A6**

Donald Stuart Marsh

Donald Marsh was born in Akron, Ohio, in 1923. He was educated at Westland Maryland University, the University of Houston, Texas, and the famous Theodora Irvine School of Drama, New York. For 13 years he was involved in the theatre, concert and television world of New York as an actor, choreographer and teacher. He also became musical director at First Presbyterian Church, Port Jervis, a small city near New York, where he spent 30 years as a colleague of **Richard Avery** with whom he wrote more than 120 religious songs, carols and hymns and toured the United States and Europe leading workshops. At the Port Jervis church Marsh directed over 75 plays and musicals and conducted three choirs. He eventually retired to Santa Fe, New Mexico. In the famous partnership between Marsh and Avery (see Avery's biography) Marsh's role was principally that of musician; Avery wrote of his work, 'Don does all sorts of things to the chords and rhythms that add a vital life-blood to them.' — **W 675**

Christopher John Marshall

Oldest son of New Zealand hymn writer **Jocelyn Marshall** and Professor Fred Marshall, Christopher Marshall was born in Paris on 18 July 1956. Christopher was raised in New Zealand and spent his formative years here, attending schools in Wellington, Hamilton and Auckland. He received his early education in music at Armidale, New South Wales, Australia, then at Auckland University, where he completed a BMus (1978) and an MMus with Honours (1989). He became a Fellow of Trinity College, London, in Music Composition in 1988, and holds a Teaching Licentiate in Piano from the same institution (1983). He went on to develop a career as a professional composer and teacher.

He ran a Continuing Education Music Programme at the University of the South Pacific, Samoa, from 1991-2, then tutored in Music Theory and Composition at the University of Waikato (1993). From 1994-5 he held a Mozart Fellowship at the University of Otago, Dunedin, where he won the 1995 Philip Neill Memorial prize in composition. Then a Fulbright Scholarship gave him the opportunity to become Composer in Residence over the following two years at the Eastman School of Music, New York. In 2000 he won the Douglas Lilburn prize for his composition *Hikurangi Sunrise*. He is currently Composer in Residence at the University of Central Florida, Orlando, Florida and in 2009 also became Adjunct Professor of Composition there.

He has written numerous choral works, among them carols, anthems and hymn tunes, pieces for chamber ensemble, orchestral music and works for wind ensembles, for which he has gained a considerable international reputation; his music has been performed throughout Europe, North America and Asia.* He is the winner of numerous national and international prizes and awards. Some of his writing incorporates aspects of Māori chant and other Polynesian music: a formative influence was his years spent in Western Samoa. — C27; H39, 48

*For fuller details see the SOUNZ website.

Jane Manton Marshall

Jane Marshall, born 5 December 1924, was a distinguished American composer of choral music and hymns tunes. A natural musician, she began composing as a teenager. After graduating from Southern Methodist University, Dallas, with a Masters degree in music (1945), she served as a church musician in a number of United Methodist churches in Texas and taught in both public schools and at Southern Methodist University, Dallas, where she was a long-serving Professor of Music at the Sacred Music graduate faculty at Perkins School of Theology. She regularly taught in the Church Music summer continuing education program there (1975-2010) and was active in promoting congregational singing through choral workshops held around the United States. She received the Roger Desehner Award, given by the Fellowship of United Methodist Musicians, and was honoured twice by the Southern Baptist Musicians Conference for her contribution to church music. She is the author of a collection of homilies and essays, *Grace Noted* (Hope Publishing Company, 1992). She was a long-time member of the Fellowship of United Methodists in Worship, Music and the Other Arts, also of the American Guild of Organists and the American Choral Directors' Association. She composed over 200 anthems, hymns and other sacred music, hymn texts and tunes, including several settings for **Shirley Murray** hymns, and was a consultant to the hymnal revision committee of the *United Methodist Hymnal*. She died at Dallas, Texas, on 29 May 2019.

'I rank her as the most sensitive and text-oriented hymn tune composer of the late 20th century. She was that good,' said Dr Carlton Young, editor of *The United Methodist Hymnal* and American Editor for *The Canterbury Dictionary of Hymnology*. — **A16, 158; F65, F68; H102, 118, 132, 148, 154**

Jocelyn Mary Marshall (née Crabtree)

Jocelyn Marshall was born on 15 September 1931 at Morrinsville in the Waikato. She was educated at Hamilton West School, Epsom Girls' Grammar School, and the Auckland and Christchurch Teachers' Colleges, graduating in 1951. She worked initially as a Speech Therapist in Auckland schools. Brought up first in the Presbyterian and then the Methodist Church she was involved in the Auckland Methodist Youth Council, the Student Christian Movement and occasional radio broadcasting. In 1954 she married Fred Marshall (later Professor of French at Waikato University), after which she spent four years in Paris, studying at the Institute of Phonetics while teaching children at the British Embassy and giving English lessons. In 1958 the couple returned to New Zealand and after an interval in Armidale, New South Wales, Australia, finally settled in 1970 in Hamilton, where she held the positions of City Councillor (1998-2004), Justice of the Peace (1999), Docent at the Waikato Museum of Art and History and Lay Canon for 30 years (later Canon Emeritus) of Waikato Cathedral Church of St Peter. She was associate editor of the Waikato Anglican newspaper *Church Alive* for 15 years, and was made a life member for her work for the Save the Children Fund. In 2007 she was awarded the New Zealand Order of Merit for services to the community. She died on 26 September 2019.

Her first hymn was written in response to a request from the Dean of St Peter's for a patronal hymn. She went on to publish four collections amounting to over 100 hymns, *A Singing Faith: Incorporating Occasional Hymns* (1996), *Additional Hymns* (1999), *More Hymns by Jocelyn Marshall* (2001) and *Hymns for All Seasons* (2007). An in-house collection of 11 hymns written after 2001 was given limited distribution in 2004: they were incorporated in *Hymns for All Seasons*. Jocelyn Marshall's hymns have appeared in *Sing Glory* and *Anthems for Two Voices* (Kevin Mayhew, 1999 and 2002), *Christ's College, Canterbury* (2009), *Carol our Christmas* (1996) and *Hope is our Song* (2009). One of her carols, set by her son Christopher, won the Auckland RSCM carol competition in 1993. Her text, 'God of Ages' (H39), was among the finalists for the worldwide 1998 Millennium Hymn Competition organised by St Paul's Cathedral, London. Some of her hymn texts are listed on the *Hymnquest 2000* and *Oremus* data bases.

Many of her hymns arose out of her own personal experiences, to mark significant events such as a visit to New Zealand by the Archbishop of Canterbury, or in response to sermons; others are the result of commissions to celebrate patronal saints, church festivals and anniversaries. In her own words, she writes 'to fill the need for [texts] that are written in inclusive language, are poetic in structure and are relevant to contemporary theology and a forward-looking faith.' Her hymns are also deeply-rooted in the social concerns, the spirituality and the imagery of the natural world of her own country. They are usually set to well-established tunes in *Hymns Ancient and Modern Revised*, but a number of them have received new and original settings by English and New Zealand composers, including **Christopher Marshall**, Anita Banbury, Len Schroeder, Nigel Williams and **Ronald Dellow**. — C27; H5, 32, 34, 39, 42, 47, 48, 152

Kathleen Mary Mayson (née Irving)

Kathleen Mayson was born in Wanganui on 25 December 1913. She attended primary school in Marton and won a scholarship to Wanganui Technical College where she remained as a student teacher while doing university papers extramurally. Moving to Auckland, she studied at the University of Auckland, gaining an MA with honours in English and co3mpleted her training as a teacher at the Auckland Teachers' College. In Auckland she met her future husband, who was then in training for the Methodist ministry. She brought up a family of four children and moved about following her husband's stationing appointments and later his teaching positions, for he became a teacher too, doing his country service near Wanganui and Dannevirke.

Kathleen herself returned to teaching, relieving at Dannevirke High School and then Wanganui Boys' College. She had already begun writing short stories when she joined a women's writing society in 1959 and she continued to write and publish poetry and short stories. She had work accepted by the Oxford University Press for *A Second Australian Poetry Book* (1983) and a 1987 *Miscellany* of women writers' prose and poetry. Between 1965 and 1987 seven of her short stories were published in *The Listener*, and other poems and stories were published in *Landfall* and *The School Journal*. In 1991 she brought out a collection of her poetry, *Kate in the Lemon Tree* (Blackwood), named after her granddaughter Kate Saywood. Until 2010 she contributed book reviews to radio and newspapers. She died at Whanganui on 5 September, 2015.

Kathleen Mayson wrote a number of hymns, which were put to music by the composer and church musician Alan Johnston of Whanganui. They are now deposited in the Colin Gibson

Hymnology Collection of the Dunedin Public Library. Alan Johnston's setting of her hymn 'How marvellous the human mind' was published in *New Zealand Praise* (1988). — **H124**

Mechtild Of Magdeburg

Little is known about the German medieval mystical writer Mechtild (=Matilda) of Magdeburg. Her name comes from her book (see below): references it contains to court custom and courtly literature suggest she was from an educated family, as does the fact that she could read and write German (although she acknowledges that she does not know Latin). She had at least one brother, who became a Dominican. In her early 20s, she left her home to go to Magdeburg (on the Elbe River); she appears to have lived most of her life there as a beguine, that is as a member of a Christian lay order – apparently in a community, perhaps as its superior. Near the end of her life, about 1270, she entered a monastery at Helfta which followed Cistercian custom.

She may have gone to Helfta because of the increasing restrictions being placed on beguines in Germany and the Low Countries. The women had received statements of papal approval in 1215 and 1233, but with approval went a requirement for clerical direction and eventually for ecclesiastical control. In 1261, a synod meeting in Magdeburg ordered the local beguines to obey their parish priests, rather than rely on the mendicant orders (such as the Dominicans) for spiritual advice.

In her mid-30s, on the advice of her Dominican confessor, Mechtild began to write down her spiritual love songs and visionary experiences. Some of these writings were circulated and she speaks of the harsh criticism she received as a woman writing about spiritual matters. But she continued to write until her death. Her work was collected in *Fliessende licht der Gottheit* (originally *Vliessende lieht miner gotheit*, often translated as 'Flowing light of the Godhead'). The manuscript is divided into seven books: Books 1-5 were written during the 1250s, Book 6 in the 1260s, and Book 7 in the 1270s at Helfta. Within the seven books are 267 sections, ranging in length from a few lines to several pages long. They include not only Mechtild's visionary experiences, but also letters of advice and criticism, allegories, reflections, and prayers; they use prose and verse, dramatic dialogue and lyric.

Mechtild wrote in the dialect used in the north of Germany; fragments remain of this original, but the surviving complete text is a translation made in the language of southern Germany about 60 years after her death. However, scholars assume that the text as we have it reflects Mechtild's words and – at least for the first six books – a structure determined by herself and her confessor. — **A56, 65**

Hirini (Sydney) Melbourne

Hirini Melbourne, composer, singer, university lecturer, poet and writer, was born in the Ureweras on 21 July 1949. His tribal affiliations were with Ngāi Tūhoe and Ngāti Kahungunu. He won a scholarship to the Auckland Teachers College, then taught at a secondary school in Whakatane. He next moved to Wellington to edit Māori-language school publications for the Department of Education, writing a number of stories and joining Ngā Tamatoa, which petitioned the New Zealand Government to have Māori taught in schools as part of its focus on Māori identity. He studied at Auckland University where he completed an MA on the appropriation of Tūhoe land, then held the position of Lecturer and Senior Lecturer in Māori at Waikato University, before being appointed Dean and Associate Professor of Māori and Pacific development there.

A chance meeting on a marae with a Radio New Zealand reporter led to some of his songs and waiata being recorded. His music was welcomed by schools and proved to be an effective teaching aid. Melbourne went on to become a significant figure in the revival of the Māori language, with dozens of his now classic songs sung in classrooms throughout New Zealand.

In the last two decades of his life his musical interests extended to traditional Māori instruments. Initially intrigued by instruments found only in museum glass cases, he subsequently met ethnomusicologist and performer Richard Nunns and from 1989 onwards the two travelled the country collecting and recording stories and memories from old people who remembered the sounds of their childhood. They amassed a body of knowledge of the ritual and ceremonial use of Māori instruments, virtually creating a map of Māori music in New Zealand. They regularly performed together on marae and in schools, galleries and concerts and recorded an album, Toiapiapi, featuring the sounds of the rediscovered instruments. Their partnership lead to the release of Te Ku Te Whe, a CD of original and traditional compositions for a variety of Māori flutes, which was given a Gold Disc Award. A second CD together with a DVD, Te Hekenga-a-rangi, was released in 2003.

SOUNZ lists over 78 musical works by Hirini Melbourne; they include the film scores for *Māori* and *Once Were Warriors*, and the collections of songs and waiata *Te Wao Nui a Tane* (1999) and *He Waiata ma te Katoa: Songs for Everyone* (2004) In 2002 Hirini was awarded an Honorary Doctorate by the University of Waikato and received the Te Waka Toi Exemplary Award in recognition of his leadership and service to Māori arts and culture. He was made an Officer of the New Zealand Order of Merit in the 2003 New Year's Honours, just before his death at Hamilton on 6 January 2003. In 2009 Hirini Melbourne and Richard Nunns were inducted into the New Zealand Music Hall of Fame in recognition of their contribution to the revival of interest in and understanding of *taonga puoro* (the treasure of Māori music and musical sounds). — A115

Douglas Christopher Mews

Douglas Mews, composer, classical organist and harpsichordist, was born in Cheam, Surrey, England, on 7 March 1956, and emigrated to New Zealand in 1969 with his family, when his father **Douglas Mews** took up a position in the Department of Music at the University of Auckland. He was educated at St Peter's College, and began playing the organ at St Patrick's Cathedral, where his father (and first organ teacher) was choir conductor in the 1970s. He graduated in 1979 from the University of Auckland with an MA in organ and harpsichord performance, then continued his harpsichord studies at the Royal Conservatory in the Hague, gaining that institution's Royal Certificate. At the Hague, Mews also expanded his interest in historical keyboards to include the fortepiano. As a church musician, he has directed choirs at St Patrick's Cathedral, Auckland, the English-speaking International Roman Catholic Church in the Hague and St Mary's Church, Nelson, New Zealand.

He holds the position of Artist Teacher at the New Zealand School of Music, Victoria University of Wellington, teaching the organ, harpsichord and fortepiano as well as keyboard harmony. He regularly broadcasts for Radio New Zealand's Concert programme and tours for Chamber Music New Zealand. Until recently he was the Wellington City Organist and is presently choir director at St Teresa's church, Karori, Wellington; in 2009 he toured Europe, giving concerts in Edinburgh, Oxford, Salzburg and Béziers in the south of France.

In 1991 the CD *Carols in Summer*, recorded by the Polyhymnos Choir of the Nelson School of Music under his direction, included his 1988 set of 'Snow-free Carols.' Two CDs of his playing on the organ have been issued, in 2010 and 2012. In 2010 he wrote a well-received unison setting of the Mass based on the new translation into English of the Roman Missal, 'Mass of St Teresa.' — A45

Eric Douglas Kelson Mews

Douglas Mews* was born at St Johns in Newfoundland on 22 September 1918. He was educated at St Johns Methodist College and St Johns Memorial University College. He studied at Trinity College, London from

1936 to 1939, graduating FRCO (1938) and BMus in 1939. He later completed a DMus (London) in 1961. Following wide-ranging military service in World War II, he became a professor and examiner at Trinity College of Music, London (1946-63) and a lecturer at Colchester Technical College (1963-8). Mews emigrated to New Zealand in 1969, to join the staff of the Music Department at the University of Auckland where he was made Associate Professor of Music in 1974. He held the position of Director of Music at St Patrick's Catholic Cathedral, Auckland, from 1970-82. He retired from the University of Auckland in 1984. He joined the Editorial Board of the New Zealand Hymnbook Trust, bringing an experienced classical and church musician's judgement to its decisions. He also contributed a number of settings for new texts. In 1990 Douglas Mews was awarded a Papal Knighthood for his services to music and the Roman Catholic Church. He died at Auckland 3 August 1993.

Douglas Mews was well known as a teacher, a performing musician, radio broadcaster and composer of much orchestral and choral music, particularly for the Roman Catholic Church; his appointment to St Patrick's Cathedral coincided with the introduction of the New Rite in English, for which he wrote extensively. His choral writing includes settings of liturgical texts such as the Gloria, Sanctus, Crucifixus and Magnificat, three operas and an oratorio on biblical subjects, a short setting of the Mass, and various anthems, psalms, prayers, carols and hymns. There are also several instrumental and orchestral pieces with biblical titles. In 1982 he published a well-received textbook, *The Young Musician's Introduction to Harmony*. His religious choral compositions are well represented in the New Zealand publications *The New Community Mass Book* (Dunedin: New Zealand Tablet (1970), *Holy Week for the Choir* (Auckland Diocesan Liturgical Commission, 1972) for which he was musical editor, *Sing Praise* (1981), and *Alleluia Aotearoa* (1993). But there were also international publications in England, Holland and America. — **A14, 23, 27, 28, 35, 41, 48, 49, 54, 58, 74, 84, 104, 111, 144. 160; C9(ii), 14 (i)**

*See further the entries on Mews in John Mansfield Thomson's *Biographical Dictionary of New Zealand Composers*, Wellington: Victoria University Press (1990) 104-5, and in the 12th edition of *Who's Who in New Zealand*, Wellington: Reed (1991) 435-6.

Charles Austin Miles

American composer and gospel songwriter Charles Austin Miles was born at Lakehurst, New Jersey, on 7 January 1868. He was educated at the Philadelphia College of Pharmacy and the University of Pennsylvania to pursue a career as a pharmacist, but after successfully submitting his first gospel song to the Hall Mack Publishing Company of Philadelphia he was accepted into the firm and remained there for 37 years as editor and manager, continuing as editor when the firm merged with the Rodeheaver Publishing Company. He became a well-known music director for camp meetings, conventions and churches, and wrote nearly 400 gospel songs and choruses, including the popular 'I come to the garden alone' and 'Wide, wide as the ocean.' — **A5; H16**

Edward Miller

Edward Miller was born at Norwich, England, on 30 October 1735. He abandoned an apprenticeship as a paver for his father to study music with Dr Charles Burney at Lynn and for a time played the German flute in Handel's London orchestra. He held the position of organist at Doncaster parish church, Yorkshire, from 1756 to 1807.

An enthusiastic composer and music editor, he published among other collections *The Psalms of David set to new Music* (1776), *Thoughts on the Present Performance of Psalmody* (1791), *The Psalms of Watts and Wesley* (1801), *Sacred Music* (1802) and *Elements of Thorough-bass and Composition* (1787). His most important publication was *The Psalms of David for the Use of Parish Churches* (1790) a collaborative work which provided a programme of psalms for the whole of the Church Year. In the manner of the time, it was financed by 5,000 subscribers and was awarded a gift of money from no less a person than King George III. In 1786 Miller received an honorary Doctorate in Music from Cambridge University. As well as writing numerous hymn tunes, he composed six sonatas for harpsichord and wrote a history of Doncaster. He died on 13 September 1807. — **W646**

Monastery of Chevetogne

This Roman Catholic Benedictine monastery, also known as the Monastery of the Holy Cross, is located in the Belgian village of Chevetogne, in the province of Namurs, halfway between Brussels and Luxembourg. The community was founded in 1925 and is dedicated to Christian unity. Its main buildings consist of two churches, one where the Latin Mass of the Roman Catholic Church is celebrated daily and another where the Byzantine Catholic liturgical rite used in many Eastern Orthodox churches is celebrated. The monks worship separately but share meals and meet regularly. The monastic choir has made several recordings of church music, including the simple plainchant 'alleluia' text, published in *With One Voice*. Their austere singing style is readily accessible through live performances recorded on the internet. — **W674(i)**

Monk of Gethsemani

See 'Make me an instrument' (**W666**).

William Henry Monk

William Henry Monk was born in London on 16 March 1823. Trained as an organist he first held appointments in London churches (St Peter's, 1841, St George's, 1843 and St Paul's, 1845). In 1852 he became organist and choir director at St Matthew's, Stoke Newington, London, concurrently with a similar position at King's College, London, leading to a professorship of vocal music there in 1874. He held other professorships in London, at a school for the Indigent Blind, at the National Training School for Music and at Bedford College.

A talented composer, arranger and editor, he was music assessor for the 1875 and 1889 editions of *Hymns Ancient and Modern*, and edited *The Parish Choir* from 1846 to 1851. A supporter of the High Church Oxford Movement, he edited collections and composed anthems, hymn tunes and other choral works for both English Anglican and Scottish Presbyterian musicians. His tune EVENTIDE for the hymn 'Abide with Me' became the most popular of several of his much-used hymn tunes.

In 1882 Durham University awarded Monk an honorary DMus, He died at Stoke Newington, on 1 March 1889. — **W633; A128; H2**

Richard Michael Moyle

Richard Moyle was born in Paeroa on 23 August 1944 and educated at Auckland Grammar and Avondale College. He gained an LTCL (piano) in 1965 before studying at the University of Auckland, where he completed the University's first PhD in ethnomusicology in 1971. He then held teaching positions at Indiana University and the University of Hawaii at Manoa, and for 8 years was a Research Fellow at the Australian Institute of Aboriginal Studies in Canberra, publishing 3 books on the music of Central Australia. He took up an appointment in anthropology at Auckland University in 1985, and in 2007 became Director of Pacific Studies, where – in retirement – he is now Honorary Research Professor and Director of the Centre for Pacific Studies. During this same time he adjudicated and composed music for more than 100 Samoan and Tongan choir competitions in Auckland, Wellington and Samoa. From 1993 to 2010 he directed Auckland University's Archive of Māori and Pacific Music. He is also Adjunct Professor at the Queensland Conservatorium of Music Research Centre, Griffith University. His 40 years as an ethnomusicologist researching music in performance and dance has included some ten years of fieldwork in Aboriginal Australia and the Pacific, including Samoa,

Tonga, Niue, Lau and the Cook Islands. He is the author of some 16 books, including (for Polynesia) *Tongan Music* (Auckland University Press, 1987), *Traditional Samoan Music* (Auckland University Press, 1988), *Polynesian Sound-Producing Instruments* (Aylesbury: Shire Publications, 1990), *Polynesian Music and Dance* (Aylesbury: Shire Publications, 1991), *The Sounds of Oceania: An Annotated Catalogue of the Oceanic Musical Instruments in the Auckland Museum* (Auckland: Auckland Institute and Museum, 1989). He has also published bilingual editions of oral tradition from Samoa, Tonga, and an ongoing series of books on the oral tradition, music, language and belief system of the Polynesian island of Takū in Papua New Guinea. For Aboriginal Australia, he authored a trilogy on the musics of the Pintupi, Alyawarra and Kukatja peoples. — A6

Charlotte Alexander Murray

Charlotte Murray, the third daughter of **Shona Murray**, was born 11 February 1974. Married and with 3 children, she now teaches Music and Japanese at Tawa College, as well as directing two highly successful harmony barbershop choruses there. She coaches the well-known New Zealand men's singing quartet, the Musical Island Boys, the first international group to win the intercollegiate Barbershop international competition in the United States, and Vocal FX, who gained a high placing in the International Men's Chorus competition in the USA in 2011. She has been awarded a Master Director of Music in the Barbershop world, one of only nine, and the first woman and the first director outside the USA. — F12(ii)

John Stewart Murray

The son of a pioneer Scottish settler family, John Murray was born in Invercargill on 5 November 1929. He was educated at King's High School and the University of Otago, Dunedin. After graduating with an Otago MA (1952) he studied at King's College, Cambridge, from 1952 to 1955, completing an MA in Divinity there in 1954, followed by a period of study at the Graduate School, Bossey Ecumenical Institute, Geneva, where he was awarded a Diploma in Ecumenical Studies. He married Shirley Erena Cockcroft in Cambridge, England, in 1954 and on his return to New Zealand he became an ordained minister of the Presbyterian Church. Appointments at Taihape (1956-62) and Knox Church, Christchurch (1967-75), and an ecumenical chaplaincy at Victoria University – the first of its kind there – and Wellington Teachers' College (1962-7), were followed by a long and significant preaching ministry at St Andrew's on the Terrace, Wellington (1975-1993), which he made a national centre for political, environmental and social justice debate and action. In 1990 he became the Moderator of the Presbyterian Church of Aotearoa New Zealand, and on his retirement in 1993 he presided over Frederic Wallis House, an ecumenical retreat centre, and became chairperson of Abolition 2000 NZ, a movement to eliminate nuclear weapons. In 1994 he went to South Africa as a World Church peace monitor. In 2000 he was made an Officer of the New Zealand Order of Merit for services to the community. After his retirement to the Kāpiti Coast in 1993 he continued to promote local and national environmental, social and international peace concerns, taught U3A courses, and vigorously espoused the welfare of Māori and other racial groups. John Murray died at Wellington on 17 February 2017.

In 1978, John Murray founded the New Zealand Hymnbook Trust, which brought together representatives of the Anglican, Baptist, Methodist, Presbyterian Churches and the Associated Churches of Christ, chairing it for 30 years and retiring in 2003 after overseeing the publication and distribution of the New Zealand supplement to *With One Voice* and the first four of the Trust's hymnbooks 'for all Churches.' He not only ceaselessly promoted the work of New Zealand composers and hymn writers, he drove policies of inclusiveness of language – he was instrumental in gathering contemporary poetry and Māori and Pacific Island texts for publication – and he himself wrote a number of short liturgical texts and encouraged their writing by others. That New Zealand now has a vigorous tradition of ecumenical and socially-focussed hymn writing is largely due to his dynamic leadership. — **F4, 7, 19, 23, 49, 58, 66, 71; HP20, 23**

Shirley Erena* Murray (née Cockcroft)

New Zealand's most distinguished hymn-writer, Shirley Murray, was born into a musical Methodist family in Invercargill on 31 March 1931. At her primary school she met a young teacher who encouraged her to write poetry. When he was sent off to war, before his death on the front he wrote a treasured letter urging her to continue doing so. She was educated at Southland High School, where she became Head Girl, and the University of Otago, where she studied classics, French and music and completed an MA with honours in Latin and French (1952) then went on to become for a time a teacher of languages. She had already gained her LTCL in piano in 1947, and later served as a church pianist and organist. She married Presbyterian minister **John Stewart Murray** in Cambridge, England, in 1954, and together the couple brought up a family of three sons. Murray's fourth collection of hymns, *Faith Makes the Song* (2003) is dedicated to three of her six grandchildren, 'for granddaughters Isabella, Anna and Rachel, to find a faith worth singing.'

Her own faith journey saw a steady progression towards a broadly-based ecumenism, which began with her involvement with the Student Christian Movement at Otago University, continued through her contacts with the World Council of Churches in Geneva and the National Council of Churches in New Zealand and led to the writing of theme songs for World Council of Churches Assemblies and the Christian Conference of Asia.

Following her husband's appointments to Taihape, Wellington and Christchurch – with an intervening term as an ecumenical chaplain to Victoria University and Wellington Teachers' College – the Murray family returned to begin a long and influential ministry at St Andrew's on the Terrace, Wellington (1975-93). From 1981 to 1988 Shirley worked as a researcher for the Labour Party (New Zealand's Parliament is located in Wellington) and, briefly, as a national radio hymn programme producer. It was at St Andrew's that she began regularly writing hymns: 'Being married to a lively theologian, who is also a Presbyterian minister, I became engaged with the difficulties of constructing a liturgy in which the Word preached had no hymns to support or reflect it. To be theologically adventurous was to be bereft of anything relevant to sing.' Murray's principled support for Amnesty International (she became its New Zealand Religious Affairs Co-ordinator) and for groups working for greater equality for women in church and society provided further prompts to hymn-writing. In 1993 she and her husband retired to Raumati, a small coastal village north of Wellington, where she became for a time a member of the Kāpiti Chamber Choir, singing under the direction of **Peter Godfrey,** and where until the end of her life she continued to write hymns and manage a now international network of correspondents and friends.

In 1978, when her husband founded the ecumenically-based New Zealand Hymn Book Trust to promote and publish New Zealand hymn-writing, Shirley Murray became secretary to its editorial board. She contributed one carol to its first publication, the New Zealand Supplement to the Australian hymnbook *With One Voice* (1982). But her calling as a hymn writer soon came to dominate her creative life. In 1987, with the aid of a grant from the Church Worship Committee of the Presbyterian Church, she published a collection of 28 of her hymns, titled *In Every Corner Sing: New Hymns to Familiar Tunes in Inclusive Language*. Successive hymnbook publications by the Trust – *Alleluia Aotearoa* (1993), *Carol Our Christmas* (1996), *Faith Forever Singing* (2000), *He Came Singing Peace* (2002) and *Hope is our Song* (2009) – included nearly 200 of her hymns and carols. Her writing was drawn to the attention of American congregations, when, on the recommendation of English-born hymn-writer Brian Wren and American editor and composer **Carlton Young,** Hope Publishing brought out a collection of her hymns, *In Every Corner Sing: The Hymns of Shirley Erena Murray* (1992), following that with five more collections spanning her hymn-writing from 1992 to 2019, *Every Day in Your Spirit* (1996), *Faith Makes the Song* (2003), *Touch the Earth Lightly* (2008), *A Place at the Table* (2013) and, *Life into Life: New and Collected Hymns* (2019). Murray's presentation of her own work at the Conference of the Hymn Society of America and Canada held at Washington in 1992 confirmed her high-standing among mainstream liberal American churches. Her hymns now regularly appear in major North American hymnals (over 30 of them, according to her publishers for three decades, Hope Publishing), together with special collections such as *Sing for Peace: The Hymns of Shirley Erena Murray set to the Tunes of Jane Marshall and Carlton R. Young* (Abingdon Press, 2004). She has an increasing presence in British hymnals, too; indicated by the inclusion of 22 of her hymn texts in the fourth edition of the *Church Hymnal* (2002) and 11 in *Singing the Faith* (2011).

Asian recognition began with *Sound the Bamboo* (1990), for which she supplied original hymns, paraphrases and some translations, working closely with I-to Loh, its editor. Beyond New Zealand, America and Asia, her hymn texts are now regularly found in Australian, Canadian, English, Scottish, European and South American hymnals; they have been translated into many languages, including sign language and Braille. Special anthologies and religious resource compilations, such as *Voices Found: Women in the Church's Song* (New York, 2003) and *Dare to Dream: A Prayer and Worship Anthology* (London 1995), extend the international and national publication of her texts. Together with her own writing on her hymns and attitude to hymn-writing as an expression of Christian faith, such publications amount to a major corpus of creative and self-critical work, which led one American commentator to describe her as 'the most important of all living hymn writers.' A full bibliography of her hymns and other writings, together with the record of its critical reception and performance history is now an urgent need, beyond the scope of this *Companion.***

The themes of her hymns have been pursued with admirable consistency over a writing career of nearly 40 years. They include the rejection of war, the search for peace, justice and human rights, the acceptance of racial, social and sexual difference, the honouring of women and the feminine element in spirituality, celebration of the natural world – particularly New Zealand's unique environment – and its need for human protection rather than exploitation, a call to social responsibility and concern for each other and a summons to a life lived out with compassion and hopefulness. Her theology is Christ and Spirit-centred, honouring the God-presence in every individual, particularly the powerless, the oppressed and abused. There are many hymns celebrating the Church's seasons and ceremonies, its rituals and festivals, but there is also a body of work addressing private needs: less community-minded and more inward-looking, mindful of personal meditation and quiet reflection.

All in all, her writing displays a remarkable range of tones, from tender carols to solemn litanies of confession, from anguished expressions of social concern to outpourings of confident faith and sheer joy. Her texts are distinguished by their intentional inclusiveness and their innovative introduction of Māori language, as well as by their bold appropriation of secular, especially scientific imagery and the poetry of nature and domestic life. Few hymn-writers have more boldly experimented with poetic forms and metrical patterns, or more directly confronted issues of faith and society.

Her command of rhythm and control of metrical shape have made her words attractive to musicians world-wide, to the point where there is almost an embarrassment of settings by New Zealand and overseas composers of Shirley Murray texts. They include **Jillian**

Bray, Barry Brinson, David Dell, Nigel Eastgate, Colin Gibson, Peter Godfrey, Guy Jansen, **Shona Murray**, Ian Render, Douglas Mews, **Roy Tankersley** and Americans Charles Damon, **Rusty Edwards**, Marty Haugen, Jane Holstein, Hal Hopson, **Amanda Husberg**, Donald Hustad, Austin Lovelace, **Jane Marshall**, **Joy Patterson**, Allen Pote, Carl Schalk, **Jack Shrader**, **Jim Strathdee** and **Carlton Young**, as well as **Ron Klusmeier** (Canada), **I-to Loh** (Taiwan), **Per Harling** (Sweden) and **Swee Hong Lim** (Singapore). She has welcomed this richness of music, saying, 'Each interpretation by a composer has brought different colouring to the words.' Her third American collection, *Faith Makes the Song* thanks her 'composer-friends' for 'setting, interpreting and illuminating my words.'

Shirley Murray has been much honoured both in her own country and internationally. In 2001 she was made a Member of the New Zealand Order of Merit for her services to community through hymn-writing (the first New Zealander to be so recognized), in 2005 she received the Mahara Gallery Trust award for literature and in 2009 she was awarded an honorary Doctorate in Literature from the University of Otago. In 1996 she was Erik Routley Fellow of the Presbyterian Church of the United States; in 2006 she was made an honorary Fellow of the Royal School of Church Music, London, and in 2009 she was named a Fellow of the Hymn Society in the United States and Canada in recognition of her contribution to the international community of congregational song.

Shirley Murray died at Wellington on 25 January 2020; a full biography is in preparation. Much of her adventurous thinking is exposed in her contribution to Janet Wootton's *This is our Song: Women's Hymn Writing* (Epworth Press: London, 2010) pages 295-307. Her incalculable contribution to New Zealand hymnology is suggested by the sheer number of her hymns in all the publications of the New Zealand Hymnbook Trust. — W645; A1, 7, 9, 10, 12 14, 15, 16, 17, 19, 22, 23, 24, 25, 26, 28, 36, 39, 41, 42, 43, 44, 45, 49, 50, 52, 54, 60, 61, 62, 63, 69, 79, 81, 86, 87, 94, 96, 99, 100, 105, 106, 108, 113, 118, 119, 122, 123, 125, 126, 127, 130, 140, 143, 149, 151, 153, 154, 155, 158, 159; C3, 7, 8, 9, 13, 14, 16, 30, 33, 35, 35*, 37, 38, 39, 40, 48, 50, 51; F1, 3*, 5, 8, 9, 10, 11, 12, 14, 16, 17, 19(ii)*, 20, 22, 25, 29, 30, 34, 35, 37, 38, 41, 44, 45, 46, 52, 54, 56, 57, 59, 60, 65, 68, 69, 70, 72, 73, 74, 75, 76, 79*; HP1, 2, 3, 4, 5, 6, 7, 8, 9, 010, 11, 18, 19, 21, 22, 24, 25; H6, 7, 10, 13, 15, 28, 29, 35, 37, 44, 49, 53, 56, 61, 64, 77, 78, 83, 85, 87, 89, 91, 93, 95, 96, 100, 102, 105, 106, 107, 108, 111, 112, 118, 122, 129, 130, 131, 132, 133, 139, 148, 153, 154, 155, 156

*Erena is the Māori form of Helen, a name gifted to Shirley Murray by her mother, who in turn received it from a South Island Māori chief and friend of Shirley Murray's Scottish grandfather.

**See the Appendices 'A Finding List of New Zealand Hymnody,' and 'Writing about New Zealand Hymn-writers and New Zealand hymnody' for an overview of such material.

Shona Marjory Murray (née Duncan)

Shona Murray was born in Xshuchang, China, on 22 September 1943. She arrived in New Zealand with her family in 1950 and was educated at Gore High School; Mana College, Porirua; Wellington Teachers' College (where she gained a Diploma of Teaching with distinction); and Victoria University of Wellington (1961-2, 1972-4), where she gained a BMus, majoring in performance on the pipe organ. She also became a Licentiate in piano of both the Royal Schools of Music and Trinity College, London. She married Bruce Murray in 1964, and became the mother of four children, Johanna, Susannah, **Charlotte** and Duncan.

After working as a primary school teacher she joined the staff of Tawa College in 1977 and in 1982 became Head of its Music Department, a position which she held until 2006. Shona continued to teach part-time at Tawa College until December 2011, and still assists with accompanying students for their performances for NCEA. She was an outstanding teacher in the fields of composing and performance, and for ten years acted as Chief Moderator for both School Certificate and University Bursaries Music examinations. For ten years she was also the accompanist for the NZ Secondary Students' Choir, travelling to international choral festivals on numerous occasions.

The Tawa Dawn Chorus and Twilight Tones became well-known school choirs under her leadership, with the Twilight Tones winning a Gold award at a Music Festival in San Francisco in 2006. She also directed many musicals in the Wellington area including the widely performed original rock musical *Saultalk*. For ten years she was the assistant director of the Wellington Bach Choir. From 1979 to 2010 she was the main driving force and Musical Director of the Tawa Schools and Community Festivals, a multi-media show with up to 700 singers and dancers. She has been a member of the music team at Tawa Linden Baptist Church playing both pipe organ and piano for more than 50 years. She particularly enjoys playing in instrumental groups within the church with young people she taught at Tawa College. She was a member of the New Zealand Hymnbook Trust from its inception until her duties as Head of Music at Tawa College compelled her to withdraw.

Shona received a Sir Woolf Fisher Memorial Award (1984) for Outstanding Teacher of the Year; the NZ 1990 Commemoration Medal; a Rotary Paul Harris Medal; and a Wellington City Council Civic Award in 1995 for her services to community music. In 2013 she was awarded the Queen's Service Medal for services to music and education. — **W645, 675; C37, 39, 52; F29**

Sydney Hugo Nicholson

Sydney Nicholson was born at London on 9 February 1875. Named after the Australian city where his English father had made a considerable fortune as a business man and had helped to found the University of Sydney, he was educated at Rugby school, New College, Oxford (where he completed an MA and BMus) and the Royal College of Music, London. He became a Fellow of the Royal College of Organists and in 1903 was appointed organist at Lower Chapel, Eton College, in 1904 organist at Carlisle Cathedral and in 1908 at Manchester Cathedral. While at Manchester be was made chief musical adviser to *Hymns Ancient & Modern*, editing the music for the 1916 *Supplement*. In 1919 he was appointed organist at Westminster Abbey and became the choral director there, responsible for the music for the great national services held in the Abbey. He founded the Westminster Abbey Special Choir, and, as chairman of the Church Music Society, campaigned enthusiastically to improve Anglican church music throughout the country and abroad.

In 1928 he retired from the Abbey to found and administer the St Nicholas College of Church Music, London, which eventually developed into the now world-wide organisation, the Royal School of Church Music, with its centre at Canterbury, to which it moved in 1954 under a Royal Charter. Nicholson continued his editorial work for *Hymns Ancient & Modern* until near the end of his life. He co-authored a *Manual of English Church Music* (1923), and wrote *Church Music: A Practical Handbook* (1920), *Boys Choirs* (1922), *The Parish Psalter* and *Quires and Places where they sing* (both 1923), *Peter: The Adventures of a Chorister* (1944) and various essays and articles on church music. He also composed a number of fine hymn tunes, a service in D Flat, a still popular communion service in G and several anthems. He became a member of the Royal Victorian Order in 1926, received the Archbishop of Canterbury's DMus in 1928, and was knighted for his services to church music in 1938. He died at Ashford, Kent, 30 May 1947. — **A87**

Christopher Garth Norton

Christopher Norton* was born on 22 June 1953 at Tauranga, New Zealand. Educated at Otago Boys' High School, he began composing at the age of 14, and by 16 had an orchestral work performed and broadcast. In

1974, already a talented pianist studying under Maurice Till, he gained first-class Honours in Music from the University of Otago, and had some success as a concert pianist, playing with the New Zealand Symphony orchestra and broadcasting over Radio New Zealand. He went on to teach music in two Wellington high schools, Scots and Tawa, and worked as a composer-in-residence for a year before launching as a freelance composer, arranger and performer, regularly playing keyboard in a rock band involved with gospel music. In 1977 Norton traveled to Britain on a University Scholarship to study composition at York University. His interest was still in gospel music, and he registered for a DPhil, but emerged with an MMus, having discovered himself to be 'resolutely anti-academic.'

In 1980 he began a freelance career in England as a rock band player, prolific composer and arranger – working particularly in popular and jazz idioms, and later as a music educationalist and writer. His earliest publications included *Carol Jazz*, a set of improvisations on Christmas music; and his stage musical *Daniel,* which included 'a rock symphony of psalms,' toured the United Kingdom. In 1983 he began a long association with the English music publishers Boosey & Hawkes, publishing *Microjazz*, a highly successful series of graded piano pieces in a variety of popular styles, and an award-winning set of guides to Pop, Latin and Jazz music. The *Microjazz* series has now expanded to include music for all the major instruments, with sales of over a million copies. Norton has gone on to launch substantial piano courses in Canada (*Connections*) and America (*American Popular Piano*) and has led workshops and teaching sessions around the world, including most recently New Zealand and Australia (2012).

In addition to much religious music, including choral anthems, an *Agnus Dei*, his *St Nicholas Mass* and a setting of the *New Zealand Liturgy* for choir, organ and guitar, his compositions include musicals, ballet scores, orchestral, chamber, instrumental and piano music, popular songs and advertising jingles. He composes for film and television and is a very active record producer, with many albums of gospel and Christian music to his credit as well as a series of praise and worship songs popular in New Zealand and elsewhere, and he has founded his own highly successful publishing companies.

Carol Jazz (1987) was followed by *Christian Classics* (1990), containing piano arrangements of 30 standard hymn tunes. He took an important role in editing and arranging the music for *Songs from the Psalms* (1990) and *Hymns for the People* (1993) and he contributed a number of arrangements to *Let's Praise 2* (1994). In 1995 he published nine new tunes for classic 18th century hymn texts in *The Hymn Makers I,* and the successive volumes of *Mission Praise* contain many of Norton's arrangements of classic and contemporary hymn tunes, together with some of his own music, particularly that written in association with Graham Kendrick. Other international hymnals containing his work include *Voices United* (Canada, 1997), *Common Ground* (Scotland, 1998) and the 4th edition of *Church Hymnary* (2005). — **A88, 117, 135, 139**

*See further the entry on Christopher Norton in John Mansfield Thomson's *Biographical Dictionary of New Zealand Composers*, Wellington: Victoria Press (1990) 107-9 and the biographical entry on the SOUNZ website.

Frederick Arthur Gore Ouseley

Ouseley – more properly Sir Frederick Arthur Gore Ouseley, Baronet – was born in London on 12 August 1825. He was an infant musical prodigy (he wrote an opera at the age of eight) who eventually became Professor of Music at Oxford University (1855-9). In 1844, having succeeded to his father's baronetcy he entered Christ Church College, Oxford, graduating MA in 1849. He was ordained in the same year, and after serving several curacies eventually became Precentor of Hereford Cathedral. In 1850 he graduated MusB at the University of Oxford, and four years later took the degree of MusD. In 1856, with his own funds he founded at Tenbury Wells a choir school intended to serve as a model for Anglican church music. A major figure in the mid-19th century revival of English church music, and the composer of a large quantity of church and chamber music, he was closely associated with the first edition of *Hymns Ancient & Modern*. He died at Hereford on 6 April 1889. — **W650**

James (Jimmy) Lloyd Owens

Jimmy Owens was born at Clarksdale, Mississippi on 9 December 1930, and educated at Millsaps College, Southwestern College, Memphis, Tennessee, Cathedral School of the Bible, Oakland, California and Cabot College, San Leandro, California. A jazz band music arranger, he went on between 1951 and 1969 to direct music at several Californian evangelical churches. Beginning in 'the Jesus Movement,' he married Carol Owens in 1954 and formed a husband and wife Christian song writing team. An early success was their musical *Ants'hillvania*, which was nominated for the 1982 Grammy Awards. They went on to do music missions for the Los Angeles Church of the Way. In 1991 they established in Singapore the School of Music Ministries International and have continued to teach and publish books about the craft of prayer and religious song writing. As performers, they have worked with many other singers, including Pat Boone, Jack Hayford, Darlene Zscheck and **Graham Kendrick.** They have published collections and albums of their own music, including long-running musicals such as *The Witness* (1978) and *Heal our Land: Praise and Prayer to Heal a Nation* (1995). They received the Christian Artists' Music Achievement Award in 1986, and Jimmy was inducted into the Mississippi Musicians Hall of Fame in 2001.

Forty-nine of their songs appear on the SongSelect site, and in 2020 Jimmy published the second volume of his *Bee Attitudes* album. They are currently working on a collection of songs drawn from the writings of the apostle Paul. — **W673**

*Carol Sue Owens was born in El Reno, California on 30 October 1931. She attended San Jose State College and the Oakland Cathedral School of the Bible. Like her husband, a talented creative artist, she wrote Christian novels as well as musicals.

Durward John Paisley

This Dunedin poet was born on 14 June 1938, probably at Wellington, and died in 1985. For most of his life he was afflicted with a serious and crippling mental disability, and was for some time a patient at Cherry Farm psychiatric hospital, near Dunedin. Despite this handicap, he studied at the University of Otago, completing a BA (1963) and an MA in English (1966). He later became a competent artist and wrote much poetry, several plays, two unfinished novels and other prose. He published one collection of his own work, *This Night in Winter* (1982); *Vigils* (1985) was published after his death, with an extensive memoir by John Caselberg. His sister, Agnes Dawn Ross, who attended Wellington Girls College and Otago Girls High School and trained at the Dunedin Teachers College (now the College of Education) gathered and published his *Collected Poems* in 1990. His poetic output includes a number of religious poems, hymns and carols.

In his *Collected Works*, the editor prints a commentary prepared by the poet for a reading of some of his own religious poems. There he says of himself, 'I make no claims to be a religious poet myself. If anything, I am perhaps a poet who writes the occasional religious poem. But while most of the time my attention and my writing is taken up with other and more secular concerns, my religious poetry is important and significant to me and my development, both as a person and as a writer. It is not without significance that when many years ago I lost contact with reality for a few weeks, I attended a party at the house of a friend and for sometime recited a long religious poem (spontaneously composed) to a room full of surprised and eventually indifferent guests. The poem is not among my papers, and I have no memory of having ever written it. But the fact that even in the state of insanity my preoccupation was a religious one, speaks volumes in itself…God, the source of all truth, is also the source of all beauty. If we turn our backs upon the world, we turn our backs also upon its maker. The poet is one who celebrates the beauty of the world, and the religious poet looks at the world and its beauty and looks beyond to the God who is the source of creativity and who gave the poet his gift and his vision.' — **H94**

Charles Hubert Hastings Parry

Sir Charles Hubert Hastings Parry (to give him his full name and title) was the second son of a successful English painter and patron of the arts. He was born at Bournemouth on 27 February 1848 and educated at Eton, Oxford University and the Royal Academy of Music. He was composing by the age of eight and completed an Oxford BMus degree while still at Eton. He went on to become in 1883 Professor of Composition and Music History (later Director) at the Royal College of Music. From 1900-1908 he held the position of Professor of Music at Oxford University. He was knighted in 1898 and made a baronet in 1902; Cambridge, Dublin and Oxford all awarded him the degree of honorary MusD.

As an undergraduate at Exeter College, Oxford, he helped to found the Oxford Music Club, but he was equally interested in yachting and other sporting activities. As Scholes' *Oxford Companion to Music* put it, 'He was prominent in almost every branch of athletics and constantly ran into every kind of danger that land and water afford, suffering all possible injuries short of the immediately fatal.' His many compositions included hymn tunes, organ works, and now famous anthems—such 'I was glad when they said unto me' and 'Jerusalem.' His books on music and musical style were influential and these together with his own distinguished and popular compositions helped to raise the standards of English music in the late 19th century. After he died at Rustington, Sussex, on 7 October 1918, his ashes were placed in the crypt of St Paul's Cathedral. — **W665; A41; F55; H50**

Joy Florence Patterson

Joy Patterson was born in 1931 in Lansing, Michigan, and raised in LaGrange, Illinois. She holds a B.A. in French Studies and an M.A. in French Literature from the University of Wisconsin. A Fulbright Scholar, she taught French at college level and worked for the United States Social Security Administration. A resident of Wausau, Wisconsin, she is an elder of the Presbyterian Church there and has been active at local, presbytery and national levels. She was a member of the committee that prepared *The Presbyterian Hymnal* (1990).

Although she describes herself as 'a middling musician,' she writes both texts and tunes which have been published widely in America. Her concerns as a hymn writer are for the unity and inclusiveness of the church, peace, justice, and the stewardship of the earth. Her collected hymns were published in 1994 under the title *Come, You People of the Promise: The Collected Hymns of Joy F. Patterson* (Carol Stream, Illinois: Hope Publishing). Her next collection, *Teach Our Eyes New Ways of Seeing* (Pittsburgh: Selah, 2005), contained settings of five **Shirley Murray** texts. She has 21 hymns on the SongSelect website, and some of her latest hymns were published in *Assembled for Song: An Anthology of New Hymns* (Chicago: GIA, 2011). — **F44, 69; H87, 133**

Ta Upu Pere

As well as becoming a prominent church and community leader among Pacific Islanders, Ta Upu Pere was a school teacher, a baker and fisherman, a choir-master and sports person. He was born on 21 September 1918 in the Cook Islands, marrying Ngakai Tiananga of Aitutaki on 17 July 1937. He was educated at Takamoa Congregational Bible School, Raratonga, 1946-51, and Mt Eden Congregational Theological College, Auckland, 1952-3, completing a LTheol there. Ordained as a Congregational minister in 1953, he became Matavera Ekalasei at Rarotonga, from 1954-55. In 1956 he attended Selly Oak Theological College, Birmingham, England. From 1957-58 he lectured at Takamoa Theological College, establishing a Christian Youth development programme around the Cook Islands. In 1964, with the Reverend Pepe Nokise, he was appointed associate leader of the Pacific Islanders Congregational Church at Newtown, Wellington, and when that church became part of the Presbyterian Church in 1969 he became a Presbyterian minister. He continued to minister at Newtown until 1978 when he moved to St Luke's Pacific Island Church, Tokoroa, from which he retired in 1985.

Ta Upu Pere exercised a wide pastoral ministry, regularly visiting Cook Islands people in Christchurch, Dunedin, Invercargill and Bluff, as well as families all over Wellington and in the Manawatu and Hawkes Bay. An enthusiastic supporter of children's and youth work, he also directed choirs and composed special hymns and arranged music for Cook Islands choirs. With **Taria Kingstone** he authored a course in Cook Islands Māori for the Auckland Unitech in 1992 and contributed to the foundation of the Pacific Conference of Churches in 1961. He was awarded an MBE on 31 December 1985 for his services to the Pacific communities of New Zealand. He died on 2 September 2002. — **A142**

Michael Arnold Perry

Michael Perry was one of the leading English hymn writers of the 20th century. He was born in Beckenham, Kent, on 8 March 1942, and educated at Dulwich College (1952-60) where he sang with the college choir and played in the orchestra. He went on to University College, London, intending to read physics, but made a career change which took him to Oak Hill Theological College, London, Ridley Hall, Cambridge and a BD from the University of London (1964). Following his ordination in the Church of England Diocese of Liverpool, and a first ministry at St Helens, Merseyside, he became curate then vicar of Bitterne, Southampton (1968-72). During this time he served on the committees that produced *Psalm Praises* (1973) and *Hymns for Today's Church* (1982). He also completed an MPhil in theology at the University of Southampton.

From 1981 to 1989 Perry served as Rector of Eversley, Hampshire. In 1982 he became Secretary of Jubilate Hymns, and was involved in editing most of their books. In addition, he worked as Chaplain and lecturer at the National Police Staff College at Bramshill, and was elected to the Church of England's General Synod in 1985 and again in 1994. From 1989 until his death in 1996 he was Vicar of Tonbridge, Kent, and during that time he was made a canon of Rochester Cathedral and was appointed chairman of the Church Pastoral Aid Society. He died on 9 December 1996

Perry wrote over 300 hymns, psalms and religious songs; his most famous, the Calypso Carol, was written in 1964 for a student concert when he was at Oak Hill, and became popular after Cliff Richards substituted it for a missing recording in a radio show. A collection of his hymns was later published as *Singing for God* (Hope Publishing, 1995). He launched the periodical *Words and Music* in 1982 to encourage budding hymn writers, edited *Carols for Today* (1986) and *Carol Praise* (1987), was involved in writing 3 religious musicals, and editing *The Daily Bible, Prayers for the People, The Dramatised Bible, The Wedding Book*, and *Songs from the Psalms. Preparing for Worship* (Zondervan, 1995) was another of his many books. — **A88, 117, 135, 139; F3**

Ethel Oliver Doreen Potter

Doreen Potter was born in Panama 28 March 1925, the daughter of a Jamaican Methodist family. On their return to Jamaica in 1931 she received her primary and secondary education there, studying the piano and violin. She then moved to England where she trained as a teacher of music. In 1968 she began to write settings for texts by **Fred Kaan**, several of them appearing in his *Pilgrim Praise* (1972). The Potters relocated to Geneva in 1967, and there she became associated with Kaan again in the production of two significant ecumenical hymnbooks, *New Songs of Asian Cities* (CCA, 1972) and *Cantate Domino* (WCC, 1975). In 1975, 20 of her tunes matched with Kaan's texts appeared in the American publication *Break Not the Circle*: they included 'Let Us Talents and Tongues Employ,' which rapidly gained world-wide popularity. Her hymn tunes were also published in Jamaican, Swedish, American and English hymnals. Towards the end of her life she worked on the music edition of *Cantate Domino*, which was published one month before her death from cancer on 24 June 1980. — **W658**

Roland Huw Pritchard (Prichard)

Roland Pritchard was born at Graienym, near Bala in Merioneth, Wales, on 14 January 1811. He worked as a weaver for most of his life. He is said to have written his single well known tune HYFRYDOL when he was 20, and published it in a songbook for children, *The Singers' Friend*, in 1844. He died at Holywell, where he had moved to find work in a flannel manufacturing company, on 25 January 1887. — **F32**

Betty Jane Pulkingham (née Carr)

American choir director, arranger and composer Betty Pulkingham was born on 25 August 1928 at Burlington, North Carolina. She was educated in various public schools in North Carolina and in 1949 completed a BSc in Music at Women's College, University of North Carolina in Greensboro. She went on to graduate study at the Eastman School of Music, Rochester, New York, and for four years taught music theory at the University of Texas. Following her marriage in 1951 to the Reverend William Graham Pulkington she became increasingly involved in church music, and directed the choir at the Church of the Redeemer at Houston, Texas, from 1965 to 1971. There she was also involved in the production of a number of church music recordings.

In 1971 she and her husband, together with other leaders from the Houston church moved to Britain to begin a series of church revival ministries in the United Kingdom. They established the Community of Celebration in the Isle of Great Cumbrae off the coast of Scotland (1974-85), and sent out evangelical teams known as the Fisherfolk. Later this form of ministry was extended to England, America, Germany, Sweden, Australia and New Zealand.

Betty Pulkingham co-edited three songbooks, *Sound of Living Waters* (1974), *Fresh Sounds* (1976) and *Cry Hosanna* (1980), as well as a hymnal supplement, *Come Celebrate!* (1990), arranging much of the music in these collections. She followed this with a collection of anthems, *Be Known to Us*, and descants, *Hosanna in the Highest*. Other published works include two books, *Little Things in the Hands of a Big God* (1977) and *Sing God a Simple Song (1986)*; a responsorial Psalter for Years A, B, and C; hymns and octavo anthems, music for children; and four settings of music for the Eucharist. She helped produce more than 40 recordings and served on the Episcopal Church's Standing Commission on Church Music.

In 2006 she received an honorary Doctor of Humane Letters degree from the Protestant Episcopal Theological Seminary in Virginia, and in 2007 she received the degree of Doctoris in Sacris Litteris from Wycliff College, University of Toronto. From 1993 she lived in her home town, Burlington, North Carolina, remaining a Companion of the Community of Celebration in Aliquippa, Pennsylvania. She published her autobiography, *This is My Story, This is My Song*, in 2011. She died on 9 May 2019. — **W674(iii)**

Henry Purcell

Now acknowledged as one of England's greatest composers, Purcell was born in Westminster, London, in 1659. His father and his uncle were both Gentlemen of the Chapel Royal, but his father died when the boy was only four and he was given a musical education by his uncle Thomas Purcell. Precociously talented (he was writing songs from the age of eight), he sang at the Chapel Royal until his voice broke in 1673, when he was apprenticed to an organ builder. For the next few years he tuned the organs and copied music at Westminster Abbey, but in 1677 on the death of Matthew Locke he was appointed composer of the King's violins and in 1679 he succeeded John Blow as organist of the Abbey. He was in charge of music for the coronations of James II (1685) and William and Mary (1689) as well as the music for Queen Mary's funeral in 1694. He composed a huge range of church, theatre and secular music, ranging from what is probably the first English organ prelude on a hymn tune to bawdy inn songs and the earliest English operas. Recognized as a genius in his lifetime, on his untimely death on 11 November 1695 he was buried in Westminster Abbey. A collected edition of his works begun in 1878 was only completed in 1965. — **H34**

Silvia Ellen Purdie (nèe Crane)

Silvia Purdie was born in Suva, Fiji, on 14 June 1968, the daughter of a Methodist missionary teacher. As a child she also lived in Kaikohe, Ruatoria (north of Gisborne), then for two years in Tonga before settling in Lower Hutt, Wellington. She completed a BA at Victoria University, Wellington, in 1988, followed by a year as a lay chaplain at the same university. She then spent five years working for the Methodist Church, sharing the role of national Youth Co-ordinator.

Following her marriage to Christopher Purdie in 1995 the couple worked for 2 years in youth and family ministry at Taupo. Five years at Wainuiomata, Wellington, followed, which Sylvia describes as a time of 'having babies' – the couple have three sons – 'and doing Playcentre.' She also completed a Diploma in Counselling from the Wellington Institute of Technology in 2001. The family then moved to Dunedin, where both she and her husband trained for Presbyterian ministry; Silvia completed a BTheol degree through the University of Otago in 2007 and the Diploma of Ministry from Knox College in 2008.

The couple moved to Linton when her husband became a New Zealand army chaplain. Silvia was ordained in 2010 into the Foxton-Shannon Co-operating Parish. In 2012 she became the minister of the Milson Combined Church (Anglican-Methodist-Presbyterian) in Palmerston North. In 2016 she moved to Christchurch as minister of the Cashmere Presbyterian Church, where she launched her website, *Conversations*, containing original worship and prayer resources.

She says of herself, 'I have been writing songs all of my adult life, I experience it as a gift of the Holy Spirit. But I am lately more into non-musical writing, and am currently working on reflections on the Psalms.' This activity resulted in a set of Biblical studies, *For God so loved the World:…exploring God's heart for our Environment* (A Rocha, 2018) and an ebook, *Let's Say a Psalm* (Philip Garside Publishing: Wellington, 2019). She writes a web blog for Kids Friendly, creates worship resources, and has contributed articles to the Presbyterian journal *Candour* on the subjects of children's faith development and marriage. — **H119**

Lewis Henry Redner

Lewis Redner was born at Philadelphia, Pennsylvania, on 15 December 1831. Redner was a wealthy real estate broker who was also active in church work as a composer, organist and Sunday School leader. He served as organist in four Philadelphia churches and is said to have increased Sunday School attendance at Holy Trinity Episcopal church from 36 to over 1,000 during his 19 years as organist and superintendent there. He is best known as the composer of the hymn tune ST LOUIS, the music for 'O Little town of Bethlehem,' used in *Alleluia Aotearoa* for Marnie Barrell's hymn 'We thank you for the gift of life' (A148). Redner never married, and died on 29 August, 1908, in Atlantic City, New Jersey.

The circumstances of the composition of ST LOUIS are well documented. In 1868 the rector of Holy Trinity Church, Philadelphia, Phillips Brooks, presented the children of the parish Sunday School with a hymn inspired by his previous Christmas week journey on horseback from Jerusalem to Bethlehem. He asked Redner to set it. According to the composer, 'the simple music was written in great haste and under great pressure almost on the Eve of Christmas. It was after midnight that a little angel whispered the strain [melody] in my ears, and I roused myself and jotted it down.' The Sunday School children sang it in their Christmas Day programme; it first appeared with Brooks' now-famous hymn in *The Sunday School Hymnal* (1871). — **A148**

Alexander Robert Reinagle

Alexander Reinagle was born at Brighton, England, on 21 August 1799, the son of a cellist and composer of Austrian descent. He was brought up in Oxford, where he became a music teacher, and from 1822 to 1853 organist of the Anglican church of St Peter in the East. He was heavily involved in music-making in Oxford, working closely with fellow organist and composer John Stainer. He retired to Kidlington, where he died on 6 April 1877. He published a few sacred works, two books of psalm tunes and instruction books for both the violin and the cello. — **H2**

Ian Philip Render

Ian Render is an Anglican priest whose hymn texts and sensitive musical settings of other writers' work have mostly appeared in the publications of the New Zealand Hymnbook Trust, *Alleluia Aotearoa*, *Carol Our Christmas* and *Faith Forever Singing*. He was born in Southampton, England, on 15 May 1954, and emigrated with his family to Nelson, New Zealand, in 1965. Educated at Nelson College and Wellington Teachers' College, and a teacher for seven years, during which time he began writing music and performing on stage with various Christian bands, in 1982 he became team leader of Youth for Christ's Y-One outreach and toured New Zealand. The following year he began to further develop his ministry skills and in 1984 was selected for training for the priesthood at St John's College, Auckland. He completed the degree of LTheol with Honours, was ordained deacon in Nelson Cathedral in 1986 and priested at Blenheim the following year. In 1988 he moved to the Diocese of Wellington to serve the congregation of St Michael and All Angels, Newlands-Paparangi, In the mid 1990s he moved to the Diocese of Waiapu where he served first as the Vicar of St Augustine's, Napier, then as Diocesan Ministry Advisor. He moved to Auckland in the mid-2000's to take up a position within the Auckland Diocese as Social Work Manager for the Mangere East Family Service Centre, and for three years acted as Ministry Enabler, supporting small Anglican communities in that city. In 2017 he was installed as Dean of Waiapu Cathedral, Napier, and has since given presentations on 'The Power of Music to form Community.'

While in Wellington, he joined the editorial committee of the New Zealand Hymnbook Trust, a position he held for seven years (1988-95), during which time he wrote most of his 22 hymns and hymn settings. There are also some 30 unpublished Christian songs for a contemporary folk/pop band, 2 musicals, *The Prodigal* and *All Fall Down*, a setting of the Liturgy of the Eucharist and other settings of liturgical material. His best-known works are his farewell to his own parents as they returned home to England after visiting their son, 'When we lift our pack and go' (A153), and his settings of texts by **Joy Cowley** and **Marnie Barrell**, as well as a number of hymns by **Shirley Murray**. Some of his hymns and hymn tunes have been published in England, the United States and Japan.

He says of himself, 'I've always had a gift for putting notes together, somehow. It's just the notation part I dislike!' and 'I believe that music for congregations should include some element of challenge, since once mastered it will remain longer in the congregation's repertoire.' — **A14, 63, 77, 82, 95, 96, 131, 136, 147, 153, 157, 158; C4(i), 9(i), 13(ii); F3, 13, 19, 30, 35, 45, 74**

Mona Riini

A member of a group of Māori gospel hymn-writers, including **Hoki Tawa, Kitty Temara** and **Reginald (Reg) Wharekura**, working co-operatively in the late 1980s. See under 'Whakatau mai te Atua.' — **A32, 150**

Caradog Roberts

Caradog Roberts was born on 30 October 1878 at Rhosllanerchrugog, Denbighshire, Wales. He showed a talent for music when very young and won several prizes at eisteddfods. He gave up an apprenticeship in carpentry for a musical career, eventually taking a doctorate in music at Oxford University, the youngest Welshman and the first from North Wales to do so. He held various posts as organist and choirmaster in Welsh churches; from 1914 to 1920 he was director of music at Bangor University College. He conducted the Rhosllanerchrugog and Llandudno choral societies, as well as a number of hymn festivals. In addition to other works, he composed or arranged several hymn tunes included in Welsh hymnals. He died on 3 March 1935, and was buried at his birthplace. — **W641**

Katharine Emily Roberts

Katharine Emily Roberts was born in Leicester, England, in 1877, and after a private school education studied singing in London and Paris. Following her marriage to R.E. Roberts, she became organizing secretary for the Rutland Community Council. In addition to the four translations of Welsh carols she contributed to the *Oxford Book of Carols*, she wrote plays, pageants and a history of Peterborough. She died at Ashford, Middlesex, on 12 April 1962. — **W641**

George Frederick Root

This American revivalist musician, who in the 19th century became famous on both sides of the Atlantic, was born on 30 August 1820 at Sheffield, Massachusetts. He was a talented farm boy who could boast at the age of 13 of being able to play on 13 instruments. In 1838 he moved to Boston, Massachusetts where he studied music under George Webb. In 1845 he moved again, to New York City, playing the organ at the Church of the Strangers, and teaching music at the Abbott Institute for Young Ladies. There he met Fanny Crosby, with whom he went on to compose a number of sentimental popular songs. In 1850 he toured Europe and shortly afterwards started teaching music at Boston's Academy of Music. He began composing in 1851, both secular songs and gospel songs in the style of Moody and Sankey, both of whom were active at this time. His many publications include collections of choral music for singing schools, Sunday Schools, church choirs and musical institutes, cantatas, music for the organ, hymn collections and an autobiography. In 1859 he moved to Chicago to work for his brother's musical publishing house and became particularly successful during the time of the American Civil War writing martial and patriotic songs. In 1872 the University of Chicago awarded him an honorary doctorate in music. He died on 6 August 1895, at his summer house in Bailey, Maine. In 1970 he was inducted into the American Songwriters' Hall of Fame. His Civil War tune 'Tramp, tramp, tramp, the boys are marching' later became the setting for both 'Jesus loves the little children' and 'God save Ireland.' — **W659**

William Henry Rudd

Other than his long lifespan (1869-1963), little is known about this American gospel song composer, except that he is thought to have written an enormously popular gospel song tune, SAVIOUR'S NAME, also known as O HOW I LOVE JESUS from its association with an equally famous gospel hymn by Frederick Whitfield, 'I love to hear the Saviour's name.' The attribution is questionable, since many hymnals cite the composer as anonymous and simply describe the tune as a 19th century American melody. In the *Companion* to the *United Methodist Hymnal* (1989), which includes the original text and tune, **Carlton Young** cites scholarly opinion that the melody may be a combination of two camp-meeting tunes attached to various 'mother-hymns' by Watts and Wesley. It seems to have been popular among American black congregations and its earliest appearance in print has been traced to the 1869 edition of *The Revivalist*. The fact that Rudd's melody (if it is in fact his) has continued to be printed in hymnals as recent as *Worship and Rejoice* (2001) and the

American *Baptist Hymnbook* (2008) and that it was released as a recording in the Hymn Makers series, *Hymns of Redemption* (2011), suggests that it had an accessible and attractive musical character which made it equally popular among Pacific congregations at an early date. — **A3**

Rosemary Meredith Russell (née Keith)

Rosemary Russell was born in Wellington on 28 December 1953. She grew up in a series of vicarages where family hymn singing was enjoyed, and remembers being exposed at an early age to the choral music of the Auckland Cathedral under Sir Peter Godfrey. She was educated at Nelson College for Girls and completed a BA in music at Canterbury University, followed by a Dip Teaching (Hons) from Christchurch College of Education. 'Through school and university I was always part of a choir or musical ensemble of some sort. Creating tape loops and multimedia musical events with John Cousins and exploring the music of Debussy and Messiaen with David Sell at Canterbury University are particular memories. I learned the piano from Wallace Woodley and Rae de Lisle [Rosemary has an LTCL and LRSM in piano] and have always enjoyed accompanying, whether for a soloist or a choir.'

In 1973 she married John Russell, a fellow teacher and later Head of Naenae College; she has 3 daughters, Elizabeth, Rebecca and Miriam. She has worked for many years in Wellington as a school music teacher, leading and accompanying choirs, writing musicals, assisting students with their compositions and musical studies. She taught at Naenae College (1975-8), Tawa Primary School (1990-2000), 'which was very arts focused, and where I wrote many songs for those students,' Queen Margaret College (2007-2010), and is currently Head of Music studies at Sacred Heart College, Lower Hutt.

A long-time member of the Titahi Bay Community Church (formerly the Titahi Bay Gospel Chapel) in Porirua City, north of Wellington, she regularly leads, plays or sings in the church's music groups and writes for the congregation or choir 'for special occasions or when the spirit moves.' In 1976 she became a foundation member of the Festival Singers of Wellington and was their Director from 2008 to 2012. She is currently engaged in many musical occupations: 'Singing, playing the piano, conducting, composing all seem to be interwoven within my Wellington network of musical friends. I sing with Nota Bene and the Orpheus choir and am a member of the Voices Chamber Choir pool of singers.' She is Assistant Director of Wellington Young Voices, a children's choir, and after participating as composer in residence and committee member in a number of International Summer Schools in Choral Conducting with Guy Jansen and Karen Grylls, in 2012 she led the inaugural Convention of the Association of Choral Directors.

Rosemary Russell says, 'For me, the voice is the way to access the soul. I have had so much pleasure from singing with other people. The whole is always greater than the sum of the parts. As a composer, you know that a piece is often created as a result of a significant experience as a human. Also much toil is required to bring it into the light. This creates an interest in and a respect for each composition you are engaged with, and a special joy in the performance of it.'

Her choral and worship songs and arrangements appear in *Festive Sounds* (1979), *Servant Songs: Psalms, Hymns and Spiritual Songs for God's People* (1987), *New Zealand Praise* (1988) and its second update (1993), *Alleluia Aotearoa* (1993), *Songs of Life: Songs to celebrate the Special Moments of Life*, by **Felicia Edgecombe** and Rosemary Russell (Wellington: Festivity Productions, 1996) and *Sounds of Grace: Music of Seven Original Songs from Titahi Bay Gospel Chapel* (2004). Other works – the Sounz website lists 18 of them include *A Shining Light: A Christmas Musical* (1995), *A Wellington Christmas: or Christmas Eve Reflections* (2000), two psalm settings, a *Magnificat* (2002), 'Let us go in peace,' a modern version of the Nunc Dimittis (2011) and settings of religious poems by Gerald Manley Hopkins. With Felicia Edgecombe she wrote a group of songs for the Scripture Union's Supakidz programme in primary schools, published in 2014 as *Godsongz 1*. — A7

John (Jack) Albert Schrader

Jack Schrader, distinguished American musical arranger, composer, conductor, vocalist and keyboard player, was born in St. Louis, Missouri, on 16 July 1942. He graduated in 1964 from the Moody Bible Institute of Chicago, where he majored in voice and organ; he also completed a Bachelor of Music Education degree from the University of Nebraska in 1966. Further studies in theology led to his ordination by the Evangelical Free Church of America in 1975. He joined the Hope Publishing Company in 1978 as music editor, retiring in January 2009. As well as composing many hymns and choral works he has published collections of instrumental and solo song music. As music editor for **Shirley Murray's** American publishers, he arranged one of her hymns in *Alleluia Aotearoa* (1993), published one year before in her American collection *In Every Corner Sing*. — **A19, 25, 49, 158; F10**

Martin Philip Setchell

This internationally famous concert organist and composer was born on 16 February 1949 in Blackpool, England. He took Honours degrees in French and Music at the University of Exeter, and was awarded both the Limpus and Shinn prizes when he was given a Fellowship of the Royal College of Organists in London. He subsequently studied classical organ technique in France, Holland and England.

He came to New Zealand in 1974 to take up an appointment to the University of Canterbury Music School, where he taught for 40 years and became Associate Professor of Music as well as University organist, tutoring in organ, conducting and performance, musicological research and composition. In 1997 he was appointed curator of the Rieger pipe organ in the Christchurch Town Hall, and for a time he directed the choirs of St Barnabas Church, Fendalton, Christchurch. In 2006 he received a Civic Award from the City of Christchurch for his services to music in the community. He founded the Jubilate Singers in that city and directed the University of Canterbury Chamber Choir. He became a Trinity Guildhall Examiner and a well-respected music critic. In 2014 he resigned his University position to work full time as a professional freelance musician, performing, conducting, writing, speaking, editing and teaching.

Before the onset of the Covid pandemic he regularly gave concert tours which took him to Australia, America, Europe, the United Kingdom and the Far East. He has an impressive list of published organ and choral music and transcriptions for organ of music from Bach to Souza. There are also several CDs of his performances, including the highly successful Bonbons for Organ series and *Pink and White Terraces*, an anthology of New Zealand organ music. Following the destruction of the Christchurch Cathedral in the earthquakes of 2011, he released two CDs, *Cardboard Cathedral Organ Capers* and *Resounding Aftershocks*. — **H126**

Martin Edward Fallas Shaw

Martin Shaw, as he is usually known, was born in Kennington, Lambeth, on 9 March, 1875. He studied at the Royal College of Music under Stanford, Parry and Walford Davies. After conducting for Ellen Terry and Isadora Duncan, as well as composing some religious music and directing music in various London churches, he took up a post as musical director at St Mary's Anglican Church, Primrose Hill, London, where from 1908 to 1920 he worked with the resident priest, Percy Dearmer, to improve the quality of the liturgy and raise the standard of church music and congregational hymn-singing. He went on to become organist at St Martin's in the Fields and the Guildhall, London, director of music for the diocese of Chelmsford and one of the founders of the Plain-Song and Mediaeval Music Society.

A staunch advocate of English music and particularly English folk music (he once urged a bonfire of pianos, classical music and drawing room songs, the 'painless extinction' of all concert 'artistes,' and the compulsory singing of English nursery rhymes to all children in their nurseries), he collaborated with **Ralph Vaughan Williams** on the music for *Songs of Praise* and *The Oxford Book of Carols* (1928). This involved, in his own words, 'spending hours at the British Museum finding and copying tunes.' He also edited *The English Carol Book* and other hymnals and many collections of British folksongs; his own compositions included hymn tunes (many of them published in *Additional Tunes in Use at St Mary's, Primrose Hill*, 1915) and more than 100 songs. His lively book of musical reminiscences, *Up to Now,* was published in 1929. He was awarded the Lambeth DMus in 1932, an OBE in 1955 and was honoured as a Fellow of the Royal College of Music in 1958. He died later in the same year on 24 October 1958. — **W652; A19; F27**

Cecily Annette Sheehy

Cecily Sheehy, Dominican sister, musician and composer, was born on 20 July 1938 at Balclutha. She was educated at Teschemakers, Tuapeka West and Lawrence primary schools before completing her secondary school education at St Dominic's College, Dunedin. She entered a postulancy for the Dominican Order in 1957 and took her final vows in 1961. During that time she passed a preliminary examination for a Diploma of Fine Arts, but music became her main interest and she completed an ATCL and LTCL in piano and violin (1960-1), and later studied the flute and classical guitar. In 2000 she completed a Bachelor of Music degree at the University of Auckland. Since 2003 she has taught music privately, composed for students and congregations on demand and occasionally played for celebrations of the mass at Ferndale House and the Marist College, Auckland. In 2011 she completed the piano realization of a friend's opera and, with Philippa Gravatt, prepared a book of duets for young flautists.

She has now resumed her interest in art while continuing to teach music and support elderly members of her Order.

In 1962 she had gained a Trained Teacher's Certificate Class C from the New Zealand Department of Education, and became a Registered Teacher of piano and music theory. From 1961 to 1977 she exercised a teaching ministry in various South Island Dominican priories and convents, and when Vatican II required change from a Latin language liturgy to a vernacular language liturgy she translated Compline hymns and responses into English and rewrote (simplifying) their ancient but elaborate melodies.

From 1980-5 she worked at the Auckland Catholic Religious Education Centre, preparing copy and writing religious songs for the monthly magazine of the Family Living Programme. This large body of work is remarkable for its distinctive freshness and directness of thought, and the engaging musical settings, while created for children, are equally enjoyable for adults overfed with stuffy lectures on traditional theology. In 1986-7 a year spent studying Creation Spirituality under Matthew Fox and the staff of the Institute in Culture and Creation Spirituality, Holy Name College, California, freshly inspired her to write religious songs about care for the planet and its creatures, and these are characterized by the passionate concern of their author.

Cecily Sheehy privately published a collection of her creation songs, *Songs for a Blue-Green Planet* (1990), and 27 of her hymns and songs have been published by the New Zealand Hymn Book Trust. A number of her hymns and songs have also appeared in *New Zealand Praise* (1988). In 2011 she wrote a hymn in honour of Dominican Fra Anton Montesin which has been circulated internationally. And her religious music has been in constant use by members of the New Zealand Dominican order. A complete edition of her hymns, songs and liturgical music is under preparation and is due to be released in 2021. — **A21, 35, 38, 64, 74, 101, 109, 111, 116, 134, 137, 144, 162,**

163; C1, 25, 46; F4, 7, 23, 33, 42, 58, 61, 71; HP14; H142

Christopher Lawrence Skinner

Father Chris Skinner was born in Hamilton on 13 December 1958, the ninth of ten children. During his college years, the family moved to Tokoroa and it was there that he learned to play the guitar and discovered his composing gift. After working in Auckland he joined an older brother on a rosary crusade which took the pair to Whangarei, where he met members of the Marist Order and in 1978 he entered the Marist Seminary at Greenmeadows, Napier.

Following his ordination as a Marist priest at St Mary's, Taradale, in 1985, he taught at Catholic schools in Timaru and Hastings. He went on to become chaplain of De la Salle College, Mangere, Auckland, and was involved with a community in West Auckland, dealing with youth at risk. In 2007 he became an assistant priest at St Mary of the Angels and part-time chaplain at St Patrick's College, Kilbirnie, Wellington. He also supported Challenge 2000, a youth and family community agency based in Johnsonville. He continues to perform at concerts and lead workshops and retreats around New Zealand, working at schools, colleges and conferences as an animator, and is involved in the formation of Marist priests at the Marist Seminary, Auckland.

In 1995 he travelled with a Tongan group to Italy where he performed some of his songs in local villages; he later travelled Europe, America and Ireland, giving performances of his own compositions and returning several times to work with young people and run workshops. He sees himself as enabling others 'to honour and celebrate the gift of life, the gift of faith and the gift of belonging.' His songs reflect a deep love of nature, respect for life and the dignity of the human person, together with a strong commitment to peace and justice.

A talented guitar player with a fine tenor voice, he has written and performed many religious songs and hymns, and since 1990 has published 22 albums and a number of songbooks, most of them featuring his own compositions. They have been collected in *Chris Skinner: A Collection of his Songs* 1990-1996 (CD, 1996) and *Truly Blessed under Southern Skies* (2008). In 1993 he won the Aotearoa Spirituality Songwriter's Award with his song, 'God of our Island Home.' In 2007 he was voted artist of the year on Southern Star Radio and his version of 'You raise me up' won Song of the Year 2008 on the same network. In 2011 he created the Hopetown Mass, a fresh setting of the new English translation of the Roman Mass. In 2014 his song, 'Sons of Gallipoli' was performed before an audience of veteran soldiers at Government House at the invitation of the Governor General. His latest album, *Light in the Lockdown* (a reference to the national lockdown against the Covid pandemic), was released in 2020. — H43

George Thomas Smart

An extraordinary musician with connections to several of the greatest composers of the age, Smart was born in Westminster, London, on 10 May 1776, son of a music and instrument seller who had seen Handel conduct. He became a chorister in the Chapel Royal, and at the age of 15 was appointed organist at St James' Chapel, Hampstead Road, the first of several such appointments. He played as a violinist in the London impresario Salomon's concerts, some of them under Haydn's personal direction. Famed as a conductor himself, he was appointed music director at Covent Garden, and was knighted in 1811 by the Lord Lieutenant of Ireland after conducting a series of concerts in Dublin. He became conductor of the Royal Philharmonic Society and one of the organists at the Chapel Royal. A personal friend of Carl Maria von Weber, he visited Beethoven in Vienna to consult with him about his interpretation of the 9th Symphony, and promoted Mendelssohn's music. He conducted the music for the coronations of William IV and Queen Victoria, edited music by Gibbons and Handel, and himself wrote much religious music, including hymn tunes and organ music. As D'Arcy Woods in his Companion to the Australian hymnbook *Together in Song* notes, when he died at Bloomsbury, London, on 23 February 1867, he had been a knight for 55 years and a professional organist for 75 years. — **W651**

Henry Thomas Smart

Born in London on 26 October 1813, Smart was the son of an accomplished violinist, music publisher and piano manufacturer. He showed an early aptitude for music and an interest in the organ – he attached pedals to the family piano so that he could 'fiddle away' at Bach fugues. He turned down a commission in the Indian Army and studied law, but soon gave this up for a career in music.

Largely self-taught but naturally talented, he became one of the finest organists of his day. At the age of 18 he was made organist of Blackburn Parish Church, Lancashire, where he wrote his first important work, a Reformation anthem. He then held positions as the organist of four London churches, including St Philip's, Regent Street (1838-44). In his final years he went blind, but his phenomenal memory and talent as an extemporizer enabled him to hold the post of organist at St Pancras New Church for nearly five years.

Smart composed over 300 secular works and an oratorio, *Jacob* (Glasgow, 1873), but his reputation rests on his organ and church choral music and his hymn tunes. He edited the *Chorale Book* in 1858, the English Presbyterian *Psalms and hymns for Divine Worship* in 1867 and the *Presbyterian Psalter and Hymnal* for the United Presbyterian Church of Scotland (1877-8). In 1879, shortly before his death, he was granted a Civil List pension in recognition of his services to music. He died at Hampstead, London, on 6 July 1879. — **W651; H51**

Alfred Morton Smith

Smith was born at Jenkintown, Pennsylvania, on 20 May 1879. He studied at the University of Pennsylvania and the Philadelphia Divinity School, graduating BA (1901) and BD (1905). He was ordained an Episcopalian priest in 1906 and briefly served churches in Pennsylvania and California before spending 10 years at St Matthias' Church, Los Angeles. He became an army chaplain during World War I, in France and with the Army of Occupation in Germany. On returning to America in 1919, he commenced a ministry lasting 35 years with the Episcopal City Mission of Philadelphia, and during this time held a number of chaplaincies, including positions at the Eastern State Penitentiary, Valley Forge Military Academy and several city hospitals.

It was not until his adult years that he began formal music studies, but he discovered an aptitude for the cello and for composition, and was soon playing in a community orchestra. He published three communion settings, including a *Mass of St Matthias* (1936) and a *Mass of St Clement* (1948), several carols and a number of hymn tunes. He retired in 1954, first to Jenkintown, then to Philadelphia and finally to Brigantine, New Jersey, where he died on 26 February 1971. — **A105; HP18**

Elizabeth Joyce Smith

Elizabeth Smith was born on 27 February 1956 at Stawell, Victoria, Australia. She was educated at Euroa High School, Monash University (BA (Hons)), Melbourne University (DipEd) and the Melbourne United Faculty of Divinity (BD, 1986). Ordained a deacon in the Anglican Church of Australia in 1987 she served as a curate in Altona (1987-88) and Mount Waverley (1989-90) where she began writing hymns, before completing a doctorate at the Graduate Theological Union, Berkeley, California (1991-1995). She was ordained a priest in 1993 and served as vicar of St John's Anglican Church, Bentleigh, Victoria, from 1995 to 2007. She is currently Mission Plan Co-ordinator for the diocese of Perth. Since 1996 she has been a member of the Liturgical Commission of the Anglican General Synod and the Anglican/Roman Dialogue in Australia.

Her published work includes *Praise the God of Grace: Hymns for Inclusive Worship* (1990), *Rejoice! For God has Called us: Hymns for Inclusive Worship* (1993), *God Loves a Cheerful*

Giver: Sixty One-Minute Stewardship Sermons (2005) and *Prayers and Plays for Christmas and Holy Week* (2007). Her hymns were collected in *Songs for a Hopeful Church* (1997). They have also appeared in *The Hymnal* (1940 and 1982), *The Covenant Hymnal* (1996), *All Together OK* (1996), *Together in Song* (1999), *Faith Forever Singing* (2000), *The Lutheran Service Book* (2006), *Hymns Old and New* (2008) and *Singing the Faith* (2011). She has a research interest in feminist biblical studies, and published *Bearing Fruit in Due Season: Feminist Hermeneutics and the Bible in Worship* in 1999. In 2020 she was made a Member (AM) in the General Division of the Queen's Birthday 2020 Honours for significant service to the Anglican Church of Australia, and to liturgical scholarship.

Author of more than 80 hymns, she says 'I started writing hymns because some of them aren't up to scratch for 21st century people… It was a feminist issue [of sexist language] that got me going, and a theological issue that kept me going.' She set out her manifesto in *Songs for a Hopeful Church*: 'I want the words of my songs to be clear, not tangled up in confusing sentences or 18th century vocabulary. I want the words to be fresh, saying things that haven't been said in hymns a hundred times before. I want the words to be true, faithful to the astonishing good news of God in Jesus Christ. And I want the words to be inclusive.' — **F2**

John Smith

John Smith is the brother-in-law of **Richard Gillard**, and was a fellow member of the congregation of St Paul's Anglican Church, Auckland, where he collaborated with Richard Gillard and also wrote independently a number of melodies for religious songs and liturgical texts which have appeared in the St Paul's Outreach Trust publications *Arise my love: Song Book* (1974), *Thusia Mass* (1974), *New Glory: Songs of Renewal* (1976) and *New Harvest* (1979). — **W676, A112**

Shirley Gibson Smith

Shirley Smith was born in Dunedin on 8 July 1924, the daughter of Horace and Nellie Fawcett; her father was a teacher and Presbyterian Elder who became principal of Matamata College. She attended Otago University (1942-5), graduating MA with double Honours in English and French. After a year at Auckland Teachers' College she taught at Whangarei Girls' High School (1947-8), then at Otago Girls' High School, Dunedin, until her marriage in 1949 to Robin Smith, a Presbyterian minister. With their five children, she accompanied him to a number of South and North Island parishes. She resumed teaching in 1963 at Ranfurly District High School, and taught at Hamilton Girls' High School and Hillcrest High School. In 1991 the couple retired to Waikouaiti where they took an active part in church and wider community activities before returning to Dunedin in 2005. Shirley Smith died on 16 January 2008. Although she inspired much creative writing among her students, and wrote poems and occasional verse, she herself wrote only one hymn. — **H147**

Va'alotu Solofa

Nothing is known of this Samoan musician other than that he was responsible for the choral arrangement of William Rudd's 19th century tune SAVIOUR'S NAME, used for 'Alofa mai ia, afio mai.' — **A3**

Charles Henry Steggall

Steggall was born in London on 3 June 1826. He was educated at Trinity College, Cambridge, where he took a DMus before studying at the Royal College of Music, where he subsequently became Professor of organ and harmony, teaching there for 50 years. A talented player, while still a student he began a career as a church organist in a number of London churches, and was one of the founders of the Royal College of Organists. For over 20 years he was the secretary of the newly-established Bach Society (later to become the Bach Choir) and held a life-long interest in hymnody. As well as composing anthems and other church music he edited *Hymns for the Church of England* in 1868 and succeeded **William Henry Monk** as music editor of *Hymns Ancient and Modern*. He died in London on 7 June 1905. — **A19**

Joan Francis Stevens (née Ross)

Joan Francis Stevens (1921-2006), was a New Zealand primary school teacher, musician and composer. She published settings for voice and piano of Willow Macky's 'Waitangi Anthem' (1990), and an arrangement of her 'Peace to the World' song, as well as *Jingle Bells: Descants for Voice and Chime Bars* (1966), *Hurrah for Christmas Morning* (undated), a collection of carols titled *Christmas Music* (1972) and several sets of fun songs for children. She founded the Joan Francis Stevens award for excellence in classical singing. Her life, like her musical heritage, is still to be studied; some of her papers are deposited in the National Library. — **H114**

Stanley (Stan) James Stewart

Stan Stewart was born at Melbourne on 14 September 1937. Educated at Dandenong High School and Swinburne Technical School, he went on to study at the Baptist Theological College, Melbourne, and the Melbourne College of Divinity, completing a LTh degree and a Diploma of Religious Studies. He began a Gospel singing and evangelical group, the Proclaimers, in Melbourne in the 1960s, and was ordained in 1974. He married Pauline Hubner in 1982 and the couple worked as consultant ministry team leaders in Australia, Canada, New Zealand and the United States, developing all age worship and initiating festivals and special events reaching well beyond ordinary church life. Their North American ministry took them into United Methodist, Lutheran, United Presbyterian and Episcopalian churches. From 1988 to 1991 they led the St Ives Uniting Church, Sydney, where Stan and Pauline created musicals on such topics as *Nehemiah, Jesus Folk* and *Stars*. *Nehemiah* was later published in the United States, and two songs from the show, 'Shake off the Dust' and 'God be With You,' reached still wider publication.

In 1991 the Stewarts transferred from the Uniting Church of Australia to the Presbyterian Church of New Zealand and began a supply ministry at Paeroa in the Waikato Presbytery. They shared a joint ministry at Te Aroha and Paeroa until 1993. From that date the pair served the Paeroa and Mercury Bay Co-operating Ventures until Stan officially retired in 2004. He has now retired from a second ministry in partnership with his wife begun in 2005 at the St Heliers Presbyterian Church and Community Centre, Auckland.

In addition to his musical leadership, Stan has taken a special interest in assisting churches develop as a People to Belong To, and has written and taught in the area of children in worship and community exhibitions. Two of his articles are found in *Candour*, May, 2006, and April, 2010; he has also published a book on *How to keep the Young People You Have, and Get More* (1998). — **H16**

Suzanne Stewart

See 'There is no child so small' (**H133**) *for the little known about this New Zealand musician.*

Charles Edward Strange

Strange, who was born at Headington, Oxfordshire in 1902 and died in 1984, was an English musician and arranger. His version of the traditional English folk song 'See saw saccara down' is matched with **Shirley Murray's** 'Come into the streets with me.' — **A22**

Jim Strathdee

Born in 1941, this American Methodist folk-singer and writer formed a partnership with his wife Jean in composition and performance that has taken them to many parts of the world, including New Zealand and Australia. In 1976 they set up their own recording and publishing company, Caliche records/Desert Flower Music, dedicated to 'a message of unity, compassion, justice and healing;' in the 1980s they formed New Wine, a pioneering project in the development of religious folk music which grew from the worship life of Temple United Methodist Church, a congregation dedicated to serving the needs of children and families in Pico-Union, a low-income multicultural neighbourhood in the inner city of Los Angeles.

They are presently based in California where they are joint directors of music at St Mark's United Methodist Church, Sacramento. Their congregation has encouraged them to exercise a travelling ministry, and they have visited much of the United States, Canada and South America, as well as India, Australia and New Zealand. In 2009 they were keynote presenters at the National Hymn Conference held in Wesley Broadway Church, Palmerston North. They have published more than 20 songbooks and recordings, many choral pieces and hymn settings, for which Jim Strathdee writes the texts, composes and arranges the music. Jim has written two sets of religious songs for children (intended for vacation schools), a Mass for the Healing of the Earth, anthems and carols as well as many hymns and religious songs. His collection *Sunshine in the Morning: Jim and Jean Strathdee Favorites* (Carmichael, Cal.: Caliche Records, 2006) covers 40 years of music ministry. — **W669, 678; A45; F30, 65; H93**

John Robson Sweney

American evangelist composer John Robson Sweney was born at West Chester, Pennsylvania (near Philadelphia), on 31 December 1837. Sweney's musical gifts showed themselves at an early age. While still a boy, he began to teach music in the public schools and lead Sunday school performances. At the age of 19 he started studying music in earnest under a celebrated German teacher. He took violin and piano lessons, and about this time became a choir leader. He was also in demand for children's concerts and conducting glee clubs.

At the age of 22 Sweney took up music teaching in Dover, Delaware. When the American Civil War broke out in 1861 he took charge of the band of the Third Delaware Regiment. After the war, Sweney became Professor of Music at the Pennsylvania Military Academy in West Chester, Pennsylvania. He worked there for over 25 years, and received the degrees of Bachelor of Music (1876) and Doctor of Music (1886). He also became Music Director and song leader at the famous Bethany Presbyterian Church.

He originally composed secular songs, but went on to write music for more than 1,000 gospel songs, and collaborated with William Kirkpatrick, Fanny Crosby and others on nearly 30 collections of Sunday School and gospel music, including such titles as *Goodly Pearls, Sunlit Songs, Songs of Joy and Gladness, Radiant Songs* and *The Bow of Promise*. Nearly all the leading song writers of the day are represented in those books, and Sweney is credited with discovering several of them, by first publishing their work and often writing music for their texts. He died at Chester on 10 April 1899. — **W630**

Kelemete Ta'ale

Samoan musician and songwriter Kelemete Ta'ale grew up playing instruments such as the ukelele, guitar and mussolini which his father Ta'ale Touli taught him to play, together with his brother Fofoga Touli, who himself was to become a renowned Samoan composer and music teacher. At Poutasi, Samoa, in 1963, Kelemete and his wife Kiligi formed a band called Lupe Ulu Iva ('the nine-headed pigeon') which played in and around Apia, and recorded several of Kelemete's first songs. He was brought up in the local Catholic Church and became the choirmaster there, with his youngest daughter Julie* playing the piano. He and his wife went on to study at the Moamoa Theological College (Samoa) and became catechists of the Catholic Church.

In the early 1980s the couple with their nine children migrated to New Zealand. They continued to serve their church as musicians and performers – he and his daughter are currently choir leaders at St Joseph's Catholic Church, Grey Lynn, Auckland – and in

2011 Kelemete was ordained as a Deacon by Bishop Patrick Dunn of Auckland. Fame came when his ballad celebrating Samoan culture and beliefs, 'O Le Atua Lava (=God Is),' was included in his daughter's first album, *Love Changes Everything* (2011), in a second composite album, *Gospel Gold Songs for your Soul* (2011), and featured in the film *Sione's Wedding 2: Unfinished Business* (2012). — **A90**

> *Their youngest child, Julie, has become a well known singer, a former member of Pacific Soul, and twice winner of the Tui Award for best Pacific Album and Group with Pacific Soul (2003) and Mount Vaea Band (2005).

Roy Bruce Tankersley

A passionate enthusiast for the organ and for church music, Roy Tankersley was born on 25 January 1945 at Ashburton. After secondary schooling at Feilding Agricultural High School, he undertook an apprenticeship in organ building with John A. Lee of Feilding before graduating BMus (Hons) in organ performance at Victoria University and completing Postgraduate Studies in the organ and harpsichord at the Guildhall School of Music and Drama, London. He returned to New Zealand in 1974 to forge a career as a musician, music educator and choir director, becoming Head of Music at Tawa College, Wellington (1975-84), and later Director of Music at Marsden School in the same city (1994-2003). He has directed numerous choirs over the years, including ten years with the Wellington Bach Choir and Bel Canto, and since 1988 has been involved with Winter Choir Schools for the Royal College of Music, to which he has belonged for over 45 years. He has been organist and choirmaster in the Presbyterian parishes of St John's in the City and St Andrew's on the Terrace in Wellington, Knox Church in Dunedin and the Anglican parishes of St Michael and All Angels in Wellington and Holy Trinity, Hampstead, in London.

Since 2003, when he retired from school teaching, Roy Tankersley has worked as a freelance performer, teacher and adjudicator, now based in Palmerston North. Until 2020 he held the position of Musical Director of the Parish of St Marks and St Andrews, Palmerston North, and directed the Schola Sacra Choir and Youth Chorus of Wanganui. He is President of the New Zealand Organ Preservation Trust and Chairman of the Manawatu/Wanganui branch of the New Zealand Choral Federation. In 2005 he was made a Fellow of the NZ Association of Organists and in 2010 an Associate of the Royal School of Church Music, in a ceremony held at Durham Cathedral. In 2011 he was honoured as a Member of the New Zealand Order of Merit for services to music.

His compositions include choral, instrumental and musical theatre pieces; his work has been widely used in schools and churches throughout New Zealand. He is a member of the Editorial Board of the New Zealand Hymn Book Trust, which he joined in 2007. Tankersley is the featured keyboard player on the 2005 New Zealand Hymnbook Trust CD *Singing Faith: Hymns and Songs by Shirley Erena Murray* of instrumental music to accompany the singing of 18 of Murray's hymns in churches where no organist or pianist is available. In 2013 he recorded on CD a variety of classical organ music pieces, played on the organ of the Hawera Wesley Methodist Church, *Brake Forth*. Since 2005 he has given an astonishing 132 organ concerts ('Organ Blasts') at Central Baptist Church. — **A7, 23(ii); C14(ii); H23, 43**

Hoki Tawa

A member of a group of Māori gospel hymn writers, including **MONA RIINI, HOKI TAWA KITTY TEMARA** and **REGINALD (REG) WHAREKURA** working cooperatively in the late 1980s. See under 'Whakatau mai te Atua.' — **A32, 150**

Joye Wilhelmina Taylor (nèe Eggars)

Joye Taylor* was born in Newtown, Wellington in 1898, the third of seven children in a musical family with Salvation Army associations. At the age of five she wrote a hymn which her proud father took to a Salvation Army band practice where the little girl played and sang her own work. She was given piano lessons at St Anne's Convent, Newtown, then went on to two private schools, returning later to one of them, St Catherine's, as a pupil teacher. In 1911 her father went bankrupt, and she left school to support the family. She set up her own private school where she wrote plays and songs for the children to further their studies; a number of them were published in the three volumes of *Twelve Graded Plays for Children*, which attracted attention from the Department of Education.

In 1922 she married Charles Taylor and gave up running her own school. However, she spent one year as a teacher at Otaki Māori Boys' School, where she became interested in Māori culture and music. One of her pupils was the famous Māori bass, Inia Te Waiata. In 1946 the couple purchased a neighbouring house and Joye set up a school for local children, teaching them Māori chants and legends and her own songs. Some of those written for her own children were broadcast over 2YA.

Throughout her life she published verse in Wellington papers and elsewhere. Her songs and compositions achieved a degree of fame, particularly 'Song of the River,' and the distinguished New Zealand tenor Peter Dawson sang this and other songs on a national tour in 1949. By 1950 she had published some 150 poems and 130 musical compositions. Towards the end of her life her eyesight failed, but she continued to write and compose, using an amanuensis. She died in 1979. Her publications included *Verses for Children* (1939) and *Little Bells and Other Verses for Children* (written with her daughter Elizabeth) (1947). Both books were illustrated by Australian artist Betty (Elizabeth) Paterson; it is probable that Joye Taylor spent some time in Australia. — **C46**

> *For further details see Judith May, 'Joye Taylor (1898-1979): A Lifetime of Music,' *Music in New Zealand,* Spring 1993, 22, pp 72-5.

Kitty Temara

A member of a group of Māori gospel hymn writers, including **MONA RIINI, HOKI TAWA, HOKI TAWA** and **REGINALD (REG) WHAREKURA** working cooperatively in the late 1980s. See under 'Whakatau mai te Atua.' — **A32, 150**

Sebastian Temple (Tempelhof)

Sebastian Temple was one of the most influential folk Mass composers from the era immediately following the Second Vatican Council. He was born in 1928 near Pretoria, South Africa and grew up in an Afrikaans culture. However, childhood friendships with young black Africans acquainted him with the tunes and rhythms of their tribes. By the age of 15 he had published one novel and two books of poems. He studied anthropology at the University of South Africa and pre-Renaissance art in Italy. In 1951 he moved to London, where he worked for the BBC on news broadcasts relating to South Africa. About this time he converted to Roman Catholicism and began composing worship music. For a time he became a monk in a Yoga monastery in India, but he found a successful career as a songwriter and performer after moving to America in 1958. Based in Los Angeles, he began composing music, both secular and religious, including music for the Roman Catholic folk Mass. By 1978 he had released a dozen record albums. 'The Prayer of St. Francis' (Make Me a Channel of Your Peace), was part of his first collection of liturgical music, *Happy the Man, songs about St. Francis of Assisi.* Sebastian Temple died in 1997 in Tucson, Arizona, on 10 December 1997.— **W666**

John Harrison Tenney

Born at Rowley, Massachusetts, on 22 November 1840, Tenney was named after American President William Henry Harrison. His father was a choir leader and his mother the leading soprano in her husband's choir. Tenney was a precocious musician: he attended a local singing school, and by the age of eight he was reading music at sight, and composing melodies to some of the hymns he found in fellow Congregational hymn writer Isaac Watts' *Psalms, Hymns and Spiritual Songs* (1841). 'He would write out these melodies on his slate or a piece of paper,' says his biographer. He went on to become a deacon in the Congregational Church in Linebrook, Massachusetts, where for many years he was organist and choir leader.

Tenney edited or was associate editor of over 30 books of religious music and contributed as a composer to hundreds more. A contemporary wrote of him, 'He delights in farm life, and to spend the evenings in giving vent to his musical nature in musical compositions.' Some of the book titles suggest the nature of his compositions: *Gems of Gospel Song, Bells of Victory, Sharon's Dewy Rose, Sweet Fields of Eden, Songs of promise: for Sunday Schools, Prayer, Praise and Conferences, Songs of Faith… adapted for devotional, revival and camp meetings, Temperance Jewels* and *The Crown of Praise*. He became immensely popular in America and beyond: 'In addition to the many books he has edited, his name appears in almost every Sunday-school, church or anthem book that has been issued for the last 30 or 40 years, and some of his gospel songs are sung by all the prominent evangelists in the field,' remarked a contemporary. Tenney died in 1918. — **W627**

Wi-Patene Te Pairi

Wi Patene was born in Ruatoki in the Bay of Plenty region of the North Island (the actual date is unknown) and adopted by his close relatives in the Waimana Valley, the Te Pairi whānau. He grew up steeped in the traditions of the local Presbyterian, Anglican and Ringatū churches. From a young age he showed an unusual musical talent, singing and playing the guitar. On the outbreak of war in Korea he enlisted in the armed forces and spent time in that country (1950-3). Years of sheep shearing in Australia followed in company with his good friend Te Waaka Palmer of Matakana Island in Tauranga (later General Secretary of the Rātana Church),

and on his return to New Zealand he joined a Māori showband, touring the North Island and frequently playing back-up to other bands and performers, including famed Māori baritone singer Deane Waretini and the equally famous Howard Morrison Quartet. Wi become known as 'Rocky' among his friends and fellow musicians.

As his musical career came to an end, he spent some time as a travelling salesman until his retirement to Rotorua in the late 1990s. There, encouraged by the Rev Wayne Te Kaawa, he studied towards a BTheol through the local Anglican Theological College. In 2008 he became a Māori Synod representative on the Takawaenga O Te Haahi Committee of the General Assembly of the Presbyterian Church. He exercised a ministry in the Rotorua Māori Pastorate from 2009 until his death, and regularly played as a guitarist in a local band as well as assisting with services in the Ruatoki Anglican Church. A colourful personality, he was known to attend Waitangi Day celebrations dressed from head to foot in red when Helen Clarke, Prime Minister of the Labour government, spoke there, and a blue suit to respect the National Prime Minister, John Key. He died on 16 September 2015.

He composed a setting of the waiata 'E te ariki' (H23) which became widely popular among Māori singing groups and was eventually published in *Hope is our Song* (2009) in a piano arrangement by **Roy Tankersley**. The song was also recorded by Steve Apirana for his album *No Turning Back* (1992) and Dennis Marsh for the album *Māori Songs 2* (Sony Music, 2015). The latest recording (2018) is by Mama Mihirangi and the Mareikura, a contemporary Māori female group advocating for indigenous cultural values. — **H23**

*In the first edition of *Hope is our Song* his name is given erroneously as Patena.

Richard Runciman Terry

Richard Terry was born at Ellington, near Ashington and the seaport of Amble, Northumberland, on 3 January 1865. The family, who were Church of England adherents, moved to South Shields, where as a boy of 11 Terry played the parish church organ for midweek services, an experience that gave him a lasting fear of church bells, 'for when they stopped I knew the awful moment had arrived for the voluntary, and was invariably seized with stage fright.' He was educated at local schools in South Shields and St Albans, then attended Battersea Grammar School and the University of Oxford as a non-collegiate student of St Catherine's Society. In 1889 he won a choral scholarship to King's College, Cambridge, where he founded the Cambridge University Music Club and became music critic for *The Cambridge Review*. He did not complete his degree, but began a professional career when in 1890 he accepted an organ appointment at Elstow School near Bedford, then at St John's Cathedral, Antigua, Leeward Islands (1892-3).

A bout of malaria led to his return to the United Kingdom. There he briefly held school posts at Margate and Leatherhead. In 1896 he was received into the Roman Catholic Church, and after a few months at St Dominic's School, Newcastle, was appointed organist and choirmaster at the Benedictine Abbey, Downside, Somerset, and music master at the Abbey school (1896-1901). He later published collections of Downside motets and masses. While London's new Roman Catholic Westminster Cathedral was still under construction, he was next made its Director of Music, a position he held until 1924. During his time at Westminster, he achieved a high standard of choral music and edited the first official Roman Catholic hymnal in English, *The Westminster Hymnal* (1912). He also published *Catholic Church Music* [for the Roman rite] (1907), was for a time Chairman of the *Tudor Church Music* series, and brought out editions of Calvin's 1539 Strasbourg *Psalter* and the 1635 Scottish *Psalter* as well as a collection of *Two Hundred Folk Carols* (1933). He resigned his position at Westminster, however, after being criticised for his over-bold choice of music for the *Westminster Hymnal*.

From 1913-21 Terry conducted the Western Madrigal Society, was President of the Union of Music Directors in Secondary Schools (1911), examined for the University of Birmingham and the National University of Ireland and joined the staff and Board of Trinity College of Music, London. He was awarded an honorary Fellowship of the Royal College of Organists, an Honorary Doctorate of Music by Durham University (1911) and in 1922 was knighted for his services to music. He died at Kensington, London, on Easter Day, 18 April 1938. In addition to his work as editor, organist and choral director, he composed 5 settings of the mass, a requiem, many motets and several hymn tunes, some of them now regarded as classics of their kind. — **W665**

Reginald Sparshatt (or Sparshott) Thatcher

This distinguished English musician, teacher and administrator was born at Midsomer Norton, Somerset, on 11 March 1888, one of 17 children. By the age of 12, 'when his feet could scarcely reach the pedals,' he became the regular organist of the local parish church, his early musical education being funded by a doting spinster aunt. He then studied at the Royal College of Music and Worcester College, Oxford, holding simultaneous organ scholarships at both colleges. In 1911 he became assistant music master at Clifton College, Bristol, then, in 1914 director of music at the Royal Naval College, Osborne, on the Isle of Wight. He served in France during World War I and was awarded an MC for bravery in the field. From 1919 to 1928 he was director of music at the famous English school Charterhouse and from 1928 held the same position at Harrow. In the same year he became President of the Music Masters' Association. In 1935 – having turned down the offer of the Directorate itself – he became Deputy Director of Music at the BBC where his Oxford friend Adrian Boult was in charge. In 1943 he joined the staff of the Royal Academy of Music and became a Fellow in 1948 and President of the institution (from 1949 to 1955). He also served as President of both the Royal College of Organists (1954-6) and the Incorporated Society of Musicians (1956).

He was awarded the OBE and later knighted (1952) for his services to music. He died at Cranleigh, Surrey, on 6 May 1957.

Thatcher wrote school songs and some fine hymn tunes, which were later taken into English, American and Australian hymn books such as *The Hymnal* (1940), *The Book of Common Prayer and Hymnal* (1982), *The Seventh-Day Adventist Hymnal* (1985) and *The Australian Hymnbook* (1999). — **W653**

Judith Thornley

This Christchurch musician has collaborated with **Bill Wallace**, supplying both original hymn tunes and piano harmonisations of Wallace's own tunes. The collaboration began in 1990 with the publication of the three volumes of *Singing the Circle*, to which Thornley contributed three hymn tunes, TARANAKI, DARKNESS AND LIGHT and GOD HAS MERCY, and piano harmonies for three of Bill Wallace's melodies, WOW, CENTRE AND CIRCLE and SHALOM. Two more harmonisations appeared in *The Mystery Telling* (2001) and *Singing the Sacred*, volume 1 (2011), together with an original setting, GOD HAS MERCY, of the text 'God has mercy' by Wallace. — **H134**

Jaroslav John Vajda

Jaroslav Vajda was born at Lorain, Ohio, America, on 28 April, 1919. The son of a Lutheran pastor of Slovakian descent he received an early musical training from his father and mother and began translating classical Slovak poetry at the age of 18, much of it critically acclaimed and published in the United States and Europe. He entered the Lutheran ministry himself after training at Concordia Theological Seminary, St. Louis, Missouri, from which he graduated with a BA and a Masterate in Divinity (1944). He was to exercise ministry at several bi-lingual Lutheran churches in Pennsylvania and Indiana for the next 18 years.

He commenced writing hymns at the age of 49, demonstrating a remarkable poetic style. From that time until his death in 2008 at the age of 89, he wrote over 200 original and translated hymns that appear worldwide in more than 65 hymnbooks. He recorded his reflections on the art of hymn writing in *Now the Joyful Celebration* (1967). He published two collections of his own hymn texts, as well as numerous religious books, translations, and articles. The most complete collection of his work as a hymnist is *Sing Peace, Sing Gift of Peace: The Comprehensive Hymnary of Jaroslav J. Vajda* (Concordia, 2003).

Vajda served on editorial committees for the Lutheran *Hymnal Supplement* (1969) and *The Lutheran Book of Worship* (1978). He was also a member of two commissions on worship for the Lutheran Church (1960-78, 1967-78), and from 1963 edited *The Day*, a Lutheran monthly family religious and cultural magazine. He was made a Fellow of the Hymn Society in America and Canada in 1988 and received a number of honorary doctorates recognizing his contribution to hymnody. From 1971 he became a book editor and project developer for the Lutheran Concordia Publishing house, a position he gave up in 1986. He died on 10 May 2008. — **H104**

William (Bill) Lawrence Wallace

The son of a mid-Canterbury Methodist farming couple, Bill Wallace was born on 9 March 1933 in Christchurch. After early schooling at Fendalton Primary School and St Andrews' College, Christchurch, he completed a Diploma of Education at the University of Otago, and a BA in Philosophy at the University of Auckland. He was active in the Student Christian Movement, and as a student experienced working class life. He trained at Trinity College, Auckland, for the Methodist ministry, which he entered in 1961, working as a parish minister mainly in poorer urban areas in Dunedin, Christchurch, Palmerston North and Wainuiomata (Wellington) until his retirement in 1995. For a time he chaired the organisation Contemporary Hymns (NZ), and was hymn selector for a national television programme, Praise Be.

A prolific hymn writer, some of his early texts were written for service organisations and local congregations and circulated in church newspapers and journals. His first personal collection, *Something to Sing about: Hymns and Reflections in search of a Contemporary Spirituality* (Melbourne, 1981), brought together 27 hymns set to traditional or folk tunes with a number of reflective poems. In 1988 his hymn 'O threefold God of tender unity' won the Hymn Society of America's Search for New Hymns. Three volumes of hymns, poems and liturgical materials, *Singing the Circle*, were privately published in 1990 with a number of the author's tunes harmonised by New Zealand musicians **Alison Carey**, Suzanne Lennon and **Judith Thornley**. New hymns set to traditional or original tunes appeared in the American publications *The Mystery Telling: Hymns and Songs for the New Millennium* (Selah, 2 volumes, 2001 and 2006) and *Singing the Sacred: Psalms, Hymns and Spiritual Songs* (World Library, 2011). A major collection of his work, including 43 religious songs for children, has been added to the website of the United States Centre for Progressive Christianity (2013), and the website of the Methodist Church of Aotearoa/New Zealand carries a further collection of his hymns.

His *Sacred Energy: Mass of the Universe* (2005) contained a number of his hymns; others have been published in more than 20 New Zealand, Australian, American, Latin American, Asian, British and Canadian hymnals, including the Brethren and Mennonite *Hymnal* (1992), *Church Hymnary* (2005), the *Covenant Hymnal* (1996), the United Methodist *The Faith we Sing* (2000), the *Presbyterian Hymnal* (1990), *Hymnal of a Faith Journey* (United Church of Christ in the Philippines), *Hymns from the Four Winds* (1983), *Sound the Bamboo* (1990 and 2000), *Thuma Mina* (1995) and *Church Hymnary 4* (2005). His hymn texts and poems have appeared in 14 anthologies, among them *Gifts of Many Cultures* (Cleveland: United Church Press, 1995), *The Way of Peace* (Oxford: Lion Publishing, 1999), *Global Praise 2* (2000) and *Eternal Springs* (London: Canterbury Press, 2006). More than 30 contemporary composers, including several New Zealanders, have set his words or composed arrangements for Bill Wallace's original melodies. He continues to compose hymn texts and tunes and invite collaborators to harmonise his melodies.

Wallace is a poet and artist as well as a hymn writer and composer. His hymns have a strong mystical and prophetic strain; they address the events of the Church's year and ecumenism, ecological and social concerns, but also the mystery of God, the sanctity and unity of creation and the possibility of interfaith communion. Their theological thought is fresh and vigorous; their imagery equally adventurous.* 'Darkness is my mother,' 'Deep in the human heart,' 'May we all live as grains of rice,' 'O three-fold God of tender unity,' 'Why has God forsaken me?' and 'We are an Easter people' are some of his best-known hymn texts. 'Sound a mystic bamboo song' has achieved particular resonance among Asian congregations. — **A110, 146; H4, 8, 19, 69, 134, 140, 146, 149**

*See also the interview 'Hymn writer seeks nature's guide on spiritual path,' *Touchstone* (April 2004), and Wallace's article, 'Christian worship in a world of dying and emerging images of God,' *The Ground of Faith* (April 2006).

Rhadha Wardrop (also known as Saher)

Rhadha Wardrop was born on 14 June 1949 at Dunedin. A multi-talented artist now based in Levin, she has a varied background in studio production, tutoring at the Nelson School of Music, kindergarten teaching, music therapy, interactive performance work, painting and installation art. She sometimes performs with her brother Graham Wardrop, an internationally famous guitarist and guitar maker who was inducted into the Rock on New Zealand Hall of Fame in 2010.

Now a prolific composer and the audio producer of numerous albums for Universal

Children's Audio music shop, Radha is known by her maiden name for much of her children's work, and by her married name for her adult music and art work. She is the musical director books of 16 *Kiwi Kidsongs* albums, issued to all New Zealand junior schools and numerous songbooks with teaching notes published by Universal Children's Audio. She has served on the New Zealand Virtue Trust for many years, her company publishing several character-education resources during that time.

In addition to many albums of classical and popular songs and music, she has published a number of religious music compositions and arrangements for children and adult choirs, including *A Celtic Christmas, Carols by Candlelight, Christmas Bells* and *Still the Night*. There are also several albums of spiritual songs: *One Earth Songs, One Earth Chants* and *A Pace of Grace* (2004), included in the *One Earth Singing* collection. In 2011, in the aftermath of the terrorist attack on the Twin Towers, New York, she created the Sacred Site website, to promote harmony between people of different beliefs, declaring that 'my life's work has been to promote interconnectedness.' She has won a number of industry awards, including the Rainbow Ribbon Award (1995) and New Zealand Music Industry Awards in 1995 and 1996 for Best Children's Album. Her album *Children of our Earth* won the World Peace Music Award, initiated at the World Judiciary Summit in India (2007). Another of her albums, *Virtues in Me*, was highly commended. — **A82**

Norman Leonard Warren

Norman Warren was born in London on 19 July 1934. He was educated at Dulwich College and Corpus Christi College, Cambridge, where he studied Music and Theology, graduating MA in 1962. He studied at Ridley Hall, Cambridge (1958-59) in preparation for his ordination into the Church of England. In the course of his following career he became rector of Morden, one of the largest parishes in England, and eventually archdeacon of Rochester, Kent (1989-2000).

He was a founding member of Jubilate Hymns, and was involved with the publication of their collection *Youth Praise* (1966 and 1969). He was a contributing member of the committee for *Psalm Praise* (London: Pastoral Aid Society,1973), and his hymn tunes appear in *Church Family Worship* (1988) and *Sing Glory* (1999). A composer of several anthems and three musical plays, his hymns and hymn tunes have had a world-wide circulation, including publication in *Hymns II* (Downers Grove, Illinois: Intervarsity Press, 1976), *Worship and Rejoice* (Carol Stream, Illinois: Hope Publishing, 2001). He co-edited *Jesus Praise: A Songbook for All Occasions* (London Scripture Union, 1982) and is the author of the hugely popular evangelical booklet *Journey into Life* (1984, revised 2005). — **F3**

Philip Begbie Watson

Welsh musician Philip Begbie Watson was born at Cardiff in 1936. He was educated at the University of Wales (BA, ARCM Diploma), then taught music in a variety of Welsh secondary schools. He served for some years as an Elder and the chief organist at Emmanuel Evangelical Church in Newport. He played a major part in the compilation of *Christian Hymns* (Evangelical Movement of Wales, 1977), which includes six of his hymn tunes and 11 arrangements. His harmonization of the melody O STORE GUD was provided at the request of the Reverend Graham Harrison, editor of the Welsh hymnal, for which Watson was the Musical Editor and remains the best known of the many arrangements of that melody. — **W628**

Isaac Watts

Known later as the Godfather of English hymnody, Isaac Watts was born on 17 July 1674 at Southampton, England, the son of a deacon of the Above Bar Congregational church. His early talent for language and poetry was fostered by the headmaster of the local grammar school, who taught him Greek, Latin and Hebrew. He turned down the offer of a university education which would have fitted him for ordination in the Church of

England, entering instead a nonconformist academy at Stoke Newington. After an interval of two years back home, during which he is said to have written a new hymn for every Sunday, later collected in his *Horae Lyricae* (1706) and *Hymns and Spiritual Songs* (1707-9), he became tutor and chaplain to the family of a wealthy nonconformist. In 1699 he became first a teacher, then an assistant-pastor at Mark Lane Independent Chapel, London, where he was ordained, and in 1702 became its senior pastor. However, in 1712 his health was destroyed by a fever and he was left a permanent invalid until his death on 28 November 1748.

Many of his early hymns were written in response to a challenge from his father to improve the quality of hymn singing, and he broke away from the Calvinist tradition of singing severe metrical versions of the biblical psalms by writing many now famous paraphrases which he later published as *The Psalms of David Imitated in the Language of the New Testament and applied to the Christian State and Worship* (1719). Watts was one of the first hymn writers to create a body of hymns for children, *Divine Hymns Attempted in Easy Language for the Use of Children* (1715); a number of them express his own harsh Calvinist theology of punishment for sin. A distinguished scholar as well as a poet, he was honoured in his own lifetime by the University of Edinburgh, which awarded him an honorary Doctorate in Divinity in 1728, and though he was buried in the Puritan cemetery at Bunhill Fields a monument was erected to his memory in Westminster Abbey. — **W626, 646, 647; A48, 93; H12, 144**

Ngapo Wehi

Ngapo ('Bub') Wehi was born in Waihirere, Gisborne in 1934. He is the leader of the Ngapo *whanau* (family), whose tribal affiliations are with Tūhoe, Te Whakatōhea, Ngā Pui, Te Whānau-ā-Apanu and Ngāti Kahu. He was educated at Auckland University. He married **Muriel Pimia Wehi** in 1955, and they raised a family of three sons and three daughters. From 1984 to 1996 Ngapo Wehi was a lecturer in Māori studies and education at the Auckland Institute of Technology and the UNITEC Institute of Technology. In 1997 he became a lecturer in Māori Studies at Auckland University, researching *kapa haka* (Māori arts performing groups) and Māori tourism.*

Ngapo Wehi's association with the arts developed through performances with several Māori kapa haka groups. He worked with Waihirere and Te Waka Huia** (which he and his wife founded in 1981) and performed at New Zealand, Polynesian and Aotearoa Festivals with Pounamu, a family-oriented cultural and entertainment group. With his family he lived and worked in Auckland, often giving cultural performances for international conferences and visits by foreign dignitaries. He and his wife Dr Pimia Wehi are the only people who have won the Aotearoa Traditional Māori Performing Arts Festival six times (and come second 5 times): in 1972 and 1979 with Waihirere, and in 1986, 1992, 1994 and 2009 with Te Waka Huia. Both of them spent a lifetime living and working in the field of Māori Performing Arts as performers, tutors and composers.

Ngapo Wehi's choral works are performed regularly by New Zealand choirs and he developed a number of projects with the Tower New Zealand Youth Choir and composers such as Helen Fisher. With various performing groups he represented New Zealand at four South Pacific Festivals, the opening of the 1988 Seoul Olympics and the closing of the 1994 Commonwealth Games in Canada. In the 1990s he served as chair of Te Waka Toi, the Māori Arts Board of the Arts Council of New Zealand. In 2001 he received an honorary doctorate from Massey University. In 2007 he and his wife were honoured at the inaugural Māori Music Awards ceremony, and in 2011 he was awarded the QSM for services to Māori. In 2012 he was awarded an honorary BA in Māori Performing Arts by Māori tertiary institution Te Whare Wānanga o Awanuiārangi for his 'outstanding involvement in kapa haka.' He died at Gisborne on 31 July 2016: his tangi (funeral) was attended by the Māori King and his family. — **H84**

*A fuller biography is provided in *Ka Mau Te Wehi: Taking Haka to the World*, by Bradford Haami. Auckland: Ngapo and Pimia Wehi Whanau Trust, 2013. The SOUNZ website lists choral works and recordings.

**The name was given to the cultural club by its founder and means 'the container of precious treasures.' In 1986, under the leadership and training of Ngapo and Pimia Wehi the group won the national Aotearoa Māori Performing Arts Festival—the first time any such group had become overall winners on their first appearance at national level. They went on to win the National Kapa Haka championships twice and become runner up three times. But they also take pride in nurturing the hundreds of young Māori who join them, fostering an environment of self-respect and pride in personal identity and Māori cultural and spiritual values.

Muriel Pimia Wehi (Te Ua)

Muriel Pimia Wehi*, known as 'Nen,' was born in 1929 in Waihirere, Gisborne. Her tribal affiliations were Te Aitanga a Mahaki, Te Whānau-ā-Apanui, Rongowhakaata, Te Whakatōhea, and Ngāti Ruapani. She married Ngapo Wehi in 1955 and later moved with him from Waihirere to Auckland. She went on to complete 60 years of performing, composing, tutoring and training young Māori in their cultural performing arts.

She worked with her husband tutoring the Waihirere *kapa haka* group and won the national championships (now known as Te Matatini) in 1972 and 1979. In 1981 the pair founded a new cultural group in Auckland, Te Waka Huia, winning in their first year of competition in 1986, and again in 1992, 1994 and 2009. No-one else has won six national titles in this way; Dr Pita Sharples has commented that 'this is an artistic achievement, but a *kapa haka* is much more than that. Success comes from building confidence, knowledge and teamwork among the performers, and directing their passion and energy into developing the cultural heritage of their ancestors, as a gift to New Zealand and the world.'

As well as raising a family of six children, and helping form it into Pounamu, a cultural and entertainment performing group, she and her husband represented New Zealand overseas, from the first Festival of Pacific Arts in 1972 in Fiji, and in supporting government and official delegations to all corners of the world. As Pita Sharples has said, 'They have welcomed royalty, heads of state and international icons to these shores, on behalf of all New Zealanders.' They led performance groups representing New Zealand at four South Pacific festivals, the opening of the 1988 Seoul Olympic Games and the closing of the 1994 Commonwealth Games in Canada.

For her lifetime of service to Māori culture, Pimia Wehi received an honorary doctorate from Massey University in 2001, was awarded a QSM in 2002 and was honoured at the inaugural Māori Music Awards ceremony in 2007. She died on 7 February 2011 and was awarded a posthumous MNZM. — H84

*A fuller biography is provided in *Ka Mau Te Wehi: Taking Haka to the World*, by Bradford Haami. Auckland: Ngapo and Pimia Wehi Whanau Trust, 2013.

John Edward Weir

John Weir was born in Nelson on 25 April 1935. He was a pupil at St Joseph's Convent School, then boarded at St Patrick's College, Silverstream, Heretaunga (1949-53). After a year in Wellington working for the Ministry of Works and attending lectures in English, French and Latin at Victoria University, he studied for the Catholic priesthood at Mount St Mary's Seminary, Greenmeadows, Hawkes Bay. He became a professed member of the Society of Mary on 24 January 1958 and was ordained a priest on 4 July 1961. Afterwards he taught at St Bede's College, Christchurch, and resumed part-time university studies. After completing a BA at the University of Canterbury he studied full-time for an MA in English Language and Literature and was awarded First-Class Honours (1968). His programme of studies included a thesis, *Man Without a Mask; a Study of the Poetry of James K. Baxter.*

After six months teaching at St Patrick's College, Silverstream, and a further six months at St Patrick's College, Wellington, he was appointed Lecturer in English at the University of Canterbury. During his tenure there he completed a PhD in English (1974, a study titled *Five New Zealand Poets; a Bibliographical and Critical Account of Manuscript Material.* In 1975 he left the University to become Rector of St Patrick's College, Wellington (1976-82) and, for a short time, Managing Editor of *Zealandia,* a Catholic newspaper based in Auckland. Subsequently he held various chaplaincy positions within the Catholic Church. He has published four collections of his own poetry (for instance *Three Pagan Poems,* 2020) and numerous academic writings, most of them focused on the poetry and other writings of **James K. Baxter** (1926-72). He is New Zealand's most distinguished scholar of Baxter's work, publishing in 1980 the *Collected Poems* (Auckland: Oxford University Press) and 2015 a four-volume set, *The Complete Prose* (Wellington: Victoria University Press, 2012).

In 1981, Weir, at the time a priest in the Society of Mary and Rector of St Patrick's College, Wellington, met **Gerard Crotty,** a Marist Brother teaching at the Brothers' intermediate school at Miramar. The pair collaborated in the writing of hymns for congregational use, Weir creating strictly metrical pieces in plain English, set to tunes by Crotty which congregations could easily pick up after only one or two hearings. Together, between 1981 and 1984 the pair composed some 60 songs, the collaboration virtually ceasing when Weir moved to Auckland. When he was rejoined there by Crotty, who had taken up a position as Head of Music at Sacred Heart College in 1987, a number of these hymns were recorded and sent to Dove Publications in Melbourne, but the tapes were lost in transit and the hymns survived only through their use by a parish music group in Hamilton and the circulation of 'bootleg' copies. They were brought to the attention of the editorial board of *Alleluia Aotearoa* and eventually four of them were published in that hymnal. — **A67, 152, 157, 160**

Betty Wendelborn

Betty Wendelborn was born in Invercargill in 1939. She attended Southland Girl's College and completed a Diploma of Teaching at the Dunedin Teachers College, and a BMus begun at the University of Otago and completed at Waikato University. In 1986 she studied under Matthew Fox at the Institute of Culture and Creation Spirituality at Oakland, California, completing a certificate of Creation Spirituality there. She also has an ATCL in piano. On her return to New Zealand she worked as a teacher, composer, arranger, choreographer and dramatist. She was for a time a vocal and drama, mime and movement tutor at the Nelson School of Music, and has now retired to Auckland to be closer to her grandchildren.

In 1969 she composed, produced and directed a dramatic and dance presentation of Māori creation myths, *From the Nothing.* Her researches into the writings of European medieval mystics led to three books of sayings set to her own music, *Sing Green* (1988, revised 1990), *Dancing the Peace* (1989) and *Homecoming* (1990). In 1992 she produced and directed *Young Messiah,* a modern dance-drama interpretation of Handel's *Messiah,* following that with a nativity musical, *Starchild* (1993), performed at Masterton and St Paul's Cathedral, Wellington. In 1996 she composed and produced a St Matthews Youth Mass, as part of the Wellington fringe festival. Beyond these major events she has created a large number of songs and instrumental pieces, many of which have been published. — **A2, 56, 71, 145**

Charles Wesley

Charles Wesley, the youngest son and 18th child of Samuel and Susannah Wesley, was born at Epworth, Lincolnshire on 18 December

1707. He was educated at Westminster School, where his brother Samuel was an usher, and won a studentship to Christ College, Oxford, graduating MA and becoming a Fellow of the college. With George Whitfield and his own brother John he formed the Holy Club and instituted the disciplined practice of work and worship which led to their being nicknamed 'Methodists.' In 1735 he took orders in the Anglican Church, and travelled with John to Georgia, America, as secretary to General Oglethorpe. But he soon returned to England, and in 1738 experienced a Whitsuntide 'conversion.' In the same year he was made curate at St Mary's, Islington, London, but when he was refused permission to preach there he became an itinerant field preacher. He was to travel the length and breadth of England, his last nationwide tour undertaken in 1756.

Unlike his brother John, he remained loyal to the Anglican Church, and first settled with his family in Bristol, where, despite fierce opposition from church authorities, he devoted himself to the care of the Methodist societies there and in London. In 1771 he shifted his base to the capital, preaching, supporting Methodist societies and giving spiritual care to the prisoners in Newgate. He died at Marylebone, London, on 29 March 1788.

He became the poetic voice of the new movement and its doctrines, writing more than 6500 hymns published in 56 volumes, among them some of the finest Christian hymns in English. The compiler of the massive *Dictionary of Hymnology*, John Julian, concluded that 'perhaps, taking quantity and quality into consideration, [Charles Wesley was] the greatest hymn-writer of all ages.' — **A5**

Samuel Sebastian Wesley

Samuel Sebastian Wesley, an illegitimate son of the brilliant musician Samuel Wesley, Charles Wesley's second son, was born at St Pancras, London 14 August 1810. He was named after his father and his father's idol, Johann Sebastian Bach. His father was his first music teacher, and at the age of ten he became a chorister at the Chapel Royal. From 1826 he served as organist at three London churches, before becoming the organist of Hereford Cathedral (1832-35). Appointments followed at Exeter Cathedral (1835-41), Leeds Parish Church (1842-49), Winchester Cathedral (1849-65) and Gloucester Cathedral (1865), a post he held until his death at Gloucester on 19 April 1876. He was awarded the MusB and MusD by Oxford University in 1839 without examination, and became Professor of Organ at the Royal Academy of Music in 1850. Gladstone offered him the choice between a knighthood and a Civil List Pension; he chose the latter.

A brilliant organist, he eventually succeeded his father as the acknowledged leading player and extemporiser in England. He also had a fine reputation as a music teacher and conductor; in 1871 for a Three Choirs Festival at Gloucester Cathedral he led the first performance in England of Bach's *St Matthew Passion*. He was also one of the first organists in England to insist on the provision of a full pedal-board, and he worked tirelessly to improve both the general standard of Anglican church music and the standing of church musicians, mainly through the publication of his outspoken *A Few Words on Cathedral Music and the Musical System of the Church, with a Plan of Reform* (1849). However, the *Oxford Dictionary of Music* remarks that 'His genius as an organist was such that church authorities overlooked his often questionable conduct in personal and professional affairs.' He is credited with many hymn tunes notable for their quality and unconventional writing, four church services, works for the organ and piano, two psalm settings and a number of splendid anthems. Several of his hymn tunes and other compositions are still sung and played today; he also undertook the musical editorship of Kemble's *Psalms and Hymns* (1864). His compilation *The European Psalmist* (1872) contained more than 700 hymn tunes, 130 of them his own composition. — **W662**

Reginald (Reg) Wharekura

A member of a group of Māori gospel hymn writers, including **Mona Riini**, **Hoki Tawa**, and **Kitty Temara**, working cooperatively in the late 1980s. See under 'Whakatau mai te Atua.' — **A32, 150**

Ralph Vaughan Williams

The great English composer was born on 12 October 1872, at Down Ampney, Gloucestershire, the son of the local vicar. He studied at the Royal College of Music under Parry, Stanford and Charles Wood. In 1892 he entered Trinity College, Cambridge and took degrees in Arts and Music. In 1895 he returned to the Royal College of Music, where he became the close friend of Gustav Holst. After further study in Berlin with Max Bruch and in Paris with Maurice Ravel he devoted himself to the study of the English Tudor composers and the collection of English folk-tunes, and became a professional teacher and composer.

With Percy Dearmer he edited *The English Hymnal* (where a number of his most famous hymn-tunes and harmonisations appeared), and went on to co-edit with **Martin Shaw** *Songs of Praise* (1925) and *The Oxford Book of Carols* (1928). His wide range of compositions included nine symphonies, three concertos, the opera *The Pilgrim's Progress*, songs and song cycles, choral works with orchestra, folk-song arrangements, music for ballet, film and theatre, organ works, chamber music, fantasias and other pieces for strings or full orchestra. Many of these works were based on or drew from religious texts or earlier religious music, including his Mass in G minor, his oratorio *Sancta Civitatis*, the masque *Job* and the *Five Mystical Songs*. He wrote 15 hymn-tunes, 13 of them included in the enlarged edition of *Songs of Praise* (1931).

At the close of World War I, in which he served in the Army Medical Corps and the Artillery, he was awarded an honorary Doctorate by the University of Oxford (1919), was appointed Professor of Composition at the Royal College of Music (1920) and in 1935 was awarded the Order of Merit by King George V in 1935, in recognition of his services to British music. He died in London on 26 August 1958. — **W657; A24, 96, 106, 129; F47, 55; H139**

William Williams

William Williams, the 'sweet singer of Wales,' also known as William Williams Pantycelyn (Welsh=hollytree hollow) to differentiate him from the many Welshmen of the same name, was born on 11 February 1717, the son of a prosperous farmer at Cefn Coed, in the parish of Llanfair-ar-y-bryn, Carmarthenshire. He was sent to study medicine in Carmarthen, but underwent a religious conversion while listening to one of George Whitfield's revivalist preachers, Howel Harris. He took deacon's orders in the Church of England in 1740, and was licensed to a curacy, but when because of his Methodist sympathies he was refused ordination as an Anglican priest he became an itinerant preacher, establishing local Methodist fellowships for his converts. Working at first in an evangelistic team with Howel Harris and David Rowlands, then independently, he continued such fieldwork for over 50 years, becoming the leader of the Methodists in Wales in the 18th century.

He was encouraged by Harris to write hymns in his native language, and his first collection, *Halleluia* (1744), proved such a success that he continued to write until he had composed more than 800 hymns in Welsh and a further 100 hymns in English, issued in nine books. His hymns were collected by his son John in 1811, and they continued to be widely known and sung. He also wrote two long religious poems, a number of poetic elegies on contemporary Christian leaders, and several prose tracts. He died at Pantycelyn, Llandovery, Carmarthen, on 11 January 1791. — **W661**

Mark Wilson

Mark Wilson was born at Invercargill on 7 June, 1968, the son of an Anglican vicar, Boyd Wilson, and his wife Lesley. Blind from birth, Mark began his education at the age of five at Homai College for the Blind, Auckland, then studied at Manurewa High School. In 1992 he completed a BMus in Musical Performance (piano) at the University of Auckland, becoming the first braille reader to be awarded such a degree. He married Emma Sykes in 2012. *Love at First Sound*, a film profiling his life as a musician and Queenstown identity was made by Joey Bania and Amy Anderson; it was broadcast on a Sky television channel on 2 February 2014.

From the age of 11 he has played for religious services on church organs. In 1984 Mark gained distinction in Grade 3 of the Royal Schools of Music performance examinations; at the same time he joined a big jazz band and has since pursued his interests in both classical and jazz music. Following his family's shift in 1992 to the Dunstan Parish in Central Otago, he played the organ at St Aidan's Church in Alexandra and joined a Queenstown group of musicians named the Jive Pranksters (later the Master Blasters). In 1998 he moved to Queenstown, becoming the principal organist at St Peter's Anglican Church, which he has made his special faith community. At the same time he was increasingly involved in local gigs, shows and reviews; in 2002 he became Musical Director of Showbiz Queenstown's production of *Joseph and his Amazing Technicolour Dreamcoat*, followed by a further three large-scale musicals.

Mark's hymn-writing career began in 1995 with the 'Dunstan Carol' (C52). He has since written other hymns, and has also composed and recorded two albums of original solo piano pieces, *Untamed* (1998) and *The Rhythms of Nature* (2012). He says of himself, 'I am not aiming to be a jazz pianist, a classical artist or a devotional organist, but simply, a musician,' and sees music as his form of Christian ministry. 'I regard all of my music-making as devotional. Whether I am playing the organ for church on Sunday, or playing music in a bar, I am aiming to give glory and thanks to the Lord of limitless life and love.' Under the title *Seeds of Faith* a further collection of 16 of his religious songs was published in 2014 (Queenstown: Rendall Music). **C52**

Jacqueline (Jackie) Denise Wise

On 13 December 1948, Jackie Wise was born in Lower Hutt to a Christian family in which music was very important. Living in Tawa, she was part of the Tawa-Linden Baptist Church, and was greatly encouraged there, both in her faith and in her use of her musical abilities. She attended Tawa College, then completed a BA at Victoria University, majoring in Music. After moving to Auckland in 1971, she began work as a piano teacher at St Cuthbert's College, Epsom, a Christian day and boarding school for girls, joining the staff there the following year, and teaching senior school examination music, and some primary school classes. She also studied part-time at Auckland University, where she gained an MA in Music (focusing on the Baroque period and music education). After some years, her focus changed to younger children, and she taught classroom music to New Entrants up to Year 6 and led junior choirs and instrumental ensembles.

Most of her songs were written for the Junior Black Watch Singers, the Year 5-6 choir for school occasions such as St Cuthbert's Day services, family chapel services, carol services and prize-givings. In 2000 they sang in a concert for the partners of Apec leaders gathered in Auckland for a Pacific Conference. Many of her songs grew out of a desire to help the children understand about God and his love, and what faith means. One of them was written for a staff member who was dying. Since writing two nativity carols, the second in 1994, she has written songs for each part of the Nativity service (except a lullaby for the baby), most of them for young children to sing, together with a few sacred songs for older people. Apart from two carols published in *Carol Our Christmas* (1996) the songs have not been published (a collection is planned), but 16 of them were recorded at St Cuthbert's school, sung by the different St Cuthbert choirs, by year-level groups and staff members, to make a CD titled *Songs for Celebrations*.

Now semi-retired, Jackie Wise teaches computer music and multi-media creative work as an enrichment activity for small groups of St Cuthbert children, and says that she loves it! — **C12, 41**

Joseph (Joe) Edward Wise

Joe Wise was born at Louisville, Kentucky, on 19 August 1939. He was educated at St Mary's College, Baltimore, where he gained a BA in Philosophy and an STB in Theology; he went on to complete an M.Ed in Counselling and Guidance from Spalding College (Louisville, Kentucky), and an MA in Religious Education from Catholic University (Washington). He launched a career in Christian songwriting and took a leading role in the revitalization of Roman Catholic congregational song in America in the 1960s, 70s, and 80s, leading liturgies, conducting workshops, and giving concerts and lectures across the United States. He also toured Canada, Europe, Australia, and New Zealand. His work was included in most religious songbooks of that period, and he has recorded his music on 19 albums, which include *Music for the Spirit, Gonna Sing, my Lord* and *Songs for the Journey*. His collected recorded works, *Most Requested Music for the Spirit,* appeared in 2003 (volume 1) and 2005 (volume 2, and there are also collections for children. *The Truth in Twenty and then some: Entries from my Journal, A Rolling Memoir* (2013), is part memoir, part reflection, based on his own journals. Wise is also a poet and a recognized painter whose award-winning work hangs in private and corporate collections. In addition to his religious songs, he has published three books, a film score, and a video. His writings have appeared in various magazines and journals, including a humorous piece in *Sports Illustrated*.

He and his wife Maleita now live in Cottonwood, Arizona, where they lead retreats and workshops, using journaling techniques as a tool for increasing spiritual awareness. — **W656**

Olive Wood (née Roberts)

This New Zealand writer and composer of scriptural songs was born at Wigan, Greater Manchester, on 25 April 1921, the ninth child of ten children. Her parents were of Wesleyan and Primitive Methodist stock; her father and both her brothers became Methodist Lay Preachers. The family emigrated to New Zealand in 1923 and settled in Shannon, where the three men worked on the Mangahao Power Station and her father preached at the local Methodist Church. She was a talented, at times eccentric woman; she married Gordon Wood and brought up a family of seven, of whom three died in childhood. She was a good singer and a competent musician who wrote a number of settings of biblical and liturgical texts in the late 1960s and early 70s.

One of her children recalls that 'music was a daily activity in our house and there was always a ukelele or a piano accordion in the car to accompany singing wherever we went. Mum had a real gift with music, considering that she never had a formal music lesson in her life. She was mostly self-taught, though her father would answer any questions she had. Having perfect pitch she was able to hear different and beautiful harmonies... [Her] faith and love of God made Scripture the focus of her music writing. Over a period of approximately three years she produced more than 30 pieces of music. Unfortunately, some of them have been lost...and only 'Now unto Him' was ever published.' Olive Wood died on 23 November 1976.

Her husband's second wife, Norma Wood, later made a collection of 25 of her religious songs and privately published them from Paeroa under the title, '*My Glorious Redeemer': Songs by Olive Wood*. — **A102**

John Joseph Woods

The composer of the music for New Zealand's national anthem* was born in 1849 in what is now Tasmania, then known as Van Diemen's Land, one of a family of 15 children, their father an Irish-born soldier. After teaching in Tasmania for nine years, Joseph Woods migrated to New Zealand, where he continued to teach at Roman Catholic schools in Nelson, Christchurch, Dunedin and Invercargill. In 1874 he was appointed to the position of head teacher of St Patrick's school in Lawrence, Central Otago. There, on 9 September 1874, he married an Irish widow, Harriet Conway, and they raised a family of four children, in addition to Harriet's two children by her first husband. In 1877 Woods gave up teaching and became the County Clerk for the Tuapeka County Council. He held this position for 55 years, until illness forced him to retire at the age of 83. In 1902 Woods built a house in Lawrence in which the family lived until his death on 9 June 1934; it is now under the care of the Historic Places Trust.

Woods was a talented musician, a good singer, a fine violin player, the choirmaster of the local Catholic church and the first president of the local choral society. He was later made an Honorary Freeman of New Zealand, the first such award in the British Empire. It was made for 'his efficiency, integrity and devotion to duty.'

In June 1876, after meeting the coach that delivered the daily newspapers in the main street of Lawrence, Woods read in the Dunedin *Saturday Advertiser* of a competition to find a national anthem. It was 9pm, but Woods found a poem by **Thomas Bracken** printed in the newspaper which so excited him that he immediately composed a setting which he then submitted under the *nom de plume* of 'Orpheus.' With eleven other entries, it was sent to Melbourne, where it won the first prize of ten guineas.

The *Saturday Advertiser*, which had sponsored the competition, gave the task of publication to the Dunedin music company Charles Begg, but the result took so long and was so shoddy—it contained only one verse—that the *Advertiser* returned the copyright to Woods, who with Bracken's agreement organised publication by the London firm of Hopwood and Crew. The popularity of the new anthem grew rapidly, and when Premier George Grey visited Lawrence in 1878 he was greeted by 600 local schoolchildren singing 'God of nations.' Grey was delighted and immediately sent a telegram congratulating Bracken as well: 'have just heard for the first time, sung by 600 children at Lawrence, your New Zealand anthem. I admire it exceedingly.' It became the national hymn of this country in 1940, and the national anthem (with 'God save the Queen') in 1977. — **W677, A51**

*See further Max Cryer, *Hear Our Voices We Entreat: The Extraordinary story of New Zealand's National Anthems* (Auckland: Exisle Publications, 2004).

William Worley

William Worley was born in Newcastle, England on 17 August 1937. He studied at the University of Hull (1956-60) from which he holds a Joint BSc Honours degree in Pure and Applied Mathematics. He taught mathematics in several English schools before travelling to Jamaica, where he taught at Munro College. In 1974 he emigrated to New Zealand, and lived for a number of years in Winton, Southland, teaching mathematics at Central Southland College. In 1962 he became an accredited Methodist Lay Preacher and in 2012 achieved his 50 years Long Service Certificate. He married in 1963 and now has a family of five. In Winton he became a member of the Winton Chapter of the full Gospel Business Men's Fellowship, with whom he shared many of his religious songs. In 1996 he returned to England where he taught in various colleges and continued to preach in the Weardale Circuit. He returned to New Zealand in 2006 and was employed as a mathematics tutor at the University of Canterbury until the Canterbury earthquake struck in 2011. He has now resumed his teaching career in Christchurch. He is the author of three privately printed books, *Listen for a Word from God* (1996), *Song of Southland: A Collection of Songs of Praise* (1992) and *Nehushtan* (2008).

William Worley began writing hymns and spiritual songs in the 1990s and has continued to do so, acknowledging the assistance of Colin Hendry (Winton) and Geoffrey Kitching (Barnsley). He says of his own hymnal, 'This is not just another hymnbook, as it is aimed at the wider church. *Song of Southland* does contain conventional hymns but it also contains a number of ballads and songs. These may be best interpreted by a soloist. The choruses could well be sung through as an expression of worship, but often the chorus will stand repeating until the tune and the message stick. My hope is that my novel tunes will bring a new spark of life into the Christian's heart, so "breaking the power of darkness with a song." Many friends say to me that they only like the old hymns. Well, these hymns may be old one day if the Lord doesn't come first, so enjoy them while you can!' — **A78**

Carlton Raymond Young

Teacher, editor, composer and conductor, Carlton Young (known to his friends as 'Sam') was born on 25 April 1926 at Hamilton, Ohio and educated at the Cincinnati College Conservatory of Music (BME), Boston University School of Theology (STB), with further study at Union Theological Seminary, New York and in Vienna and Prague. He served in the Air Force during World War II. He went on to teach church music at Perkins School of Theology, Southern Methodist University, Scarritt College and Candler School of Theology, Emory University, of which he is an Emeritus Professor of church music. From 1969 to 1972 he was choral director and lecturer in music at Graz University, Austria. He is a Past-President and Fellow of The Hymn Society in the United States and Canada; and the first American to be named an honorary member of The British Methodist Church Music Society.

He tutored computer music-setting at Africa University, Mutare, Zimbabwe, in 1996 and was visiting professor of church music at Taiwan Presbyterian College and Seminary from 1995-2004, and at the Methodist School of Theology, Sibu, Sarawak, Malaysia, in 2004, and 2007. He has lectured and directed choir and hymn festivals throughout the United States and at conferences, churches and schools in England, Germany, Austria, Taiwan, China, Korea, Singapore, Malaysia, and New Zealand.

Since 1971 he has been consultant and editor (now Emeritus) for the Hope Publishing Company, for whom he edited *Ecumenical Praise* (1877), *Duty and Delight: Routley Remembered* (1985), *Our Lives Be Praise* (1990), *Music of the Heart, John and Charles Wesley on Music and Musicians* (1995) and a Carlton Young Anthem series. His extensive editorial work includes the editorship of two major American Methodist hymnals, *The Methodist Hymnal*, 1966, and *The United Methodist Hymnal*, 1989, for which he prepared an extensive and scholarly *Companion* (1993). He co-authored *Psalms for Praise and Worship*: *A Complete Liturgical Psalter* (Abingdon Press, 1992), and he is American Editor for the major online *Canterbury Dictionary of Hymnology* (2013). In addition, there is an impressive number of articles and essays on church music and hymnody. Carlton Young's own compositions, mostly choral and organ works, number more than 150, including many hymn, psalm and carol settings, which have attracted thirty-six awards from the American Society of Composers and Publishers.

Carlton Young has received honorary doctorates from four American universities. A Past President and Fellow of The Hymn Society in the United States and Canada, he was the first American to be named an honorary member of the Music Society of the British Methodist Church. He continues to write and compose in retirement in Nashville, Tennessee. — **W656, 667; C30, 40(ii); F35, 38; H35, 78, 114, 122,124**

Appendix — 1
A Finding List of
New Zealand Hymn Writing

Items in this list are arranged alphabetically by title. The following terms are used throughout:

- **Hymn** — text and musical setting, either in a full harmony or melody-only form.
- **Standard source** — major hymnbook published overseas.
- **Standard hymn** — hymn of international authorship, commonly used within world-wide Christian worship.

This list does not include material on websites or digital or other recordings of performances of New Zealand-authored hymns.

New Zealand Publications

1A – Hymn Books

Alleluia Aotearoa: Hymns and Songs for all Churches. Christchurch: The New Zealand Hymnbook Trust (1992), xxx+169pp [unpaged]. 163 hymns, rounds and liturgical pieces by New Zealand writers and composers.

All Heaven Declares: Songs of the People, compiled by David and Dale Garrett. Auckland: Scripture in Song (1991), 42pp [unpaged)]. 20 praise songs by New Zealand writers Bruce Bremner, Robert Burrell, Brent Chambers, Wayne Drain, Bob Fitts (2) Ian Gall, David and Dale Garrett (3), Bruce McGrail, Rob Packer, Ramon Pink (2), Joseph Vogels (2) and others.

Arise my Love Song Book. Auckland: St Paul's Outreach Trust (1974).

Camp Songbook: Inter School Christian Fellowship. Wellington: Scripture Union in New Zealand (undated), 19pp.

Carol our Christmas: A Book of New Zealand Carols. Raumati: The New Zealand Hymnbook Trust (1996), xv+113pp [unpaged]. 52 carols by New Zealand writers and composers.

Catholic Hymn Book: Melodies harmonised for singing in two, three or four Parts. Vernon Griffiths. Auckland, Wellington, Dunedin: Catholic Supplies New Zealand (1947), [unpaged].

Catholic Prayer Book and Hymnal. Dunedin: The Tablet (undated), 95pp.

Christmas Carols, selected by Karl Schulte. Dunedin: Charles Begg (?1942), 35pp. 20 standard carols.

The Community Mass Book. Dunedin: New Zealand Tablet (1975), 288pp. Includes 84 standard hymn texts in English and five Māori hymn texts.

Conference Songbook. Manukau: Methodist Conference (2008), 40pp [unpaged]. 58 hymn and song texts, including texts by Bill Bennett, Colin Gibson (8), John Murray, Shirley Murray (6), and three Māori hymns, two Fijian hymns, one Samoan hymn and two Tongan hymns.

Contemporary Praise: A Collection of Hymns and Ballads for the 20th Century. Taranaki Methodist Education Council (undated) 16pp. 56 hymn texts from standard sources.

Congregational Hymnal for Christian Life Week 22 to 29 January 1967. Auckland: (publisher unnamed) (1967), 16pp. 13 hymns compiled from standard Roman Catholic sources.

Country Conversations Handbook. Paihia and Russell: Bay of Islands Co-operating Parish (2000), 47pp. 24 hymns in English and six Māori hymns. Texts and settings include those by Bill Bennett (3), Colin Gibson (11), Doug Grierson, Dave Mullan, Shirley Murray (8), Ian Render, Cecily Sheehy, and Bill Wallace (4).

The Dominion Songbook no. 8: Twelve Well-known Songs, Sacred and Secular, for Four-part Choir. Christchurch et al: Whitcombe and Tombs (undated), 44pp. Includes six standard hymns arranged for choral singing by Vernon Griffiths.

The Dominion Songbook no. 12: Twelve Well-known Hymns. Christchurch et al: Whitcombe and Tombs (undated), 36pp. 12 standard hymns arranged for choral singing by Vernon Griffiths.

The Dominion Songbook no. 14: Twenty Well-known Hymns. Christchurch et al: Whitcombe and Tombs (undated), 36pp. 20 standard hymns arranged for choral singing by Vernon Griffiths.

Dunedin Revival Centre Songbook. Dunedin: Dunedin Revival Centre (undated), 32pp.

The Europa Book of Christmas Carols. Wellington: Europa Oil (NZ) (1964), 12pp. 12 standard carol texts and tunes from Chappell's *Standard Book of Christmas Carols* (1953).

Faith Forever Singing: New Zealand Hymns and Songs for a New Day. Raumati: The New Zealand Hymnbook Trust (2000), xxii+176pp [unpaged]. 80 hymns by New Zealand writers and composers.

Festive Praise One. Wellington: The Festival Singers (1983).

Festive Praise Two. Wellington: The Festival Singers (1983), 17pp. Eight folk-hymns and songs by New Zealand authors and composers, David Wood, Joy Ryan, John Franklin, Eileen Rounthwaite, Colin Gibson, Taryn Calyton, Janet Carter and Kim Doust.

A Festival of Music arranged by the Presbytery of Dunedin. Dunedin: Presbyterian Church of New Zealand (1969), 2pp.

Festive Sounds: Twenty Choral Arrangements of Contemporary Folk-Hymns. Wellington: Festivity Productions (1979), 24pp [unpaged]. Includes texts by Richard Gillard and Merla and Mervyn Watson, and music by Richard Gillard, Christopher Norton (7), Rosemary Russell, John Hendren, Guy E. Jansen (13), Merla and Mervyn Watson.

Fonomarae Songbook. Auckland: The Girls' Brigade (1973), 56pp. 65 hymns, choruses and spirituals from traditional sources, includes four items by New Zealand or Pacific island writers.

Funeral Service Hymns. Masterton: St Matthews Parish (1986).

Glory Be. Christchurch: Christchurch Cathedral (2000), [unpaged]. 106 hymns including texts by Marnie Barrell (4), Colin Gibson (2), Shirley Murray (12) Frank Nichol, and five traditional Māori hymns.

Harvest of Praise, comp. Sue and Richard Gillard and Clyde Whitechurch. Auckland: St Paul's Outreach Trust (1975), 31pp.

He Came Singing Peace: Songs to overcome Violence. Raumati: The New Zealand Hymnbook Trust (2002), 31pp [unpaged]. 27 hymn texts reprinted from *Alleluia Aotearoa* and *Faith Forever Singing*, with three settings by Colin Gibson and one by Cecily Sheehy.

He Himene mo te Karakia ki te Atua. Napier: Na te Haaringii ta ki Tona Whare Perehi Pukapuka (1890), 135pp. 172 Māori hymn texts.

Himene: Waiata Tapu, e Tahi Inoi, te Inoi a te Ariki, te Whakapono a Naihia me Nga. Kingi Ihaka. Rotorua: Te Pitopatanga o Aotearoa (1983), vii+56pp.

Holy Week for the Choir. Auckland: Auckland Diocesan Liturgical Commission (1972), 48pp. 39 hymns, psalms, carols, songs and other liturgical pieces with settings and arrangements (in manuscript) by David Jillett and Douglas Mews.

Hope is our Song; New Hymns and Songs from Aotearoa New Zealand. Palmerston North: The New Zealand Hymnbook Trust (2009), xxiii+316pp. 158 hymns and songs by New Zealand writers and composers.

Hymn Book. Napier: Spiritualist Church of New Zealand (1989), [unpaged]. 'Come to this Christmas singing,' 'Sing Hosanna,' 'Sing a song for peace and justice' and 'Let's praise the Creator' by Shirley Murray and *E Koutou katoa, kia oho rapea, E te ariki toku nei Atua, E te Aroha kaha rawa, Te ariki, hei a au koe noho ai, Tanumia tou pouri, Ko Ihowa toku hepara, I tetahi ahiahi, Haere mai ra koutou, E nga hoa hei a koutou na.*

Hymn Book: Trans-Pacific Crusade 12th to 16th September 1965. Baptist Union of New Zealand (1965), 32pp. 126 texts compiled from standard sources.

Hymn Book. Baptist Union of New Zealand (undated), 34pp. 128 hymn and chorus texts compiled from standard sources.

Hymns and Notes for Worship for the Ecumenical Youth Conference Palmerston North, N.Z. 1956-57. Palmerston North: National Council of Churches (1956), 31pp. 28 hymns from standard sources.

Hymns and Prayers. Christchurch. Rangi Ruru Girls' School (undated), 92pp. Includes hymn texts by Joy Cowley, Felicia Edgecombe, Colin Gibson (2), Barbara Gillard, Richard Gillard, Willow Macky, Shirley Murray (9), Cecily Sheehy (3), Bill Wallace (2), and 4 Māori hymns.

Hymns and Songs (In Process) 2002-2003. Jane Simpson and Peter Low. Christchurch: Godzone Hymns NZ (2003). Five hymns by Jane Simpson, Peter Low, Bill Ahlers and Barry Brinson.

Hymns and Songs Manukau 1986. Manukau, Auckland: New Zealand Methodist Church (1986), 20pp.

Hymns and Waiata. The Hymnbook of the 1990 Dunedin Conference of the Methodist Church of New Zealand, comp. Colin Gibson. Dunedin: Methodist Church of New Zealand (1990), 56pp.

Hymns from the Holy Coast: A Supplementary Hymnbook for the Parishes of Port Chalmers and Warrington. Port Chalmers and Warrington: Parish Vestry (undated), 84pp. 67 hymn texts and liturgical pieces, including hymns by Marnie Barrell (2), Joy Cowley, Colin Gibson (6), Richard Gillard, Shirley Murray (15), Cecily Sheehy and three Māori hymn texts.

Hymns in Māori and English. Auckland: Methodist Literature and Colporteur Society (undated), 40pp. 72 Māori hymns and 30 hymns from standard sources.

Hymns in Māori and English. Methodist Church of New Zealand (undated), 44pp. 112 texts in Māori (52) and English (60) drawn from the *Methodist Māori Service Book*, the *Methodist Hymn Book* (1933), and the Alexander and Sankey songbooks.

ISCF (International Student Christian Fellowship) Songbook Wellington: Scripture Union (undated), 25pp [unpaged]. 30 hymns, songs and graces with melodies. Includes texts by Felicia Edgecombe, Mervyn and Merle Watson, Richard Gillard and an arrangement by Guy Jansen.

Knox Church Song Book. Dunedin: Knox Church (undated), [unpaged].

Ko ngā karakia o te miha me ngā himene: Māori-English Mass Book. Auckland: Mill Hill Missionaries (1999), 67pp. 86 Māori hymn texts and acclamations, including 18 English or bi-lingual texts.

Ko te Pukapuka A Ngā Inoi me era Atu Tikanga a te Hai Weteriana (Methodist) ngā Himene me ngā Hakarameta me era Atu Ritenga hoki a te Hahi. London: The Epworth Press (1938), 258pp. Includes 121 Māori hymns.

'*Let's Sing.*' Wellington: Methodist Department of Christian Education (undated), 29pp. Compilation of 98 hymns, spirituals and choruses from standard sources.

The Little Blue Hymn Book. Napier: St Peter's Presbyterian Church (c.1975), 32pp. 103 hymns and songs compiled from standard sources.

Māori Himene & Waiata. Compiled by Adrienne Bruce. Papamoa: Diocese of Waiapu (2010) 11pp. Ten Māori hymns with English translations.

Methodist Conference Manawatu 1988. Hymns and Songs. Palmerston North: Conference Arrangements Committee Methodist Church (1986), 44pp.

The Minerva Hymnal, compiled by R.H. Marryatt. Auckland: Minerva (1958), 56pp.

Mornington Methodist Church Hymn Book, compiled by Evan Lewis and Colin Gibson. Dunedin: Mornington Methodist Church (undated), 134pp.

Music 1957: New Zealand Broadcasting Service. Wellington: Department of Education, 29pp. Includes a carol and a hymn, both traditional.

Music for a New Millennium. Auckland: Millennium Music, 64pp. Includes Psalm 67/68 by Suzanne Gasson and settings of Psalms 32/33, 33/34, 97/98 and 114/116 by Anthony Mullany.

Music for Moving Through the Silence. Wellington. Festivity Productions (undated), 58pp. Includes hymns and songs by Felicia Edgecombe (4), Colin Gibson (2), Henry Milne, Monica Jack, Shirley Murray (2), Ian Render, John Weir (2) and settings or arrangements by Gerard Crotty (2), Colin Gibson, Guy Jansen (6) and Christopher Norton.

Nelson Conference Songbook. Nelson 1987. Nelson: New Zealand Methodist Conference Arrangements Committee (1987), 27pp.

The New Community Mass Book. Dunedin: New Zealand Tablet Company (1970), 128pp. 56 hymns from standard sources and two Māori hymns (also printed as a separate issue). Includes liturgical settings by Douglas Mews and 'O Mary, mother of our joy,' by James K. Baxter, to music by Vernon Griffiths.

The New Community Mass Book. Dunedin: New Zealand Tablet (1976), 8pp.

New Glory: Songs of Renewal. Auckland: St Paul's Outreach Trust (1976), 20pp. 186 hymns and praise songs compiled from standard sources.

New Harvest, Music Edition. Auckland: St Paul's Outreach Trust (1979), 244pp [unpaged]. 235 hymns and praise songs, including items by Christine Allan, Chris Benge, Patsy Burton (3), Brent Chambers (3), Chris Donaldson, Dale Garratt, John Harris, Maryse Ingley (2), Bruce McGrail, John McNeill, Kim Miller (2), Barbara Gillard, Richard Gillard (8), Jules Riding (6), John Smith (5), Tapu Moata, Jenny Thorne, Merla and Mervyn Watson (2) and Kathy Wood. Musical arrangements by Christine Allan (47), Barry Clewett, Edward Dagnes (2), Val Fleetwood (39), Charles High (1). Martin Hurricks (10), Bruce McGrail, Richard Pether, Rod Wallace and others

New Harvest. Auckland: St Paul's Outreach Trust (1979), 56pp [unpaged]. 235 hymns and praise song texts. Words only.

The New Zealand Hymnal compiled under the Authority of the General Synod of the Branch of the United Church of England and Ireland, sessions 1862 and 1863 (edited by Arthur Guyan Purchas). London: William Collins (1872), 241pp. 322 hymns and doxologies compiled from standard sources.

New Zealand Hymns to Well-known Tunes. Norman E. Brookes and Jan Chamberlin.

Auckland: Publishing Press (2004). 50 hymns.

New Zealand Praise: A Book of Contemporary New Zealand Christian Songs and Hymns written by and for the people of New Zealand. Compiled by David R.S. Dell. Hastings: New Zealand Christian Resource Trust (1988). One 125 hymns, songs and arrangements by New Zealand writers and composers. *Update One* (1990) and *Update Two* (1993), also compiled by David Dell and published at Hastings by the New Zealand Christian Resource Trust contained further material by New Zealand writers.

New Zealand Praise. Words Edition. Compiled and edited by David R.S. Dell. Hastings: New Zealand Christian Resource Trust (1988), 42pp [unpaged]. 177 hymn texts by New Zealand writers. See *New Zealand Praise*.

The New Zealand Radio Hymn Book. Wellington: A.H. and A.W. Reed (1962), 107pp. 309 texts in English (302) and Māori (7), compiled from standard sources.

The New Zealand Radio Hymn Book. Wellington: A.H. and A.W. Reed (second enlarged edition, 1963), 110pp. 313 texts in English (305) and Māori (8), compiled from standard sources.

The New Zealand Radio Hymn Book. Wellington: A.H. and A.W. Reed (sixth edition, 1975), 110pp. 313 texts in English (305) and Māori (8), compiled from standard sources.

Nga Himene. Auckland: Methodist Māori Division (undated), 140pp. 52 texts in Māori and 62 English hymns from traditional sources.

Nga Himene Hunga Tapu. No publication information (undated, c.1918). 134 hymns in Māori, translated from English traditional hymns, together with the English original texts. Includes 'Dear old M. A. C' (Māori Agricultural College) by Walter Smith.

North Canterbury Methodist Bible Class Fellowships. Hymns ad Choruses. Christchurch: North Canterbury Bible Class Fellowship (undated), 378pp.

Pilgrim Praise. Centennial Committee of the Baptist Union of New Zealand (1982), 74pp. 40 hymns drawn from standard sources.

Psalms and Hymns of the Reformed Churches, compiled by the Liturgical Committee of the Reformed Churches of New Zealand. Wellington: Reformed Churches of New Zealand (1966), 240pp.

Roys Songs of Praise, compiled by Royale Milmarnisque. Wellington: Enam Press (1976), 8pp.

St Patrick's Cathedral Hymn Book. Auckland: B.F. Arahill, 43pp.

St Mary's Song Book, compiled by Carol Spain. Addington: St Mary the Virgin, (unpaged). 63 hymns. Includes hymns by Marnie Barrell (15), Colin Gibson (6), Richard Gillard, Shirley Murray (2), Chris Skinner, Carol Spain (2), Bill Wallace, John Weir and three Māori hymns.

'Sacred Energy/Mass of the Universe (For Congregation and/or Choir),' William L. (Bill) Wallace. *Music in the Air: Song and Spirituality*, (Winter/Spring 2009), 12-18. This text includes a number of hymn texts by Bill Wallace.

The Salvation Soloist Volume 1…for use in New Zealand. Compiled by Authority of W. Bramwell Booth for use in New Zealand. Wellington and London: The Salvation Army (1927), 192pp. 262 hymns and songs compiled from standard sources.

Secondary School Hymnary: 112 Selected Hymns. Auckland: Unity Books (1952), 110pp. The New Zealand national anthem ('God of Nations') and 111 hymns from standard hymn books.

The School Book of Services. Wellington: New Zealand Council for Christian Education (revised edition, 1962), 56pp.

38 hymn texts compiled from standard sources, and three Māori translations.

Scripture in Song Music Book. Edition One. Auckland: Scripture in Song (undated), 16pp.

Scripture in Song: Songs of Praise. Combined Music Edition, compiled by David and Dale Garrett. Auckland: Scripture in Song (1976, 1979), 252pp [unpaged]. 205 praise songs by New Zealand writers and musicians Brent Chambers, Bruce McGrail (3), Dale Garrett (11), Richard Gillard, Nick Ridings (4) Tapu Moala (2), Olive Wood, Val Cash and others.

Scripture in Song. Book One: Songs of Praise (words only edition of *Songs of Praise: Book 1*). Auckland: Scripture in Song (1976, 1979), 24pp. 205 texts. Also issued with the title *Scripture in Song. Volume One: Songs of Praise.*

Scripture in Song. Book Two: Songs of the Kingdom (words only edition of *Songs of Praise: Book 2*). Auckland: Scripture in Song (1976, 1979), 40pp. 245 texts numbered 206-451. Also issued with title *Scripture in Song. Volume Two: Songs of the Kingdom.*

Scripture in Song. Volume Two: Songs of the Kingdom, compiled by David and Dale Garrett. Auckland: Scripture in Song (1981), 294pp [unnumbered]. 246 praise songs by Bruce Bremner, Leigh Briggs, Richard Britton, Hoard Carter, Brent Chambers (9), Ken Chant, Jackie Edwards, David Fellingham, Ross Fleming, Hilary Foged (2), Dale Garratt (14), Gary Garratt, Richard Gillard, Naida Hearn (2), Mike and Viv Hibbert, Roy Hicks (3), Adrienne Hoggarth, Tony Hopkins, Dale and Evelyn Hunter, Beverley Jack, Peter Jordan, Graham Kelly (2), Bonnie Low (4), Bruce McGrail, Tom McLain (2), Richard Oddie (2), Nolene Prince, Dave Richards, Jules Riding (2), Rick Ridings (4), Neil Riley (3), Steve Smith, Linda Spencer, Steve Stewart, Dan Stradwick, Merla Watson (2), Ted Watson and others.

Scripture in Song. Book Three: Songs of the Nations, compiled by David and Dale Garrett. Auckland: Scripture in Song (1988), 417pp [unnumbered]. 230 praise songs, numbered 452-682, by David Baumstark (2), Bruce Bremner (2), Brent Chambers (10), Bruce Clewett, Dale Cox (2), Wayne Drain (21), Bob Fitts (5), Ian Gall (4), Dale Garratt (11), David Garratt (2), Jan Garrett, Stephen Hampton (2), Mike Harris, Maurie Hooper, Dale Jackson, Charlie Matthews, Jim and Ann Mills, Richard Oddie (3), Rob Packer (6), Shirley Pavy (4), Ramon Pink (5), Shirley Powell (2), Jules Riding, Rick and Patti Ridings (3), Deanne Rutledge, Shona Sauni (2), Dan Stradwick, Kevin Taylor, Joseph Vogels (6), Gill Watson, Dave Watson (2), Merla Watson. Musical arrangements by Chrissy Badger, Yvonne Bartlett, Raewyn Fraser, Gayla Traylor, Matthew Raymond, Meryl and Ray Watson.

Scripture in Song. Book Three: Songs of the Nations, compiled by David and Dale Garrett. Auckland: Scripture in Song (1988), [unpaged]. 230 praise songs, numbered 452-682. Words only.

Secondary School Hymnary: 112 Selected Hymns. Auckland: Unity Press (undated), 110pp. Compiled from standard sources.

Second Book of Songs. Christchurch. New Zealand Girl Guides Association (1956), 86pp. Includes 26 hymns, spirituals, graces and other material compiled from standard sources.

Servant Songs: Psalms, Hymns and Spiritual Songs for God's People, compiled by Guy E. Jansen and Felicia Edgecombe. Sutherland, Australia: Albatross Books (1987), 324pp [unpaged]. 166 hymns and songs, including texts by Chris Benge, Jillian Bray, Janet Carter, Brent Chambers, A.J. Duncan and P.H.C. Lucas, Felicia Edgecombe (5), John Franklin, Colin Gibson (6), Richard Gillard (2), Bonnie Low (3), Christopher Norton, Rosemary Russell, and Merla Watson (2), and settings and musical arrangements by Jillian Bray, Janet Carter, Ron Dellow, Janet Elder, Felicia

Edgecombe, John Gibson, Nicola and Guy E. Jansen, Shona Murray, Christopher Norton. Rosemary Russell, John Smith and William Southgate. Two Māori and one Samoan hymns are included.

Servant Songs: Psalms, Hymns and Spiritual Songs for God's People, compiled by Guy E. Jansen and Felicia Edgecombe. Sutherland, Australia: Albatross Books (1987), [unpaged]. 166 hymns and songs. Words only.

Services of Worship (Undenominational) for Use in the Public Schools of New Zealand. Wellington: Bible in Schools League (1901), 512pp.

Sing a Psalm: Methodist Women's Fellowship Convention '88. Methodist Women's Fellowship (1988), 39pp [unpaged]. 26 hymns and songs from standard sources, including texts by Norman Brookes, Les R.M. Gilmore, Kathleen Mayson, Shirley Murray (2) and a setting by Jillian Bray.

Singing the Faith. London: The Methodist Church (2011), 840 hymns, psalms and canticles, including texts by Marnie Barrell, Richard Gillard, Shirley Murray (11), Bill Wallace (2), and a setting by Colin Gibson.

Singing the Truth: Songs for Praise and Meditation. Waikanae: Os Guiness Conference, Scripture Union (1975), 18pp.

Singing to the Lord! Wellington: Baptist Union of New Zealand (1974), 32pp. 150 choruses, hymns and spiritual song texts drawn from standard sources, including nine hymns in Māori.

Sing Praise Supplement: Accompaniments not previously published for Hymns and Liturgical texts in Sing Praise, edited by Charles Cooper. Wellington: Price Milburn Music (1981), 38pp. 33 accompaniments by New Zealand composers Cyril Crabtree, Charles Cooper, David Dobson (2), A. Maxwell Fernie, Edward Forsman, Vernon Griffiths (3), David Jillett (3), Paul Katene, Michael McConnell, L.B. Mannes (2), Douglas Mews (7), Evan Roberts (2), Stephen Somerville, Robert Stamps, Henare Tate (2), F.H. Walsh, Alan Woodcock (2) and David Wright.

Sing Praise: Words and Music for Liturgical Worship Compiled and Edited by Charles Cooper. Wellington: Price Milburn Music (1981), 260pp. 367 hymns and psalms, including texts by James K. Baxter, Thomas Bracken, Edward Forsman, and William Kerekere, music by Charles Cooper (4), Maxwell A. Fernie, Vernon Griffiths (3), David Jillett (3), Paul Katene, Douglas Mews (7), Michael F. McConnell, Henare Tate (2) and John Woods.

Sing Sing Sing. Wellington: Education Committee of the Sisters of Mercy (undated), 52pp [unpaged]. Compilation of 72 hymns and songs from standard sources.

Sing to the Lord: Hymns for Mass and Benediction. Auckland: Auckland Diocesan Liturgical Centre (1975), 131pp. A compilation of liturgical material, including 24 hymns in English or Latin from standard sources, and five Māori and one Samoan hymn.

Songs of Praise 2nd edition. Auckland: Scripture in Song (1972), 48pp [unpaged]. 118 unattributed praise song texts.

Songs of Praise 3rd edition. Auckland: Scripture in Song (undated), 12pp [unpaged]. 122 unattributed praise song texts.

Songs of Praise, 5th edition. Auckland: Scripture in Song (1976), 24pp [unpaged]. 205 unattributed praise song texts.

Songs of Praise Music Book, 2nd edition. Auckland: Scripture in Song (1972), 52pp [unpaged]. Melody only arrangements by Bruce McGrail of 118 praise songs.

Songs of Praise Music Book, 3rd edition. Auckland: Scripture in Song (1973), 131pp [unpaged]. Musical arrangements by Ena Thompson and Bruce McGrail of 122 praise songs.

Songs of Praise Music Book, supplementary 4th edition. Auckland: Scripture in

Song (1974), 156pp [unpaged]. Musical arrangements by Barry Clewett of 44 praise songs numbered 123-167

Songs of Praise Music Book, 5th edition. Auckland: Scripture in Song (1976), 82pp [unpaged]. Musical arrangements by Barry Clewett and Rod Wallace 69 praise songs, numbered 136-205.

A Supplementary Hymnbook. Dunedin: Mornington Methodist Church (1976), [unpaged]. 98 hymns and psalms, including 30 psalms and 11 hymns by Colin Gibson.

A Second Supplementary Hymnbook. Dunedin: Mornington Methodist Church (1999), [unpaged]. Includes texts by Dorothy Ballantyne, Marnie Barrell (2), Helen Clyde, Joy Cowley, John Franklin, Marion Kitchingman (2), Kathleen Mayson, Shirley Murray (33), John Paisley, Mary Pearson and Annette Wells, and hymns or settings by Malcolm Gould (2), Colin Gibson (47) and Ian Render.

Spiritualist Church of New Zealand Hymn Book. Napier and Petone: Spiritualist Church of New Zealand (1989), [unpaged]. 'Ask and keep on asking' by Dale Garrett, 'Sing Hosanna,' 'A Song for Human rights,' 'Come to this Christmas singing' and 'Let's praise the Creator' by Shirley Murray, 'Who shines through the sun?,' 'Inner Light' and 'Everyone is special' by Radha Wardrop and *E ngahei a koutou na*, *E te Aroha kaha rawa*, *E te Atua, ko koe nei ra*, *Haere mai ra koutou*, *I tetahi ahiahi*, *Ko Ihowa toku hepara* and *Tanumia toui*.

Tenei Matou. Christchurch: Christchurch (Roman Catholic) Pastoral Diocesan Council (undated), 80pp [unpaged]. 100 hymns and songs compiled from standard sources, including seven Māori hymns.

The Tune Book of the New Zealand Hymnal. Compiled and arranged by Arthur Guyan Purchas. Auckland: Wayte and Batger (1866), 97pp. 212 four-part hymn settings compiled from standard sources, together with eight original settings by the author (unidentified).

Tussocks Dancing: Hymns and Songs 2000-2001. Christchurch: Godzone Hymns (2002), 35pp [unpaged]. Ten hymn texts by Jane Simpson; music by Jane Simpson and Bill Ahlers, Barry Brinson, Chris Graham, Denis Guyan and Peter Low.

Untitled, undated collection of 74 hymn texts) (c.2005). Includes texts by Colin Gibson, Stan Stewart, Shirley Murray and Bill Wallace.

Waiata original: Sing a New Song, compiled by Carolyn Ann Aish and Joyce C. Straub. Inglewood: privately printed (1984).

The Word made Flesh: A Christmas Resource Pack, edited by Rosemary Neave. Auckland: St Paul's Outreach Trust (1982).

Worship Book. Christchurch: Knox Church, Christchurch (undated), 29pp.

Worship the Lord in the Beauty of Holiness. Lyttleton: Lyttleton Harbour Union Parish (1983), [unpaged]. 368 hymns and songs compiled from standard sources.

1B – Individual Author Collections

Additional Hymns: A Supplement to A Singing Faith. Jocelyn Marshall. Hamilton: F. W. Marshall (1999). 24 hymn texts.

Advent Carols for SATB. Maurice Faulknor. Raumati South: privately printed (2003), [unpaged]. Three carol texts by Shirley Erena Murray and one by Charles Wesley; settings by Maurice Faulknor.

Beautiful Blue-green Planet: and other Songs of Cosmic Connection. Cecily Sheehy. Auckland. Cecily Sheehy (undated), 8pp. 14 hymns, songs, graces and liturgical pieces.

Chants for Silence. Chris Skinner. Auckland: Reta Publishing (1994), 24pp. 16 hymns and chants; words and music by the author.

The Christian Year Beneath the Southern Cross. F.R. Inwood. Lyttleton: privately printed (1906), 130pp.

Dancing the Peace: Words from the audiocassettes Sing Green and Dance Peace. Betty Wendelborn. Auckland: Pyramid Press (1989).

Gradual Praise (Ngā Waiata Whakapono). Bill Bennett. Napier: Bill Bennett (2010), iii+134pp. 131 hymns; words and music by the author.

Hymns for all Seasons: A Singing Faith Revised and Enlarged. Hamilton: F. W. Marshall (2007), vi+151pp. 121 hymn texts by Jocelyn Marshall; 13 are provided with settings by New Zealand composers Anita Banbury (2), Ronald Dellow (2), Len Schroeder (2), Christopher Marshall (4), Fred Marshall and Charles Tyrell.

Hymns. Helen Watson-White. Dunedin. (Undated). Four texts.

Hymns. Music by W.V. Ashton. Auckland. W.V. Ashton (undated), 43pp. Original settings by the author of 27 standard hymn texts.

Hymns from the Holy Coast: A Supplementary Hymn Book for the Parishes of Port Chalmers and Warrington. (Undated), 84pp. 63 hymns and three Māori hymns. Includes texts by Joy Cowley, Marnie Barrell (2) Joy Dine, Colin Gibson (3), Richard Gillard, Shirley Murray (14) and Cecily Sheehy (2).

Hymns set to Easy Guitar Chords. Ray Galvin. Auckland: Department of Parish Development and Mission of the Presbyterian Church (1981), 35pp. 20 hymn tunes.

In Every Corner Sing: New Hymns to Familiar Tunes in Inclusive Language by Shirley Murray. Shirley Erena Murray. Wellington (1987), [unpaged]. 28 hymn texts.

Job and other Sacred Poems. Dugald Ferguson. Dunedin: James Horsburgh (1898), 128pp.

Kindle a Flame: Songs, Prayers & Poems – Creative Worship Volume 1. Philip Garside. Wellington: Philip Garside Publishing (2017, revised 2020), 31pp. Includes 11 hymns and religious songs by the author.

Mass of the Universe. See *Sacred Energy*

More Simply Different Hymns. Manurewa: Audrey Dickinson (2001), 46pp [unpaged]. 23 hymn texts by Audrey Dickinson with 19 settings by Trevor Cox.

My Book of Prayer and Māoriland Hymns. Wellington: A.H. & A.W. Reed (1942), 20pp. Contains four hymns by A.H. Reed set to standard tunes.

My Book of Prayer and Māoriland Hymns. Wellington: A.H. & A.W. Reed (second enlarged edition, 1944), 20pp. Contains four hymns by A.H. Reed set to standard tunes.

My Book of Prayer and Māoriland Hymns. Wellington: A.H. & A.W. Reed (third edition, 1952), 20pp. Contains four hymns by A.H. Reed set to standard tunes.

'*My glorious Redeemer'; Songs by Olive Wood.* Paeroa. Norma Wood (1972), 57pp [unpaged]. 25 hymns; words and music by the author.

The Mystery Telling: Hymns and Songs for the New Millennium. William L. Wallace. Kingston, NY. Selah Publishing (2001), 64p. 49 hymn texts by the author, with settings by New Zealand composers Alison Carey (8), David Childs, Graham Hollebon (2), Suzanne Lennon (5 arrangements), Richard Madden, Robert Perks, Carol Spain, Judith Thornley, and Bill Wallace(13).

New Sacred Music by Alan H. Spinks. Words by Albert E West and Others. Porirua: Alan H. Spinks (2003), 38pp [unpaged]. 23 hymn texts by Albert E West (21) and two others; settings by Alan. H Spinks.

'Sacred Energy/Mass of the Universe (For Congregation and/or Choir),' William L. (Bill) Wallace. *Music in the Air: Song and Spirituality*, (Winter/Spring 2009), 12-18. This text includes several hymn texts by Bill Wallace, with settings or arrangements by Alison Carey, Barry Brinson, David Childs, Graham Hollobon and Suzanne Lennon.

Second Book of Ten New Carols for Christmas. Words and Music by H.W. Hitchcock. Waiheke Island: H.W. Hitchcock (1975), 12pp [unpaged]. Ten carols with settings by the author.

Seeds of Faith Hymnbook. Queenstown: Mark Wilson (2014), 20pp [unpaged]. 16 hymn texts by the author.

Seeds of Faith: A Collection of original hymns and songs by Mark Wilson. Queenstown: Rendall Music (2014), 58pp. 16 hymn texts by the author.

Sing Green; Songs of the Mystics. Words and Music (by) Betty Wendelborn, Art (by) Rae Minogue. Auckland: Betty Wendelborn (1988), 63pp. 62 hymns, songs and rounds, texts and music by the author.

Simply Different Hymns. Manurewa: Audrey Dickinson (2001), 39pp [unpaged]. 20 hymn texts by Audrey Dickinson with 19 settings by Trevor Cox.

A Singing Faith: Incorporating Occasional Hymns, Jocelyn Marshall (1996). Hamilton: F. W. Marshall (1996), 82pp. 70 hymn texts by the author.

Singing Love: A Collection of New Hymns, Songs and Carols for today's Church. Colin Gibson. London, Auckland and Melbourne: Collins Liturgical (1988), 143pp. 57 hymns and their tunes by the author.

Singing the Circle Book 1: Sacred Earth, Holy Darkness. Hymns, Poems and Reflections for Aotearoa. Christchurch: Bill Wallace (1990), 84pp. 26 hymn texts by Bill Wallace, with settings by Alison Carey, Colin Gibson (2), Jocelyn Naylor (2), Judith Thornley (3), Bill Wallace (5), and arrangements by Alison Carey, David Childs and Suzanne Lennon.

Singing the Circle Book 2: Darkness and Light. Hymns and Reflections. Christchurch: Bill Wallace (1990), 69pp. 25 hymn texts by Bill Wallace, with settings by Alison Carey (2), Richard Madden, Jocelyn Naylor, Judith Thornley, Sue Van Royen, Bill Wallace (6), and arrangements by Alison Carey, Beverley Jones and Suzanne Lennon.

Singing the Circle Book 3: Broken Bread, Broken Chains. Hymns, Reflections and other Resources for the Celebration of the Sacrament of Life. Christchurch. Bill Wallace (1990), 84pp. Includes 21 hymn texts and 5 liturgical pieces by Bill Wallace, with settings by Alison Carey (3), Colin Gibson, Judith Thornley, Suzanne Lennon, Bill Wallace (11), and arrangements by Alison Carey, Colin Gibson, Suzanne Lennon and Judith Thornley.

Singing the Sacred: Psalms, Hymns and Spiritual Songs, volume 1, by William L. Wallace. Franklin Park, IL. (2011), 88pp. 36 hymn texts, with 21 melodies by the author, and settings or harmonisations by Barry Brinson (7), David Childs (2), Francis Dennis (3), Graham Hollobon (12), Judith Thornley and Wallace Woodley.

Singing the Sacred: Psalms, Hymns and Spiritual Songs, volume 2, by William L. Wallace. Franklin Park, IL. (2014), 88pp. 32 hymn texts, with 20 melodies by the author, and settings or harmonisations by Alison Carey, Barry Brinson (5), David Childs, Francis Dennis (4), Graham Hollobon (8), and Wallace Woodley.

Singing to the Lord. Wellington: The Baptist Union of New Zealand (1974), 33pp. 150 hymns from traditional sources, including five Māori hymns.

Somehow, the light comes to me: 20 more songs by Jonathan Berkahn. Wellington: Little Fish Productions (2013), 36pp. 20 hymns, songs and liturgical pieces with text and piano accompaniment by the author.

Something to sing about: Hymns and Reflections in search of a Contemporary Spirituality by Bill Wallace. Melbourne: Joint Board of Christian Education of Australia and New Zealand (1981), 65pp. 40 hymn texts by the author.

Song of Southland: A Collection of Songs of Praise by William Worley. Winton,

Southland: William Worley (1992), viii+132pp. 141 hymns, ballads and songs set to the writer's tunes.

Songs for Aotearoa. Graham Horne. Ten texts and tunes by the author. Auckland: Friends of St Barnabas (1981).

Songs of Expectation: 20 Songs by Jonathan Berkahn. Wellington: Little Fish Productions (2013), 36pp. 20 hymns, songs and liturgical pieces with text and piano accompaniment by the author.

Songs of Life: Songs to Celebrate the Special Moments of Life. Felicia Edgecombe and Rosemary Russell. Wellington: Festivity Productions (1996), 104pp. 43 hymns, songs and carols by Felicia Edgecombe (20) and Rosemary Russell (23) with 18 piano arrangements by Glenys Chiaroni.

Sounds of Grace: Music of 7 original Songs from Titahi Bay Gospel Chapel. Jillian Bray, Felicia Edgecombe and Rosemary Russell. (2004), 22pp. Texts and music by Felicia Edgecombe (7), Rosemary Russell (2) and Jillian Bray's setting of Shirley Murray's 'We are the singers who celebrate Jesus.'

Sun Festival Carols. Jenny McLeod. Wellington: Educational Music/Jenny Mcleod (1983). Eight carols with settings by the author.

Ten New Carols for Christmas. Words and Music by H.W. Hitchcock. Waiheke lsland. H.W. Hitchcock (1975), 12pp [unpaged]. Ten carols with settings by the author.

Third Book of Ten New Carols for Christmas. Words and Music H.W. Hitchcock. Waiheke lsland: H.W. Hitchcock (1980), 12pp [unpaged]. Ten carols with settings by the author.

Three Christmas Carols. Richard Madden. Dunedin. Musicke Fyne (1992), 11pp (unpaged). Three traditional carols with original choral settings by Richard Madden.

Truly Blessed under Southern Skies; Chris Skinner Songbook. Wellington: Chris Skinner Music (2008), 74pp. 31 hymns and songs by the author.

Two Hymns: (settings by) Mozart, edited by Raymond White. Dunedin: Musicke Fyne (1992), 12pp [unpaged]. 'O Gottes Lamm' and 'Als aus Aegypten Israel' (K. 343, K. 336c) edited and supplied with standard English texts.

Under the Southern Cross. Bruce Cockburn. Mangakino: Bruce Cockburn (2010), 64pp. 80 hymns and songs by the author.

Vocal Music. Robyn Allen Goudge. Seven sacred songs by the author. 1996-1997.

With a Song in our Heart: Forty-three new hymns, some to new tunes, many to popular tunes. Norman E. Brookes, Norman Goreham and Jeremy F. Whimster. Auckland: BGW Press (2019). 43 hymns.

With Heart and Voice, by Norman E Brookes and Jan Chamberlin. Pukekohe: Euroa Farms (2004), iv+121pp [unpaged]. 63 hymns and liturgical pieces by Norman Brookes (23) and Jan Chamberlin (20); with arrangements of standard tunes by William Chessum and original settings by Frank Dennis, Roger Hey and Marjorie Spicer (6).

1C – Hymns in Periodicals and Other Publications

Birthed from the Womb of God: A lectionary for Women. Edited by Dorothy Harvey. Wellington: Department of Communication, Presbyterian Church of New Zealand (1987), 73pp. 'Come celebrate the women' by Shirley Murray.

Job and Other Sacred Poems. Dugald Ferguson. Dunedin: James Horsburgh (1898).

Lifesparks. Auckland: Methodist Writers' Guild (1992-). Issue 1 Easter (1992) 8 'Two Crosses,' Norman E Brookes, 'Easter Resurrection Hymn,' Rob Ferguson'; Issue 2 Christmas (1992) 1 'Children's Christmas Hymn, Kathleen Mayson, 2 'Pohutukawa promise,' Norman E Brookes, 15-16 'Brightly Shines the Summer Sun,' text Rosalie Sugrue, music Troy Sugrue; Issue 3 Creation (1993) 12 'Loving Spirit,' Joy Dine, 11 'There's Beauty all around us,'

June Gibson; 'Anniversary Hymn' Joy Dine, 13-14 'Little Child from God,' Annette Wells; 5 Beginnings and Endings (1994) 17-18 'Little Child from God,' Annette Wells; Issue 6 Seasons (1994) 'Song of Spring'; Annette Wells, 10-11 'A Christmas Carol,' text Lucy G Henry, music Helen Williamson, 12 'Summertime Christmas,' Norman E Brookes; Issue 7 In the Biblical Tradition (1995) 9-10 'Song of Harvest,' Annette Wells.

1D — Single Hymns

'Awake O sleeper,' Nicola Sutherland. *On the Move* 26 (October 1979) 23.

Bellbird from a Forest Tree. By Christopher Jarman: A New Zealand Carol. (Wellington: Cosette Jarman) (1963), 2pp (unpaged). Text Cosette Jarman, music by Christopher Jarman.

Benedicite Otago Peninsula. Macandrew Bay, Dunedin: Shirley Mavis Mackenzie (undated), 5pp [unpaged]. Five sectionalised hymns by Shirley Mackenzie and Elizabeth Purdie, set to tunes by Shirley MacKenzie.

Haddon of Glen Leith: An Ecumenical Pilgrimage. Murray J. Savage. Dunedin: Associated Churches of Christ in New Zealand (1970), 88pp. Includes one hymn text by A.L. Haddon, 'Lord God, from Whom we all have life' (p88).

Hymn for Anzac Day/Himene mō te rā o Anzac. Palmerston North: The New Zealand Hymnbook Trust (2008), 7pp. Text by Shirley Murray, music by Colin Gibson, with Māori translation by Rangi McGarvey, adapted by Whirimako Black.

I Sing of a Maiden. Richard Madden. Dunedin: St Paul's Cathedral (1983), 3pp [unpaged]. A setting by Richard Madden of the 15th century English carol text.

The Kauri and the Carol. By Christopher Jarman. Wellington: Cosette Jarman (undated), 2pp [unpaged]. Text by Cosette Jarman, music by Christopher Jarman.

A Pohutukawa Carol. E.A. Forsman, musical arrangement by Moor-Karoly. Auckland: Franciscan Missionaries of the Divine Motherhood (undated), 4pp.

Pohutukawa Promise: Resources for the Season of Advent and Christmas. Auckland: Trinity Methodist Theological College (undated). Includes 'Pohutukawa promise' by Norman Brookes and Marjorie Spicer.

Said the Robin to the Sparrow. By Christopher Jarman. Wellington: Cosette Jarman (undated), 2pp [unpaged]. Text by 'anon,' probably Cosette Jarman, setting by Christopher Jarman.

'We claim the heritage of Christ,' by Colin Gibson. *"A Kind of Opening": A Tribute to Dame Phyllis Guthardt.* Edited by Lynne Frith and Susan J. Thompson, Proceedings of the Wesley Historical Society, 94 (July 2012), pp56-7.

'Wind of God, blow on me,' Nicola and Alex Sutherland. *On the Move* 27 (January 1980), p23. Reprinted in *Experiments with Bible Study*, Hans Ruedi-Weber. Geneva: World Council of Churches (1981), 256.

New Zealand Hymns Published Overseas

2A – In Hymnbooks And Other Collections

100 Hymns of Hope. Carol Stream, Il: Hope Publishing Company (1992), 126pp [unpaged]. 101 hymns, including 'God of our every day' and 'Here is the place,' texts by Shirley Murray and settings by Colin Gibson, and five other texts by Shirley Murray.

Agape: Songs of Hope and Reconciliation. Oxford: Oxford University Press and the Lutheran World Federation (2003), 220pp. 'Loving Spirit' by Shirley Murray.

The AILM Collection of Hymns, Psalms and Songs for Worship ed. Francisco Feliciano. Quezon City: Asian Institute for Liturgy and Music (2005). Includes 'Stranger standing at my door' and 'Touch the earth lightly' by Shirley Murray.

Ancient & Modern: Hymns and Songs for Refreshing Worship. London: Hymns Ancient & Modern (2013), c+847pp. Includes 'Brother, sister, let me serve you' by Richard Gillard, 'Come to a wedding,' 'For the music of creation,' 'God of freedom, God of justice,' 'Touch the earth lightly' and 'When human voices cannot sing,' by Shirley Murray, and tunes by Colin Gibson, Richard Gillard, Vernon Griffiths and Christopher Norton (4).

Asian Songs of Worship: CCA Hymnal Supplement III. Manila: Asian Institute for Liturgy and Music and World Council of Churches (1988), [unpaged]. Contains three hymn paraphrases and 'He came singing love' by Colin Gibson, two paraphrases by Shirley Murray and *Tama ngākau mārie*.

As One Voice for Kids. Manly Vale, NSW: Willow Connection and Adelaide: Openbook (2002), [unpaged]. Includes 'Touch the earth lightly' by Shirley Murray and Colin Gibson and 'And did you see him, little star,' by Helen Clyde and Colin Gibson.

Assembled for Song: An Anthology of New Hymns. Chicago: GIA (2011), 126pp. Includes 'Christ Jesus, in your name,' and 'Everything that has voice' by Shirley Murray.

The Australian Hymnbook. Blackburn: Victoria (1977), 679pp+xxxivpp. Includes 'Give praise and thanksgiving' adapted by Colin Gibson

The Australian Hymnbook with Catholic Supplement. Blackburn: Victoria (1977), 744pp+xxxiv. Includes 'Give praise and thanksgiving' adapted by Colin Gibson

Baptist Praise and Worship. Oxford: Oxford University Press/Psalms and Hymns Trust (1991), 1087pp. Includes 'The Servant Song' by Richard Gillard, 'God of Freedom' by Shirley Murray, DUNEDIN by Vernon Griffiths.

BBC Songs of Praise. Oxford: Oxford University Press/BBC Books (1997), 785pp. Includes 'The Servant Song' by Richard Gillard, and 'Star-child' by Shirley Murray.

The Book of Praise 1996. North York, Ontario: Presbyterian Church in Canada (1996). Includes 'The Servant Song' by Richard Gillard, and 'Give thanks for life' by Shirley Murray.

Cantos de Alabanza y Adoración (Songs of Praise and Worship). El Paso, Texas: Mundo Hispano (1997), 320pp. Includes 'Star-Child' by Shirley Murray.

C.C.A. Hymnal Supplement 1. Singapore: Christian Conference of Asia (1981), [unpaged]. Includes 'The God of us all is our Father' and 'Jesus the Lord stands with the poor' by Ron O'Grady, and 'Tell my people I love them' adapted, arranged with additional verses by Guy E. Jansen.

Celebrating Grace Hymnal for Baptist Worship. Macon, Georgia: Celebrating Grace (2010), 756pp. Includes 'The Servant Song' (two versions) by Richard Gillard, and 'Star-Child,' 'Come teach us,' 'Holy Presence, Holy teacher' and 'Take my Gifts' by Shirley Murray.

Celtic Hymnbook. Selected by Ray Simpson. Buxhall, Stowmarket: Kevin Mayhew (2005), [unpaged]. Includes 'Come and find the quiet centre,' God of freedom, God of justice,' and Touch the Earth Lightly' by Shirley Murray and Colin Gibson,

Chalice Hymnal. St Louis, Missouri: Chalice Press, 852pp. Includes 'The Servant Song' by Richard Gillard, 'The God of us all is our father' by Ron O'Grady, and 'Touch the earth lightly,' 'Loving Spirit,' 'Take my gifts,' 'Who is my mother,' 'Come and find the quiet centre,' 'Give thanks for life,' 'Community of Christ,' 'God of freedom, God of justice,' 'O God, we bear the imprint of your face' and 'Of women and of women's hopes we sing' by Shirley Murray, with two settings by Colin Gibson.

Children's Hymnbook of the United Church of Christ in Japan. Tokyo: (2003), 213pp. Includes 'With a hoot and a toot' by Colin Gibson, 'How is Jesus present' by Cecily Sheehy, and 'Small things count' by Shirley Murray and Jillian Bray.

Church Hymnary: Fourth Edition. Norwich: Canterbury Press. 825 hymns and doxologies. Includes hymns by Marnie Barrell (2), Richard Gillard, Colin Gibson (6), Shirley Murray (22) and Bill Wallace (2).

Come Celebrate! Pacific, Mo.: Cathedral Press (1990), [unpaged]. Includes 'In the presence of your people,' 'Let our praise to you be as incense' by Brent Chambers, 'Worthy the Lamb' and 'The Servant Song' by Richard Gillard.

Come, you People of the Promise: The Collected Hymns of Joy F. Patterson. Carol Stream, Ill.: Hope Publishing (1994), [unpaged]. 'To Christ, whose hands will bless' and 'I am standing waiting' by Shirley Murray.

Common Ground: A Song Book for All the Churches. Edinburgh: Saint Andrew Press (1998), 320pp. Includes hymns texts by Richard Gillard and Shirley Murray and settings by Richard Gillard and Colin Gibson.

Come, you People of the Promise: The Collected Hymns of Joy F. Patterson. Carol Stream, Ill: Hope Publishing (1994), [unpaged]. Includes settings of 'To Christ whose hands will bless' and 'I am standing waiting' by Shirley Murray.

Community of Christ Sings. Independence, Missouri: Community of Christ (2013), 864pp. Includes 'He came singing love' by Colin Gibson, 'We are pilgrims on a journey' by Richard Gillard, 'Between our thoughts,' 'Let this mind be in you,' 'Come let us dwell,' 'Why has God forsaken me?' by Bill Wallace, 31 hymns by Shirley Murray, and tunes by Barry Brinson, David Childs, Colin Gibson (3) and Christopher Norton.

The Covenant Hymnal: A Worship Book. Chicago: Covenant Publications (1996), 1045pp. Includes 'The Servant Song' by Richard Gillard, 'Loving Spirit,' 'To Christ whose hands will bless,' 'Here in the busy city,' 'I am standing waiting' by Shirley Murray and 'Why has God forsaken me' by Bill Wallace.

CPWI Hymnal, Church in the Province of the West Indies (Anglican (2010), xcii+1661pp. Includes 'The Servant Song' by Richard Gillard and 'God of Freedom' and 'Great God of earth and heaven' by Shirley Murray.

The Door is Open: Hymns and Tunes for Today's Church. Tunes by Carlton R. Young. Nashville: Abingdon Press (2002), 75pp. Includes 'Carol of Dreams,' 'Original Blessing,' 'More than we know' (Shirley Murray) and 'The Ho-hum Hymn' (Colin Gibson).

Drawn to the Wonder: Hymns and Songs from Churches Worldwide. London: Council for World Mission (1995), xxv+74pp. Includes 'He came singing love' by Colin Gibson,

'Loving Spirit' and 'Son of a peaceful heart' by Shirley Murray, and *Tama ngākau mārie*.

E.A.C.C. Hymnal. Tokyo: East Asia Christian Conference (1994), [unpaged]. Includes 'Father, Son and Spirit' *(Tama ngākau mārie)* and 'The sower's seed is swiftly sown' *(E te Atua)* paraphrased by D.T. Niles.

Each Breath, Every Heartbeat: New Hymns by Rusty Edwards. Nashville: Abingdon Press (2004), 62pp. Includes 'Come and find the quiet centre' and 'More than we know, God works within us' by Shirley Murray.

Evangelical Lutheran Worship. Minneapolis: Augsburg Fortress (2006), 1211pp. Includes 'The Servant Song' by Richard Gillard, 'Touch the earth lightly' by Shirley Murray and Colin Gibson, and 'Loving Spirit' and 'In the singing' by Shirley Murray.

Forward Together Songs. Melbourne: The Joint Board of Christian Education (1991), 15pp. Includes 'Hymn to Christ the Companion' by Colin Gibson.

Gather (Comprehensive Edition). Chicago: GIA Publications (1994), [unpaged]. Includes 'The Servant Song' by Richard Gillard.

Gather (Third Edition). Chicago: GIA Publications (2011), 1229pp. Includes 'The Servant Song' by Richard Gillard, and 'Dream a dream,' 'Star-Child,' 'Fresh as the morning,' 'Touch the earth lightly' and 'A Place at the table' by Shirley Murray.

Global Praise 1. Edited by S.T. Kimborough and Carlton R. Young, New York: United Methodist Church (1996). Includes 'Child of joy and peace' and 'When our lives know sudden shadow' by Shirley Murray.

Global Praise 2. Edited by S.T. Kimborough and Carlton R. Young, New York: United Methodist Church (1996). Includes 'For everyone born a place at the table,' 'In the singing' by Shirley Murray, 'Sound a mystic bamboo song' by Bill Wallace and *E toru ngā mea*.

Glory to God: The Presbyterian Hymnal. Louisville: Westminster John Knox Press (2013), vi+1018pp. Includes 'In the presence of your people,' by Brent Chambers, 'The Servant Song' by Richard Gillard, 'Son of God whose heart is peace' (*Tama ngākau mārie*) with nine other original hymns by Shirley Murray, 'Sound a mystic bamboo song' and 'Why has God forsaken me?' by Bill Wallace, and tunes by Colin Gibson and Christopher Norton.

God's Mission, God's Song. Joyce de Sohl. New York: The United Methodist Church (2006), 150pp. Includes 'Gentle God, when we are driven' by Shirley Murray and Jillian Bray, 'Every day I will offer you' by Shirley Murray and Colin Gibson, 'I am your mother,' 'God of our foremothers, make plain the vision' and 'Child of joy and peace' by Shirley Murray.

Grateful Praise: Hymns and Songs by Rusty Edwards. Kingston, New York: Selah (1998), [unpaged]. 'Dream a dream,' 'Wise men came journeying' and 'Forgive us, forgive us' by Shirley Murray.

Hymnal 21. Tokyo: United Church of Christ in Japan (2012), 1007pp. Includes 'For the man and for the woman' by Colin Gibson and DUNEDIN by Vernon Griffiths.

Hymnal: A Worship Book. Elgin, Illinois: Brethren Press (1992), 919pp. Includes 'The Servant Song' by Richard Gillard.

Hymnal of a Faith Journey. Quezon City, Philippines: United Church of Christ in the Philippines (2002), 482pp. Includes 'The Servant Song' by Richard Gillard, 'Spirit who broods' and 'Christ is our peace' by Shirley Murray and 'Sing praise to God for life' by Bill Wallace and Alison Carey.

The Hymnal of Nippon Sei Ko Kai (Anglican Episcopal Church of Japan): Tokyo (2008). Includes '*Tama ngākau mārie,*' 'In the name of Christ we gather' by Shirley Murray and DUNEDIN by Vernon Griffiths.

Hymns for Our Time: The Collected Hymn Tunes of Hal H. Hopson. Carol Stream: Il.: Hope Publishing (2009). Settings of 'Loving Spirit,' 'Take my gifts,' 'Through all the world' 'Forgive! Forgive us, Holy God,' 'Wounded world that cries for healing,' 'Song of faith that sings forever,' 'Creation sings,' 'Give thanks for life' and 'Teach us, O loving heart of Christ' by Shirley Murray.

Hymns for Today. Brian Wren. Louisville, Kentucky: Westminster John Knox Press (2009), 142pp. Includes 'Brother, Sister, let me serve you' by Richard Gillard, 'Come and find the quiet centre,' 'Loving Spirit,' 'O God, we bear the imprint of your face' and 'Touch the earth lightly' by Shirley Murray, and 'Why has God forsaken me?' by Bill Wallace.

Hymns for Worship. Grand Rapids: Calvin Institute for Christian Worship. Faith Alive Christian resources (2010), 340pp. 'For the music of creation' by Shirley Murray.

Hymns from the Four Winds: A Collection of Asian American Hymns. Nashville: Abingdon (1983), [unpaged]. Includes 'The God of us all is our Father' and 'Jesus the Lord stands with the poor' by Ron O'Grady and 'Why has God forsaken me?' by Bill Wallace.

Hymns of Heritage and Hope. Charlotte, N.C.: Advent Christian Conference (2001), 823pp. Includes 'The Servant Song' by Richard Gillard, 'Not on a snowy night' by Willow Macky, 'Come to a wedding,' 'To Christ, whose hands will bless,' 'Give thanks for life,' by Shirley Murray, and 'Now as we go' by Shirley Murray and Colin Gibson.

Hymns of Praise (revised edition). Hong Kong: Taosheng Publishing House (1994), 101pp. Includes 'Child of joy and peace' and 'Honour the earth' by Shirley Murray.

Hymns of Praise (New revised edition). Hong Kong: Chinese Christian Literature Council (2002), 976pp. Includes 'For the music of creation,' 'Church of the living Christ,' 'Stranger standing at my door,' 'Community of Christ,' 'Celebrate all human beauty,' 'O God, we bear the imprint of your face,' 'God weeps at love withheld' by Shirley Murray, 'The Spring has come' by Shirley Murray and Colin Gibson, 'Come now Lord Jesus' and 'Child of Joy and peace' by Shirley Murray and Douglas Mews.

Hymns of Universal Praise: Supplement. Hong Kong: Chinese Christian Literature Council (2002), 326pp. Includes 'For the music of creation,' 'Church of the living Christ' by Shirley Murray, 'Come now Lord Jesus,' 'Child of Joy and Peace' by Shirley Murray and Douglas Mews.

Hymns for Worship. Grand Rapids, Miss.: Calvin Institute of Christian Worship (2010), 340p. Includes 'For the music of creation' by Shirley Murray.

Hymns Old and New. 790 hymns. [unpaged]. Eastbourne: Kevin Mayhew (2004). Includes 'The Servant Song' by Richard Gillard, and DUNEDIN by Vernon Griffiths,

In our Own Voice: Hymns of Pullen Memorial Baptist Church. Raleigh, N.C.: Pullen Memorial Baptist Church (2009), 31pp. 'Includes 'Raise up new hope' by Shirley Murray.

In the Circle of faith: Worship Resource Book for the 2002 Asia Pacific Conference on Music and Worship. Ed. Lillibeth Nacion Puyot. Quezon City: Asian Institute for Liturgy and Music (2002), 72pp. Includes 'Repaying Force with Counterforce' and 'Mass of the Universe' by Bill Wallace.

Lambeth Praise. Harrisburg, Pennsylvania: Morehouse Publishing (1998). Includes 'God of freedom, God of justice' by Shirley Murray, 'He came singing love' by Colin Gibson, 'The Servant Song' by Richard Gillard and *Tama ngākau mārie*.

Lift up your Hearts: Songs for creative worship. Louisville, Kentucky: Geneva Press (1999), 208pp. Includes 'In the singing' by Shirley Murray.

Living Praise (Words Edition). Basingstoke: Marshall, Morgan & Scott (1983), [unpaged]. Includes 'I will give thanks to thee' by Brent Chambers.

The Lord's Supper: Choral Settings for Communion. Carol Stream, Illinois: Hope Publishing (2009), 69pp. Includes 'In the singing' by Shirley Murray.

Meet and Sing. New Market, England: Anglia Guides (1995), 88pp. Includes 'Upside down Christmas' by Shirley Murray and Colin Gibson.

Moravian Book of Worship. Bethlehem, Pennsylvania: Moravian Church in America (1995), 954pp. Includes 'He came singing love' by Colin Gibson and 'Loving Spirit' 'Touch the earth lightly' and 'When we lift our pack and go' by Shirley Murray and Ian Render.

More Voices. Toronto: United Church of Canada (2007), 288pp. Includes 'God in the darkness' (setting by Colin Gibson), 'God of the Bible,' 'Because you came,' 'God weeps,' 'Dream a dream' and 'Who is my mother' by Shirley Murray.

New Apostolic Church Hymnal. Zurich: New Apostolic Church (2008), 883pp. Includes 'And Jesus said' by Shirley Murray.

New Journeys Songbook (Music Edition). Melbourne: Joint Board of Christian Education (1991), 319pp. 176 hymns and songs, including texts and settings by John Aston, Patsy Burton, Brent Chambers (3), John Franklin, Colin Gibson (3), Barbara Gillard, Richard Gillard (2), Shirley Murray (4), Ian Render, Joy Ryan, Cecily Sheehy (8), John Smith (3), Jenny Thorne (2), Bill Wallace, Merv and Mera Watson (2) and Betty Wendelborn (5),

New Songs of Asian Cities. Tainan, Taiwan: East Asia Christian Conference (1972), iv+98pp. 62 hymns and songs, including two settings by Colin Gibson.

New Songs of Rejoicing. Kingston, New York: Selah (1994), 224pp. Includes 'Of women and of women's hopes' by Shirley Murray.

A Panorama of Christian Hymnody by Erik Routley, edited and expanded by Paul A Richardson. Chicago: GIA Publications (2005), 708pp. 982 hymns, including hymns by Marnie Barrell (2), Shirley Murray (8), Colin Gibson (4), Richard Gillard, Kathleen Mayson), Ron O'Grady (2) and Bill Wallace (4).

PCT Hymnal. Taipei: The Presbyterian Church in Taiwan (2009), 1205pp. Includes *Tama ngākau mārie, E toru ngā mea,* and texts and settings by Colin Gibson, Shirley Murray (2) and Ron O'Grady.

Praise Worship: New Songs for Worshiping Churches. Mobile, AL: Integrity Music (1987). 'Victory Song (Through our God)' by Dale Garratt.

The Presbyterian Hymnal: Hymns, Psalms and Spiritual Songs. Louisville: Westminster John Knox Press (1990), 716pp. Includes 'Why has God forsaken me?' by Bill Wallace and 'Because you live, O Christ,' 'Loving Spirit,' 'O God, we bear the imprint of your face,' 'Now to your table spread,' and 'Give thanks for life' by Shirley Murray.

Puls: Y's Men's Sangbog. Frederiksberg, Sweden: Unitas (2009), [unpaged]. Includes 'Star-Child' by Shirley Murray.

Renewing Worship Songbook. Minneapolis: Augsburg Fortress (2003), 253pp. Includes 'The Servant Song' by Richard Gillard, 'Touch the earth lightly' by Shirley Murray and Colin Gibson, and 'A Place at the table' by Shirley Murray.

Rejoice and Sing. Oxford: Oxford University Press (1991), 1171pp. Includes 'The Servant Song' by Richard Gillard, 'Loving Spirit' and 'God of freedom' by Shirley Murray.

Report of the 1987 Asian Workshop on Liturgy and Music. Manila: Asian Institute for Liturgy and Music (1987). 'He came singing love' by Colin Gibson and *Tama ngākau mārie*.

Resoundings! New Hymn Tunes by Perry Nelson. Schiller Park, Ill: World Library Publications (1998), 47pp. Includes 'Loving Spirit' by Shirley Murray.

Ritual Song: A Hymnal and Service Book for Roman Catholics (Choir Edition). Chicago: GIA Publications (1996), [unpaged]. Includes 'The Servant Song' by Richard Gillard.

Seeing Christ in Others: An Anthology for Worship, Meditation and Mission, ed. Geoffrey Duncan. Norwich: Canterbury Press (1998), 356pp. Includes 'Because You came,' 'Celebrate all Human Beauty,' 'Every Day I will offer You' and 'The Justice Tree has bloomed' by Shirley Murray.

Shepherd Songs. Kingston, New York: Selah (2002). Includes 'Christ Jesus, in your name' by Shirley Murray.

Sing Alleluia: More Hymns to sing with One Voice (Harmony Edition). London: Collins Liturgical Publications (1987), 247pp. 126 hymns and liturgical pieces, including hymn texts and settings by Brent Chambers, Helen Clyde, Colin Gibson, Richard Gillard, Vernon Griffiths and Shirley Murray.

Sing a New Song. Melbourne: Methodist Federal Board of Education (1970), iv+67pp [unpaged]. 67 hymns, including hymn texts and settings by Colin Gibson (5), Iris McCoy, Jim Cropp and Wallace Woodley.

Sing for Peace. Independence, Miss.: Temple Worship Centre (1994), [unpaged]. Includes 'Gentle God, when we are driven,' 'How happy you who work for peace,' 'I am standing waiting' and 'O Christ, who by a cross' by Shirley Murray.

Singing the Faith. London: Hymns Ancient & Modern (2011), [unpaged]. 839 hymns and psalms. Includes 'The Servant Song' by Richard Gillard, 11 hymns by Shirley Murray and two hymns by Bill Wallace.

Singing Peace. Geneva: World Council of Churches (2011), 119pp. 'Let the earth be peaceful' by Shirley Murray and 'Nothing is lost on the breath of God' by Colin Gibson.

Sing Justice! Do Justice! A Collection of New Hymns and Songs to New and Familiar Tunes. Kingston, NY: Selah Publishing (1998), 48pp. Includes 'Dream a dream' and 'For everyone born a place at the table' by Shirley Murray (text), the tune by Colin Gibson (See review by Sue Mitchell-Wallace in The *Hymn: A Journal of Congregational Song*, 52.1 (April 2000), 47).

Sing Praise: Hymns and Songs for refreshing Worship. London: Hymns Ancient & Modern and the RSCM (2010), xxvi+287pp [unpaged]. Includes 'We do not hope to ease our minds' by Marnie Barrell, 'Brother, sister, let me serve you' by Richard Gillard, and 'When human voices cannot sing.' 'In the name of Christ we gather,' 'God of freedom, God of justice' and 'For the music of creation' by Shirley Murray.

Sing! Prayer and Praise. Cleveland: Pilgrim Press (2009), 262pp. Includes 'God weeps,' 'Star-Child' and 'Who is my mother' by Shirley Murray.

Sing the Faith. Louisville, Kentucky: Geneva Press (2003), [unpaged]. Includes 'Brother, sister' let me serve you' by Richard Gillard, 'Come and find the quiet centre,' 'Earth prayer,' 'For our great peace,' 'God weeps,' 'I am your mother,' 'In the singing,' 'Star-child,' 'This thread I weave,' 'Who is my mother' and 'Wounded world that cries for healing' by Shirley Murray.

Sing the Journey: Hymnal: A Worship Book Supplement I. Scottdale, Pennsylvania: Faith & Life Resources (2005), iv+174pp. Includes 'God of the bible,' 'Give thanks for life' and 'Loving spirit' by Shirley Murray,

Sing the Story: Hymnal: A Worship Book Supplement II. Scottdale, Pennsylvania: Faith & Life Resources (2007), iv+208pp. Includes 'Here to the House of God we come' by Shirley Murray and Colin Gibson, 'Gentle God, when we are driven' by Shirley

Murray and Jillian Bray, 'Nothing is lost on the breath of God' by Colin Gibson

Songs for the People of God 4 (revised edition). Adelaide: Pilgrim Church (1996), 102pp [unpaged]. 101 and liturgical pieces, including 'Take my gifts' by Shirley Murray and Colin Gibson.

Songs for Worship. Melbourne: The Joint Board of Christian Education for Australia and New Zealand (1968), vii+72pp [unpaged]. Contains texts and settings by Helen Clyde, Jim Cropp, Colin Gibson (4), Len Harwood (2), Iris McCoy, Frank Nichol, Mervyn Rosser (2).

Songs of Faith. Melbourne: The Joint Board of Christian Education for Australia and New Zealand (1962), ii+93pp [unpaged]. Contains two texts and settings by Colin Gibson.

Songs of Rejoicing. Kingston, New York: Selah (2011), 364pp. Includes 'Great and deep the Spirit's purpose' by Marnie Barrell and 'O beauty ever ancient' by Shirley Murray and 'Easter Chant, O threefold God of tender unity' and 'Why has God forsaken me' by Bill Wallace, with settings by Barry Brinson, Judith Thornley and Bill Wallace.

Songs of Our People: A Collection of Songs from Asia and South Pacific. Hongkong: Asia Alliance of YMCAs (1987), 59pp. Includes 'Christ is our peace,' 'Peace has a price,' by Shirley Murray, 'Our Task' by Allison O'Grady and 'For the man and for the woman' by Colin Gibson.

Sound the Bamboo: CCA Hymnal 1990. Manila: Christian Conference of Asia and AILM (1990), 442pp. 'Although a man, yes, Mary's son,' 'Why has God forsaken me,' 'In nature as in Jesus,' 'Deep in the human heart,' 'Sing praise to God for life,' 'Why has God forsaken me' by Bill Wallace; 'The God of us all,' 'Living in Christ with people' by Ron O'Grady'; 'Child of Christmas story,' 'Honour the earth,' 'Loving Spirit,' 'Child of joy and peace,' 'Christ is our peace,' 'The grain is ripe,' 'Song to the Spirit,' 'Come to this Christmas singing' by Shirley Murray, Douglas Mews, and Colin Gibson; 'Upside-down Christmas' and 'Sing to celebrate the city' by Shirley Murray and Colin Gibson; 'For the man and for the woman,' 'He came singing love' by Colin Gibson; 'Tell my people, I love them' by Jan Harrington and Guy E. Jansen; and *Tama ngākau mārie*.

Supplement 96. Carol Stream, Ill.: Hope Publishing (1999), 224pp. Includes hymns or settings by Jillian Bray (2), Colin Gibson (5) and Shirley Murray (13).

Supplement 99. Carol Stream, Ill.: Hope Publishing (1999), 224pp. Includes hymns or settings by Jillian Bray (2), Colin Gibson (3), Peter Godfrey (1), and Shirley Murray (17).

Synghap: Sanger og bonner fra den verdensvide kirke. Oslo: IKO (2006), 202pp. Includes 'Star-child' and 'I am your mother' by Shirley Murray, and *E toru ngā mea*.

Thuma Mina: Internationales Okumenisches Liederbuch. Basle and Munich: Basileia and Strube 1995), 432pp. Includes 'Deep in the human heart' (Bill Wallace), *Tama ngākau mārie* and 'The God of us all' (Ron O'Grady).

Together in Song: Australian Hymn Book II. Melbourne: HarperCollins (1999), 1114pp. Includes 'Loving Spirit (FELICITY) and 'Touch the earth lightly' (TENDERNESS) by Shirley Murray and Colin Gibson and 'Community of Christ,' 'God of Freedom, God of Justice,' 'When human voices cannot sing' by Shirley Murray, 'Brother, sister, let me serve you' by Richard Gillard and 'Sing praise and thanksgiving' by Colin Gibson.

Total Praise: Songs and Other Worship Resources for Every Generation. Chicago: GIA Publications (2011), [unpaged]. Includes 'Star-Child' by Shirley Murray.

Unidentified modern Japanese children's hymn book. Includes hymns by Colin Gibson 'With a hoot and a toot,' Cecily Sheehy 'How is Jesus present?' and Shirley Murray and Jillian Bray 'Small things count.'

Upper Room Worshipbook: Music and Liturgies for Spiritual Formation. Nashville: Upper Room Books (2006), 467pp. Includes 'The Servant Song' by Richard Gillard, 'Sound a mystic bamboo sound' by Bill Wallace and 'For the music of creation,' 'Give thanks for life,' 'Touch the earth lightly' and 'Loving Spirit' by Shirley Murray.

Voices United. Etobicoke, Ontario: United Church of Canada (1996), 1078pp. Includes 'The Servant Song' by Richard Gillard, 'He came singing love,' 'God is the One whom we seek together,' 'Lord of all love' by Colin Gibson, 'Because you live, O Christ,' 'The Spring has come,' 'Sing a happy hallelujah.' 'Touch the earth lightly,' 'Christ, let us come with you' by Shirley Murray and Colin Gibson, 'Small things count' by Shirley Murray and Jillian Bray, 'Come and find the quiet centre,' 'Loving Spirit' 'Now to your table spread,' 'For the music of creation,' 'God freedom,' 'Give thanks for life' by Shirley Murray.

Voices Found. New York: Church Publishing (2003), 277pp. Includes 'The Servant Song' by Richard Gillard, 'Litany for Sisters of the Christ,' 'The grain is ripe,' Star-child, earth-child,' 'Loving Spirit,' 'One small child Jesus called,' 'God of all time, all seasons of our living,' 'God freedom, God of justice,' 'In the name of Christ we gather,' and 'Sing to celebrate the city' by Shirley Murray with a setting by Colin Gibson.

Will You Come and Follow Me: Resources for Corporate Worship and private devotion considering Faith, Vocation and Learning, in support of Samford in Mission. Ed Paul A Richardson. Birmingham, Al.: Samford University (2007), unpaged. Includes 'Wisdom far beyond our knowledge,' 'May the anger of Christ be mine' and 'He came singing love' by Colin Gibson, and 'Holy Presence, holy teacher,' 'Come teach us, Spirit of our God,' 'God of our every day,' 'Come and find the quiet centre,' 'Go gently, go lightly' and 'This thread I weave' by Shirley Murray.

With One Voice: A Hymn Book for all the Churches with New Zealand Supplement. London and Auckland: Collins (1982), lxii+800pp. Includes 27 hymns by New Zealand and Pacific authors and composers.

With One Voice: A Lutheran Resource for Worship. Minneapolis: Augsburg Fortress (1995), 288pp. Includes 'In the presence of your people' by Brent Chambers, DUNEDIN by Vernon Griffiths and 'Loving Spirit' by Shirley Murray.

Wonder, Love and Praise: A Supplement to the Hymnal 1982. New York: Church Publishing (1997), 262pp. Includes 'Loving Spirit' and 'Give thanks for life' by Shirley Murray, 'O threefold God of tender unity' by Bill Wallace, and DUNEDIN by Vernon Griffiths.

Worship (Fourth edition). Chicago: GIA Publications (2011), [unpaged]. Includes DUNEDIN (Vernon Griffiths), 'Touch the earth lightly' by Shirley Murray and Colin Gibson, and 'Everything that has voice' and 'Let's praise the Creator' by Shirley Murray.

Worship & Rejoice. Carol Stream, Ill.: Hope Publishing (2001). Includes 'The Servant Song' by Richard Gillard, 'Touch the earth lightly' and 'Christ, let us come with you' by Shirley Murray and Colin Gibson, 'He came singing love' by Colin Gibson, and 'Loving Spirit,' 'Star-Child,' 'Because you live,' 'Come and find the quiet centre,' 'Come to a wedding,' 'Give thanks for life,' 'God of all time,' 'A Place at the Table,' 'And Jesus said,' 'For the Music of Creation' and 'Little One, born to bring' by Shirley Murray.

Worship & Song. Nashville: Abingdon Press (2011), [unpaged]. Includes 'Creation sings,' 'God of the Bible,' 'O Christ you hang upon a cross' (setting by Colin Gibson), 'Let the earth be peaceful' by Shirley Murray.

Worship: Called to Prophesy, Reconcile and Heal. Kuala Lumpur: Christian Conference of Asia (2010), 88pp. Includes 'Gentle God, when we are driven,' 'Out of strange, unlikely places,' 'Jesus, saviour, Spirit, sun' by Shirley Murray, 'Let justice roll down like a river,' 'He came singing love' by Colin Gibson and 'Yes, as the clay in the potter's hand' by Cecily Sheehy.

Worship in the City: Prayers and Songs for Urban Settings. Comp. Nancy E. Hardy. Toronto: United Church Publishing House (2015). Includes 'Sing to celebrate the city' by Shirley Murray.

Worship Together. Fresno, Cal.: Mennonite Brethren Churches (1995), 773pp. Includes 'The Servant Song' by Richard Gillard and 'Come to a Wedding,' 'When human voices cannot sing' and 'Gentle God, when we are driven' by Shirley Murray.

Wort Laute: Liederheft zum Evangelischen Gesangbuch. Cologne: German Evangelical Church (2007), 127pp. Includes 'Love is your way,' and 'Honour the earth' by Shirley Murray and Douglas Mews.

The Yes of the Heart: Faith, Hope and Love Songs by Rusty Edwards. Carol Stream, Ill.: Hope Publishing (1993), 65pp. Includes 'Loving Spirit' by Shirley Murray.

Zion still Sings for Every Generation. Nashville, Tenn.: Abingdon Press (2007), 239pp. Includes 'Star-Child,' 'God weeps' and 'Who is my mother' by Shirley Murray.

2B – In Individual Author Collections

Every Day in Your Spirit: New Hymns written between 1992 and 1996. Shirley Erena Murray. Carol Stream, ill.: Hope Publishing (1996), [unpaged]. 41 hymn texts by the author, with settings by Jillian Bray (4), Colin Gibson (6), Vernon Griffiths (1) and David Dell (1).

Faith Makes the Song: New Hymns written between 1997 and 2002. Shirley Erena Murray. Carol Stream, ill.: Hope Publishing (2003), [unpaged]. 50 hymn texts by the author, with settings by Jillian Bray (4), Nigel Eastgate (1), Colin Gibson (4), Peter Godfrey (1), and Jenny Mcleod (6).

A Greener Place to Grow: 50 More Hymn Texts, Adam M.L. Tice. Chicago: GIA Publications (2011). Includes four settings by Colin Gibson.

In Every Corner Sing: The Hymns of Shirley Erena Murray. Shirley Erena Murray. Carol Stream, ill.: Hope Publishing (1992), [unpaged]. 85 hymn texts by the author, with settings by Jillian Bray (3), Nigel Eastgate (3), Colin Gibson (26), Douglas Mews (4) and Ian Render 91).

Life into Life: New and Collected Hymns. Shirley Murray. Carol Stream, ill.: Hope Publishing (2019), [unpaged]. 70 texts by the author, with settings by Jillian Bray (8), Vivien Chiu (1), Colin Gibson (6), and Douglas Mews (1).

Love's Open Door: Hymns and Songs 2004-2008. Brian Wren. London: Stainer & Bell and Carol Stream, Illinois: Hope Publishing (2009). Includes six settings by Colin Gibson.

The Mystery Telling II: Hymns and Songs for the New Millennium. William L Wallace. Pittsburgh: Selah Publishing Company (2008), 22pp [unpaged]. 14 hymns and songs by Bill Wallace; settings and harmonisations by Barry Brinson, David Child, Francis Dennis and Graham Hollobon.

Pieces of our Lives. Jim and Jean Strathdee. Carmichael, California: Desert Flower Music (1998). Settings of 'Every day,' 'This Thread I weave' and 'God weeps at love withheld' by Shirley Murray.

A Place at the Table: New Hymns written between 2009 and 2013. Shirley Erena Murray. Carol Stream, Ill.: Hope Publishing (2013), 163pp. 47 hymn texts by the author, with settings by Jillian Bray (8), Colin Gibson (3) and Shona Murray (1).

Pulse and Breath: 50 More Hymn texts by Adam M.L. Tice. Chicago: GIA (2009). Includes one setting by Colin Gibson.

Reading the Signature: New Hymns and Songs by Colin Gibson. Carol Stream, Ill.: Hope

Publishing (1994), 56pp. 29 hymns; words and music by the author.

Sing for peace: The Hymns of Shirley Erena Murray set to the Tunes of Jane Marshall and Carlton Young. Nashville: Abingdon Press (2004), 75pp.

Singing the Sacred: A Collection of Psalms, Hymns and Spiritual Songs. William L Wallace. Franklin Park, Il. World Library Publications (2011).

Something to Sing About: Hymns and Reflections in Search of a Contemporary Spirituality. Bill Wallace. Melbourne: Joint Board of Christian Education of Australia and New Zealand (1981). 27 hymn texts by the author and one setting each by Dorothy Buchanan and Bill Wallace.

Songs for a Rainbow people: New hymns and Songs by Colin Gibson. Carol Stream, Il: Hope Publishing (1998), 32pp. 33 hymns; words and music by the author.

Stand for What is Right. Jim and Jean Strathdee. Carmichael, California: Desert Flower Music (2006), [unpaged]. Includes 'I am standing waiting,' 'Summer sun or winter skies,' 'Make spaces for Spirit' and 'Sing a Happy Alleluia' by Shirley Murray.

Touch the earth Lightly: New Hymns written between 2003 and 2008. Shirley Erena Murray. Carol Stream, Ill.: Hope Publishing (2008), 171pp. 60 hymn texts by the author, with settings by Jillian Bray (8), Barry Brinson (4), Colin Gibson (8) and Charles Naylor (1).

2C – Single Hymns and Hymn Tunes

Christ our Hope. Brian Wren. Carol Stream, Illinois: Hope Publishing (2004). 39 hymns, includes OAKHURST SESSION, by Colin Gibson.

Complete Anglican Hymns Old and New. Stowmarket, Suffolk: Kevin Mayhew (2000). 920 hymns and songs. Includes DUNEDIN by Vernon Griffiths.

Each Breath, Every Heartbeat: New Hymns by Rusty Edwards. Nashville: Abingdon Press (2004), 58pp. Preface and 'Come and find the quiet centre,' 'More than we know' by Shirley Murray.

'For the Music of Creation,' Shirley Murray. Music by Larry Harris. Illinois: Hope Publishing (1998).

'For the Music of Creation,' Shirley Murray. Music by Sally Ann Morris. Chicago: GIA Publications (1992)

'For the Music of Creation' (Shirley Erena Murray). The *Hymn: A Journal of Congregational Song,* 49.3 (July 1998), 503.

God in your Grace transform the World. San Fernando, Trinidad: St Andrews Theological College (2006), 54pp. 'God in your Grace transform the World' by Shirley Murray.

Grateful Praise: Hymns and Songs by Rusty Edwards. Accord, New York: Selah (1998). Unpaged. Includes settings of 'Dream a dream,' 'Forgive us,' and 'Wise men came journeying' by Shirley Murray.

'The God of us all,' Ron O'Grady. *Jesus Christ the Life of the World: A Worship Book for the Sixth Assembly of the World Council of Churches.* Geneva: World Council of Churches (1983), 151.

A Handful of Light: A Companion for Advent, Christmas and New Year. Edited by Lynda Patterson and Craufurd Murray. Christchurch: Theology House (2008). Includes 'Carol for a Hard Winter' by Colin Gibson.

Hymns for Our Time: The Collected Hymn Tunes of Hal H. Hopson. Carol Stream, Ill.: Hope Publishing (2009), [unpaged]. Includes settings for 'Loving Spirit,' 'Take my gifts,' 'Through all the world,' 'We light a candle for life,' 'Forgive, forgive us holy God,' 'Wounded world that cries for healing,' 'Song of faith that sings forever,' 'Creation sings' and 'Give thanks for life' by Shirley Murray.

Let the Peoples Sing vol 3. An International Christmastide: Advent, Christmas, Epiphany. Ed. Marian Dolan. Minneapolis: Augsburg Fortress (2005), includes 'Peace child by Shirley Murray and Colin Gibson, 6-7.

'Made in God's Image: Two new Hymns on healing Sexual Identity,' Robert Bayley. *Reformed Worship* 91 number 24 (March 2009), 30-32. Two hymn texts by Robert Bayley, 'O God, who made us in your image,' 'Fan into flame, Lord, creation's sixth day.'

Merrily at Christmas: A Book of Christmas Songs and Poems for Children. Nunawading, Australia: Nursing Mothers Association of Australia (1986). Includes 'And did you see him, little star' by Helen Clyde and Colin Gibson.

Spirit Anew: Singing Prayer & Praise, ed. Alan C. Whitmore. Kelonia, British Columbia: Woodlake Books, [unpaged]. Includes 'The Spring has come' by Shirley Murray and Colin Gibson.

Te Harinui (Tay-Ha(h)-ree-noo-ee): A New Zealand Christmas Carol Arranged for Two Parts, Willow Macky. London: Chappell (1959), 2pp.

Touching the Altar: The Old Testament for Christian Worship. Edited by Carol M. Bechtel. Grand Rapids and Cambridge, England: W.B. Eerdmans (2008), 211pp. Includes 'Touch the earth lightly' by Shirley Murray.

With One Voice: A Lutheran Resource for Worship. Minneapolis: Augsburg Fortress (1995), 288pp. Includes 'Loving Spirit' by Shirley Murray.

Appendix — 2
Writing About New Zealand Hymns and Hymn writers

Books

A Bibliography of Writings about New Zealand Music published to the End of 1983. D.R. Harvey. Wellington: Victoria University Press (1985), 222pp. (Items 1930-1939.)

A Brief History of Christian Music from Biblical Times to the Present. Andrew Wilson-Dickson. Oxford: Lion Publishing (1997). (Chapter 39: Christian Music in Australasia.)

A Companion to Sing Alleluia. Wesley Milgate. Sydney: The Australian Hymn Book Company (2000), 164pp. (Colin Gibson, Richard Gillard, Vernon Griffiths, Shirley Murray.)

A Companion to Rejoice and Sing. Norwich: Canterbury Press (1999), 1289pp. (Richard Gillard, Shirley Murray.)

A Companion to Together in Song: Australian Hymn Book II. Wesley Milgate and D'Arcy Wood. Sydney: The Australian Hymn Book (2006), 862pp. (Brent Chambers, Colin Gibson, Richard Gillard, Vernon Griffiths, Bonnie Low, Douglas Mews, Shirley Murray, Christopher Norton.)

A Biographical Dictionary of New Zealand Composers. John Mansfield Thomson. Wellington: Victoria University Press (1990), 168pp. (Gerard Crotty, Ronald Dellow, Vernon Griffiths, Jenny McLeod, Richard Madden, Douglas Mews, Christopher Norton.)

Gather into One: Praying and Singing Globally, C. Michael Hawn. Grand Rapids: William B. Eerdmans (2003), 308pp. (Shirley Murray.)

Hymnal Companion prepared by Churches in the Believers Church Tradition. Joan Fyock and Lani Wright. Elgin, Il.: Brethren Press (1996). (Richard Gillard.)

Hymnal Companion to Evangelical Lutheran Worship. Paul Westermeyer. Minneapolis: Augsburg Fortress (2010), 944pp. (Colin Gibson, Richard Gillard, Shirley Murray.)

Hymnal Companion to Sound the Bamboo: Asian Hymns in Their Cultural and Liturgical Contexts. I-to Loh. Chicago: GIA Publications (2011), 616pp. (Colin Gibson, Janet Gibbs, Richard Gillard, *Tama ngākau marie*, Shirley Murray, Ron O'Grady, Bill Wallace.)

Hymns for Today, Brian Wren. Louisville: Westminster John Knox Press (2009), 142pp. (Richard Gillard, Shirley Murray.)

Joy in the Singing: The Choral Commitment of St Paul's Cathedral Choir, Dunedin, New Zealand 1859-1989, Raymond White. Dunedin: Musick Fyne (1989), 148pp. (Richard Madden.)

Music Ministry. Mike and Viv Hibbert. Christchurch: Mike and Viv Hibbert (1982), 84pp.

The Oxford History of New Zealand Music, John Mansfield Thomson. Auckland: Oxford University Press (1991), 315pp.

A Panorama of Christian Hymnody, Erik Routley, edited and expanded by Paul A. Richardson. Chicago: GIA Publications (2005), 708pp. (Marnie Barrell, Colin Gibson, Richard Gillard,

New Zealand hymn writing, Ron O'Grady, Shirley Murray, Bill Wallace.)

Sing New Zealand: The Story of Choral Music in Aotearoa. Guy E. Jansen. Auckland: Massey University Press (2019), 384pp.

Songs of the People of God: A Companion to the Australian Hymn Book/With One Voice. Wesley Milgate. London: The Australian Hymn Book (1982), 364pp. (Colin Gibson.)

Sunday Best: How the Church Shaped New Zealand and New Zealand Shaped the Church. Peter Lineham. Auckland: Massey University Press (2017), 463pp. (Chapter 4: The Music and Words of Faith).

Theology in Aotearoa New Zealand: An Annotated Bibliography under Subject Headings. Neil Darragh, 2007 ('an amended and updated version of an earlier 2002 article, "Contextual Theology in Aotearoa New Zealand." *Asian Christian Theologies: a research guide to authors, movements, sources.* J.C. England *et al.* Maryknoll, New York, ISPCK/Claretian Publishers/Orbis Books (2002) volume 1: 541-598)

This is Our Song: Women's Hymn-Writing. Edited by Janet Wootton. London: Epworth Press (2010), 379pp. (Shirley Erena Murray.)

Wonder Reborn: Creating Sermons on Hymns, Music and Poetry, Thomas H. Troeger. New York: Oxford University Press (2010), 208pp. (Colin Gibson.)

Articles and Reviews

'60 Hymns, Carols and Songs for a Public Theology,' John Thornley. *Music in the Air: Song and Spirituality*, (Summer/Autumn 2010), 18-19.

'*Alleluia Aotearoa: Hymns and Songs for All Churches*,' a review by Margaret Clarkson. The *Hymn: A Journal of Congregational Song*, 45.1 (January 1994) 44-45.

'*Alleluia Aotearoa*: Why I Like It,' a review *by* Hilary Revfeim. *Music in the Air: Song and Spirituality*, (Winter 1998), 7-9.

'All will be well,' William (Bill) Wallace. *Word & Worship*, 4.3 (Winter 2006) 24-6.

'Always there's a Carol,' [Colin Gibson]. *Word & Worship*, 4.3 (Summer 2005/06), 23-6.

'Be opened, my soul,' Colin Gibson. *Word & Worship*, 6.3 (Winter 2008) 257-8.

'Bill Wallace: Hymns of a prophetic Mystic,' Terry Wall. *Music in the Air: Song and Spirituality*, (Summer/Autumn 2015), 2-9.

'Blessed Assurance: Beyond Fanny Crosby,' Shirley Erena Murray. *The Hymn: A Journal of Congregational Song*, 60.4 (Autumn 2009), 10-15.

'Bless all the dear children in thy tender care,' Colin Gibson. *Word & Worship*, 14.2 (Autumn 2016) 13-15.

'Bones in search of flesh: a worship-song writer reflects,' Karel Van Helden-Stevens. *Stimulus*, 9.4 (November 2001) 7-8.

'Bonfire Praise,' Joan Lees. *Word & Worship*, 2.4 (Spring 2004), 29-30.

Bringing in a New world,' Colin Gibson. *Word & Worship*, 14.1 (Summer 2015-16) 21-3.

'Building Jerusalem: New Zealand Hymns on Social Issues,' Colin Gibson. *Music in the Air: Song and Spirituality*, (Winter/Spring 2011) 6-16.

'Building Jerusalem: New Zealand Hymns on Social Issues,' Colin Gibson. *Tui Motu Interislands*, (July 2012), 12-13.

'Carol our Christmas,' Colin Gibson. *Word & Worship*, 6.2 (Spring 2007) 22-4.

'The catching of values,' John Thornley. *Sound Ideas: The Church and Music Education* 4.2 (January 2001) 6-15.

'Choosing Hymns for a New Century: The Dunedin Methodist Experience,' Evan Lewis. *Music in the Air: Song and Spirituality*, (Winter 1996), 10-13.

'Chris Skinner, Priest and Songwriter of Aotearoa,' Lisa Beech. *Music in the Air: Song and Spirituality*, (Winter 1996), 17-22.

'Christians are all kinds of people,' Stan Stewart. *Word & Worship*, 5.3, (Winter 2007), 25-67.

'Colin Gibson: Hymn writer Extraordinaire,' John Murray. *Music in the Air: Song and Spirituality*, (Summer 1998), 21-25.

'Company of Clowns and Cripples: Personal Confession about Writing Hymn Texts,' Shirley Murray. *Music in the Air: Song and Spirituality*, (Summer 1996), 16-19.

'Contemporary New Zealand Church Music: An Interview with Dianne Halliday,' Maureen Geering. *The Bulletin of the Church Service Society*, (29 April 1999), 5-9

'Drafting Pens, Compass Points and Westerlies,' Bill Bennett. *Music in the Air: Song and Spirituality*, (Summer 1998), 10-13.

'Easter City,' Colin Gibson. *Word & Worship*, 5.2, (Autumn 2007), 23-7.

'Easter City: "For the crowd another busy day", a Hymn for Easter,' Colin Gibson. *Music in the Air: Song and Spirituality*, (Winter 2006), 30.

'Finding a Voice Down-Under: The Story of a Developing Hymnody in Australian and New Zealand,' Colin Gibson. *Music in the Air: Song and Spirituality*, (Winter/Spring 2008), 5-15. Also reprinted in *The Bulletin of the Hymn Society of Great Britain and Ireland*, 19.3 (July 2009), 1-74.

'The Folksong of the Church,' Shirley Erena Murray. *Candour: A Magazine for Ministers*, 2 (March 2004), 10-11; *Music in the Air: Song and Spirituality*, (Summer/Autumn 2009), 29-30; *Word & Worship*, 2.3, (Winter 2004), 3-8.

'The Folly of Love,' Colin Gibson. *Word & Worship*, 1.1, (Summer 2002), 19-21.

'"For everyone born, a place at the table", Hospitality and Justice in the Hymns of Shirley Erena Murray,' Deborah Carlton Loftis. *Music in the Air: Song and Spirituality*, (Winter 2004), 17-21.

'For Everyone Born, a Place at the Table,' Lauren Hall, *The Hymn*, 6.3 (Summer 2012) 42-4.

'For the blast of creation,' Colin Gibson. *Word & Worship*, 11.3, (Winter 2013), 24-6.

'Friend in Christ,' Colin Gibson. *Word & Worship*, 3.4, (Spring 2005), 28-9.

'The Gift of Music,' Colin Gibson. *Music in the Air: Song and Spirituality*, (Winter/Spring 2012), 2-4.

'God, come now to explore my heart,' Marnie Barrell. *Word & Worship*, 8.2, (Autumn 2010), 24-6.

'God dancing in the rain,' Joy Cowley. *Word & Worship*, 6.2, (Autumn 2008), 24-5.

'God of our every day,' Shirley Murray. *Word & Worship*, 11.1, (Spring 2012), 23-4.

'Gradual Praise by Bill Bennett,' a review by Colin Gibson. *Music in the Air: Song and Spirituality*, (Winter/Spring 2011), 619-20.

'The Greening of Hymnody, Part 1: "Touch the earth lightly,"' William L. Wallace. *The Hymn: A Journal of Congregational Song*, 60.1 (Winter 2009), 24-26.

'The Greening of Hymnody? Touching the Earth Lightly through Congregational Song,' David Buley. *The Hymn: A Journal of Congregational Song*, 60.1 (Winter 2009), 27-28.

'The Greening of Hymnody, Part 2: "Charge our Hearts with Wonder,"' William L. Wallace. *The Hymn: A Journal of Congregational Song*, 60.2 (Spring 2009), 43-45.

'The Greening of Hymnody, Part 3: "Come join the Cosmic Family,"' William L. Wallace. *The Hymn: A Journal of Congregational Song*, 60.3 (Summer 2009), 24-25.

'The Greening of Hymnody, Part 4: Greening the Eucharist,' William L. Wallace. *The Hymn: A Journal of Congregational Song*, 60.4 (Autumn 2009), 47-49.

'God who sets us on a Journey: The Life, Liturgy and Hymns of Joy Dine,' Mervyn Dine. *Music in the Air: Song and Spirituality*, (Winter 2003), 7-11.

'Happy 10th Birthday to *Alleluia Aotearoa*: Messages of Appreciation from New Zealand, Australia, Scotland and USA.' *Music in the Air: Song and Spirituality*, (Winter 2003), 2-7.

'"The heart is greater than the head": Gospel songs, Christian belief and practice,' Brian Gilling. *Stimulus* 9.4 (November 2001) 9-26.

'Here in the busy city,' Shirley Murray and Barry Brinson. *Word & Worship*, 9.2, (Autumn 2011), 24-6.

'"His Songs were a Thousand and Five": The Waiata of Canon Wiremu Wi te Tau Huata, 1917-1991, Ngāti Kahungunu, Anglican Priest, Military Chaplain and Songwriter,' Richard Spence. *Music in the Air: Song and Spirituality*, (Winter 2002), 20-24.

'Hope is our Song,' review by Linda Cowan. *Word & Worship*, 8.1, (Summer 2009/10), 21-6.

'Hope is our Song,' review by Catherine Macdonald. *Candour: A Magazine for Ministers*, (October 2010), 15; reprinted *Music in the Air*, Summer/Autumn, 2011, 34-5.

'Hope is Our Song CD,' review by Maureen Smith. *Tui Motu Interislands*, May 2011, 28.

'Hope is Our Song CD,' review by Stuart Grant. *Candour: A Magazine for Ministers*, (May 2011), 10-11.

'How does hymnody influence worship?,' Janet Sim Elder. *Candour: A Magazine for Ministers*, number 2 (July 2008), 15-18

'A Hymnbook for the Churches in New Zealand,' John Murray. *The Bulletin of the Church Service Society*, (28 September 1979), 3-4.

'A Hymn for Anzac Day,' Shirley Erena Murray. *Word & Worship*, 4.2, (Autumn 2006), 24-7.

'Hymn for Anzac Day,' Shirley Erena Murray. *Music in the Air: Song and Spirituality*, (Winter/Spring 2007), 2.

'Hymn Interpretations: Carols for grown-ups – "All over Creation,"' Shirley Erena Murray. *The Hymn: A Journal of Congregational Song*, 58.2 (Autumn 2007), 49-51.

'Hymns for All Seasons: Jocelyn Marshall,' a review by Peg Riley. *Music in the Air: Song and Spirituality*, (Winter/Spring 2007), 19.

'Hymns for Sunday Morning: A Religious Expression in a Secular Society,' Maureen Garing. *Music in the Air: Song and Spirituality*, (Summer 1996), 20-23.

'Hymns of Shirley Erena Murray, Part I: Notes for an Incarnational Theology: "My community has grown as the Church has shrunk,"' John Thornley. *Music in the Air: Song and Spirituality*, (Winter 2004), 3-9

'Hymns of Shirley Erena Murray, Part II: "Down to Earth" – Hymns for Sunday Worship,"' John Thornley. *Music in the Air: Song and Spirituality*, (Winter 2004), 31-3.

'Hymn writer stresses the power of words,' Amanda Wells. *Spanz* 41, (December 2009), 16 (Shirley Erena Murray.)

'*In Every Corner Sing* (by Shirley Erena Murray),' review by Edith B. Card. *The Hymn: A Journal of Congregational Song*, 45.2 (April 1994), 50-51.

'In Recognition of Distinguished services to Church Music: Shirley Erena Murray FRSCM,' John Murray, *Music in the Air: Song and Spirituality* 22 (Winter 2006), 35.

'In the singing,' Shirley Erena Murray. *Word & Worship*, 1.4, (Spring 2003), 24-5.

'I've never seen an elephant,' Colin Gibson. *Word & Worship*, (September 2002), 15-17.

'Jean Andrewes, Kerikeri Composer: Hymns and Musicals for Church Folk,' Joy Bolkey. *Music in the Air: Song and Spirituality*, (Winter 2000), 23-29.

'Jumping Jesus,' Colin Gibson. *Refresh: A Journal of Contemplative Spirituality*, Encountering Jesus, 7.1 (Winter 2007), 4-5.

'Knocking on Heaven's Door: Rock Music and Redemption,' Mike Riddell. *Music in the Air: Song and Spirituality*, (Winter 1996), 23-27.

'Kyrie Eleison,' (Colin Gibson). *Word & Worship*, 3.1, (Autumn 2005), 20-3.

'Let Metaphor speak: hymns as subversive text,' Jane Simpson. *Women-Church* 33, (Spring 2003), 16-42.

'Let my Spirit always Sing,' Catherine Russ and Shirley Murray. *Music in the Air: Song and Spirituality*, (Winter 1999), 32-33.

'Let the Number Eight Wire Sing,' John Thornley. *Music in the Air: Song and Spirituality*, (Summer/Autumn 2015), 26-35.

'"Lift high the Cross": Reflecting on "good words" with Shirley Erena Murray,' John Thornley. *Music in the Air: Song and Spirituality*, (Summer 2005), 25-27.

'Lift up your voices,' Marnie Barrell. *Taonga*, (Advent 2015), number 50, 26-7.

'Look with the eyes of love,' Colin Gibson. *Word & Worship*, 14.3 (Winter 2016) 20-3.

'Love's Feast for All to Share: Hymns for an Inclusive Sexuality,' Colin Gibson. *Music in the Air: Song and Spirituality*, (Summer 2004), 22-25.

'Martha and her Music: Reflections on Feminism and Music,' Faith Williamson. *Music in the Air: Song and Spirituality*, (Summer 2001), 2-7.

'Music at Mass – Keep it simple!,' Cecily Sheehy. *Tui Motu Interislands* (June 1998), 23-24.

'Music in Prayer and Worship,' Colin Gibson. *Tui Motu Interislands* (June 1998), 20-21.

'Music in the Air,' review by Gavin Drew. *Stimulus*, 4.1 (February 1996) 42-43

'Music in the Air,' review by Phil Bettany. *Candour: A Magazine for Ministers,* number 2 (March 2004) 14

My Musico-Autobiography,' Greg Hughson. *Music in the Air: Song and Spirituality*, (Summer 1997), 2-7.

'Natalie Yeoman Yule: Singer/Songwriter from Mosgiel,' John Thornley and Natalie Yule. *Music in the Air: Song and Spirituality*, (Winter 2003), 25-32.

'"New Creation": Theology in the Hymns of Colin Gibson,' Terry Wall. *Music in the Air: Song and Spirituality*, (Summer 2003), 25-28.

'New hymnbook [*Hope is our Song*] wins praise,' review by Catherine McDonald. *Candour: A Magazine for Ministers,* number 9 (October 2010) 15.

'New Wine Old Bottles,' Rob Ferguson. *Music in the Air: Song and Spirituality*, (Summer 1997), 25-28.

'New Words to Old Tunes,' Mary Pearson and Audrey Dickinson. *Music in the Air: Song and Spirituality*, (Winter 2002), 11.

'New Zealand Hymnbook,' L.J. Reid. *The Bulletin of the Church Service Society*, (23 October 1982), 1-5

'New Zealand Hymnbook Trust: A Short History,' John Murray. *Music in the Air: Song and Spirituality*, (Summer 1999), 2-6.

'New Zealand Hymnbook Trust: an Introduction,' John Thornley. *Stimulus* 8.4 (November 2000) 21-24.

'New Zealand Hymns of the very highest Standard' [review of *Hope is our Song*], Charles Cooper. *Tui Motu Interislands*, (March 2010), 28.

'The New Zealand Landscape in our Hymns,' Colin Gibson. *Music in the Air: Song and Spirituality*, (Winter 1998), 10-13.

'Nothing, nothing in all creation,' Shirley Murray. *Word & Worship*, 9.3, (Winter 2011), 24.

'Nothing is lost,' Colin Gibson. *Word & Worship*, (June 2002), 17-19.

'"Now where did that come from?": Colin Gibson talks about the origin of some of his hymns,' Colin Gibson. *Music in the Air: Song and Spirituality*, (Summer 2005), 8-12.

'On writing a hymn for Anzac Day,' Shirley Murray. Kāpiti Coast: *Kapiti Independent News*, (25 April 2014).

'Open your eyes, open your ears: an Easter meditation,' (Colin Gibson). *Word & Worship*, 2.2, (Autumn 2004), 25-8.

'Peace Child,' [Colin Gibson]. *Word & Worship*, 3.1, (Summer 2004-5), 24-7.

'Peace Child,' Colin Gibson. *Word & Worship*, 18.1 (Summer 2019-20), 14-16.

'People, Pathways and Power: Reflections on a Bicultural Journey,' Jenny McLeod. *Music in the Air: Song and Spirituality*, (Winter 1996), 2-9.

'"Praise the Spirit": the Hymns, Carols and Songs of Colin Gibson.' Helene Mann. *Music in the Air: Song and Spirituality*, (Winter 2001), 2-9.

'*Reading the Signature*' (Colin Gibson), review by Dolores Hruby. *The Hymn: A Journal of Congregational Song*, 47.1 (January 1996), 63.

'Review of *Hope is our Song*: New Hymns and Songs from Aotearoa New Zealand,' Geoff King. *Music in the Air: Song and Spirituality*, (Summer/Autumn 2010), 18-19.

'Review of Music in the Air,' Richard Lawrence. *Candour: A Magazine for Ministers*, 6.3 (1996), 13

'A savour of songs: the place of hymns in New Zealand worship,' Colin Gibson. *Stimulus* 9.4 (November 2001), 30-33.

'See the bursting: A springtime carol,' Colin Gibson. *Word & Worship*, 14.4, (Spring 2016), 20-22.

'"Shall we have a shot at this?": Working with Shirley Murray,' Colin Gibson. *Music in the Air: Song and Spirituality*, (Summer 2000), 2-5.

'"Simply Different": Manurewa Methodist Hymnwriting,' Audrey Dickinson. *Music in the Air: Song and Spirituality*, (Winter 2002), 15-19.

'Simply to be,' Shirley Murray. *Word & Worship*, 5.4, (Spring 2007), 26.

'Sing for Peace: The Hymns of Shirley Erena Murray Set to the Tunes of Jane Marshall and Carleton R. Young,' review by Mary Louise Bringle. *The Hymn: A Journal of Congregational Song*, 56.2 (Spring 2005), 64.

'Singing a Public Theology of Peace, Justice and Creation,' Clive Pearson *Music in the Air: Song and Spirituality*, (Summer/Autumn 2010), 24-32.

'A Singing Faith,' Jocelyn Marshall. *Music in the Air: Song and Spirituality*, (Winter 2000), 13-18.

'Singing the Sacred (Bill Wallace),' review by Philip Baldwin, *Anglican Life* 17, (February/March 2012), reprinted in *Tui Motu Interislands*, (May 2012), 12-13.

'Singing the Sacred,' review by Terry Wall, *Touchstone* (March 2012), 13.

'Snap us out of it, Lord' (The Ho-Hum Hymn),' by Colin Gibson. *Word & Worship*, 9.4, (Spring 2011), 25-6.

'Some Goals in Church Music for New Zealand Presbyterians,' J.M. Bates. *The Bulletin of the Church Service Society*, (18 May 1988), 8-12

'A Song and a Sermon,' Colin Gibson and Bruce Scamell. *Music in the Air: Song and Spirituality*, (Winter 2000), 2-7.

'Songs and Poems for Peace, Justice, Creation,' John Thornley. *Candour: A Magazine for Ministers*, number 9 (October 2009), 11-12.

'Songs of Justice: The New Zealand Tradition,' Colin Gibson. *Music in the Air: Song and Spirituality*, (Summer/Autumn 2010), 2-10.

'Songs of the incarnation: An Introduction to the Hymns of Marnie Barrell,' Terry Wall. *Music in the Air: Song and Spirituality*, (Winter/Spring 2015), 2-7.

'Songs of the Spirit for a Twenty-first Century Faith Journey: New Zealand Hymn Writers respond,' John Thornley. In *Why Weren't We Told? A Handbook on 'Progressive Spirituality*, compiled and edited by Rex A.E. Hunt and John W.H. Smith. Salem, Oregon, Polebridge Press (2013), 196-202. (Shirley Murray, Colin Gibson and Bill Bennett.)

'"Sound a Mystic Bamboo Song": Sounds and Images of Christ in Asian Hymns,' I-toh Loh. *The Hymn: A Journal of Congregational Song*, 64.1 (Winter 2013), 19-27.

'Sounds of Grace 2004,' review by Roy Tankersley. *Music in the Air: Song and Spirituality*, (Summer 2005), 34.

'So What's New?,' Colin Gibson. *Candour: A Magazine for Ministers*, number 2 (March 2004), 3

'Te Harinui: New Zealand's first Christmas Service,' Patricia Bawden and John Thornley, Music in the Air 24 (Winter/Spring 2007), 28-33.

'Theology off the Wall,' Brian Smith. *Stimulus* 9.4 (November 2001), 2-6.

'*Together in Song*: An Ecumenical Si(g)n?,' review by Sarah Mitchell. *The Ecumenical Review*, 53.3 (July 2002), 353-368. See further the review of this article by Anne Bagnall Yardley in The *Hymn: A Journal of Congregational Song*, 54.3 (July 2003), 30.

'Thank you, Shirley and John,' Colin Gibson. *Music in the Air: Song and Spirituality*, (Summer 2004), 2.

'Theology in the Hymns and Carols of Shirley Erena Murray,' Helene Mann. *Music in the Air: Song and Spirituality*, (Summer 2000), 6-13.

'This is our faith,' Marnie Barrell. *Word & Worship*, 7.2, (Winter 2009), 23-6.

This is our Song: Women's Hymn Writing, edited Janet Wootton. London: Epworth Press, (2010). 'Shirley Erena Murray' (by Shirley Erena Murray) pp195-307.

'Three faiths, one carol,' Shirley Murray. *Word & Worship*, 7.1, (Summer 2008/09), 20-3.

'To sing the Gospel: *A Place at the Table* by Shirley Erena Murray,' review by Cecily Sheehy and Gavin Rennie. *Tui Motu Interislands*. (March 2014), 28

'*Touch the Earth Lightly: Hymns 2003-2008* (Shirley Erena Murray),' review by Robin Knowles Wallace. The *Hymn: A Journal of Congregational Song*, 60.3 (Summer 2009), 51.

'Tradition and change in church music,' Simon Tipping. *Stimulus* 9.4 (November 2001), 21-26.

'Tussocks Dancing: Hymns and Songs by Jane Simpson, sung by Poiema Voices,' review by Jenny Boyack. *Music in the Air: Song and Spirituality*, (Summer 2003), 35.

'Tussocks Dancing: the story from divine encounter to CD,' Jane Simpson. *Stimulus* 10.4 (November 2002), 26-29.

'Willow Macky: Balladeer for a New Country,' interview by Robin Nathan, Music in New Zealand 26 (Spring 1944) 37-43.

'When angels rove the restless skies,' Colin Gibson. *Word & Worship*, 11.1 (Summer 2012), 24-6.

'When evenings shorten,' Shirley Smith. *Word & Worship*, 11.2, (Autumn 2013), 25-6.

'When human voices cannot sing': A Hymn for a Funeral Liturgy (by Shirley

Erena Murray),' Bernadette Gasslein and Gordon Johnston. *The Hymn: A Journal of Congregational Song*, 50.2 (April 1999), 43-44.

'When is a Hymn Contemporary?,' William (Bill) L. Wallace. *Music in the Air: Song and Spirituality*, (Winter 2002), 25-33.

'When our lives know sudden shadow,' Shirley Erena Murray. *The Hymn: A Journal of Congregational Song*, 58.2 (Spring 2007), 48-50.

'Where are the Voices for the Earth?' Colin Gibson. *Word & Worship*, 19.2, (2021), 14-16.

'Where is the room?,' David Bell and Shirley Murray. *Word & Worship*, 2.1, (Summer 2003-4), 26-8.

'Where mountains rise to open skies,' Shirley Erena Murray. *The Hymn: A Journal of Congregational Song*, 58.1 (Winter 2007), 51-54.

'"Who is my mother?": Origins and Biblical Sources of a Hymn,' Shirley Erena Murray. *Music in the Air: Song and Spirituality*, (Summer 2007), 7-9.

'Will you offer me compassion,' Shirley Erena Murray. *The Hymn: A Journal of Congregational Song*, 58.3 (Summer 2007), 46-47.

'With One Voice,' John Murray. *The Bulletin of the Church Service Society*, (31 March 1982), 12

Theses

Anglican Church Music in Canterbury, 1850-1900. C.P. Bornet. MA, University of Canterbury, 1973.

A History of Music in Dunedin to 1925. Ethel Margaret Campbell Pearson. MA (Hons), University of Otago, 1941

The History of School Music in New Zealand, Guy E. Jansen. MA, Victoria University of Wellington, 1966.

How Shall We Sing the Lord's Song in a Strange Land? Robert (Rob) Ferguson. MA, Massey University, 1989

An Exploration of the Similarities and Differences between the Works of Two Welsh Methodist Hymn-writers and those of Two Contemporary Hymn-writers in Aotearoa New Zealand, with Special Reference to Celtic Characteristics. Helene Vicary Mann. MA, University of Wales, Lampeter, 2000

Appendix — 3
The New Zealand Hymnbook Trust

The following survey of the history of the New Zealand Hymnbook Trust is the work of its two long-term chairmen to date, The Reverend Dr John Murray (1979-2000) and John Thornley (2000-14). John Murray's contribution is an edited version of his article 'New Zealand Hymnbook Trust: A Short History,' published in Music in the Air: Song and Spirituality, (Summer 1999), 2-6. See also John Thornley's 'New Zealand Hymnbook Trust: An Introduction,' Stimulus 8.4 (November 2000) 21-24.

Part One: 1979-2000

Broodings of a Sixties Dreamer

When I realised that it was taking me as long, or longer, to choose the hymns as to prepare the sermon each Sunday, I knew something had to be done about it. Where was I – and surely a multitude of ministers – to find words to sing that would be relevant to the late 1960s, let alone the next millennium?

What we all needed were new hymns, in new words, for a world of social protest, theological revolution, ecumenical encounter, and bicultural community, and in a language both inclusive and indigenous.

Ah, but where to find them?

It was in the early 1970s, while minister of Knox Church, Christchurch, that I got together with a small group of musicians and put the question – where can we find a new hymnbook? At Knox, some of us had already put together a 'Worship Book,' having already passed through several editions and revisions. You remember the Medical Mission Sisters, Taizé songs, Fred Kaan, Sydney Carter, Geoffrey Ainger and others? But these were all, gladly, borrowed from outside our country. What of our own?

As I remember, four of us gathered: Guy Jansen, Roy Tankersley, Wallace Woodley, each of eminent ability in church music, and myself. We had a few meetings to explore the possibility of a new hymnbook, and then I was off to Wellington, to a new appointment to St Andrew's on the Terrace. I was soon followed to Wellington by Guy Jansen.

The idea of a new hymnbook lay restless in me for a little while, and I began to look for ways to forward the concept. I put it to my friend, Cliff Reed, then managing director of Reed Books, who was helpful but not enthusiastic.

I then put a proposal to the Joint Commission on Church Union for their backing. Surely they would see this idea as a God-given way of promoting ecumenical worship, and so the goal of church union itself? They were very friendly, listened to me, as some sort of diversion, it seemed to me, from the real work of creeds and statements of faith. They thanked me, wished me well, and moved on to the next item of business.

Where was I to turn? It seemed a stalemate.

A Publisher as the Angel Gabriel

But, one afternoon, as I sat at my desk, my 'New Hymnbook' file gathering dust beside me, the phone rang, and an English voice said, 'I'm Geoff Chapman of Collins Liturgical. I'm in Wellington seeing the Catholics about a new prayer book. I hear you are interested in publishing a hymnbook for New Zealand. I've got an hour to spare, so can I come and see you?' You can imagine how I felt! An answer to prayer?

Actually, it happened this way: I had been in tentative touch with the Australian Hymnbook Committee, who were in process of putting together a grand, comprehensive ecumenical hymnbook to serve their progress towards church union. I had visited a Presbyterian member of that committee, C.L. Fouvy, and somehow the names of New Zealand and John Murray got passed on to Geoff Chapman.

So into my modest vestry bounced the cigar-smoking boss of Collins Liturgical. I was overwhelmed by this entrepreneur, but seized the opportunity as an act of faith. The question of what sort of hymnbook for New Zealand took new directions.

New Zealand, without the support of the Churches – a situation I had seen as a real loss at the time, but later came to realise was an act of deliverance for us, as I saw more of the Australian process of protracted negotiations among the Churches – could not possibly publish a new hymnbook as a business venture, comprehensive of all centuries and denominational traditions. It would be beyond our resources and our market.

The alternative presented to me by Chapman was to 'piggy-back' on the Australian Hymn Book (AHB), and maybe add a supplement of our own, as in Australia the Catholics were to add their supplement.

Our Supplement to *With One Voice*

We got to it, Guy Jansen, Roy Tankersley – now my organist and Musical Director at St Andrew's, and myself, and set up the New Zealand Hymnbook Trust. Alan Woodley, the Methodist Connexional Secretary, began laboriously to prepare a constitution. Five churches – Anglican, Baptist, Associated Churches of Christ, Methodist and Presbyterian – willingly, but offering no funding, became the foundation members of the Trust as an incorporated body. Their chief national executives, Bill Best, Jenny Cotterell (replacing her husband), Stan Edgar, Alan Woodley and D'Arcy Woolf were the trustees.

We could now get down to business.

About this time, in 1979, we set up our first Editorial Committee. They were: Jillian Bray, Rob Elder, Tony Georgantis, Colin Gibson, Jock Hosking, Guy Jansen, Shona Murray, Lester Reid, Roger Williams, and D'Arcy Woolf, with myself as chairman. We were all nominated by our Churches. Professor Colin Gibson acted as words editor and Guy Jansen as music editor.

We worked on preparing 'our supplement' as an addendum to the *Australian Hymn Book*. It was the only way to get started. We decided on three principles of selection: to be contemporary, to be ecumenical, and to be 'multicultural.' Though we wanted to emphasize New Zealand writers and composers, this did not eventuate – except for Colin Gibson's 'He Came Singing Love' (which had been a prize-winner in a TVNZ programme, 'Sing a New Song,' produced by John Terris in 1974), Helen Clyde's 'And Did You See Him, Little Star?,' Shirley Murray's 'Come Now, Lord Jesus,' and Gibson's 'Where the Road Runs Out.'

However, a real breakthrough came with the inclusion of 20 hymns in Māori and Pacific Island languages. These were not contemporary, but well-known and often-sung hymns in those churches, and so, for the first time, Pākehā – that is, European and Pacific Islands – worshippers could share in multi-cultural services.

Sing Praise, a Catholic hymnbook edited by Father Charles Cooper, was published with some Māori hymns about this time, but for use only in the Catholic Church. It should be noted that, during this period, I had made several approaches to the Catholic Bishops' Conference inviting them to join the Trust, but on each occasion this was declined.

For the selection of Māori and Pacific Island hymns, a number of clergy in various churches were approached, and the top favourites from their lists were chosen for *With One Voice*. The question of translation into English was solved by providing a literal and non-singable translation, interlined with the original words. Those who helped me prepare these English translations were Tawhao Tioke, Setu Masina, Lagi Sipeli and Jim Kiriau.

As for the English-language hymns included, they were quite a hotch-potch, certainly not all contemporary, and some we called 'gap-fillers,' hymns we felt should have been included, but had been left out by the Australian Hymnbook Committee.

Indeed, the Australians were somewhat suspicious of our abilities in adding to their book! To overcome their anxieties and to draw up a mutual contract with Collins Liturgical, their two top people, Canon Lawrence Bartlett and Professor Wesley Milgate, were brought to Wellington, and over one Anzac holiday we were able to allay their fears and enter into a joint venture here in New Zealand.

When *With One Voice*, plus its New Zealand Supplement, was released in New Zealand in 1982, Collins Liturgical made a killing. Tens of thousands of copies were sold because most of our churches were using hymnbooks dating from the 1920s, and we were all longing for something modern.

It's interesting to note that nowadays *With One Voice*, though about 20 percent of its hymns were written in this century, seems out-of-date. But, at the time, and for the next decade, it opened up a whole new range of songs and became widely acceptable.

All this brought to the Editorial Committee a tremendous sense of achievement, a great load of exhaustion and very little money! Out of the hundreds of thousands of dollars from New Zealand sales of *With One Voice*, the Trust earned only between $5,000 and $6,000.

We had bridged the gap between the old denominational British hymnals and a modern ecumenical hymnbook. But we wanted to do more. We wanted to produce a really authentic New Zealand collection.

1993: *Alleluia Aotearoa*

So was born, in 1993, after a long gestation over two decades since those first meetings, *Alleluia Aotearoa*.

Some changes were necessary in order to proceed. First, some of us wanted to choose our own Editorial Board members rather than take the nominations of the churches. The Trust member churches were not very obviously interested in the work of the Trust, evidenced by the few who bothered to turn up at our annual meetings. And we wanted to broaden the range of talent on the Board. So we chose a new group: Jillian Bray, Colin Gibson, Guy Jansen, Douglas Mews senior, Shirley Murray, Sister Cecily Sheehy, for a short while William Southgate, later to be replaced by Ian Render, and myself. This proved to be an excellent, talented and broadly ecumenical team. As work progressed, we enjoyed working with each other and did so to great effect. And we were independent of the Churches!

Second, we wanted to revive the project of a totally New Zealand collection. New Zealand had been becoming a 'nest of hymning birds,' known worldwide for songs and choruses by such people as David and Dale Garrett, Brent Chambers and Richard Gillard, and more recently, by authors and composers such as Colin Gibson, Shirley Murray and Douglas Mews senior. Now we felt was the time to publish 'our own book' in every sense, and leave comprehensive hymnbooks to the Australians, who were already working on a revision of their 1977 *Australian Hymn Book*, to be published in 1999 as *Together in Song: Australian Hymnbook II*.

Third, we wanted to concentrate on hymns for today's world in today's language and imagery and not relapse into traditionalism. 'Inclusive' became the key guideline.

Fourth, we wanted to broaden the inclusion of hymns in languages other than English and so be more representative of our church society. On this point, I admit that we have mostly failed. We failed to find new hymns as distinct from translations of earlier missionary hymns. This remains a goal we still hope to achieve but, as far as we can find, even today, there are few if any new hymns being produced in these languages. In 1987, some five years after the publication of *With One Voice*, we were ready to begin making real our dream.

The Dream Comes True

At the beginning we had little money and that was spent in bringing together the editors, from Auckland and Dunedin to Wellington, on infrequent occasions. However, thanks to the generosity of the Methodist Church of New Zealand – Te Hahi Weteriana O Aotearoa, and a grant of $15,000 through the Prince Albert College Fund, the future of our work was secured. Other smaller donations and loans, including $5,000 from the Alfred and Isobel and Marian Reed Trust, made the dream possible.

We called for contributors through church papers, and a steady stream of offerings were received, several hundred in fact. As we met to consider and sing all of these – a mammoth task of great labour and, sometimes, moments of discovery – we found that many were so wedded to past styles of theology and music that they eliminated themselves.

Then we would find what we considered to be writers and composers of real talent and promise, such as, to mention only a few, Marnie Barrell, David Dell, Nigel Eastgate, Radha Wardrop, John Weir and Gerard Crotty. All our editors proved to be producing excellent material in words and music as well. So good were they, that, at one of our last editorial selection meetings, I challenged all of them, except myself as neither writer or composer, to go away and compose an 'acclamation' on the words 'Alleluia Aotearoa'!

These words had now become the title of our book in the making, thus linking the traditional sung cry of the faith – the word 'Alleluia' comes from the Hebrew 'halaluyah,' meaning 'praise ye Jehovah' – with the indigenous name for our own country in which we express our praise to God!

With regard to the format of *Alleluia Aotearoa*, after we had decided on the superb artwork of the cover, we settled two further details. One was that, for ease of use in the hand as well as on the piano or organ holder, the book should be spiral-bound. Very few hymnbooks had used this format but its advantages need no explanation. And the other was that it should be arranged alphabetically rather than in traditional sections. This annoyed traditional clergy and musicians who complained and had to be pointed to the more than adequate theme indexes!

When it came to layout, we found that in order not to have to turn the pages of any hymn, there would have to be empty pages. How annoying these are to accompanists! Out of this came the inspirational idea of 'fillers.' The Lord's Prayer in seven New Zealand languages and a couple of poems by no less a writer than Joy Cowley were inserted to enhance the book.

The process of compiling a hymnbook, even a comparatively small one of only 163 songs, is always more exhilarating and tedious than is expected. *Alleluia Aotearoa* was no exception.

As months turned to years, people began to clamour, 'Where is your book?' And so we decided to do another 'new thing' and prepare a cassette of some of the songs before the book was published. That was in 1992. In those days, Radio New Zealand was a creative body with recording facilities. So, together with Gavin McGinley, National Programme Manager, we contracted to record 22 of the songs. This proved to be a wonderful appetiser for our waiting market.

Among other by-products of the tape was the chance to get our best-known New Zealand churchman, Archbishop Paul Reeves, to write our Foreword, while running through the streets of New York with his Walkman: 'The issue for those who compose sacred songs, hymns, (call them what you will) is to match the energy and vibrancy of the world and give us something real to sing. *Alleluia Aotearoa* does that…for years we have lacked a good hymnbook…the banal has tended to triumph over the worthwhile. There is no reason why this should continue. I commend *Alleluia Aotearoa* as a very significant contribution.'

And the Churches now think this too. Already, five years after publication, *Alleluia Aotearoa* is well into its second reprint and continues to sell steadily. It sells well in Australia too, and its songs may be heard even in the USA, Canada and Britain. With *Alleluia Aotearoa* the Trust became in every way independent and able to make its own future. (Since that time, *Alleluia Aotearoa* has become the Trust's most successful publication, with nine reprintings and sales of over 9,500 copies.)

1996: The Birth of *Carol our Christmas*

The Editorial Board was still restless. The restlessness was centred on the celebration of our main annual festival in which church and community join forces – Christmas.

This had been the easiest and the hardest time of the year for clergy to choose appropriate carols. Easiest because everyone wants to sing again 'Silent Night, Holy Night' and 'Once in Royal David's City'; but you can't sing 'In the Bleak Mid-Winter' and celebrate Christ's birth in our summertime. Already in *Alleluia Aotearoa* there had been printed a handful of New Zealand, carols, including that first of all New Zealand carols, 'Te Harinui' by Willow Macky, from way back in the 1950s. But surely we could expand to something more!

Shirley Murray's words and Colin Gibson's music to 'Carol our Christmas/An Upside Down Christmas,' published in *Alleluia Aotearoa,* had caught on and was being more and more sung. So, taking these opening words, a new book was born to the Trust in 1996. It has 52 authentic New Zealand carols for us to sing in our churches, our schools, our end-of-the-year parties and concerts.

Again it was the same editorial team, now with the addition of former editor, Shona Murray, but alas, without the jovial and learned presence of Professor Douglas Mews, who had died in 1993 – though two of his very singable tunes are included. We who worked with him came to love and treasure him and his innately religious and musical spirit.

Again we called for contributions, many of which as before were in fact imitations of traditional carols with an added sprig of pohutukawa or the chime of a bellbird. But again there were also 'finds,' including work by Bill Bennett, Jocelyn and Christopher Marshall, Jackie Wise and Mark Wilson, as well as by the editors themselves. And, to fill the gaps, we chose six poems by Joy Cowley, Shirley Murray, Peter Cape and Eileen Duggan. *Carol our Christmas* is the first ever book of New Zealand carols for all churches and for all who want to sing Christmas here in a southern sunny summer season.

Following the success of the *Alleluia Aotearoa* cassette, the editors decided on a recording of 24 carols, this time, in the march of electronic media, in both cassette and CD format. The release of the recording in 1997, to accompany the book, has been yet a further illustration of the Trust's creative work – and arguably one of its brightest lights.

This has opened the book to many more people, as we listen to Christmas in a woolshed, on a beach, at a time for picking cherries, or sing a four-part Gloria with the angels, in English, Latin and Māori!

Joy Cowley, in her introduction to this book writes, 'For this country and its people, the prevailing symbol of the Christmas season is not snow but light. The star that heralds the Christ child in our midst is the sun, and even the sound of its name is symbolic blessing… in this volume of New Zealand carols…not only do the words and the music here reflect Christmas in Aotearoa, they offer us a wide experience of music and rejoicing.'

We have achieved what had been our goal since the Trust was set up 20 years ago, and our vision, a decade before that.

The Trust, and in particular the Editorial Board, after the success – and the labour – of our three books, which have changed the voice of singing in our churches and wider even than here in New Zealand, have now become an experienced team with much to offer. Forgotten are the days when no-one wanted to own us. A New Zealand hymnody, contemporary, ecumenical, indigenous, is now a unique fact and something to be proud of.

Recently, one of the Editors was invited to speak at a world ecumenical conference on music and liturgy in Asia. She recalls how proud she was to represent the only country of the many attending, which had produced three uniquely indigenous books of worship, *Alleluia Aotearoa, Carol our Christmas*, and the third, *A New Zealand Prayer Book of the Anglican Church*.

End of Story?

Not really! It's one of those never-ending stories. Recently, the Trust has been able to set aside $10,000 as an Endowment Fund in honour of our own writer/composer, Professor Colin Gibson, for students wanting to write or research hymns in New Zealand. And, with the millennium approaching, we are planning a new project, *Songs 2000* (published in 2000 as *Faith Forever Singing*) providing new hymns and songs for congregational singing, 'small songs,' refrains, responses – all to help us sing our faith and hope in a new and very different century.

We look forward to finding new insights and inspiration, and to be able to sing in English and Māori and the languages of the Pacific Island communities, and maybe of Asia too.

We know that the opportunity is there, and that we are here to take it!

Part Two: 2000-2014

The Editor briefly takes up the tale.

2000: *Faith Forever Singing*

In 1998, under the chairmanship of John Murray, a re-assembled Editorial Board began work on a further collection of New Zealand hymns to celebrate the dawn of the second Christian Millennium. The Board was a mixture of former and new members: Jillian Bray, Charles Cooper, Colin Gibson, Ian Render, Shirley Murray, Shona Murray and Cecily Sheehy brought their previous experience of preparing earlier hymnbooks. They were joined by Wellington Methodist minister Craig Forbes and commenced sifting through several hundred submitted hymns, a process which included a rigorous Queen's Birthday weekend 'Sing Hui' at Wallis House, Wellington. The Editorial Board were encouraged to provide a range of 'small songs' and the chairman led the way by offering several short liturgical texts to be set for singing. The model for these pieces was *The Wee Worship Book* from the Iona Community, which had been recently published (1999) and was already in circulation among some of the New Zealand churches.

In the event, *Faith Forever Singing* was published in May 2000, heralded by a TV One/Praise Be video of a number of the hymns, and accompanied by a CD of 27 items recorded by Wellington choirs. The hymnbook, in the by now well-established ring-bound format, contained 80 hymns and songs, most them by New Zealanders, though Shirley Murray's increasing international status brought in settings by American composers Rusty Edwards, Jim Strathdee and Carlton Young. Following a practice established in *Alleluia Aotearoa* of including some religious poems, in this book were included psalm-poems by Joy Cowley and poetry by James K. Baxter and Shirley Murray. The preface was written by the then Governor-General of New Zealand, Sir Michael Hardie-Boys. The focus was firmly on the future: in his foreword John Murray described the collection as 'a compendium of song for all Christians and seekers, as we travel new roads, find God in new forms, realise the relevance of Jesus in new places, and are blown by the Spirit into the new future.'

2002: *He Came Singing Peace*

Murray was convinced that some of the material being published by the Trust needed to reach a new generation of singers through exposure in schools rather than in churches. And 2002, declared by the World Council of Churches to be the start of a Decade to Overcome Violence and by the United Nations the beginning of an international Decade for a Culture of Peace and of Non-violence for the Children of the World, provided such an opportunity.

The result was the publication in 2002 of *He Came Singing Peace: Songs to Overcome Violence*, a booklet distributed free to schools and similar institutions, containing 27 hymn and songs texts on the theme of peace and non-violence, selected from *Alleluia Aotearoa*, *Carol Our Christmas* and *Faith Forever Singing*. Four of the items were accompanied by their musical settings.

Now John Thornley, next co-chairman of the Trust with his wife Gillian Thornley, resumes the story.

Handover to New Co-Management

On Tuesday, 4 November 2003, a truckload of hymn books and CD recordings, along with assorted files and cardboard cartons, pulled in to the back of 15 Oriana Place, Highbury, Palmerston North, the home of John and Gillian Thornley, the new Management Team for the New Zealand Hymnbook Trust. The load was uplifted and moved into its new residence, in rooms on the second floor for the archival and on-going records, and the rear of the garage for books and CD stocks.

I attended my first AGM of the Trust on 4 September 2003, held in the vestry at Wesley Church, Taranaki Street, Wellington, later venue for all subsequent AGMs we have attended. Gillian and I would serve as 'Co-Managers' for the Trust, bringing different and complementary skills to the role. These were clearly set out at the 2004 AGM, as recorded in the Minutes: 'Role division: Gillian handles all accounts/finances, which includes preparation of annual accounts for auditing prior to AGM, payment of GST, and attending to royalty payments. John attends to sales, promotion and oversight of editorial or new products. Both share in the following tasks: periodic stocktaking, protection of copyright, decisions about reprints.'

Under the new accounting regime of the Charities Commission, set up in 2005, a full audit is no longer needed for voluntary associations. In its place, a 'review' by an appropriate person is sufficient. This provides some relief and cost-saving, though in today's climate of compliance requirements for non-profit organisations, maintaining full and transparent annual financial statements remains paramount. I myself and the Trust Board annually record in the AGM minutes our thanks to Gillian for her meticulous keeping of the books. (How John Murray combined every role including this one in his 30 years of stewardship never ceases to amaze us!)

Hymn-Singing 'Happenings' throughout Aotearoa

'Hymn festivals,' 'hymnfests,' or 'hymn workshops,' that is, ecumenically organised public hymn singing occasions, have continued to promote and spread the knowledge of our New Zealand hymns, songs and carols in the opening decades of this millennium. These began with several workshops held during 2003/2004, marking the tenth anniversary of the publication of *Alleluia Aotearoa*—a good introduction for the new Management Team to the Trust's work, and for church folk interested to meet them. Venues visited included Auckland, Napier, twice in Palmerston North, Masterton, Nelson, Invercargill, Ashburton and Gisborne. Written by Colin Gibson, a tribute to the contribution that John and Shirley Murray had made to the place of hymns in worship (and continue to make) was shared at one of the Palmerston North events, with John and Shirley present. (This tribute is printed in full as 'Thank you, Shirley and John,' in *Music in the Air*, (Summer 2004), 2).

The close of our first decade as Trust managers ended strongly in further New Zealand hymn singing occasions in the Spring season for 2012, with leadership coming from local churches supported by enthusiastic 'outsiders.' Rev Sally Carter of St Paul's Presbyterian Church, Napier, and Rev Adrian Skelton of St Andrew's Presbyterian Church in Hastings, joined by Roy Tankersley, Gillian and myself, led a Spring Sing at St Andrew's Church on the afternoon of Sunday 16 September. During the last week of October 2012 Colin Gibson presented four workshops in Auckland/Northland, at St John's Golden Church in Whangarei, Warkworth Methodist Church, Mairangi and Castor Bays Presbyterian Church, and St Matthew-in-the-City, Auckland. A similar tour taking in the Southland towns of Invercargill, Owaka and Gore followed in 2013, and 2014 sees a workshop tour to the Chinese Christian community and St David's Presbyterian Church, Auckland, as well as Tokoroa, Thames and Opotiki. Gaynor McCartney, Chair of the These Hills Workshops in Music and Ministry, has given sterling service in organising these events, in partnership with the New Zealand Hymnbook Trust.

Also popular are 'down-under' Kiwi carol singalongs. Palmerston North has organised such events for over 10 years, with three inner city churches – Presbyterian, Methodist and Anglican – sharing the venue. This may be the only annual church event some people attend. Churches easily gain media coverage and public attention with the sharing of New Zealand's own carols ('You mean there *are* New Zealand-born carols?' is the common reporter response). The carols are mostly drawn from *Carol our Christmas* (1996), but they are now supplemented by 'Dream a dream' from *Faith Forever Singing*, and 'Always there's a carol' and 'Bring in your new world,' among others, from *Hope is our Song*.

Two Karaoke CDs

In the course of 2004 two 'singalong' CDs were recorded. One, titled *Singing Love*, featured Colin Gibson playing 27 of his hymns from *Alleluia Aotearoa* and *Faith Forever Singing*. These were recorded in Dunedin, with a Yamaha grand piano as the keyboard instrument. The second, titled *Singing Faith*, presented 18 of Shirley Murray's hymns played by Palmerston North-based Roy Tankersley on his Roland digital keyboard. Each musician plays the tune first then plays the whole hymn, observing pauses between verses, helping to link the pace of the singers and the accompaniment., The two new karaoke CDs were launched at the morning services held on Sunday 22 May 2005 at the small rural Methodist churches of Ashhurst and Pohangina in the Manawatu, exactly the settings where such resources can be a creative aid to worship.

Learning to sing to CDs is a new skill churches are having to pick up. Encouragement and support must be given, assuring the congregations that they start quietly, listen intently and keep pace with the CD tempo. Voices can be raised once everyone feels confident they are all together and in time with the CD player. The Trust has heard of churches who also find helpful the choral CDs that complement all four of the books.

In reality, the CD can never replace the live musician on keyboard, and churches must continue working at the recruitment of younger accompanists for the New Zealand songs which provide tuneful and lively melodies for worship. But as a temporary or relief measure, the karaoke CDs fill a gap where the live accompanist is not available.

Changes in the Editorial Group

Along with Management, it is this group that makes the greatest contribution to the Trust's work. Thanks are given to those who served on the first Editorial Group, responsible for the first three titles: *Alleluia Aotearoa*, *Carol our Christmas* and *Faith Forever Singing*. John and Shirley Murray, Sister Cecily Sheehy, Jillian Bray, Guy Jansen and Ian Render.

With a new generic hymnbook in mind, we sought some changes in the Editorial Group. Joining Colin Gibson, whose membership continued, were newcomers Roy Tankersley from Palmerston North, Sarah Mitchell from Dunedin, and Barry Brinson and Marnie Barrell from Christchurch.

Roy Tankersley, Music Director for St Andrews in the City in Palmerston North, was nationally known for his leadership in church music, notably as organist and choir leader. Marnie Barrell was a fine lay theologian, well-illustrated in her hymn texts combining traditional theological emphases with contemporary words and images. Along with Bill Wallace, Colin Gibson and Shirley Murray, she joined the four named as our internationally published New Zealand hymn writers. Barry Brinson was a Christchurch organist and harpsichordist with interests ranging from classical organ and jazz piano to composition of hymn tunes, 18 of them featuring in *Hope is our Song*. Sarah Mitchell was minister at Knox Church, Dunedin, where she delighted in preparing liturgies which take seriously 21st century theologies. Gillian and I, from Palmerston North, made up the seven-member team working towards the fourth book, *Hope is our Song*, launched at the National Hymn Conference held in Palmerston North, in October 2009.

2009: *Hope is our Song*

The title of the book, suggested to the Editorial Board by Marnie Barrell, came from Shirley Murray's text 'Nothing, nothing in all creation':

> Never alone,
> though human error,
> turmoil or terror
> shake every bone,
> hope is our song:
> hope that is joyous,
> born with Christ Jesus,
> where we belong.

Shirley Murray's, with a little bit of inspiration from St Paul, Romans 8!

Selected from several hundred submissions from a wide range of New Zealand authors and composers, many of them previously unknown, 158 hymns made up the new book. It provided new reference aids: a total of nine Indices gave guidance to worship leaders to the contents of the book. These indices included The Church's Year ('Advent' to 'All Saints'), Themes (41 in total, including 'Children/Youth,' 'Aotearoa,' 'Dance,' 'Hospitality,' 'Family' and 'Hope'), The Worship Service (from 'Adoration' to 'Benediction'), and indices covering Pastoral/Sacramental Services, Biblical references, Māori words, as well as the usual Authors/Composers, Tunes, and First line titles and subtitles indexes. Sarah Mitchell played a key role in preparing all of these indices.

55 names appear under the Index of Authors, Translators, Composers and Arrangers. Alongside Colin Gibson, Shirley Murray, Marnie Barrell, Bill Wallace, and Bill Bennett – all significant contributors to earlier titles – new contributors of at least two texts included Rob Ferguson of Christchurch, Robyn Allen-Goudge of Auckland, Margaret Bond of Hamilton, Joy Cowley of Wellington and Timothy Hurd of Dunedin. The work of the pioneer folksinger of the 1960s, Willow Macky, also contributed two songs, one of them, 'Peace to the world,' an anthem, 'We shall overcome,' for the people of Aotearoa/New Zealand. A significant change to earlier policy not to include texts sung to traditional hymn tunes occurred with the acceptance of eight texts by Jocelyn Marshall, of Hamilton, whose hymns, which re-create traditional theologies in contemporary context and language, are given the support of a standard and familiar tune. Already mentioned is Barry Brinson's contribution as a new composer to the Trust contributors, setting tunes to 18 texts. Further individual gems include Jenny McLeod's 'Thank you for the night,' Helen Fisher's 'Karakia ki te Wairua Tapu,' and Stan Stewart's fun song, 'Christians are all kinds of people.'

Earlier titles by the Trust had been printed in Hong Kong. A shift in currency rates against Asian economies and more in favour of the local economy, together with the advantage of easier delivery and faster reprints led to the decision to print *Hope is our Song* 'in our own neighbourhood' at the Massey University Printery. Giving jobs to locals was a further plus!

The Auckland chamber choir, Viva Voce, conducted by John Rosser and with Michael Bell of St Matthew-in-the-City as accompanist on organ and piano, later recorded 27 songs from the new book. This CD, released in 2010, received positive reviews from church and choral publications, and is a valuable resource in helping spread the new songs through church and community groups. A new feature of this CD was the inclusion of a booklet supplying the hymn texts, making this a complete-in-itself personal or group resource

The 2009 National Hymn Conference in Palmerston North

When the World Council of Churches' Decade to Overcome Violence (DOV) programme was nearing its end, those New Zealand churches who set the programme up had unspent funds. Applications from interested parties were invited and the New Zealand Hymnbook Trust was successful in obtaining a generous sum of $10,000, tagged to the organisation of a national hymn conference.

The main title given to the event, 'Hope is our Song,' corresponded to the new hymnbook which Jono Naylor, Mayor of Palmerston North, launched at the opening session. The subtitle 'Peace-Justice-Creation' highlighted key issues facing church and the wider society, issues at the centre of the World Council of Churches' Decade. The conference was held over Labour Weekend, 23 to 26 October 2009, at Wesley Broadway Church in Palmerston North.

Including those who attended individual day sessions and those from outside the region who stayed over for the full conference, some 80 persons came to the event. Among them were six international attendees: Jim and June Strathdee from California, USA; Susan Jacobs from South India; Clive Pearson, Michael Earl and Ann Perrin, all from the United Theological College of the Uniting Church in Australia; and Deborah Carlton-Loftis, newly elected Executive Director of the Hymn Society in the United States and Canada.

Jim and June Strathdee's keynote presentation, 'The Power of Song in Transformational Faith Communities in USA, Canada, Central America and India,' reflected their far-reaching ministry in music. At the Saturday night worship conducted in the Cathedral of the Holy Spirit, Jim led the singing of the Shirley Murray text 'Look in Wonder,' found in *Hope is our Song*, singing the tune he had himself written for Shirley's words. Two other keynote talks were Clive Pearson's opening address, 'A Public Theology of Peace/Justice/Creation' on the Friday night, followed on the Saturday by Colin Gibson's talk on 'Justice in the hymns of Indigenous Pākehā Hymn Writers.' Flying in from the States on the Sunday morning, Deborah Carlton-Loftis was guest speaker for the Sunday evening dinner. She presented a citation to Shirley Murray inducting her as a Fellow of the Hymn Society in the United States and Canada.

Panel presentations were given by John Murray, founder of the Hymnbook Trust, hymn writers Bill Bennett, Shirley Murray and Marnie Barrell, liturgists Sarah Mitchell and Helene Mann, and local church music leader, Roy Tankersley. Ten workshop options were offered in three sessions. Those leading included: Roy Tankersley, John Murray, Bill Wallace, Helene Mann, Jim and June Strathdee, Ann Perrin, Brian Dawson, Graham Parsons, Pamela Tankersley, Bill Bennett, and Marnie Barrell with Colin Gibson.

A DVD of the occasion was mailed to all attendees as souvenir of the conference. For the historical record, 24 songs were included in the Conference Songbook: 'Honour the Dead,' 'Christ has changed the world's direction,' 'Where the light of Easter Day,' 'God bless our land,' 'Look in wonder,' 'Bring in your new world,' 'Everything that has voice,' 'God of the northerlies,' 'Rockin' the boat,' 'No, I've never seen an angel,' 'Let our earth be peaceful,' 'Jumping Jesus,' 'From this holy time,' 'This is our faith,' 'My heart is leaping,' 'Simply to be,' 'What does our God require of us?,' 'Who sweeps the stable?, 'Wisdom far beyond our knowledge,' 'Peace be with you,' 'Leftover people in leftover places, 'Thank you for the night,' 'Mary's son, my friend,' and 'We are children of God, children of God.'

New Zealand Hymns in an audiovisual world

John Murray has already mentioned the partnership between the Trust and Radio New Zealand who in 1992 recorded 22 of the songs to appear in *Alleluia Aotearoa*. A further partnership with TV One/Praise Be led, in 1999, to the publication of a video, *Songs of Praise from Aotearoa*, with 24 hymns and carols from the Praise Be library. Today's products will no longer be in video format, though the compact disc continues to complement the Trust's books. CDs for *Alleluia Aotearoa, Carol our Christmas, Faith Forever Singing* and *Hope is our Song* have all appeared and continue to find a market, though with smaller sales than the books. How long before a DVD – or some newer audiovisual technology still to emerge – is produced?

Choirs performing on the Trust's CDs include church and civic-based singing groups, mainly drawn from the major cities, though smaller provincial centres are represented by Colla Voce from Havelock North High School on the *Alleluia Aotearoa* CD. School choirs participating on the same CD include the Aorere College from South Auckland and Sacred Heart College from Lower Hutt. Regional and national youth choirs are represented with the Wellington Secondary Students Choir and Wellington Youth Choir on *Carol our Christmas*, and The New Zealand Secondary Student Choir and Friends on *Faith Forever Singing*. Well-known civic choirs are the Orlando singers from Auckland, Christchurch City Choir and Festival Singers from Wellington, all three on *Alleluia Aotearoa*. The Porirua City Choir is heard on *Faith Forever Singing*, and the Auckland chamber choir Viva Voce cover all songs on *Hope is our Song*. Church choirs include Wellington Cathedral Choir, who feature on three CDs, *Alleluia Aotearoa, Carol our Christmas* and *Faith Forever Singing*, while the Wellington City Songsters are included on *Faith Forever Singing*. Finally, individual and small group singers include Rachel Gillon and Mike Wespel-Rose, who sing 'You are born in us again' on *Carol our Christmas*, the Wellington-based Sings Harry have four songs on *Carol our Christmas*, and Kiwikids with Radha Wardrop, also from Wellington, have two songs on *Alleluia Aotearoa* and four children's songs on *Carol our Christmas*.

Such resources make it possible for New Zealand hymns, songs, and carols published by the Trust to be played on radio and television networks. Two key remaining programmes were Hymns for Sunday Morning and Television New Zealand's Praise Be on their Channel One. We acknowledge the contribution made by presenter Maureen Garing (1993-2011) during her long service on the former programme. Churches had a more direct input to Praise Be, as the programme traveled and recorded ecumenical congregations and local choirs. We acknowledge the commitment that Graeme Thomson (1939 to 2008) made to ensure New Zealand hymn writers were included in such broadcast programmes.

With restructuring and resourcing issues always a threat to public broadcasting, constant vigilance is needed to ensure New Zealand hymn texts and tunes, as well as the choirs and congregations who sing them, remain as voices on air.

The Trust Website
www.hymns.org.nz

With the Trust up and running in the 1990s a website, under the operation of Jeff Simmons of Paraparaumu, was set up in 2001. Initially the site gave information on products and prices, with a website order form for direct sales from the Trust office. Subsequently a full listing of all songs found in the books and on the CDs was added to the site. Following the National Hymn Conference of 2009, a Noticeboard was added by Gaynor McCartney of Piopio, King Country. This includes lectionary lists of New Zealand hymns for each Sunday in four quarterly or three-month periods annually. Information and reports on Trust events are also included on this site.

Asia comes to Aotearoa July 2012

The international spread of the hymns by New Zealanders is mentioned by John Murray, and this has continued through further publication of individual hymns in overseas collections, appearance of New Zealanders at conferences, and – hugely significantly – via the digital revolution underway in a networked global world.

I conclude this brief survey with a report on the Trust's appearance at the 21st annual conference of the World Association of Chinese Church Music (WACCM). Over 400 delegates attended the event which took place in the Baptist Tabernacle, Auckland, from 12-15 July 2012. Delegates came from the diaspora of Chinese living now in America, Australia and New Zealand, as well as from Malaysia, Hong Kong, Thailand, Indonesia, Singapore, Philippines and mainland China.

To honour the host country, the Trust was given two sessions on Friday morning, 13 July. A group of eight Methodists from Devonport and Mt Albert churches, joined by Rev Robyn Allen-Goudge from Devonport Methodist Church as conductor, Prudence Bell, my younger sister on grand piano, led the singing of 16 hymns taken from the Trust's four books. Robyn played the harp for 'E te Ariki,' sung in Māori; after her solo presentation all joined in a repeat. PowerPoint projected the words in English, while simultaneous translation from English to Mandarin was available. Despite the fact that the songs were new to many, and in a new language for some, the singers joined in enthusiastically. Many commented on the singability of the tunes and the relevance of the words for today's faith journey.

A letter from Shirley Murray, printed in the Conference handbook, welcomed the delegates to New Zealand, and challenged them to sing hymns 'relevant to the changing world of the present time,' songs relevant for the 21st century Asia, where 'rice fields and lotus flowers which grow in muddy waters give you symbols of life and resurrection.' The same challenge exists for all us who live in Aotearoa/New Zealand, and we can surely take on board Shirley's challenge and invitation, with our own hymn writers as inspirers and energizers for the Way ahead.

Coda: 2014-2021

John and Gillian Thornley retired from their dedicated leadership of the Editorial Board of the New Zealand Hymnbook Trust in October 2014. They were followed by two relatively short-lived appointments, Stuart Weightman (October 2014 – March 2015) and James Mist (May 2016 – April 2020). No new publications were undertaken during that time.

However, James Mist, working with Philip Garside Publishing Ltd, successfully transferred the printing of the *Alleluia Aotearoa*, *Faith Forever Singing* and *Hope is Our Song* music books to a print-on-demand basis with Wellington printers – Printing.com. This will enable smaller, more economical reprint runs of these books to be produced as needed in future.

In 2020, during the COVID-19 lockdown when delivery of physical books and CDs was not possible, Philip Garside Publishing Ltd converted the Trust's music books and CDs into digital PDF and MP3 formats to be sold and supplied online. The digital products are appreciated by overseas customers who avoid the otherwise high postage costs to send print books and CDs to their country.

The Trust plans to appoint a new manager in 2021 to guide day-to-day operations, promote its resources and initiate new collections, publications and recordings.

Philip Garside Publishing Ltd of Wellington, who handled design and printing of this present Companion, also handles sales and distribution of the Trust's publications.

Indexes

The following short references are used in the Hymn Names and First Lines index and the Tune Names index: **W**–*With One Voice* (1982); **A**–*Alleluia Aotearoa* (1993); **C**–*Carol Our Christmas* (1996); **F**–*Faith Forever Singing* (2000); **HP**–*He Came Singing Peace* (2002); **H**–*Hope Is Our Song* (2009).

Hymn Names and First Lines

A

Abba, Matua, we ask you – H3 16
Above the peaks the angels sing – C2 17
A child was born in Bethlehem – C1 14
Advent I – facing C48 17
Advent Triptych III – facing C35 18
Agaaga Tapu – W649 18
A great and mighty wonder 14
Alive to God – A133 216
Alleluia, alleluia, alleluia! – W674(i) 22
Alleluia, alleluia, give thanks to the risen Lord (Alleluia No 1) – W674 (ii) 22
Alleluia Amen Aotearoa! – A163 22
Alleluia Aotearoa! – A1 21
Alleluia Aotearoa! – A13 21
Alleluia Aotearoa! – A34 21
Alleluia Aotearoa! – A53 21
Alleluia Aotearoa! – A92 21
Alleluia Aotearoa! – A121 21
Alleluia Aotearoa! – A131 22
Alleluia Aotearoa! – A163 22
Alleluia, Jesus, saviour – W674 (iii) 22
All over creation – C3 18
All poor men and humble – W641 19
All who would see God's greatness – C4 19
All will be well – A2 20
All will be well – H4 20
Alofa mai ia, afio mai – A3 23
Always there's a carol – H6 23
And did you see him, little star – A4, C5, W644 24

And Jesus said – F1 24
Another Servant Song – H154 (i) and (ii) 263
Aʻou manatu ifo nei – W647 16
A pinch of salt – H1 15
Arahina, e Ihowa – W661 24
Arohanui Blessing – A95 165
A Song for Epiphany – C37 196
As sisters, brothers, called by Christ – H5 25
As the sun beats down – F2 25
As the wind-song through the trees – H7 26
A stranger met by chance – H2 15
As we walk along beside you – F3 26
Au, e Ihu, tirohia – W631 27
Aue te tu aroa – A5 28
Autumn comes in all its fullness – H8 28
Ave lou ola – A6 28
Awake before sunrise – C6 29
A Wedding Song – facing A25 16

B

Beautiful presence – H9 30
Because you came – facing F19 (ii) 31
Because you live, O Christ – A7 32
Be still my heart – F4 (i) and (ii) 30
Be their names remembered – F5 30
Beyond all accidents of chance and change – H12 32
Blessing for a House, A – H54 103
Blessings on the buildings – H11 33
Blow through the valleys and sing in the rimu – F6 33

Blue Sky, Lord of Creation – F77 259
Born in the night, Mary's child – W642 34
Bring in your new world – H13 34
Bring peace to us – F7 (i) and (ii) 35
Broken the body – F8 35
Brother, sister, let me serve you – A8 36

C

Can You Drink the Cup I Drink? F55 195
Caring – A20 46
Carol for Advent – W645 49
Carol for a Hard Winter – H120 202
Carol of Cold Comfort – A141, C44 225
Carol of Dreams – F12 (i) and (ii) 58
Carol of the Least Child – H133 (i) and (ii) 225
Carol our Christmas – A9, C7 37
Celebrate each generation – A10 37
Celebration Song, The – A70 128
Child of blessing, child of promise – A11 38
Child of Christmas story – A12 39
Child of joy and peace – A14 (i) and (ii) 39
Children's Saviour, The – A66 120
Christ ascends to God! – H14 40
Christ has changed the world's direction – H15 41
Christians are all kinds of people – H16 44
Christ is alive – A15 41
Christ is our peace – A16 42
Christ, let us come with you – A17 44
Christmas in the picture book – A18 44
Christ of darkness, Christ of light – C10 43
Christ of the sad face – F9, HP2 43
Church of the living Christ – A19 45
'Click, click,' how the needles fly – A20 46
Colour me free! – A21 46
Come and find the quiet centre – F10 (i) and (ii) 47
Come celebrate the gift of life – H17 47
Come, come, come to the feast – H20 53
Come, fill our cup with the water of life – H18 54
Come in, come in, New Year – C13 (i) and (ii) 48
Come into the streets with me – A22 48
Come now, Lord Jesus – W645, A23 (i) and (ii), C14 (i) and (ii) 49
Come now where we least expect you – C15 49
Come on this wedding day – A24 50
Come, teach us, Spirit of our God – F11 50
Come to a wedding – A25 51
Come to our land – A26 51
Come to the celebration – A27 52
Come to the feast – H20 53
Come to this Christmas singing – A28, C16 53
Communion Meditation – H80 137
Companions, let us pray together – H21 55
Cradle Song – H59 111
Creation sings – H29 55
Creator God – H34 103
Creator God, we give you thanks – H22 56

D

Deep in the human heart – H19 56
Don't tell anyone – C17 57
Do this in remembrance of me – A29 57
Dream a dream – F12 (i) and (ii) 58

E

E aere rekareka mai – W627 58
Easter City – F18 71
Easter New Zealand – facing F3 62
Easter Song – A15 41
E Ihoa Atua – W677, A51 59
Ephphatha, be opened my soul – H25 62
E te Ariki – A30 59
E te Ariki – F13 59
E te Ariki – H23 59
E te Atua – A31 60
E te Atua, kua ruia nei – W650 60
E te Iwi – A32 61
E Te Koru, te Wairua Tapu – H84 141
E te Matua – H24 61
Eternal God, beyond the reach of mystery – H26 62

Eternal Spirit of the living Christ – A33 63
Even if you're small – A35 63
Every day I will offer you – A36 63
Every hair upon your head – H27 64
Every star shall sing a carol – W640 65
Everything that has voice – H28 65

F

Faafetai i le Atua – W629 66
Faith has set us on a journey – F14 66
Fancy Noah sailing in the ark – F15 67
Farewell, A – H78 131
Father, I have seen Your Kingdom – A157 261
First set your mind on the kingdom of God – W635 67
Fofoga mai ma Iesu – W651 68
Follow the Way – F16 68
Food is given for us all – A37 69
For all small children – A38 69
For everyone born, a place at the table – F17, HP3 69
Forgive, forgive us, Holy God – F20, HP4 73
Forgive us, O God – F21 72
For the bread and wine and blessing – A39 70
For the crowd another busy day – F18 71
For the hurt that I create – F19 (i) and (ii) 71
For the man and for the woman – A40 71
For the music of creation – A41 72
Fresh as the Morning – F25 92
Friend in Christ – H30 74
From pastures green – C18 74
From the apple in the garden – A42 74
From the waiting comes the sign – A43 75
From this holy time – H31 75
Fruits of the Spirit, The – H127 212

G

Gentle God – A44 76
Gentle is the way of Jesus – F22 77
Get up, get up, no time to yawn – C19 77
Give thanks for life – A45 77
Gloria – C20 77

Gloria – C21 78
Gloria – C22 78
Gloria in excelsis – C23 78
Glorious are you – H33 78
Glory be to the Father – W675 79
Glory! Glory! – C24 80
Glory to God – F23 80
God be in, around, above me – H36 81
God bless our land – H37 81
God, come now to explore my heart – H38 102
God comes to us as one unheard – H42 82
God, companion of our journey – H32 102
God, composer and conductor H34 103
God Dancing in the rain – F24 205
God defend New Zealand – A51 88
God gave to man the woman – A46 82
God in Everything – H42 82
God in the darkness – F24 83
God is the One whom we seek together – A47 83
God is working his purpose out – W652 84
God of ages, times and seasons – H39 85
God of all beauty – A48 85
God of all time – A49 86
God of diversity – H40 86
God of freedom, God of justice – A50, HP7 87
God of growth and recreation – H41 87
God of nations, at thy feet – A51, W677 88
God of our every day – A52 89
God of our island home – H43 90
God of our workplace – H44 90
God of solemnity, God of festivity – H47 91
God of the ages, by whose hand – W662 91
God of the Bible – F25 92
God of the galaxies – A54 92
God of the northerlies – H45 93
God of the past – F26 94
God of unexplored tomorrows – F27 94
God of work and rest and play – H46 95
God our father, mother, lover – H48 95
God rest us – F28 96

God's grace upon this house – H54 103
Godspeed Song – F29 96
God speed you on your way – F29 96
God was in Christ – H49 97
God weeps – F30 97
God, when I was a child – facing F73 194
God who births us fully gifted – H51 98
God who carved this timeless landscape – F31 99
God who granted faith and vision – H50 99
God who sets us on a journey – F32 100
God who weeps – H52 101
God within our deepest thought – H53 101
Go gently, go lightly – H35 (i) and (ii) 80
Good Friday is a dying here – facing F3 62
Good Friday Lament – F70 248
Grace before Meals – A37 69
Grace before Meals – facing F61 104
Great and deep the Spirit's purpose – A55 104
Great is the Love – A56 105
Great ring of light – A57 105
Greetings, little child of Bethlehem – C25 105

H

Hail Mary, full of grace – A58 106
Heav'n is ringing – C26 107
He came singing love – A59 106
Here in the busy city – H56 108
Here is a night that's bleak and raw – H57 109
Here I stand among God's people – H55 108
Here is the place, now is the time – A60 109
Here to celebrate God's loving – H58 110
Here to the house of God we come – A61 110
Here we bring small or great – A62 111
Heritage of Faith – H144 244
He rongo pai te oranga – W634 107
Ho-hum Hymn, The – H121 203
Hold him tenderly – H59 111
Holy day, holiday – C27 112
Holy! Holy! Holy! – F33 112
Honour the dead – H61 113

Honour the Earth – A54, HP8 92
How happy you who work for peace – A63 114
How is Jesus present? – A64 115
How much am I worth – H63 115
How small a spark – H64 116
Hymn for a Confirmation – A60 109
Hymn for a New Ministry, A – H145 245
Hymn for Ascension, A – H14 40
Hymn for a Wedding – A24 50
Hymn for Bible Sunday – A42 74
Hymn for the Church after Easter – A19 45
Hymn for the Funeral of a Small Child – F44 152
Hymn for Waitangi Day – A155 256
Hymn of Approach to Communion – H148 249
Hymn of Thanks for our Pets, A – H22 56
Hymn on Growing Older – F41 145
Hymn to Celebrate a Long Life – F56 199

I

I am standing waiting – F34 116
I am the light of the world – W669 117
I am the vine – F35 118
I arise this day – H65 118
Ia tatou vivii atu nei – A65 125
I cannot dance, O dancing Love – H66 119
I come where trust and faith are tried – H67 119
I didn't hear the angels sing – C28 120
If I take the wings of the morning – A68 125
If one could speak – H73 126
If you shut your eyes – H74 126
I know someone who watches over me – A66 120
I'm a fishbowl Christian – F36 123
I'm a living stone – H70 123
I'm gonna take another step – H72 123
Indigo II – A89 152
In the beginning was Love – facing A25 16
In the name of Christ – H75 117, 127
In the name of Christ we gather – A69 127
In the presence of your people – A70 128
In the quiet of this day – F37 128

In the shaking of God's mantle – A71 129
In the Shelter of My Hand – A152 253
In the singing – F38 129
In this familiar place – A72 130
Into the hands – H78 131
In trust we come – H76 130
Invitation to Communion – H131 217
In what strange land – H77 131
I sing the grace of God within you – H68 121
Is there no other way? – A73 132
Is this the end of the world? – A74 133
It all depends on where I'm going – F39 133
I toou arataa tikai – W663 121
I've got knees – A75 124
I've never seen an elephant – A76 124
I will comfort you – A67 122
I will talk to my heart in the stillness – H69 122

J
Jesus comes to me as a springtime tree – A77 133
Jesus, come to our hearts – A78 134
Jesus, I come – A79 134
Jesus, I sing your praise – A80 135
Jesus, our sun – H79 135
Jesus, Saviour, Spirit, Sun – A81 136
Jesus, stand among us – W637 137
Jesus, touch us – H80 137
Join hands in the Spirit – A82 138
Jumping Jesus – H81 138
Just a cup of water – A83 139
Just a mustard seed of faith will do – H82 140
Just as a mother sings her baby to sleep – H83 140

K
Karakia ki te Wairua Tapu – H84 141
Ka tirohia te ripeka – W646 140
Ke tau fakafeta'i – A84 142
Kindness, a Children's Song – F40 144
Ko tei anoano aere ua mai – W668 142
Koutou katoa ra, mea iti nei – W659 142

L
Learning to Fly – facing F44 143
Leftover people in leftover places – H85 143
Let justice roll down – A85 144
Let me be kind to you – F40 144
Let me turn your light on – H86 145
Let my spirit always sing – F41 145
Let our earth be peaceful – H87 145
Let our love shine out – H88 146
Let's praise the creator – A86 149
Let there be light – W671 146
Let there be peace – F42 and HP14 147
Let there be respect for the earth – F43 147
Let us go in your peace – H89 148
Let us talents and tongues employ – W658 148
Life into life, the threads are woven – H91 149
Life is like a river – H60 150
Life of ages, richly poured – W660 150
Lift high the cross – A87 151
Lift up your hearts to the Lord – A88 152
Light of lights beholden – A89, C29, HP16 152
Litany for a Spirit-filled Planet – A38 69
Little one, born to bring us such love – F44 152
Living Christ, you call us here – H90 153
Living Creatively – H152 272
Lo matou Tama e – A90 153
Look around you – H92 154
Look in wonder – H93 154
Look now! It is happening again – facing C28 167
Look toward Christmas! – C30 (i) and (ii) 155
Lord, have mercy – F13 59
Lord Jesus, look on this we do – H94 155
Lord of all being, throned afar – W626 156
Lord of all love – A91 156
Lord of the living, in your name assembled – W657 157
Lord, turn our grieving into grace – F45 158
Love is your way – H95 158
Lover of creation – H98 159
Love to the world – A93 159

Loving Spirit, Loving Spirit – A94 (i) and (ii) 160
Lullaby Carol – F46 161
Lullaby, sing lullaby – F46 161

M

Magnificat – facing H62 166
Magnificat Now – W643 202
Make me, O Lord, an instrument of thy peace – W666 162
Maker of mystery – F47 163
Make spaces for Spirit! – H96 162
Many-Faceted God, The – H47 91
Mary's Song – H101 166
Mary's son, my friend – H97 163
Ma te marie a te Atua – W679 161
Matthew was a lonely man – H99 164
May the anger of Christ be mine – F48 164
May the mystery of God enfold us – A95 165
Mercy Tree, The – A160 265
Merry Christmas Rag – C26 107
More than we know – H100 165
My heart is leaping – H101 166
My soul sings in gratitude – facing H62 166

N

Nativity – facing C28 167
Nativity – facing C42 167
New Beginnings – H32 102
New child of God, come to be blest – A96 168
Night in Bethlehem, A – H57 109
No, I've never seen an angel – H103 169
No Room! No Room! – C46 236
No te aroa maata noou – A97 169
Nothing is lost on the breath of God – F50 170
Nothing, nothing in all creation – H102 171
Not on a snowy night – A98 170
Now as we go – A99 172
Now Jesus came among us – A101 172
Now the silence – H104 172
Now the star of Christmas – H105 173
Now to your table spread – A100 174
Now unto him – A102 174

O

O beauty ever ancient – H107 175
O be joyful in God – A103 175
O Bread of joy – A104 176
O Christ who by a cross – A105 176
O Christ, you hang upon a cross – H108 177
O God, beyond our knowledge H71
O God, beyond our knowledge – H71 178
O God, our God, disabled God – H112 179
O God, to you I cry in pain – H106 179
O God we bear the imprint of your face – A106 178
O he is born – A107, C32 180
O little love who comes again – A108 (i) and (ii), C33 (i) and (ii) 180
O living Word – H109 181
O Lord my God, I stand and gaze in wonder – W628 181
O mai, Iesu, tai meitaki – W638 183
On a cool and autumn dawn – H110 185
One Day…Right Now – A116 194
One small child – F52 185
One, two, three, alleluia! – A111 186
Open, open, open the stable door – C34 186
Open your Eyes, open your Ears – H74 126
Ordinary People – H156 266
O spring in the desert – F51 183
O the Spirit she moves on the water – A109 183
O threefold God of tender unity – A110 184
Our Father in heaven – W676, A112 187
Our life has its seasons – A113 187
Out of such sun and air – A114 188
Out of the storms – F53 188

P

Palm Sunday Song – A22 48
Parting Blessing, A – F72 249
Pāuatahanui Blessing – H89 148
Peace be with you – H111 189
Peace Carol – A108 (i) and (ii), C33 (i) and (ii) 180
Peace Child – C35 189

Peace Hat Song, The – H113 190
Peace is not fighting – H113 190
Peace to the world – H114 190
Peace to you, sisters, brothers – F54 190
Pentecost Song – H96 162
Piko nei te matenga – W655 191
Pilgrimage Song – H143 243
Praise facing – A135 192
Praise God, from whom all blessings flow – W678 192
Praise God, I am welcome at the table – H115 192
Praise the all-sustaining Word – H116 192
Praise to God, whose Holy Spirit – C36 193
Prayer for Discernment – facing F73 194
Prayer for the Presence – F51 183
Prayer to the Holy Spirit – H84 141
Psalm 151 – A161 267
Purea nei e te hau – A115 194

R

Rainbow People – F15 67
Real Christmas – C41 211
Rejoice, be glad – A116 194
Relentless lover, God in Christ – F55 195
Responses for Communion – F33 112
Rockin' the boat – H117 195

S

Safe in the hands of God – A117 196
Selkirk Grace – A124 204
Servant Song, The – A8 36
Set the sun dancing – C37 196
Simply to be – H118 197
Sing a carol for summer – C38 197
Sing a happy alleluia! – A118 198
Sing alleluia, Sing alleluia – A34 21
Sing alleluia, sing alleluia – A53 21
Sing for Peace – H28 65
Sing green – A119, HP19 199
Sing no sad songs today – F56 199

Sing of the saints – A120 200
Sing out a song – H119 200
Sing to celebrate the city – A122 201
Sing we a song of high revolt – W643 202
Sing with the angels, Gloria! – C39 202
Sisters and brothers, gather around – H120 202
Small Carol – A12 39
Small things count – A123 203
Snap us out of it, Lord – H121 203
So is the Love of God – H83 140
Some hae meat – A124 204
Something beautiful for God – H122 204
Something's dead inside me – facing F24, H123 (i) and (ii) 205
Sometimes the boundless beauty – H124 205
Song for Epiphany – C51 267
Song for Quaker Friends – H129 264
Song for Travellers – A153 254
Song in Times of Drought, A – F2 25
Song of Letters – H3 16
Song of Light, A – F48 164
Song of Southland – A78 134
Song of the Wilderness – H150 254
Song to the Lord Jesus – A80 135
Son of a peaceful heart – W633, A128 213
Spirit of love – A125 208
Spirit of love – H125 207
Spirit of peace – F58 (i) and (ii), HP20 (i) and (ii) 209
Spirit of springtime – F59 209
Spring Song – F59 209
Star-Child, earth-Child – C40 (i) and (ii) 210
St Joseph facing – C8 241
Stranger, standing at my door – F60 211
Summer's a time to discover – C41 211

T

Take a grape – H127 212
Take my gifts – A127 212
Take our bread, we ask you – W656 212
Tama ngakau marie – W633, A128 213

Teach us, O loving heart of Christ – A130 214

Te Atua mou o Betela – A129 214

Tell my people I love them – A132 215

Thanks be to God – A134 216

Thank you for the night – H128 215

Thank you God – A133 216

The Blessing of water and light and air – H130 217

The bread is blessed, the wine is poured – H131 217

The food we have here is a gift – facing F61 104

The Gamble facing – F79 217

The God of heaven thunders – A135 218

The grace of God has appeared – F61 218

The grace of our Lord Jesus Christ – A136 218

The heavens are telling the glory of the Lord – W625 219

The jersey cow came mooing – C42 219

The journey of life may be easy, may be hard – W670 220

The Kingdom is within you – A137 220

The light begins to shine – facing C35 18

The light, the Christmas light – H132 221

The Lord bless you and keep you – A138 221

The Lord God walked in Paradise – F62 222

The love of God is broad like beach and mountain – W667 222

The majesty of mountains – A139 223

There is no child so small – H133 (i) and (ii) 225

There's a Time – A113 187

There's a wideness in God's mercy – H135 226

There shall be life and love – H134 226

There's straw in the manger – C45 227

The River – H60 150

These hills where the hawk flies lonely – F63 228

The Sevenfold Passion Mysteries – H138 235

The spring has come – A140 223

The stars danced, the angels sang – C43 224

The Tenth Leper facing – F37 224

The wind blew keen – A141, C44 225

They were set for the home – facing C42 167

This is our faith – H136 228

This is the day – W653 229

This table is the Lord's – F64 230

This thread I weave – F65 230

This year, this year, who comes – facing C48 17

Thou art the peace – H137 231

Three Faiths Carol – H105 173

Through winter cold – H139 231

To compassion and to justice – F66 232

Today my God, I came back to thank you - facing F37 224

To God the process – H140 233

Toku wairua, oho mai – W664 234

To matou Metua – A142 233

Touch the earth lightly – A143 234

Tree of Eve and Adam's blame – H138 235

Tree of Peace – H151 257

Treksong – H72 123

Twelve disciples Jesus had – H141 236

Two tired people asked for rest – C46 236

U

Ua soona olioli nei – W630 237

Upside down Christmas – A9 37

W

Wake up! – A144 238

Wake up! You're special! – A144 238

We are an Easter people – A146 238

We are a wheel – A145 238

We are children of God – H142 239

We are heirs of the Father – W673 239

We are many, we are one – F67 240

We are the singers who celebrate Jesus – F68 240

Weaver Spirit – A125 208

We could not love you more – facing C8 241

We do not hope to ease our minds – A147 (i) and (ii) 242

Welcome the child – F69 (i) and ii) 246

We praise our country's saints of old – H143 243

We stand with Christ – A147 (i) and (ii) 242

We thank you for the gift of life – A148 243

We thank you for the heritage – H144 244

We thank you, God, for this beginning – H145 245

We turn to you, O God of every nation – W665 245

We wait for you – A149 246

Whakarongo ki te kupu – W648 247

Whakatau mai te Atua – A150 247

What does our God require of us – H146 247

Whatever is true and honest and good – F71 249

Whatever this life has been – F72 249

What have we done to you? – F70 248

When at this table – H148 249

When evenings shorten – H147 250

When human voices cannot sing – A151 250

When I was a child – F73 251

When Joseph and Mary were turned from the inn – C47 251

When our lives know sudden shadow – F74 (i) and (ii) 252

When the child is at the centre – H149 252

When the storm winds blow – A152 253

When we go into the night – H150 254

When we lift our pack and go – A153 254

Where are the voices for the earth? – F75 255

Where is the room? – A154 255

Where mountains rise to open skies – A155 256

Where shall be found – H151 257

Where the light of Easter Day – H153 257

Where the love of God is guiding – F76, HP25 258

Where the road runs out – W672, A156 259

While soldiers threw a dice – facing F79 217

Whispering gently – F77 259

Who are these strangers – F78, HP26 260

Who are these who ride by starlight – C49 261

Who is moving through the silence? – A157 261

Who is my mother – A158 262

Who is the child that is to be born – C50, A159 263

Who sweeps the stable? – H154 (i) and (ii) 263

Who will carry the cross with me? – F79 264

Who would walk cheerfully – H129 264

Will you offer me compassion? – A160 265

Wind on the water – H155 266

Wisdom be our Guide – H156 266

Wisdom far beyond our knowledge – H157 266

Wise men came journeying – C51 267

With a hoot and a toot – A161 267

With grateful hearts our faith professing – W654 268

Wounded world – F80 269

Y

Yahweh, breathe the breath of God – H158 269

Yes, as the clay – A162 270

You are born in us again – C52 271

You can Walk Tall – A35 63

You hold us with a tender parent's hand – H152 272

Scripture

Old Testament

Genesis 1 16, 177, 255
Genesis 1:1 24, 157, 184
Genesis 1:1-31 154
Genesis 1-2 199, 206
Genesis 1:2 94, 165, 208, 210, 236
Genesis 1:3 48, 67, 147, 226
Genesis 1:3-5 230
Genesis 1:6-7 236
Genesis 1:20 178
Genesis 1:20-25 56
Genesis 1:26 64, 85, 88, 90, 138
Genesis 1:27 198
Genesis 1:27-31 93
Genesis 1:28 66
Genesis 1:29 69
Genesis 1:31 85, 159
Genesis 2:1-25 154
Genesis 2-3 75
Genesis 2:3 230
Genesis 2:7 54, 58, 66, 79, 138, 184, 199, 201, 245, 269
Genesis 2:8-14 209
Genesis 2:8-15 93
Genesis 2:16-17 235
Genesis 2:17-19 75
Genesis 2:21-24 82
Genesis 2:23-4 121
Genesis 3:17-19 226
Genesis 3:19 132, 170, 199
Genesis 4:8-10 235
Genesis 6 235
Genesis 6:19 15
Genesis 7-8 193
Genesis 8 75
Genesis 8:8-11 32
Genesis 8:10-11 67
Genesis 8:22 216
Genesis 9:8-17 26, 32, 67, 166, 226, 240
Genesis 9:12-17 26
Genesis 11 136, 245
Genesis 12 100
Genesis 12:1 100
Genesis 12:1-3 267
Genesis 12:1-4 66
Genesis 12:8 100
Genesis 12:10 259
Genesis 15:18-21 95
Genesis 18:1-8 211
Genesis 18:12-15 198
Genesis 28:20-22 214
Genesis 43:23 189

Exodus 2, 15 36
Exodus 3:1-12 222
Exodus 3:2 136
Exodus 3:5. 49
Exodus 5:1-9 222
Exodus 13:18-22 254
Exodus 13:20-22 167
Exodus 13:21 94, 100
Exodus 13:21-22 100
Exodus 14 236
Exodus 15:25 236
Exodus 16 75
Exodus 21:23 132
Exodus 24:20 52
Exodus 33:14 160

Leviticus 27:30-33 111

Numbers 6:24-26 221
Numbers 21:16-17 135
Numbers 23:12 109

Deuteronomy 1:11 195
Deuteronomy 6:6-9 157
Deuteronomy 8:3 68
Deuteronomy 14:2 193
Deuteronomy 16:16 52
Deuteronomy 28:2-8 193
Deuteronomy 32:2 129
Deuteronomy 33:27 33

Judges 6:23 189

1 Samuel 2:1-10 166
1 Samuel 11:14 83
1 Samuel 18:10-11 235
1 Samuel 21:1-9 250

2 Samuel 8:14 198
2 Samuel 14:14 236

1 Kings 4:24-5 257
1 Kings 4:24-25 257
1 Kings 8:12 83
1 Kings 8:30 253
1 Kings 8:57 214
1 Kings 18:44 188
1 Kings 19: 9-18 26
1 Kings 19:11-18 178
1 Kings 19:12 47
1 Kings 22:27 75

2 Chronicles 6:1 83

Nehemiah 1:6 59
Nehemiah 9:6 103

Job 1:21 132, 153
Job 4:9 216
Job 10:12-13 229
Job 11:7 165

Job 12:12 165
Job 14:7-9 38
Job 19:26 33
Job 37:10 179, 216
Job 38:1-7 140
Job 38:7 42, 65
Job 38:37 55

Psalm 8 125
Psalm 8:6 158
Psalm 8:6-8 188
Psalm 16:1 33
Psalm 17:8 214
Psalm 18:2 96
Psalm 18:11 83
Psalm 19 135
Psalm 19:1-6 219
Psalm 19:4 84
Psalm 19:5 219
Psalm 19:14 153, 271
Psalm 22:22-25 128
Psalm 23 137, 217
Psalm 23:3 103
Psalm 23:3, 5 169
Psalm 23:4 55, 170
Psalm 24:1 209
Psalm 27 196
Psalm 27:1 139
Psalm 28:7 139
Psalm 30:11-12 201
Psalm 30:12 169, 233
Psalm 33:18 166
Psalm 34:8 53
Psalm 35:28 22
Psalm 39:12 59
Psalm 40:3 109, 131, 220
Psalm 40:4 169
Psalm 42:7 24
Psalm 46 122
Psalm 46:1 103, 216

Psalm 46:10 47, 197
Psalm 47:9 88
Psalm 51:2 134
Psalm 51:15 147
Psalm 54:4 216
Psalm 59:17 186
Psalm 61:1-4 59
Psalm 62:5 259
Psalm 63 131
Psalm 63:1 252
Psalm 63:8 229
Psalm 68:19 202
Psalm 68:34 192
Psalm 72:6 134
Psalm 76:3 89
Psalm 79:13 204
Psalm 80:3 181
Psalm 80:5 176
Psalm 85:8 152
Psalm 86:5 227
Psalm 89:14 227
Psalm 90 153
Psalm 90:14 137
Psalm 91:4 214
Psalm 91:14-16 169
Psalm 95:1 48
Psalm 95:6 152
Psalm 96:1 240
Psalm 96:2-3 22
Psalm 97:2 83, 85
Psalm 98 14, 152, 268
Psalm 98:7 192
Psalm 100 125, 161, 162
Psalm 100:1 268
Psalm 100:4 28
Psalm 100:5 52, 183
Psalm 103:1-5 179
Psalm 103:11-12 227
Psalm 103:15 170
Psalm 104 223

Psalm 105 154
Psalm 106:1-3 149
Psalm 107:1 59
Psalm 107:29 188
Psalm 107:30 266
Psalm 109:5, 10-28 159
Psalm 118:22 252
Psalm 118:24 230, 268
Psalm 119:50 160
Psalm 121 99
Psalm 121:1 216
Psalm 122:1 169
Psalm 130 180, 248
Psalm 134 161, 162
Psalm 136:1-2 146
Psalm 137:4 131
Psalm 139:1-18 197
Psalm 139:7-12 125
Psalm 145:16 44
Psalm 147:3 102
Psalm 147:5 165
Psalm 148 135, 239
Psalm 149:3 229
Psalm 149:4 233
Psalm 150 267, 268

Proverbs 1:20-33 267
Proverbs 11:14 245
Proverbs 15:3 166
Proverbs 17:1 130

Ecclesiastes 3:1-6 187

Song of Solomon 2:6 21
Song of Solomon 8:6 85

Isaiah 2:4 258
Isaiah 2:4, 9:6 152
Isaiah 4:6 183
Isaiah 6:8 29

Isaiah 7-8 14
Isaiah 9:2 68, 271
Isaiah 9:5 41
Isaiah 9:6 189
Isaiah 11:3-9 35
Isaiah 11:6 53
Isaiah 25:6 53
Isaiah 30:18 252
Isaiah 30:21 45
Isaiah 32:18 249
Isaiah 35:1 135
Isaiah 35:1-2 253
Isaiah 35:6 178
Isaiah 35:10 253
Isaiah 40:9 243
Isaiah 40:11 153
Isaiah 40:29 183
Isaiah 41:10 271
Isaiah 42:7 112
Isaiah 43:1 252, 271
Isaiah 43:4 88, 271
Isaiah 43:9 147
Isaiah 43:19 183
Isaiah 47:5 85
Isaiah 49:1 102
Isaiah 50:8 147
Isaiah 51:16 253
Isaiah 52:7 90
Isaiah 53:3 43, 49
Isaiah 53:3-6 247
Isaiah 55:3 143
Isaiah 55:12 135
Isaiah 60:6 224
Isaiah 61 57
Isaiah 65:14 201
Isaiah 66:13 122

Jeremiah 17:7 183
Jeremiah 18:6 241, 271
Jeremiah 32:3 75

Lamentations 3:22-23 92
Lamentations 3:41 94, 152
Lamentations 5:21 83

Ezekiel 6:4 14
Ezekiel 11:19 109
Ezekiel 16:2 135
Ezekiel 33:11 85
Ezekiel 36:26 18, 60, 98, 111
Ezekiel 37:10 201
Ezekiel 47 21

Joel 2:28-29 201

Amos 5:24 144

Micah 4:4 190
Micah 6:8 76, 248, 261

Habakkuk 2:14 84
Habakkuk 3:18 104

Malachi 4:2 134

New Testament

Matthew 1:1-16 193
Matthew 1:18-21 180
Matthew 1:18-25 237, 241
Matthew 1:22-23 14
Matthew 1:23 148, 180, 186, 237
Matthew 2 40, 57, 75, 221, 224, 225
Matthew 2:1 186
Matthew 2:1-2 37, 181
Matthew 2:1-10 169
Matthew 2:1-11 53
Matthew 2:1-12 45, 227, 267
Matthew 2:2 267

Matthew 2:9 17, 23
Matthew 2:9-11 120
Matthew 2:11 37
Matthew 2:13-14 261
Matthew 2:16 105
Matthew 2:16-18 20, 181, 227, 260, 261
Matthew 2:18 127
Matthew 3:1-6 155
Matthew 3:16 32
Matthew 3:17 193
Matthew 4:1-11 254
Matthew 4:4 68, 108
Matthew 4:16 58, 68
Matthew 4:18-19 49
Matthew 4:18-22 127, 169, 264
Matthew 5:1-12 195
Matthew 5:6 271
Matthew 5:7 265
Matthew 5:9 114, 257
Matthew 5:13 15, 108
Matthew 5:13-14 15
Matthew 5:14 241, 244
Matthew 5:15 123, 146, 258
Matthew 5:16 197
Matthew 5:22 147
Matthew 5:23-24 249
Matthew 5:24 122
Matthew 5:38-39 132
Matthew 5:39 76, 146
Matthew 5:41 37
Matthew 5:44-45 67
Matthew 6:8 171
Matthew 6:9-13 187
Matthew 6:10 193
Matthew 6:19-20 111
Matthew 6:19-21 111
Matthew 6:33 67, 68
Matthew 7:7 68, 124
Matthew 7:9 111, 131
Matthew 7:24-27 94

Matthew 8:20 110
Matthew 8:22 52
Matthew 8:23-27 121, 188, 231
Matthew 9:9 164
Matthew 9:16-17 45
Matthew 9:17 232, 241, 246
Matthew 9:20-22 79
Matthew 10:2-4 236
Matthew 10:13 43
Matthew 10:29 254
Matthew 10:29-31 115, 203
Matthew 10:30 64
Matthew 10:31 271
Matthew 10:42 203
Matthew 11:5 253
Matthew 11:15 124
Matthew 11:25-30 230
Matthew 11:28 61, 222
Matthew 11:29 102
Matthew 11:30 80, 220
Matthew 12:10-14 115
Matthew 12:46-50 263
Matthew 13:1-9 163
Matthew 13:1-23 60
Matthew 13:31-3 140
Matthew 13:31-32 220, 232, 257
Matthew 13:33 26, 108, 203, 212, 239, 258
Matthew 13:44 241
Matthew 13:55-56 241
Matthew 14:13-21 17
Matthew 14:22-33 79
Matthew 15:11 145
Matthew 15:16-19 169
Matthew 15:30 183
Matthew 16:15 39, 231
Matthew 16:21-28 264
Matthew 16:24 151
Matthew 16:25 234
Matthew 16:25-26 205

Matthew 16:28. 76
Matthew 17:1-8 47
Matthew 17:20 140
Matthew 18 110
Matthew 18:1-4 105
Matthew 18:2 253
Matthew 18:12-14 153
Matthew 18:14 153, 217
Matthew 18:18 236
Matthew 18:20 127
Matthew 19:13-14) 168
Matthew 19:13-15 105, 198
Matthew 19:14 38, 143, 216, 246
Matthew 19:21 135
Matthew 19:21-22 193
Matthew 20:16 49, 52
Matthew 20:17-23 195
Matthew 21:6-11 49
Matthew 21:12-13 164
Matthew 22 52
Matthew 22:1-10 52
Matthew 22:1-14 230, 253
Matthew 22:32 157
Matthew 22:34-39 201
Matthew 23:37 46, 140
Matthew 24 43
Matthew 24:29 158
Matthew 24:44 49
Matthew 25:1-10 52
Matthew 25:14-30 212, 265
Matthew 25:14-39 89
Matthew 25:15-30 148
Matthew 25:31-46 203, 211, 225, 250
Matthew 25:34 221
Matthew 25:35 231
Matthew 25:35-36 244
Matthew 25:40 104, 109, 110, 115, 143
Matthew 25:40-46 240

Matthew 25:41 67
Matthew 26:10 180
Matthew 26:17-30 213
Matthew 26:26 115, 264
Matthew 26:27-29 239
Matthew 26:36 69
Matthew 26:51-54 20
Matthew 26:52 147
Matthew 27:15-26 235
Matthew 27:38 36
Matthew 27:45 177
Matthew 27:46 98, 105, 242
Matthew 27:47-56 49
Matthew 27:51-54 247
Matthew 27:57-60 111
Matthew 28 154
Matthew 28:2 32
Matthew 28:6 239
Matthew 28:7-8 157
Matthew 28:16-20 262
Matthew 28:18-20 183, 267
Matthew 28:19 22
Matthew 28:19-20 15, 79, 148
Matthew 28:20 40, 115, 139, 140, 220, 231
Matthew 28-30 46
Matthew 30:24 139
Matthew 36:69-75 164

Mark 1:9-10 169
Mark 1:12-13 254
Mark1:14-20 195
Mark 1:15 258
Mark 1:16-20 127, 169
Mark 2:6-12 169
Mark 2:14 164
Mark 2:15 31
Mark 2:22 232
Mark 3:16-19 236
Mark 3:31 262
Mark 3:33-35 262

KNOWING THE SONG

Mark 3:35 81
Mark 4:26-22 258
Mark 4:30-32 140, 220, 232
Mark 4:30-42 165
Mark 4:35-40 128, 135, 169
Mark 4:35-41 121, 231
Mark 5:1-20 179
Mark 5:2-20 169
Mark 5:24-34 174
Mark 6:3 241
Mark 6:8-11 80
Mark 6:15 45
Mark 6:17 75
Mark 6:30-44 17, 169
Mark 7:25-30 203
Mark 7:31-7 62
Mark 7:34 62
Mark 8:29 231
Mark 8:34 109
Mark 8:34-9:1 264
Mark 8:35-36 75
Mark 9:30-50 110
Mark 9:33-37 185
Mark 9:36-37 105
Mark 9:41 139
Mark 9:50 53
Mark 10:13 46
Mark 10:13-16 105
Mark 10:14 31, 38, 143
Mark 10:16 132
Mark 10:21 135
Mark 10:29-30 237
Mark 10:35-38 195
Mark 11:1-10 49
Mark 11:1-11 71
Mark 11:7-10 220
Mark 12:16-17 166
Mark 12:28-31 201
Mark 12:30-31 100
Mark 12:31 121, 139, 245

Mark 12:41-44 166, 213
Mark 13:11 109
Mark 13:26-27 104
Mark 14:3-9 73
Mark 14:15 44
Mark 14:22-24 249
Mark 14:32 69
Mark 14:43-50 49
Mark 14:66-72 164
Mark 15:29-32 71
Mark 15:33 75, 253
Mark 15:34 105, 270
Mark 16 230
Mark 16:1-4 75
Mark 16:3-4 32
Mark 16:7 44
Mark 16:15 66, 105, 108, 148
Mark 16:15-16 15
Mark:16-17 49

Luke 1:26-38 169, 237, 241
Luke 1:27-30, 46-53 106
Luke 1:31 180
Luke 1:35 193, 220
Luke 1:38 193, 205
Luke 1:46-7, 49-50 22, 152
Luke 1:46-55 166, 198
Luke 1:47-55 19, 166
Luke 1:54-55 166
Luke 1:76 53
Luke 2 57, 171, 221, 224, 225
Luke 2:1-5 241
Luke 2:1-16 161
Luke 2:1-18 236
Luke 2:6-7 40
Luke 2:7 46, 50, 127, 190, 252, 255
Luke 2:7-16 227
Luke 2:8-14 37, 58
Luke 2:8-16 120
Luke 2:8-20 29

Luke 2:10 58, 80, 171, 243
Luke 2:11 189
Luke 2:13-14 20, 23, 43, 107, 169
Luke 2:14 14, 77, 80, 189, 190, 202
Luke 2:16 186, 219
Luke 2:21-38 48
Luke 2:31 181
Luke 2:34 19
Luke 2:35 237
Luke 3:22 210, 254
Luke 4:1-13 254
Luke 4:16-21 222
Luke 4:18 112, 136
Luke 4:18-19 56
Luke 5:1-11 196
Luke 5:11 206
Luke 5:27 164
Luke 5:39 232
Luke 6:12-19 236
Luke 6:20 126, 178, 195
Luke 6:27 76
Luke 7:31-32 36
Luke 8:19-21 263
Luke 8:22-25 121
Luke 9:10-17 17
Luke 9:20 231
Luke 9:22-27 264
Luke 9:23 132
Luke 9:35 193
Luke 9:51 166
Luke 9:57-62 151
Luke 9:58 252
Luke 9:62 221
Luke 10:1-6 195
Luke 10:5 104, 189
Luke 10:29-37 71, 264
Luke 10:38-42 164
Luke 11:1-4 63
Luke 11:4 76

Luke 12:6-7 115
Luke 12:7 170
Luke 12:24-28 111
Luke 12:27-28 46
Luke 12:32-34 100
Luke 12:37 271
Luke 13 43
Luke 13:18-19 140, 232
Luke 13:18-21 239
Luke 13:20-21 46, 253
Luke 13:21 258
Luke 13:34 43, 46, 92, 140
Luke 14:12-24 143
Luke 14:13 231
Luke 14: 15-24 253
Luke 14:15-24 126
Luke 14:23 52
Luke 15 165
Luke 15:1-7 112, 170
Luke 15:3-4 261
Luke 15:3-6 115
Luke 15:8-9 115
Luke 15:11-32 128, 229, 252
Luke 15:20 229
Luke 16:19-31 143
Luke 17:11-19 224
Luke 17:20-21 220
Luke 17:21 122
Luke 18:9 59
Luke 18:15-17 120
Luke 18:16 143
Luke 18:16-17 38
Luke 18:22 135
Luke 19:12-8 212
Luke 19:28-40 49
Luke 19:34 98
Luke 19:40 151
Luke 19:41-42 151
Luke 19:41-44 87
Luke 20:38 157

Luke 21:1-4 213
Luke 21:2-3 29
Luke 22-3 40
Luke 22:12 44
Luke 22:19 40, 172
Luke 22:19-20 57, 148
Luke 22:24-47 264
Luke 22:42 194, 250
Luke 22:47-53 49
Luke 22:54-62 164
Luke 23:26 177
Luke 23:34 36, 185, 214, 236
Luke 23:35 248
Luke 23:42-43 195
Luke 23:44 75, 185, 206
Luke 23:44-45 248
Luke 23:46 105
Luke 23:50-53 185
Luke 24 75, 154
Luke 24:1 136, 258
Luke 24:1-2 75
Luke 24:1-5 215
Luke 24:1-35 27
Luke 24:2 32, 42, 158
Luke 24:13-15 135
Luke 24:13-25 79, 103
Luke 24:13-27 37, 136
Luke 24:13-32 89
Luke 24:13-35 15, 45, 62
Luke 24:13-50 82
Luke 24:15-24 53
Luke 24:28-31 86, 136
Luke 24:31 27
Luke 24:32 159
Luke 24:45 147
Luke 24:51 172

John 1 177
John 1:1 110, 267
John 1:1-3, 14 73

John 1:1-5 123, 153, 180, 193
John 1:1-5, 9-11 225
John 1:1-9 221
John 1:1-14 14
John 1:1-18 181
John 1:4-5 35, 85, 231, 261
John 1:4-8 245
John 1:5 100, 105, 135, 145, 146, 183, 189, 212
John 1:9 43, 265
John 1:11 253
John 1:14 18, 42, 49, 66, 85, 106, 127, 193, 227
John 1:29 168, 216
John 2:1-11 26, 50, 51, 52, 54, 158, 169, 212, 253
John 2:10 52
John 3:1 159
John 3:1-7 260
John 3:1-8 224, 262
John 3:1-21 226
John 3:3 18
John 3:3-6 229
John 3:3-8 184, 271
John 3:5 244
John 3:6 132
John 3:7 204
John 3:8 26, 62, 184, 223, 266
John 3: 16 111
John 3:16 49, 74, 79, 85, 120, 135, 180, 203, 208, 217, 218, 230, 261
John 3:17 253
John 3:29 52
John 3:34 227
John 4:1-26 184
John 4:7-15 54, 94, 182
John 4:10 66
John 4:10-12 212
John 4:14 38, 52
John 4:24 208
John 5:24 186

John 6:1-14 201
John 6:16-21 169
John 6:33, 35 148
John 6:35 26, 54, 156
John 6:38 66
John 6:48-58 174
John 6:53-54 153
John 6:56-59 153
John 6:63 209
John 7:37-38 150
John 7:38 85, 184
John 8: 1-14 17
John 8:12 100, 117, 145, 158, 160, 166, 181, 231, 271
John 10:1-6 136
John 10:3 252
John 10:9 179, 221, 231
John 10:10 57, 165
John 10:11 29, 120, 156, 227
John 11:25-26 157
John 11:35 98
John 11:44 157
John 12:12-15 49
John 12:24 77, 205
John 12: 32 32
John 13:1-15 153
John 13:2-9 36
John 13:2-15 269
John 13:2-17 264
John 13:34-5 158
John 13:34-35 214
John 13:35 271
John 14:1 24, 152
John 14:1-3 220, 249
John 14:2 124, 229
John 14:4-7 239
John 14:6 24, 59, 84, 94, 95, 101, 102, 124, 153, 156, 190, 231, 244, 253, 258
John 14:8 76
John 14:8-11 236

John 14:15-17 79, 133
John 14:16 153, 259
John 14:16-17 59
John 14:17 82, 210
John 14:18 31
John 14:20 213
John 14:23 135
John 14:23-26 100
John 14:25-27 23
John 14:26 18, 66, 105, 193, 215, 261
John 14:27 35, 43, 44, 151, 189, 239
John 15:1 156
John 15:1-5 240
John 15:1-9 118
John 15:5 241
John15:5 163
John 15:5, 20-21 148
John 15:12-13 115
John 15:14 44
John 15:16 160
John 16:13 79, 209, 258
John 16:14 80
John 16:20 183
John 16:22 120
John 16:32 133
John 16:69 271
John 17 44
John 17:11 148
John 17:20-23 222
John 17:21 36, 44, 73, 153, 210, 221, 234
John 17:21-22 240
John 17:22 18, 100, 136, 174
John 18:1-12 49
John 18:12-14 185
John 18:15-27 102, 164
John 18:28 185
John 19:13 242
John 19:14 185

John 19:23-24 218
John 19:23-25 73
John 19:29 195
John 19:30 185, 247
John 19:33-34 235
John 19:34 87, 214
John 19:39 50, 224
John 20 71, 154
John 20:1 32, 250
John 20:2 236
John 20:11-16 32
John 20:19 55
John 20:19-23 189
John 20:19-31 93
John 20:24-25 120
John 20:24-29 135, 136, 156, 164, 236
John 20:26 76, 137
John 20:26-9 115
John 21:1-14 136, 222
John 21:15-17 231
John 21:16 234
John 24:16 103

Acts 1:3-11 40
Acts 1:8 26
Acts 1:9 172
Acts 1:9-11 76
Acts 1:13 236
Acts 2 162
Acts 2:1-3 134
Acts 2:1-4 79, 166, 178
Acts 2:1-11 230
Acts 2:1-13 62
Acts 2:1-28 75
Acts 2:2 91, 209
Acts 2:3 54, 105, 184, 258
Acts 2:5-6 245
Acts 2:5-11 91
Acts 2:7 33
Acts 2:17 188, 201

Acts 2:39 38
Acts 2:44 174
Acts 2:46 176
Acts 4:11 252
Acts 9:2 110
Acts 16:14-15, 40 129
Acts 17:18 103

Romans 1:25 258
Romans 5:5 210
Romans 6:4, 8 22
Romans 6:5-11 244
Romans 6:53 42
Romans 7:19 71
Romans 8:1-2 184
Romans 8:17 239
Romans 8:22 55, 179
Romans 8:26-27 23, 63
Romans 8:35 44
Romans 8:36-39 171
Romans 8:38 171
Romans 8:38-39 42
Romans 8:39 171
Romans 10:1-4 227
Romans 10:18 84
Romans 12:1 29, 156
Romans 12:6-8 148
Romans 12:6-18 208
Romans 12:8 245
Romans 14:11 103
Romans 15:13 210

1 Corinthians 1:10-17 75
1 Corinthians 1:23-5 227
1 Corinthians 1:25 198
1 Corinthians 2:7-10 104
1 Corinthians 2:9 104
1 Corinthians 6:19 50
1 Corinthians 9:24 55
1 Corinthians 10:31 146

1 Corinthians 11:23-25 75
1 Corinthians 11:23-26 148
1 Corinthians 11:24 50, 75
1 Corinthians 12:1-11 98, 102
1 Corinthians 12:1-31 162
1 Corinthians 12:4-11 208
1 Corinthians 12:7-11 26
1 Corinthians 12:12 36
1 Corinthians 12:14-26 86
1 Corinthians 12:27 45
1 Corinthians 13 15, 112, 126, 268
1 Corinthians 13:1-2 126
1 Corinthians 13:4-6 83
1 Corinthians13:4-10 126
1 Corinthians 13:5 51
1 Corinthians 13:5-6 210
1 Corinthians 13:6 148
1 Corinthians 13:8 51, 83, 117, 127
1 Corinthians 13:8-13 149
1 Corinthians 13:11 131
1 Corinthians 13:11-13 194, 251
1 Corinthians 13:12 17, 104, 108, 184
1 Corinthians 13:13 50, 107, 187, 222, 229
1 Corinthians 14:15 210
1 Corinthians 15:3 22
1 Corinthians 15:23 104
1 Corinthians 15:51-56 157
1 Corinthians 15:56 189
1 Corinthians 15:58 145

2 Corinthians 2:15 165
2 Corinthians 3:1 41
2 Corinthians 3:17 210
2 Corinthians 5:17 22, 48
2 Corinthians 5:17, 19 258
2 Corinthians 5:19 86, 97
2 Corinthians 5:20 41

2 Corinthians 6:18 127
2 Corinthians 13:11-14 148
2 Corinthians 13:14 218

Galatians 2:20 22, 30
Galatians 3:16 209
Galatians 3:26 138, 239
Galatians 3:26-7 168
Galatians 3:26-28 178
Galatians 3:28 74, 148, 150, 160, 262
Galatians 5:22 76, 130, 208, 212
Galatians 5:22-23 80, 186, 208, 209, 212, 224, 264
Galatians 6:2 37, 98, 202
Galatians 6:10 135, 168, 241

Ephesians 1:4 160
Ephesians 1:7-9 17
Ephesians 1:10, 20-22 22
Ephesians 1:17 79
Ephesians 2:4-7 157
Ephesians 2:7 135
Ephesians 2:12 127
Ephesians 2:14 42
Ephesians 2:19 111
Ephesians 3:7-10 40
Ephesians 3:16-19 54
Ephesians 4:3-15 244
Ephesians 4:4 209
Ephesians 5:8 227
Ephesians 5:14 96
Ephesians 5:25 173
Ephesians 5:32-3 83

Philippians 1:20-21 29
Philippians 2:8 79
Philippians 2:9 216
Philippians 3:14 55, 88, 100
Philippians 3:20 253
Philippians 4:4 224

KNOWING THE SONG

Philippians 4:7 165
Philippians 4:7-8 190
Philippians 4:7-9 161
Philippians 4:8 86, 249
Philippians 4:11-13 133
Philippians 4:19 160, 244

Colossians 1:10 146
Colossians 1:12 271
Colossians 1:15-17 22
Colossians 1:15-19 193
Colossians 1:17 207
Colossians 1:18-20 227
Colossians 1:19 54
Colossians 2:2-3 165
Colossians 3:19 198

1 Thessalonians 5:5 67

2 Thessalonians 3:2 66

1 Timothy 1:1 70
1 Timothy 6:15 220
1 Timothy 6:19 230

2 Timothy 1:7 208
2 Timothy 2:20-1 241
2 Timothy 4:1 221
2 Timothy 4:2 127

Titus 2:11 218

Hebrews 2:11 81
Hebrews 4:2 48
Hebrews 6:19 81
Hebrews 12:1 124

James 2:14-17 263
James 3:18 98

1 Peter 1:3 157
1 Peter 2:5 123
1 Peter 2:9 198, 227, 240
1 Peter 3:9 81
1 Peter 3:15 49
1 Peter 3:18-20 45

1 John 1:1-2 45
1 John 1:3 262
1 John 1:5 165
1 John 1:7 33
1 John:1-7 76
1 John 2:20 135
1 John 3:1 28, 38
1 John 3:2 234
1 John 4 181
1 John 4:7-8 16
1 John 4:7-12 144
1 John 4:8 51, 125, 158, 160, 165, 169, 229
1 John 4:11 148
1 John 4:16 138
1 John 4:19 229
1 John 5:13 235

Jude 1:24-25 174

Revelation 1:8 259
Revelation 1:12-16 176
Revelation 3 211
Revelation 3:20 147, 201, 254, 261
Revelation 4:3 156
Revelation 4:8 207
Revelation 5:9-14 136
Revelation 5:12 134, 161
Revelation 7:13-14 182
Revelation 7:14 213
Revelation 14:3 136
Revelation 17:14 178
Revelation 17-18 201
Revelation 19:7 52
Revelation 19:10 40
Revelation 21:1-2 91
Revelation 21:1-5 165
Revelation 21:3-4 40
Revelation 21:4 229
Revelation 21:5 26, 73, 83, 85, 95, 148, 178, 250
Revelation 22:1-2 135, 190
Revelation 22: 2 265
Revelation 22:2 146, 237, 257
Revelation 22:3 183
Revelation 22:3-4 195
Revelation 22:13, 21 85
Revelation 22:17 182
Revelation 22:20 188, 233

Tune Names

A

ABBEYFIELD
– F57* 207
– H55 108
ABERYSTWYTH – W631 27
ACROSTIC – H3* 17
ADIEU – H78* 132
ADORATION – C13 (i and ii) 48
AFFLICTION – H106* 180
AGAAGA TAPU – W649* 18
AGINCOURT – W643* 202
AHIMELECH – H148* 250
ALDERSGATE 88 – H64* 116
ALIVE – A146 239
ALIVE TO GOD# – A133* 216
ALL CREATURES – A76 125
ALLELUIA AOTEAROA 3 – A34 21
ALLELUIA AOTEAROA 4 – A53 21
ALLELUIA AOTEAROA 5 – A92 21
ALLELUIA AOTEAROA 6 – A121 21
ALLELUIA AOTEAROA 7 – A131 22
ALLELUIA AOTEAROA 8 – A163 22
ALLELUIA NO 1 – W674 (ii)* 22
ALLELUIA# – W674 (iii)* 23
ALOFA MAI IA# – A3 23
AMICITIA – H30* 74
ANAURA BAY – C19* 77
ANGEL – F44* 153
ANGELSONG# – C28* 120
ANGELUS – H112* 179
ANTIOCH – A93 159
ANZAC – H61* 114
ARGYLE STREET – A33* 63
ARNSTADT – A14*, C9 40
ASHBURTON – C4(ii)* 20
ASHLEY – A62* 111
AUCKLAND – C15* 49
AU CLAIR DE LA LUNE – F34* 116
AUSTRIA – H39 85
AVE – A58* 106
AVE LAU OLA# – A6* 29
AWAKE BEFORE SUNRISE# – C6* 29

B

BALLYHERKIN – H6* 23
BARRELL# – A147 (i) and (ii)* 242
BARR STREET – H58* 205
BATH STREET – H154* 264
BEAUTIFUL PRESENCE – H9* 30
BECKENHAM – H20* 53
BEFORE THE THRONE OF GOD ABOVE – A147 (i and ii)* 243
BENEDICTION – A99* 172
BENISON – F72* 249
BENSON – W652* 84
BE STILL# – F4(i)* 30
BETHLEHEM# – C1* 14
BITHYNIA – H8 28
BLESSING – A11* 38
BLESSINGS – H11* 33
BLESSING SONG# – A138 222
BLUE SKY – F77 259
BOOM, BOOM# – A111* 186
BRANDENBURG – W660* 151
BREAD AND WINE – A39* 71
BREAD OF JOY# – A104* 176
BREAD OF PEACE – F38* 130
BRIGHT DAY – H136 229
BRING PEACE I# – F7(i)* 35
BRING PEACE II# – F7(ii)* 35
BRITTANY – A48* 85
BROAD BAY – H100* 166
BROAD STREET – A73 132
BROMELL – F18* 71
BRONWEN – A158* 263
BRUNEL – A55* 104
BRYANT STREET – H59 111

BRYN CALFARIA – H52 101
BUD OF HOPE – A10* 38
BUNESSAN – A25* 51
BURNSIDE – H137* 231
BUSHBURN – C37* 197

C

CAMBRIDGE – F9* 43
CAMPANE – C30 (i) and (ii)* 155
CANA – A27* 52
CARDRONA – H131* 217
CARING – A20* 46
CAROL OF DREAMS – F12 (i)* 58
CATHEDRAL SQUARE – H56* 109
CAVELL STREET – H147* 250
CELEBRATION SONG – A70* 128
CHAPEAU DE PAIX – H113* 190
CHEAM – A54* 93
CHERRY FARM – H94* 156
CHEVETOGNE – W674(i) 22
CHILCOMBE – H139* 232
CHILDREN OF GOD – H142* 239
CHILDREN'S SAVIOUR, THE – A66 120
CHILTON FOLIAT – H71* 179
CHRISTCHURCH – A19* 45
CHRISTE SANCTORUM – W657* 157
CHRIST IS BORN# – C32* 180
CLIPPETY-CLOP# – C12* 46
CLONBERN PLACE – H116* 193
COLOMBO – F25* 92
COLOUR ME FREE# – A21* 47
COLUMBUS – W672, A156* 259
COME TO THE SAVIOUR – W659* 143
COMPANIONS – H21* 55
CONCORD
  – A154*, C48 256
  – W671* 147
CONNECT – H85* 144
CONSECRATION – A6 29
CONTEMPLATION – W650* 60
CONVERSE – W648* 247

CORNELIA – H49* 97
CORONATION ROAD – H157* 267
CRASHAW – A7* 32
CREATION SINGS – H29 55
CREATION – W625* 219
CREDO – H136* 229
CROMWELL – F27* 95
CROSS OF JESUS – H23 103
CRUCIFER – A87* 151
CRUSADER – H153* 258
CUP OF WATER# – A83* 139
CWM RHONDDA – W661* 25

D

DANIELL – H36* 81
DANSEY – F31* 99
DARK CHRIST# – C10* 43
DEDICATIO MEA – H122* 205
DIADEMATA – H19* 57
DIVA SERVATRIX – W657 157
DIVERSITY – A19 45
DO THIS IN REMEMBRANCE* – A29 57
DOWN AMPNEY
  – A24* 50
  – F47 163
DREAM A DREAM – F12(ii)* 58
DUBLIN – H42* 82
DUNEDIN – A155* 256, 388, 390, 395, 397
DUNSTAN – C52* 271
DURHAM STREET – F15* 67

E

EASTER SUNRISE – H79* 136
EATON – F48* 164
EDITH – H140* 233
EDUCARE – F11* 51
EISENACH – C33 (i and ii) 181
ELIZABETH – C3* 18
EMMAUS ROAD – H2* 15
EMPATHY – F30* 98
ENGELBERG – A45 77

EPHPHATHA – H25* 62
ERENA – H96* 162
ERIKSSON – H139 232
ESKDALE – F35* 118
ESTHER – C49* 261
E TE ARIKI# – H23* 60
E TE IWI – A32* 61
EVERY STAR – W640* 65
EXPECTATION – A149* 246

F

FELICITY – A94(ii)* 160, 394
FERNER – H128* 216
FINLANDIA – H12 33
FISHBOWL – F36* 123
FIVE SCRUPLES – F19(ii)* 71
FOLLOW MY LEADER – W670* 220
FOLLY OF LOVE – C45* 228
FOOD IS GIVEN – A37 69
FOR ALL THY MERCIES – W650 60
FOR EVERYONE BORN – F17, HP3 70
FORGIVNESS – F19(ii),* H10 31
FRANKLIN WEST – A42* 75
FREELAND – A72* 130

G

GABBATHA – A147(i)* 242
GAELIC AIR – F10 (i)*, H41 88
GAELIC TRADITIONAL MELODY – F10(i)* 47
GALLOWAY – H104* 173
GALLOWAY STREET – H81* 139
GERALDINE – C16*, A28 53
GETHSEMANE
 – F16* 69
 – W648* 247
GIFT OF LIFE – H17* 48
GLENROSS – H150* 254

GLORIA
 – C20* 77
 – C21* 78
 – C22* 78
 – W675* 80
GLORIA IN EXCELSIS – C23* 78
GLORY TO GOD – F23 80
GOD DEFEND NEW ZEALAND – W677, A51* 89
GOD, IN YOUR GRACE – H95* 159
GOD OF FREEDOM – A50 87
GOD OF NEW BEGINNINGS# – F49 165
GODPOINT – A47* 84
GOD'S CREATURES – H22* 56
GOD'S GIFT# – A46* 83
GOMA – F78* 260
GONFALON ROYAL – A63, HP10 115
GOOD FRIDAY – H108* 177
GOSPEL OF PEACE – A63* 115
GOTHENBURG – F64* 230
GRACELAND – H68* 121
GRACE OF GOD# – F61 218
GRACE, THE# – A136 219
GRAFTON – H14 41
GREAT LOVE# – A56* 105
GREEN ISLAND – A60* 110
GREENLANE – F50* 170
GREENSLEEVES – H109 181
GREETINGS# – C25* 106
GUDS KÄRLEK – W667* 223

H

HADLEY CLOSE – H120* 203
HAEREMAI – A26* 52
HAIRSONG – H27* 65
HALLEY – A57* 105
HAMILTON AVENUE – H8* 28
HAMILTON – F67* 240
HARMONY – A91* 157
HAVELOCK – F73* 251
HEALING SPIRIT – F80 269

HEARTBEAT# – A15 42
HE ATAAHUA KOEI# – A30* 59
HE IS BORN# – A107 180
HEREFORD – W662* 92, 169
HIGHFIELD – F69(ii)* 247
HIGHWOOD
  – 665* 245
  – A9* 86
  – W653* 230
HILDEGARD – A71 129
HILDEGARD'S WHEEL# – A145* 238
HIVA HOSANNA – A84* 142
HOANI – F70* 248
HO HUM – H121* 204
HOLLY LEA – H31* 76
HOLY HOLY – F33 112
HONOUR THE EARTH – A54, HP8 93
HOW GREAT THOU ART – W628 181
HUARAHI – H90* 153
HUSH-A-BYE BABY – F69(i)* 246
HYDE PARK – F25* 92
HYFRYDOL
  – F32 100
  – H8 28
  – H48 96

I

I AM TRUSTING – W638* 183
I ARISE – H65* 118
IA TATOU VIVII ATU NEI – A65* 125
ILLUMINATION – F54* 191
INCARNATION – A12,* C8 39
IN DULCI JUBILO – C1 14
INFINITE – A49* 86
INHERITANCE – W673* 239
IN TIMES OF DROUGHT# – F2* 26
IRISH – H42* 82
ISLAND HOME# – H43* 90
IT'S A SURPRISE# – C17* 57
I'VE GOT KNEES# – A75* 124

J

JANSEN – A51* 90
JENNIFER'S GIFT – A14(i),* C9(i) 40
JESU, MEINE FREUDE – H98* 160
JESUS AMONG US# – A101* 172
JESUS PRESENT# – A64 115
JEWEL – H133 225
JOIN HANDS# – A82* 138
JOY – A77* 134
JULIAN (I) – A2 20
JULIAN (II) – H4 21
JUSTICE VOICE – F80* 269

K

KAIKOURA – F63* 228
KAPITI – H118* 197
KARAKIA A TE WAIRUA TAPU – H84* 141
KEY UP – F68* 241
KHANDALLAH – A130* 215
KHAO I DANG – A61 111
KINDNESS – F40* 145
KINGDOM WITHIN# – A137* 221
KINGSFOLD – F55 195
KINGSLAND – C35* 190
KNOX COLLEGE – A69 128
KORU – F44* 153
KO TEI ANOANO – W668* 142
KOTUKU – A113* 187
KREMSER – A86* 149
KUM BA YAH – A31* 60
KUPE – H105* 173

L

LACE – F1* 24
LACRIMAE RERUM – F20 73
LACRIMOSA – H52* 101
LALA MNTWANA – W645,* A23(i), C14(ii) 50
LANGLEY – H63* 115
LANGSTON – H70* 123
LAUGHTON – W634 107
LEAST CHILD – H133 (i) and (ii)* 226

LEGÈRE – H35* 80
LENITER – H35* 80
LEONARD – A153* 254
LEULUMOEGA FOU – W647 16
LIAM – A159, C50* 263
LIFT UP YOUR HEARTS – A88* 152
LIGHT OF LIGHTS# – A89*, C29, HP16 152
LIGHT OF THE WORLD – W669* 118
LINSTEAD (or LINSTEAD MARKET) – W658* 148
LITANY# – A38* 69
LITTLE CORNARD – A19 45
LITTLE ONE – F52* 186
LITTLE VENICE – A79* 135
LIVING WORD – H109* 181
LLANGWYM – F74(i)* 252
LOFTIS – H13 35
LO MATOU TAMA E# – A90* 154
LONELY MAN – H99* 164
LOOK IN WONDER – H93* 154
LOVE TO THE WORLD# – A93* 159
LOVE UNKNOWN – A100* 174
LOVING SPIRIT – A94(i)* 160
LULLABY CAROL# – F46* 161
LYDIA – F37* 128
LYNNEFRITH – A36* 64

M

MAKER OF MYSTERY# – F47* 163
MAKILING – A40* 72
MAKORA STREET – C30(ii)* 155
MALCOLM AVENUE – H103* 169
MALPASS – H75* 117, 127
MANOR PLACE – H107* 175
MARCHING
 – 27* 95
 – F14 67
MARGARET – H40* 86
MARLBOROUGH SOUNDS – A95* 165
MARYLANDS – C2* 17
MARY MORRISON – A147 (i) and (ii)* 243

MARY'S CHILD – W642* 34
MARY'S SONG – H101* 166
MARY'S SON – H97* 163
MATANGI – H45* 93
MECHTILDE – H66* 119
MENSA – F17* 70
MERRY CHRISTMAS RAG – C26* 107
MEWS# – W645*, A23, C14 50
MICAH – H146* 248
MICHAELA – C48*, A154 256
MICHAEL – C15 49
MICHAELMAS – H14* 41
MILLENNIUM 1 – H39* 85
MILLENNIUM 2 – H48* 96
MILLENNIUM – F43 148
MIRACULUM MAGNUM – W639* 14
MIRIAM – F8* 36
MISERICORDIA – A160* 265
MISTERIOSO# – A139* 223
MITCHELL – H124* 206
MONK'S GATE – H129* 265
MORNINGTON – C34* 187
MOVING THROUGH THE SILENCE – A157* 262
MUSIC OF CREATION# – A41* 72
MYLOR – H38* 102
MY REDEEMER – W631* 27
MYSTERIUM – H77* 131
MYSTERY 79

N

NEW BEGINNINGS – H51* 98
NEWBURY – H42* 82
NEW DIRECTIONS – H15* 41
NEW FERN – A119, HP19* 199
NEWLANDS ROAD – F13* 59
NEW WORLD CHILD – H13 35
NEW YEAR SAMBA – C13(ii)* 48
NGAKURU – C39* 202
NGA TUPUNA – A5* 28
NIMBUS – H123* 205

NO ROOM# – C46* 237
NORTHBROOK – W653* 230
NORTHLAND – A114* 188
NORTHVIEW – H26* 62
NOW UNTO HIM# – A102* 174
NUN DANKET – F56* 199

O

OAKHURST SESSION 397
OBEISANCE – C4(i)* 20
O BE JOYFUL# – A103* 175
ODE TO JOY – A43* 72
OLD 100TH – W679* 161
OLD SHED DOOR – C42* 220
O LE FAAFETAI – W629* 66
O LE VAIPUNA – W632* 183
OLWYN – W641* 19
OMBERSLEY – W626* 156
ONE TWO THREE ALLELUIA – A111 186
OOM-PAH-PAH – H16* 44
ORIANA – H57* 109
O STORE GUD – W628* 182
OTAGO – F53* 189
OUR FATHER – W676, A112* 187
OUTRAM – H46* 95

P

PASTURES GREEN# – C18* 74
PATATAG – H19* 56
PATMOS – A6* 29
PAUATAHANUI – H89* 148
PAX VOBISCUM – H111* 189
PEACE CAROL – A108 (ii), C33 (ii) 181
PEACE SONG – H114* 190
PEACE TREE – H151* 257
PELENISE – H83* 140
PENTECOST SONG – H96 163
PEOPLE FIRST – H126 207
PHILIPPIANS 4 – F71* 249
PICARDY – A50*, HP7 87
PIKO NEI – W655* 191

PILOT – W663 121
PORTENT – F75* 255
POTTER'S HAND – A162 271
POULTNEY – H145 245
POWERPOINT – H86* 145
PRESENCE – F51* 183
PSALM 27 – A117 196
PSALM 98 – A88 152
PSALM 100 – A103 175
PSALM 104 – A139 223
PUER NOBIS – C1 14
PUREA NEI – A115* 194
PURPOSE – W652* 84

Q

QUI CRUCIFER# – F79* 264
QUILTINGS – F74 (ii)* 252

R

RAIN DANCE – H123* 205
RANGIMARIE – H87* 146
RANGI RURU – H73* 126
RAUMATI – C30 (ii) and (ii)* 155
REAL CHRISTMAS – C41* 212
REASSURANCE – H102* 171
REBECCA – C36* 193
REBEKAH – F41* 145
RECOGNITION – F3* 27
RECONCILIATION – F76* 258
REDHEAD 27 – W655 191
REGENT SQUARE
  – H14 41
  – H34 103
  – H51 98
  – W651 68
REMEMBRANCE – A29 57
REPTON – F55 195
RESTING – F28* 96
RESURRECTION – A19* 45
REVERSI – A9*, C7 37
RIGHT NOW# – A116* 195

RIO GRANDE – W639* 14
RIVERTON – F21* 73
ROCKINGHAM – W646* 141
ROSETTA ROAD – H54* 104
ROTORUA – H133* 225
ROYAL TERRACE – H28* 66
ROY CRESCENT – H82* 140
RUAHINE – F6* 34
RUH – A67* 122
RUSTINGTON – H50* 100

S

SACRA – H80* 138
SAFE IN THE HANDS – A117 196
SAINT SONG# – A120* 200
SAL – H1* 15
SALISBURY STREET – H13* 35
SANCTUM – F10 (ii)* 47
SARABAND AVENUE – C13(i)* 48
SAVIOUR'S NAME – A3* 23
SEASTRANDS – H155 266
SEEK YE FIRST – W635* 68
SEE SAW SACCARA DOWN – A22* 49
SELKIRK GRACE# – A124* 204
SERENAM – H156 266
SERVANT LIFE – H154* 264
SERVANT SONG# – A8* 37
SHELTER – C47* 252
SHERIDAN – H133 (i) and (ii)* 226
SHINING – H88* 146
SHINING THREAD – H132* 221
SHIPSTON – A10* 38
SHIRLEY – A81* 136
SIGNUM – A43* 75
SINE NOMINE
  – A45 77
  – H37 82
  – H73 126
SING FOR PEACE – H28* 66
SINGING LOVE – W636*, A59 107
SMALL THINGS – A123* 203

SMILE – C38* 198
SMOKEY MOUNTAIN – A14*, C9 40
SOLOMON'S MEMORY – F45* 158
SOMS STRANDEN – W667* 223
SONG 1 – A106* 178
SONG 1 – H152* 272
SONG OF THE POOR – H74* 126
SONG TO THE LORD JESUS – A80* 135
SONG TO THE SPIRIT – A126* 210
SOON EE – A81 137
SOROMUNDI – F5* 30
SOUTHERLY – A141, C44 225
SOUTHLAND – A78* 134
SPIRIT OF PEACE I# – F58 (i), HP20* 209
SPIRIT OF PEACE II# – F58(ii)* 209
SPIRIT SONG# – 109* 184
SPIRITUS VITAE – W654* 269
SPONTANEITY – C24* 80
SPRING CAROL – H92* 154
ST AIDANS – A108(i), C33(i)* 181
STANLEY STREET – H91 150
STANMORE – H125 208
STANSFIELD – A118* 198
STAR-CHILD (i) – C40 (i) 210
STAR-CHILD (ii)# – C40 (ii) 210
STAR DANCE# – C43* 224
STARSIGHT – W644*, A4, C5 24
ST BEES – W664* 234
ST CATHERINE'S COURT – A27 53
ST COLUMBA – A151* 250
ST DUNSTAN – W655 191
ST FRANCIS – W666* 162
ST HELEN'S – H14 41
ST HELIERS – H119 201
STILLNESS – F4 (ii) 30
STILLNESS – H69* 122
ST JOHN – C13 (i) and (ii) 48
ST KILDA – H88* 146
ST LOUIS – A148 243
STORM WINDS# – A152* 253

ST PETER – H5* 25
ST PRISCA – W655 191
STRANGER – F60 211
STRATHDEE – W678* 192
STRINGER – F31 99
SUANTRAI – A16* 42
SUMMER CAROL – C27* 112
SUNSHINE – W630* 237
SUPPLIANT – F19 (i)* 71
SURSUM CORDA – A105* 177
SUSSEX – H32* 103
SYCAMORE CLOSE – H58* 110

T

TAKE OUR BREAD – W656* 213
TALAVERA TERRACE – A127* 212
TAMA NGAKAU MARIE# – W633, A128* 213
TANGI-TUAKANA – A97* 169
TANNENBAUM – W643* 202
TARANAKI – H134* 226
TAWA – A44*, HP5 76
TE ATUA MOU O BETELA# – A129* 214
TEESDALE STREET – F62* 222
TE HARINUI# – A98, C31* 171
TE HORO – F39 133
TELL MY PEOPLE# – A132* 215
TE MOANA – H130 217
TENDERNESS – A143* 234, 394
TENNEY – W627* 59
TE PIRINGA – F37* 128
TE RAHUI – H158 270
TE RANGIMARIE# – F42, HP14 147
TE RIPEKA – H110* 185
TE WAKA – H117* 196
THANKS BE TO GOD 216
THANKS FOR LIFE# – A45* 77
THE CHILDREN'S SAVIOUR# – A66* 120
THE GRACE# – A136 219
THE MAJESTY OF MOUNTAINS – A139* 223
THEO – A18*, C11 45

THE STAR OF THE COUNTY DOWN – F55* 195
THREAD# – F65* 231
THUNDER# – A135 218
TITUS# – F61* 218
TO COMPASSION – F66*, HP23 233
TOKOTORUTAPU – H24* 61
TO MATOU METUA# – A142* 233
TOOTING – A161* 268
TRARALGON – F24* 83
TREDEGAR# – A50*, HP7 87
TREGURTHA – H135* 227
TREKSONG – H72* 124
TUGWOOD – W643* 202

U

UNDE ET MEMORES – H2 15
UNITY – A110* 185
UTRECHT – A14(ii)*, C9(ii) 40

V

VENANTIUS – H138* 236
VENTURE – F14* 67
VERDURE – F59* 209
VERITAS – H53* 102
VERVACITY – A140* 224
VINEYARD – F35* 118
VIVACE – H44 91
VRUECHTEN – A7 32
VULPIUS – H14 41

W

WAIAPU 243
WAIRUA TAPU – H7* 26
WAITAKI – A85* 144
WAITANGI DAY – H37* 82
WAIWHETU – H141* 236
WAKARI – H67* 120
WAKE UP# – A144* 238
WALK TALL# – A35* 63
WALLIS HOUSE – F55* 195
WALY WALY – H112* 179

WANDERING – H149* 253
WAS LEBET — H47 91
WATER'S EDGE – A96* 169
WE ARE A WHEEL – A145 238
WEAVER – A125* 208
WELCOME – H115* 192
WELLINGTON – A122* 201
WE STAND WITH CHRIST – A147(ii) 242
WESTMINSTER ABBEY
  – A69 128
  – H34 103
WHAKAKI – H18* 54
WHAKATAU MAI TE ATUA# – A150* 247
WHAKATEITEI – H76* 130

WHANAU O WAIAPU – F26* 94
WHERE IS THE ROOM – A154 255
WHISPERING GENTLY# – F77* 260
WHITBY STREET – H144* 244
WHO WILL CARRY# – F79 264
WINGATE WAY – C51* 267
WINGS OF THE MORNING# – A68* 125
WORLD'S END# – A74* 133
WROSLYN ROAD – A17* 44

Y
YAMSONG – H127* 212
YORK – W637* 137

www.ingramcontent.com/pod-product-compliance
Lightning Source LLC
Chambersburg PA
CBHW081342070526
44578CB00005B/695